西行漫记
Red Star Over China

英汉对照
有声纪念版

[美] Edgar Snow 著

董乐山 译

外语教学与研究出版社
FOREIGN LANGUAGE TEACHING AND RESEARCH PRESS
北京 BEIJING

京权图字：01-2003-6877

Copyright © 1938, 1944 by Random House, Inc.
Copyright © 1968 by Edgar Snow
Copyright © 1961, 1993 by John K. Fairbank
Copyright © 1993 by Lois Snow

Licensed edition for sale in the mainland territory of China only. Not for sale elsewhere.
仅限中国大陆地区销售。不得在香港、澳门、台湾地区销售，不得出口。

图书在版编目（CIP）数据

西行漫记：有声纪念版：英汉对照 /（美）埃德加·斯诺（Edgar Snow）著；董乐山译. -- 北京：外语教学与研究出版社，2025.6. -- ISBN 978-7-5213-6380-7

I. H319.4

中国国家版本馆 CIP 数据核字第 2025DK0335 号

出 版 人	王　芳
项目策划	周渝毅
责任编辑	郭芮萱
责任校对	宋微微
装帧设计	奇文云海
出版发行	外语教学与研究出版社
社　　址	北京市西三环北路 19 号（100089）
网　　址	https://www.fltrp.com
印　　刷	天津善印科技有限公司
开　　本	710×1000　1/16
印　　张	49.5
字　　数	1030 千字
版　　次	2025 年 6 月第 1 版
印　　次	2025 年 6 月第 1 次印刷
书　　号	ISBN 978-7-5213-6380-7
定　　价	88.00 元

如有图书采购需求，图书内容或印刷装订问题，侵权、盗版书籍等线索，请拨打以下电话或关注官方服务号：
客服电话：400 898 7008
官方服务号：微信搜索并关注公众号"外研社官方服务号"
外研社购书网址：https://fltrp.tmall.com

物料号：363800001

毛泽东在保安。这张著名的照片是 1936 年斯诺于保安期间拍摄的。
Mao Tse-tung at Pao An. This famous photo was taken by Edgar Snow at Pao An in 1936.

▲ 朱德在训练一个红军分队
Chu Teh Training a Detachment of Red Army Soldiers.

▶▶ 周恩来在保安（1936 年斯诺摄）
Chou En-lai at Pao An. Photo by Edgar Snow in 1936.

▶▶▶ 1936 年斯诺在保安，时年 31 岁。斯诺所戴的这顶红军军帽后来在他为毛泽东拍摄那张著名照片时，被他戴在了毛泽东的头上。这顶军帽被洛伊丝·斯诺捐赠给了北京的中国革命历史博物馆（今中国国家博物馆）。
Edgar Snow, Age 31, at Pao An, 1936. He was wearing the Red Army cap he later placed on Mao Tse-tung's head when he took the famous photo of Mao. The cap was donated by Lois Snow to the National Museum of Chinese Revolution and History in Beijing (now the National Museum of China).

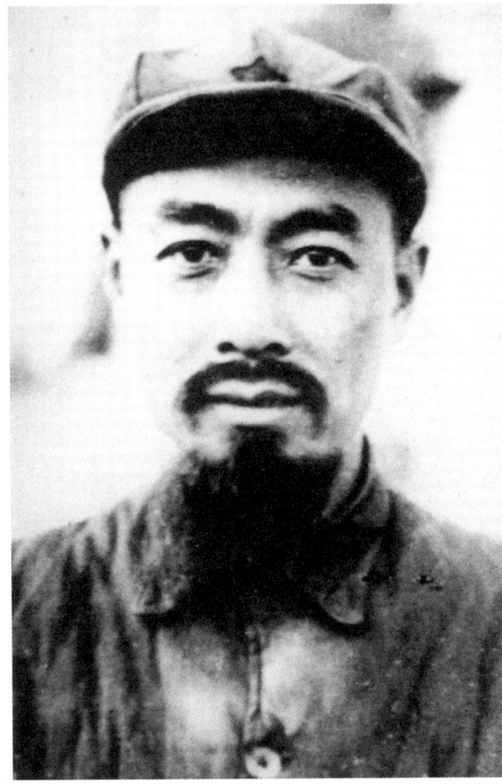

▸▸

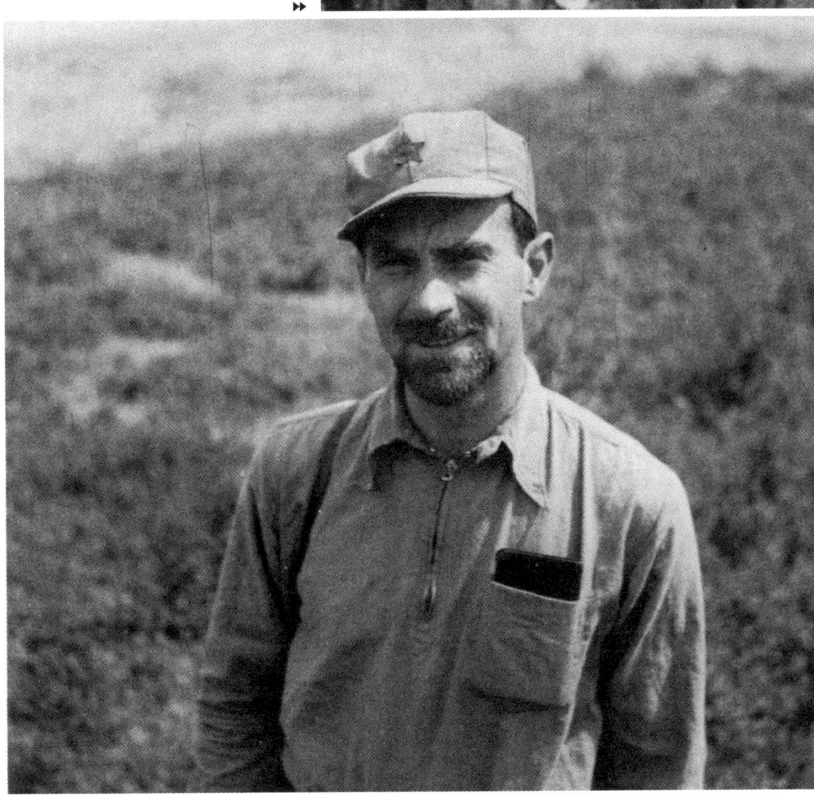

▸▸▸

▲ 毛泽东在陕北向战士讲话（1936 年斯诺摄）
Mao Tse-tung Addressing His Troops in North Shensi. Photo by Edgar Snow in 1936.

▲ 毛泽东与夫人贺子珍在保安（1936 年斯诺摄）
Mao Tse-tung and His Wife, Ho Tzu-chen, at Pao An. Photo by Edgar Snow in 1936.

陕北苏维埃边区附近哨所门口的红色哨兵（1936年斯诺摄）
A Red Sentry Framed in the Doorway of an Army Outpost near the Soviet Frontier in North Shensi. Photo by Edgar Snow in 1936.

▲ 斯诺与林祖涵（林伯渠）在保安（1936 年摄）
Edgar Snow and Lin Tsu-han (Lin Po-chu) at Pao An in 1936.

▲ 黄华（左二）与斯诺在保安，另两人为谢觉哉（左一）和王林（左三）（1936 年摄）
Huang Hua (Second from Left) and Edgar Snow at Pao An in 1936, with Hsieh Chueh-tsai (First from Left) and Wang Lin (Third from Left).

▲ 蔡畅（左，李富春夫人，蔡和森之妹）在保安。时任妇女部部长。（1936 年斯诺摄）
Ts'ai Ch'ang (Left), Wife of Li Fu-ch'un and Sister of Ts'ai Ho-sen at Pao An. She was Head of Women's Federation. Photo by Edgar Snow in 1936.

▲ ▲ 邓颖超等人在保安
Teng Ying-ch'ao et al. at Pao An.

陕北的红军机关枪班（1936年斯诺摄）
Red Army Machine Gun Squad in North Shensi. Photo by Edgar Snow in 1936.

▲ 保安贫农子女在学习认字（1936年斯诺摄）
Poor Peasant Children Learning to Read at Pao An. Photo by Edgar Snow in 1936.

▲ 保安的"红小鬼"（1936年斯诺摄）
"Little Red Devils" at Pao An. Photo by Edgar Snow in 1936.

▲ 陕北的工厂女工（1936年斯诺摄）
Girl Workers in Factories in North Shensi. Photo by Edgar Snow in 1936.

"土匪"网球手:保安的红军大学学员(1936年斯诺摄)
"Bandit" Tennis Players: Red Army University Cadets at Pao An. Photo by Edgar Snow in 1936.

女子大学的露天教室（1936年斯诺摄）
Open-air Classroom of Women's University. Photo by Edgar Snow in 1936.

保安的抗大校门
Entrance to "K'ang Ta"—Military Academy—at Pao An.

▲ 保安的红军军校学员（1936年斯诺摄）
Red Army Cadets at Pao An. Photo by Edgar Snow in 1936.

▲ 红军军校学员在保安聆听林彪讲话（1936年斯诺摄）
Red Army Cadets Listening to a Lecture by Lin Piao at Pao An. Photo by Edgar Snow in 1936.

▲ 保安的露天剧社（1936年斯诺摄）
Outdoor Theater at Pao An. Photo by Edgar Snow in 1936.

◀◀ 危拱之（人民抗日剧社社长）在保安（1936年摄）
Wei Kung-chih, Director of the People's Anti-Japanese Dramatic Society at Pao An in 1936.

中国西北的八路军哨兵
An 8th Route Army Sentry in Northwest China.

斯诺于 1965 年从中国内地抵达香港后接受记者提问
Edgar Snow Being Questioned by Press in Hongkong
as He Arrives from Chinese Mainland in 1965.

出版前言

1936 年 6 月，中国人民的老朋友、美国著名新闻记者埃德加·斯诺在战火纷飞中不畏艰险、只身深入红都保安（今陕西志丹县），实地采访了英勇的中国共产党人和苏区人民，亲历了苏区的斗争、生产和生活，收集了大量珍贵的历史资料和图片。后来斯诺回到北平，为英美报刊撰写了许多轰动一时的通讯报道，并突破敌人的重重封锁，向全世界澄清了关于红色中国的种种谜团，客观公正地传达了红色中国的声音。1937 年 10 月，这些报道被汇集成书，取名 *Red Star Over China*，由英国伦敦戈兰茨公司出版，随即轰动世界。1938 年初，经斯诺同意，在胡愈之等同志的推动下，本书中译本于上海以"复社"名义出版。鉴于当时的环境，中译本使用了比较隐晦的书名——《西行漫记》。从此，《西行漫记》和埃德加·斯诺便成了中国家喻户晓的名字。

2025 年是中国人民抗日战争暨世界反法西斯战争胜利 80 周年，也是埃德加·斯诺诞辰 120 周年。为纪念这一重要时刻，外语教学与研究出版社（以下简称"外研社"）对本社 2005 年出版的《西行漫记》（英汉对照版）（以下简称"2005 年版"）进行升级，推出《西行漫记》（英汉对照·有声纪念版）（以下简称"有声纪念版"）。

有声纪念版沿用 2005 年版文字内容，其中英文部分采用埃德加·斯诺 1968 年修订本内容；中文部分则采用著名翻译家董乐山先生的译本，其底本为 1937 年英国戈兰茨公司出版的英文初版。

董氏译本今已成为经典，有声纪念版尽可能保留了董氏译文的完整性，尽量为广大读者呈现原译文的大家风范。然而由于中英版本的差异，本书呈现的中英文内容无法完全对照，译文与原文有明显出入之处皆以不同字体标出。尽管如此，我们有时仍不得不忍痛割爱，对译文（包括部分脚注）作必要的删改，或安排补译。其中，"费正清序"、

"修订版序"、第二篇第二章中关于周恩来生平的内容、第三篇第二章"共产党的基本政策"的前半部分、第十篇第四章"关于朱德"、"后记（1944年）"和"深访毛泽东"便是由外研社副编审车云峰翻译的。

需要注意的是，《西行漫记》是新闻报道类作品，不同于历史著作。由于采访时的交流问题、叙述者的记忆偏差以及辗转传闻中的信息衰减等诸多因素，其中难免有失实之处，有些事实已经无从考证。然而，正如斯诺在"修订版序"中所说，"文中可以进行许多改进，最大限度地减少它的不足——不过同时也会使其丧失它可能拥有的原有价值"，所以我们原则上采用了斯诺1968年修订本的全部内容。我们深信，广大读者会以鉴别的眼光看待书中所述内容。

值此中国人民抗日战争暨世界反法西斯战争胜利80周年、埃德加·斯诺诞辰120周年之际，外研社对2005年版《西行漫记》进行了全面升级：修订个别疏漏，重新设计版式与封面，增加全书配套英文音频。此次升级既拓展了经典作品的多元使用场景，也为读者带来了更为丰富的阅读体验，更是对那段峥嵘岁月的重要纪念。

最后，我们要特别感谢埃德加·斯诺先生的家人Sian Snow女士、董乐山先生的家人凌励君女士对本书的倾力支持；感谢北京广播电视台外语广播中心副主任刘智嘉女士的热心相助；感谢Eric Foster先生的古道热肠。正是诸位的不懈努力与全力支持，这部经典才得以以新的面貌走近读者。

目录

费正清序　XXVIII
修订版序　XXXIV

第一篇
探寻红色中国

一、一些未获解答的问题　002
二、去西安的慢车　012
三、汉代青铜　024
四、通过红色大门　040

第二篇
去红都的道路

一、遭白匪追逐　056
二、造反者　068
三、贺龙二三事　084
四、红军旅伴　094

第三篇
在保安

一、苏维埃掌权人物　104
二、共产党的基本政策　120
三、论抗日战争　136
四、悬赏200万元的首级　152
五、红军剧社　162

第四篇
一个共产党员的由来

一、童年　178
二、在长沙的日子　198
三、革命的前奏　218

contents

Introduction by Dr. John K. Fairbank   XXIX
Preface to the Revised Edition   XXXV

Part One:
In Search of Red China

1. Some Unanswered Questions   003
2. Slow Train to "Western Peace"   013
3. Some Han Bronzes   025
4. Through Red Gates   041

Part Two:
The Road to the Red Capital

1. Chased by White Bandits   057
2. The Insurrectionist   069
3. Something About Ho Lung   085
4. Red Companions   095

Part Three:
In "Defended Peace"

1. Soviet Strong Man   105
2. Basic Communist Policies   121
3. On War with Japan   137
4. $2,000,000 in Heads   153
5. Red Theater   163

Part Four:
Genesis of a Communist

1. Childhood   179
2. Days in Changsha   199
3. Prelude to Revolution   219

　　　　　　　　　　　　四、国民革命时期　230

　　　　　　　　　　　　五、苏维埃运动　242

　　　　　　　　　　　　六、红军的成长　258

第五篇　　　　　　　　　一、第五次"围剿"　278

长征　　　　　　　　　　二、举国大迁移　288

　　　　　　　　　　　　三、大渡河英雄　296

　　　　　　　　　　　　四、过大草地　308

第六篇　　　　　　　　　一、陕西苏区：开创时期　324

红星在西北　　　　　　　二、死亡和捐税　334

　　　　　　　　　　　　三、苏维埃社会　344

　　　　　　　　　　　　四、货币解剖　360

　　　　　　　　　　　　五、人生五十始！　372

第七篇　　　　　　　　　一、同红色农民谈话　384

去前线的路上　　　　　　二、苏区工业　394

　　　　　　　　　　　　三、"他们唱得太多了"　402

第八篇　　　　　　　　　一、"真正的"红军　412

同红军在一起　　　　　　二、彭德怀印象　424

　　　　　　　　　　　　三、为什么当红军？　432

　　　　　　　　　　　　四、游击战术　442

　　　　　　　　　　　　五、红军战士的生活　454

　　　　　　　　　　　　六、政治课　464

第九篇　　　　　　　　　一、红色窑工徐海东　478

同红军在一起（续）　　　二、中国的阶级战争　490

　　　　　　　　　　　　三、四大马　500

　　　　　　　　　　　　四、穆斯林和马克思主义者　508

4. The Nationalist Period   231

5. The Soviet Movement   243

6. Growth of the Red Army   259

Part Five:
The Long March

1. The Fifth Campaign   279

2. A Nation Emigrates   289

3. The Heroes of Tatu   297

4. Across the Great Grasslands   309

Part Six:
Red Star
in the Northwest

1. The Shensi Soviets: Beginnings   325

2. Death and Taxes   335

3. Soviet Society   345

4. Anatomy of Money   361

5. Life Begins at Fifty!   373

Part Seven:
En Route
to the Front

1. Conversation with Red Peasants   385

2. Soviet Industries   395

3. "They Sing Too Much"   403

Part Eight:
With the
Red Army

1. The "Real" Red Army   413

2. Impression of P'eng Teh-huai   425

3. Why Is a Red?   433

4. Tactics of Partisan Warfare   443

5. Life of the Red Warrior   455

6. Session in Politics   465

Part Nine:
With the Red
Army (Continued)

1. Hsu Hai-tung, the Red Potter   479

2. Class War in China   491

3. Four Great Horses   501

4. Moslem and Marxist   509

第十篇 ── 一、再谈马　520
战争与和平 　二、"红小鬼"　526
　　　　　　　　三、实践中的统一战线　538
　　　　　　　　四、关于朱德　548

第十一篇 ── 一、路上的邂逅　564
回到保安 　二、保安的生活　574
　　　　　　　　三、俄国的影响　582
　　　　　　　　四、中国共产主义运动和共产国际　592
　　　　　　　　五、那个外国智囊　600
　　　　　　　　六、别了，红色中国　606

第十二篇 ── 一、兵变前奏　618
又是白色世界 　二、总司令被逮　632
　　　　　　　　三、蒋、张和共产党　644
　　　　　　　　四、"针锋相对"　656
　　　　　　　　五、《友谊地久天长》？　666
　　　　　　　　六、红色的天际　674

后记（1944 年）　692
深访毛泽东　708
尾注　关于朱德　722

Part Ten:
War and Peace

1. More About Horses   521
2. "Little Red Devils"   527
3. United Front in Action   539
4. Concerning Chu Teh   549

Part Eleven:
Back to Pao An

1. Casuals of the Road   565
2. Life in Pao An   575
3. The Russian Influence   583
4. Chinese Communism and the Comintern   593
5. That Foreign Brain Trust   601
6. Farewell to Red China   607

Part Twelve:
White
World Again

1. A Preface to Mutiny   619
2. The Generalissimo Is Arrested   633
3. Chiang, Chang, and the Reds   645
4. "Point Counter Point"   657
5. "Auld Lang Syne"?   667
6. Red Horizons   675

Epilogue (1944)   693
Further Interviews with Mao Tse-tung   709
Endnote   Concerning Chu Teh   723

费正清序

《西行漫记》之所以是一部经典之作，在于它成书的方式。埃德加·斯诺当年只有30岁，在中国已经做了7年的记者。1936年，中国共产党人刚刚完成了他们从中国东南部到西北地区的胜利大逃亡，正在着手推行他们的统一战线策略。他们准备将自己的故事讲给外部世界听。斯诺有报道这个故事的能力。本书读者应该注意到这一多种因素的综合作用。

埃德加·斯诺于1905年生于堪萨斯城，他的先辈从北卡罗来纳逐渐地向西部迁移，先是到了肯塔基州，之后又到了堪萨斯州。1928年，斯诺开始环游世界。他到了上海，成了一名记者，从此13年间都没有离开过远东地区。在踏上报道中国共产党人的旅途之前，他已经走遍了西北的饥荒地区，在滇缅公路通车10年之前便穿过了它的路线，报道了1932年不宣而战的战争，成为了《星期六晚邮报》的一名记者。当时他已经成为孙夫人（宋庆龄）的朋友，结识了无数的中国知识分子和作家。1932年在北平安顿下来之后，他与夫人居住在燕京大学附近，这是一所一流的基督教大学，是在美国教会的资助下成立的。作为活力四射、高度清醒的美国年轻一代，斯诺夫妇广泛了解了1935年末中国学生抗击日本侵略者的运动。他们学过汉语，口语比较流畅。除了发表描写日本侵略的《远东前线》之外，埃德加·斯诺还编辑了一部现代中国短篇小说译文集，即《活的中国》。

因此，在日本在东北扩张势力进而侵入华北这些事件占据报刊标题位置的这样一个时期，这位年轻的美国人不仅报道了当时所发生的事件，而且深入这些事件之后，在某种程度上触及了中国爱国青年的精神和情感。事实证明，他是一位具有博大的人类同情心的年轻人，他意识到了中国知识分子中间革命的脉动，能够利用一些基本的汉语知识与他们交流。不仅如此，埃德加·斯诺还是一位活动家，时刻准备帮助各种

Introduction by Dr. John K. Fairbank

Red Star Over China is a classic because of the way in which it was produced. Edgar Snow was just thirty and had spent seven years in China as a journalist. In 1936 the Chinese Communists had just completed their successful escape from Southeast China to the Northwest, and were embarking upon their united-front tactic. They were ready to tell their story to the outside world. Snow had the capacity to report it. Readers of the book today should be aware of this combination of factors.

Edgar Snow was born in Kansas City in 1905, his forebears having moved westward by degrees from North Carolina to Kentucky and then into Kansas territory. In 1928 he started around the world. He reached Shanghai, became a journalist, and did not leave the Far East for thirteen years. Before he made his trip to report the Chinese Communists, he had toured through famine districts in the Northwest, traversed the route of the Burma Road ten years before it was operating, reported the undeclared war at Shanghai in 1932, and become a correspondent for the *Saturday Evening Post*. He had become a friend of Mme. Sun and had met numerous Chinese intellectuals and writers. Settling in Peking in 1932, he and his wife lived near Yenching University, one of the leading Christian colleges which had been built up under American missionary auspices. As energetic and wide-awake young Americans, the Snows had become widely acquainted with the Chinese student movement against Japanese aggression in late 1935. They had studied Chinese and developed a modest fluency in speaking. In addition to publishing his account of the Japanese aggression, *Far Eastern Front*, Edgar Snow had also edited a collection of translations of modern Chinese short stories, *Living China*.

Thus in the period when the Japanese expansion over Manchuria and into North China dominated the headlines, this young American had not only reported the events of the day but had got behind them into some contact with the minds and feelings of Chinese patriotic youth. He had proved himself a young man of broad human sympathy, aware of the revolutionary stirrings among China's intellectuals, and able to meet them with some elementary use of the Chinese language. More than this, Ed Snow was an activist, ready to encourage worthy causes rather than be a purely passive

可敬的事业，而不是做一名袖手旁观的看客。最难得的是，他以行动证明了自己是一位热诚的事实报道者，能够评价时局的大趋势，又绘声绘色地呈现给广大美国读者。

1936 年，他站立在美国跨越太平洋向亚洲扩张的西部前沿，经过美国整整一个世纪在商业、外交和传教方面的努力，这个扩张当时已经达到顶峰。本世纪（20 世纪）美国与各个通商口岸的联系日渐紧密，外国人在通商口岸仍然保留着他们的种种特权。传教士已经深入中国不计其数的村庄中间的农村内陆地区，启蒙并参与了旨在现代化的初始尝试。20 世纪 30 年代初，美国的基金会和传教士在"农村重建"运动中都非常活跃，这项运动旨在通过将科学技术应用于土地问题而重塑农村生活。与此同时，留学美国及其他西方国家的中国学生站立在那些日益坚定地不惜一切代价抗击日本侵略的现代爱国者的最前列。就这样，西方式的民族主义与西方技术结合了起来，成为中国舞台上的一股现代力量，而二者都是由于美国的关系而促成的。

虽然取得了所有这些进展，但是，在新成立的南京国民政府的保护之下，中国农村最严重的问题才刚刚开始受到冲击。困于日本侵略的烦恼，蒋介石和国民党被迫集中精力进行防御，重点集中在沿海通商口岸和长江下游各省，根本就没有要在农村地区进行革命性变革的想法或动机。与此同时，1936 年，中国共产党人一般都被称为"赤匪"，没有哪位西方观察家直接接触过他们的领导层，也没有谁将它报道给外部世界。以 1/3 个世纪的后见之明来看，现在我们似乎会觉得几乎不可思议，毛泽东及其领导的运动为外界所知的竟如此之少。当埃德加·斯诺抵达中国共产党的总部时，她已经有了 15 年的历史，但是 20 年代突然袭向她的那场灾难使她陷入了风雨飘摇之中。

1936 年 6 月，当斯诺带着孙逸仙夫人的一封引见信踏上前往被封锁的红区的旅途时，他已经熟悉了中国的国情和中国青年的情绪，这使他几乎可以独一无二地来洞察中国共产主义运动仍在不断增强之中的强大吸引力。凭借西安的东北军（在心理上这支军队是准备与共产党结成某种形式的统一战线的）的善意，斯诺得以穿越封锁线，到达了红色首都，当时的保安（比后来的首都延安还要偏向西北），刚好在毛泽东准备让人对自己进行报道的时候见到了他。

斯诺在保安度过了 4 个月，记录下了毛泽东作为革命者的生平，于 1936 年 10 月离开被封锁的红区。他以文章的形式将他令人大开眼界的故事讲给新闻界，并于 1937 年 7 月在笔记的基础上写成了《西行漫记》。

spectator. Most of all, he had proved himself a zealous factual reporter, able to appraise the major trends of the day and describe them in vivid color for the American reading public.

In 1936 he stood on the western frontier of the American expansion across the Pacific toward Asia, which had reached its height after a full century of American commercial, diplomatic, and missionary effort. This century had produced an increasing American contact with the treaty ports, where foreigners still retained their special privileges. Missionaries had pushed into the rural interior among China's myriad villages and had inspired and aided the first efforts at modernization. In the early 1930's American foundations and missionaries both were active in the movement for "rural reconstruction," the remaking of village life through the application of scientific technology to the problems of the land. At the same time, Chinese students trained in the United States and other Western countries stood in the forefront of those modern patriots who were becoming increasingly determined to resist Japanese aggression at all costs. Western-type nationalism thus joined Western technology as a modern force in the Chinese scene, and both had been stimulated by the American contact.

Despite all these developments, however, the grievous problems of China's peasant villages had only begun to be attacked under the aegis of the new Nationalist Government at Nanking. Harassed by Japanese aggression, Chiang Kai-shek and the Kuomintang were absorbed in a defense effort which centered in the coastal treaty ports and lower Yangtze provinces, with little thought or motive for revolutionary change in the rural countryside. Meanwhile, in 1936, the Chinese Communists were known generally as "Red bandits," and no Western observer had had direct contact with their leadership or reported it to the outside world. With the hindsight of a third of a century, it may seem to us now almost incredible that so little could have been known about Mao Tse-tung and the movement which he headed. The Chinese Communist Party had a history of fifteen years when Edgar Snow journeyed to its headquarters, but the disaster which had overtaken it in the 1920's had left it in a precarious state of weakness.

When he set out for the blockaded Red area in the Northwest in June, 1936, with an introduction from Mme. Sun Yat-sen, he had an insight into Chinese conditions and the sentiments of Chinese youth which made him almost uniquely capable of perceiving the powerful appeal which the Chinese Communist movement was still in the process of developing. Through the good will of the Manchurian army forces at Sian, who were psychologically prepared for some kind of united front with the Communists, Snow was able to cross the lines, reach the Communist capital, then at Pao An (even farther in the Northwest than the later capital at Yenan), and meet Mao Tse-tung just at the time when Mao was prepared to put himself on record.

After spending four months and taking down Mao Tse-tung's own story of his life as a revolutionist, Snow came out of the blockaded Red area in October, 1936. He gave his eye-opening story to the press in articles, and finished *Red Star Over China* on the basis of his notes in July, 1937.

《西行漫记》的非凡之处在于，它不仅第一次呈现了关于毛泽东及其同志们的生平、他们的出身，而且描绘了这场鲜为人知的运动的前景，后来事实证明这是极具预言性的。由于埃德加·斯诺的努力，本书在这两个方面都经受住了时间的考验——一是作为对历史的记录；二是作为对历史趋势的预见。

The remarkable thing about *Red Star Over China* was that it not only gave the first connected history of Mao and his colleagues and where they had come from, but it also gave a prospect of the future of this little-known movement which was to prove disastrously prophetic. It is very much to the credit of Edgar Snow that this book has stood the test of time on both these counts — as a historical record and as an indication of a trend.

修订版序

本书所记旅行及事件发生于 1936 和 1937 年间，身居北平的我，在城墙之外日本军队的炮火声中于 1937 年 7 月完成了手稿。中国那年 7 月的枪炮声拉开了 8 年抗战的序幕，这场战争与第二次世界大战融为一体。同样是这些枪炮声预示着共产主义在中国的最终胜利，从而深刻地改变了过去所谓的"共产主义阵营"内外的力量对比。

在时间和空间上，这份报告报道的是远离处于极度灾难前夕的西方的一片土地上的一支孤立的作战力量。国际联盟在 1931 至 1933 年间未能阻止日本占领中国东北之后便宣告破产。1936 年，西方"盟国"允许羽翼未丰的希特勒不费一枪一弹便重新占领了莱茵兰地区。它们眼睁睁地看着墨索里尼强占了埃塞俄比亚。之后又打着中立的虚伪旗号，对西班牙实施了武器禁运，断绝了西班牙共和国用以抵抗以佛朗哥为首的反动军官的进攻的途径，而后者却拥有国外涌入的成千上万的纳粹士兵和飞机的公然支持。它们就是这样纵容希特勒和墨索里尼结成了联盟。这个联盟表面上是针对着俄国，但是却明白无疑地意在征服整个西欧。1938 年，它们听任希特勒吞并了奥地利。之后，希特勒又得到了张伯伦和达拉第的酬谢，捷克斯洛伐克被当作"我们这个时代的和平"的代价。作为回报，它们很快拿到了希特勒和斯大林签订的协约。

这便是此行开始时中国所面临的国际环境。那个支离破碎的社会的内部形势在正文中有详细说明。1936 年，我在中国已经生活了 7 年，作为一名外国记者我到过许多地方，掌握了汉语的一些知识。这是我对中国进行的最长的一段报道。如果说这段报道比大多数新闻文章更为有用的话，那就在于它不仅仅是"抢报"转瞬即逝的新闻，而且它同样报道了许多历久弥新的历史事实。它之所以赢得人们同情的眼光，或许还在于当时西方列强出于自身利益考虑，还期望中国会出现奇迹。它们幻想民族主义会获得新生，使日本陷入泥淖，从而再也无力进攻西方的殖民地——日本的真正目标。

Preface to the Revised Edition

Travels and events described in this book took place in 1936 and 1937 and the manuscript was completed in July, 1937, to the sound of gunfire by Japanese troops outside the walls of Peking, where I lived. Those guns of July in China opened eight years of Sino-Japanese battle which merged with the Second World War. The same guns also heralded the ultimate Communist victory in China which profoundly altered the balance of power, both inside and outside what was formerly called "the Communist camp."

In time and space this report concerned an isolated fighting force in an area far removed from the West on the eve of its greatest catastrophe. The League of Nations had been destroyed when it failed to halt Japan's conquest of Manchuria in 1931 - 1933. In 1936 the Western "Allies" permitted Hitler, still a cardboard Napoleon, to reoccupy the Rhineland without a fight. They impotently watched Mussolini seize Ethiopia. They then imposed an arms embargo against Spain under the hypocrisy of neutralism, which denied the Republic the means to defend itself against reactionary generals led by Franco, who had the open support of thousands of imported Nazi and Fascist troops and planes. They thus encouraged Hitler and Mussolini to form an alliance ostensibly aimed at Russia but clearly intended to subjugate all of Western Europe. In 1938 Hitler was allowed to swallow Austria. He was then rewarded, by Chamberlain and Daladier, with Czechoslovakia as the price of "peace in our time." In compensation they soon received the Hitler-Stalin pact.

Such was the international environment of China when this journey was undertaken. Domestic conditions inside that disintegrating society are defined in the text. In 1936 I had already lived in China for seven years and I had, as a foreign correspondent, traveled widely and acquired some knowledge of the language. This was my longest piece of reportage on China. If it has enjoyed a more useful life than most journalism it is because it was not only a "scoop" of perishable news but likewise of many facts of durable history. It won sympathetic attention also perhaps because it was a time when the Western powers, in self-interest, were hoping for a miracle in China. They dreamed of a new birth of nationalism that would keep Japan so bogged down that she would never be able

《西行漫记》意在展示中国共产党人的确能够提供那种有效抵抗日本侵略所需的民族主义领导才能。

其他一些情况也延长了本书的使用价值。我在一个特别有利的时刻——长年战争的间歇期——见到了毛泽东及其他领导人。他们给了我大量的时间，空前坦率地提供了个人及非个人的信息，信息量之大是任何外国记者都无法完全吸收的。我在1939年再次拜访毛泽东的时候，中国西北的所有红军根据地都被它们后方的国民党军队封锁了，游击区周围也被日本占领区给切断了。在接下来的5年里，由于没有外国记者能够到达红都延安，所以这些报道仍然是独家新闻。

当然，本书所讲述的多半是从党派的观点来看的历史，但是这是创造了它的那些男男女女们所亲身经历过的历史。它不仅为非中国的读者，而且也为全中国人民——包括除了共产党领导人自身以外的所有人——提供了对中国共产党第一手的真实描述，提供了第一手关于他们为在中国3,000年的历史中实现最彻底的社会革命而长期斗争的事迹。中国出版了许多版本，在成千上万的汉语译作之中，一些完全是在游击区产生的。

我并不觉得自己与赋予本书如此之多的国际教益有多大关系。因为有许多页我只是记下我从那些非凡的年轻男女那里所听到的，30岁的时候我有幸与他们生活在一起，从他们那里了解到（或者有机会了解到）许多东西。

1937年，当《西行漫记》首次在英格兰面世时，对于这里提供的大部分材料几乎没有可供参考的资料来源。今天许多外国的中国问题专家——在不同政治色彩的中国学者的帮助或引导下——已经创作了数十部分量和质量参差不齐的著作。如今有了大量的新信息，在我本人及其他人的后见之明的帮助下，文中可以进行许多改进，最大限度地减少它的不足——不过同时也会使其丧失它可能拥有的原有价值。因此除了对印刷错误和拼写错误或者事实细节谬误进行更正之外，我有意保留其当初写就时的原貌。事实表明，这种希望并不是完全行得通，对于希望的偏离谨收录于下。

…………

自从在战火中完成《西行漫记》之后，我一直没有机会看到或纠正第一版的长条校样。对于其后其他的版本我也是直到现在才有机会这么做。

to turn upon the Western colonies—her true objectives. *Red Star Over China* tended to show that the Chinese Communists could indeed provide that *nationalist* leadership needed for effective anti-Japanese resistance.

Other circumstances contributed to prolong the utility of this book. I had found Mao Tse-tung and other leaders at an especially favorable moment, in a lull between long years of battle. They gave me a vast amount of their time, and with unprecedented frankness provided more personal and impersonal information than any one foreign scribe could fully absorb. After my second visit to see Mao Tse-tung, in 1939, all the Red bases in Northwest China were blockaded by Nationalist troops, in their rear, and cut off by Japanese occupation around the guerrilla areas. For another five years, while no foreign newsmen were able to reach Yenan, the Red capital, these reports remained a unique source.

Much of this work is history seen from a partisan point of view, of course, but it is history as lived by the men and women who made it. It provided not only for non-Chinese readers, but also for the entire Chinese people—including all but the Communist leaders themselves—the first authentic account of the Chinese Communist Party and the first connected story of their long struggle to carry through the most thorough going social revolution in China's three millenniums of history. Many editions were published in China, and among the tens of thousands of copies of the Chinese translations some were produced entirely in guerrilla territory.

I do not flatter myself that I had much to do with imparting to this volume such lessons of international application as may be drawn from it. For many pages I simply wrote down what I was told by the extraordinary young men and women with whom it was my privilege to live at age thirty, and from whom I learned (or had the chance to learn) a great deal.

In 1937, when *Red Star Over China* first appeared, in England, there were practically no sources of documentation for most of the material presented here. Today many foreign China specialists—helped or led by Chinese scholars of different political colorations—have produced dozens of works of varying importance and quality. With an abundance of new information available, aided by my own and others' wisdom of hindsight, many improvements might be made in the text to minimize its limitations—and yet deprive it of whatever original value it may possess. Therefore it was my intention to leave it as first written except for corrections of typographical errors and mistakes of spelling or of factual detail. That hope has not proved wholly practicable and departures from its fulfillment are acknowledged below.

. . .

Since *Red Star Over China* was completed under conditions of war I did not have the opportunity to see or correct galley proofs of the first edition. Nor have I been able to do so with subsequent editions until now.

本书引用或者转述他人的话语时，原话的措辞一般都被保留了下来——以免篡改**先验的**历史材料——即便是它与更为可信的现有信息相冲突。在个别二手材料已被明确证明不准确的地方，我已作了删除或更正，而不是让明知的错误谬种流传。对于这两种情况，读者均可以参阅"人物小传"或者本版的注释，以补充或修正正文事实或观点。偶尔（怀着一种回首往昔的肃穆）我改写了某些句子，因为时间的流逝——或是因为第一种情况字迹模糊——已经使我无法理解了。本书的绝大部分，所有的事件、主要的旅行笔记、采访以及传记——包括毛泽东的传记——均未作改动。

我缩短、压缩或者删节了对一些不再重要的事件的冗长而乏味的描述，这使我得以有空间来插入"中国革命年表"、"后记"、新的脚注、一些至今尚未发表的文件、章节评论以及一些以传记续篇的形式出现的引人注目的历史文献[1]。段落甚至整页的删节使安排新的过渡段落成为必需。由此而产生的插入部分仅限于1937年之前我的知识范围，页面脚注也同样如此——但是这一点当然不适用于本书末尾的材料。

毫无疑问，即便我删去几个完整的章节，也不会给这个大部头造成什么损失（而且读者也会从中受益）。然而修订并非易事，想必让与这个主题不太相关的人删减起来，可能给他造成的痛苦会小一些，对读者也会有更大的裨益。

埃德加·斯诺

1968年2月14日于日内瓦

---

1. 由于种种原因，本对照版并未收录"中国革命年表"、章节评论等内容。——编注

Where the book quotes or paraphrases the testimony of others, the wording of the original text has generally been preserved—to avoid tampering with *a priori* historical material—even when it conflicts with more believable information now available. In a few instances where secondary material has been proved manifestly inaccurate I have cut or corrected, rather than perpetuate known errors. In either case readers may refer to the Biographical Notes or the Notes to this edition to supplement or modify some textual facts or opinions. Here and there (with a certain macabre sense of looking backward on myself) I have reworked lines which the passage of time—or murky writing in the first instance—has made unintelligible to me. The great bulk of the volume, all the happenings, the main travel notes, interviews, and biographies — including Mao Tse-tung's — remain intact.

Such liberties as I have taken in shortening, condensing, or discarding tedious accounts of a few matters no longer of importance helped to make room for the chronology, an epilogue, new footnotes, some heretofore unpublished documents, chapter commentaries, and some fascinating lessons of history in the form of biographical sequels. Cuts of paragraphs and even whole pages necessitated composing new transitional passages. Such "spin-ins" are confined to knowledge available to me no later than 1937, and the same applies to page footnotes—but not to the end-of-book materials, of course.

Doubtless this tome would not have suffered (and the reader would have profited) if I had omitted several whole chapters. Revision was not easy, and I daresay someone less connected with the subject could have done it with less pain to himself and with more grace for the reader.

Edgar Snow

Geneva, February 14, 1968

PART ONE
In Search of Red China

第一篇
探寻红色中国

一、　　一些未获解答的问题

我在中国的 7 年中间，关于中国红军、苏维埃和共产主义运动，人们提出过很多很多问题。热心的党人是能够向你提供一套现成的答案的，可是这些答案始终很难令人满意。他们是怎么**知道**的呢？他们可从来没有到过红色中国呀。

事实是，在世界各国中，恐怕没有比红色中国的情况是更大的谜，更混乱的传说了。中华天朝的红军在地球上人口最多的国度的腹地进行着战斗，9 年以来一直遭到铜墙铁壁一样严密的新闻封锁而与世隔绝。千千万万敌军所组成的一道活动长城时刻包围着他们。他们的地区比西藏还要难以进入。自从 1927 年 11 月中国的第一个苏维埃在湖南省东南部茶陵成立以来，还没有一个人自告奋勇，穿过那道长城，再回来报道他的经历。

哪怕是最简单的事情，也是有争议的。有些人否认红军的存在，认为根本没有这么一回事。只不过有几千名饥饿的土匪罢了。有些人甚至否认苏维埃的存在。这是共产党宣传的捏造。然而，亲共的人却称颂红军和苏维埃是中国要摆脱一切弊害祸患的唯一救星。在这样的宣传和反宣传中，要想了解真相的冷静的观察家就得不到可信的证据。关心东方政治及其瞬息万变的历史的人，都有这样一些感到兴趣而未获解答的问题：

中国的红军是不是一批自觉的马克思主义革命者，服从并遵守一个统一的纲领，受中国共产党的统一指挥的呢？如果是的，那么那个纲领是什么？共产党人自称是在为实现土地革命，为反对帝国主义，为争取苏维埃民主和民族解放而斗争。南京却说，红军不过是由"文匪"领导的一种新式流寇。究竟谁是谁非？还是不管哪一方都是对的？

1   SOME UNANSWERED QUESTIONS

During my seven years in China, hundreds of questions had been asked about the Chinese Red Army, the Soviets, and the Communist movement. Eager partisans could supply you with a stock of ready answers, but these remained highly unsatisfactory. How did they *know*? They had never been to Red China.

The fact was that there had been perhaps no greater mystery among nations, no more confused an epic, than the story of Red China. Fighting in the very heart of the most populous nation on earth, the Celestial Reds had for nine years been isolated by a news blockade as effective as a stone fortress. A wall of thousands of enemy troops constantly surrounded them; their territory was more inaccessible than Tibet. No one had voluntarily penetrated that wall and returned to write of his experiences since the first Chinese soviet was established in southeastern Hunan, in November, 1927.

Even the simplest points were disputed. Some people denied that there was such a thing as a Red Army. There were only thousands of hungry brigands. Some denied even the existence of soviets. They were an invention of Communist propaganda. Yet Red sympathizers extolled both as the only salvation for all the ills of China. In the midst of this propaganda and counterpropaganda, credible evidence was lacking for dispassionate observers seeking the truth. Here are some of the unanswered questions that interested everyone concerned with politics and the quickening history of the Orient:

Was or was not this Red Army of China a mass of conscious Marxist revolutionaries, disciplined by and adhering to a centralized program and a unified command under the Chinese Communist Party? If so, what was that program? The Communists claimed to be fighting for agrarian revolution, and against imperialism, and for soviet democracy and national emancipation. Nanking said that the Reds were only a new type of vandals and marauders led by "intellectual bandits." Who was right? Or was either one?

在 1927 年以前，共产党员是容许参加国民党的，但在那年 4 月，开始了那场著名的"清洗"。共产党员，以及无党派激进知识分子和成千成万有组织的工人农民，都遭当时在南京夺取政权的右派政变领袖蒋介石的大规模处决。从那时起，做一个共产党员或共产党的同情者，就是犯了死罪，而且确实有成千成万的人受到了这个惩罚。然而，仍有成千成万的人继续甘冒这种风险。成千成万的农民、工人、学生、士兵参加了红军，同南京政府的军事独裁进行武装斗争。这是为什么？有什么不可动摇的力量推动他们豁出性命去拥护这种政见呢？国民党和共产党的基本争论究竟是什么？[1]

中国共产党人究竟是什么样的人？他们同其他地方的共产党人或社会党人有哪些地方相像，哪些地方不同？旅游者问的是，他们是不是留着长胡子，是不是喝汤的时候发出咕嘟咕嘟的响声，是不是在皮包里夹带土制炸弹。认真思索的人想知道，他们是不是"纯正的"马克思主义者。他们读过《资本论》和列宁的著作没有？他们有没有一个彻底的社会主义经济纲领？他们是斯大林派还是托洛茨基派？或者两派都不是呢？他们的运动真是世界革命的一个有机部分吗？他们是真正的国际主义者吗？或"不过是莫斯科的工具"，或者主要是为中国的独立而斗争的民族主义者？

这些战士战斗得那么长久，那么顽强，那么勇敢，而且——正如各种色彩的观察家所承认的，就连蒋介石总司令自己的部下私下也承认的——从整体说来是那么无敌，他们到底是什么样的人？是什么使他们那样地战斗？是什么支持着他们？他们的运动的革命基础是什么？是什么样的希望，什么样的目标，什么样的理想，使他们成为顽强到令人难以置信的战士的呢？说令人难以置信，是同中国的那部充满折中妥协的历史比较而言的，但他们却身经百战，经历过封锁、缺盐、饥饿、疾病、瘟疫，最后还有那 6,000 英里的历史性"长征"，穿过中国的 12 个省份，冲破千千万万国民党军队的阻拦，终于胜利地出现在西北的一个强大的新根据地上。

他们的领导人是谁？他们是不是对于一种理想、一种意识形态、一种学说抱着热烈信仰的受过教育的人？他们是社会先知，还是只不过是为了活命而盲目战斗的无知农民？例如，毛泽东，南京通缉名单上的第一号"赤匪"，蒋介石悬赏 25 万元

---

1. 国民党是孙逸仙博士等人所建立，掌握 1924—1927 年所谓国民革命的领导权。共产党创建于 1921 年，在国民革命中是国民党的主要盟友。

Before 1927, members of the Communist Party were admitted to the Kuomintang, but in April of that year there began a great "purgation." Communists, as well as unorganized radical intellectuals and thousands of organized workers and peasants, were executed on an extensive scale under Chiang Kai-shek, the leader of a Right *coup d'état* which seized power, to form a "National Government" at Nanking. Since then it had been a crime punishable by death to be a Communist or a Communist sympathizer, and thousands had paid that penalty. Yet thousands more continued to run the risk. Thousands of peasants, workers, students, and soldiers joined the Red Army in armed struggle against the military dictatorship of the Nanking regime. Why? What inexorable force drove them on to support suicidal political opinions? What were the fundamental quarrels between the Kuomintang and the Kungch'antang?[1]

What were the Chinese Communists like? In what way did they resemble, in what way were they unlike, Communists or Socialists elsewhere? The tourist asked if they wore long beards, made noises with their soup, and carried homemade bombs in their briefcases. The serious-minded wanted to know whether they were "genuine" Marxists. Did they read *Capital* and the works of Lenin? Had they a thoroughly Socialist economic program? Were they Stalinites or Trotskyites? Or neither? Was their movement really an organic part of the World Revolution? Were they true internationalists? "Mere tools of Moscow," or primarily nationalists struggling for an independent China?

Who were these warriors who had fought so long, so fiercely, so courageously, and—as admitted by observers of every color, and privately among Generalissimo Chiang Kai-shek's own followers—on the whole so invincibly? What made them fight like that? What held them up? What was the revolutionary basis of their movement? What were the hopes and aims and dreams that had made of them the incredibly stubborn warriors—incredible compared with the history of compromise that is China—who had endured hundreds of battles, blockade, salt shortage, famine, disease, epidemic, and finally the Long March of 6,000 miles, in which they crossed twelve provinces of China, broke through thousands of Kuomintang troops, and triumphantly emerged at last into a new base in the Northwest?

Who were their leaders? Were they educated men with a fervent belief in an ideal, an ideology, and a doctrine? Social prophets, or mere ignorant peasants blindly fighting for an existence? What kind of man was Mao Tse-tung, No. 1 "Red bandit" on Nanking's list, for whose capture, dead or alive, Chiang Kai-shek offered a reward of a quarter of a million

---

1. The Kuomintang, or "National People's Party," founded by Dr. Sun Yat-sen and others, held the hegemony of power in the so-called Great Revolution, 1924—1927. The Kungch'antang, "Share Production Party," or the Communist Party of China, founded in 1921, was the chief ally of the Kuomintang, 1924—1927.

银洋[1]不论死活要缉拿到他，他是怎样的人呢？那个价值这么高昂的东方人脑袋里到底有些什么名堂呢？或者像南京官方宣布的那样，毛泽东真的已经死了吗？朱德，称作红军总司令的这个人的生命在南京看来具有同样的价值，他又是怎样的人呢？林彪[2]这个28岁的红军天才战术家，据说在他率领下的红军一军团从来没有打过一次败仗，他又是谁？他的来历如何？还有其他许多红军领导人，多次报道已经毙命，可是又在新闻报道中重新出现，不但毫毛无损，而且仍旧在指挥着新的军队同国民党对抗，他们又是些什么人呢？

红军抗击优势极大的军事联合力量达9年之久，这个非凡的记录应该拿什么来解释呢？红军没有任何大工业基地，没有大炮，没有毒气，没有飞机，没有金钱，也没有南京在同他们作战时能利用的现代技术，他们是怎样生存下来并扩大了自己的队伍的呢？他们采用了什么样的军事战术？他们是怎样训练的？是谁给他们当顾问的？他们里面有一些俄国军事天才吗？是谁领导他们在谋略上不但胜过所有被派来同他们作战的国民党将领，而且胜过蒋介石重金聘请来的、以前由希特勒已故的国防军头目冯·泽克特将军[3]领导的大批外国顾问？

中国的苏维埃是怎样的？农民支持它吗？如果不支持，那么是什么力量在维系住它的？共产党在他们的权力已经巩固的地区实行"社会主义"达到什么程度？为什么红军没有攻占大城市？这是不是证明红军不是真正由无产阶级领导的运动，而基本上仍然是农民的造反呢？中国有80%以上的人口仍然是农业人口，工业体系即使不说是患小儿麻痹症，也还是穿着小儿衫裤，在这样的国家怎么谈得上"共产主义"或"社会主义"呢？

共产党怎样穿衣？怎样吃饭？怎样娱乐？怎样恋爱？怎样工作？他们的婚姻法是怎样的？他们的妇女真的像国民党宣传所说的那样是被"共妻"的吗？中国的"红色工厂"是怎样的？红色剧团是怎样的？他们是怎样组织经济的？公共卫生、娱乐、教育和"红色文化"，又是怎样的？

红军的兵力有多少？真像共产国际出版物所吹嘘的那样有50万人吗？果真如此，他们为什么没有能夺取政权呢？他们的武器和弹药是从哪里来的？它是一支有纪律的军队吗？它的士气怎么样？官兵生活真是一样吗？如果像蒋介石总司令在

---
1. 元当时被外国人称为"dollar"，约合0.35美元。
2. 林彪后来叛党叛国，于1971年9月13日私乘飞机外逃，摔死在蒙古的温都尔汗。——译注
3. 后来是冯·法尔肯豪森。

silver dollars?[1] What went on inside that highly priced Oriental head? Or was Mao really already dead, as Nanking officially announced? What was Chu Teh like—the commander-in-chief of the Red Army, whose life had the same value to Nanking? What about Lin Piao, the twenty-eight-year-old Red tactician whose famous First Red Army Corps was said never to have suffered a defeat? Where did he come from? Who were the many other Red leaders repeatedly reported dead, only to reappear in the news—unscathed and commanding new forces against the Kuomintang?

What explained the Red Army's remarkable record of resistance for nine years against vastly superior military combinations? Lacking any industrial base, big cannon, gas, airplanes, money, and the modern techniques which Nanking had utilized in its wars against them, how had these Reds survived, and increased their following? What military tactics did they use? How were they instructed? Who advised them? Were there some Russian military geniuses among them? Who led the outmaneuvering, not only of all Kuomintang commanders sent against them but also of Chiang Kai-shek's large and expensive staff of German advisers, headed first by General von Seeckt and later by General von Falkenhausen?

What was a Chinese soviet like? Did the peasants support it? If not, what held it together? To what degree did the Reds carry out "socialism" in districts where they had consolidated their power? Why hadn't the Red Army taken big cities? Did this prove that it wasn't a genuine proletarian-led movement, but fundamentally remained a peasant rebellion? How was it possible to speak of "communism" or "socialism" in China, where over 80 per cent of the population was still agrarian, where industrialism was still in infant garments—if not infantile paralysis?

How did the Reds dress? Eat? Play? Love? Work? What were their marriage laws? Were women "nationalized," as Kuomintang publicists asserted? What was a Chinese "Red factory"? A Red dramatic society? How did they organize their economy? What about public health, recreation, education, "Red culture"?

What was the strength of the Red Army? Half a million, as the Comintern publications boasted? If so, why had it not seized power? Where did it get arms and munitions? Was it a disciplined army? What about its morale? Was it true that officers and men lived alike?

---

1. The Chinese *yuan*, then called a "dollar" by foreigners, was worth about U. S. $.35.

1935年所宣布的那样，南京已经"消灭了'共匪'的威胁"，那么共产党到1937年在中国战略地位最重要的西北占领了一块比以前更大的整块土地，又怎样解释呢？如果共产党真的是完蛋了，那么，为什么日本在著名的广田弘毅[1]第三点中要求南京同东京和纳粹德国缔结反共协定以"防止亚洲布尔什维克化"呢？共产党是真正"反帝"的吗？他们真要同日本交战吗？在这场战争中，莫斯科会帮助他们吗？或者，像著名的胡适博士拼命说服他在北平的情绪激昂的学生那样，他们的激烈的抗日口号只不过是争取公众同情的诡计和绝望的挣扎，是亡命的汉奸和土匪的最后呼号？

中国共产主义运动的军事和政治前景如何？它的具有历史意义的发展是怎样的？它能成功吗？一旦成功，对我们意味着什么？对日本意味着什么？这种巨大的变化对世界1/5的人口会产生什么影响？它在世界政治上会引起什么变化？在世界历史上会引起什么变化？它对英、美等外国在中国的巨额投资会产生什么后果？说真的，共产党究竟有没有"对外政策"呢？

最后，共产党倡议在中国建立"民族统一战线"，停止内战，这到底是什么意思？

相当一个时期以来，竟没有一个非共产党观察家能够有把握地、准确地，或是用亲身调查过的事实解答这些问题，这似乎是荒唐可笑的。因此，这里有一个日益使人感到兴趣和日益变得重要的值得采访的消息，正如记者们在无关紧要的枝节问题上发出电讯之余相互承认的一样，这是中国的**唯一**值得采访的消息。然而，我们大家对它却一无所知，实在令人可悲。要在"白"区同共产党人发生联系极为困难。

共产党人的头顶上随时笼罩着死刑的威胁，不论在上等社会里，或者在非上等社会里，他们都是不会暴露自己身份的。哪怕在外国租界里，南京也有出高价雇用的侦探网在那里活动，其中有C.帕特里克·吉文斯那样热心的反共分子，他原来是上海公共租界英国警务处中主要负责侦缉共产党的人。据说吉文斯督察每年要逮捕好几十个共产党嫌疑犯，大多数年龄在15岁到25岁之间，然后由国民党当局从租界引渡过去加以监禁或处死。1934年南京为了酬答这个有名警察的效劳，授给他一枚宝玉勋章和大量现款作为礼物。中国为了要缉拿本国的激进青年，雇用了不少外国侦探，吉文斯不过是其中的一个罢了。

---

1. 1933—1936年任日本外相。——译注

If, as Generalissimo Chiang announced in 1935, Nanking had "destroyed the menace of Communist banditry," what explained the fact that in 1937 the Reds occupied a bigger single unified territory (in China's most strategic Northwest) than ever before? If the Reds were finished, why did Japan demand, as the famous Third Point of Koki Hirota (Foreign Minister, 1933—1936), that Nanking form an anti-Red pact with Tokyo and Nazi Germany "to prevent the bolshevization of Asia"? Were the Reds really "anti-imperialist"? Did they want war with Japan? Would Moscow support them in such a war? Or were their fierce anti-Japanese slogans only a trick and a desperate attempt to win public sympathy, the last cry of demoralized traitors and bandits, as the eminent Dr. Hu Shih nervously assured his excited students in Peking?

What were the military and political perspectives of the Chinese Communist movement? What was the history of its development? Could it succeed? And just what would such success mean to us? To Japan? What would be the effect of this tremendous mutation upon a fifth (some said a fourth) of the world's inhabitants? What changes would it produce in world politics? In world history? How would it affect the vast British, American, and other foreign investment in China? Indeed, had the Reds any "foreign policy" at all?

Finally, what was the meaning of the Communists' offer to form a "National United Front" in China, and stop civil war?

For some time it had seemed ridiculous that not a single non-Communist observer could answer those questions with confidence, accuracy, or facts based on personal investigation. Here was a story, growing in interest and importance every day; here was *the* story of China, as newspaper correspondents admitted to each other between dispatches sent out on trivial side issues. Yet we were all woefully ignorant about it. To get in touch with Communists in the "White" areas was extremely difficult.

Communists, over whose heads hung the sentence of death, did not identify themselves as such in polite—or impolite—society. Even in the foreign concessions, Nanking kept a well-paid espionage system at work. It included, for example, such vigilantes as C. Patrick Givens, former chief Red-chaser in the British police force of Shanghai's International Settlement. Inspector Givens was each year credited with the arrest—and subsequent imprisonment or execution, after extradition from the Settlement by the Kuomintang authorities—of scores of alleged Communists, the majority of them between the ages of fifteen and twenty-five. He was only one of many foreign sleuths hired to spy upon young Chinese radicals and hunt them down in their own country.

我们都知道，要对红色中国有所了解，唯一的办法就是到那里去一趟。但我们推托说"没有法子"。有少数人尝试过，但失败了。这就被看成是做不到的事。大家都认为没有谁能够进了红区后活着回来的。在报纸受到像意大利或德国那样严格检查和管制的国家里，长年累月的反共宣传就有那么大的力量。

后来，到 1936 年 6 月，我的一位中国好友带给我中国西北出现了使人惊讶的政治局面的消息——这后来终于导致蒋介石总司令被扣的惊人事件，扭转了中国历史的潮流。但是，当时对我来说更重要的是，我在得到上述消息的同时，了解到我可能有办法进入红区。这需要我立即动身。机会千载难逢，不能错过。我决定抓住这个机会，设法打破这一已经持续了 9 年的新闻封锁。

我那样做，确实是有危险的，不过后来报上发表我的死讯，说是"已遭土匪杀害"，那又太夸张了。但是多年来关于共产党暴行的恐怖故事层出不穷地充斥于中国那些领津贴的本国报纸和外国报纸，在这种情况下，我在旅途上很少有什么东西可以叫我感到放心的。说实在的，除了带着一封给苏维埃政府主席毛泽东的介绍信，确实没有什么东西可以叫我感到放心。我只要找到他就行了。这要经过怎样的冒险呢？我不知道。但是，在这些年的国共内战中，已经有千千万万的人牺牲了生命。为了要探明事情的真相，难道不值得拿一个外国人的脑袋去冒一下险吗？我发现我同这个脑袋正好有些联系，但是我的结论是，这个代价不算太高。

就是怀着这种冒险的心情，我出发了。

We all knew that the only way to learn anything about Red China was to go there. We excused ourselves by saying "*Mei yu fa-tzu*"—"It can't be done." A few had tried and failed. It was believed impossible. People thought that nobody could enter Red territory and come out alive.

Then, in June, 1936, a close Chinese friend of mine brought me news of an amazing political situation in Northwest China—a situation which was later to culminate in the sensational arrest of Generalissimo Chiang Kai-shek, and to change the current of Chinese history. More important to me then, however, I learned with this news of a possible method of entry to Red territory. It necessitated leaving at once. The opportunity was unique and not to be missed. I decided to take it and attempt to break a news blockade nine years old.

It is true there were risks involved, though the reports later published of my death—"killed by bandits"—were exaggerated. But against a torrent of horror stories about Red atrocities that had for many years filled the subsidized vernacular and foreign press of China, I had little to cheer me on my way. Nothing, in truth, but a letter of introduction to Mao Tse-tung, Chairman of the Soviet Government. All I had to do was to find him. Through what adventures? I did not know. But thousands of lives had been sacrificed in these years of Kuomintang-Communist warfare. Could one foreign neck be better hazarded than in an effort to discover why? I found myself somewhat attached to the neck in question, but I concluded that the price was not too high to pay.

In this melodramatic mood I set out.

二、　　去西安的慢车

　　那是6月初，北平披上了春天的绿装，无数的杨柳和巍峨的松柏把紫禁城变成了一个迷人的奇境；在许多清幽的花园里，人们很难相信在金碧辉煌的宫殿的大屋顶外边，还有一个劳苦的、饥饿的、革命的和受到外国侵略的中国。在这里，饱食终日的外国人，可以在自己的小小的世外桃源里过着喝威士忌酒掺苏打水、打马球和网球、闲聊天的生活，无忧无虑地完全不觉得这个伟大城市的无声的绝缘的城墙外面的人间脉搏——许多人也确实是这样生活的。

　　然而，在过去的一年里，就连北平这个绿洲，也难免那弥漫于全中国的战斗气氛的侵袭。日本征服的威胁，在人民中间，特别是在愤怒的青年中间，激起了盛大的示威抗议。几个月以前，我曾经站在那弹痕累累的内城城墙下，看到上万名学生在那里集合，他们不顾宪警的棍棒，齐声高呼："一致抗日！反对日本帝国主义分割华北的要求！"

　　北平的全部砖石屏障都阻挡不住中国红军试图穿过山西向长城挺进的这一惊人之举引起的反响。这次远征号称要对日作战，收复失地，但未免有些堂吉诃德味道，立即被蒋介石总司令十一个师的精锐新军所拦截，但是，这却阻止不了那些爱国学生，他们不怕坐牢，也不怕可能丢脑袋，大批走向街头，喊出了那被禁的口号："停止内战！国共合作抗日救国！"[1]

　　一天午夜，我登上了一列破败不堪的火车，身上有点不舒服，可是心里却非常

---

1. 1935年12月9日的学生示威运动，即"一二·九"运动，是一个有利于共产党的历史"转折点"。其领导者包括黄敬和黄华。

2   Slow Train to "Western Peace"

It was early June and Peking wore the green lace of spring, its thousands of willows and imperial cypresses making the Forbidden City a place of wonder and enchantment, and in many cool gardens it was impossible to believe in the China of breaking toil, starvation, revolution, and foreign invasion that lay beyond the glittering roofs of the palaces. Here well-fed foreigners could live in their own little never-never land of whisky-and-soda, polo, tennis, and gossip, happily quite unaware of the pulse of humanity outside the great city's silent, insulating walls—as indeed many did.

And yet during the past year even the oasis of Peking had been invaded by the atmosphere of struggle that hovered over all China. Threats of Japanese conquest had provoked great demonstrations of the people, especially among the enraged youth. A few months earlier I had stood under the bullet-pitted Tartar Wall and seen ten thousand students gather, defiant of the gendarmes' clubbings, to shout in a mighty chorus: "Resist Japan! Reject the demands of Japanese imperialism for the separation of North China from the South!"

All Peking's defensive masonry could not prevent reverberations of the Chinese Red Army's sensational attempt to march through Shansi to the Great Wall—ostensibly to begin a war against Japan for recovery of the lost territories. This somewhat quixotic expedition had been promptly blocked by eleven divisions of Generalissimo Chiang Kai-shek's crack new army, but that had not prevented patriotic students from courting imprisonment and possible death by massing in the streets and uttering the forbidden slogans: "Cease civil war! Cooperate with the Communists to resist Japan! Save China!"[1]

One midnight I climbed aboard a dilapidated train, feeling a little ill, but in a state of

---
1. The December 9, 1935 student demonstration was a historic "turning point" favorable to the Communists. Among its leaders were Huang Ching and Huang Hua.

兴奋。我所以兴奋，是因为摆在我面前的这次旅行是要去探索一个跟紫禁城的中世纪壮丽豪华在时间上相隔千百年、空间上相距千百里的地方：我是到"红色中国"去。我所以"有点不舒服"，是因为我身上注射了凡是能够弄到的一切预防针。用微生物的眼睛来看一下我的血液，就可以发现一支令人毛骨悚然的队伍；在我的臂部和腿部注射了天花、伤寒、霍乱、斑疹伤寒和鼠疫的病菌。这五种病在当时的西北都是流行病。此外，最近还流传着令人吃惊的消息，说淋巴腺鼠疫正在陕西省蔓延开来，陕西省是地球上少数几处流行这种风土病的地方之一。

而我的第一个目的地就是西安府。这个地名有"西方平安"的意思，是陕西省的省会，要从北平向西南坐两天两夜劳累的火车，才能到达陇海路西端的这个终点站。我的计划是从那里向北走，进入位于大西北中心的苏区。在西安府以北大约150英里的一个市镇——洛川，当时是陕西红区的起点。洛川以北的地区，除了公路干线两旁的几个狭长地段以及下文将要提到的几个地点外，已经全部染红了。大致说来，陕西红军控制的地区南到洛川，北到长城；东西两边都以黄河为界。那条宽阔的浊流从西藏边缘往北流经甘肃和宁夏，在长城北面进入内蒙古的绥远省，然后曲曲折折地向东流行许多英里，又折而向南，穿过长城而构成陕西、山西两省的分界线。

当时苏维埃活动的地方，就在中国这条最容易闹灾的河流的这个大河套里——陕西北部、甘肃东北部和宁夏东南部。这个区域同中国诞生地的最初疆界差不多相符，真可谓历史的巧合。数千年前，中国人当初就是在这一带形成统一的民族的。

第二天早晨，我观察一下我的旅伴，看见一个青年人和一个面目端正、留着一绺花白胡子的老人，坐在我对面呷着浓茶。那个青年很快就跟我攀谈起来，先是客套一番，后来就不免谈到了政治。我发现他妻子的叔叔是个铁路职员，他是拿着一张免票证乘车的。他要回到离开7年的四川老家去。不过他不能肯定究竟能不能到家。据说他家乡附近有土匪在活动。

"你是说红军吗？"

"哦，不，不是红军，虽然四川也有红军。我是说土匪。"

high excitement. Excitement because before me lay a journey of exploration into a land hundreds of years and hundreds of miles removed from the medieval splendors of the Forbidden City: I was bound for "Red China." And a little ill because I had taken all the inoculations available. A microbe's-eye view of my bloodstream would have revealed a macabre cavalcade; my arms and legs were shot with smallpox, typhoid, cholera, typhus, and plague germs. All five diseases were prevalent in the Northwest. Moreover, alarming reports had lately told of the spread of bubonic plague in Shensi province, one of the few spots on earth where it was endemic.

My immediate destination was Sianfu—which means "Western Peace." Sianfu was the capital of Shensi province, it was two tiresome days and nights by train to the southwest of Peking, and it was the western terminus of the Lunghai railway. From there I planned to go northward and enter the soviet districts, which occupied the very heart of Ta Hsi-pei, China's Great Northwest. Lochuan, a town about one hundred fifty miles north of Sianfu, then marked the beginning of Red territory in Shensi. Everything north of it, except strips of territory along the main highways, and some points which will be noted later, was already dyed Red. With Lochuan roughly the southern, and the Great Wall the northern, extremities of Red control in Shensi, both the eastern and western Red frontiers were formed by the Yellow River. Coming down from the fringes of Tibet, the wide, muddy stream flows northward through Kansu and Ninghsia, and above the Great Wall into the province of Suiyuan—Inner Mongolia. Then after many miles of uncertain wandering toward the east it turns southward again, to pierce the Great Wall and form the boundary between the provinces of Shensi and Shansi.

It was within this great bend of China's most treacherous river that the soviets then operated—in northern Shensi, northeastern Kansu, and southeastern Ninghsia. And by a strange sequence of history this region almost corresponded to the original confines of the birthplace of China. Near here the Chinese first formed and unified themselves as a people, thousands of years ago.

In the morning I inspected my traveling companions and found a youth and a handsome old man with a wisp of gray beard sitting opposite me, sipping bitter tea. Presently the youth spoke to me, in formalities at first, and then inevitably of politics. I discovered that his wife's uncle was a railway official and that he was traveling with a pass. He was on his way back to Szechuan, his native province, which he had left seven years before. But he was not sure that he would be able to visit his home town after all. Bandits were reported to be operating near there.

"You mean Reds?"

"Oh, no, not Reds, although there are Reds in Szechuan, too. No, I mean bandits."

"可是红军不也就是土匪吗？"我出于好奇心问他，"报纸上总是把他们称为'赤匪'或'共匪'的。"

"啊，可是你一定知道，报纸编辑不能不把他们称作土匪，因为南京命令他们这样做，"他解释说，"他们要是用共产党或革命者的称呼，那就证明他们自己也是共产党了。"

"但是在四川，大家害怕红军不是像害怕土匪一样吗？"

"这个嘛，就要看情况了。有钱人是怕他们的，地主、做官的和收税的，都是怕的。可是农民并不怕他们。有时候他们还欢迎他们呢。"说到这里，他不安地望了那老人一眼，那老人坐在那里留心地听着，却又显得并不在听的样子。"你知道，"他接着说，"农民太无知了，他们不懂得红军不过是要利用他们。他们以为红军说话是当真的。"

"那么他们说话不是当真的了？"

"我父亲写信给我，说红军在松潘取缔了高利贷和鸦片，重新分配了那里的土地。所以，你看，他们并不完全是土匪。他们有主义，这没有问题。但是他们是坏人。他们杀人太多了。"

这时，那花白胡子忽然抬起他那温和的脸孔，十分心平气和地说出一句惊人的话来："杀得不够！"我们两人听了都不禁目瞪口呆地望着他。

不巧火车这时已经快到郑州，我在那里得换乘陇海路的车，因而不得不中断讨论。可是，从那时起，我心里一直在纳闷，这位模样儒雅的老先生有什么确凿的证据来支持他那骇人听闻的论点呢。在这第二天的旅途上，火车（这列火车还新，很舒适）在河南和陕西的景象奇异、层层叠叠的黄土山中缓慢地爬行，最后开进西安府新建的漂亮车站，我却整天都在纳闷这件事。

我到西安府不久，就去拜访陕西省绥靖公署主任杨虎城将军。杨将军在一两年以前，在陕西那些未被红军控制的地区，还是个惟我独尊的土皇帝。他当过土匪，后来经由中国那条许多极有才能的领导人由此上台的途径而掌握了权势，据说也在这条大道上照例发了大财。但是在最近，他不得不同西北的其他几位先生分享他的权力了。因为在1935年，以前满洲的统治者张学良"少帅"，带着他的东北军开到了陕西，在西安府就任这一带的最高红军征剿者——全国剿匪总部副司令。而为了

"But aren't the Reds also bandits?" I asked out of curiosity. "The newspapers always call them Red bandits or Communist bandits."

"Ah, but you must know that the editors must call them bandits because they are ordered to do so by Nanking," he explained. "If they called them Communists or revolutionaries that would prove they were Communists themselves."

"But in Szechuan don't people fear the Reds as much as the bandits?"

"Well, that depends. The rich men fear them, and the landlords, and the officials and tax collectors, yes. But the peasants do not fear them. Sometimes they welcome them." Then he glanced apprehensively at the old man, who sat listening intently, and yet seeming not to listen. "You see," he continued, "the peasants are too ignorant to understand that the Reds only want to use them. They think the Reds really mean what they say."

"But they don't mean it?"

"My father wrote to me that they did abolish usury and opium in the Sungpan [Szechuan], and that they redistributed the land there. So you see they are not exactly bandits. They have principles, all right. But they are wicked men. They kill too many people."

Then surprisingly the graybeard lifted his gentle face and with perfect composure made an astonishing remark. "*Sha pu kou!*" he said. "They don't kill enough!" We both looked at him flabbergasted.

Unfortunately the train was nearing Chengchow, where I had to transfer to the Lunghai line, and I was obliged to break off the discussion. But I have ever since wondered with what deadly evidence this Confucian-looking old gentleman would have supported his startling contention. I wondered about it all the next day of travel, as we climbed slowly through the weird levels of loess hills in Honan and Shensi, and until my train—this one still new and very comfortable—rolled up to the new and handsome railway station at Sianfu.

Soon after my arrival I went to call on General Yang Hu-ch'eng, Pacification Commissioner of Shensi province. Until a couple of years before, General Yang had been undisputed monarch of those parts of Shensi not controlled by the Reds. A former bandit, he rose to authority via the route that had put many of China's ablest leaders in office, and on the same highway he was said to have accumulated the customary fortune. But recently he had been obliged to divide his power with several other gentlemen in the Northwest. For in 1935 the "Young Marshal," Chang Hsueh-liang, who used to be ruler of Manchuria, had brought his Tungpei (Manchurian) Army into Shensi, and assumed office in Sianfu as supreme Red chaser in these parts—Vice-Commander of the National Bandit-Suppression

监视这位少帅，又派来了蒋介石总司令的侍从邵力子。这位邵先生便是陕西省的省主席。

在这些人物——还有其他一些人——之间，维持着一种微妙的均势。而在所有这些人的背后牵线的，就是那位手段厉害的总司令本人，他力图把他的独裁统治扩大到西北去，不但要消灭正在奋斗中的苏维埃民主，而且要把老杨和小张两人的军队都消灭掉，用的就是使他们互相残杀这个简单的办法——这是政治军事方面一出出色的三幕剧，而戏中的主要谋略，蒋介石显然认为只有他自己才懂得。正是这种估计错误——在追求上述目的时有些操之过急，在肯定对手的愚蠢时又有些过分自信——导致蒋介石几个月以后在西安府成了阶下囚，听由这三方面发落！我在下文中要谈到总司令被逮的这一惊人事件，说明它怎样把中国的历史引导到了新的方向。

我在一所新近竣工、耗资5万的巨石宅第里会见了杨将军[1]。当时他没有带着太太而是单身住在这所有着多间寝室的拱顶建筑物——绥靖公署主任的官邸里。原来杨虎城也同这个过渡时期的许多中国人一样，为家庭纠纷所苦，因为他有两个太太。第一个太太是他年轻时娶的小脚女人，是他的父母在蒲城给他娶的。第二个是像蒋介石夫人那样的一位活泼而勇敢的女性，年轻貌美，已经是5个孩子的母亲，既摩登又进步，据说从前参加过共产党，是杨将军自己看中的。据传教士们说，在杨将军这个新居落成的时候，两个太太看来都向他提出了相同的最低要求。她们互相憎恨；她们都为他生育了儿子，都有权做他的合法妻子；双方都坚决不肯搬到那巨石营建的宅第里去住，除非对方不住在里面。

在一个局外人看起来，事情好像很简单：显而易见的解决办法是，离去一位太太或者另娶第三位太太。但是杨将军还没有打定主意，因而他还是单身住着。他的这种尴尬处境，在现代中国并不少见。蒋介石同那位有钱的、美国留学的、相信基督教的宋美龄结婚的时候，也曾遇到同样的问题，他最终与第一位夫人（蒋经国之母）离了婚，给资遣散了他的两位老式太太，解决了这个问题。这一决定受到了传教士们的高度赞许，他们从此以后一直在为他的灵魂祈祷。然而这样的解决办法是从西方输入的新颖思想，许多中国人对之仍然要皱眉头。至于出身草莽的老杨，对于自己的灵魂的归宿，大约是不如对祖宗的传统那么关心的。

---

1. 我是由王炳南引见给杨将军的，王炳南当时和他的夫人安娜住在杨的官邸里。王是杨的政治秘书和西安中共中央与杨将军和张少帅之间的首席联络员。

Commission. And to watch the Young Marshal had come Shao Li-tzu, an acolyte of Generalissimo Chiang Kai-shek. The Hon. Shao was Governor of Shensi.

A delicate balance of power was maintained between these figures—and still others. Tugging strings behind all of them was the redoubtable Generalissimo himself, who sought to extend his dictatorship to the Northwest and liquidate not only the Communist-led revolution but also the troops of old Yang Hu-ch'eng and young Chang Hsueh-liang, by the simple process of using each to destroy the other—three acts of a brilliant politico-military drama the main stratagem of which Chiang evidently believed was understood only by himself. And it was that error in calculation—a little too much haste in pursuit of the purpose, a little too much confidence in his adversaries' stupidity—which was in a few months to land Chiang Kai-shek a prisoner in Sianfu, at the mercy of all three.

I found General Yang[1] in a newly finished stone mansion, just completed at a cost of $50,000. He was living in this many-chambered vault—the official home of the Pacification Commissioner—without a wife. Yang Hu-ch'eng, like many Chinese in this transitional period, was burdened with domestic infelicity, for he was a two-wife man. The first was the lily-footed wife of his youth, betrothed to him by his parents in Pucheng. The second, as vivacious and courageous a woman as Mme. Chiang Kai-shek, was a pretty young mother of five children, modern and progressive, a former Communist, they said, and the girl that Yang had chosen himself. It seemed, according to the missionaries, that when he opened his new home each of his wives had presented him with the same minimum demand. Each detested the other; each had borne him sons and had the right to be legal wife; and each resolutely refused to move into the stone mansion unless the other stayed behind.

To an outsider the case looked simple: a divorce or a third wife was the obvious solution. But General Yang had not made up his mind and so he still lived alone. His dilemma was a not uncommon one in modern China. Chiang Kai-shek had faced a similar issue when he married rich, American-educated Soong Mei-ling, who as a Methodist was not prepared to accept polygamy. Chiang had finally divorced his first wife (the mother of his son Ching-kuo) and pensioned off his two concubines. The decision was highly approved by the missionaries, who had ever since prayed for his soul. Nevertheless, this way out—a newfangled idea imported from the West—was still frowned upon by many Chinese. Old Yang, having risen from the people, was probably less concerned over the disposal of his soul than the traditions of his ancestors.

---

1. I was introduced to General Yang by Wang Ping-nan, who with his wife, Anna, was then living in Yang's home. Wang was Yang's political secretary and was chief liaison in Sian between the CCP CC and General Yang and Marshal Chang.

决不要以为杨虎城将军早年当过土匪，就必然没有资格做领袖了。这样的假定在中国是不适用的。因为在中国，一个人青年时当过土匪，往往表示他有坚强的性格和意志。翻一翻中国的历史，就可以发现中国有些极能干的爱国志士，都曾一度被人贴上土匪的标签。事实上，许多罪大恶极的无赖、流氓、汉奸，都是以正人君子的面目，陈腐的诗云子曰的伪善，中国经书上的愚民巫术，爬上显赫的地位的，尽管他们常常也要利用一个纯朴的土匪的有力臂助来达到这一目的——今天多少也仍是如此。

杨将军反正在大多数外国传教士中间名声不佳，因此他不可能真的是个坏人。他的革命历史，说明他原来是个粗鲁的农民，可能一度有过崇高的梦想，要大大改变自己的世界，但是他掌了权以后，却没有找到什么办法，他听着他周围那些食客的进言，也逐渐感到腻味和混乱起来了。不过，他假如有过这样的梦想的话，他并没有向我吐露。他拒绝讨论政治问题，客气地委派他的一个秘书陪我参观市容。再说，我见他的时候，他害着严重的头痛和关节炎，在他这样多灾多难的当口，我当然不想坚持向他提出为难的问题。相反，对于他所处的困境，我倒是十分同情的。因此，我对他作了简短的访问之后，便知趣地告辞了，打算去找省主席邵力子阁下，向他寻求一些答案。

邵主席在他那宽敞的衙门的花园里接见我，经过尘土飞扬的西安街头的酷热之后，分外觉得那里凉爽舒适。我上次见到他是在6年前，当时他是蒋介石的私人秘书，他帮助我访问了总司令。从那时起，他就在国民党里飞黄腾达起来。他是一个能干的人，受过良好的教育，现在总司令赐给了他省主席的殊荣。但是可怜的邵力子，也同其他许多文官当省主席的一样，他统治的地盘不出省会的灰色城墙——城外的地方是由杨将军和张少帅瓜分的。

邵力子阁下自己一度当过"共匪"，现在再提这件事未免有些不恭。他事实上是中国共产党的一个创始者。但是我们不应当对他太严厉，在那些日子里，当共产党是一桩时髦的事情，没有人十分明白入党究竟意味着什么，只知道许多有才华的青年都是共产党。后来邵力子反悔了；因为在1927年以后，当共产党是怎么一回事，已经可以看得十分清楚了，那是可以叫你脑袋搬家的。此后邵力子便成了一个虔诚的佛教徒，再也没有表现出信仰异端的痕迹了。

"现在红军怎么样了？"我问他。

And it must not be supposed that Yang's early career as a bandit necessarily disqualified him as a leader. Such assumptions could not be made in China, where a career of banditry in early youth often indicated a man of strong character and purpose. A look at Chinese history showed that some of China's ablest patriots were at one time or another labeled bandits. The fact was that many of the worst rogues, scoundrels, and traitors had climbed to power under cover of respectability, the putrid hypocrisy of Confucian maxims, and the priestcraft of the Chinese Classics—though they had very often utilized the good strong arm of an honest bandit in doing so.

General Yang's history as a revolutionary suggested a rugged peasant who might once have had high dreams of making a big change in his world, but who, finding himself in power, looked vainly for a method, and grew weary and confused, listening to the advice of the mercenaries who gathered around him. But if he had such dreams he did not confide them to me. He declined to discuss political questions, and courteously delegated one of his secretaries to show me the city. He was also suffering from a severe headache and rheumatism when I saw him, and in the midst of his sea of troubles I was not one to insist upon asking him nettling questions. On the contrary, in his dilemma he had all my sympathy. So after a brief interview with him I discreetly retired, to seek some answers from the Honorable Governor, Shao Li-tzu.

Governor Shao received me in the garden of his spacious yamen, cool and restful after the parching heat of Sian's dusty streets. I had last seen him six years before, when he was Chiang Kai-shek's personal secretary, and at that time he had assisted me in an interview with the Generalissimo. Since then he had risen rapidly in the Kuomintang. He was an able man, well educated, and the Generalissimo had now bestowed upon him the honors of a governorship. But poor Shao, like many another civil governor, did not rule much beyond the provincial capital's gray walls—the outlying territory being divided by General Yang and the Young Marshal.

The Hon. Shao had once been a "Communist bandit" himself. He had played a pioneer role in the Chinese Communist Party. In those days it was fashionable to be a Communist and nobody was very sure exactly what it meant, except that many bright young men were Communists. Later on he had recanted; after 1927 it had become very clear what it meant, and one could have one's head removed for it. Shao then became a devout Buddhist, and subsequently displayed no further signs of heresy. He was one of the most charming gentlemen in China.

"How are the Reds getting along?" I asked him.

"没有留下多少了。在陕西的不过是些残余。"

"那么战事还在继续？"我问。

"不，现在陕北没有多少战斗。红军正在转移到宁夏和甘肃去。他们似乎要跟外蒙古取得联系。"

他把话题转到西南的局势，当时那里的反叛的将领正在要求出兵抗日。我问他，中国应不应该同日本打仗。他反问道："我们能打吗？"接着，这位信佛的省主席将他对日本的看法如实地对我说了，但不允许我发表，正像那时所有的国民党官员那样，他们对日本的看法可以告诉你，但是不能发表。

这次访问以后几个月，可怜的邵力子和他的总司令一起，就为这个抗日问题，被张学良少帅部下的一些反叛的年轻人弄得狼狈不堪，他们不再讲理了，不再接受"也许有一天"这样的答复了。而邵力子的那位小胖子夫人——从莫斯科回来的留学生，后来也"叛变"的前共产党员——则受到一些反叛分子的围困，奋勇拒捕。

可是，在我们那次谈话的时候，邵力子对于这一切并没有透露出半点预感来，我们经过交换意见，在看法上已有极为接近之处，我该向他告别了。我已经从邵力子那里弄明白我要知道的事情。他已经证实了我在北平的熟人通知我的消息：陕北方面的战斗已暂时停止。因此，如果有适当的安排，到前线去应当是可能的。于是我就着手进行这些安排。

"There are not many left. Those in Shensi are only remnants."

"Then the war continues?" I asked.

"No, at present there is little fighting in north Shensi. The Reds are moving into Ninghsia and Kansu. They seem to want to connect with Outer Mongolia."

He shifted the conversation to the situation in the Southwest, where insurgent generals were then demanding an anti-Japanese expedition. I asked him whether he thought China should fight Japan. "Can we?" he demanded. And then the Buddhist governor told me exactly what he thought about Japan—not for publication—just as every Kuomintang official would then tell you his opinion of Japan—not for publication.

A few months after this interview poor Shao was to be put on the spot on this question of war with Japan—along with his Generalissimo—by some rebellious young men of Marshal Chang Hsueh-liang's army, who refused to be reasonable and take "maybe some day" for an answer any longer. And Shao's diminutive wife—a returned student from Moscow and a former Communist herself—was to be cornered by some of the insurrectionists and make a plucky fight to resist arrest.

But Shao revealed no premonition of all this in our talk, and, an exchange of views having brought us perilously near agreement, it was time to leave. I had already learned from Shao Li-tzu what I wanted to know. He had confirmed the word of my Peking informant, that fighting had temporarily halted in north Shensi. Therefore it should be possible to go to the front, if properly arranged.

三、 汉代青铜

西北的危机在我到达西安府大约 6 个月后就要令人意想不到地爆发，富有戏剧性地使全世界都知道，张学良少帅统率下的大军同他以"剿共"军副总司令身份奉命要去剿灭的"匪军"令人惊诧地结成了联盟。但是在 1936 年 6 月，外界仍完全蒙在鼓里，不知道这些奇怪的发展，甚至在蒋介石自己控制西安府警察的蓝衣社宪兵总部，也没有人知道到底要发生什么事情。西安府的监牢里关着大约 300 名共产党员，蓝衣社还在继续搜捕。当时空气极度紧张。到处是特务和对方的特务。

但是现在已经没有必要秘而不宣这些兴奋紧张的日子里发生的事情，和当初不得已才让我知道的秘密了，因此可以在这里报道出来。

我在到西安府之前从来没有见到过一个红军战士。在北平为我用隐色墨水写了一封介绍信给毛泽东的人，我知道是个红军指挥员，但是我没有见到过他。这封介绍信是通过第三者，我的一个老朋友给我的。但是除了这封介绍信以外，我在西北要取得联系，只有一个希望。我得到的指点就是到西安府某家旅馆去，要了一个房间住下来，等一个自称姓王的先生来访，除此之外，我对他一无所知。确实是一无所知，除了他会设法给我安排搭乘——他们这样答应我——张学良的私人座机去红区！

我在旅馆里住下来后过了几天，有一个身材高大，胖得有点圆滚滚的，但是体格结实，仪表堂堂的中国人，身穿一件灰色绸大褂，穿过打开着的房门进来，用一口漂亮的英语向我打招呼。他的外表像个富裕的商人，自称姓王，提到了我在北平的那个朋友的名字，并且还以其他方式证实了他就是我等的那个人。

3   SOME HAN BRONZES

Some six months after my arrival in Sianfu the crisis in the Northwest was to explode in a manner nobody had anticipated, so that the whole world was made dramatically aware of an amazing alliance between the big army under Marshal Chang Hsueh-liang and the "bandits" whom he had been ordered, as deputy commander-in-chief of the Communist-Suppression Forces, to destroy. But in June, 1936, the outside world was still in complete ignorance of these strange developments, and even in the headquarters of Chiang Kai-shek's own Blueshirt gendarmes, who controlled the Sianfu police, nobody knew exactly what was taking place. Some 300 Communists were imprisoned in the city's jail, and the Blueshirts were hunting for more. An atmosphere of extreme tension prevailed. Spies and counterspies were everywhere.

But there is no longer any necessity to remain covert about those exciting days, with the secrets of which I was perforce entrusted, so here it can be told.

I had never seen a Red Army man before I arrived in Sianfu. The man in Peking who had written for me in invisible ink the letter addressed to Mao Tse-tung was, I knew, a Red commander; but I had not seen him. The letter had reached me through a third person, an old friend; but besides this letter I had only one hope of a connection in the Northwest. I had been instructed simply to go to a hotel in Sianfu, take a room there, and await a visit from a gentleman who would call himself Wang, but about whom I knew nothing else. Nothing—except that he would arrange for me to enter the Red districts by way of the private airplane, I was promised, of Chang Hsueh-liang!

A few days after I put up in the hotel a large, somewhat florid and rotund, but strongly built and dignified Chinese, wearing a long gray silk gown, entered my open door and greeted me in excellent English. He looked like a prosperous merchant, but he introduced himself as Wang, mentioned the name of my Peking friend, and otherwise established that he was the man I awaited.

在这以后的那个星期里，我发现即使仅仅为了王一个人，也值得我到西安府一行。我每天花四五个小时听他聊天，回忆往事，还听他对政局作比较严肃的解释。他是我完全意想不到的一个人。他曾经在上海一所教会学校里受教育，在基督教圈子里颇有地位，一度自己有个教堂，我后来知道，在共产党中间，大家都叫他王牧师[1]。像上海的许多发达得意的基督教徒一样，他参加过操纵该市的青帮[2]，从蒋介石（也是青帮中人）到青帮头子杜月笙，他都认识。他一度在国民党中担任过高级官员，但是我现在也不能泄露他的真实姓名。

一些时候以来，王牧师就丢官弃教，同共产党合作。这样有多久了，我不知道。他成了一种秘密的、非正式的使节，到各种各样的文武官员那里去进行游说，帮助共产党把他们争取过来，使他们了解和支持共产党的成立"抗日民族统一战线"的建议。至少在张学良那里，他的游说是成功的。这里就需要介绍一些背景情况，才能说明当时已经达成的秘密谅解的基础是什么。

大家知道，张学良在1931年之前还是受人爱戴、为人慷慨、有现代化思想、能打高尔夫球、却又喜好赌博、吸毒成瘾这样一个性格矛盾的主宰满洲3,000万人民的军阀独裁者。南京的国民党政府承认了他从他土匪出身的父亲张作霖那里继承下来的职务，并且还给了他中国军队副总司令的头衔。1931年9月日本一开始征服东北，张学良的厄运就开始了。侵略开始时，张少帅在长城以南的北平协和医院治疗伤寒，无法独力应付这场危机。他只有依靠南京，依靠和他歃血为盟的"大哥"蒋介石总司令。但是蒋介石要不惜一切代价避免打仗，主张不抵抗，向后撤，依赖国际联盟。张学良当时有病在身，年轻（只有33岁），没有经验，又受到腐败无能的食客的包围，于是接受了蒋介石的意见和南京的命令，结果就坐失了他的老家满洲，几乎没有放一枪来进行保卫。这样的牺牲使得总司令能够在南京维系他自己的摇摇欲坠的政权，开始对红军发动新的"围剿"。

---

1. 这位"王牧师"的真名是董健吾。——译注
2. 青帮，流氓黑社会组织，在国际租界和法国租界当局的保护下，操纵着利润丰厚的鸦片走私、赌博、娼妓、绑架等行业。1927年青帮帮助蒋介石摧毁了共产党领导的工会，进行了"上海大屠杀"。参见第二篇第二章。

In the week that followed I discovered that Wang alone was worth the trip to Sianfu. I spent four or five hours a day listening to his yarns and reminiscences and to his more serious explanations of the political situation. He was wholly unexpected. Educated in a missionary school in Shanghai, he had been prominently identified with the Christian community, had once had a church of his own, and (as I was later to learn) was known among the Communists as Wang Mu-shih—Wang the Pastor. Like many successful Christians of Shanghai, he had been a member of the Ch'ing Pang,[1] and he knew everyone from Chiang Kai-shek (also a member) down to Tu Yueh-sheng, the Ch'ing Pang chieftain. He had once been a high official in the Kuomintang, but I cannot even now disclose his real name.

For some time, Pastor Wang, having deserted his congregation and officialdom, had been working with the Reds. How long I do not know. He was a kind of secret and unofficial ambassador to the courts of various militarists and officials whom the Communists were trying to win over to understanding and support of their "anti-Japanese national front" proposals. With Chang Hsueh-liang, at least, he had been successful. And here some background is necessary to illuminate the basis of the secret understanding which had at this time been reached.

Chang Hsueh-liang was until 1931 the popular, gambling, generous, modern-minded, golf-playing, dope-using, paradoxical warlord-dictator of the 30,000,000 people of Manchuria, confirmed in the office he had inherited from his ex-bandit father Chang Tso-lin by the Kuomintang Government at Nanking, which had also given him the title Vice-Commander-in-Chief of the Armed Forces of China. In September, 1931, Japan set out to conquer the Northeast, and Chang's reverses began. When the invasion commenced, Young Marshal Chang was in the Peking Union Hospital, below the Wall, recovering from typhoid, and in no condition to meet this crisis alone. He leaned heavily on Nanking and on his blood-sworn "elder brother," Chiang Kai-shek, the Generalissimo. But Chiang Kai-shek, who lacked adequate means to fight Japan—and the Reds—urged reliance on the League of Nations. Chang Hsueh-liang took the Generalissimo's counsel and Nanking's orders. As a result he lost his homeland, Manchuria, after only token resistance was offered by his retreating troops. Nanking propaganda had made it appear that the nonresistance policy was the Young Marshal's idea, whereas the record showed that it was the government's explicit order. The sacrifice enabled the Generalissimo to hold his own shaky regime together in Nanking and begin a new annihilation campaign against the Reds.

---

1. The Ch'ing Pang, a gangster secret society, controlled the profitable traffic in opium, gambling, prostitution, kidnaping, etc., under the protection of the International Settlement and French Concession authorities. In 1927 it helped Chiang Kai-shek destroy Communist-led unions and carry out the "Shanghai Massacre." See Part Two, Chapter 2.

这就是在中国叫做东北军的满洲军队的大部转移到长城以南中国本土来的背景。日本侵略热河时又发生了同样的情况。张学良当时没有在医院里，其实他是应该住院的。南京没有给他任何支援，也没有做抵抗的准备。总司令为了要避免打仗，准备让热河也沦于日本之手——结果就是这样。张学良背了黑锅，驯服地扮演了替罪羊的角色，在全国义愤填膺的情况下，总得有人辞职以谢国人。本来这不是蒋介石就是张学良，结果是张学良屈服下台，他到欧洲去"考察"一年。

张学良在欧洲所经历的最重要的一件事，不是他见了墨索里尼和希特勒，会晤了麦克唐纳[1]，也不是苏俄愚蠢地不让他去访问，而是他治愈了吸毒恶习。他像许多中国将领一样，几年前在作战间隙染上了吸鸦片的恶习。要戒烟不是件易事；他没有时间进行必要的长期治疗，他天真地盲目相信的一个医生告诉他可以用打针的办法治愈。他固然戒掉了烟瘾，可是等到疗程结束时，这位少帅却成了一个吗啡鬼了。

我在1929年在沈阳第一次见到张学良时，他是全世界最年轻的独裁者，当时他的气色还不错。他人很瘦，脸色清癯发黄，但是思想敏捷活跃，看上去精神饱满。他是公开激烈反日的，他很想实现把日本赶出中国和把满洲现代化这两个奇迹。几年后他的健康状况大为恶化。他在北平的一位医生告诉我，他一天用"药"要花200元钱——这种药是特别调制的吗啡，从理论上来说能够"逐步减少用量"。

但是在欧洲，张学良取得了一个大胜利，他戒了吸毒恶习。到1934年他回国时，他的朋友们看到他又惊又喜：他的体重增加了，肌肉结实了，脸色红润，看上去年轻了10年，人们在他身上又看到了年轻时代那个杰出有为的领袖的痕迹。他本来思想敏捷，讲究现实，现在他就给他这种头脑一个发展的机会。他到汉口重掌东北军的统率权，当时为了打红军，东北军已调到了华中。尽管他过去犯有错误，他的部下仍旧热烈地欢迎他回来，由此可见他人望之高。

张学良实行了新的生活习惯——6时起床，锻炼身体，每日练武读书，吃的是粗茶淡饭，过的是简朴生活。当时东北军还有14万人，他除了同军官以外，还同部下直接接触。东北军开始出现了新面貌。怀疑派逐渐相信，少帅又成了一个值得注意的人，因此认真对待他在回国时立下的誓言：他要把毕生精力用于收复满洲，为人民雪耻。

---

1. 当时英国工党领袖（1866—1937年）。——译注

That was how the Manchurian troops, known in China as the Tungpei (pronounced "Dungbei," and meaning "Northeastern") Army, moved south of the Great Wall into China proper. The same thing happened when Japan invaded Jehol. Chang Hsueh-liang was not in the hospital then, but he should have been. Nanking sent no support to him, and made no preparations for defense. The Generalissimo, to avoid war, was ready to see Jehol fall to Japan, too—and so it did. Chang Hsueh-liang got the blame, and docilely played the goat when somebody had to resign to appease an infuriated populace. It was Chiang or Chang—and the latter bowed and departed. He went to Europe for a year "to study conditions."

The most important thing that happened to Chang Hsueh-liang while he was in Europe was not that he saw Mussolini and Hitler and met Ramsay MacDonald, but it was that for the first time in several years he found himself a healthy man, cured of the dope habit. Some years before he had taken up opium, as many Chinese generals did, between battles. To break himself of the habit was not easy; his doctor assured him he could be cured by injections. He was freed of the craving of opium, all right, but when the doctor got through with him the Young Marshal was a morphine addict.

When I first met Chang at Mukden, in 1929, he was the world's youngest dictator, and he still looked fairly well. He was thin, his face somewhat drawn and jaundiced-looking, but his mind was quick and energetic, he seemed full of exuberance. He was openly anti-Japanese, and he was eager to perform miracles in driving Japan from China and modernizing Manchuria. Several years later his physical condition was much worse. One of his doctors in Peking told me that he was spending $200 a day on "medicine"—a special preparation of morphine which theoretically could be "tapered off."

But in Shanghai, just before he left for Europe, Chang Hsueh-liang began to cure himself of the drug habit. When he returned to China in 1934 his friends were pleased and amazed: he had put on weight and muscle, there was color in his cheeks, he looked ten years younger, and people saw in him traces of the brilliant leader of his youth. He had always possessed a quick, realistic mind, and now he gave it a chance to develop. At Hankow he resumed command of the Tungpei Army, which had been shifted to Central China to fight the Reds. It was a tribute to his popularity that, despite his errors of the past, his army enthusiastically welcomed him back.

Chang adopted a new routine—up at six, hard exercise, daily drill and study, simple food and Spartan habits, and direct personal contact with the subalterns as well as officers of his troops, which still numbered about 140,000 men. A new Tungpei Army began to emerge. Skeptics gradually became convinced that the Young Marshal had again become a man worth watching, and took seriously the vow he had made on his return: that his whole life would be devoted to the task of recovering Manchuria, and erasing the humiliation of his people.

与此同时，张学良对总司令还没有失去信心。在他们的全部交往的关系中，张学良对那个长者始终忠心耿耿，从未动摇，他曾经3次拯救那个长者的政权免于崩溃，而且充分信任那个长者的识见和诚意。他显然相信蒋介石所说的要收复满洲，决不再未经抵抗就让出一寸领土的话。但是，1935年日本军国主义者继续进行侵略，成立了冀东傀儡政权，并吞了一部分察哈尔，提出了华北脱离南方的要求，对此，南京已经默认了一部分。少帅麾下的官兵甚为不满，特别是在调到西北继续对红军打不受欢迎的内战，而对日本却不开一枪以后，更是普遍啧有怨言。

在南方同红军打了几个月的仗以后，少帅和他的一些军官开始有了几点重要的认识：他们所打的"土匪"实际上是由抗日爱国的能干指挥员领导的；"剿共"这件事可能要继续好几年；一边同红军打仗，一边要抗日是不可能的；而在这期间东北军却在同自己毫不相干的战事中很快地消耗兵力，土崩瓦解。

尽管如此，张学良把他的司令部迁到西北以后，仍开始大举进攻红军。有一阵子他打了几次胜仗，但是到1935年10月和11月间，东北军吃了大败仗，据说丢了整整两个师（一○一师和一○九师）和另外一个师（一一○师）的一部分。成千上万的东北军士兵"投向了"红军。也有许多军官被俘，扣了一阵子受"抗日教育"。

这些军官释放回到西安以后，大肆赞扬地向少帅作了关于苏区士气和组织的报告；特别是关于红军有诚意要停止内战，用和平民主方法统一全国，团结起来抵抗日本帝国主义。这给了张学良很深刻的印象。使他印象更为加深的是，他的部队送上来的报告说，全军都有反对与红军作战的情绪，红军的"中国人不打中国人"和"同我们一起打回老家去"的口号影响到了东北军的全体官兵。

与此同时，张学良本人也受到了强烈的左倾影响。他的东北大学的许多学生来到西安，在他手下工作，其中有些是共产党员。1935年12月日本在北平提出要求以后，他传话到北方去，凡是抗日的学生，不论政治信仰如何，都可以投奔到西安府来。在中国其他地方，进行抗日宣传的人都遭到南京的逮捕，惟独在陕西，他们

Meanwhile, Chang had not lost faith in the Generalissimo. In their entire relationship Chang had never wavered in his loyalty to the older man, whose regime he had three times saved from collapse, and in whose judgment and sincerity he placed full confidence. He evidently believed Chiang Kai-shek when he said he was preparing to recover Manchuria, and would yield no more territory without resistance. In 1935 Japan's militarists continued their aggression: the puppet regime of east Hopei was set up, part of Chahar was annexed, and demands were made for the separation of North China from the South, to which Nanking partly acquiesced. Ominous discontent rumbled among the Young Marshal's officers and men, especially after his troops were shifted to the Northwest to continue to wage an unpopular civil war against the Red Army, while Japanese attrition continued almost unopposed.

After months of fighting the Reds in the South, several important realizations had come to the Young Marshal and some of his officers: that the "bandits" they were fighting were in reality led by able, patriotic, anti-Japanese commanders; that this process of "Communist extermination" might last for many more years; that it was impossible to resist Japan while the anti-Red wars continued; and that meanwhile the Tungpei Army was rapidly being reduced and disbanded in battles which were to it devoid of meaning.

Nevertheless, when Chang shifted his headquarters to the Northwest, he began an energetic campaign against the Reds. For a while he had some success, but in October and November, 1935, the Tungpei Army suffered serious defeats, reportedly losing two whole divisions (the 101st and 109th) and part of a third (110th). Thousands of Tungpei soldiers "turned over" to the Red Army. Many officers were also taken captive, and held for a period of "anti-Japanese tutelage."

When those officers were released, and returned to Sian, they brought back to the Young Marshal glowing accounts of the morale and organization in the soviet districts, but especially of the Red Army's sincerity in wanting to stop civil war, unify China by peaceful democratic methods, and unite to oppose Japanese imperialism. Chang was impressed. He was impressed even more by reports from his divisions that the sentiment throughout the whole army was turning against war with the Reds, whose slogans—"Chinese must not fight Chinese!" and "Unite with us and fight back to Manchuria!"—were infecting the rank and file of the entire Tungpei Army.

In the meantime, Chang himself had been strongly influenced to the left. Many of the students in his Tungpei University had come to Sian and were working with him, and among these were some Communists. After the Japanese demands in Peking of December, 1935, he had sent word to the North that all anti-Japanese students, regardless of their political beliefs, could find haven in Sianfu. While anti-Japanese agitators elsewhere in China were being arrested by agents of the Nanking government, in

却受到了鼓励和保护。张学良的一些年轻军官也受到学生的很大影响，当被俘的军官从红区回来，谈到那里到处都有公开的抗日群众团体和红军在人民中间的爱国宣传时，张学良开始越来越把红军当作天然的盟友而不是敌人了。

据王牧师告诉我，就是在这当儿，也就是1936年初，有一天他去拜访张学良，开门见山地说："我是来向你借飞机到红区去的。"

张学良吃了一惊，跳起来瞪着眼睛说："什么？你敢到这里来提出这样的要求？你不知道凭这一点就可以把你押出去枪毙吗？"

王牧师详细作了解释。他说他同共产党有联系，知道许多张学良应该知道的情况。他谈了很久，谈到他们政策的改变。谈到中国需要团结抗日，谈到红军为了使南京抗日愿意作出很大的让步，因为这一政策，红军认识到他们单方面是不能实现的。他建议，由他来安排一次会见，请张学良和某些共产党领导人进一步讨论这些问题。张学良开始时很惊异，后来却留心地听了这一些话。他有一个时期以来就一直在想他可以利用红军；现在看来他们也显然认为可以利用他；那么好吧，也许咱们可以在结束内战团结抗日的共同要求的基础上互相利用一下。

最后王牧师还是坐了张少帅的私人座机飞到了陕北的延安。他进了苏维埃中国，带回来一个谈判方案。过了不久，张学良本人飞到延安去，见了红军指挥员周恩来（关于他的情况下文还要述及）。在经过了同周恩来长时间的详细讨论以后，张学良相信了红军的诚意，相信了他们的统一战线建议的合理可行。

东北军与共产党之间的协议的第一步执行就是停止陕西境内的战事。双方未经通知对方都不得调动兵力。红军派了好几个代表到西安府去，穿上东北军的制服，参加了张学良的参谋部，帮助改组他的军队的政治训练方法。在王曲镇开办了一所新学校，张学良把他部下的低级军官送去集训，课程有政治、经济、社会科学和日本如何征服满洲以及中国因此受到什么损失的详细统计。另外又有成百上千的激进学生纷纷来到西安，进了另外一个抗日政治训练学校，少帅也经常去作演讲。东北军中采用了苏俄和中国红军所采用的政治委员那种制度。从满洲时代遗留下来的一些头脑封建的年老高级军官给撤换了，张学良提拔了激进的年轻军官来代替他们，

Shensi they were encouraged and protected. Some of Chang's younger officers had been much influenced by the students also, and when the captured officers returned from the Red districts and reported that open anti-Japanese mass organizations were flourishing there, and described the Reds' patriotic propaganda among the people, Chang began to think more and more of the Reds as natural allies rather than enemies.

It was at this point, early in 1936, Pastor Wang told me, that he one day called on Chang Hsueh-liang and opened an interview by declaring: "I have come to borrow your airplane to go to the Red districts."

Chang jumped up and stared in amazement. "What? You dare to come here and make such a request? Do you realize you can be shot for this?"

The Pastor elaborated. He explained that he had contacts with the Communists and knew things which Chang should know. He talked for a long time about their changing policies, about the necessity for a united China to resist Japan, about the Reds' willingness to make big concessions in order to influence Nanking to resist Japan, a policy which the Reds realized they could not, alone, make effective. He proposed that he should arrange for a further discussion of these points between Chang and certain Red leaders. And to all of this, after his first surprise, Chang listened attentively. He had for some time been thinking that he could make use of the Reds: they also evidently believed they could make use of him; very well, perhaps they could utilize each other on the basis of common demands for an end to civil war and united resistance to Japan.

The Pastor did, after all, fly to Yenan, north Shensi, in the Young Marshal's private airplane. He entered Soviet China and returned with a formula for negotiation. And a short time later Chang Hsueh-liang himself flew up to Yenan, met Chou En-lai, and after long and detailed discussion with him became convinced, according to Wang, of the Reds' sincerity, and of the sanity and practicability of their proposals for a united front.

First steps in the implementation of the Tungpei-Communist agreement included the cessation of hostilities in Shensi. Neither side was to move without notifying the other. The Reds sent several delegates to Sianfu, who put on Tungpei uniforms, joined Chang Hsueh-liang's staff, and helped reorganize political training methods in his army. A new school was opened at Wang Ch'u Ts'un, where Chang's lower officers went through intensified courses in politics, economics, social science, and detailed and statistical study of how Japan had conquered Manchuria and what China had lost thereby. Hundreds of radical students flocked to Sian and entered another anti-Japanese political training school, at which the Young Marshal also gave frequent lectures. Something like the political commissar system used in Soviet Russia and by the Chinese Red Army was adopted in the Tungpei Army. Some aging higher officers inherited from the Manchurian days were sacked; to replace them Chang Hsueh-liang promoted radical younger officers,

指望依靠这些年轻军官作为建设新军的主要支柱。在张学良"花花公子"时代包围他的一些腐败的阿谀谄媚之徒也由东北大学的热心认真的学生所代替。

但是这种改革都是在极端秘密的情况下进行的。虽然东北军不再同红军作战，在陕晋交界处，在甘肃、宁夏，仍有南京军队驻扎，激战仍在进行。张学良与共产党真正关系的消息没有泄露给报界。蒋介石在西安的特务虽然知道有什么事情正在酝酿之中，但是他们无法得悉确切的内容。偶尔有卡车开到西安来，载着一些共产党乘客，但是他们外表上是看不出来的，因为他们都穿着东北军制服。偶尔有其他卡车离开西安去红区，也没有引起怀疑；因为这些卡车同其他东北军去前线的卡车没有什么两样。

在我到了不久之后，王牧师有一次告诉我，我就是要搭这样的卡车到前线去。坐飞机的计划告吹了：这样做很有可能引起少帅难堪，因为如果有一个外国人丢在前线不回来，他的美国飞行员可能嘴快说出来。

一天早晨，王牧师同一个东北军军官，或者至少是个穿着东北军军官制服的年轻人一起来见我。他建议我们到西安城外汉朝古城遗址一游。在旅馆外面有一辆挂着窗帘的汽车等着我们，我们进了汽车以后，我看到里边坐着一个头戴一副墨镜，身穿一套国民党官员穿的中山装的人。我们驱车前往汉朝一个皇宫的遗址[1]，在那里，我们走上了有名的汉武帝坐在他的御殿里君临天下的隆起的土堆。你在这里还能拾到一些两千多年以前大屋顶上的碎瓦片。

王牧师和那个东北军军官有几句话要说，所以他们站在一旁去说话了。那个国民党官员在我们坐汽车出来的尘土飞扬的路上一直坐在那里没有说话，这时向我走了过来，卸下墨镜，摘掉白帽。我这才看出他相当年轻。他的一头黑油油的浓发下面，一双闪闪发光的眼睛紧紧地盯着我，他的青铜色的脸上露出了恶作剧的笑容，在他卸掉那副墨镜以后，你一眼就可以看出，他的制服是件伪装，他并不是个坐办公室的官僚，而是个户外活动的人。他中等身材，看上去力气不大，所以当他走近过来，突然一把抓住我的胳膊时，我没有想到他的手像铁爪子似的那么有力，不禁痛得退缩了一步。我后来注意到，这个人的行动有一种黑豹的优美风度，在那套硬邦邦的制服底下，一点也不失轻巧矫捷。

---

1. 兴盛的汉朝统治"中央王国"的时期（前202—公元220）与罗马帝国重叠，汉朝与罗马帝国有一些贸易和文化交流。

to whom he now looked for his main support in building a new army. Many of the corrupt sycophants who had surrounded Chang during his "playboy" years were also replaced by eager and serious-minded students from the Tungpei University.

Such changes developed in close secrecy, made possible by Chang's semiautonomy as a provincial warlord. Although the Tungpei troops no longer fought the Reds, there were Nanking troops along the Shansi-Shensi border and in Kansu and Ninghsia, and some fighting continued in those regions. No word of the truce between Chang and the Communists crept into the press. And although Chiang Kai-shek's spies in Sian knew that something was fermenting, they could get few details of its exact nature. Occasional trucks arrived in Sian carrying Red passengers, but they looked innocuous; they all wore Tungpei uniforms. The occasional departure of other trucks from Sian to the Red districts aroused no suspicion; they resembled any other Tungpei trucks setting off for the front.

It was on just such a truck, Pastor Wang confided to me soon after my arrival, that I would myself be going to the front. The journey by plane was out: too much risk of embarrassment to the Young Marshal was involved, for his American pilots might not hold their tongues if a foreigner were dumped on the front and not returned.

One morning the Pastor called on me with a Tungpei officer—or at any rate a youth wearing the uniform of a Tungpei officer—and suggested a trip to the ancient Han city outside Sian. A curtained car waited for us in front of the hotel, and when we got in I saw in a corner a man wearing dark glasses and the Chung Shan uniform of a Kuomintang official. We drove out to the site of the old palace of the Han Dynasty,[1] and there we walked over to the raised mound of earth where the celebrated Han Wu Ti once sat in his throne room and "ruled the earth." Here you could still pick up fragments of tile from those great roofs of over 2,000 years ago.

Pastor Wang and the Tungpei officer had some words to exchange, and stood apart, talking. The Kuomintang official, who had sat without speaking during our long dusty drive, came over to me and removed his dark glasses and his white hat. I saw that he was quite young. Under a rim of thick, glossy hair a pair of intense eyes sparkled at me. A mischievous grin spread over his bronzed face, and one look at him, without those glasses, showed that the uniform was a disguise, that this was no sedentary bureaucrat but an out-of-doors man of action. He was of medium height and looked slight of strength, so that when he came close to me and suddenly took my arm in a grip of iron I winced with surprise. There was a pantherish grace about the man's movements, I noticed later, a lithe limberness under the stiff formal cut of the suit.

---

1. The illustrious Han Dynasty governed the "Central Kingdom" for a period (202 B.C.–220 A.D.) that overlapped with the life span of the Roman Empire, with which it had some trade and cultural exchanges.

他把脸凑近我，露出笑容，锐利的眼光紧紧地盯着我，把我的两条胳膊紧紧地握在他的那双铁爪子中，然后摇摇脑袋，滑稽地撅起了嘴，向我眨着眼！"瞧瞧我！"他低声说，好像一个有什么秘密的孩子一样高兴。"瞧瞧我！瞧瞧我！你认出我来了吗？"

我不知道这个人是怎么回事。他兴奋地不知在说些什么东西，结果这种兴奋情绪也感染了我，但是我觉得很尴尬，因为我不知说什么才好。认出他来了吗？我这一辈子从来没有遇到过像他那样的中国人！我抱歉地摇摇头。

他从我的胳膊上松开一只手，用手指指着他的胸膛。"我以为你可能在什么地方见过我的照片，"他说。"我是邓发，"他告诉我说——"邓发！"他的脑袋向后一仰，看着我对这个炸弹的反应。

邓发？邓发……哦，邓发是中国共产党秘密警察的头子。而且还有，悬赏5万元要他的首级！

邓发泄露了他的身份以后高兴得跳了起来。他按捺不住自己，对目前这种情况感到好玩：他，这个鼎鼎大名的"共匪"，就生活在敌营中心，不把到处追缉他的特务放在眼里。他看到我，一个自告奋勇到"匪"区去的美国人感到很高兴——不断地拥抱我。他什么都愿意给我。我要他的马吗？啊，他的马好极了，红色中国最好的马！我要他的照片吗？他收集得不少，都可以给我。我要他的日记吗？他会带信到仍在苏区的妻子，把这一切，还有别的东西都给我。他后来真的没有食言。

真是个你意想不到的中国人！真是个你意想不到的"赤匪"！

邓发是个广东人，出身工人阶级家庭，曾经在一艘来往于广州与香港之间的轮船上当西餐厨师。他是香港海员大罢工的一个领导人，被一个不喜欢罢工的英国警察打伤了胸口，折断了几乎全部肋骨。他接着就成了共产党，进了黄埔军校，参加了国民革命，1927年以后到江西参加了红军。

我们在那个土堆上站了一个多小时，一边谈话，一边看着下面绿草掩盖的皇城遗址。我无法向你形容那一时刻在我感情上引起的奇怪冲击——由于我们所在的环境而这么强烈，又是这么奇怪地富有预兆性质，这么奇怪地超脱于我、超脱于中国的那部分变化无穷的历史；因为这些共产党人把这个地方当作我们四个人可以安然无事地碰面的安全场所，似乎是很不协调的，但是又是很合乎逻辑的，而且毕竟是在这里，在两千多年以前，

He put his face close to mine and grinned and fixed his sharp, burning eyes on me and held my two arms tightly in that iron grip, and then wagged his head and comically screwed up his mouth—and winked! "Look at me!" he whispered with the delight of a child with a secret. "Look at me! Look at me! Do you recognize me?"

I did not know what to think of the fellow. He was so bubbling over about something that his excitement infected me, and I felt foolish because I had nothing to say. Recognize him? I had never met a Chinese like him in my life! I shook my head apologetically.

He released a hand from my arm and pointed a finger at his chest. "I thought maybe you had seen my picture somewhere," he said. "Well, I am Teng Fa," he offered—"*Teng Fa!*" He pulled back his head and gazed at me to see the effect of the bombshell.

Teng Fa? Teng Fa . . . why, Teng Fa was chief of the Chinese Red Army's Security Police. And something else, there was $50,000 on his head!

Teng danced with pleasure when he disclosed his identity. He was irrepressible, full of amusement at the situation: he, the notorious "Communist bandit," living in the very midst of the enemy's camp, thumbing his nose at the spies that hovered everywhere. And he was overjoyed at seeing me—he literally hugged me repeatedly—an American who was voluntarily going into the "bandit" areas. He offered me everything. Did I want his horse? Oh, what a horse he had, the finest in Red China! His pictures? He had a wonderful collection and it was all mine. His diary? He would send instructions to his wife, who was still in the soviet areas, to give all this and more to me. And he kept his word.

What a Chinese! What a Red bandit!

Teng Fa was a Cantonese, the son of a working-class family, and had once been a foreign-style cook on a Canton-Hongkong steamer. He had been a leader of the great Hongkong shipping strike, when he was beaten in the chest and had had some ribs broken by a British constable who did not like pickets. And then he had become a Communist, and entered Whampoa, and taken part in the Nationalist Revolution, until after 1927 he had joined the Red Army in Kiangsi.

We stood for an hour or more on that height, talking and looking down on the green-shrouded grave of an imperial city. How incongruous and yet how logical it was that this place should seem to the Communists the one rendezvous where we four could safely

当时已经够激进的大汉族统治着一个统一的、当时是进步的中国，成功地在战国的混乱中巩固了一个民族和文化，使得后代从此以后以汉族子孙自称，就在这样的地方会见这个令人惊讶的现代革命年轻战士，又是多么合适啊。

就是在这里，邓发告诉我由谁护送我去红区，我一路怎么走，我在红色中国怎么生活，并且向我保证在那里会受到热烈欢迎。

"你不怕丢掉你的脑袋吗？"我们坐车回城里去的时候我问他。

"不比张学良更怕，"他笑道。"我同他住在一起。"

meet, the exact spot where, two millenniums ago, Han Wu Ti had ruled a united China, and so successfully consolidated a people and a culture from the chaos of warring states that their descendants, ever since, had been content to call themselves Sons of Han.

It was here that Teng told me who would escort me to the Red districts, how I would travel, how I would live in Red China, and assured me of a warm welcome there.

"Aren't you afraid for your head?" I asked as we drove back to the city.

"Not any more than Chang Hsueh-liang is," he said. "I'm living with him."

四、　　通过红色大门

我们在黎明之前离开西安府,那一度是"金城汤池"的高大的木头城门在我们的军事通行证魔力前面霍地打了开来,拖着门上的链条铛铛作响。在熹微的晨光中,军用大卡车隆隆驶过飞机场,当时每天都有飞机从那个机场起飞,到红军防线上空去侦察和轰炸。

对于一个中国旅客来说,在这条从西安府北去的大道上,每走一里路都会勾起他对本民族丰富多彩的绚烂历史的回忆。中国最近发生的历史性变化——共产主义运动,竟然选择在这个地方来决定中国的命运,不可不谓恰当。1小时以后,我们摆渡过了渭河,在这个肥沃的渭河流域,孔子的祖先[1]、肤色发黑的野蛮的人发展了他们的稻米文化,形成了今天在中国农村的民间神话里仍是一股力量的一些传说。快到正午的时候,我们到了蒲城县。大约2,200年前,那个最先"统一"中国的威赫一时的人物秦始皇就是在这个筑有雉堞的城池附近诞生的。秦始皇第一个把他的国家的古代边境城墙都连接起来,成了今天仍然是地球上最宏伟的砖石工程——中国的万里长城。

在那条新修的汽车路上,沿途的罂粟摇摆着肿胀的脑袋,等待收割。新修的路面经过水冲车压,到处是深沟浅辙,因而我们那部载重6吨的道奇卡车,有时也甚至无法通行。陕西长期以来就以盛产鸦片闻名。几年前西北发生大饥荒,曾有300万人丧命,美国红十字会调查人员,把造成那场惨剧的原因大部分归咎于鸦片的种植。当时贪婪的军阀强迫农民种植鸦片,最好的土地都种上了鸦片,一遇到干旱的年头,西北的主要粮食作物小米、麦子和玉米就会严重短缺。

---

1. 前3000—前551年期间。

4   THROUGH RED GATES

We left Sianfu before dawn, the high wooden gates of the once "golden city" swinging open and noisily dragging their chains before the magic of our military pass. In the half-light of predawn the big army trucks lumbered past the airfield from which expeditions set out for daily reconnaissance and bombing over the Red lines.

To a Chinese traveler every mile of this road northward from Sianfu evokes memories of the rich and colorful pageant of his people. It seemed not inappropriate that the latest historical mutation in China, the Communist movement, should choose this locale in which to work out a destiny. In an hour we were being ferried across the Wei River, in whose rich valley Confucius' ancestors[1] developed their rice culture and formulated traditions still a power in the folk myth of rural China today. And toward noon we had reached Ts'un Pu. It was near this battlemented city that the towering and terrible figure who first "unified" China—the Emperor Ch'in Shih Huang Ti—was born some 2,200 years ago. The Emperor Ch'in first consolidated all of the ancient frontier walls of his country into what remains today the most stupendous masonry on earth—the Great Wall of China.

Opium poppies nodded their swollen heads, ready for harvest, along the newly completed motor road—a road already deeply wrinkled with washouts and ruts, so that at times it was scarcely navigable even for our six-ton Dodge truck. Shensi had long been a noted opium province. During the great Northwest Famine, which a few years before had taken a toll of 3,000,000 lives, American Red Cross investigators attributed much of the tragedy to the cultivation of the poppy, forced upon the peasants by provincial monopolies controlled by greedy warlords. The best land being devoted to the poppy, in years of drought there was a serious shortage of millet, wheat, and corn, the staple cereals of the Northwest.

---

1. During 3000 B.C.–551 B.C.

那天晚上，我在洛川一间肮脏的茅屋里的土炕[1]上过了一夜，隔壁屋里关着猪和毛驴，我自己屋里则有老鼠，闹腾得大家都睡不了多少觉。第二天早上刚出城数英里，那片黄土地面便逐层升高，险峻起来，地势古怪地变了样。

这一令人惊叹的黄土地带，广及甘肃、陕西、宁夏、山西四省的大部分地区，雨量充分的时候异常肥沃，因为这种黄土提供了无穷无尽的、有几十英尺深的多孔表土层。地质学家认为，这种黄土是有机物质，是许多世纪以来被中亚细亚的大风从蒙古、从西方吹过来的。这在景色上造成了变化无穷的奇特、森严的形象——有的山丘像巨大的城堡，有的像成队的猛犸，有的像滚圆的大馒头，有的像被巨手撕裂的岗峦，上面还留着粗暴的指痕。那些奇形怪状、不可思议有时甚至吓人的形象，好像是个疯神捏就的世界——有时却又是个超现实主义的奇美的世界。

在这里，虽然到处可以看见田畴和耕地，却难得看见房屋。农民们也是在那些黄土山里藏身的。在整个西北，多少世纪以来已成了习惯，都是在那坚硬的淡褐色的山壁上掘洞而居的，中国人称之为"窑洞"。可是这种窑洞同西洋人所说的洞穴并不是一回事。窑洞冬暖夏凉，易于建造，也易于打扫。就连最富有的地主，也往往在山上挖洞为家。有些是有好几间屋子的大宅，设备和装饰华丽，石铺的地板，高敞的居室，光线从墙上的纸窗透进室内，墙上还开有坚固的黑漆大门。

在那辆颠簸的卡车里，一位年轻的东北军军官坐在我身旁，在离洛川不远的地方，他将那样一个"窑洞村"指给我看。那地方离汽车路只有1英里左右，中间只隔着一个深谷。

"他们是红军，"他向我透露说，"几个星期以前，我们派一队人到那里去买小米，村子里的人一斤也不肯卖给我们。当兵的笨蛋就动手抢了一些。他们退出村子的时候，农民便开枪打他们。"他用双臂画了一条大弧线，把国民党军队驻守的许多堡垒——构筑在山顶上的机枪阵地——严密保护下的公路两边的一切都包括在里面。"赤匪，"他说，"在那边，全部都是'赤匪'的地盘。"

我怀着更加浓厚的兴趣凝望他指出的地方，因为几小时之内，我就要踏进那莫测究竟的山丘和高地的那一边去了。

---

1. 中国房屋中土垒的平台，一头有灶，下面有迷宫一样的弯弯曲曲的烟道，可以把土炕烧暖。

I spent the night on a clay *k'ang*,[1] in a filthy hut at Lochuan, with pigs and donkeys quartered in the next room, and rats in my own, and I'm sure we all slept very little. Next morning, a few miles beyond that city, the loess terraces rose higher and more imposing, and the country was weirdly transformed.

The wonderful loess lands, which cover much of Kansu, Shensi, Ninghsia, and Shansi provinces, account for the marvelous fertility of these regions (when there is rainfall), for the loess furnishes an inexhaustible porous topsoil tens of feet deep. Geologists think the loess is organic matter blown down in centuries past from Mongolia and from the west by the great winds that rise in Central Asia. Scenically the result is an infinite variety of queer, embattled shapes—hills like great castles, like rows of mammoth, nicely rounded scones, like ranges torn by some giant hand, leaving behind the imprint of angry fingers. Fantastic, incredible, and sometimes frightening shapes, a world configurated by a mad god—and sometimes a world also of strange surrealist beauty.

And though we saw fields and cultivated land everywhere, we seldom saw houses. The peasants were tucked away in those loess hills also. Throughout the Northwest, as has been the habit of centuries, men lived in homes dug out of the hard, fudge-colored cliffs—*yao-fang*, or "cave houses," as the Chinese call them. But they were no caves in the Western sense. Cool in summer, warm in winter, they were easily built and easily cleaned. Even the wealthiest landlords often dug their homes in the hills. Some of them were many-roomed edifices gaily furnished and decorated, with stone floors and high-ceilinged chambers, lighted through ricepaper windows opened in the walls of earth also athwart the stout, black-lacquered doors.

Once, not far from Lochuan, a young Tungpei officer, who rode beside me in the cavorting truck, pointed to such a *yao-fang-ts'un*—a cave village. It lay only a mile or so distant from the motor road, just across a deep ravine.

"They are Reds," he revealed. "One of our detachments was sent over there to buy millet a few weeks ago, and those villagers refused to sell us a catty of it. The stupid soldiers took some by force. As they retired the peasants shot at them." He swung his arms in an arc including everything on each side of the highway, so carefully guarded by dozens of *pao-lei*—hilltop machine gun nests—manned by Kuomintang troops. "*Hung-fei*," he said, "everything out there is Red-bandit territory."

I gazed toward the spaces indicated with keener interest, for it was into that horizon of unknown hill and upland that I intended, within a few hours, to make my way.

---

1. A *k'ang* is a raised earthen platform built in Chinese houses, with a fireplace at one end. The flue is arranged in a maze beneath, so that it heats the clay platform, if desired.

在路上，我们遇见了一〇五师的一些部队，他们都是东北人，正从延安回到洛川去。他们是瘦削而结实的青年，大多数比一般中国士兵的身材高些。我们在路边的一家小客店歇下来喝茶，有几个士兵在那里休息，我在他们的附近坐了下来。他们是刚从陕北的瓦窑堡回来的，在那里曾经和红军发生过遭遇战。我听到了他们相互间谈话的一些片断。他们是在那里谈论红军。

"他们吃的比我们好得多，"一个说。

"是的，他们吃的是老百姓[1]的肉呀！"另一个答道。

"那没有关系，不过是少数地主，反而有好处。我们到瓦窑堡去，有谁感谢我们呢？是地主！你说是不是？我们为什么要为那些有钱人送命呢？"

"他们说现在有3,000多东北军已经加入他们一边了……"

"这又是他们有理的一件事。我们除了打日本人，同谁也不想打的，为什么我们要打起自己人来呢？"

一个军官走了过来，于是这番引人入胜的谈话就中止了。那个军官命令他们上路。他们拣起了他们的枪，拖着脚步走上了公路。不久我们也坐车走了。

第二天午后不久，我们到达延安，在长城以南约400华里[2]，陕北唯一可以通车的道路到这里便是终点。延安是一个历史名城，在过去几个世纪里，从北方来的游牧部落曾经通过这里入侵中原，成吉思汗的蒙古铁骑也曾经通过这里南征西安府。

延安是个理想的要塞，它位于一个深谷中间，四周都是岩石嶙峋的高山，坚固的城墙一直延伸到山巅。现在，城墙上新建了许多工事，像蜂窝一样，工事里一挺挺机枪都对着不远地方的红军。公路以及与公路直接毗连的地方，那时仍然在东北军手里，可是直到最近，延安是完全被切断联系的。蒋介石总司令对红军进行了封锁，红军利用封锁来对敌人进行反封锁，据说有数以百计的人活活地饿死。

就是用飞机来对付周围的红军也证明是不起作用的。红军把机关枪架在山顶——因为他们没有高射炮——结果很有效，以致南京的飞行员来给城里空投供应时，不得不飞得极高。事实上，大多数的供应品都落在红军手里，他们就在延安城外开了一个市场，将食物卖回给城里

---

1. 老百姓字面的意思就是"100个姓氏"，中国口语中指乡下人。
2. 1华里约等于1/3英里。

On the road we passed part of the 105th Division, all Manchurians, moving back from Yenan to Lochuan. They were lean and sturdy youths, most of them taller than the average Chinese soldier. At a roadside inn we stopped to drink tea, and I sat down near several of them who were resting. They were just returning from Wa Ya Pao, in north Shensi, where there had been a skirmish with the Reds. I overheard scraps of conversation between them. They were talking about the Reds.

"They eat a lot better than we do," one argued.

"Yes—eat the flesh of the *lao-pai-hsing!*"[1] another replied.

"Never mind that—a few landlords—it's all to the good. Who thanked us for coming to Wa Ya Pao? The landlords! Isn't it a fact? Why should we kill ourselves for these rich men?"

"They say more than three thousand of our Tungpei men are with them now. . . ."

"Another thing on their side. Why should we fight our own people, when none of us want to fight anybody, unless it's a Japanese, eh?"

An officer approached and this promising conversation came to an end. The officer ordered them to move on. They picked up their rifles and trudged off down the road. Soon afterwards we drove away.

Early in the afternoon of the second day we reached Yenan, where north Shensi's single road fit for wheeled traffic came to an end—about 400 *li*,[2] more or less, south of the Great Wall. It was a historic town: through it, in centuries past, had come the nomadic raiders from the north, and through it swept the great Mongol cavalry of Genghis Khan, in its ride of conquest toward Sianfu.

Yenan was ideally suited for defense. Cradled in a bowl of high, rock-ribbed hills, its stout walls crawled up to the very tops. Attached to them now, like wasps' nests, were newly made fortifications, where machine guns bristled toward the Reds not far beyond. The road and its immediate environs were then held by Tungpei troops, but until recently Yenan had been completely cut off. The Reds had turned upon their enemy the blockade which the Generalissimo enforced against themselves, and hundreds reportedly had died of starvation.

---

1. *Lao-pai-hsing*, literally "old hundred names," is the colloquial Chinese expression for the country people.
2. One Chinese *li* is about a third of a mile.

被困的居民。连张学良自己的外国驾驶员，因怕机关枪的高射，也有点胆怯起来，有一个美国人竟因此而辞职。后来我在西安府看见少帅的漂亮的波音式私人座机满身都是弹孔，我对那飞行员深表同情。

红军对延安[1]的长期包围，是在我到达那里以前几个星期才解除的，但是从居民的面有菜色，从店铺里的货架空空如也或者店门紧闭，还可以明显地看到围城的迹象。食品极少，价格高昂。可以买到的那一点东西，都是因为同红军游击队达成暂时的休战而得到的。当时曾达成协议，东北军不在这条战线上向苏区发动攻势，作为交换条件，苏区的农民开始出售粮食和蔬菜给那饥饿的"剿共"军队。

我有到前线访问的证件。我的计划是第二天一早离开延安，到"白军"前线去，那里的军队限于防守阵地，没有前进的意图。到了前线后，我打算岔入一条据说是商贩偷运货物出入苏区的山道。

我如愿以偿，安然通过最后一个岗哨，进入无人地带——这个经历，我要是如实地叙述出来，就可能给那些帮助我前去的国民党方面的人造成严重困难。现在我只消说，我的经历再次证明在中国任何事情都可能办到，只要照中国的方式去办。因为到了第二天早上7点钟的时候，我确实已经把最后一架国民党的机关枪抛在后边，走过那个把"红""白"两区分开的狭长地带了。

跟着我的，只有一个骡夫，他是我在延安雇来的。他答应把我简单的行李——铺盖卷、一点吃的、两架照相机和24卷胶片，运到红军游击队的第一个前哨。我不知道他本人是赤匪还是白匪，不过他的样子的确像个土匪。几年以来，这一带反复被那两种颜色的军队交替控制，所以他很可能不是做过赤匪就是做过白匪——也许两者都做过。我决定最好是不要问莽撞的问题，只是乖乖地跟着他走，希望一切顺利。

我们沿着一条弯弯曲曲的小溪走了4个小时，一路没有见着一个人影。那里根本没有路，只有小溪的溪床，两边岩壁高耸，溪水就在中间湍急地流过，在岩壁上面就是险峻的黄土山。要结果掉一个过分好奇的洋鬼子，这是个好去处。使我惴惴不安的一个因素，是那个骡夫对我的牛皮鞋子多次表示羡慕。

"到啦！"他突然转过头来大声说。这里，岩壁终于消失，一个狭小的山谷展现在我们面前，山谷里一片绿油油的麦苗。"我们到啦！"

---

1. 延安后来为红军所占领，现在（1937年）是红区临时首都。参见第十二篇。

The long Red siege of Yenan[1] had been lifted a few weeks before I arrived, but signs of it were still evident in the famished-looking inhabitants and the empty shelves or barred doors of shops. Little food was available and prices were alpine. What could be bought at all had been secured as a result of a temporary truce with the Red partisans. In return for an agreement not to take the offensive against the soviet districts on this front, the soviet peasants now sold grain and vegetables to the hungry anti-Red troops.

I had my credentials for a visit to the front. My plan was to leave the city early next morning, and go toward the "White" lines, where the troops were merely holding their positions, without attempting any advance. Then I meant to branch off on one of the mountain lanes over which, I had been told, merchants smuggled their goods in and out of the soviet regions.

To state precisely the manner in which, just as I had hoped, I did pass the last sentry and enter no man's land, might have caused serious difficulties for the Kuomintang adherents who assisted me on my way. Suffice it to say that my experience proved once more that anything is possible in China, if it is done in the Chinese manner. For by seven o'clock next morning I had really left the last Kuomintang machine gun behind, and was walking through the thin strip of territory that divided "Red" from "White."

With me was a single muleteer, who had been hired for me by a Manchurian colonel in Yenan. He was to carry my scant belongings—bedding roll, a little food, two cameras and twenty-four rolls of film—to the first Red partisan outpost. I did not know whether he himself was a Red bandit or a White bandit—but bandit he certainly looked. All this territory having for several years alternately been controlled by armies of both colors, it was quite possible for him to have been either—or perhaps both.

For four hours we followed a small winding stream and did not see any sign of human life. There was no road at all, but only the bed of the stream that rushed swiftly between high walls of rock, above which rose swift hills of loess. It was the perfect setting for the blotting-out of a too inquisitive foreign devil. A disturbing factor was the muleteer's frequently expressed admiration of my cowhide shoes.

"*Tao-la!*" he suddenly shouted around his ear, as the rock walls at last gave way and opened out into a narrow valley, green with young wheat. "We have arrived!"

---

1. Yenan was later occupied by the Red Army and became the provisional Red capital. See Part Twelve.

我放下了心，朝着他的前面望去，看见一座小山的山边有一个黄土村落，缕缕青烟从村里那些高大的泥烟囱里袅袅上升，那些烟囱像长长的手指一样竖立在峭壁的面前。几分钟之后，我们就到了那里。

一个年轻的农民，头上包着一条白毛巾，腰间插着一支左轮手枪，从村里走出来，惊愕地望着我，问我是谁，到那里去干什么？

"我是个美国记者，"我说，"我要见这里的贫民会主席。"

他面无表情地看着我，回答说："hài // pà！"

我过去听到中国人说"hài // pà"就只有一个意思："我害怕！"我心里想，如果他感到害怕，那我该感到怎么样呢？但是，他神色泰然自若，看来他的话不是这个意思。他回过头问那骡夫我是什么人。

那骡夫把我说过的话重说了一遍，还添枝加叶地说了些他自己的话。我放心地看到那位青年农民的脸色和缓下来了。这时我发现他确实是个长得很英俊的小伙子，皮肤黝黑发亮，牙齿整齐洁白。他好像同中国其他地方的胆怯的农民不属于一个族类。他那一双炯炯有神的快乐的眼睛含着一种挑战的神情，他还有一定的吓人气派。他的手慢慢地从枪柄上移开，脸上露出了笑容。

"我就是你要见的人，"他说，"我就是主席。请进来喝口热茶吧。"

这些陕西山区的居民有自己的方言，尽是发音含混的口语，但是他们懂得"白话"——中国的官话，他们自己的话有一大部分是外地人很容易听懂的。我同那位主席又作了几次谈话的努力之后，他渐渐地现出能够领会的神情，我们的谈话就有了顺利的进展。不过在我们的谈话当中，偶尔又会出现 hài // pà 一词，我一时顾不上问他到底害怕什么。等到我最后问清这个问题时，我这才发现陕西山区方言中的 hài // pà 等于官话中的 bù zhī dào（不知道）。这个发现使我感到很满意。

我坐在铺着炕毡的炕上，向我的主人进一步谈到我自己和我的计划。过了不久，他就显得没有什么疑虑了。我想去县政府所在地安塞，当时我以为苏维埃主席毛泽东就在那里。他能不能给我找一个向导和一个骡夫？

他答应说，没有问题，没有问题，不过我不能在大热天赶路。太阳已经升到当空，天确实是非常热，我看上去很疲倦，再说，我吃了东西没有呢？说实在的，我

Relieved, I gazed beyond him and saw in the side of a hill a loess village, where blue smoke curled from the tall clay chimneys that stood up like long fingers against the face of the cliff. In a few minutes we were there.

A young farmer who wore a turban of white toweling on his head and a revolver strapped to his waist came out and looked at me in astonishment. Who was I and what did I want?

"I am an American journalist," I said in conformance with the instructions Wang the Pastor had given me. "I want to see the local chief of the Poor People's League."

He looked at me blankly and replied, "*Hai p'a!*"

Hai p'a in any Chinese I had ever heard had only one meaning: "I'm afraid." If he is afraid, I thought to myself, what the devil am I supposed to feel? But his appearance belied his words: he looked completely self-assured. He turned to the *lofu* and asked him who I was.

The muleteer repeated what I had said, adding a few flourishes of his own. With relief, I saw the young farmer's face soften and then I noticed that he was really a good-looking young man, with fine bronzed skin and good white teeth. He did not seem to belong to the race of timid peasants of China elsewhere. There was a challenge in his sparkling merry eyes, and a certain bravado. He slowly moved his hand away from his revolver butt and smiled.

"I am that man," he said. "I am the chief. Come inside and drink some hot tea."

These Shensi hill people had a dialect of their own, full of slurred colloquialisms, but they understood *pai-hua*, or mandarin Chinese, and most of their own speech was quite comprehensible to an outlander. After a few more attempts at conversation with the chief, he began to show understanding, and we made good progress. Occasionally into our talk, however, would creep this *hai p'a* business, but for a while I was too disconcerted to ask him just *what* he feared. When I finally did probe into the matter, I discovered that *hai p'a* in the dialect of the Shensi hills is the equivalent of *pu chih-tao* in mandarin Chinese. It simply means "don't understand." My satisfaction at this discovery was considerable.

Seated on a felt-covered *k'ang* I told my host more about myself and my plans. In a short time he seemed reassured. I wanted to go to An Tsai—the county seat—where I then believed Soviet Chairman Mao Tse-tung to be. Could he give me a guide and a muleteer?

Certainly, certainly, he agreed, but I should not think of moving in the heat of day. The sun had already climbed to its zenith, it was really very hot, I looked tired, and, meanwhile, had I eaten? Actually I was ravenous, and without any further ceremony I

饿极了，因此我不再跟他客气，接受了他的邀请，第一次同一个"赤匪"一道吃饭。我的骡夫急于回延安去，我把钱付了给他，跟他告别。这也是我同白色世界的最后一个联系环节告别，从此要有许多星期不跟它发生接触。我已破釜沉舟，决心跨进红区了。

我现在已经完全落入刘龙火先生（我后来知道这就是那位青年农民的姓名）的掌握之中，也同样落在他的那些外貌强悍的同志的掌握之中，他们开始从附近的窑洞里陆续过来。他们穿着同样的装束，带着同样的武器，好奇地看着我，听见我说话的怪腔怪调，都呵呵大笑。

刘龙火拿烟、酒、茶来招待我，向我提出无数的问题。他和他的朋友们非常好奇地翻看我的照相机、鞋子、毛袜、我的布短裤的质料，不时发出赞美的声音；对于我的卡其布衬衫的拉链，更是赞不绝口。总的印象似乎是：我的行头不论看起来是多么可笑，显然非常实用。我不知道"共产主义"在实践上对这班人意味着什么，我准备眼看我的这些东西很快地被"共产"——但是当然没有发生这种事情。我几乎可以肯定，我受到严密检查的目的（比你在其他边境所受到的海关检查要愉快得多）是为了要证实他们以前的一种看法：洋鬼子不可思议。

不到一个小时，他们端来了一大盘炒鸡蛋，还有蒸卷、小米饭、一些白菜和少量烤猪肉。我的主人为饭菜简单而表示歉意，我则为我的食量不同寻常而表示歉意。其实后面这一点完全没有必要，因为我必须飞快运用我的一双筷子，才能赶上贫民会的那些好汉呢。

龙火告诉我，说安塞离那里不过"几步路"，尽管我不大放心，但是除了照他说等一等以外，没有其他办法。等到一个年轻的向导和一个骡夫终于到来的时候，已经过了下午4点钟了。临走时，我想把饭钱付给刘先生，可是他怂然拒绝了。

"你是一位外国客人，"他解释说，"而且你是来找我们的毛主席的。再说，你的钱也没有用处。"他对我手里拿着的纸币瞟了一眼，问道："你没有苏区的钱吗？"听我回答说没有，他就数了共值1元钱的苏区纸币说，"这个你拿去，你路上会用得着的。"

我拿1元国民党的钱和刘先生交换，他接受了；我再一次向他道谢，然后跟在我的向导和骡夫后边爬上山道。

accepted this invitation to a first meal with a "Red bandit." My muleteer was anxious to return to Yenan, and, paying him off, I bade him goodby. It was a farewell to my last link with the "White" world for many weeks to come. I had crossed the Red Rubicon.

I was now at the mercy of Mr. Liu Lung-huo—Liu the Dragon Fire, as I learned the young peasant was called—and likewise at the mercy of his toughlooking comrades, who had begun to drift in from neighboring *yao-fang*. Similarly clad and armed, they look at me curiously and laughed at my preposterous accent.

Liu offered me tobacco, wine, and tea, and plied me with numerous questions. He and his friends examined with close interest, interrupted by exclamations of approval, my camera, my shoes, my woolen stockings, the fabric of my cotton shorts, and (with lengthy admiration) the zipper on my khaki shirt. The general impression seemed to prevail that, however ridiculous it might look, the ensemble evidently served its purposes well enough. I did not know just what "communism" might mean to these men in practice, and I was prepared to see my belongings rapidly "redistributed"—but instead I was given the foreign-guest treatment.

In an hour a vast platter of scrambled eggs arrived, accompanied by steamed rolls, boiled millet, some cabbage, and a little roast pork. My host apologized for the simplicity of the fare, and I for an inordinate appetite. Which latter was quite beside the point, as I had to punt my chopsticks at a lively pace to keep up with the good fellows of the Poor People's League.

Dragon Fire assured me that An Tsai was "only a few steps," and though I was uneasy about it I could do nothing but wait, as he insisted. When finally a youthful guide appeared, accompanied by a muleteer, it was already past four in the afternoon. Before leaving, I ventured to pay Mr. Liu for his food, but he indignantly refused.

"You are a foreign guest," he explained, "and you have business with our Chairman Mao. Moreover, your money is no good." Glancing at the bill I held out to him, he asked, "Haven't you any soviet money?" When I replied in the negative, he counted out a dollar's worth of soviet paper notes. "Here—you will need this on the road."

Mr. Liu accepted a Kuomintang dollar in exchange; I thanked him again, and climbed up the road behind my guide and muleteer.

"好啊，"我一边气喘喘地爬山，一边对自己说。"到现在为止，一切顺利。"我已闯进了红色大门。这件事多么简单！

但是在前面等待着我的是一场险遭不测的事件，以致后来谣传我被土匪绑架杀掉了。其实，土匪早已在那寂静的黄土山壁后边跟踪着我了——只不过不是赤匪而是白匪而已。

Ahead of me was a narrow escape and an incident which was later to nourish the rumor that I had been kidnaped and killed by bandits. And as a matter of fact, bandits—not Red but White—were already trailing me behind those silent walls of loess.

PART TWO
The Road to the Red Capital

第二篇
去红都的道路

一、　　遭白匪追逐

"打倒吃我们肉的地主！"

"打倒喝我们血的军阀！"

"打倒把中国出卖给日本的汉奸！"

"欢迎一切抗日军队结成统一战线！"

"中国革命万岁！"

"中国红军万岁！"

我就是在这些用醒目的黑字写的、多少有些令人不安的标语下面度过我在红区的第一夜的。

但是，这不是在安塞，也不是在任何红军战士的保护之下。因为，不出我的所料，我们当天并没有到达安塞，到太阳下山的时候，我们才走到一个坐落在河湾上的小村庄，四周都是阴森森地俯瞰着的山峦。有好几排石板屋顶的房子从溪口升起，标语就写在这些房子的土坯墙上。五六十个农民和目不转睛的儿童拥出来迎接我们这个只有一匹驴子的旅队。

我的那位贫民会的年轻向导，决定把我安顿在这里。他说，他的一头母牛最近下了仔，附近有狼，他得回去照应。安塞离这里还有 10 英里路，要摸黑赶到那里是不容易的。于是他把我交托给当地贫民会分会主席照料。我的向导和骡夫都拒绝接受任何报酬，不管是白区的钱，还是红区的钱。

1 — Chased by White Bandits

"Down with the landlords who eat our flesh!"

"Down with the militarists who drink our blood!"

"Down with the traitors who sell China to Japan!"

"Welcome the United Front with all anti-Japanese armies!"

"Long live the Chinese Revolution!"

"Long live the Chinese Red Army!"

It was under these somewhat disturbing exhortations, emblazoned in bold black characters, that I spent my first night in Red territory.

But it was not in An Tsai and not under the protection of any Red soldiers. For, as I had feared, we did not reach An Tsai that day, but by sunset had arrived only at a little village that nestled in the curve of a river, with hills brooding darkly on every side. Several layers of slate-roofed houses rose up from the lip of the stream, and it was on their mud-brick walls that the slogans were chalked. Fifty or sixty peasants and staring children poured out to greet my caravan of one donkey.

My young emissary of the Poor People's League decided to deposit me here. One of his cows had recently calved, he said; there were wolves in the neighborhood, and he had to get back to his charges. An Tsai was still ten miles distant and we could not get there easily in the dark. He turned me over for safekeeping to the chairman of the local branch of the Poor People's League. Both guide and muleteer refused any compensation for their services—either in White money or in Red.

分会主席是位20出头的青年，脸色黝黑开朗，身上穿着褪了色的蓝布褂子和白裤，露出一双牛革似的赤脚。他很客气地招待我。他请我到村公所的一间屋子里去睡，派人送来热水和一碗小米粥。但是我谢绝住在这间有臭味的黑屋子里，请他让我使用两扇拆卸下来的门板。我把这两扇门板搁在两条板凳上，摊开毯子，就睡在露天里。这是一个美丽的夜晚，晴朗的夜空闪耀着北方的繁星，在我下面的一个小瀑布流水淙淙，使人感到和平与宁静。因为长途跋涉的疲乏，我倒头就睡着了。

当我再睁开眼睛时，天已破晓。分会主席站在我的身边，摇摇我的肩膀。我当然吃了一惊，连忙翻身坐起，完全醒了过来。

"什么事？"我问。

"你最好早一点动身，这里附近有土匪，你得赶紧到安塞去。"

土匪？我的话已到嘴边上，正要回答我正是来找这些所谓土匪的，这时我才明白他的话是什么意思。他说的土匪，不是指红军，而是指"白匪"。我不用他再劝说就翻身而起。我不想闹出在苏维埃中国给白匪掳去这样的笑话。

这里需要向读者作一些解释。白匪，用国民党的名词来说就是民团，正如"赤匪"用苏维埃的名词来说就是游击队一样。国民党为了要镇压农民起义，纷纷组织民团。现在国民党在中国、日本人在"满洲国"都普遍实行保甲制度这个控制农民的古老办法，民团就是作为保甲制度的一个有机部分进行活动的。

保甲的字面含义就是"保证盔甲"。这个制度规定每10户农民必须有个甲长，保证他们循规蹈矩，使当地县长满意。这是一种连保制度，一个保甲里的任何一个人如果犯了罪，整个保甲的人都要负责任。当初蒙古人和满洲人就是用这个办法统治中国的。

用这方法来防止农民组织反叛，几乎是无往而不胜。因为保甲长几乎总是富农、地主、开当铺或放债的，他们是最最积极的，自然不愿"担保"任何具有叛逆倾向的佃户或债户。无人担保是一件十分严重的事情。一个无人担保的人，可以用任何借口，当作"嫌疑分子"投入牢狱。

The chairman was a youth in his early twenties who wore a faded blue cotton jacket under a brown, open face, and a pair of white trousers above a pair of leathery bare feet. He welcomed me and was very kind. He offered me a room in the village meeting house, and had hot water brought to me, and a bowl of millet. But I declined the dark, evil-smelling room and petitioned for the use of two dismantled doors. Laying these on a couple of benches, I unrolled my blankets and made my bed in the open. It was a gorgeous night, with a clear sky spangled with northern stars, and the waters in a little fall below me murmured of peace and tranquillity. Exhausted from the long walk, I fell asleep immediately.

When I opened my eyes again dawn was just breaking. The chairman was standing over me, shaking my shoulder.

"What is it?"

"You had better leave a little early. There are bandits near here, and you ought to get to An Tsai quickly."

Bandits? He was not talking about Reds, he meant "White bandits." I got up without further persuasion. I did not want anything to happen to me so ridiculous as being kidnaped by White bandits in Soviet China.

White bandits were in the Kuomintang's terminology called *min-t'uan*, or "people's corps," just as Red bandits were in soviet terminology called *yu-chi-tui*, "roving bands"—Red partisans. In an effort to combat peasant uprisings, the *min-t'uan* forces had increasingly been organized by the Kuomintang. They functioned as an organic part of the *pao-chia* system, an ancient method of controlling the peasantry which was now being widely imposed by both the Kuomintang in China and the Japanese in Manchukuo.

Pao-chia literally means "guaranteed armor." One *chia* consisted of approximately ten families, with a headman supposedly elected but usually appointed by the local magistrate. One *pao* was made up of approximately ten *chia*. The combined *pao-chia* was held collectively responsible to the district magistrate (*hsien chang*), a government appointee, for any offense committed by any member of the roughly hundred-family unit. It was the *chia* headman's duty to report any "rebel son" in his group, otherwise he would be punished for any irregularity. By such means the Mongols and Manchus had pacified rural China—and it was not a popular means, especially among the poor.

As a measure for preventing the organization of peasant protest it was almost unbeatable. Since headmen of the *pao-chia* were nearly always rich farmers, landlords, pawnbrokers, or moneylenders—most zealous of subjects—naturally they were not inclined to "guarantee" any tenant or debtor peasants of a rebellious turn of mind. Yet not to be guaranteed was a serious matter. An unguaranteed man could be thrown in jail on any pretext, as a "suspicious character."

实际上这就是说，整个农民阶级的命运是操在乡绅阶级的手中，后者随时可以用拒绝担保的方法来毁掉一个人。保甲制度的重要作用之一，就是征收捐税维持民团。民团是由地主和乡绅挑选、组织和指挥的。它的主要任务是反对共产主义，帮助收租交谷，包讨欠债本息，帮助县长勒索苛捐杂税。

所以，每当红军占领一个地方，它的第一个，也是最后一个敌人就是民团。因为除了出钱供养他们的地主外，民团没有什么基础，红军一到，他们当然就失去了这个基础。中国的真正阶级战争，从民团和红军游击队的斗争上，可以看得最清楚，因为这一个斗争往往就是地主和他们以前的佃农债户之间的直接武装冲突。民团的人数有几十万，是中国200万左右名义上反共的军队的最重要的辅助部队。

如今红军和国民党军队在这一条战线上虽已停战，民团对于红军游击队的袭击还是继续不断。在西安、洛川和延安等处，我听说有许多逃到这些城市里的地主，出钱供养或亲自领导白匪在苏维埃边区活动。他们常常利用红军主力不在的机会，侵入红区，烧村劫寨，杀戮农民，把农民领袖带到白区去，作为"共产党"俘虏向地主和白军军官邀功领赏。

民团从事冒险活动，主要是为了进行报复和很快地到手钱财，他们在红白战争中以最富于破坏性著称。无论如何，我个人是不愿在自己的身上试验白匪的"外交政策"的。我的行李虽然不多，但我觉得如果只需干掉一个孤零零的洋鬼子就可以把我的一点点现钱、衣服和照相机据为己有的话，这些东西还是有足够引诱力，使他们不会放过的。

匆匆地吞下了几口热茶和麦饼以后，我跟分会主席所派的另外一个向导兼骡夫一同出发。我们沿着一条河床走了一个钟头，有时经过一些窑洞组成的小村落，便有毛茸茸的狗恶狠狠地朝我吠叫，站岗的儿童走出来查问我们的路条。接着我们走到了一个巨石围绕、自然形成的可爱的水潭旁边，在这里我遇见了第一个红军战士。

除了一匹身上披着绣有一颗金星的天蓝色鞍毯的白马在河边吃草以外，只有他一个人。这个青年正在洗澡；我们走近时，他很快地跳了出来，披上天蓝色的裤子，

This meant in effect that the whole peasantry was placed at the mercy of the gentry, who at any time could ruin a man by refusing to guarantee him. Among the functions of the *pao-chia*, and a very important one, was the collection of taxes for the maintenance of the *min-t'uan*, or militia. The *min-t'uan* was selected, organized, and commanded by the landlords and gentry. Its primary duties were to fight communism, to help collect rents and share-crop debts, to collect loans and interest, and to support the local magistrates' efforts to gather in the taxes.

Hence it happened that, when the Red Army occupied a territory, its first as well as its last enemy was the *min-t'uan*. For the *min-t'uan* had no base except in the landlords who paid them, and they lost that base when the Reds came in. Class war in China was best seen in the struggles between *min-t'uan* and Red partisans, for here very often was a direct armed conflict between landlords and their former tenants and debtors. *Min-t'uan* mercenaries numbered hundreds of thousands and were most important auxiliaries of the some 2,000,000 nominally anti-Red troops of China.

Now, although there was a truce between the Red Army and the Kuomintang Army on this front, attacks by the *min-t'uan* on the Red partisan brigades continued intermittently. In Sian, Lochuan, and Yenan I had heard that many landlords who had fled to these cities were now financing or personally leading the White bandits to operate in the soviet border districts. Taking advantage of the absence of the main Red forces, they made retaliatory raids into Red territory, burning and looting villages and killing peasants. Leaders were carried off to the White districts, where generous rewards were given for such Red captives by the landlords and White officers.

Interested primarily in *revanche* and quick cash returns on their adventures, the *min-t'uan* were credited with the most destructive work of the Red-White wars. I, at any rate, had no wish to test out the White bandits' "foreign policy" on myself. Although my belongings were few, I feared that the little cash and clothing I had, together with my cameras, would prove prizes too tempting for them to overlook, if it required only the erasure of a lone foreign devil to possess them.

After hastily swallowing some hot tea and wheat cakes, I set off with another guide and muleteer contributed by the chairman. For an hour we followed the bed of the stream, occasionally passing small cave villages, where heavy-furred dogs growled menacingly at me and child sentinels came out to demand our road pass. Then we reached a lovely pool of still water set in a natural basin hollowed from great rocks, and there I saw my first Red warrior.

He was alone except for a white pony which stood grazing beside the stream, wearing a vivid silky-blue saddle-blanket with a yellow star on it. The young man had been bathing; at our approach he jumped up quickly, pulling on a sky-blue coat and a turban of white

和白布的头巾，上面有一颗红星。一支毛瑟枪挂在他腰际，木盒子柄上垂着一绺红缨绸带。他手按着枪，等着我们走近，问向导我们有什么事情。后者拿出他的路条，简单地说明了我是怎么被交给他的，那个战士好奇地看着我，等我进一步解释。

"我是来见毛泽东的，"我说。"我知道他在安塞。我们还得走多远？"

"毛主席吗？"他慢吞吞地问，"不，他不在安塞。"接着他看了看我们的后面，问我是不是没有别人。他弄清楚确实只有我一人之后，态度才自然起来，他微笑着，好像有什么秘密的好玩的事情似的。他对我说："我正要到安塞去。我和你一块到县政府去吧。"

他牵着马在我身边走，我自动地更详细地介绍了我自己，也问了一些关于他的情况和问题。我弄清楚了他是在政治保卫局里工作，在这一带边境上值班巡逻。那匹马？这是张学良少帅的"礼物"。他告诉我，最近在陕北的战争中，红军从张学良的军队方面俘获了1,000多匹马。我又进一步知道他姓姚，22岁，当红军已经6年了。6年！他该有什么样的故事可以讲啊！

我很欢喜他。他是一个外貌诚实的青年，长得很匀称，红星帽下一头乌亮的黑发。在寂寞的山谷中遇见了他，令人安心。真的，我甚至忘记了问他关于土匪的事情，因为我们很快就谈到红军在春天的东征山西。我告诉他那次东征在北平所发生的影响，他也告诉我，他在那次惊人的"抗日东征"中的个人经验，据说红军在一个月内增加了15,000人。

两小时后，我们到了安塞，它位于黄河支流肤水的对岸。从地图上看来，安塞是一个大城，实际上则很小，徒有空墙。街上阒无人迹，到处都是断垣残壁。我的第一个想法是，这是劫掠和破坏的证据。但再仔细一看，并没有放火的痕迹，很明显这些废墟年代久远，不可能是红军造成的。

姚解释说："10年前安塞给大水完全冲毁，全城都泡在水里了。"

安塞的居民没有再把原来的城厢建筑起来，他们如今都住在城外不远石崖上蜂巢似的窑洞里。我们到了以后才发现，驻扎在那里的红军一个支队，已经派去追击白匪，县苏维埃的委员都已到附近的一个小村庄百家坪[1]去向省里的一位委员报告工作。姚自告奋勇，护送我去百家坪，我们在黄昏时候到达。

---

1. 经查证，"百家坪"疑为"白家坪"。——编注

toweling on which was fixed a red star. A Mauser hung at his hip, with a red tassel dangling bravely from its wooden combination holsterstock. With his hand on his gun he waited for us to come up to him, and demanded our business from the guide.

"I have come to interview Mao Tse-tung," I said. "I understand he is at An Tsai. How much farther have we to go?"

"Chairman Mao?" he inquired slowly. "No, he is not at An Tsai." Then he peered behind us and asked if I were alone. When he convinced himself that I was, his reserve dropped from him, he smiled as if at some secret amusement, and said, "I am going to An Tsai. I'll just go along with you to the district government."

He walked his pony beside me and I volunteered more details about myself, and ventured some inquiries about him. I learned that he was in the political defense bureau, and was on patrol duty along this frontier. And the horse? It was a "gift" from Young Marshal Chang Hsueh-liang. He told me that the Reds had captured over 1,000 horses from Chang's troops in recent battles in north Shensi. I learned further that he was called Yao, that he was twenty-two years old, and that he had been a Red for six years.

In a couple of hours we had reached An Tsai, which lay opposite the Fu Ho, a subtributary of the Yellow River. A big town on the map, An Tsai turned out to be little but the pretty shell of its wall. The streets were completely deserted and everything stood in crumbling ruins.

"The town was completely destroyed over a decade ago by a great flood," Yao explained. "The whole city went swimming."

An Tsai's inhabitants had not rebuilt the city, but lived now in the face of a great stone cliff, honeycombed with *yao-fang*, a little beyond the walls. Upon arrival we discovered, however, that the Red Army detachment stationed there had been dispatched to chase bandits, while members of the district soviet had gone to Pai Chia P'ing, a nearby hamlet, to render a report to a provincial commissioner. Yao volunteered to escort me to Pai Chia P'ing—"Hundred Family Peace"—which we reached at dusk.

我在苏区境内已经有一天半了，可是还没有看见一点战时紧张的迹象，只遇到过一个红军战士，所看见的老百姓，似乎毫无例外地都在从容不迫地从事田间劳动。不过，我是不会给外表所欺骗的。我记得，在1932年的中日淞沪战争中，中国农民就在炮火交加之中也毫不在乎地继续种他们的田。所以，当我们转一个弯刚要走进百家坪，就听到头顶上传来令人胆战心惊的呐喊声时，我不是完全没有准备的。

我抬头向传来凶狠的呐喊声的地方看去，只见大路上面山坡上有十几个农民站在一排营房似的房子前，挥舞着长矛短枪和几支步枪，神情非常坚决。他们要把我当作一个帝国主义者交给行刑队吗？还是当作一个真正的访问者来欢迎？看来我这一个闯封锁线的人的命运是立刻就要决定了。

我对姚一定露出很滑稽的脸色，因为他忽然大笑起来。他咯咯地笑着说："不怕！不怕！他们不过是几个游击队——正在操练。这里有一个红军游击队学校，不要惊慌！"

后来我才知道游击队的课程里，有这中国古代战争厮杀呐喊的演习，就好像在《水浒传》[1]中所描写的封建时代比武的那样。在无意中作了这种战术的对象，亲自尝到了脊梁凉了半截的滋味以后，我可以证明这用来恫吓敌人还是非常有效的。游击队喜欢夜间出动，在天黑突袭时发出这种叫喊一定是很怕人的。

姚在百家坪介绍给我一个苏维埃工作人员。我刚刚坐下，准备和他开始谈话，忽然一个束着军官皮带的青年指挥员骑了一匹汗流浃背的马疾驰而到，跨下马背。他好奇地端详着我。我从他口中才知道我自己这段冒险经历的详细情形。

新来这个人姓卜，他是安塞赤卫队队长。他说，他刚和100多个民团打了一场遭遇战回来。原来有一个农民的儿童——一个少年先锋队员——跑了好几里路，筋疲力竭到了安塞，来报告民团已经侵犯县境。据他报告，民团的头子是一个真正的**白匪**！——一个洋鬼子——就是我自己！

卜接下去说："我马上领了一队骑兵，上山抄了近路，一个小时后，我们就看见了白匪。他们都跟随着你"——他指一指我——"离你只有两里地。可是我们在一个山谷中把他们包围起来，进行袭击，俘获了几个人，其中有两个他们的头子和几匹

---

1. 字面含义为"水边"，一部著名的16世纪中国传奇小说。赛珍珠曾翻译过《水浒传》，译名为 *All Men Are Brothers*。

I had already been in soviet territory a day and a half, yet I had seen no signs of wartime distress, had met but one Red soldier, and a populace that universally seemed to be pursuing its agrarian tasks in complete composure. Yet I was not to be misled by appearances. I remembered how, during the Sino-Japanese War at Shanghai in 1932, Chinese peasants had gone on tilling their fields in the very midst of battle, with apparent unconcern. So that when, just as we rounded a corner to enter "Hundred Family Peace," and I heard blood-curdling yells directly above me, I was not entirely unprepared.

Looking toward the sound of the fierce battle cries, I saw, standing on a ledge above the road, in front of a row of barracklike houses, a dozen peasants brandishing spears, pikes and a few rifles in the most uncompromising of attitudes. It seemed that the question of my fate as blockade runner—whether I was to be given the firing squad as an imperialist, or to be welcomed as an honest inquirer—was about to be settled without further delay.

I must have turned a comical face toward Yao, for he burst into laughter. "*Pu p'a*," he chuckled. "Don't be afraid. They are only some partisans—*practicing*. There is a Red partisan school here. Don't be alarmed!"

Later on I learned that the curriculum for partisans included this rehearsal of ancient Chinese war cries, just as in the days of feudal tourneys described in one of Mao Tse-tung's favorite books, the *Shui Hu Chuan*.[1] And having experienced a certain frigidity of spine as an unwitting subject of the technique, I could testify that it was still very effective in intimidating an enemy.

I had just sat down and begun an interview with a soviet functionary to whom Yao had introduced me in Pai Chia P'ing, when a young commander, wearing a Sam Browne belt, stumbled up on a sweating horse and plunged to the ground. He looked curiously at me. And it was from him that I heard the full details of my own adventure.

The new arrival was named Pien, and he was commandant of the An Tsai Red Guard. He announced that he had just returned from an encounter with a force of about a hundred *min-t'uan*. A little peasant boy—a "Young Vanguard"—had run several miles and arrived almost exhausted at An Tsai, to warn them that *min-t'uan* had invaded the district. And that their leader was a really *white* bandit! —a foreign devil—*myself*!

"I at once took a mounted detachment over a mountain short cut, and in an hour we sighted the bandits," Pien recounted. "They were following you"—he pointed at me—"only about two *li* behind. But we surrounded them, attacked in a valley, and captured some, including two of their leaders, and several horses. The rest escaped toward the frontier."

---

1. Literally *The Water Margin*, a celebrated Chinese romance of the sixteenth century. Pearl Buck has translated it under the title *All Men Are Brothers*.

马。其余的人都向边境逃去。"他简单地报告完毕后,他的几个部下鱼贯走进院子,牵着几匹俘获的马。

我开始担心他会不会真的把我当作带领那些民团的头子。我刚从白党——他们如果在无人地带捉住了我,一定会叫我是赤党——那里逃身出来,仅仅是为了要给赤党抓住叫我是白党吗?

但是这时突然出现了一个清瘦的青年军官,他长着一脸黑色大胡子。他走上前来,用温和文雅的口气向我招呼:"哈啰,你想找什么人吗?"

他是用**英语**讲的!

我马上就知道了他就是那个"鼎鼎大名"的周恩来,红军指挥员,他曾经是个教会学校的高材生。这时如何接待我的问题终于决定了。

As he concluded his brief report, some of his command filed into the courtyard, leading several of the captured mounts.

I began to wonder if he really thought I *was* leading the *min-t'uan*. Had I escaped from Whites—who, had they seized me in no man's land, undoubtedly would have called me a Red—only to be captured by the Reds and accused of being a White?

But presently a slender young officer appeared, ornamented with a black beard unusually heavy for a Chinese. He came up and addressed me in a soft, cultured voice. "Hello," he said, "are you looking for somebody?"

He had spoken in *English*!

And in a moment I learned that he was the notorious Chou En-lai.

二、　造反者

我和周恩来谈了几分钟，向他说明了我的身份以后，他就替我安排在百家坪过夜，叫我在第二天早晨到他设在附近的一个村庄里的司令部去。

我坐下来和驻扎在这里的交通处的一部分人员一起吃饭，见到了十几个宿在百家坪的青年。他们有些人是游击队学校的教员，一个是无线电报务员，有几个是红军军官。我们吃的有炖鸡、不发酵的保麸馒头、白菜、小米和我放量大吃的马铃薯。可是像平常一样，除了热开水以外，没有别的喝的，而开水又烫得不能进口。因此我口渴得要命。

饭是由两个态度冷淡的孩子侍候的，确切地说是由他们端来的，他们穿着大了好几号的制服，戴着红军八角帽，帽舌很长不断掉下来遮住他们的眼睛。他们最初不高兴地看着我，可是在几分钟后，我就想法惹起了其中一个孩子的友善的微笑。这使我胆子大了一些，他从我身边走过时，我就招呼他："喂，给我们拿点冷水来。"

那个孩子压根儿不理我。几分钟后，我又招呼另外一个孩子，结果也是一样。

这时我发现戴着厚玻璃近视眼镜的交通处长李克农在笑我。他扯扯我的袖子，对我说，"你可以叫他'小鬼'，或者可以叫他'同志'，可是，你不能叫他'喂'。这里什么人都是同志。这些孩子是少年先锋队员，他们是革命者，所以自愿到这里来帮忙。他们不是佣仆。他们是未来的红军战士。"

正好这个时候，冷水来了。

2   THE INSURRECTIONIST

After I had talked for a few minutes with Chou En-lai and explained who I was, he arranged for me to spend the night in Pai Chia P'ing, and asked me to come next morning to his headquarters in a nearby village.

I sat down to dinner with a section of the communications department, which was stationed here, and met a dozen young men who were billeted in Pai Chia P'ing. Some of them were teachers in the partisan school, one was a radio operator, and some were officers of the Red Army. Our meal consisted of boiled chicken, unleavened whole-wheat bread, cabbage, millet, and potatoes, of which I ate heartily. But, as usual, there was nothing to drink but hot water and I could not touch it. I was parched with thirst.

The food was served—delivered is the word—by two nonchalant young lads wearing uniforms several sizes too large for them, and peaked Red caps with long bills that kept flapping down over their eyes. They looked at me sourly at first, but after a few minutes I managed to provoke a friendly grin from one of them. Emboldened by this success, I called to him as he went past.

"*Wei* [hey]!" I called, "bring us some cold water."

The youth simply ignored me. In a few minutes I tried the other one, with no better result.

Then I saw that Li K'e-nung, head of the communications section, was laughing at me behind his thick-lensed goggles. He plucked my sleeve. "You can call him 'little devil'," he advised, "or you can call him 'comrade' [*t'ung-chih*]—but you cannot call him *wei!* In here everybody is a comrade. These lads are Young Vanguards, and they are here because they are revolutionaries and volunteer to help us. They are not servants. They are future Red warriors."

Just then the cold (boiled) water did arrive.

"谢谢你——同志！"我道歉说。

那个少年先锋队员大胆地看着我。"不要紧，"他说，"你不用为了这样一件事情感谢一个同志！"

我想，这些孩子真了不起。我从来没有在中国儿童中间看到过这样高度的个人自尊。可是，这第一次遭遇不过是少年先锋队以后要使我感到意外的一系列事情的开端而已，因为我深入苏区以后，我就会在这些脸颊红彤彤的"红小鬼"——情绪愉快、精神饱满，而且忠心耿耿——的身上发现一种令人惊异的青年运动所表现的生气勃勃的精神。

第二天早晨护送我到周恩来的司令部去的，就是列宁儿童团的一个团员。司令部原来是一个不怕轰炸的小屋，四面围着许多同样的小屋，农民都若无其事地住在那里，尽管他们是处在战区中间，而且他们中间还有个东路红军司令[1]。我心里不由得想，红军能够这样不惹人注目地开进一个地方，是不是红军受到农民欢迎的原因？附近驻扎一些军队似乎一点也没有破坏农村的宁静。蒋介石悬赏8万元要周恩来的首级，可是在周恩来的司令部门前，只有一个哨兵。

我到屋子里以后看到里面很干净，陈设非常简单。土炕上挂的一顶蚊帐，是唯一可以看到的奢侈品。炕头放着两只铁制的文件箱，一张木制的小炕桌当作办公桌。哨兵向他报告我到来的时候，周恩来正伏案在看电报。

"我接到报告，说你是一个可靠的新闻记者，对中国人民是友好的，并且说可以信任你会如实报道，"周恩来说。"我们知道这一些就够了。你不是共产主义者，这对于我们是没有关系的。任何一个新闻记者要来苏区访问，我们都欢迎。不许新闻记者到苏区来的，不是我们，是国民党。你见到什么，都可以报道，我们要给你一切帮助来考察苏区。"

给我这样自由活动的诚意，我是有一点惊奇和怀疑的。我原来以为即使允许我到苏区去旅行，对于拍照、收集材料或访问谈话等总会对我加以一定的限制的。他的话听起来太理想了；总归有什么地方会出毛病的……

关于我的"报告"，显然来自共产党在西安的秘密总部。共产党同中国的所有重

---

1. 叶剑英时任周的参谋长。

"Thank you," I said apologetically, "—comrade!"

The Young Vanguard looked at me boldly. "Never mind that," he said, "you don't thank a comrade for a thing like that!"

I had never before seen so much personal dignity in any Chinese youngsters. This first encounter was only the beginning of a series of surprises that the Young Vanguards were to give me, for as I penetrated deeper into the soviet districts I was to discover in these red-cheeked "little Red devils"—cheerful, gay, energetic, and loyal—the living spirit of an astonishing crusade of youth.

It was one of those Sons of Lenin, in fact, who escorted me in the morning to Chou En-lai's headquarters. That turned out to be a bomb-proof hut (half cave) surrounded by many others exactly like it, in which farmers dwelt undismayed by the fact that they were in a battle area, and that in their midst was the Red commander of the Eastern Front.[1] The quartering of a few troops in the vicinity did not seem to have disturbed the rustic serenity. Before the quarters of Chou En-lai, for whose head Chiang Kai-shek had offered $80,000, there was one sentry.

Inside I saw that the room was clean but furnished in the barest fashion. A mosquito net hanging over the clay *k'ang* was the only luxury observable. A couple of iron dispatch boxes stood at the foot of it, and a little wooden table served as desk. Chou was bending over it reading radiograms when the sentry announced my arrival.

"I have a report that you are a reliable journalist, friendly to the Chinese people, and that you can be trusted to tell the truth," said Chou. "This is all we want to know. It does not matter to us that you are not a Communist. We will welcome any journalist who comes to see the soviet districts. It is not we, but the Kuomintang, who prevent it. You can write about anything you see and you will be given every help to investigate the soviet districts."

Evidently the "report" about me had come from the Communists' secret headquarters

---

1. Yeh Chien-ying was Chou's chief of staff.

要城市，包括上海、汉口、南京、天津等处，都有无线电的交通。他们在白区城市内的无线电台虽然经常被破获，国民党要想长期切断他们与红区的通讯联系，却从来没有成功过。据周恩来告诉我，自从红军用白军那里缴获的设备成立了无线电通讯部门之后，他们的密码从来没有给国民党破译过。

周恩来的无线电台设在离开他的司令部不远。他靠了这个电台和苏区里所有各个重要地方，各个战线都保持联系。他甚至和总司令朱德直接通讯，那时朱德的部队驻扎在西南数百英里外的川藏边境。在西北的苏区临时首都保安有一个无线电学校，大约有90个学生正在那里受无线电工程的训练。他们每天收听南京、上海和东京的广播，把新闻供给苏区的报纸。

周恩来盘腿坐在小炕桌前，把无线电报推开一边——据他说，其中大多数是对面山西省黄河沿岸红军东线各地驻军的报告。他动手替我起草一个旅程。写完以后，他交给我一张纸，开列着为时共需92天的旅程中的各个项目。

"这是我个人的建议，"他说，"但是你是否愿意遵照，那完全是你自己的事情。我认为，你会觉得这次旅行是非常有趣的。"

但需要92天！而且几乎一半的日子要花在路上。那里究竟有什么可以看呢？难道红区有这样辽阔吗？我嘴里没有作声，但是心里对这旅程是有保留的。可是，实际结果是，我花的时间比他所建议的还长得多，最后我还舍不得离开，因为我看到的太少了。

周恩来答应让我骑马到保安去，有3天的路程，并且给我安排好第二天早晨就动身，因为我可以跟着回到临时首都去的一部分通讯部队同行。我听说毛泽东和苏区其他干部都在那里，周恩来同意打一个电报给他们，告诉他们我就要来到。

我一边和周恩来谈话，一边深感兴趣地观察着他，因为在中国，像其他许多红军领袖一样，他是一个传奇式的人物。他个子清瘦，中等身材，骨骼小而结实，尽管胡子又长又黑，外表上仍不脱孩子气，又大又深的眼睛富于热情。他确乎有一种吸引力，似乎是羞怯、个人的魅力和领袖的自信的奇怪混合的产物。他讲英语有点迟缓，但相当准确。他对我说已有5年不讲英语了，这使我感到惊讶。

in Sian. The Reds had radio communication with all important cities of China, including Shanghai, Hankow, Nanking, and Tientsin. Despite frequent seizures of Red radio sets in the White cities, the Kuomintang had never succeeded in severing urban-rural Red communications for very long. According to Chou, the Kuomintang had never cracked the Red Army's codes since they first established a radio department, with equipment captured from the White troops.

Chou's radio station, a portable wireless set powered by a manually operated generator, was erected only a short distance from his headquarters. Through it he was in touch with all important points in the soviet areas, and with every front. He even had direct communication with Commander-in-Chief Chu Teh, whose forces were then stationed hundreds of miles to the southwest, on the Szechuan-Tibetan border. There was a radio school in Pao An, temporary soviet capital in the Northwest, where about ninety students were being trained as radio engineers. They picked up the daily broadcasts from Nanking, Shanghai, and Tokyo, and furnished news to the press of Soviet China.

Chou squatted before his little desk and put aside his radiograms—mostly reports (he said) from units stationed at various points along the Yellow River, opposite Shansi province, the Reds' Eastern Front. He began working out a suggested itinerary for me. When he finished he handed me a paper containing items covering a trip of ninety-two days.

"This is my recommendation," he said, "but whether you follow it is your own business. I think you will find it an interesting journey."

But ninety-two days! And almost half of them to be spent on foot or horseback. What was there to be seen? Were the Red districts so extensive as that? As it turned out, I was to spend much longer than he had suggested, and in the end to leave with reluctance because I had seen so little.

Chou promised me the use of a horse to carry me to Pao An, three days distant, and arranged for me to leave the following morning, when I could accompany part of the communications corps that was returning to the provisional capital. I learned that Mao Tse-tung and other soviet functionaries were there now, and Chou agreed to send a radio message to them telling of my arrival.

As we talked I had been studying Chou with deep interest; like many Red leaders, he was as much a legend as a man. Slender and of medium height, with a slight wiry frame, he was boyish in appearance despite his long black beard, and had large, warm, deep-set eyes. A certain magnetism about him seemed to derive from a combination of personal charm and assurance of command. His English was somewhat hesitant and difficult. He told me he had not used it for five years. The account below is based on notes of our conversation at that time.

周恩来，祖籍浙江绍兴，1898年出生于江苏淮安一个"破落的官僚家庭"（周恩来语）。母亲是清河县知事万青选的女儿。周（不满半岁时）被过继给叔父。当时叔父病危，尚无子嗣，生父为了使他放心自己（在家族牌位上）有男性后人，便将恩来过继给他为子。"我还是个婴儿时，婶婶就成了我真正的母亲，"周说道。"10岁之前，我几乎一天都没有离开过她——10岁那年，她和我的生母都去世了。"

周的祖父曾任山阳县（今淮安市）知事。周恩来在淮安度过了自己的童年，而他通过了科举考试的父亲（叔父）周贻淦，则空等着上面的任命；周还是个婴儿时他便去世了。他的嗣母（周称其为"母亲"）才学出众，这在当时的官太太中间并不普遍。更不寻常的是，她喜欢小说和有关旧时叛乱的"禁书"，[1]并将这些书介绍给了儿时的周恩来。他的早期教育是在家塾中完成的，跟着私塾先生学习古典文学和哲学，为"官僚"生活做准备。"两个母亲"去世后，周被送到东北的奉天（今沈阳），与另一位伯母和同为官员的伯父同住。他开始读梁启超之类的改良主义者撰写或者受其启示的非法书籍和文章。

1913年15岁时，周恩来进入天津南开中学。这时清王朝已被推翻，周充分"受到了孙逸仙博士创建的国民党的影响"。[2]孙逸仙煽动反清期间，日本表现出了友善之意。孙在准备推翻窃取了共和国的腐败军阀时，仍以日本为避风港。周于1917年自南开中学毕业后便东渡日本。他一边学习日语，一边在东京早稻田大学和京都大学做"旁听生"。在日本的18个月期间，他还广泛结识了倡导革命思想的留日中国学生，并通过书信和读书时刻了解北京的时局。

1919年，原南开中学校长张伯苓成为新组建的天津南开大学的校长。周恩来在张的邀请下离开日本，进入南开大学。与此同时，他的亲戚们——"一群败家子"（周恩来语）——已经一贫如洗，无力供他读大学。张伯苓给周安排了一份工作，薪

---

1. 因此他也读了大多数同样影响过童年毛泽东的激动人心的书。参见第四篇第一、第二章。
2. 与史实有出入。——编注

Chou was born in 1898 in Huai-an, Kiangsu, in what he called a "bankrupt mandarin family." His mother was a native of Shaohsing, Chekiang province. Chou was given (at the age of four months) to the family of his father's younger brother. The brother was about to die without issue when Chou's father, to assure him of male posterity (on the family tablets), presented him with En-lai to rear as his own son. "My aunt became my real mother when I was a baby," said Chou. "I did not leave her for even one day until I was ten years old—when she and my natural mother both died."

Chou's paternal grandfather was a scholar who served as a magistrate in Huai-an county, north Kiangsu, during the Manchu Dynasty. It was there that Chou spent his childhood, while his father, Chou Yun-liang, who had passed the imperial examinations, vainly waited for a magistry; he died while Chou was still an infant. His foster mother (whom Chou called "mother") was highly literate, and that was not general then among officials' wives. Still more uncommon, she liked fiction and "forbidden"[1] stories of past rebellions, to which she introduced Chou as a child. His early education was in a family school under a private tutor who taught classical literature and philosophy, to prepare one for official life. After his "two mothers" died Chou was sent to live with another aunt and uncle—his father's older brother, who was also an official—in Fengtien (Mukden, Shenyang) Manchuria. He began to read illegal books and papers written or inspired by such reformists as Liang Ch'i-ch'ao.

At the age of fourteen Chou entered Nankai Middle School, in Tientsin. The monarchy had been overthrown and Chou now fully "came under the influence of the Kuomintang" or Nationalist Party founded by Dr. Sun Yat-sen. Japan had provided hospitality to Sun Yat-sen during his agitation against the monarchy. Sun still found refuge there as he prepared to overthrow corrupt warlords who had seized the republic. Chou himself went to Japan in 1917, the year he graduated from Nankai Middle School. While learning Japanese, Chou was an "auditor student" at Waseda University in Tokyo, and at the University of Kyoto. He also became widely acquainted with revolution-minded Chinese students in Japan during his eighteen months there, and kept in touch, through letters and reading, with events in Peking.

In 1919 the former director of Nankai Middle School, Chang Po-ling, became chancellor of the newly organized Nankai University of Tientsin. Chou left Japan to enroll there at Chang's invitation. Meanwhile his relatives—"a spendthrift lot," Chou called them—had become so impoverished that they could provide no support for Chou's college plans. Chang Po-ling gave Chou a job that paid enough to meet costs of tuition, lodging, and

---

1. Thus he read most of the exciting books that also affected Mao Tse-tung as a boy. See Part Four, Chapters 1 and 2.

水足以支付学费、住宿费和书本费。"我在南开中学的最后两年，没有得到过家里的帮助。我依靠作为全班最优秀的学生所赢得的奖学金生活。在日本期间我靠向朋友借钱过活。这时在南开大学我成了《学生联合会报》的编辑，这帮助解决了一些开支。"1919年，五四运动[1]爆发。

在此期间，周恩来参与创建了觉悟社。这是一个激进的团体，其成员后来所走的道路各不相同，有无政府主义者，有国民党员，也有共产党人。（其中一个成员便是邓颖超，1925年与周恩来结了婚。）1920年上半年，周恩来领导南开学生进行了抗暴斗争，因而入狱5个多月。同年，作为华法教育会组织的半工半读计划的一部分，觉悟社的几位创建者在周恩来的带领下前往欧洲留学考察。

"在去法国之前，"周恩来说道，"我读了《共产党宣言》的翻译本、考茨基的《阶级斗争》和《十月革命》。这些书是在陈独秀主编的《新青年》的资助下出版的。我还亲自拜会了陈独秀和李大钊——中国共产党的创始人。"[2]（周没有提及当时与毛泽东有任何会面。）

"我于1920年11月乘船前往法国。在路上我遇到了许多湖南学生，他们是毛泽东创办的新民学会的成员。在这些人当中有蔡和森和他的妹妹蔡畅，他们于1921年在法国创建了第一个中国社会主义青年团。[3]1922年，我成了（中国）共产主义青年团的创始成员，开始为团全职工作。两年后，我去了伦敦，[4]在伦敦呆了两个半月。我不喜欢伦敦。之后我去了德国，在那里工作了1年，参与做组织工作。[5]我们的共产主义青年团在1922年已经向上海派了代表，要求加入1年前成立的党。我们的请求获得了批准，共产主义青年团正式成为党的附属机构，于是我便成了一名共产党员。[6]在法国的共产主义青年团创始成员以这种方式成为党员的还有蔡和森、蔡畅、赵世炎、李富春、李立三、王若飞和陈独秀的两个儿子——陈延年和陈乔年。后来为了组织上海的人力车夫，陈延年化装成了一名人力车夫。在反革命期间，他被俘后惨遭酷刑杀害。他的弟弟1年后——1928年——在上海龙华遇害。"

---

1. 五四运动的诱因是波及全国的反对日本的"二十一条"和反对《凡尔赛条约》将德国在中国青岛的殖民地转让给日本的爱国浪潮。
2. 周这时未见过陈独秀。——编注
3. 与史实有出入，周并未与这几个人同行。——编注
4. 周1921年初到的伦敦。——编注
5. 周1922年3月到德国，经常往来于巴黎和柏林之间（——编注）。朱德就是由周恩来介绍入党的。
6. 周恩来1921年经张申府、刘清扬介绍加入中国共产党。——编注

books. "During my last two years at Nankai Middle School I had received no help from my family. I lived on a scholarship which I won as best student in my class. In Japan I had lived by borrowing from my friends. Now at Nankai University I became editor of the *Hsueh-sheng Lien-ho Hui Pao* (*Students' Union Paper*), which helped cover some expenses." Chou managed to do that despite five months spent in jail in 1920, as a leader of Nankai's student rebellion which grew out of the May 4th Movement.[1]

During that period Chou helped to form the Chueh-wu Shih, or Awakening Society, a radical group whose members later became, variously, anarchists, Nationalists, and Communists. (One of them was Teng Ying-ch'ao, whom Chou was to marry in 1925.) The Awakening Society existed until the end of 1920, when four of its founders, led by Chou, went to France as part of the Work-Study program organized by Ch'en Tu-hsiu and other Francophiles.

"Before going to France," said Chou, "I read translations of the *Communist Manifesto*; Kautsky's *Class Struggle*; and *The October Revolution*. These books were published under the auspices of the *New Youth* (*Hsin Ch'ing-nien*), edited by Ch'en Tu-hsiu. I also personally met Ch'en Tu-hsiu as well as Li Ta-chao—who were to become founders of the Chinese Communist Party." (Chou made no reference to any meeting with Mao Tse-tung at that time.)

"I sailed for France in October, 1920. On the way I met many Hunanese students who were members of the Hsin-min Hsueh-hui (the New People's Study Society), organized by Mao Tse-tung. Among these were Ts'ai Ho-sen and his sister, Ts'ai Ch'ang, who organized the first China Socialist Youth Corps in France in 1921. In 1922 I became a member-founder of the [Chinese] Communist Youth League and began to work full time for that organization.[2] After two years I went to London, where I spent two and a half months. I did not like it. Then I went to Germany and worked there for a year, helping to organize.[3] Our Communist Youth League had sent delegates to Shanghai in 1922, to request admission to the Party, formed the year before. Our petition being granted, the CYL became formally affiliated with the Party, and thus I became a Communist. Foundermembers of the CYL in France who became Party members in this way included Ts'ai Ho-sen, Ts'ai Ch'ang, Chao Shih-yen, Li Fu-ch'un, Li Li-san, Wang Jofei, and the two sons of Ch'en Tu-hsiu—Ch'en Yen-nien and Ch'en Ch'iao-nien. Ch'en Yen-nien later became a ricksha puller in order to organize rickshamen in Shanghai. During the counterrevolution he was captured and badly tortured before he was killed. His brother was executed at Lunghua a year later—1928.

---

1. Inspired by nation-wide resistance to Japan's "Twenty-one Demands" and to the *Versailles Treaty* award, to Japan, of Germany's colony in Tsingtao, China.
2. The CYL was an outgrowth of the Socialist Youth Corps.
3. Chu Teh was one of Chou's recruits to communism.

"在留法的中国学生联合会的成员中，有 400 多人加入了共产主义青年团。有不足 100 人成了无政府主义者，有约 100 人加入了国民党。"

留法中国学生的财力支持来自华法教育会与蔡元培和李石曾。"许多爱国的老先生，"周恩来说道，"私下里都帮助我们学生，不带个人政治目的。"周恩来在欧洲期间的资助人是严修，南开大学的创建者之一。与一些中国学生不同的是，周恩来在法国期间除了研究劳工组织时在雷诺汽车厂短暂地呆过一段时间之外，没有从事过体力劳动。跟随私人老师学了 1 年法语之后，[1] 他将自己的全部精力都倾注于政治之中。"后来，"周恩来告诉我，"当朋友说我用严修的钱做了共产党时，严修引用了一句中国谚语，叫做'人各有志'！"

在法国、伦敦和德国，周恩来度过了 3 年。在返回中国的途中，他在莫斯科作了短暂停留，接受指示。[2] 1924 年末，他到达广州，在黄埔军校成了蒋介石的政治部主任。（周远在巴黎时就已被选入国民党中央执行委员会。在广州他还被选为中共广东省委书记——一个奇怪的联盟造就的一件怪事！）在黄埔军校，周的真正上司是俄国顾问瓦西里·布留赫尔将军，在广州人称"加林"。

在加林和俄国人的首席政治顾问鲍罗廷的巧妙指导下，周恩来构筑了一个学员圈子，被称为"青年军人联合会"，其中就包括林彪和其他未来的红军将领。1925 年，他被委任为国民党第一师政治委员，[3] 平息了汕头附近的一场叛乱，并借机在汕头组织了工会，这使他的影响力进一步得到了加强。1926 年 3 月，国共之间的紧张关系导致了蒋介石反共的第一击。蒋介石成功地结束了双重党籍的做法，将许多共产党人排挤出了黄埔军校的领导岗位。然而，在蒋介石的授意下，周恩来留了下来。[4]

1926 年，北伐开始，由蒋介石任总司令，这是国共两党联合推选的。周恩来奉命去上海准备起义，协助国民军攻占上海。共产党在 3 个月之内组织了 60 万工人，可以举行一次总罢工，但是起义失败了。工人们没有武装和训练，不知道如何"占领城市"。

北洋老军阀低估了第一次罢工和接着第二次罢工的意义，只砍了几个脑袋，却

---

1. 与史实有出入。——编注
2. 当时大多数奉命回国的干部是先到莫斯科东方大学学习一段时间，再回国参加斗争。周没有到莫斯科去，而是从法国直接回国。——编注
3. 周时任国民革命军第一军政治部主任。——编注
4. 与史实有出入。——编注

"Among members of our Chinese Students Union in France more than four hundred joined the CYL. Fewer than a hundred joined the anarchists and about a hundred became Nationalists."

Financial support for Chinese students in France came from the Sino-French Educational Association and from Ts'ai Yuan-p'ei and Li Shih-tseng. "Many old and patriotic gentlemen," said Chou, "privately helped us students, and with no personal political aims." Chou's own financial backer while in Europe was Yen Hsiu, a founder of Nankai University. Unlike some Chinese students, Chou did no manual labor in France, except for a brief period at the Renault plant, when he studied labor organization. After a year with a private tutor, learning the French language, he devoted his entire time to politics. "Later on," Chou told me, "when friends remarked that I had used Yen Hsiu's money to become a Communist, Yen quoted a Chinese proverb, 'Every intelligent man has his own purposes!'"

In France, London, and Germany, Chou spent three years. On his return to China he stopped briefly for instructions in Moscow. Late in 1924 he arrived in Canton, where he became Chiang Kai-shek's deputy director of the political department of Whampoa Academy. (While still in Paris Chou had been elected to the Central Executive Committee of the Kuomintang. In Canton he was also elected secretary of the Kwangtung provincial Communist Party—paradox of a strange alliance!) At Whampoa, Chou's real boss was the Russian adviser, General Vasili Bluecher, known in Canton as Galin.

Under the skillful guidance of Galin, and of the Russians' chief political adviser, Mikhail Borodin, Chou En-lai built up a circle of cadet disciples known as the League of Military Youth, which included Lin Piao and other future generals of the Red Army. His influence was further enhanced when, in 1925, he was appointed political commissar of the Nationalists' first division, which suppressed a revolt near Swatow—an occasion Chou utilized to organize labor unions in that port. In March, 1926, Kuomintang-Communist tension resulted in Chiang's first anti-Communist blow. He succeeded in ending the practice of dual-party membership and removed many Communists from Whampoa posts. Chou En-lai remained, however, on Chiang Kai-shek's orders.

During 1926 the Northern Expedition got under way, with Chiang Kai-shek as commander-in-chief selected jointly by the Kuomintang and the Communists. Chou En-lai was ordered to prepare an insurrection and help the Nationalist Army seize Shanghai. Within three months the Communist Party had organized 600,000 workers and was able to call a general strike, but it was a fiasco. Unarmed and untrained, the workers did not know how to go about "seizing the city."

Underestimating the significance of the first and then of a second strike, the northern warlords cut off a number of heads but failed to halt the labor movement, while Chou

没有制止工人运动，而周恩来则在实践中明白了"如何领导起义"。周恩来和赵泽炎（译音）[1]、赵世炎、顾顺章、罗亦农等工人领袖终于成功组织了5万名纠察队，把毛瑟枪偷运到市里，训练了300名枪手，成为上海工人唯一的武装力量。

1927年3月21日，这些革命者下令举行总罢工，关停了上海的所有行业。他们先占领了警察局，又占领了兵工厂，接着占领了警备司令部，最后取得了胜利。有5,000工人被武装起来，编成6营革命军，军阀军撤出了上海，"人民政府"宣布成立。"两天之内，"周恩来说，"我们攻占了除外国租界之外的所有地区。"

在第三次武装起义中，毗邻的国际租界（由英、美、日联合控制）和法国租界从未受到过攻击；否则胜利将是彻底的——也将是短命的。国民军在白崇禧将军的率领下被工人武装欢迎入城。接着在4月12日国共合作便突然破裂了，蒋介石在南京建立了一个独立的政权，领导了历史上最为惨烈的一次反革命行动。

在法国租界和国际租界内，蒋介石的特使秘密地与各国列强进行了谈判。他们达成协议共同反共及其俄国盟友——当时也是蒋的盟友。除了上海财阀的大笔资金和外国当局的支持——包括枪炮和装甲车——之外，蒋介石还得到了租界黑社会头目的帮助。他们动员了数百名职业流氓。流氓们开着外国人的装甲车，穿着国民党的制服，与蒋介石的军队联合开展了一次夜间行动，从背后和其他侧翼进入。工人武装被认为是友军的蒋军打了个完全不知所措，遭到了大屠杀，"人民政府"在血腥中解体。

于是周恩来在经历了一次奇迹般幸运的脱险之后，开始了躲避国民党暗杀的流亡生涯，开始成为最后在中国高举红色大旗的那次革命的领导人。

在上海起义中，周恩来的数十位亲密战友被捕遇害。周估计"上海大屠杀"的死难人数高达5,000。他本人也被蒋介石的第二师逮捕，白崇禧（后来成为桂系军阀头子）下令将他处决。但是该师师长的弟弟在黄埔曾是周的学生，他帮助周逃脱了。

---

1. 原文为Chao Tse-yen，似无此人。——编注

En-lai learned by practice "how to lead an uprising." Chou and such Shanghai labor leaders as Chao Tse-yen, Chao Shih-yen, Ku Shun-chang, and Lo Yi-nung now succeeded in organizing 50,000 pickets. With Mausers smuggled into the city an "iron band" of 300 marksmen was trained, to become the only armed force these Shanghai workers had.

On March 21, 1927, the revolutionists called a general strike which closed all the industries of Shanghai. They first seized the police stations, next the arsenal, then the garrison, and after that, victory. Five thousand workers were armed, six battalions of revolutionary troops created, the warlord armies withdrew, and a "citizens' government" was proclaimed. "Within two days," said Chou, "we won everything but the foreign concessions."

The International Settlement (jointly controlled by Britain, the U. S., and Japan) and the French Concession which adjoined it were never attacked during the third insurrection; otherwise the triumph was complete—and short-lived. The Nationalist Army, led by General Pai Chung-hsi, was welcomed to the city by the workers' militia. Then on April 12 the Nationalist-Communist coalition abruptly ended when Chiang Kai-shek set up a separate regime in Nanking, to lead one of history's classic counterrevolutions.

In the French Concession and the International Settlement, Chiang's envoys had secretly conferred with representatives of the foreign powers. They reached agreements to cooperate against the Chinese Communists and their Russian allies—until then also Chiang's allies. Given large sums by Shanghai's bankers, and the blessings of the foreign authorities, including guns and armored cars, Chiang was also helped by powerful Settlement and Concession underworld leaders. They mobilized hundreds of professional gangsters. Installed in the foreigners' armored cars, and attired in Nationalist uniforms, the gangsters carried out a night operation in coordination with Chiang's troops, moving in from the rear and other flanks. Taken by complete surprise by troops considered friendly, the militiamen were massacred and their "citizens' government" bloodily dissolved.

And thus it happened that Chou En-lai, after a remarkably lucky escape, began his life as a fugitive from Kuomintang assassins and a leader of the revolution which finally raised the Red banner in China.

Dozens of Chou En-lai's close co-workers in the Shanghai Uprising were seized and executed. Chou estimated the toll of the "Shanghai Massacre" at 5,000 lives. He himself was captured by Chiang Kai-shek's Second Division, and General Pai Chung-hsi, (later ruler of Kwangsi) issued an order for his execution. But the brother of the division commander had been Chou's student at Whampoa, and he helped Chou to escape.

这个造反者先逃到了武汉[1]，后又到南昌，参与组织了八一起义。周恩来当时是中央政治局的高级委员，担任指挥起义的前敌委员会书记，这次起义最后也失败了。接着他去了汕头，坚守了10天，抵御外国炮舰和地方军阀部队的进攻。广州公社失败后，周恩来只得转入地下活动——一直到1931年，他终于"闯破封锁"，到了江西和福建的苏区。他在那里担任红军总司令朱德的政委，后来任革命军事委员会副主席，在我见到他时他仍担任着这一职务。他们在南方进行了多年的艰苦斗争，接着又是长征……但是关于周恩来更多的故事和上述事件，我不久就会从毛泽东及其他人那里了解到更多，背景也会更广阔一些。

周恩来给我的印象是，他头脑冷静，富于逻辑，讲究实际经验。在南开期间（我从他的一位同学那里了解到），周恩来在学校的戏剧表演中经常饰演旦角。我在百家坪见到的这个留着胡须的冷峻的硬汉，身上却没有丝毫柔弱的气息。但是他确有一种魅力——这种魅力和其他因素融合在一起，共同造就了红色中国的头号外交家。

---

1. 武汉是汉阳、汉口、武昌三镇的合称，位于汉江和长江的交汇处。

The Insurrectionist fled to Wuhan[1] and then to Nanchang, where he helped organize the August First Uprising. Senior member of the Politburo at the time, Chou was secretary of the Front Committee that directed the uprising, which was a fiasco. Next he went to Swatow and held it for ten days against assaults from both foreign gunboats and the native troops of militarists. With the failure and defeat of the Canton Commune, Chou was obliged to work underground—until 1931, when he succeeded in "running the blockade" and entered the soviet districts of Kiangsi and Fukien. There he was made political commissar to Chu Teh, commander-in-chief of the Red Army. Later Chou became vice-chairman of the revolutionary military council, an office he still held when I met him. There had been years of exhausting struggle in the South, and then the Long March. . . . But of Chou's further story, and of the scenes and events already mentioned, I was shortly to learn more, and in a broader context, from Mao Tse-tung and others.

Chou left me with an impression of a cool, logical, and empirical mind. In his days at Nankai (I had heard from one of his classmates there) Chou had often taken feminine leads in school plays. There was nothing effeminate about the tough, bearded, unsentimental soldier I met in Pai Chia P'ing. But there was charm—one quality in the mixed ingredients that were to make Chou Red China's No. 1 diplomat.

---

1. Wuhan is the collective name for the triple cities—Hanyang, Hankow, Wuchang—at the confluence of the Han and Yangtze rivers.

三、　　贺龙二三事

第二天早晨 6 点钟，我就同一队大约 40 名青年一起出发，他们是属于通讯部队的，正要护送一批物资到保安去。

我发现只有我自己、外交部的一个人员傅锦魁（译音）[1]和一个红军指挥员李长林[2]有坐骑。也许这话说得并不完全确切：傅锦魁在一头壮实的，但是负担已经过重的骡子背上挤了一个栖身的地方。李长林骑的一头驴子，负担同样过重；我像腾云驾雾似的跨在仅有的一匹马上，它是不是真的在我胯下，有时我也没有多大把握。

我的这头牲口的弓背像一弯新月，迈步像骆驼一样缓慢，瘦腿软弱发抖，随时可能倒下不起，咽下最后一口气。我们顺着河床爬到河边悬崖上的羊肠小道时，它使我特别担心。要是我在它的瘦骨嶙峋的背上稍微挪动一下重心，我们俩就会一起掉向下面岩石嶙峋的峡谷中去。

李长林高高地跨在他的一堆行李上，看到我的狼狈相，不禁大笑。"你坐的马鞍倒不错，同志，不过马鞍下面是什么东西？"

我没有抱怨的份儿，因为毕竟我算老几，能够骑马；但是对他的玩笑，我禁不住说道："请你告诉我，李长林，你们怎么能够骑着这种瘦狗去打仗呢？你们的红军骑兵就是这样的吗？"

"不是！你会看到的！你的牲口'坏啦'？就是因为我们把这种坏牲口留在后方，我们的骑兵在前线才不可战胜！要是有一匹马又壮又能跑，就是毛泽东也不能把它

---

1. 经查证，"傅锦魁"疑为"胡金魁"。——编注
2. 经查证，"李长林"疑为"李湘舲"。——编注

3   SOMETHING ABOUT HO LUNG

Next morning at six I set out with a squad of about forty youths of the communications corps, who were escorting a caravan of goods to Pao An.

I found that only myself, Fu Chin-kuei, an emissary from the Waichiaopu—the Reds' own "Foreign Office"—and Li Chiang-lin, a Red commander, were mounted. It may not be precisely the word: Fu had a privileged perch on a stout but already heavily laden mule; Li Chiang-lin rode an equally overburdened ass; and I was vaguely astride the lone horse, which at times I could not be quite sure was really there at all.

My animal had a quarter-moon back and a camel gait. His enfeebled legs wobbled so that I expected him at any moment to buckle up and breathe his last. He was especially disconcerting as we crept along the narrow trails hewn from steep cliffs that rose up from the river bed we followed. It seemed to me that any sudden shift of my weight over his sunken flanks would send us both hurtling to the rocky gorge below.

Li Chiang-lin laughed down from his pyramid of luggage at my discomfiture. "That's a fine saddle you are sitting, *t'ung-chih*, but what is that underneath it?"

At his gibe I could not resist commenting: "Just tell me this, Li Chiang-lin, how can you fight on dogs like these? Is this how you mount your Red Cavalry?"

"*Pu-shih!* No, you will see! Is your steed *huai-la*?[1] Well, it's just because we have bad ones like this at the rear that our cavalry is unbeatable at the front! If there is a horse that is fat and can run, not even Mao Tse-tung can keep him from the front! Only the worn-out

---

1. "Broken" or "useless."

留下不送前线！我们在后方只用快死的老狗。什么事情都是这样：枪炮、粮食、衣服、马匹、骡子、骆驼、羊——最好的都送去给我们的红军战士！如果你要马，同志，请到前线去！"

"我，'坏啦'？决不是！但是前线少一个好人比少一匹好马好办！"

真的，指挥员李长林看来是个好人，好布尔什维克，而且还是说故事的好手。他当红军已有10年了，曾经参加过著名的1927年南昌起义，从那时候起，共产主义在中国成了一支独立的力量。我在李指挥员旁边，一边在陕西的山沟沟里爬上爬下，有时骑着马，有时下来步行，喘着气，忍着渴，一边就听着他讲一个接着一个的趣闻逸事，有时在再三要求和追问之下，他甚至也赏面子说一说自己。

李长林是湖南人，大革命开始时还是个中学生。他加入了国民党，一直留在党内，到1927年政变后才加入共产党。他在香港在邓发领导下做过一段时期的工会组织者，后来到江西苏区，成为游击队领导人。他在1925年时曾奉国民党之命同一个宣传队去做一项很重要的工作，那就是去见"土匪头子"贺龙，贺龙现在在国民党报纸上被称为"劣迹昭著的"贺龙，但当时却是个极力要争取的领袖人物。李长林奉命同他的宣传队去把贺龙争取过来，参加国民党的国民革命。

"即使在那个时候，贺龙的部下也不是土匪，"有一天，我们坐在一条清凉的溪流旁边几棵树下休息时，李对我说。"他的父亲是哥老会[1]的一个领袖，他的名望传给了贺龙，因此贺龙在年轻时就闻名湖南全省。湖南人都传说他年轻时的许多英勇故事。

"他的父亲是清朝一个武官，一天别的武官请他去赴宴。他把儿子贺龙带去。做爸爸的吹嘘自己儿子如何勇敢无畏，有个客人想试他一下，在桌子底下开了一枪。他们说贺龙面不改色，连眼睛都没有眨一下！

"我们见到他时，他已在省军中任职。他当时控制的地区是云南运鸦片烟到汉口去的必经之道，他就靠抽烟税为生，不抢老百姓。他的部下也不像许多军阀的军队那样强奸民女、大吃大喝，他也不让他们抽大烟。他们都把枪擦得亮亮的。但是当时习惯用大烟敬客。贺龙本人不抽大烟，但我们到时他把烟具和大烟送上炕来，我们就在烟炕上谈革命。

---

1. 哥老会是个规模很大的秘密团体，在全国农村都有分支。该团体反对清朝，对孙逸仙有用。在结构上它与中共地下党极为相似。

dogs we use in our rear. And that's how it is with everything: guns, food, clothing, horses, mules, camels, sheep—the best go to our Red fighters! If it's a horse you want, *t'ung-chih,* go to the front!"

But men? Li explained that it was easier to spare a good man from the front than a good horse.

And Commander Li was a good man, a good Bolshevik and a good storyteller. He had been a Red for ten years, and was a veteran of the Nanchang Uprising of 1927, when communism first became an independent force in China. As I rode, walked, panted and thirsted up and down the broken hills of Shensi beside Commander Li, he recounted incidents and anecdotes one after another, and sometimes, when pressed again and again, even stooped to talk about himself.

A Hunanese, Li had been a middle-school student when he joined the Kuomintang and began to take part in the Great Revolution. He must have entered the Communist Party in the early 1920's; he had worked as a labor organizer with Teng Fa in Hongkong during the great seamen's strike of 1922. He said that in 1925 he had been sent, as part of a Communist-led delegation, to see Ho Lung, who already had a reputation as a bandit leader. Li's reminiscences are here presented as part of the Red Army legend.

"Ho Lung's men were not bandits, even then," Li told me, as we sat resting one day beneath some trees that stood beside a cool stream. "His father had been a leader in the Ke Lao Hui,[1] and Ho Lung inherited his prestige, so that he became famous throughout Hunan when still a young man. Many stories are told by the Hunanese of his bravery as a youth.

"His father was a military officer in the Ch'ing Dynasty, and one day he was invited to a dinner by his fellow officers. He took his son, Ho Lung, with him. His father was boasting of Ho Lung's fearlessness, and one of the guests decided to test it out. He fired off a gun under the table. They say that Ho Lung did not even blink!

"When we met him he had already been commissioned in the provincial army. He then controlled a territory through which rich opium caravans had to pass from Yunnan to Hankow, and he lived by taxing them, and did not rob the people. His followers did not rape or carouse, like the troops of many warlord armies, and he did not let them smoke opium. They kept their rifles clean. But it was the custom there to offer opium to guests. Ho Lung himself did not smoke, but when we arrived he had opium pipes and opium brought to the *k'ang,* and over these we talked about revolution.

---

1. The Elder Brother Society, an ancient secret organization which fought the Manchus and was useful to Sun Yat-sen. In structure it strikingly resembled the cell system adopted by the Chinese Communist Party underground.

"我们的宣传队长是周逸群，他是个共产党员，同贺龙有些亲戚关系。我们同他谈了3个星期。贺龙除了在军事方面以外，没有受过多少教育，但是他并不是个无知的人。他很快懂得革命的意义，但是他经过了慎重的考虑，同他的部下商量，最后才同意加入国民党。

"我们在他的军队里办了一个党的训练班，由周逸群主持，周后来牺牲了。虽然这是一个国民党的训练班，但是大多数教员都是共产党员。入学的学员很多，后来都成了政治领导人。除了贺龙的部队以外，这个学校也为第三师培养政治委员，第三师归袁祖铭统率，他当时是左路军军长，后来被唐生智的特务暗杀，第三师就交给贺龙指挥。他的部队这样扩充后就称为第二十军，成为国民党左派将领张发奎的第四集团军[1]的一部分。"

"南昌起义后贺龙怎样了？"

"他的部队失败后，他和朱德转移到汕头。他们又吃了败仗。他的残部去了内地，但是贺龙却逃到香港。后来他又偷偷地去了上海，从那里化了装回湖南。

"传说贺龙用一把菜刀在湖南建立了一个苏区。那是早在1928年。贺龙躲在一个村子里，同哥老会的兄弟们策划起义，这时有几个国民党收税的来了。他就率领村里的几个人袭击收税的，用他自己的一把刀宰了他们，解除了他们的卫队的武装。从这一事件中，他缴获了足够的手枪和步枪来武装他的第一支农民军。"

贺龙在哥老会中的名声遍及全中国。红军说，他可以手无寸铁地到全国任何哪个村子里去，向哥老会说出自己的身份后，组织起一支部队来。哥老会的规矩和黑话很难掌握，但是贺龙的"辈分"最高，因此据说曾经不止一次把一个地方的哥老会全部兄弟收编进红军。他的口才很好，在国民党中是有名的。李说他说起话来能"叫死人活过来打仗"。

贺龙的红二方面军在1935年最后从湖南苏区撤出时，据说有步枪四万多支。这支红军在它自己的去西北的长征路上所经受的艰难困苦较之江西红军主力甚至更大。在雪山上死去的有成千上万，又有成千上万的饿死或被南京方面炸死。但是由于贺

---

1. 国共北伐（1926—1927）征讨各省军阀和北京政府的一部分部队。

"The head of our propaganda committee was Chou Yi-chung, a Communist, who had some family connection with Ho Lung. We talked to him for three weeks. Ho Lung had not had much education, except in military affairs, but he was not an ignorant man.

"We established a Party training school in his army, with Chou Yi-chung—who was later killed—as leader. Although it was a Kuomintang Nationalist training school, most of the propagandists were Communists. Many students entered the school and later became political leaders. Besides Ho Lung's army, the school furnished political commissioners for the Third Division, under Yuan Tso-ming, who was then commander of the Left Route Army. Yuan Tso-ming was assassinated by agents of T'ang Sheng-chih, and the Third Division was given to Ho Lung. His enlarged command was called the Twentieth Army, which became part of the main Fourth Group Army[1] under the Left Kuomintang general, Chang Fa-kuei."

"What happened to Ho Lung after the Nanchang Uprising?"

"His forces were defeated. He and Chu Teh next moved to Swatow. They were defeated again. The remnant of his army went into the interior, but Ho Lung escaped to Hongkong. Later he smuggled himself to Shanghai, and then, disguised, he returned to Hunan.

"It is said of Ho Lung that he established a soviet district in Hunan with one knife. This was early in 1928. Ho Lung was in hiding in a village, plotting with members of the Ke Lao Hui, when some Kuomintang tax collectors arrived. Leading a few villagers, he attacked the tax collectors and killed them with his own knife, and then disarmed the tax collectors' guard. From this adventure he got enough revolvers and rifles to arm his first peasants' army."

Ho Lung's fame in the Elder Brother Society extended over all China. The Reds said that he could go unarmed into any village of the country, announce himself to the Elder Brother Society, and form an army. The society's special ritual and language were quite difficult to master, but Ho Lung had the highest "degrees" and was said to have more than once enlisted an entire Ke Lao Hui branch in the Red Army. His eloquence as a speaker was well known in the Kuomintang. Li said that when he spoke he could "raise the dead to fight."

When Ho Lung's Second Front Red Army finally withdrew from the Hunan soviet districts, in 1935, its rifles were reported to number more than 40,000, and this army underwent even greater hardships in its own Long March to the Northwest than the main forces from Kiangsi. Thousands died on the snow mountains, and thousands more starved to death

---

1. Part of the Nationalist-Communist Northern Expedition (1926—1927) against the provincial warlords and the Peking Government.

龙的个人感召力和他在中国农村的影响，据李说，他的许多部下宁可与他一起在路上死去，也不愿意离去，在长征路上有成千上万的穷人参加，填补缺额。最后他率众约两万人——大多数赤着脚，处于半饥饿和筋疲力竭状态——到达西藏东部，与朱德会师。经过几个月的休整，他的部队现在又在行军路上，向甘肃进发，预期在几个星期之内就可以到达。

"贺龙的外表怎么样？"我问李。

"他是个大个子，像只老虎一样强壮有力。他已年过半百，但仍很健康。他不知疲倦。他们说他在长征路上背着许多受伤的部下行军。即使他还在当国民党的将领时，他生活也跟他的部下一样简单。他不计较个人财物——除了马匹。他喜欢马。有一次他有一匹非常喜欢的马，这匹马给敌军俘获了。贺龙又去打仗夺回来。结果真的夺了回来！

"虽然贺龙性格很急躁，但是他很谦虚。他参加共产党后，一直忠于党，从来没有违反过党的纪律。他总希望别人提出批评，留心听取意见。他的妹妹很像他，个子高大，是个大脚女人。她领导红军作战——还亲自背伤员。贺龙的妻子也是如此。"

贺龙对有钱人的仇视，在中国是到处流传的——这似乎主要要回溯到他的红色游击队刚刚开始组成的年代，当时湖南苏区还没有处在共产党的全面控制之下。在何键"农民大屠杀"时期许多农民有亲友遭到牺牲，或者反动派在何键统治下夺回权力后，本人遭到地主的殴打和压迫，都抱着深仇大恨来投奔贺龙。据说，如果贺龙还在200里外的地方，地主士绅都要闻风逃跑，哪怕有南京军队重兵驻守的地方也是如此，因为他以行军神出鬼没著称。

有一次贺龙逮到了一个名叫波斯哈德的瑞士传教士，军事法庭因他从事所谓间谍活动——大概不过是把红军动向的情报传给国民党当局，许多传教士都是这样做的——"判处"他监禁18个月，贺龙开始长征时，波斯哈德牧师的徒刑还没有满期，因此奉命跟着军队走，最后刑期满了以后才在途中释放，给旅费前往云南府。使得大多数人感到意外的是，波斯哈德牧师对贺龙并没有讲什么坏话。相反，据说他说过，"如果农民都知道共产党是怎样的，没有人会逃走。"[1]

---

1. 由约瑟夫·F.洛克转述给我听的，他在波斯哈德到达云南府时曾与他谈过话。

or were killed by Nanking bombs. Yet so great was Ho Lung's personal magnetism, and his influence throughout rural China, Li said, that many of his men stayed with him and died on the road rather than desert, and thousands of poor men along the route of march joined in to help fill up the dwindling ranks. In the end he reached eastern Tibet, where he finally connected with Chu Teh, with about 20,000 men—most of them barefoot, half-starved, and physically exhausted. After several months of recuperation, his troops were now on the march again, into Kansu, where they were expected to arrive in a few weeks.

"What does Ho Lung look like?" I asked Li.

"He is a big man, and strong as a tiger. He never gets tired. They say he carried many of his wounded men on the march. Even when he was a Kuomintang general he lived as simply as his men. He cares nothing about personal possessions—except horses. He loves horses. Once he had a beautiful horse that he liked very much. It was captured by some enemy troops. Ho Lung went to battle to recover that horse. He got it back!

"Although he is impetuous, Ho Lung is very humble. Since he joined the Communists he has been faithful to the Party, and has never broken Party discipline. He always asks for criticism and listens carefully to advice. His sister is much like him—a big woman, with large [unbound] feet. She has led Red troops in battle herself—and carried wounded men on her back. So has Ho Lung's wife."

Ho Lung's hatred of the rich had become legendary in China. It was said that landlords and gentry used to flee without further ado, even from places well guarded by Nanking troops, if Ho Lung was reported as far away as 200 *li*—for he was famous for the swiftness of his movements.

Once Ho Lung arrested a Swiss missionary named Bosshard, and a military court "sentenced" him to eighteen months' imprisonment for alleged espionage. The Reverend Bosshard's sentence had still not been completed when Ho Lung began the Long March, but he was ordered to move with the army. He was finally released during the march, when his sentence expired, and was given traveling expenses to Yunnanfu. Rather to most people's surprise, the Reverend Bosshard brought out few harsh words about Ho Lung. On the contrary, he was reported to have remarked, "If the peasants knew what the Communists were like, none of them would run away."[1]

---

1. Related to me by Dr. Joseph F. Rock, who talked to Bosshard when he arrived in Yunnanfu.

当时正好中午要歇脚,我们决定到清凉宜人的溪水中洗个澡。我们下了水,躺在溪底一块长长的平石上,浅浅的凉水在我们身上潺潺流过。有几个农民过去,赶着一大群绵羊;头顶上蔚蓝色的天空晴朗无云。四周一片宁静、幽美,几百年来都是这样的,这种奇怪的晌午时分,只使人感到宁静、幽美和满足。

我忽然问李长林结过婚没有。

"我结过婚了,"他慢慢地说,"我的妻子在南方被国民党杀死了。"

我开始有一点点懂得中国共产党人为什么这样长期地、这样毫不妥协地、这样不像中国人地进行战斗。我以后在路上还要从其他红军旅伴那里了解到更多这方面的情况。

It was the noon halt, and we decided to bathe in the cool, inviting stream. We got in and lay on a long, flat rock, while the shallow water rippled over us in cool sheets. Some peasants went past, driving a big cloud of sheep before them; overhead the sky was clear and blue. There was nothing but peace and beauty here, and it was that odd midday moment when the world for centuries has been like this, with only peace, beauty and contentment.

I asked Li Chiang-lin if he were married.

"I was," he said slowly. "My wife was killed in the South, by the Kuomintang."

四、　　红军旅伴

陕北是我在中国见到的最贫困的地区之一，即使包括云南西部在内也是如此。那里并不真正缺少土地，而是在许多地方严重缺少真正的土地——至少缺少真正的耕地。在陕西，一个农民有地可以多达 100 亩[1]，可是仍一贫如洗。在这一带，至少要有几百亩地才称得上是一个地主，甚至按中国的标准来说，他也称不上富有，除非他的土地是在那些有限的肥沃的河谷里，可以种大米和其他有价值的作物。

陕西的农田可以说是倾斜的，有许多也可以说是滑溜溜的，因为经常发生山崩。农田大部分是地缝和小溪之间的条状小块。在许多地方，土地看来是够肥沃的，但是所种作物受到很陡的斜坡的严格限制，无论从数和质上来说都是这样。很少有真正的山脉，只有无穷无尽的断山孤丘，连绵不断，好像詹姆斯·乔伊斯[2]的长句，甚至更加乏味。然而其效果却常常像毕加索[3]一样触目，随着阳光的转移，这些山丘的角度陡峭的阴影和颜色起着奇异的变化，到黄昏时分，紫色的山巅连成一片壮丽的海洋，深色的天鹅绒般的褶层从上而下，好像满族的百褶裙，一直到看去似乎深不及底的沟壑中。

第一天以后，我很少骑马，倒不是可怜那匹奄奄待毙的老马，而是因为大家都在走路。李长林是这一队战士中最年长的，其他都是十几岁的少年，比孩子大不了多少。有一个绰号叫"老狗"，我同他一起走时问他为什么参加红军。

他是个南方人，在福建苏区参加红军 6,000 英里长征，一路走过来的。外国军

---

1. 1 华亩约等于 1/6 英亩。
2. 1882—1941 年，著名爱尔兰小说家。——译注
3. 1881—1973 年，著名西班牙画家。——译注

4   Red Companions

North Shensi was one of the poorest parts of China I had seen, not excluding western Yunnan. There was no real land scarcity, but there was in many places a serious scarcity of real land—at least real farming land. Here in Shensi a peasant could own as much as 100 *mou*[1] of land and yet be a poor man. A landlord in this country had to possess at least several hundred *mou* of land, and even on a Chinese scale he could not be considered rich unless his holdings were part of the limited and fertile valley land, where rice and other valued crops could be grown.

The farms of Shensi could have been described as slanting, and many of them also as slipping, for landslides were frequent. The fields were mostly patches laid on the serried landscape, between crevices and small streams. The land seemed rich enough in many places, but the crops grown were strictly limited by the steep gradients, in both quantity and quality. There were few genuine mountains, only endless broken hills. Their sharp-angled shadowing and coloring changed miraculously with the sun's wheel, and toward dusk they became a magnificent sea of purpled hilltops with dark velvety folds running down, like the pleats on a mandarin skirt, to ravines that seemed bottomless.

After the first day I rode little, not so much out of pity for the languishing nag, but because everyone else marched. Li Chiang-lin was the oldest warrior of the company. Most of the others were lads in their teens, hardly more than children. One of these was nicknamed "Lao Kou," the Old Dog, and walking with him I asked why he had joined the Reds.

He was a southerner and had come all the way from the Fukien soviet districts, on the

---

1. One Chinese *mou* is about a sixth of an acre.

事专家都拒绝相信长征是可能的事。但是这里却有这个"老狗",年方17,实际上看上去像14岁。他走了这次长征,并不把它当作一回事。他说,如果红军要再长征25,000里,他就准备再走25,000里。

同他一起的一个孩子外号叫"老表",他也是从差不多那么远的地方江西走过来的。"老表"16岁。

他们喜欢红军吗?我问他们。他们真的感到有些奇怪地看看我。他们两人显然都从来没有想到过会有人不喜欢红军的。

"红军教我读书写字,""老狗"说,"现在我已经能够操纵无线电,用步枪瞄准。红军帮助穷人。"

"就这么一些?"

"红军对待我们很好,我们从来没挨过打,""老表"说,"这里大家都一样。不像在白区里,穷人是地主和国民党的奴隶。这里大家打仗是为了帮助穷人,救中国。红军打地主和白匪,红军是抗日的。这样的军队为什么有人会不喜欢呢?"

有一个农村少年是在四川参加红军的,我问他为什么参加。他告诉我说,他的父母是贫农,只有4亩田(不到1英亩),不够养活他和两个姊妹。他说,红军到他村子来时,全体农民都欢迎他们,给他们喝热茶,做糖给他们吃。红军剧团演了戏。大家很快活。只有地主逃跑了。分配土地后,他的父母也分到了地。因此他参加穷人的军队时,他们并不难过,反而很高兴。

另一个少年大约19岁,在湖南当过铁匠学徒,外号叫"铁老虎"。红军到他县里时,他放下风箱、锅盘,不再当学徒了,只穿了一双草鞋、一条裤子就赶紧去参军。为什么?因为他要同那些不让学徒吃饱的师傅打仗,同剥削他的父母的地主打仗。他是为革命打仗,革命要解放穷人。红军对人民很好,不抢不打,不像白军。他拉起裤腿,给我看一条长长的白色伤疤,那是战斗的纪念。

还有一个少年是福建来的,一个是浙江来的,还有几个是江西和四川来的,但是大多数是陕西和甘肃本地人。有的已从少年先锋队"毕业",虽然看上去还像孩子,却已当了几年红军了。有的参加红军是为了打日本,有两个是为了要逃脱奴役[1],三个

---

1. 实际上是契约劳工;在那些地区就等于奴隶。汉语用词为丫头,字面意思为"轭头"。

Red Army's six-thousand-mile expedition which foreign military experts refused to believe possible. Yet here was Old Dog, seventeen years old, and actually looking fourteen. He had made that march and thought nothing of it. He said he was prepared to walk another 25,000 *li* if the Red Army did.

With him was a lad nicknamed Local Cousin, and he had walked almost as far, from Kiangsi. Local Cousin was sixteen.

Did they like the Red Army? I asked. They looked at me in genuine amazement. It had evidently never occurred to either of them that anyone could not like the Red Army.

"The Red Army has taught me to read and to write," said Old Dog. "Here I have learned to operate a radio, and how to aim a rifle straight. The Red Army helps the poor."

"Is that all?"

"It is good to us and we are never beaten," added Local Cousin. "Here everybody is the same. It is not like the White districts, where poor people are slaves of the landlords and the Kuomintang. Here everybody fights to help the poor, and to save China. The Red Army fights the landlords and the White bandits and the Red Army is anti-Japanese. Why should anyone not like such an army as this?"

There was a peasant lad who had joined the Reds in Szechuan, and I asked him why he had done so. He told me that his parents were poor farmers, with only four *mou* of land (less than an acre), which wasn't enough to feed him and his two sisters. When the Reds came to his village, he said, all the peasants welcomed them, brought them hot tea and made sweets for them. The Red dramatists gave plays. It was a happy time. Only the landlords ran. When the land was redistributed his parents received their share. So they were not sorry, but very glad, when he joined the poor people's army.

Another youth, about nineteen, had formerly been an ironsmith's apprentice in Hunan, and he was nicknamed "T'ieh Lao-hu," the Iron Tiger. When the Reds arrived in his district, he had dropped bellows, pans, and apprenticeship, and, clad only in a pair of sandals and trousers, hurried off to enlist. Why? Because he wanted to fight the masters who starved their apprentices, and to fight the landlords who robbed his parents. He was fighting for the revolution, which would free the poor. The Red Army was good to people and did not rob them and beat them like the White armies. He pulled up his trouser leg and displayed a long white scar, his souvenir of battle.

There was another youth from Fukien, one from Chekiang, several more from Kiangsi and Szechuan, but the majority were natives of Shensi and Kansu. Some had "graduated" from the Young Vanguards, and (though they looked like infants) had already been Reds for years. Some had joined the Red Army to fight Japan, two had enlisted to escape from

是从国民党军队中逃过来的，但是他们大多数人参加红军是"因为红军是革命的军队，打地主和帝国主义"。

接着我同一个班长谈话，他是个"大"人，24岁。他从1931年起就参加红军。那一年他父母在江西被南京的轰炸机炸死，他的家也被炸毁了。他从田里回到家里，发现父母都已炸死，他就马上放下耙子，同妻子告别，参加了共产党。他的一个兄弟是红军游击队，1935年在江西牺牲。

他们来历不同，但是同普通中国军队相比，是真正的"全国性"的军队，后者一般都按省份不同分别编制的。他们的籍贯和方言不一，但这似乎并不影响他们团结，只不过是时常作为开善意的玩笑的材料。我从来没有见到过他们真的吵架。事实上，我在红区旅行的全部时间中，我没有看到红军战士打过一次架，我认为这在年轻人中间是很突出的。

虽然他们几乎全体都遭遇过人生的悲剧，但是他们都没有太悲伤，也许是因为年纪太轻的缘故。在我看来，他们相当快活，也许是我所看到过的第一批真正感到快活的中国无产者。在中国，消极的满足是普遍的现象，但是快活这种比较高一级的感情，却的确是罕见的，这意味着对于生存有着一种自信的感觉。

他们在路上几乎整天都唱歌，能唱的歌无穷无尽。他们唱歌没有人指挥，都是自发的，唱得很好。只要有一个人什么时候劲儿来了，或者想到了一个合适的歌，他就突然唱起来，指挥员和战士们就都跟着唱。他们在夜里也唱，从农民那里学新的民歌，这时农民就拿出来陕西琵琶。

他们有的那点纪律，似乎都是自觉遵守的。我们走过山上的一丛野杏树时，他们忽然四散开来去摘野杏，个个装满了口袋，总是有人给我带回来一把。临走时他们好像一阵大风卷过一般又排列成行，赶紧上路，把耽误了的时间补回来。但是在我们走过私人果园时，却没有人去碰一碰里面的果子，我们在村子里吃的粮食和蔬菜也是照价付钱的。

就我所见到的来说，农民们对我的红军旅伴并无不满的流露。有些农民似乎还十分友善，非常向着他们——这同最近分配土地和取消苛捐杂税大概不无关系。他

slavery,[1] three had deserted from the Kuomintang troops, but most of them had joined "because the Red Army is a revolutionary army, fighting landlords and imperialism."

Then I talked to a squad commander, who was an "older" man of twenty-four. He had been in the Red Army since 1931. In that year his father and mother were killed by a Nanking bomber, which also destroyed his house, in Kiangsi. When he got home from the fields and found both his parents dead he had at once thrown down his hoe, bidden his wife good-by, and enlisted with the Communists. One of his brothers, a Red partisan, had been killed in Kiangsi in 1935.

They were a heterogeneous lot, but more truly "national" in composition than ordinary Chinese armies, usually carefully segregated according to provinces. Their different provincial backgrounds and dialects did not seem to divide them, but became the subject of constant good-natured raillery. I never saw a serious quarrel among them. In fact, during all my travel in the Red districts, I was not to see a single fist fight between Red soldiers, and among young men I thought that remarkable.

Though tragedy had touched the lives of nearly all of them, they were perhaps too young for it to have depressed them much. They seemed to me fairly happy, and perhaps the first consciously happy group of Chinese proletarians I had seen. Passive contentment was the common phenomenon in China, but the higher emotion of happiness, which implies a feeling of positiveness about existence, was rare indeed.

They sang nearly all day on the road, and their supply of songs was endless. Their singing was not done at a command, but was spontaneous, and they sang well. Whenever the spirit moved him, or he thought of an appropriate song, one of them would suddenly burst forth, and commanders and men joined in. They sang at night, too, and learned new folk tunes from the peasants, who brought out their Shensi guitars.

What discipline they had seemed almost entirely self-imposed. When we passed wild apricot trees on the hills there was an abrupt dispersal until everyone had filled his pockets, and somebody always brought me back a handful. Then, leaving the trees looking as if a great wind had struck through them, they moved back into order and quick-timed to make up for the loss. But when we passed private orchards, nobody touched the fruit in them, and the grain and vegetables we ate in the villages were paid for in full.

As far as I could see, the peasants bore no resentment toward my Red companions. Some seemed on close terms of friendship, and very loyal—a fact probably not unconnected with a recent redivision of land and the abolition of taxes. They freely offered for sale

---

1. Really indentured labor; in those parts it amounted to slavery. Chinese used the word *ya-t'ou*, which literally means "yoke-head."

们很自愿地把他们的一点点吃的东西卖给我们,毫不犹豫地收下了苏区的钱。我们在中午或傍晚到达一个村子时,当地苏维埃的主席就立即给我们安排住处,指定炉灶给我们使用。我常常见到农村妇女或她们的女儿自动给我们拉风箱生火,同红军战士说说笑笑——对中国妇女来说,特别是对陕西妇女来说,这是非常开通的一种现象。

在路上的最后一天,我们在一个青翠的山谷中间一个村子里歇脚吃中饭,所有的孩子们都来看他们头一次看到的洋鬼子。我决定考他们一下。

"什么叫共产党员?"我问道。

"共产党员是帮助红军打白匪和国民党的人,"一个10岁左右的孩子开腔道。

"还有呢?"

"他帮助我们打地主和资本家!"

"那么什么叫资本家呢?"这个问题可难住了一个孩子,可是另外一个孩子回答说:"资本家自己不干活,却让别人给他干活。"这个答复也许过分简单化了,不过我继续问:

"这里有地主和资本家吗?"

"没有!"他们都齐声叫道,"他们都逃跑了!"

"逃跑了?怕什么?"

"怕**我们的红军**!"

"我们的"军队,一个农村孩子说"他的"军队?显然,这不是中国,但是,如果不是中国,又是什么国家呢?我觉得这是不可信的。谁把这一切教给他们的呢?

我后来看到红色中国的教科书和遇到圣诞老人徐特立时,终于知道了是谁教给他们的。徐特立曾经担任过湖南一所师范学校的校长,现在是苏维埃教育人民委员。

事实上,那天下午我就要见到他,那是在我们这个小小的旅队走下最后一个山坡,踏进红色中国临时首都的时候。

what edibles they had, and accepted soviet money without hesitation. When we reached a village at noon or sunset the chairman of the local soviet promptly provided quarters, and designated ovens for our use. I frequently saw peasant women or their daughters volunteer to pull the bellows of the fire of our ovens, and laugh and joke with the Red warriors, in a very emancipated way for Chinese women—especially Shensi women.

On the last day, we stopped for lunch at a village in a green valley, and here all the children came round to examine the first foreign devil many of them had seen. I decided to catechize them.

"What is a Communist?" I asked.

"He is a citizen who helps the Red Army fight the White bandits and the Japanese," one youngster of nine or ten piped up.

"What else?"

"He helps fight the landlords and the capitalists!"

"But what is a capitalist?" That silenced one child, but another came forward: "A capitalist is a man who does not work, but makes others work for him." Oversimplification, perhaps, but I went on:

"Are there any landlords or capitalists here?"

"No!" they all shrieked together. "They've all run away!"

"Run away? From what?"

"From our RED ARMY!"

"Our" army, a peasant child talking about "his" army? Well, obviously it wasn't China, but, if not, what was it? Who could have taught them all this?

I was to learn who it was when I examined the textbooks of Red China, and met old Santa Claus Hsu T'eh-li, once president of a normal school in Hunan, now Soviet Commissioner of Education.

Part Three
In "Defended Peace"

第三篇
在保安

一、　　苏维埃掌权人物

小村庄在西北很多，但是城市不论大小却不常见。除了红军草创的工业以外，西北完全是个农业区，有些地方还是半游牧区。因此，纵马登上崎岖的山顶，看到下面苍翠的山谷中保安的一片古老城墙，确实使人觉得十分意外[1]。

在秦朝和唐朝的时候，保安曾是抵御北方游牧民族入侵的边防要塞。至今人们犹可在一条狭仄的隘口两旁，看到堡垒的残迹，被下午的阳光染成一片火红色。当年蒙古人的征略大军，就是通过这条隘口大举侵入这个山谷里来的。保安还有一座内城，从前驻扎过边防军；最近经过红军修缮的一道高大的用作防御的砖墙，围绕着约莫1英里见方的地方，就是现在保安城所在。

我在这里终于找到了南京同他打了10年仗的共产党领袖——毛泽东，用最近采用的正式头衔，就是"中华人民苏维埃共和国"的主席。旧名"中华工农苏维埃共和国"已在共产党开始实行争取建立统一战线的新政策的时候放弃了。

周恩来的电报已经收到，他们正等待着我，"外交部"里已替我预备好一个房间，我暂时成了苏维埃国家的客人。我到了后，保安外侨的人数顿然剧增。另外的一个西方侨民就是一个称作李德同志的德国人。关于前德军高级军官李德，中国红军的这个唯一外国顾问（这使希特勒极为恼火），下文还要提到。

---

1. 1936年12月红军占领陕北延安（肤施），迁都到了那里。参见第十二篇。

1   Soviet Strong Man

Small villages were numerous in the Northwest, but towns of any size were infrequent. Except for the industries begun by the Reds it was agrarian and in places semipastoral country. Thus it was quite breathtaking to ride out suddenly on the brow of the wrinkled hills and see stretched out below me in a green valley the ancient walls of Pao An, which means "Defended Peace."[1]

Pao An was once a frontier stronghold, during the Ch'in and T'ang dynasties, against the nomadic invaders to the north. Remains of its fortifications, flame-struck in that afternoon sun, could be seen flanking the narrow pass through which once emptied into this valley the conquering legions of the Mongols. There was an inner city, still, where the garrisons were once quartered; and a high defensive masonry, lately improved by the Reds, embraced about a square mile in which the present town was located.

Here at last I found the Red leader whom Nanking had been fighting for ten years—Mao Tse-tung, chairman of the "Chinese People's Soviet Republic," to employ the official title which had recently been adopted. The old cognomen, "Chinese Workers' and Peasants' Soviet Republic," was dropped when the Reds began their new policy of struggle for a united front.

Chou En-lai's radiogram had been received and I was expected. A room was provided for me in the "Foreign Office," and I became temporarily a guest of the soviet state. My arrival resulted in a phenomenal increase of the foreign population of Pao An. The other Occidental resident was a German known as Li Teh T'ung-chih—the 'Virtuous Comrade Li.' Of Li Teh, the only foreign adviser ever with the Chinese Red Army, more later.

---

1. In December, 1936, the Reds occupied Yenan (Fushih), north Shensi, and the capital was transferred there. See Part Twelve.

我到后不久，就见到了毛泽东，他是个面容瘦削、看上去很像林肯的人物，个子高出一般的中国人，背有些驼，一头浓密的黑发留得很长，双眼炯炯有神，鼻梁很高，颧骨突出。我在一刹那间所得的印象，是一个非常精明的知识分子的面孔，可是在好几天里面，我总没有证实这一点的机会。我第二次看见他是傍晚的时候，毛泽东光着头在街上走，一边和两个年轻的农民谈着话，一边认真地在做着手势。我起先认不出是他，后来等到别人指出才知道。南京虽然悬赏25万元要他的首级，可是他却毫不介意地和旁的行人一起在走。

关于毛泽东，我可以单独写一本书。我跟他谈了许多夜晚，谈到各种广泛的问题，我也从士兵和共产党员那里听到关于他的许多故事。我同他谈话后写的访问记录就有大约两万字。他幼年和青年时代的情形，他怎样成为国民党和国民革命的一个领袖，为什么成为一个共产主义者，红军怎样成长壮大起来，他统统告诉了我。他向我介绍了长征到西北的情形，并且写了一首关于长征的旧诗给我。他又告诉我许多其他著名的红军战士的故事，从朱德一直到那个把藏有苏维埃政府档案的两只铁制文件箱背在肩上走了长征全程的青年。

从这样丰富的未经利用、不为人知的材料中，我怎么能够用寥寥数百个字把这个农民出身的知识分子转变为革命家的故事告诉你们呢？我不想作这样压缩的尝试。毛泽东生平的历史是整整一代人的一个丰富的横断面，是要了解中国国内动向的原委的一个重要指南，我以后还要根据他所告诉我的情况，把他个人历史的那个丰富的激动人心的记录写进本书。[1] 但是我在这里想要谈一些主观的印象，还有关于他的令人感到兴趣的少数事实。

首先，切莫以为毛泽东可以做中国的"救星"。这完全是胡说八道。绝不会有一个人可以做中国的"救星"。但是，不可否认，你觉得他的身上有一种天命的力量。这并不是什么昙花一现的东西，而是一种实实在在的根本活力。你觉得这个人身上不论有什么异乎寻常的地方，都是产生于他对中国人民大众，特别是农民——这些占中国人口绝大多数的贫穷饥饿、受剥削、不识字，但又宽厚大度、勇敢无畏、如今还敢于造反的人们——的迫切要求作了综合和表达，达到了不可思议的程度。假使他们的这些要求以及推动他们前进的运动是可以复兴中国的动力，那么，在这个极其富有历史性的意义上，毛泽东也许可能成为一个非常伟大的人物。

---

1. 参见第四篇。

I met Mao soon after my arrival: a gaunt, rather Lincolnesque figure, above average height for a Chinese, somewhat stooped, with a head of thick black hair grown very long, and with large, searching eyes, a high-bridged nose and prominent cheekbones. My fleeting impression was of an intellectual face of great shrewdness, but I had no opportunity to verify this for several days. Next time I saw him, Mao was walking hatless along the street at dusk, talking with two young peasants and gesticulating earnestly. I did not recognize him until he was pointed out to me—moving along unconcernedly with the rest of the strollers, despite the $250,000 which Nanking had hung over his head.

I could have written a book about Mao Tse-tung. I talked with him many nights, on a wide range of subjects, and I heard dozens of stories about him from soldiers and Communists. My written interviews with him totaled about twenty thousand words. He told me of his childhood and youth, how he became a leader in the Kuomintang and the Nationalist Revolution, why he became a Communist, and how the Red Army grew. He described the Long March to the Northwest and wrote a classical poem about it for me. He told me stories of many other famous Reds, from Chu Teh down to the youth who carried on his shoulders for over 6,000 miles the two iron dispatch boxes that held the archives of the Soviet Government.

The story of Mao's life was a rich cross-section of a whole generation, an important guide to understanding the sources of action in China, and I have included that full exciting record of personal history, just as he told it to me.[1] But here my own impressions of him may be worth recording.

There would never be any one "savior" of China, yet undeniably one felt a certain force of destiny in Mao. It was nothing quick or flashy, but a kind of solid elemental vitality. One felt that whatever there was extraordinary in this man grew out of the uncanny degree to which he synthesized and expressed the urgent demands of millions of Chinese, and especially the peasantry. If their "demands" and the movement which was pressing them forward were the dynamics which could regenerate China, then in that deeply historical sense Mao Tse-tung might possibly become a very great man.

---

1. See Part Four.

但是我并不想宣布历史的判决。同时，除了他的政治生活以外，毛泽东作为个人也是一个使人感到兴趣的人物，因为，虽则他的名字同蒋介石一样为许多中国人所熟悉，可是关于他的情况却很少知道，因此有着各种各样关于他的奇怪传说。我是访问他的第一个外国新闻记者。

毛泽东有能够从死里逃生、大难不死的传说。南京曾经一再宣告他死了，可是没有几天以后，报上的新闻栏又出现了他的消息，而且活跃如昔。国民党也曾经好几次正式宣布"击毙"并埋葬了朱德，有时还得到有千里眼的传教士的旁证。尽管如此，这两个著名人物多次遭难，可并不妨碍他们参与许多次惊人壮举，其中包括长征。说真的，当我访问红色中国的时候，报上正盛传毛泽东的又一次死讯，但我却看到他活得好好的。不过，关于他的死里逃生、大难不死的传说，看来是有一些根据的，那就是，他虽身经百战，有一次还被敌军俘获而逃脱，有世界上最高的赏格缉拿他的首级，可是在这许多年头里，他从来没有受过一次伤。

有一个晚上，一个红军医生——一个曾在欧洲学习、精通医道的人——给他作全面体格检查，我正好在他的屋子里，结果宣布他身体非常健康。他从来没有得过肺病或任何其他"不治之症"，像有些想入非非的旅行家所谣传的那样[1]。他的肺部是完全健康的，尽管他跟大部分红军指挥员不一样，吸烟没有节制。在长征路上，毛泽东和李德（另一个烟瘾很重的人）进行了独特的植物学研究，遍尝各种叶子，要寻出烟叶的代替品来。

毛泽东现在的夫人贺子珍——从前是小学教员，现在本人也是个共产党的组织者——却不及她丈夫幸运。她受到过十多处伤，是炸弹碎片造成的，不过都是表面的伤。正当我离开保安以前，毛氏夫妇新生了一个女孩子。毛泽东的前妻杨开慧曾生了两个孩子。她是一个中国名教授的女儿，数年前被何键杀害。

毛泽东现年（1936年）43岁。在第二次中华全国苏维埃大会上，他被选为中央苏维埃临时政府主席，这次大会的出席者，代表着当时生活在红色法律[2]下的900万左右的人民。说到这里，我要附带插入几句话。据毛泽东的估计，中央苏维埃政府在1934年直接控制下的各区最高人口数字如下：江西苏区300万；鄂皖豫苏区200

---

1. 彼得·弗莱明先生在其《孤家寡人》一书中似乎大大地传播了这一谣言。
2. 参阅毛泽东等人编写的《中华苏维埃共和国的基本法律》（1934年伦敦劳伦斯书店出版）。其中包括苏区临时宪法，和关于"资产阶级民主革命"阶段的基本目标的说明。又可参阅《红色中国：毛泽东主席关于中华苏维埃共和国的发展的报告》（1934年伦敦劳伦斯书店出版）。

Meanwhile, Mao was of interest as a personality, apart from his political life, because, although his name was as familiar to many Chinese as that of Chiang Kai-shek, very little was known about him, and all sorts of strange legends existed about him. I was the first foreign newspaperman to interview him.

Mao had the reputation of a charmed life. He had been repeatedly pronounced dead by his enemies, only to return to the news columns a few days later, as active as ever. The Kuomintang had also officially "killed" and buried Chu Teh many times, assisted by occasional corroborations from clairvoyant missionaries. Numerous deaths of the two famous men, nevertheless, did not prevent them from being involved in many spectacular exploits, including the Long March. Mao was indeed in one of his periods of newspaper demise when I visited Red China, but I found him quite substantially alive. There were good reasons why people said that he had a charmed life, however; although he had been in scores of battles, was once captured by enemy troops and escaped, and had the world's highest reward on his head, during all these years he had never once been wounded.

I happened to be in Mao's house one evening when he was given a complete physical examination by a Red surgeon—a man who had studied in Europe and who knew his business—and pronounced in excellent health. He had never had tuberculosis or any "incurable disease," as had been rumored by some romantic travelers. His lungs were completely sound, although, unlike most Red commanders, he was an inordinate cigarette smoker. During the Long March, Mao and Li Teh had carried on original botanical research by testing out various kinds of leaves as tobacco substitutes.

Ho Tzu-chen, Mao's second wife, a former schoolteacher and a Communist organizer herself, had been less fortunate than her husband. She had suffered more than a dozen wounds, caused by splinters from an air bomb, but all of them were superficial. Just before I left Pao An the Maos were proud parents of a new baby girl. He had two other children by his former wife, Yang K'ai-hui, the daughter of his favorite professor. She was killed in Changsha in 1930 at the order of General Ho Chien, warlord of Hunan province.

Mao Tse-tung was forty-three years old when I met him in 1936. He was elected chairman of the provisional Central Soviet Government at the Second All-China Soviet Congress, attended by delegates representing approximately 9,000,000 people then living under Red laws.[1] Here, incidentally, it may be inserted that Mao Tse-tung estimated the maximum population of the various districts under the direct control of the Soviet Central Government in 1934 as follows: Kiangsi Soviet, 3,000,000; Hupeh-Anhui-Honan Soviet,

---

1. See Mao Tse-tung et al., *Fundamental Laws of the Chinese Soviet Republic* (London, Martin Lawrence, 1934). It contains the provisional constitution of the soviets, and a statement of basic objectives during the "bourgeois-democratic" phase of the revolution. See also Mao Tse-tung, *Red China: President Mao Tse-tung Reports on the Progress of the Chinese Soviet Republic* (London, Martin Lawrence, 1934).

万；湘赣鄂苏区100万；赣湘苏区100万；浙闽苏区100万；湘鄂苏区100万；总共900万。有些估计高达此数的十倍，令人难以置信，大概是把红军或红色游击队所活动的各个地区全部人口加在一起而得出来的。我把中国苏区人民有8,000万的数字告诉毛泽东的时候，他就笑了起来，并且说，要是他们真的有这样广大的面积，革命就差不多胜利了。不过当然，红色游击队的地区，人口还有好几百万。

毛泽东在中国的共产党势力范围内的影响，今天大概比什么人都要大。在几乎所有组织里，他都是一位委员——如革命军事委员会、中央政治局、财政委员会、组织委员会、公共卫生委员会以及其他等等。他的实际影响是通过在政治局的支配地位发挥出来的，[1]因为政治局有着决定党、政、军政策的大权。不过虽然每个人都知道他而且尊重他，但没有——至少现在还没有——在他身上搞英雄崇拜的一套。我从来没有碰到过一个中国共产党人，口中老是叨念着"我们的伟大领袖"。我没有听到过有人把毛泽东的名字当作是中国人民的同义语，但是，我却也从来没有碰到过一个不喜欢"主席"——个个人都这样叫他——或不景仰他的人。他个人在运动中的作用，显然是很大的。

在我看来，毛泽东是一个令人极感兴趣而复杂的人。他有着中国农民的质朴纯真的性格，颇有幽默感，喜欢憨笑。甚至在说到自己的时候和苏维埃的缺点的时候他也笑得厉害——但是这种孩子气的笑，丝毫也不会动摇他内心对他目标的信念。他说话平易，生活简朴，有些人可能以为他有点粗俗。然而他把天真质朴的奇怪品质同锐利的机智和老练的世故结合了起来。

我想我第一次的印象——主要是天生精明这一点——大概是不错的。然而毛泽东还是一个精通中国旧学的有成就的学者，他博览群书，对哲学和历史有深入的研究，他有演讲和写作的才能，记忆力异乎常人，专心致志的能力不同寻常，个人习惯和外表落拓不羁，但是对于工作却事无巨细都一丝不苟，他精力过人，不知疲倦，是一个颇有天才的军事和政治战略家。许多日本人都认为他是中国现有的最有才干的战略家，这是令人很感到兴趣的事。

红军正在保安盖起几所新建筑，但当我在那里的时候，住处是非常原始的。毛泽东和他的夫人住在两间窑洞里，四壁简陋，空无所有，只挂了一些地图。比这更

---

1. 参见第四篇第六章。

2,000,000; Hunan-Kiangsi-Hupeh Soviet, 1,000,000; Kiangsi-Hunan Soviet, 1,000,000; Chekiang-Fukien Soviet, 1,000,000; Hunan-Hupeh Soviet, 1,000,000; total, 9,000,000. Fantastic estimates ranging as high as ten times that figure were evidently achieved by adding up the entire population in every area in which the Red Army or Red partisans had been reported as operating. Mao laughed when I quoted him the figure of "80,000,000" people living under the Chinese soviets, and said that when they had that big an area the revolution would be practically won. But of course there were many millions in all the areas where Red partisans had operated.

The influence of Mao Tse-tung throughout the Communist world of China was probably greater than that of anyone else. He was a member of nearly everything—the revolutionary military committee, the political bureau of the Central Committee, the finance commission, the organization committee, the public health commission, and others. His real influence was asserted through his domination of the political bureau,[1] which had decisive power in the policies of the Party, the government, and the army. Yet, while everyone knew and respected him, there was—as yet, at least—no ritual of hero worship built up around him. I never met a Chinese Red who drooled "our-great-leader" phrases, I did not hear Mao's name used as a synonym for the Chinese people, but still I never met one who did not like "the Chairman"—as everyone called him—and admire him. The role of his personality in the movement was clearly immense.

Mao seemed to me a very interesting and complex man. He had the simplicity and naturalness of the Chinese peasant, with a lively sense of humor and a love of rustic laughter. His laughter was even active on the subject of himself and the shortcomings of the soviets—a boyish sort of laughter which never in the least shook his inner faith in his purpose. He was plain-speaking and plain-living, and some people might have considered him rather coarse and vulgar. Yet he combined curious qualities of naiveté with incisive wit and worldly sophistication.

I think my first impression—dominantly one of native shrewdness—was probably correct. And yet Mao was an accomplished scholar of Classical Chinese, an omnivorous reader, a deep student of philosophy and history, a good speaker, a man with an unusual memory and extraordinary powers of concentration, an able writer, careless in his personal habits and appearance but astonishingly meticulous about details of duty, a man of tireless energy, and a military and political strategist of considerable genius. It was interesting that many Japanese regarded him as the ablest Chinese strategist alive.

The Reds were putting up some new buildings in Pao An, but accommodations were very primitive while I was there. Mao lived with his wife in a two-room *yao-fang* with bare,

---

1. See Part Four, Chapter 6.

差的他都经历过了，但因为是一个湖南"富"农的儿子，他也经历过比这更好的。毛氏夫妇的主要奢侈品是一顶蚊帐。除此之外，毛泽东的生活和红军一般战士没有什么两样。做了10年红军领袖，千百次地没收了地主、官僚和税吏的财产，他所有的财物却依然是一卷铺盖，几件随身衣物——包括两套布制服。他虽然除了主席以外还是红军的一个指挥员，他所佩的领章，也不过是普通红军战士所佩的两条红领章。

我曾几次同毛泽东一起去参加过村民和红军学员的群众大会，去过红色剧院。他毫不惹眼地坐在观众的中间，玩得很高兴。我记得有一次在抗日剧社看戏，休息的时候，群众一致要求毛泽东和林彪来一次合唱。林彪是红军大学的校长，只有28岁，他以前是蒋介石参谋部里一个著名的年轻军校毕业生。林彪像一个小学生似的涨红了脸，讲了几句很得体的话，请女共产党员代替他们唱支歌，逃脱了"点名表演"。

毛泽东的伙食也同每个人一样，但因为是湖南人，他有着南方人"爱辣"的癖好。他甚至用辣椒夹着馒头吃。除了这种癖好之外，他对于吃的东西就很随便。有一次吃晚饭的时候，我听到他发挥爱吃辣的人都是革命者的理论。他首先举出他的本省湖南，就是因产生革命家出名的。他又列举了西班牙、墨西哥、俄国和法国来证明他的说法，可是后来有人提出意大利人也是以爱吃红辣椒和大蒜出名的例子来反驳他，他又只得笑着认输了。附带说一句，"赤匪"中间流行的一首最有趣的歌曲叫《红辣椒》。它唱的是辣椒对自己活着供人吃食没有意义感到不满，它嘲笑白菜、菠菜、青豆的浑浑噩噩、没有骨气的生活，终于领导了一场蔬菜的起义。这首《红辣椒》是毛主席最爱唱的歌。

他似乎一点也没有自大狂的征象，但个人自尊心极强，他的态度使人感到他有着一种在必要时候当机立断的魄力。我从来没有看见他生过气，不过我听到别人说，他有几次曾经大发脾气，使人害怕。在那种时候，据说他嬉笑怒骂的本领是极其杰出和无法招架的。

我发现他对于当前世界政治惊人地熟悉。甚至在长征途上，红军似乎也收到无线电新闻广播，在西北，他们还出版着自己的报纸。毛泽东熟读世界历史，对于欧洲社会和政治的情形，也有实际的了解。他对英国的工党很感兴趣，详尽地问我关

poor, map-covered walls. He had known much worse, and as the son of a "rich" peasant in Hunan he had also known better. The Maos' chief luxury (like Chou's) was a mosquito net. Otherwise Mao lived very much like the rank and file of the Red Army. After ten years of leadership of the Reds, after hundreds of confiscations of property of landlords, officials, and tax collectors, he owned only his blankets and a few personal belongings, including two cotton uniforms. Although he was a Red Army commander as well as chairman, he wore on his coat collar only the two red bars that are the insignia of the ordinary Red soldier.

I went with Mao several times to mass meetings of the villagers and the Red cadets, and to the Red theater. He sat inconspicuously in the midst of the crowd and enjoyed himself hugely. I remember once, between acts at the Anti-Japanese Theater, there was a general demand for a duet by Mao Tse-tung and Lin Piao, the twenty-eight-year-old president of the Hung Chung Ta-hsueh (Red Army University) and formerly a famed young cadet on Chiang Kai-shek's staff. Lin blushed like a schoolboy and got them out of the "command performance" by a graceful speech, calling upon the women Communists for a song instead.

Mao's food was the same as everybody's, but being a Hunanese he had the southerner's *ai-la*, or "love of pepper." He even had pepper cooked into his bread. Except for this passion, he scarcely seemed to notice what he ate. One night at dinner I heard him expand on a theory of pepper-loving peoples being revolutionaries. He first submitted his own province, Hunan, famous for the revolutionaries it has produced. Then he listed Spain, Mexico, Russia, and France to support his contention, but laughingly had to admit defeat when somebody mentioned the well-known Italian love of red pepper and garlic, in refutation of his theory. One of the most amusing songs of the "bandits," incidentally, was a ditty called "The Hot Red Pepper." It told of the disgust of the pepper with his pointless vegetable existence, waiting to be eaten, and how he ridiculed the contentment of the cabbages, spinach, and beans with their invertebrate careers. He ends up by leading a vegetable insurrection. "The Hot Red Pepper" was a great favorite with Chairman Mao.

He appeared to be quite free from symptoms of megalomania, but he had a deep sense of personal dignity, and something about him suggested a power of ruthless decision when he deemed it necessary. I never saw him angry, but I heard from others that on occasions he had been roused to an intense and withering fury. At such times his command of irony and invective was said to be classic and lethal.

I found him surprisingly well informed on current world politics. Even on the Long March, it seems, the Reds received news broadcasts by radio, and in the Northwest they published their own newspapers. Mao was exceptionally well read in world history and had a realistic conception of European social and political conditions. He was very

于工党目前的政策，很快就使我答不上来了。他似乎觉得很难理解，像英国那样工人有参政权的国家，为什么仍没有一个工人的政府。我的答案恐怕并没有使他满意。他对于麦克唐纳表示极端的蔑视，他说麦克唐纳是个"汉奸"——即英国人民的头号叛徒。

他对于罗斯福总统的看法是令人很感兴趣的。他相信罗斯福是个反法西斯主义者，以为中国可以跟这样的人合作。他又问到许多关于美国新政和罗斯福外交政策的问题。他所提问题表明他对于这两个政策的目标都有很明白的了解。他把墨索里尼和希特勒看做走江湖的骗子，但认为墨索里尼能干得多，一个真正的权术家，有历史知识，而希特勒，却不过是资本家的没有意志的傀儡。

毛泽东读过许多关于印度的书，对于那个国家也有一定的看法。主要的一点，就是认为印度不经过土地革命是永远不会实现独立的。他问到我关于甘地、尼赫鲁、查多巴蒂亚以及我所知道的其他印度领袖的情况。他知道一些美国的黑人问题，把黑人和美国印第安人所遭受的待遇，跟苏联对待少数民族的政策相对照。我指出美国的黑人和苏联的少数民族在历史和心理背景上有着某些很大的不同，他对此也表示有兴趣。有兴趣——但是并不同意我。

毛泽东是个认真研究哲学的人。我有一阵子每天晚上都去见他，向他采访共产党的党史，有一次一个客人带了几本哲学新书来给他，于是毛泽东就要求我改期再谈。他花了三四夜的工夫专心读了这几本书，在这期间，他似乎是什么都不管了。他读书的范围不仅限于马克思主义的哲学家，而且也读过一些古希腊哲学家、斯宾诺莎、康德、歌德、黑格尔、卢梭等人的著作。

我常常在想毛泽东自己对于武力、暴力以及"杀人的必要性"等问题的责任感。他年轻的时候，就有强烈的自由主义的和人道主义的倾向，从理想主义转到现实主义的过渡只能是在哲学上开始的。虽然他出身农民，但在年轻时候，本人却不曾怎么受过地主的压迫，像有许多共产党员那样；还有，马克思主义虽然是他思想的核心，但据我的推想，阶级仇恨对他来说大概基本上是他的哲学体系中的一种理性的产物，而不是本能的冲动。

他的身上似乎没有什么可以称为宗教感情的东西。我相信他的判断都是根据理性和必要作出的。因此我认为他在生与死的问题上，在共产主义运动中大概基本上起着一种节制的作用。我觉得他想把他的哲学，即"长期观点"的辩证法，作为任何大规模行动中的权衡标准，

interested in the Labour Party of England, and questioned me intensely about its present policies, soon exhausting all my information. It seemed to me that he found it difficult fully to understand why, in a country where workers were enfranchised, there was still no workers' government. I was afraid my answers did not satisfy him. He expressed profound contempt for Ramsay MacDonald, whom he designated as a *han-chien*—an archtraitor of the British people.

His opinion of President Roosevelt was rather interesting. He believed him to be anti-Fascist, and thought China could cooperate with such a man. He asked innumerable questions about the New Deal, and Roosevelt's foreign policy. The questioning showed a remarkably clear conception of the objectives of both. He regarded Mussolini and Hitler as mountebanks, but considered Mussolini intellectually a much abler man, a real Machiavellian, with a knowledge of history, while Hitler was a mere will-less puppet of the reactionary capitalists.

Mao had read a number of books about India and had some definite opinions on that country. Chief among these was that Indian independence would never be realized without an agrarian revolution. He questioned me about Gandhi, Jawaharlal Nehru, Suhasini Chattopadhyaya, and other Indian leaders I had known. He knew something about the Negro question in America, and unfavorably compared the treatment of Negroes and American Indians with policies in the Soviet Union toward national minorities. He was interested when I pointed out certain great differences in the historical background of the Negro in America and that of minorities in Russia.

Mao was an ardent student of philosophy. Once when I was having nightly interviews with him on Communist history, a visitor brought him several new books on philosophy, and Mao asked me to postpone our engagements. He consumed those books in three or four nights of intensive reading, during which he seemed oblivious to everything else. He had not confined his reading to Marxist philosophers, but also knew something of the ancient Greeks, of Spinoza, Kant, Goethe, Hegel, Rousseau, and others.

I often wondered about Mao's own sense of responsibility over the question of force, violence, and the "necessity of killing." He had in his youth had strongly liberal and humanistic tendencies, and the transition from idealism to realism evidently had first been made philosophically. Although he was peasant-born, he did not as a youth personally suffer much from oppression of the landlords, as did many Reds, and, although Marxism was the core of his thought, I deduced that class hatred was for him probably an intellectually acquired mechanism in the bulwark of his philosophy, rather than an instinctive impulse to action.

There seemed to be nothing in him that might be called religious feeling. He was a humanist in a fundamental sense; he believed in man's ability to solve man's problems.

而在这个思想范围内，人命的宝贵只是相对的。这在中国的领袖人物中间显然是很不平常的，因为从历史上来说，他们往往置权宜于伦理之上。

毛泽东每天工作十三四个小时，常常到深夜两三点钟才休息。他的身体仿佛是铁打的。他认为这要归因于他在少年时代在父亲的田里干过苦活，要归因于他在学校读书的刻苦时期，当时他与几个志同道合的人组织斯巴达俱乐部一类的团体。他们常常饿着肚皮，到华南山林中作长途的徒步跋涉，在严寒的日子去游泳，在雨雪中光着脊梁——这一切都是为了要锻炼他们自己。他们凭直觉知道，中国的来日需要他们有忍受最大的艰难困苦的能力。

有一次，毛泽东曾经花了整整一个夏天走遍他的家乡湖南全省。他靠挨家挨户替农家做工换饭吃，有时候甚至靠行乞。有一次他几天不吃饭，只吃些硬豆和水——这又是一种"锻炼"肠胃的方法。他早年在这次农村漫游中所结交的友谊，日后对他是有很大价值的，因为10年以后，他开始把湖南的成千上万的农民组成了有名的农民协会，这到1927年国共分裂后，成了苏维埃最初的基础。

毛泽东在我的印象中是一个有相当深邃感情的人。我记得有一两次当他讲到已死的同志或回忆到少年时代湖南由于饥荒引起的大米暴动中发生死人事件的时候，他的眼睛是润湿的。在那次暴动中他的省里有几个饥饿的农民因到衙门要粮而被砍了头。有一个战士告诉我，他曾经亲眼看到毛泽东把自己的上衣脱下来给一位在前线受伤的弟兄穿。他们又说当红军战士没有鞋穿的时候，他也不愿意穿鞋的。

然而我非常怀疑，他是否能够博得中国上层知识分子的敬仰，也许这并不完全因为他有非凡的头脑，而是因为他有农民的个人习惯。帕累托[1]的中国门徒们也许要嫌他粗鲁的吧。我记得有一天我和毛泽东谈话的时候，看见他心不在焉地松下了裤带，搜寻着什么寄生物——不过话得说回来，帕累托要是生活在同样的环境中可能也非搜寻一下不可。但我可以断定，帕累托决不会当着红军大学校长的面松下裤子的——我有一次访问林彪的时候，毛泽东却这样做过。小小的窑洞里非常闷热。毛泽东把身子向床上一躺，脱下了裤子，向着壁上的军用地图，仔细研究了20分钟——偶然只有林彪插口问他一些日期和人名，而毛泽东都是一概知道的。他随便的习惯和他完全不在乎个人外表这一点相一致，虽然他完全有条件可以打扮得同巧克力糖果匣上的将军和《中国名人录》中的政治家照片一样。

---

1. 一译博洽德（1848—1923），意大利经济学家和社会学家，《通俗资本论》的作者。——译注

I thought he had probably on the whole been a moderating influence in the Communist movement where life and death were concerned.

Mao worked thirteen or fourteen hours a day, often until very late at night, frequently retiring at two or three. He seemed to have an iron constitution. That he traced to a youth spent in hard work on his father's farm, and to an austere period in his schooldays when he had formed a kind of Spartan club with some comrades. They used to fast, go on long hikes in the wooded hills of South China, swim in the coldest weather, walk shirtless in the rain and sleet—to toughen themselves. They intuitively knew that the years ahead in China would demand the capacity for withstanding great hardship and suffering.

Mao once spent a summer tramping all over Hunan, his native province. He earned his bread by working from farm to farm, and sometimes by begging. Another time, for days he ate nothing but hard beans and water—again a process of "toughening" his stomach. The friendships he made on country rambles in his early youth were of great value to him when, some ten years later, he began to organize thousands of farmers in Hunan into the famous peasant unions which became the first base of the soviets, after the Kuomintang broke with the Communists in 1927.

Mao impressed me as a man of considerable depth of feeling. I remember that his eyes moistened once or twice when he was speaking of dead comrades, or recalling incidents in his youth, during the rice riots and famines of Hunan, when some starving peasants were beheaded in his province for demanding food from the yamen. One soldier told me of seeing Mao give his coat away to a wounded man at the front. They said that he refused to wear shoes when the Red warriors had none.

Yet I doubted very much if he would ever command great respect from the intellectual elite of China, perhaps not entirely because he had an extraordinary mind, but because he had the personal habits of a peasant. The Chinese disciples of Pareto might have thought him uncouth. Talking with Mao one day, I saw him absent-mindedly turn down the belt of his trousers and search for some guests—but then it is just possible that Pareto might have done a little searching himself if he had lived in similar circumstances. But I am sure that Pareto would never have taken off his trousers in the presence of the president of the Red Army University—as Mao did once when I was interviewing Lin Piao. It was extremely hot inside the little cave. Mao lay down on the bed, pulled off his pants, and for twenty minutes carefully studied a military map on the wall—interrupted occasionally by Lin Piao, who asked for confirmation of dates and names, which Mao invariably knew. His nonchalant habits fitted with his complete indifference to personal appearance, although the means were at hand to fix himself up like a chocolate-box general or a politician's picture in *Who's Who in China.*

在6,000英里的长征途中，除了几个星期生病以外，毛泽东和普通战士一样都是步行的。在最近几年中，他只要"叛变"投向国民党，就可以升官发财，这也适用于大部分红军指挥员。这些共产党人10年来忠于主义的坚定性，你如不知道中国收买其他造反者的"银弹"的历史，是无法充分估计的。

在我看来，他说的话是真诚、老实的。我有机会核对他的许多话，结果往往发现这些话是对的。他对我进行了几次不太过分的政治宣传，但是同我在非匪区所受到的政治宣传比起来，却算不得什么。无论对我写的文章，或拍的照片，他从来不加任何检查，对这优待，我非常感激。他尽力使我弄到能够说明苏区生活的各个方面的材料。

由于在今天中国政局上的极大重要性，他的关于共产党政策的一些主要讲话，是值得认真考虑的。因为在今天，西北全境以及其他各地武装和非武装的中国人民似乎都拥护他们的许多政策，因此，这些政策很可能成为造成中国命运发生根本变化的重要手段。

Except for a few weeks when he was ill, he walked most of the 6,000 miles of the Long March, like the rank and file. He could have achieved high office and riches by "betraying" to the Kuomintang, and this applied to most Red commanders. The tenacity with which these Communists for ten years clung to their principles could not be fully evaluated unless one knew the history of "silver bullets" in China, by means of which other rebels were bought off.

I was able to check up on many of Mao's assertions, and usually found them to be correct. He subjected me to mild doses of political propaganda, but it was interesting compared to what I had received in nonbandit quarters. He never imposed any censorship on me, in either my writing or my photography, courtesies for which I was grateful. He did his best to see that I got facts to explain various aspects of soviet life.

二、 共产党的基本政策

中国共产党人今天的基本政策是什么？关于这个问题，我和毛泽东以及共产党的其他领导人在这个问题上曾经作了十几次的谈话。但在考察他们的政策之前，我们对于共产党和南京之间长期斗争的性质，必须先有一些概念。哪怕要了解红色西北最近的情形，也必须首先看一看一些历史事实。

我在下文中有一部分转述了洛甫（张闻天）的话，他是共产党中央委员会的总负责人，会说英语，我在保安访问了他。

中国共产党在1921年才成立（后文有更为详细的交代）。她发展很快，1923年与孙逸仙博士的国民党结成两党同盟。孙博士单独与列宁领导下的俄共达成了协议，根据协议俄共向孙提供物质和政治援助。当时共产党和国民党都没有当权，但是孙拥有华南地方军阀的支持。他们允许孙在广州建立一个临时的全国政府，与一小撮北方军阀支持的并被列强承认的北京政府抗衡。从1923年起，国民党在俄国顾问帮助下，按照列宁党的方式，进行了改组。经孙逸仙同意，一些年轻的共产党员也加入了国民党。孙逸仙是一位民族主义爱国者，其志向是恢复中国的主权独立；除此之外，他对社会革命的设想（见于他的《三民主义》）只是改良资本主义和社会主义含糊的混杂。共产党支持孙实现国家独立的志向，但是他们的最终目标是实现无产阶级专政。

2 _____ BASIC COMMUNIST POLICIES

What were the fundamental policies of the Chinese Reds? I had a dozen or more talks on this subject with Mao Tse-tung and other leading Communists. But before one examined their policies it was necessary to have some conception of the nature of the long struggle between the Communists and Nanking. To comprehend even the recent events in the Reddening Northwest one had first to look at a few facts of history, as they looked to Chinese Communists.

In the following paragraphs I have paraphrased, in part, the comments of Lo Fu (Chang Wen-t'ien), the English-speaking general secretary of the Communist Party Politburo, whom I interviewed in Pao An.

The Chinese Communist Party was founded only in 1921 (an event reserved for more detailed discussion in a later context). It grew rapidly until 1923, when a two-party alliance was formed with Dr. Sun Yat-sen's Kuomintang (commonly called the Nationalist Party). Dr. Sun had independently reached an entente with the Russian Communist Party, under Lenin, which offered Sun material and political help. Neither the Kungch'antang (Chinese Communist Party) nor the Kuomintang held power at the time, but Sun was supported by provincial warlords in South China. They permitted Sun to set up a provisional all-China government in Canton, in rivalry to the Peking Government, which was backed by a coterie of northern warlords and was recognized by the foreign powers. From 1923 onward the Kuomintang was reorganized with the help of Russian political advisers, along lines of the party of Lenin. With Sun's concurrence, some members of the young Chinese Communist Party also joined the Kuomintang. Sun Yat-sen was a nationalist patriot whose ambition was to recover China's sovereign independence; beyond that, his concepts of social revolution (as expressed in his *Three Principles of the People*) were a vague mixture of reform capitalism and socialism. The Communists supported Sun's national independence aspirations but they aimed ultimately at a proletarian dictatorship.

莫斯科起初（1918—1922）试图与北京军阀合作，以此扩张俄国在远东的革命利益。1921年至1922年，共产国际代表马林[1]带回了一份看好孙逸仙博士的报告，共产国际于是重新评估了中国的潜在盟友的价值。在西方列强拒绝了孙博士关于"国际开发中国"的计划（在华盛顿会议上，1921—1922）之后，孙彻底幻灭了。现在他欢迎俄国通过共产国际的代表越飞提供援助。苏俄政策的彻底转向自《孙文越飞宣言》开始。这份联合宣言（1923年1月26日）成了三方联盟（国民党、共产党和苏俄）的基础，宣言认为"这里（中国）不存在成功实现共产主义或社会主义的条件，中国首要而且最当前的目标是实现国家统一和民族独立，"在实现这个目标的斗争中中国人民"可以依靠俄国的援助"。1922年末，鲍罗廷到达广州，担任孙的顾问和苏俄代表团团长，他身兼苏俄政治局代表和共产国际代表的双重身份，此时的共产国际已成为苏俄对外政策的工具。（从一开始便存在的这种固有的双重身份成了俄国国家利益和中国共产党的利益之间永远无法解决的矛盾。）

这种合作的基础，就共产党人而论，可以归结为孙逸仙博士和国民党接受两大革命原则。第一个原则承认有必要采取反帝政策——用革命行动收复政治上、领土上和经济上的全部主权。第二个原则要求在国内实行反封建、反军阀政策——对地主、军阀实现民主革命，建设新式的社会、经济、政治生活，共产党和国民党都认为这必须是民主性质的。

孙博士使用"民主"这个字眼是为了掩饰他的家长式革命理念，他的理念是"人民"要在他的国民党的"监护"下实现现代化。对共产党人来说，这个理念是一场"资产阶级民主"革命，在自己的党的"支配"下可资利用，渐进地走向社会主义。在广州组建的这个两党联合政府只包括国民党中央执行委员会委员——1924年至1927年期间包括共产党人。它的"合法性"和"民主性"的最为典型的体现在于它的组织结构。国民党中央机关的共产党席位被限制在总数的1/3。

当然，共产党认为"资产阶级民主"革命的胜利实现，是将来建立社会主义社

---

1. 参见第四篇第四章。

Moscow had at first (1918—1922) tried to advance Russian revolutionary interests in the Far East by working with the Peking warlords. In 1921—1922 the Comintern reassessed the value of potential allies in China after its delegate, Henricus Sneevliet,[1] returned with a favorable report on the prospects of Dr. Sun Yat-sen. Completely disillusioned after Western rejection of his plans (at the Washington Conference, 1921—1922) for the "international development of China," Dr. Sun now welcomed Russian offers of aid extended through the Comintern's agent, Adolf Joffe. A complete reorientation of Soviet policy began with the *Sun-Joffe Agreement*. In the Sun-Joffe joint statement (January 26, 1923), which became the basis of the three-way alliance (Kuomintang-Chinese Communist-Soviet Russia), it was agreed that "conditions do not exist here [in China] for the successful establishment of communism or socialism," while the "chief and immediate aim of China is the achievement of national union and national independence," in the struggle for which the Chinese "could depend on the aid of Russia." When Mikhail Borodin arrived in Canton late in 1922, to become Sun's adviser and head of the Soviet mission, he held dual positions as a delegate of the Soviet Politburo and as delegate of the Comintern, itself already an instrument of Soviet foreign policy. (Inherent in this dualism from the outset were contradictions between Russian national interests and the interests of the Chinese Communist Party, which were never resolved.)

The durability of the alliance, as far as Chinese Communists were concerned, depended upon the continued acceptance by the Kuomintang of two major objectives. The first recognized the necessity for an anti-imperialist policy—the recovery of complete political, territorial, and economic sovereignty by revolutionary action. The second demanded an internal policy of "anti-feudalism and anti-militarism"—the overthrow of landlords and warlords, and the construction of new forms of social, economic, and political life, which both the Communists and the Kuomintang agreed must be "democratic" in character.

"Democratic" was a word used by Dr. Sun to cover his paternalistic concept of a revolution in which the "people" or masses were to achieve "modernization" under the "tutelage" of his Nationalist Party. For the Communists the concept was a "bourgeois-democratic" revolution that could be manipulated, by stages, toward socialism, under the "hegemony" of their party. The two-party government formed at Canton consisted only of members of the Central Executive Committee of the Kuomintang—which from 1924 to 1927 included Communists. It was never more "legal" or "democratic" than its own organic structure. Communist membership in Kuomintang central organs was limited to one-third of the total.

The Communists regarded the successful fulfillment of Dr. Sun's "bourgeois-democratic" revolution as a necessary preliminary to the Socialist society later to be established. Their

---

1. See Part Four, Chapter 4.

会的先决条件。因此，他们采取支持"民主的民族独立和解放"运动的立场是合乎逻辑的。

不幸孙逸仙博士在1925年革命还没有完成的时候就去世了。到1927年，国共两党的合作宣告结束。从共产党的观点看来，国民革命也可说是在那时候完结了。国民党的右翼，在新军阀的控制之下，在某些外国、通商口岸[1]银行家和地主的支持之下，跟合法选出的汉口政府宣告决裂。他们在蒋介石领导下在南京另立政权，当时共产党和国民党中的大多数都认为这个政权是"反革命的"，也就是说，是反对"资产阶级民主革命"本身的。

国民党不久便顺从南京的政变，[2]但共产主义却成了杀头的罪名。共产党认为民族主义的主要两点——反帝运动和民主革命——实际上已被放弃了。接着就是军阀的内战，和后来对高涨的土地革命加紧进行镇压。成千上万的共产党员和前农会、工人领袖遭到了杀戮。工会都被解散。所谓"开明的专政"对各种形式的反对力量都进行镇压。即使这样，军队中却仍有不少共产党员保存下来，在整个大恐怖时期党没有被打垮。在内战中虽然耗资达几十亿元，可是到了1937年，红军在西北所占领的地方却是在他们完全控制下的一块最大的连成一片的地区。

自然，共产党相信，1927年以来的10年的历史，充分证明了他们的论点，那就是：对外不实行反帝政策，对内不实行土地革命，中国的民族独立和民主政治（国民党也把这定做他们的目标）是无法实现的。对于他们的论点，这里没有必要充分探讨。但是假使我们要知道共产主义为什么能够有越来越多的人拥护，特别在爱国青年中间是这样，为什么在目前它还能在历史的屏幕上投射东方大动荡、大变化的影子，我们就必须注意它的主要论点。这些论点是什么呢？

首先，共产党说，自从南京分裂了革命的有生力量以后，中国的情形是每况愈下了。妥协接着妥协。由于没有能够进行土地革命，在全国许多地方的农村人口中间引起了广大的不满和公开的造反。农村人口中间普遍存在的贫穷和困苦的情形日

---

1. 根据鸦片战争期间及其后强加给中国的不平等条约而被迫向外国商人开放的沿海及内陆港口。
2. 只有以孙中山夫人宋庆龄为首的少数左派人士拒不妥协。

position in support of a "democratic national independence and liberation" movement seemed logical.

Dr. Sun Yat-sen died in 1925, before the revolution was completed. Cooperation between the Kuomintang and the Kungch'antang came to an end in 1927. From the Communist viewpoint, the Nationalist Revolution could also be said to have ended then. The right wing of the Kuomintang, dominated by the new militarism, and supported by certain foreign powers, the treaty-port[1] bankers, and the landlords, broke away from the Left Kuomintang Government at Hankow. It formed a regime at Nanking under Chiang Kai-shek which the Communists and the majority of the Kuomintang at that time regarded as "counterrevolutionary," that is, against the "bourgeois-democratic revolution" itself.

The Kuomintang soon reconciled itself to the Nanking *coup d'état*,[2] but communism became a crime punishable by death. What the Reds conceived to be the two main points of nationalism—the anti-imperialist movement and the democratic revolution—were in practice abandoned. Militarists' civil wars and, later, intensive war against the rising agrarian revolution ensued. Many thousands of Communists and former peasant-union and labor leaders were killed. The unions were suppressed. An "enlightened dictatorship" made war on all forms of opposition. Even so, quite a number of Communists survived in the army, and the Party held together throughout a period of great terrorism. In 1937, despite the expenditure of billions of dollars in civil war against them, the Red armies occupied in the Northwest the largest (though sparsely populated) connected territory ever under their complete control.

Of course the Reds believed that the decade of history since 1927 had richly validated their thesis that national independence and democracy (which the Kuomintang also set as its objective) could not be achieved in China without an anti-imperialist policy externally, and an agrarian revolution internally. To see why communism steadily increased its following, especially among patriotic youth, and why at the moment it still projected upon the screen of history the shadows of great upheaval and change in the Orient, one had to note its main contentions. What were they?

First of all, the Reds argued that, after Nanking split the living forces of the revolution, China rapidly lost much ground. Compromise followed compromise. The failure to realize agrarian reforms resulted in widespread discontent and open rebellion from the rural population in many parts of the country. General conditions of poverty and distress among the rural populace seriously worsened. China now had some passable motor roads,

---

1. Coastal and inland ports opened to foreign commerce by treaties imposed on China during the Opium Wars and later.
2. Except for a splinter left-wing element which came to be personified by Mme. Sun Yat-sen (Soong Ch'ing-ling).

益恶化。中国现在也有了几条可以通行的公路，一队优秀的飞机和"新生活运动"，[1]但是除此之外，凡是了解一些其他情况的经济学家无不为黯淡的前途担忧。每天有天灾人祸的消息传来，这要是在大多数国家就会被认为是不得了，但是在中国已多少成了司空见惯的常事。举例说，甚至当我执笔在写本章的时候，报上就载着从华中、华西发来的这样骇人听闻的消息：

> 豫、皖、陕、甘、川、黔各省灾情，续有所闻。全国显已遭多年来最严重的灾馑，已有千万人死亡。据最近川灾救济委员会调查，该省灾区人口3,000万人，已有好几万人食树皮和观音土[2]充饥。据传陕西现有灾民40余万人，甘肃百余万人，河南约700万人，贵州约300万人。贵州灾区遍及60县，官方的中央社承认是百年来最严重的一次灾荒。[3]

在许多省份中，赋税往往已预征到60年或60年以上，农民因无力缴付地租和高利贷的利息，好几千英亩的土地都任其荒芜着。四川就是其中的一省。在我6年来所收集的材料中，有的材料说明许多别的省份也有同样的情形。但是很少迹象表明，发生这种灾荒的周期率有减缓的趋向。

当大批农村人口迅速地趋于破产的时候，土地和财富就随着个体农民的总衰落而日益集中到少数地主和高利贷者的手里。[4]据报道，李滋-罗斯爵士曾经说过，中国没有中产阶级，只有赤贫和巨富。如果此说过去不确的话，以后很可能成为事实。苛捐杂税，腐败的谷物交租制度以及像魏特夫博士称为"亚细亚生产方式"的社会、政治、经济关系的整个传统制度，弄得无地的农民经常负债累累，没有粮食储备，完全无力应付旱灾、饥馑、洪水这样的危机。

1926年，毛泽东还担任国民党农民运动委员会书记（在国共分裂之前，[5]当时他是国民党中央执行委员会候补委员）的时候，曾经负责搜集21省土地统计。据他

---

1. 蒋发起该运动旨在利用恢复封建的伦理纲常来控制人们的行为。
2. 用以缓解饥饿的泥丸和稻草，常常导致死亡。
3. 1937年5月15日北平出版的《民主》。
4. 讨论这一问题的最杰出的研究和分析的著作是陈翰笙的近著《中国的地主和农民》（1936年纽约）。
5. 毛泽东当时担任国民党宣传部副部长和农民运动讲习所所长，农民运动委员会书记是他在中共党内的职务（——编注）。他所教过的许多学员后来同他一起组建了红军。

an excellent fleet of airplanes, and a New Life Movement,[1] but reports came in daily of catastrophes which in China were considered more or less routine. Even as I was writing this chapter, for example, the press brought this appalling news from Central and West China:

Famine conditions continue to be reported in Honan, Anhui, Shensi, Kansu, Szechuan, and Kweichow. Quite evidently the country faces one of the most severe famines of many years, and thousands have already died. A recent survey by the Szechuan Famine Relief Commission discovered that 30,000,000 people are now in the famine belt of that province, where bark and "Goddess-of-Mercy" earth[2] are being consumed by tens of thousands. There are said to be over 400,000 famine refugees in Shensi, over 1,000,000 in Kansu, some 7,000,000 in Honan, and 3,000,000 in Kweichow. The famine in Kweichow is admitted by the official Central News to be the most serious in 100 years, affecting sixty districts of the province.[3]

Szechuan was one of the provinces where taxes had been collected sixty years or more in advance, and thousands of acres of land had been abandoned by farmers unable to pay rents and outrageous loan interest. In my files were items, collected over a period of six years, showing comparable distress in many other provinces. There were few signs that the rate of frequency of these calamities was diminishing.

While the mass of the rural population was rapidly going bankrupt, concentration of land and wealth in the hands of a small number of landlords and land-owning usurers increased in proportion to the general decline of independent farming. Sir Frederick Leith-Ross was reported to have said that there was no middle class in China, but only the incredibly poor and the very rich. Enormous taxes, the share-crop method, and the whole historical system of social, political, and economic relationships described by Dr. Karl August Wittfogel as the "Asiatic mode of production," contrived to leave the landless peasantry constantly heavily in debt, without reserves, and unable to meet such crises as draught, famine, and flood.

Mao Tse-tung, when a secretary of the Kuomintang's Committee on the Peasant Movement in 1926 (and a candidate to the Central Executive Committee of the Kuomintang),[4] supervised the collection of land statistics for areas in twenty-one provinces. He asserted

---

1. Launched by Chiang in an attempt to revivify certain rules of personal behavior based on Confucian teachings.
2. Balls of mud and straw eaten to appease hunger, and often resulting in death.
3. From Democracy, Peking, May 15, 1937.
4. Mao was also deputy chief of the Kuomintang propaganda department and deputy director of its Peasant Movement Training Institute, where he lectured to many cadres who later joined him in the formation of the Red Army.

说，这次调查说明了占全部农村人口 10% 的在乡地主、富农、官吏、在外地主和高利贷者，总共占有中国所有可耕地的 70%。中农占有 15%。但是占农村人口 65% 以上的贫农、佃农和雇农，却只占全部耕地的 10% 到 15%。

据毛泽东说，"自从反革命以后，这些数字被禁止发表了。在 10 年后的现在，关于中国土地分配情况，仍不能从南京方面得到任何说明。"

共产党认为，农村的破产由于放弃反帝斗争——这在大多数中国人看来即"抗日斗争"——带来的严重不利后果而加速了。由于南京对日本采取"不抵抗政策"的结果，中国把 1/5 的领土，40% 以上的铁路线，85% 的荒地，一大部分的煤，80% 的铁矿，37% 的最佳森林地带以及 40% 左右的全国出口贸易丢给了日本侵略者。日本现在还控制了中国剩下来的地方的 75% 以上的全部铣铁和铁矿企业，中国一半以上的纺织业。对满洲的征服，不仅从中国夺去了它最方便的原料来源，而且也夺去了它自己最好的市场。在 1931 年，满洲从中国其他各省的输入，占其总输入的 27% 以上，到 1935 年，中国对伪满洲国的贸易，却只占其输入的 4%。日本因此得到了中国最适于工业发展的区域——使它可以阻止这种发展，而把原料移用于它自己的工业。这给予了日本以大陆上的根据地，它可以从这里毫无顾忌地继续侵略中国。许多人觉得，即使中国其余部分不再遭侵略，这种种变化，已完全勾销了南京可以归功于自己的任何改革给后代带来的好处。

那么，南京的 9 年反共战争的结果是什么呢？西北当局最近曾在一个反对第六次反共"清剿"运动的宣言中，总结了这些结果。[1] 它告诉我们，第一次"清剿"运动时，满洲落入日本的手里，第二次上海遭到侵犯，第三次放弃了热河，第四次失去了冀东，而第五次"肃清残匪"运动中，冀、察的主权又受了很大的损害。因此，西北方面认为，蒋介石最新的"剿共"与日本侵略绥远北部发生在同一个时候，绥远必然就要丢失。

自然，只要共产党继续企图用武力推翻政府，南京是不能停止内战的。但是早在 1932 年，红军就提出媾和，愿意在抗日的共同纲领上与南京联合。他们的提议被拒绝了。现

---

1. 引自西安事变时"联合抗日委员会"发表的一项声明。参见第十二篇第二章。

that this investigation indicated that resident landlords, rich peasants, officials, absentee landlords, and usurers, about 10 per cent of the whole rural population, together owned over 70 per cent of the cultivable land in China. About 15 per cent was owned by middle peasants. But over 65 per cent of the rural population, made up of poor peasants, tenants, and farm workers, owned only from 10 to 15 per cent of the total arable land.

"These statistics were suppressed after the counterrevolution," according to Mao. "Now, ten years later, it is still impossible to get any statement from Nanking on land distribution in China."

The Communists alleged that rural bankruptcy had been accelerated by the Kuomintang's policy of "nonresistance to imperialism"—in particular, Japanese imperialism. As a result of Nanking's "no-war policy" against Japan, China had lost to Japanese invaders about a fifth of her national territory, over 40 per cent of her railway mileage, 85 per cent of her unsettled lands, a large part of her coal, 80 per cent of her iron deposits, 37 per cent of her finest forest lands, and about 40 per cent of her national export trade. Japan now controlled over 75 per cent of the total pig iron and iron-mining enterprises of what remained of China, and over half of the textile industry of China. The conquest of Manchuria also robbed China of its own best market as well as its most accessible raw materials. In 1931, Manchuria took more than 27 per cent of its total imports from other Chinese provinces, but in 1935 China could sell Manchukuo only 4 per cent of those imports. It presented Japan with the region of China best suited for industrial development—and enabled her to prevent that development and shuttle the raw materials to her own industries. It gave to Japan the continental base from which she could inexorably continue her aggression in China. Such changes, many felt, completely wiped out the benefits of any reforms that Nanking might be able to claim to its credit for generations in the future—even provided the rest of China remained intact.

And what was achieved by Nanking's nine years of war against the Reds? The Northwest junta had recently summarized the results in a manifesto opposing preparations for the sixth anti-Red "final annihilation" drive.[1] It reminded us that Manchuria had gone to Japan during one "final-annihilation" drive, Shanghai had been invaded during another, Jehol had been given up during the third, east Hopei lost during still another, and the sovereignty of Hopei and Chahar provinces had been badly impaired during the fifth "remnant-bandit extermination."

Of course Nanking could not stop civil war as long as the Reds continued to attempt to overthrow the government by force. In April, 1932, when the Chinese Soviet Republic

---

1. From a statement issued by the "United Anti-Japanese Council" at the time of the Sian Incident. See Part Twelve, Chapter 2.

在，红军在西北不断扩展地盘，占了战略上很大的有利条件，但共产党却在全国与抗日军队和爱国团体联合，又重申它原来的提议，愿意合作停止内战，建立民族"抗日统一战线"来抵抗侵略者。只要南京同意建立民主的代议制政府，对日抗战，还政于民和保障人民的公民权利，它答应把红军和苏区完全归中央政府来管辖。[1] 换句话说，共产党准备同国民党"重婚"，只要它能恢复反帝反封建的"资产阶级民族主义"纲领。在这两个基本目标中，他们认识到争取民族生存的斗争是最最重要的，甚至要不惜放弃土地问题的国内斗争去进行；而阶级矛盾可能不得不从属于外部的对日斗争的胜利解决，没有这胜利解决，阶级矛盾当然是不能满意地解决的。

把毛泽东在我访问时候所说的话，引录几段在下面：

"今天中国人民的根本问题是抵抗日本帝国主义。我们苏维埃的政策决定于这一斗争。日本军阀希望征服全中国，使中国人民成为他们殖民地的奴隶。反抗日本侵略的斗争，反抗日本经济和军事征服的斗争——这就是在分析苏维埃政策时必须记住的主要任务。

"日本帝国主义不仅是中国的敌人，而且也是全世界所有爱好和平的人民的敌人。它特别是那些在太平洋有利害关系的各国，即美、英、法和苏俄各国人民的敌人。日本的大陆政策和海上政策一样，不仅针对着中国，而且也是针对那些国家的……

"我们对于外国希望的是什么？我们希望友好各国至少不要帮助日本帝国主义，而采取中立的立场。我们希望他们能够积极帮助中国抵抗侵略和征服。"

在用"帝国主义"一词的时候，共产党把今天积极侵略中国的日本和目前友好的、不侵略的、民主的资本主义国家作了显明的区分。毛泽东解释说：

"关于总的帝国主义问题，我们认为在大国中间，有些表示不愿参加新的世界大

---

1. 不过毛泽东自然无意将共产党控制的领土及其政党的政治势力拱手送给总司令，这一点他很快就向我表明了。

declared war against Japan, it had offered to combine with anti-Japanese elements. Again in January, 1933, it had proposed to unite with "any armed force" in a "united front from below." There was no real offer, however, to compromise with Chiang Kai-shek. By mid-1936 the Communists (and the Comintern) had radically changed their position. In a search for broad national unity, they included the Kuomintang and even Chiang Kai-shek. The Chinese Communist Party now promised to unite its Red Army and the soviet districts under the sovereignty of the Kuomintang Central Government, provided that the latter would agree to "establish democratic representative government, resist Japan, enfranchise the people, and guarantee civil liberties to the masses."[1] In other words, the Reds were ready to "remarry" the Kuomintang if it would return to the "bourgeois-nationalist" program of anti-imperialism and anti-feudalism. But of these two basic aims they realized that the fight for national survival was paramount, and must be conducted even at the expense of modifying the internal struggle over the land question; that class antagonisms might have to be sublimated in, certainly could not be satisfied without, the successful solution of the external struggle against Japan.

To quote Mao in his interview with me:

"The fundamental issue before the Chinese people today is the struggle against Japanese imperialism. Our soviet policy is decisively conditioned by this struggle. Japan's warlords hope to subjugate the whole of China and make of the Chinese people their colonial slaves. The fight against the Japanese invasion, the fight against Japanese economic and military conquest—these are the main tasks that must be remembered in analyzing soviet policies.

"Japanese imperialism is not only the enemy of China but also of all people of the world who desire peace. Especially it is the enemy of those peoples with interests on the Pacific Ocean, namely, the American, British, French, and Soviet Russian nations. The Japanese continental policy, as well as naval policy, is directed not only against China but also against those countries . . . .

"What do we expect from the foreign powers? We expect at least that friendly nations will not help Japanese imperialism, and will adopt a neutral position. We hope that they will actively help China to resist invasion and conquest."

In using the word "imperialism," the Communists sharply distinguished between Japan and friendly and nonaggressive democratic capitalist powers. Mao Tse-tung explained:

"Concerning the question of imperialism in general we observe that among the great powers some express unwillingness to engage in a new world war, some are not ready

---

1. But Mao Tse-tung had no intention, of course, as he would soon make clear to me, of surrendering either Communist-held territory or the political independence of his party to the Generalissimo.

战，有些不愿坐看日本占领中国，如美、英、法、荷兰和比利时等国。此外还有永远在侵略强国威胁下的国家，如暹罗、菲律宾、中美各国、加拿大、印度、澳大利亚、荷属东印度等，这些国家，都多少在日本的威胁之下。我们都把它们当作朋友，请它们合作……

"因此，除了日本和那些帮助日本帝国主义的国家［根据毛泽东在别处所指，即意大利和德国］以外，上述范围中的各国，可以组成反战、反侵略、反法西斯的世界联盟……在过去，南京曾从美、英和其他各国接受了许多的援助。这些款项和供应品大部分用于内战。南京每杀一个红军的战士，就杀了许多的农民和工人。据银行家章乃器在最近发表一篇论文中的估计，南京每杀一个红军的战士，就花中国人民8万元钱。[1] 因此，我们看来，这样的'援助'，不能说是给中国人民的。

"只有当南京决定停止内战，对日本帝国主义发动抗战，并且与革命的人民联合起来组成一个民主的国防政府的时候——只有到了那个时候，这样的援助于中国民族才有真正的利益。"

我问毛泽东，苏维埃是否主张取消不平等条约。他指出有许多的不平等条约，实际上已为日本所破坏，特别在满洲。至于中国代议制政府将来的态度，他这样说：

"那些援助中国或者并不反对中国独立和解放战争的国家，应该请他们同中国保持密切的友好关系。那些积极援助日本的国家，自然不能给予同样的待遇：举例说，德国和意国，他们已和伪满洲国建立了特殊的关系，是不能算做中国人民的友邦的。

"对于友邦，中国愿意和平谈判互利的条约。对于其他的国家，中国准备在更广泛的范围上同他们保持合作……至于日本，中国必须以解放战争的行动，来废除一切不平等条约，没收日本帝国主义所有的财产，取消日本在我国的特权、租界和势力。关于我们对于其他国家的关系，我们共产党人并不主张采取可能使中国在抗日斗争中在国际上处于不利地位的措施。

"当中国真正获得了独立时，那么，外国正当贸易利益就可享有比从前更多的机

---

1. 人民和"游击队"被杀的要比正规红军战士多得多。章先生的估计，除了实际军事费用外，还包括劳动力的损失、庄稼的损失，村庄、城市和农田的破坏等耗费。

to see Japan occupy China: countries such as America, Great Britain, France, Holland, and Belgium. Then there are countries permanently under the menace of the aggressive powers, such as Siam, the Philippines, Central American countries, Canada, India, Australia, the Dutch Indies, etc.—all more or less under the direct threat of Japan. We consider them our friends and invite their cooperation . . . .

"So, except for Japan and those countries which help Japanese imperialism, the categories mentioned above can be organized into anti-war, anti-aggression, anti-Fascist world alliances . . . . In the past, Nanking has received much help from America, England, and other countries. Most of these funds and supplies have been used in civil war. For every Red soldier killed, Nanking has slain many peasants and workers. According to a recent article by the banker Chang Nai-ch'i it has cost the Chinese people about $80,000 for every Red soldier killed by Nanking.[1] Such 'help' therefore does not seem to us to have been rendered to the Chinese people.

"Only when Nanking determines to cease civil war and to fight against Japanese imperialism, and unites with the people's revolution to organize a democratic national defense government—only then can such help be of real benefit to the Chinese nation."

I asked Mao whether the soviets were in favor of canceling unequal treaties. He pointed out that many of these unequal treaties had, in effect, already been destroyed by the Japanese, especially in the case of Manchuria. But as for the future attitude of a representative government in China, he declared:

"Those powers that help or do not oppose China in her war of independence and liberation should be invited to enjoy close friendly relations with China. Those powers which actively assist Japan should naturally not be given the same treatment: for example, Germany and Italy, which have already established special relations with Manchukuo, and cannot be regarded as powers friendly to the Chinese people.

"With friendly powers, China will peacefully negotiate treaties of mutual advantage. With other powers China is prepared to maintain cooperation on a much broader scale . . . . So far as Japan is concerned, China must by the act of war of liberation cancel all unequal treaties, confiscate all Japanese imperialist holdings, and annul Japan's special privileges, concessions, and influence in this country. Concerning our relations with other powers, we Communists do not advocate any measure that may place at disadvantage the world position of China in her struggle against Japanese imperialism.

"When China really wins her independence, then legitimate foreign trading interests will

---

1. Far more civilians and "partisans" were killed than regular Red soldiers. Mr. Chang's estimate included costs of lost labor, lost crops, ruined villages and towns, ruined farmlands, etc., as well as actual military expenses.

会。四亿五千万人民生产和消费的力量，不是一件能完全由中国人来管的事情，而必须要许多国家来参加。我们几万万的人民，一旦获得真正的解放，把他们巨大的潜在的生产力用在各方面创造性的活动上，能够帮助改善全世界经济和提高全世界文化的水准。但中国人民的生产力在过去却很少发挥；相反，它还受着本国军阀和日本帝国主义的压制。"

最后我问："中国是否可能与民主的资本主义国家结成反帝的联盟呢？"

毛泽东回答道：

"反帝、反法西斯的联盟，性质上就是共同防御好战国家的和平联盟。中国与资本主义民主国家缔结反法西斯条约，是完全可能而且需要的。这种国家为了自卫加入反法西斯阵线，是对它们自己有利的……

"假使中国完全沦为殖民地，那么这就是一系列长期的、可怕的、毫无意义的战争的开始。因此必须作出抉择。从中国人民自己来说，我们将采取对压迫者进行抵抗的道路，我们希望外国的政治家和人民也能同我们一起走这一条路，而不要走上帝国主义的血腥历史所决定的黑暗的道路……

"要抗日成功，中国也必须得到其他国家的援助。**但这不是说，没有外国的援助，中国就不能抗日！**中国共产党、苏维埃政府、红军和中国的人民，准备同任何国家联合起来，以缩短这次战争的时期。但是如果没有一个国家加入我们，我们也决心要单独进行下去！"

但是这是多么荒谬可笑！共产党是真的认为中国可以打败日本这样强大的战争机器？我相信他们是这样想的。那么，他们认定能获得胜利所根据的，究竟是什么样的逻辑呢？这就是我向毛泽东提出的十几个问题中的一个问题。下面他的回答是有启发性的，而且也许确是有预见性的，即使正统的军事思想家可能认为它在技术上是有谬误的。

enjoy more opportunities than ever before. The power of production and consumption of 450,000,000 people is not a matter that can remain the exclusive interest of the Chinese, but one that must engage the many nations. Our millions of people, once really emancipated, with their great latent productive possibilities freed for creative activity in every field, can help improve the economy as well as raise the cultural level of the whole world. But the productive power of the Chinese people has in the past scarcely been touched; on the contrary, it has been suppressed—both by native militarists and Japanese imperialism."

Finally I asked, "Is it possible for China to make anti-imperialist alliances with democratic capitalist powers?"

"Anti-imperialist, anti-Fascist alliances," replied Mao, "are in the nature of peace alliances, and for mutual defense against war-making nations. A Chinese anti-Fascist pact with capitalist democracies is perfectly possible and desirable. It is to the interest of such countries to join the anti-Fascist front in self-defense. . . .

"If China should become completely colonized it would mean the beginning of a long series of terrible and senseless wars. A choice must be made. For itself, the Chinese people will take the road of struggle against its oppressors, and we hope also that the statesmen and people of foreign nations will march with us on this road, and not follow the dark paths laid down by the bloody history of imperialism . . . .

"To oppose Japan successfully, China must also seek assistance from other powers. *This does not mean, however, that China is incapable of fighting Japan without foreign help!* The Chinese Communist Party, the Soviet Government, the Red Army, and the Chinese people are ready to unite with any power to shorten the duration of this war. But if none join us we are determined to carry on alone."

Did the Reds really imagine that China could defeat Japan's mighty war machine? I believed that they did. What was the peculiar shape of logic on which they based their assumption of triumph? It was one of dozens of questions I put to Mao Tse-tung.

三、　论抗日战争

　　1936年7月16日，我坐在毛泽东住处里面一条没有靠背的方凳上。时间已过了晚上9点，"熄灯号"已经吹过，几乎所有的灯火已经熄灭。毛泽东家里的天花板和墙壁，都是从岩石中凿出来的；下面则是砖块地。窗户也是从岩石中凿出的，半窗里挂着一幅布窗帘，我们前面是一张没有上油漆的方桌，铺了一块清洁的红毡，蜡烛在上面毕剥着火花。毛夫人在隔壁房间里，把那天从水果贩子那里买来的野桃子制成蜜饯。毛泽东交叉着腿坐在从岩石中凿成的一个很深的壁龛里，吸着一支前门牌香烟。

　　坐在我旁边的是吴亮平，他是一位年轻的苏维埃"干部"，在我对毛泽东进行"正式"访问时担任译员。我把毛泽东对我所提出的问题的回答，用英文全部记下来，然后又译成了中文，由毛泽东改正，他对具体细节也必力求准确是有名的。靠着吴先生的帮助，这些访问记再译成了英文，经过了这样的反复，我相信这几节文字很少有报道的错误。

　　我在收集材料上多亏吴亮平给我许多的帮助。他是蒋介石在浙江的故乡奉化一个大地主的儿子。几年以前，因为他那显然有野心的父亲要叫他和蒋总司令的一个亲戚订婚，他就从家里逃出。吴是上海大夏大学的毕业生。在上海，帕特·吉文斯曾经因共产党活动逮捕他，使他在华德路监牢里关了两年。他曾经留学法国、英国和苏联，26岁，因为作为一个共产党员努力工作，领到了制服、住所和食物——后者主要是小米和面条。

3   On War with Japan

On July 16, 1936, I sat on a square, backless stool inside Mao Tse-tung's residence. It was after nine at night, "Taps" had been sounded and nearly all lights were out. The walls and ceiling of Mao's home were of solid rock; beneath was a flooring of bricks. Cotton gauze extended halfway up windows also hollowed from stone, and candles sputtered on the square, unpainted table before us, spread with a clean red-felt cloth. Mrs. Mao was in an adjoining room making compote from wild peaches purchased that day from a fruit merchant. Mao sat with his legs crossed, in a deep shelf hewn from the solid rock, and smoked a Chien Men cigarette.

Seated next to me was Wu Liang-p'ing, a young soviet "functionary" who acted as interpreter in my "formal" interviews with Mao Tse-tung. I wrote down in full in English Mao Tse-tung's answers to my questions, and these were then translated into Chinese and corrected by Mao, who is noted for his insistence upon accuracy of detail. With the assistance of Mr. Wu, the interviews were retranslated into English, and because of such precautions I believe these pages to contain few errors of reporting. They were, of course, the strictly partisan views of the leader of the Chinese Communists—views being made known to the Western world for the first time.

Wu Liang-p'ing, to whom I am indebted for much assistance in gathering material, was the son of a rich landlord in Fenghua, Chiang Kai-shek's native district in Chekiang. He had fled from there some years ago when his father, apparently an ambitious burgher, wished to betroth him to a relative of the Generalissimo. Wu was a graduate of Ta Hsia University, in Shanghai. There Patrick Givens, chief of the Criminal Investigation Department of the British-controlled police of the International Settlement, had arrested Wu Liang-P'ing. Charged with Communist activity, Wu spent two years in the Settlement's Ward Road Jail. He had studied in France, England, and Russia, was twenty-six years old, and for his energetic labors as a Communist received his uniform, room, and food—the latter consisting chiefly of millet and noodles.

毛泽东开始回答我提出关于共产党对日政策的第一个问题，我的问题是这样的："如果日本被打败了而且被逐出了中国，你是不是以为'外国帝国主义'这个大问题总的来说也就此解决了呢？"

"是的。如果别的帝国主义国家不像日本这样地行动，而且如果中国打败了日本，那就意味着中国人民大众是觉醒了，动员了起来，而且确立了他们的独立。因此，帝国主义这个主要问题也就解决了。"

"你认为在什么条件下，中国人民才能够消耗和打败日本的军队？"我问。

他回答说："三个条件可以保证我们的成功：第一，中国结成抗日民族统一战线；第二，全世界结成反日统一战线；第三，目前在日本帝国主义势力下受苦的被压迫各国人民采取革命行动。在这三个条件中，主要条件是中国人民自己的团结。"

我问："你认为这样的战争要打多久？"

毛答："这要看中国人民的民族统一战线的力量，要看中国和日本国内的许多的决定性因素，要看国际对华援助的程度以及日本内部革命发展的速度而定。如果中国人民的民族统一战线是极其一致的，如果上下左右都是有效地组织起来的，如果那些认识到日本帝国主义对自身利益威胁的各国政府给予中国的国际援助是大量的，如果日本国内很快发生革命，那么这次战争就会很短，很快就可以得到胜利。[1]但是，如果这些条件不能实现，那么战争会是很长久的，但到最后，日本还是要被打败，只不过牺牲重大，全世界都要经历一个痛苦的时期。"

问："你对这样一场战争在军事上和政治上的可能发展趋势有怎么样的看法？"

答："这里包含两个问题——外国的政策和中国军队的战略。

"现在，日本的大陆政策，谁都知道是已经确定的了。那些以为再牺牲一些中国主权，再作一些经济上、政治上或领土上的妥协让步，就可以阻止日本前进的人们，只不过是沉溺在乌托邦的幻想中。南京过去所采取的错误政策，就是根据这种的战略，我们只要看一看东亚的地图，就可知道结果是怎样了。

---

1. 共产党这时已"正式"对日本处于战争状态了，因为苏维埃政府早在 1932 年就已在江西发表的一个文告中这样宣战了。国民党扣压这个文告的发表。参看《红色中国：毛泽东主席……》第 6 页（1934 年伦敦）。

Mao began to answer my first question, about Communist policy toward Japan, which was this: "If Japan is defeated and driven from China, do you think that the major problem of 'foreign imperialism' will in general have been solved here?"

"Yes. If other imperialist countries do not act like Japan, and if China defeats Japan, it will mean that the Chinese masses have awakened, have mobilized, and have established their independence. Therefore the main problem of imperialism will have been solved."

"Under what conditions do you think the Chinese people can exhaust and defeat the forces of Japan?" I asked.

He replied: "Three conditions will guarantee our success: first, the achievement of the National United Front against Japanese imperialism in China; second, the formation of a World Anti-Japanese United Front; third, revolutionary action by the oppressed peoples at present suffering under Japanese imperialism. Of these, the central necessity is the union of the Chinese people themselves."

My question: "How long do you think such a war would last?"

Mao's answer: "That depends on the strength of the Chinese People's Front, many conditioning factors in China and Japan, and the degree of international help given to China, as well as the rate of revolutionary development in Japan. If the Chinese People's Front is powerfully homogeneous, if it is effectively organized horizontally and vertically, if the international aid to China is considerable from those governments which recognize the menace of Japanese imperialism to their own interests, if revolution comes quickly in Japan, the war[1] will be short and victory speedily won. If these conditions are not realized, however, the war will be very long, but in the end, just the same, Japan will be defeated, only the sacrifices will be extensive and it will be a painful period for the whole world."

Question: "What is your opinion of the probable course of development of such a war, politically and militarily?"

Answer: "Two questions are involved here—the policy of the foreign powers, and the strategy of China's armies.

"Now, the Japanese continental policy is already fixed and is well known. Those who imagine that by further sacrifices of Chinese sovereignty, by making economic, political, or territorial compromises and concessions, they can halt the advance of Japan, are only indulging in Utopian fancy. Nanking has in the past adopted erroneous policies based on this strategy, and we have only to look at the map of East Asia to see the results of it.

---

1. The Communists were already "officially" at war with Japan, the Soviet Government having declared such a war in a proclamation issued in Kiangsi in April, 1932. See *Red China: President Mao Tse-tung Reports...*, p. 6.

"不过我们已经知道,不仅是华北,连长江下游和我们南部的海港,都包括在日本的大陆计划里面。此外,也同样很清楚,日本的海军还想封锁中国海,夺取菲律宾、暹罗、印度支那、马来亚和荷属东印度。一旦发生战争,日本必将把这些地方作为它的战略基地,割断英、法、美和中国的联系,独占南太平洋各个海面。这些行动都包括在日本海上战略计划中,我们已看到了这种计划。而且这种海上战略,是必将与日本陆上战略相配合的。

"有许多人以为一旦日本占领了沿海的几个战略要冲而实行封锁以后,中国就将不可能继续对日抗战了。这是胡说。我们只要看看红军的历史,就可以驳倒这种看法。在有些时候,我们的力量在数量上要比国民党的军队少10倍或20倍,他们在装备上也胜过我们。他们的经济资源超过我们好几倍,他们还得到外界物资上的援助。可是,为什么红军还能节节获胜,它不仅能够存在到今天,而且还能增加它的力量?

"答案就是,红军和苏维埃政府已在他们区域内的全体人民中,造成了一种磐石般的团结,因为苏区中的每一个人,都准备为他的政府反抗压迫者而战,因为每一个人都是志愿的、自觉的,为着他本身的利益和他认为正确的信仰而战。第二,在苏区的斗争中,人民是由有能力、有力量和有决心的人领导的,他们对于自己在战略上、政治上、经济上以及军事上的需要,都有着深切的了解。红军获得了许多次的胜利——当开始的时候,有决心的革命家手中只握着几十支步枪——因为它在人民中有坚实的基础,能够从老百姓方面甚至从白军方面吸引许多朋友。敌人在军事上强过我们不知多少倍,但在政治上,它却是无法动弹的。

"在抗日战争中,中国人民会有比红军对国民党斗争时候所能利用的更大的有利条件。中国是一个很大的国家,只要还有一寸的土地没有在侵略者刺刀的下面,它就不能说是被征服。就算日本占领了一大部分中国,一块有一万万,或者甚至二万万人口的地方,要打败我们,也还差得很远。我们仍旧有很大的力量来抵抗日本军阀,而且在整个战争中,他们还得不断打一场激烈的后卫战。

"至于军火,日本不能夺取我们内地的兵工厂,而这是尽够供给中国军队用许多年的;他们也不能阻止我们从他们自己手中夺取大量的武器和军火。红军就是用这

"But we know well enough that not only North China but the Lower Yangtze Valley and our southern seaports are already included in the Japanese continental program. Moreover, it is just as clear that the Japanese navy aspires to blockade the China seas and to seize the Philippines, Siam, Indochina, Malaya, and the Dutch East Indies. In the event of war, Japan will try to make them her strategic bases, cutting off Great Britain, France, and America from China, and monopolizing the seas of the southern Pacific. These moves are included in Japan's plans of naval strategy, copies of which we have seen. And such naval strategy will be coordinated with the land strategy of Japan.

"Many people think it would be impossible for China to continue her fight against Japan once the latter had seized certain strategic points on the coast and enforced a blockade. This is nonsense. To refute it we have only to refer to the history of the Red Army. In certain periods our forces have been exceeded numerically some ten or twenty times by the Kuomintang troops, which were also superior to us in equipment. Their economic resources many times surpassed ours, and they received material assistance from the outside. Why, then, has the Red Army scored success after success against the White troops and not only survived till today but increased its power?

"The explanation is that the Red Army and the Soviet Government had created among all people within their areas a rocklike solidarity, because everyone in the soviets was ready to fight for his government against the oppressors, because every person was voluntarily and consciously fighting for his own interests and what he believed to be right. Second, in the struggle of the soviets the people were led by men of ability, strength, and determination, equipped with deep understanding of the strategic, political, economic, and military needs of their position. The Red Army won its many victories—beginning with only a few dozen rifles in the hands of determined revolutionaries—because its solid base in the people attracted friends even among the White troops as well as among the civilian populace. The enemy was infinitely our superior militarily, but politically it was immobilized.

"In the anti-Japanese war the Chinese people would have on their side greater advantages than those the Red Army has utilized in its struggle with the Kuomintang. China is a very big nation, and it cannot be said to be conquered until every inch of it is under the sword of the invader. If Japan should succeed in occupying even a large section of China, getting possession of an area with as many as 100 or even 200 million people, we would still be far from defeated. We would still have left a great force to fight against Japan's warlords, who would also have to fight a heavy and constant rear-guard action throughout the entire war.

"As for munitions, the Japanese cannot seize our arsenals in the interior, which are sufficient to equip Chinese armies for many years, nor can they prevent us from capturing great amounts of arms and ammunition from their own hands. By the latter method the

种方法从国民党手中来装备它现在的部队的：9年以来，国民党成了我们的'军火运输队'。如果全中国人民联合起来抗日，那么，运用这种战术来取得我们的军火的可能性就更加无限了！

"从经济上说，中国当然不是统一的。但是中国经济的不平衡发展，在对经济高度集中的日本抗战的时候，也是有利的。譬如将上海跟中国其他部分隔绝，对于中国并不像将纽约跟美国其他部分隔绝这样的为害严重。而且，日本要使全中国陷于孤立是不可能的：日本从大陆的观点来看，仍是一个海国，它就不能封锁中国的西北、西南和西部。

"因此，问题的中心点又要归结到全中国人民的动员和团结，统一战线的建立，这就是共产党从1932年以来所一直主张的。"

问："一旦发生中日战争，你想日本会不会发生革命呢？"

答："日本的革命不仅是可能的，而且是一定的。在日军一遭到严重的失败，革命就不可避免地马上要开始发生了。"

问："你想苏俄和外蒙古是否会卷入这场战争，是否会来帮助中国？在怎样的情势之下，才有这种可能？"

答："苏联当然也不是一个孤立的国家。它不能不顾远东的事态。它不能保持消极被动。它是坐视日本征服全中国，把中国作为进攻苏联的战略基地？还是帮助中国人民抵抗日本侵略者，争取独立，同俄国人民建立友好关系呢？我们认为俄国会采取后一条途径的。

"我们相信中国人民一旦有了他们自己的政府，开始抗战，需要跟苏联以及其他友邦建立友好联盟时，苏联一定将首先来和我们握手。反对日本帝国主义的斗争，是全世界的事，苏联既是世界的一部分，它同英、美一样不能保持中立。"

问："中国人民的当前任务是夺回丢给日本帝国主义的全部失地，还是只将日本赶出华北和长城以北的中国领土？"

Red Army has equipped its present forces from the Kuomintang: for nine years they have been our 'ammunition carriers.' What infinitely greater possibilities would open up for the utilization of such tactics as won our arms for us if the whole Chinese people were united against Japan!

"Economically, of course, China is not unified. But the uneven development of China's economy also presents advantages in a war against the highly centralized and highly concentrated economy of Japan. For example, to sever Shanghai from the rest of China is not as disastrous to the country as would be, for instance, the severance of New York from the rest of America. Moreover, it is impossible for Japan to isolate all of China: China's Northwest, Southwest, and West cannot be blockaded by Japan.

"Thus once more the central point of the problem becomes the mobilization and unification of the entire Chinese people and the building up of a united front, such as has been advocated by the Communist Party ever since 1932."

Question: "In the event of a Sino-Japanese war, do you think there will be a revolution in Japan?"

Answer: "The Japanese revolution is not only a possibility but a certainty. It is inevitable and will begin to occur promptly after the first severe defeats suffered by the Japanese Army."

Question: "Do you think Soviet Russia and Outer Mongolia would become involved in this war, and would come to the assistance of China? Under what circumstances is that likely?"

Answer: "Of course the Soviet Union is also not an isolated country. It cannot ignore events in the Far East. It cannot remain passive. Will it complacently watch Japan conquer all China and make of it a strategic base from which to attack the U.S.S.R.? Or will it help the Chinese people to oppose their Japanese oppressors, win their independence, and establish friendly relations with the Russian people? We think Russia will choose the latter course.

"We believe that once the Chinese people have their own government and begin this war of resistance and want to establish friendly alliances with the U.S.S.R., as well as other friendly powers, the Soviet Union will be in the vanguard to shake hands with us. The struggle against Japanese imperialism is a world task and the Soviet Union, as part of that world, can no more remain neutral than can England or America."

Question: "Is it the immediate task of the Chinese people to regain all the territories lost to Japanese imperialism, or only to drive Japan from North China, and all Chinese territory beyond the Great Wall?"

答:"中国的当前任务是收复全部失地,不仅仅是保卫我们长城以南的主权。这就是说,东三省是必须收复的。但我们并没有将朝鲜[1]包括在内。不过,在我们恢复了中国失地的独立以后,如果朝鲜人要想挣脱日帝国主义的锁链,我们对他们的独立斗争将加以热情的援助。至于内蒙古,那是汉人和蒙人合居的地方,我们一定要把日本从那里赶出去,帮助内蒙古建立一个自治的政府。"[2]

问:"在实际上,苏维埃政府和红军怎样才能跟国民党军队合作抗日呢?在对外战争中,所有的中国军队,是必须放在统一指挥之下的。如果最高军事会议有红军代表,红军是否愿意遵守它的政治和军事的决定?"

答:"是的。只要它是真正抗日的,我们的政府将全心全意遵守这样一个会议的决定。"

问:"红军是否同意,除了得到最高军事会议的允许或命令之外,不开入也不进攻国民党军队所驻扎的区域?"

答:"是的。我们军队当然不会开入抗日军队所驻扎的任何区域的——我们在过去也不曾这样做过。红军决不会乘机利用战时的情势。"

问:"共产党对于这样合作的交换条件是什么?"

答:"那就是坚决地、断然地坚持对日本侵略进行抗战。此外,它还要求遵守我们在呼吁建立民主共和国和国防政府的宣言中所提出的各点。"[3]

---

1. 并非真正的"中国殖民地",而是中国的邻邦,1895年中国在中日甲午战争中战败前曾对其主张宗主权。
2. 在另一次采访中回答后来的一个问题时,毛泽东就外蒙问题作了以下阐述:
   "外蒙古和苏联的关系,无论现在还是过去,一直都是建立在完全平等这个原则之上的。在中国的人民革命胜利后,外蒙古共和国将按照其意愿自动成为中华联邦的一部分。同样地,回族和藏族人民也都将在中华联邦之下组建自治的政府。"参见附录"深访毛泽东"中的"关于共产国际、中国和外蒙古"。
3. 在1935年和1936年苏维埃政府和红军发给国民党的几个宣言中提出过这几点。参见第十一篇第六章。

Answer: "It is the immediate task of China to regain all our lost territories, not merely to defend our sovereignty south of the Great Wall. This means that Manchuria must be regained. We do not, however, include Korea, formerly a 'Chinese colony,'[1] but when we have re-established the independence of the lost territories of China, and if the Koreans wish to break away from the chains of Japanese imperialism, we will extend them our enthusiastic help in their struggle for independence. As for Inner Mongolia, which is populated by both Chinese and Mongolians, we will struggle to drive Japan from there and help Inner Mongolia to establish an autonomous state."[2]

Question: "In actual practice, how could the Soviet Government and the Red Army cooperate with the Kuomintang armies in a war against Japan? In a foreign war it would be necessary for all Chinese armies to be placed under a centralized command. Would the Red Army agree, if allowed representation on a supreme war council, to submit to its decisions both militarily and politically?"

Answer: "Yes. Our government will wholeheartedly submit to the decisions of such a council, provided it really resists Japan."

Question: "Would the Red Army agree not to move its troops into or against any areas occupied by Kuomintang armies, except with the consent or at the order of the supreme war council?"

Answer: "Yes. Certainly we will not move our troops into any areas occupied by anti-Japanese armies—nor have we done so for some time past. The Red Army would not utilize any wartime situation in an opportunist way."

Question: "What demands would the Communist Party make in return for such cooperation?"

Answer: "It would insist upon waging war, decisively and finally, against Japanese aggression. In addition it would request the observance of the points advanced in the calls for a democratic republic and the establishment of a national defense government."[3]

---

1. Not really a "Chinese colony" but a neighbor over whom China claimed suzerainty before her defeat by Japan in 1895.
2. In answer to a later question, in another interview, Mao Tse-tung made the following statement concerning Outer Mongolia:
"The relationship between Outer Mongolia and the Soviet Union, now and in the past, has always been based on the principle of complete equality. When the people's revolution has been victorious in China, the Outer Mongolian republic will automatically become a part of the Chinese federation, at its own will. The Mohammedan and Tibetan peoples, likewise, will form autonomous republics attached to the China federation." See Appendices, Further Interviews with Mao Tse-tung, "On the Comintern, China, and Outer Mongolia."
3. Discussed in several proclamations issued to the Kuomintang in 1935 and 1936 by the Soviet Government and the Red Army. See Part Eleven, Chapter 6.

问:"怎样才能最好地武装人民、组织人民和训练人民来参加这样的战争?"

答:"人民必须有组织自己和武装自己的权利。这种自由,蒋介石在过去是不肯给予他们的。但这种压制可并没有完全成功——譬如就红军的情形来说,就是如此。还有,北平、上海和其他各地虽有严重的镇压,但是学生却仍开始把自己组织起来,有了政治上的准备。但是学生和革命的反日群众还没有获得他们的自由,还不能动员起来,加以训练和武装。反过来,当人民大众获得了经济的、社会的和政治的自由,他们的力量就将千百倍地增强,全国人民的真正力量就将显示出来。

"红军经过自己的斗争,从军阀手中获得了自由,成为一支不可征服的力量。抗日义勇军,也同样地从日本压迫者的手中,获得了行动自由,武装了他们自己。中国人民如果加以训练起来、武装起来和组织起来,他们也一样可以成为一支不可战胜的力量。"

问:"在这次'解放战争'中,你看应该主要采取怎样的战略和战术?"

答:"战略应该是一种在一条很长的、流动的、不定的战线上进行运动战的战略,战略的成功完全要靠在地形险阻的地方保持高度机动性,其特点是进攻和退却都要迅速,集中和分散都要迅速。这将是一种大规模的运动战,而不是深壕、重兵和坚垒的单纯阵地战。我们的战略和战术必须依作战的地形来决定,而这就决定了运动战。

"这并不是说要放弃战略要冲,只要认为有利,战略要冲还是应该用阵地战来保卫的。但中心战略却必须是运动战,而着重依靠游击队战术。深垒战必须利用,但这在战略上只是辅助的和次要的。"

这里不妨插一句,就是这种战略一般来说似乎也颇得非共产党的中国军事领导人的普遍赞成。南京由于有一支全部靠输入的空军,固然有了一支虽然开支浩大然而力量可观的对内进行镇压的力量,但大部分的专家,对于它在对外战争中的长期价值,却并不存怎样的幻想。空军和中央军的这种机械化,有许多人甚至视为是花费不赀的玩具,认为在战争初起时肯定有令人感到意外的效果和辅助性的防御作用,但在最初几个星期后,就不能维持主动的作用,因为中国几乎完全没有基本军事工业,足以维持和补充空军或现代战争中任何其他高度技术化的部队。

Question: "How can the people best be armed, organized, and trained to participate in such a war?"

Answer: "The people *must* be given the right to organize and to arm themselves. This is a freedom which Chiang Kai-shek has in the past denied to them. The suppression has not, however, been entirely successful—as, for example, in the case of the Red Army. Also, despite severe repression in Peking, Shanghai, and other places, the students have begun to organize themselves and have already prepared themselves politically. But still the students and the revolutionary anti-Japanese masses have not yet got their freedom, cannot be mobilized, cannot be trained and armed. When the contrary is true, when the masses are given economic, social and political freedom, their strength will be intensified hundreds of times, and the true power of the nation will be revealed.

"The Red Army through its own struggle has won its freedom from the militarists to become an unconquerable power. The anti-Japanese volunteers have won their freedom of action from the Japanese oppressors and have armed themselves in a similar way. If the Chinese people are trained, armed, and organized they can likewise become an invincible force."

Question: "What, in your opinion, should be the main strategy and tactics to be followed in this 'war of liberation'?"

Answer: "The strategy should be that of a war of maneuver, over an extended, shifting, and indefinite front: a strategy depending for success on a high degree of mobility in difficult terrain, and featured by swift attack and withdrawal, swift concentration and dispersal. It will be a large-scale war of maneuver rather than the simple positional war of extensive trench work, deep-massed lines and heavy fortifications. Our strategy and tactics must be conditioned by the theater in which the war will take place, and this dictates a war of maneuver.

"This does not mean the abandonment of vital strategic points, which can be defended in positional warfare as long as profitable. But the pivotal strategy must be a war of maneuver, and important reliance must be placed on guerrilla and partisan tactics. Fortified warfare must be utilized, but it will be of auxiliary and secondary strategic importance."

Here it may be inserted that this sort of strategy in general seemed to be rather widely supported also among non-Communist Chinese military leaders. Nanking's wholly imported air force provided an impressive if costly internal police machine, but few experts had illusions about its long-range value in a foreign war. Both the air force and such mechanization as had taken place in the central army were looked upon by many as costly toys incapable of retaining a role of initiative after the first few weeks, since China lacked the industries necessary to maintain and replenish either an air force or any other highly technical branch of modern warfare.

白崇禧、李宗仁、韩复榘、胡宗南、陈诚、张学良、冯玉祥和蔡廷锴都似乎相信：中国战胜日本的唯一希望，最终必须依靠把大军分成机动部队，进行优势的运动战，并且在广大的游击区域中要有能力维持持久的防御，这样先在经济上，后在军事上慢慢拖垮日本。这至少就是他们的理论。

毛泽东继续说："从地理方面来说，战场是这样的广大，因此我们有可能以最大的效率来进行运动战，这对像日本这样行动缓慢的战争机器有致命的效果，因为它为了对付后方的袭击，不得不小心翼翼地摸索着前进。如果在一条狭隘的战线上集中重兵、竭力防御一二处要镇，那就完全丢掉了我们地理上和经济组织上的战术有利条件，而重蹈阿比西尼亚的覆辙。我们的战略和战术应该注意避免在战争初期阶段进行大决战，而应该逐步打击敌军有生力量的士气、斗志和军事效率。

"阿比西尼亚的错误，除了内部政治上的弱点以外，就是在于他们想保有一条纵深战线，使得法西斯便于轰炸，便于放毒气，便于将技术上较强的战争机器对不机动的集中兵力进行袭击，使得自己受到致命的有机伤害。

"除了中国正规军之外，我们还应在农民中创建、指导并且在政治上和军事上武装大量的游击队。东三省的这种类型的抗日义勇军的成绩，只不过是全国革命农民中可以动员起来的潜在抵抗力量的极小表现。只要有适当的领导和组织，这种队伍可以弄得日本人一天 24 小时疲于奔命，愁得要死。

"必须记住，这次战争是在中国境内打的。这就是说日本人受到敌视他们的中国人民的完全包围。日本人的全部给养不得不靠从外面运进来，并且还要加以保护，在各交通线都要重兵驻守，同时在东三省和日本的基地也须重兵驻守。

"战争的进行中使中国有可能夺获许多日本的俘虏、武器、弹药、战争机器等等。到了某个时候，我们就越来越可以跟日本军队作阵地战，利用堡垒和深壕了，因为随着战争的进展，抗日军队的技术装备一定会大大地改善，**而且还由于外国的重大援助而加强起来**。在占领中国的长期负担的重压下，日本的经济是要崩溃的；在无数次胜负不决的战役的考验下，日本军队的士气是要涣散的。当日本帝国主义的浪潮在中国抗战的暗礁上冲散了以后，中国革命人民中潜藏的大量人力，却还可以输送无数为自己的自由而战斗的战士到前线来。

Pai Chung-hsi, Li Tsung-jen, Han Fu-chu, Hu Tsung-nan, Ch'en Ch'eng, Chang Hsueh-liang, Feng Yu-hsiang, and Ts'ai T'ing-k'ai were among the leading Nationalist generals who seemed to share Mao's conviction that China's sole hope of victory over Japan must rest ultimately on superior maneuvering of great masses of troops, divided into mobile units, and the ability to maintain a protracted defense over immense partisan areas.

Mao Tse-tung continued:

"Geographically the theater of the war is so vast that it is possible for us to pursue mobile warfare with the utmost efficiency and with a telling effect on a slow-moving war machine like Japan's, cautiously feeling its way in front of fierce rear-guard actions. Deep concentration and the exhausting defense of a vital position or two on a narrow front would be to throw away all the tactical advantages of our geography and economic organization, and to repeat the mistake of the Abyssinians. Our strategy and tactics must aim to avoid great decisive battles in the early stages of the war, and gradually to break the morale, the fighting spirit, and the military efficiency of the living forces of the enemy . . . .

"Besides the regular Chinese troops we should create, direct, and politically and militarily equip great numbers of partisan and guerrilla detachments among the peasantry. What has been accomplished by the anti-Japanese volunteer units of this type in Manchuria is only a very minor demonstration of the latent power of resistance that can be mobilized from the revolutionary peasantry of all China. Properly led and organized, such units can keep the Japanese busy twenty-four hours a day and worry them to death.

"It must be remembered that the war will be fought inside China. This means that the Japanese will be entirely surrounded by a hostile Chinese people. The Japanese will be forced to move in all their provisions and guard them, maintaining troops along all lines of communications, and heavily garrisoning their bases in Manchuria and Japan as well.

"The process of the war will present to China the possibility of capturing many Japanese prisoners, arms, ammunition, war machines, and so forth. A point will be reached where it will become more and more possible to engage Japan's armies on a basis of positional warfare, using fortifications and deep entrenchment, for, as the war progresses, the technical equipment of the anti-Japanese forces will greatly improve, *and will be reinforced by important foreign help.* Japan's economy will crack under the strain of a long, expensive occupation of China and the morale of her forces will break under the trial of a war of innumerable but indecisive battles. The great reservoirs of human material in the revolutionary Chinese people will still be pouring men ready to fight for their freedom into our front lines long after the tidal flood of Japanese imperialism has wrecked itself on the hidden reefs of Chinese resistance.

"这一切以及其他的因素，是决定战争的条件，使我们可以对日本的堡垒和战略根据地作最后的决定性的攻击，将日本占领军赶出中国。

"**我们将欢迎并优待被我们俘获的和解除武装的日本官兵。我们不会杀他们。我们将对兄弟一般的对待他们。我们对于日本无产阶级的士兵并无冲突，我们要用一切方法使他们站起来，反对他们本国的法西斯压迫者。我们的口号是：'联合起来反对共同的压迫者法西斯头子！'反法西斯的日本士兵是我们的朋友，我们的目标是不矛盾的。**"[1]

时间已经过了早晨两点，我精疲力竭，但在毛泽东的苍白有点发黄的脸上，我却找不出一些疲倦的表示。在吴亮平翻译和我记录的时候，他一忽儿在两个小房间之间来回踱步，一忽儿坐下来，一忽儿躺下来，一忽儿倚着桌子读一叠报告。毛夫人也还没有睡。忽然间，他们两个都俯过身去，看到一只飞蛾在蜡烛旁边奄奄一息地死去，高兴得叫起来。这确是一只很可爱的小东西，翅膀是淡淡的苹果绿，边上有一条橘黄色和玫瑰色的彩纹。毛泽东打开一本书，把这片彩色的薄纱般的羽翼夹了进去。

这样的人会是真的在认真地考虑战争吗？

我突然想起第二天早上8点有一个约会要参观红军大学——要考察中国共产党人抗日情绪的"诚意"，这个地方大概是最合适不过了。

---

1. 此处用了强调。

"All these and other factors will condition the war and will enable us to make the final and decisive attacks on Japan's fortifications and strategic bases and to drive Japan's army of occupation from China.

"Japanese officers and soldiers captured and disarmed by us will be welcomed and will be well treated. They will not be killed. They will be treated in a brotherly way. Every method will be adopted to make the Japanese proletarian soldiers, with whom we have no quarrel, stand up and oppose their own Fascist oppressors. Our slogan will be: 'Unite and oppose the common oppressors, the Fascist leaders.' Anti-Fascist Japanese troops are our friends, and there is no conflict in our aims."[1]

It was past two o'clock in the morning and I was exhausted, but I could see no signs of fatigue on Mao's thoughtful face. He alternately walked up and down between the two little rooms, sat down, lay down, leaned on the table, and read from a sheaf of reports in the intervals when Wu translated and I wrote. Mrs. Mao also was still awake. Suddenly both of them bent over and gave an exclamation of delight at a moth that had languished beside the candle. It was a really lovely thing, with wings shaded a delicate apple-green and fringed in a soft rainbow of saffron and rose. Mao opened a book and pressed this gossamer of color between its leaves.

Could such people really be thinking seriously of war?

---

1. Emphasis added.

四、 悬赏 200 万元的首级

红军大学有许多独特无二的地方。

它的校长是一个 28 岁的指挥员，据说他从来没有吃过一次败仗。红军大学自称有一个班的学员全是老战士，平均年龄是 27 岁，平均每人有 8 年作战经验，受过 3 次伤。有什么别的学校由于"纸荒"而不得不把敌人的传单翻过来当作课堂笔记本使用？或者每个学员的教育费用，包括伙食、衣着、一切在校开支，每月不到 15 元银洋？或者把那些鼎鼎大名的学员的首级赏格加起来总共超过 200 万元？

红军大学就是这样。

最后，以窑洞为教室，石头砖块为桌椅，石灰泥土糊的墙为黑板，校舍完全不怕轰炸的这种"高等学府"，全世界恐怕就只有这一家。

所以不怕轰炸是因为在陕西和甘肃，除了普通房屋以外，还有很大的住人的窑洞、供佛的岩窟、防敌的堡垒，都有几百年的历史。有钱的官吏和地主在 1,000 年前就修建了这种奇怪的建筑物，用以防御洪水、外敌、饥荒，在这些地方囤粮藏宝，挨过历次的围困。这些洞窟深挖在黄土岩或硬石岩中，有些有好几间屋子，可以容纳好几百人，是天造地设的防空洞，不怕原来是中国人民送给蒋介石去打日本人的南京新轰炸机的轰炸。红军大学就是在这种古老的洞窟中找到了奇怪而安全的校舍。

我到达后不久，他们就把红军大学校长林彪介绍给我。林彪邀我找个日子给他的学员讲话。他拟的题目是："英美对华政策"。我感到为难。我对两国的对华政策都知道得太少了。何况，我也不能用马克思主义的术语来解释。但是林彪坚持要我讲。他说他们自己可以提供马克思主义的术语。他为此安排了一次"面条宴"，使我感到盛情难却，只好勉强从命。

4 _____ $2,000,000 IN HEADS

There were many things unique about the Red Army University.

Its president was a twenty-eight-year-old army commander who (Communists said) had never lost a battle. It boasted, in one class of undergraduates, veteran warriors whose average age was twenty-seven, with an average of eight years of fighting experience and three wounds each. Was there any other school where "paper shortage" made it necessary to use the blank side of enemy propaganda leaflets for classroom notebooks? Or where the cost of educating each cadet, including food, clothing, all institutional expenses, was less than $15 silver per month? Or where the aggregate value of rewards offered for the heads of various notorious cadets exceeded $2,000,000?

Finally, it was probably the world's only seat of "higher learning" whose classrooms were bombproof caves, with chairs and desks of stone and brick, and blackboards and walls of limestone and clay.

In Shensi and Kansu, besides ordinary houses, there were great cave dwellings, temple grottoes and castled battlements hundreds of years old. Wealthy officials and landlords built these queer edifices a thousand years ago, to guard against flood and invasion and famine, and here hoarded the grain and treasure to see them through sieges of each. Many-vaulted chambers, cut deeply into the loess or solid rock, some with rooms that held several hundred people, these cliff dwellings made perfect bomb shelters. In such archaic manors the Red University found strange but safe accommodation.

Lin Piao, the president, was introduced to me soon after my arrival, and he invited me to speak one day to his cadets. He suggested the topic: "British and American Policies toward China." When he arranged a "noodle dinner" for the occasion it was too much for me, and I succumbed.

林彪是湖北省一个工厂主的儿子，生于1908年。他的父亲因苛捐杂税而破产，但是林彪还是设法读完了中学，进了广州的黄埔军校学习。他在那里成绩优秀，在蒋介石及其首席顾问俄国将军布留赫尔手下，受到了紧张的政治军事训练。他毕业后不久，北伐开始，林彪被提拔为上尉。到1927年，他刚20岁，就成了国民党张发奎领导下的著名第四军里的一个上校。同年8月，南京发生右派政变后，他率领所属的一团军队在南昌起义中参加了贺龙和叶挺领导下的第二十军，南昌起义是中国出现共产党武装夺取政权斗争的开始。

林彪和毛泽东一样，从来没有受过伤，享有这样盛名的红军指挥员并不多。他在前线身经百战，在战地指挥大军历时10年以上，凡是他的部下战士所经历的各种艰难困苦他都尝到过，他的首级的赏格高达10万元，但是他仍神奇地没有受伤，身体健康。

1932年，林彪负责指挥红军一军团，当时该军团有两万支步枪，成了红军最厉害的一部。主要由于林彪作为战术家的出众才能，奉派前来同它交战的政府军无不遭到它的歼灭，打败或者被其制胜，而它自己则从来没有被打败过。据说有时南京部队一经发现与一军团对垒，就闻风而逃。然而关于这些著名的"铁军"的事，待我到了前线以后再说。

像红军的许多能干的指挥员一样，林彪从来没有出过国，除了中文以外，不会说也不会读任何外语。但是他不到30岁就博得了红军内外人士的尊重。他在中国红军的军事刊物《斗争》和《战争与革命》上发表的文章被南京的军事刊物转载，受到他们的研究和评论，在日本和苏俄也是这样。他以"短促突击战"创始者著称，冯玉祥将军曾经就这种战术发表过评论。据说一军团的许多胜利都可归因于红军熟练地掌握了"短促突击战"。

有一天早晨，我同林彪指挥员和他的红军大学教员一起到保安城外不远的红军大学。我们是在文娱时间里到的。有的学员在两个球场上打篮球；有的在保安城外一条黄河支流旁边草地上的一个网球场上打网球。有的在打乒乓球，有的在写东西，读新到的书报，或者在他们简单的"俱乐部"中学习。

这是红军大学的第一分部，有200名左右学员。红大一共有4个分部，800名学员。在保安附近，在教育人民委员的行政管理下，还有无线电、骑兵、农业、医

Lin Piao was the son of a factory owner in Hupeh province, and was born in 1908. His father was ruined by extortionate taxation, but Lin managed to get through prep school, and became a cadet in the famous Whampoa Academy at Canton. There he made a brilliant record. He received intensive political and military training under Chiang Kai-shek and Chiang's chief adviser, the Russian General Bluecher. Soon after his graduation the Nationalist Expedition began, and Lin Piao was promoted to a captaincy. By 1927, at the age of twenty, he was a colonel in the noted Fourth Kuomintang Army, under Chang Fa-kuei. And in August of that year, after the Right *coup d'état* at Nanking, he led his regiment to join the Twentieth Army under Ho Lung and Yeh T'ing in the Nanchang Uprising, which began the Communists' armed struggle for power.

With Mao Tse-tung, Lin Piao shared the distinction of being one of the few Red commanders never wounded. Engaged on the front in more than a hundred battles, in field command for more than ten years, exposed to every hardship that his men had known, with a reward of $100,000 on his head, he was as yet unhurt.

In 1932, Lin Piao was given command of the First Red Army Corps, which then numbered about 20,000 rifles. It became, according to general opinion among Red Army officers, their "most dreaded force," chiefly because of Lin's extraordinary talent as a tactician. The mere discovery that they were fighting the First Red Army Corps was said to have sometimes put a Nanking army to rout.

Like many able Red commanders, Lin had never been outside China, and spoke and read no language but Chinese. Before the age of thirty, however, he had already won recognition beyond Red circles. His articles in the Chinese Reds' military magazines, *Struggle* and *War and Revolution*, had been republished, studied, and criticized in Nanking military journals, and also in Japan and Soviet Russia. He was noted as the originator of the "short attack"—a tactic on which General Feng Yu-hsiang had commented. To the Reds' skillful mastery of the "short attack" many victories of the First Army Corps were said to be traceable.

With Commander Lin and his faculty I journeyed one morning a short distance beyond the walls of Pao An to the Red Army University. We arrived at recreation hour. Some of the cadets were playing basketball on the two courts set up; others were playing tennis on a court laid down on the turf beside the Pao An River, a tributary of the Yellow River. Still other cadets were playing table tennis, writing, reading new books and magazines, or studying in their primitive "clubrooms."

This was the First Section of the University, in which there were some 200 students. Altogether, Hung Ta, as the school was known in the soviet districts, had four sections, with over 800 students. There were also, near Pao An, and under the administrative control of the education commissioner, radio, cavalry, agricultural, and medical-training

务等学校。此外还有 1 个党校[1]和 1 个群众文化教育中心。

有 200 多名学员集合起来听我讲"英美对华政策"。我扼要地谈了一下英美的态度，然后同意解答问题。我不久就发现，这是个大错误，请我吃的面条根本抵偿不了我遇到的难堪。向我提出的问题，即使由 H.G. 威尔斯先生[2]来回答，也要自叹智穷才竭。比如，你不妨想一想如何回答向我提出的下列问题：

"英国政府对成立亲日的冀察委员会的态度如何，对日军进驻华北的态度如何？"

"全国复兴署[3]政策在美国的结果如何，对工人阶级有什么好处？"

"如果日本与中国开战，德、意会帮助日本吗？"

"如果没有其他国家帮助，你估计日本对中国大规模作战能维持多久？"

"国际联盟为什么失败？"

"在英国和美国，共产党都是合法存在的，为什么这两个国家都没有工人政府？"

"在英国组织反法西斯阵线方面有了什么结果？在美国呢？"

"以巴黎为中心的国际学生运动的前途如何？"

"你认为李滋－罗斯访日会不会造成英日在对华政策上取得一致意见？"

"中国抗日后，美国和英国会帮中国还是帮日本？"

"请谈一谈，既然美国和英国是中国人民的朋友，为什么它们在中国驻有军舰和军队？"

"美国和英国的工人对苏联的看法如何？"

要在两个小时之内回答这些问题可不简单！而且实际上不止两个小时。从早上 10 点开始，一直到下午很晚的时候。最后得不出什么结论，暂告结束。

---

1. 董必武时任该校校长。(后由李维汉和康生先后继任。)谢富治就是该校学员。
2. 1866—1946 年，著名英国小说家。——译注
3. 罗斯福的一个新政机构。——译注

schools. There was a Communist Party school[1] and a mass-education training center.

Over 200 cadets assembled to hear me explain "British and American policies." I made a crude summary of Anglo-American attitudes, and agreed to answer questions. It was a great mistake, I soon realized, and the noodle dinner hardly compensated for my embarrassment.

"What is the attitude of the British Government toward the formation of the pro-Japanese Hopei-Chahar Council, and the garrisoning of North China by Japanese troops?"

"What are the results of the N.R.A. policy in America, and how has it benefited the working class?"

"Will Germany and Italy help Japan if a war breaks out with China?"

"How long do you think Japan can carry on a major war against China if she is not helped by other powers?"

"Why has the League of Nations failed?"

"Why is it that, although the Communist Party is legal in both Great Britain and America, there is no workers' government in either country?"

"What progress is being made in the formation of an anti-Fascist front in England? In America?"

"What is the future of the international student movement, which has its center in Paris?"

"In your opinion, can Leith-Ross's visit to Japan result in Anglo-Japanese agreement on policies toward China?"

"When China begins to resist Japan, will America and Great Britain assist China or Japan?"

"Please tell us why America and Great Britain keep their fleets and armed forces in China if they are friends of the Chinese people?"

"What do the American and British workers think of the U.S.S.R.?"

No small territory to cover in a two-hour question period! And it was not confined to two hours. Beginning at ten in the morning, it continued till late in the afternoon.

---

1. Tung Pi-wu was director of this Party school. (Li Wei-han and K'ang Sheng were to succeed him in that post.) Hsieh Fu-chih was one of the cadets.

后来我参观了各个教室，并同林彪和他的教员们谈了话。他们把学校招生条件告诉了我，并且给我看了印好的招生简章，有好几千份这样的简章秘密地发到了中国各地。4个分部招收"决心抵抗日本帝国主义和献身于民族革命事业的人，不分阶级、社会或政治背景"。年龄限制是16岁到28岁，"不分性别"。"报考者必须体格健康，不患传染病"，而且——这话有点笼统——"不染一切恶习"。

我发现，在实际上，第一分部的学员大部分是红军中的营、团、师级指挥员或政委，[1] 接受高级军政训练。为期4个月。根据红军规定，每个在役指挥员或政委每两年必须至少受4个月这样的训练。

第二分部和第三分部收的是连、排、班级指挥员，红军中有经验的战士，还有从"中学毕业生或有同等学力者、失业教员或军官、抗日义勇军干部和抗日游击队领袖、从事组织和领导工运的工人"中招来的新学员。红军在东征山西省时，山西有60多个中学毕业生参加了红军。

第二分部和第三分部上课6个月。第四分部主要"训练工兵、骑兵干部、炮兵部队"。我在这里遇到了一些以前当过机工和学徒的人。后来，我在离开红色中国时，我还遇到8个坐卡车来的新学员，他们是从上海和北平来上红军大学的。林彪告诉我，全国各地报名的有2,000多名。当时主要问题是交通问题，因为每个学员都得"潜越"入境。

红大各分部课程互不相同。第一分部的内容可以作为样品以见一斑。政治课程有：政治知识、中国革命问题、政治经济学、党的建设、共和国的策略问题、列宁主义、民主主义的历史基础、日本的政治社会状况。军事课程有：抗日战争的战略问题、运动战、抗日战争中的游击战术的发展。

有些课程有专门的教材。有些是从江西苏区出版机构带来的，据说那里的一个主要印刷厂曾经有800名印刷工人在工作。其他课程用的材料是红军指挥员和党的

---

1. 罗瑞卿便是其中之一。

Afterwards I toured the various classrooms and talked with Lin Piao and his faculty. They told me something of the conditions of enrollment in their school, and showed me printed announcements of its courses, thousands of copies of which had been secretly distributed throughout China. The four sections of the academy invited "all who are determined to fight Japanese imperialism and to offer themselves for the national revolutionary cause, regardless of class, social, or political differences." The age limit was sixteen to twenty-eight, "regardless of sex." "The applicants must be physically strong, free from epidemic diseases," and also—rather sweeping—"free from all bad habits."

In practice, I discovered, most of the cadets in the First Section were battalion, regimental, or division commanders or political commissars of the Red Army,[1] receiving advanced military and political training. According to Red Army regulations, every active commander or commissar was supposed to spend at least four months at such study during every two years of active service.

The Second and Third sections included company, platoon, and squad commanders—experienced fighters in the Red Army—as well as new recruits selected from "graduates of middle schools or the equivalent, unemployed teachers or officers, cadres of anti-Japanese volunteer corps, and anti-Japanese partisan leaders, and workers who have engaged in organizing and leading labor movements." Over sixty middle-school graduates from Shansi had joined the Reds during their expedition to that province.

Classes in the Second and Third sections lasted six months. The Fourth Section was devoted chiefly to "training engineers, cavalry cadres, and artillery units." Here I met some former machinists and apprentices. Later on, as I was leaving Red China, I was to meet, entering by truck, eight new recruits for the "bandit university" arriving from Shanghai and Peking. Lin Piao told me that they had a waiting list of over 2,000 student applicants from all parts of China. At that time every cadet had to be "smuggled" in.

The curriculum varied in different sections of Hung Ta. In the First Section political lectures included these courses: Political Knowledge, Problems of the Chinese Revolution, Political Economy, Party Construction, Tactical Problems of the Republic, Leninism and Historical Foundations of Democracy, and Political and Social Forces in Japan. Military courses included: Problems of Strategy in the War with Japan, Maneuvering Warfare (against Japan), and the Development of Partisan Warfare in the Anti-Japanese War.

Special textbooks had been prepared for some of these courses. Some were carried clear from the soviet publishing house in Kiangsi, where, (I was told) more than eight hundred printers were employed in the main plant. In other courses the materials used were

---

1. One of them was Lo Jui-ch'ing.

领导人的讲话，谈的是俄国革命和中国革命的历史经验，或者利用缴获的政府档案、文件、统计的材料。

对于"红军真的要打日本吗？"这个问题，红大的这些课程也许是个很好的答复。这足以说明红军早已预见到而且在积极计划中国如何对日本打一场"独立战争"——他们认为这场战争是不可避免的，除非出于奇迹，日本从已经处于日本军队的铁蹄下的广大中国领土上撤出去。

这不是个愉快的前景。有些在华外国资本家认为这是发疯。但是也有其他的人坦率承认，已有千百万中国人成了日本的亡国奴，在这样的情况下，就不能怪中国人现在宁死也不愿再未经一战就放弃他们的自由。

至少红军有充分决心要抗战，而且认为一打仗他们就首先上前线，这一点不仅可以从他们的领导人的热烈言论中，从军队严格的实际训练中，从他们提出要同他们十年宿敌国民党组成"统一战线"的建议中可以看出，而且也可以从苏区到处看得到的紧张宣传活动中看出。

在这种宣传教育活动中起着一个带头作用的是许多叫做人民抗日剧社的青年组成的剧团，他们在苏区不断地巡回旅行，宣传抗战，在农民中唤起尚在沉睡中的民族主义意识。

我首次参观红军大学后不久就去看了这个令人惊异的儿童剧社的一场演出。

lectures by Red Army commanders and Party leaders, dealing with historical experiences of the Russian and the Chinese revolutions, or utilizing material from captured government files, documents and statistics.

These courses at Hung Ta perhaps suggested a reply to the question, "Do the Reds really intend to fight Japan?" It sufficed to show how the Reds foresaw and actively planned for China's "war of independence" against Japan—a war which they regarded as inevitable unless, by some miracle, Japan withdrew from the vast areas of China already under the wheels of Nippon's military juggernaut.

That the Reds were fully determined to fight, and believed that the opening of the war would find them first on the front, was indicated not only in the impassioned utterances of their leaders, in grim practical schooling in the army, and in their proposals for a "united front" with their ten-year enemy, the Kuomintang, but also by the intensive propagandizing one saw throughout the soviet districts.

Playing a leading part in this educative mission were the many companies of youths known as the Jen-min K'ang-Jih Chu-She, or People's Anti-Japanese Dramatic Society, who traveled ceaselessly back and forth in the Red districts, spreading the gospel of resistance and awakening the slumbering nationalism of the peasantry.

It was to one of the performances of this astonishing children's theater that I went soon after my first visit to the Red Army University.

五、　　红军剧社

我同一个邀我前去看红军剧社演出的年轻干部出发时，人们已经纷纷朝着那个用古庙临时改建的露天剧场奔去了。那天是星期六，距日落还有两三个小时，保安似乎已经倾城而出。

学员、骡夫、妇女、被服工厂和鞋袜工厂的女工、合作社职工、苏区邮局职工、士兵、木工、拖儿带女的村民，大家都向河边那块大草地拥过去，演员们就在那里演出。很难想象有比这更加民主的场合了。不远的网球场上甚至还有几头羊在啃草。

不售门票，没有包厢，也无雅座。我看到中央委员会书记洛甫、红军大学校长林彪、财政人民委员林伯渠、政府主席毛泽东以及其他干部和他们的妻子都分散在观众中间，像旁人一样坐在软绵绵的草地上。演出一开始就再也没有人去怎么注意他们了。

台上挂着一块红色的绸制大幕布，上面有"人民抗日剧社"几个大字，还有拉丁化的新文字拼音，红军大力提倡拉丁化来促进群众教育。节目有3个小时，有短剧、舞蹈、歌唱、哑剧——可以说是一种杂耍表演，共同的地方主要是两个中心主题：抗日和革命。节目充满了明显的宣传，一点也不精致，道具都很简单。但是优点是从锣鼓铙钹和假嗓歌唱中解放出来，采用活的题材而不像腐朽的中国京剧那种没有意义的历史故事。

最后，演出生气勃勃，幽默风趣，演员和观众打成一片，这就弥补了一部分细腻精美的不足。红军剧社的观众似乎真的在听着台上的说话：同那些神情厌烦的京

5   RED THEATER

People were already moving down toward the open-air stage, improvised from an old temple, when I set out with the young official who had invited me to the Red Theater. It was Saturday, two or three hours before sunset, and all Pao An seemed to be going.

Cadets, muleteers, women and girl workers from the uniform and shoe factory, clerks from the cooperatives and from the soviet post office, soldiers, carpenters, villagers followed by their infants, all began streaming toward the big grassy plain beside the river, where the players were performing. It would be hard to imagine a more democratic gathering—something like old-time Chautauqua.

No tickets were sold, there was no "dress circle," and there were no preferred seats. Goats were grazing on the tennis court not far beyond. I noticed Lo Fu, general secretary of the Politburo of the Central Committee, Lin Piao, Lin Po-chu (Lin Tsu-han), the commissioner of finance, Chairman Mao Tse-tung, and other officials and their wives scattered through the crowd, seated on the springy turf like the rest. No one paid much attention to them once the performance had begun.

Across the stage was a big pink curtain of silk, with the words "People's Anti-Japanese Dramatic Society" in Chinese characters as well as Latinized Chinese, which the Reds were promoting to hasten mass education. The program was to last three hours. It proved to be a combination of playlets, dancing, singing, and pantomime—a kind of variety show, or vaudeville, given unity chiefly by two central themes: anti-Nipponism and the revolution. It was full of overt propaganda and the props were primitive. But it had the advantage of being emancipated from cymbal-crashing and falsetto singing, and of dealing with living material rather than with meaningless historical intrigues that are the concern of the decadent Chinese opera.

What it lacked in subtlety and refinement it partly made up by its robust vitality, its sparkling humor, and a sort of participation between actors and audience. Guests at

剧观众相比，这真使人惊奇，因为在中国，看戏的把时间主要花在吃水果、嗑瓜子、聊天、把热毛巾扔来扔去、到别的包厢里去访客上面，只是偶尔才看一下台上的戏。

第一个短剧叫《侵略》，以1931年满洲一村庄为背景，幕启时日军到达，把"不抵抗的"中国军队赶走。第二幕中，日本军官在一个农民家设宴，把中国人当作椅子坐，喝醉了酒污辱中国人的妻女。下一幕是日本毒贩在叫卖吗啡和海洛因，强迫每一农民买一份。一个青年拒绝，就被叫出来讯问：

"你不买吗啡，你不遵守满洲国卫生条例，你不爱你的'圣上'溥仪，"拷打他的人这么说。"你不好，你是抗日的匪徒！"那个青年就马上给处决了。

接着一场戏是农村集市，有些小商人在太平的气氛中叫卖货物。突然来了日本兵，搜查"抗日匪徒"。他们要当场查看身份证，忘记带在身上的就被枪决了。接着两个日本军官大吃一个小贩的猪肉。吃完后他要他们付钱时，他们奇怪地看着他说："你要我们付钱？可是蒋介石把满洲、热河、察哈尔、塘沽停战、何应钦—梅津协定、冀察委员会都给了我们，也没有要一个铜板！为了一点点肉，你却要我们付钱！"他们立刻把他当作"匪徒"用刺刀捅死了。

当然，最后村子里的人忍无可忍了。商贩们把货摊和遮阳的大伞推倒，农民们拿起长矛，妇女儿童拿起菜刀赶来，大家都宣誓要同日本鬼子"血战到底"。

这个短剧很幽默风趣，用了本地方言。观众不时哄堂大笑，或者对日本人表示厌恶和仇恨的咒骂，他们情绪很激动。对他们来说，这不仅仅是政治宣传，也不是滑稽戏，而是深刻的真理。演员大多数是十几岁的少年，而且是陕西和山西的本地人，但是观众由于全神贯注于剧中的思想，就把这一点完全给忘记了。

这场以滑稽戏为形式的表演所蕴藏的残酷的现实意义，并没有因为剧中的风趣和幽默而模糊起来，至少对一个在场的年轻战士是如此。他在演剧结束时站了起来，用感情激动的嗓子大声喊道："打死日本强盗！打倒杀害中国人民的凶手！打回老家去！"全场观众都齐声高喊他的口号。我后来打听到这个少年是个东北人，他的父母都被日本人杀死了。

the Red Theater seemed actually to *listen* to what was said: a really astonishing thing in contrast with the bored opera audience, who often spent their time eating fruit and melon seeds, gossiping, tossing hot towels back and forth, visiting from one box to another, and only occasionally looking at the stage.

The first playlet was called *Invasion*. It opened in a Manchurian village in 1931, with the Japanese arriving and driving out the "non-resisting" Chinese soldiers. In the second scene Japanese officers banqueted in a peasant's home, using Chinese men for chairs and drunkenly making love to their wives. Another scene showed Japanese dope peddlers selling morphine and heroin and forcing every peasant to buy a quantity. A youth who refused to buy was singled out for questioning.

"You don't buy morphine, you don't obey Manchukuo health rules, you don't love your 'divine' Emperor P'u Yi," charged his tormentors. "You are no good, you are an anti-Japanese bandit!" And the youth was promptly executed.

A scene in the village market place showed small merchants peacefully selling their wares. Suddenly Japanese soldiers arrived, searching for more "anti-Japanese bandits." Instantly they demanded passports, and those who had forgotten them were shot. Then two Japanese officers gorged themselves on a peddler's pork. When he asked for payment they looked at him in astonishment. "*You* ask for payment? Why, Chiang Kai-shek gave us Manchuria, Jehol, Chahar, the Tangku Truce, the Ho-Umetsu Agreement, and the Hopei-Chahar Council without asking a single copper! And *you* want us to pay for a little pork!" Whereupon they impaled him as a "bandit."

In the end, of course, all that proved too much for the villagers. Merchants turned over their stands and umbrellas, farmers rushed forth with their spears, women and children came with their knives, and all swore to "fight to the death" against the *Jih-pen-kuei*—the "Japanese devils."

The little play was sprinkled with humor and local idiom. Bursts of laughter alternated with oaths of disgust and hatred for the Japanese. The audience got quite agitated. It was not just political propaganda to them, nor slapstick melodrama, but the poignant truth itself. The fact that the players were mostly youths in their teens and natives of Shensi and Shansi seemed entirely forgotten in the onlookers' absorption with the ideas presented.

The substratum of bitter reality behind this portrayal, done as a sort of farce, was not obscured by its wit and humor for at least one young soldier there. He stood up at the end, and in a voice shaking with emotion cried out: "Death to the Japanese bandits! Down with the murderers of our Chinese people! Fight back to our homes!" The whole assembly echoed his slogans mightily. I learned that this lad was a Manchurian whose parents had been killed by the Japanese.

就在这个时候，漫游的羊群引起了哄堂大笑，缓和了气氛。原来它们正在满不在乎地啃球网，那是开场前忘记收起来的。一些学员赶去追逐羊群，把文娱部门这一重要财产抢救下来，引起了观众一阵哄笑。

第二个节目是《丰收舞》，由剧社的十几个女孩子优美地演出。她们光着脚，穿着农民的衣裤和花背心，头上系着绸头巾，跳起舞来动作整齐优美。我后来知道，其中有两个姑娘是从江西一路走过来的，她们原来在瑞金的红军戏剧学校学习舞蹈。她们是真正有才华的。

另外一个独特而好玩的节目叫做《统一战线舞》，表演中国动员抗日。我不知道他们是用什么魔术变出这些服装来的，忽然之间有一群群青年穿着白色的水手服，戴着水手帽，穿着短裤——先是以骑兵队形，后来以空军队形，步兵队形，最后以海军队形出现。中国人是演哑剧的天生艺术家，他们的姿态十分写实地传达了舞蹈的精神。接着是一个叫做《红色机器舞》的节目。小舞蹈家们用音响和姿势，用胳膊、大腿、头部的相互勾接和相互作用，天才地模拟了气缸的发动、齿轮和轴辘的转动、发动机的轰鸣——未来的机器时代的中国的远景。

在演出之间，观众中不时有人叫喊，要请别人即兴唱歌。在大家的要求下，五六个陕西本地姑娘——工厂女工——唱了本省的一个古老民歌，由一个陕西农民用土制琵琶伴奏。另一个"点名"演出是一个学员吹口琴，又有一个学员唱一首南方人爱唱的歌。接着，使我感到完全手足无措的是，有人要求外国新闻记者独唱！

他们不肯放过我。天晓得，我除了狐步舞、圆舞曲、《波希米》和《圣母马利亚》以外，什么也不会，而这些乐曲对这批斗志昂扬的观众来说是很不合适的。我甚至已记不起《马赛曲》是怎么唱的了。他们仍继续要求。我在极度尴尬的情况下终于唱了《荡秋千的人》。他们很有礼貌。没有叫我再来一个。

看到幕布升起演下一个节目，我这才感到心头一块大石落地。这个节目是一个有革命主题的社会剧——一个管账的同他的房东太太谈恋爱。接着又是舞蹈，舞蹈之后是一个关于西南方面新闻的活报剧和儿童们合唱《国际歌》。从灯光集中的一个圆柱上拉出绳子来挂着万国旗，周围伏着许多舞蹈演员。她们慢慢地跟着歌词抬起身来，挺立着，最后在歌声结束时高举着紧握的拳头。

Comic relief was provided at this moment by the meandering goats. They were discovered nonchalantly eating the tennis net, which someone had forgotten to take down. A wave of laughter swept the audience while some cadets gave chase to the culprits and salvaged this important property of the recreation department.

Second number on the program was a harvest dance, daintily performed by a dozen girls of the Dramatic Society. Barefoot, clad in peasant trousers and coats and fancy vests, with silk bandannas on their heads, they danced with good unison and grace. Two of these girls, I learned, had walked clear from Kiangsi, where they had learned to dance in the Reds' dramatic school at Juichin. They had genuine talent.

Another unique and amusing number was called the "United Front Dance," which interpreted the mobilization of China to resist Japan. By what legerdemain they produced their costumes I do not know, but suddenly there were groups of youths wearing sailors' white jumpers and caps and shorts—first appearing as cavalry formations, next as aviation corps, then as foot soldiers, and finally as the navy. Their pantomime and gesture, at which Chinese are born artists, very realistically conveyed the spirit of the dance. Then there was something called the "Dance of the Red Machines." By sound and gesture, by an interplay and interlocking of arms, legs, and heads, the little dancers ingeniously imitated the thrust and drive of pistons, the turn of cogs and wheels, the hum of dynamos—and visions of a machine-age China of the future.

Between acts, shouts arose for extemporaneous singing by people in the audience. Half a dozen native Shensi girls—workers in the factories—were by popular demand required to sing an old folk song of the province, accompaniment being furnished by a Shensi farmer with his homemade guitar. Another "command" performance was given by a cadet who played the harmonica, and one was called upon to sing a favorite song of the Southland. Then, to my utter consternation, a demand began that the *wai-kuo hsin-wen chi-che*—the foreign newspaperman—strain his lungs in a solo of his own!

They refused to excuse me. Alas, I could think of nothing but fox trots, waltzes, "La Bohème," and "Ave Maria," which all seemed inappropriate for this martial audience. I could not even remember "The Marseillaise." The demand persisted. In extreme embarrassment I at last rendered "The Man on the Flying Trapeze." They were very polite about it. No encore was requested.

With infinite relief I saw the curtain go up on the next act, which turned out to be a social play with a revolutionary theme—an accountant falling in love with his landlord's wife. Then there was more dancing, a "Living Newspaper" dealing with some late news from the Southwest, and a chorus of children singing "The International." Here the flags of several nations were hung on streamers from a central illuminated column, round which reclined the young dancers. They rose slowly, as the words were sung, to stand erect, clenched fists upraised, as the song ended.

演出结束了，但是我的好奇心仍旧未减。因此第二天我去访问人民抗日剧社的社长危拱之女士。

危女士于1907年生于河南，参加红军已有10年。她原来参加"基督将军"冯玉祥的国民军的宣传队[1]，1927年冯玉祥与南京的政变妥协以后，她就同许多年轻学生一起离开那里，在汉口加入共产党。1929年共产党派她去欧洲，在法国学习了一个时期以后又到莫斯科去，1年后回国，闯过国民党对红色中国的封锁，开始在瑞金工作。

她把红军剧社的历史向我作了一些介绍。演剧团体最初是在1931年在江西组织起来的。据危女士说，在那里，在瑞金的著名的高尔基学校[2]里，从苏区各地招来了1,000多名学员，红军训练了大约60个剧团。他们在各个村子里和在前线巡回演出。每个剧团都收到各村苏维埃要求去演戏的邀请。农民们由于文化生活贫乏，对于任何娱乐都是很欢迎的，他们自动安排交通、吃饭、住宿的问题。

危女士在南方时任副社长，到了西北以后负责全部戏剧工作。她在江西参加长征，是极少数经历长征而仍活下来的妇女之一。在南方的军队到西北之前，陕西苏区就已有了剧社，但在江西的演员到达以后，戏剧艺术显然有了新的生命。危女士告诉我，现在一共约有30个这样的巡回剧社，甘肃也有一些。我以后旅行时还会碰到。

危女士继续说："每个军都有自己的剧团，几乎每个县也都有。演员几乎都是在当地招来的。我们从南方来的有经验的演员现在都已成了导演了。"

我遇到好几个少年先锋队员，他们还只有十几岁，可是已经过长征，现在负责组织和训练各个村子里的儿童剧社。

"农民们老远来看我们红军演出，"危女士自豪地告诉我，"有时，我们临近白区边界，国民党士兵偷偷地带信来要求我们的演员到边界的集市上去。我们去后，红军和白军都不带武器前来集市看我们表演。但是国民党高级军官如果知道是决不答应的，因为国民党士兵一旦看了我们演出后就不愿再打红军了！"

---

1. 属中山军事学校，邓小平时任该校政治部主任。
2. 叶剑英时任该校技术主任。

The theater was over, but my curiosity remained. Next day I went to interview Miss Wei Kung-chih, director of the People's Anti-Japanese Dramatic Society.

Miss Wei was born in Honan in 1907 and had been a Red for ten years. She originally joined a propaganda corps of the political training school (where Teng Hsiao-p'ing was director) of the Kuominchun, "Christian General" Feng Yu-hsiang's army, but when Feng reconciled himself to the Nanking *coup d'état* in 1927 she deserted, along with many young students, and became a Communist in Hankow. In 1929 she was sent to Europe by the Communist Party and studied for a while in France, then in Moscow. A year later she returned to China, successfully ran the Kuomintang blockade around Red China, and began to work at Juichin.

She told me something of the history of the Red Theater. Dramatic groups were first organized in Kiangsi in 1931. There, at the famous Gorky School (under the technical direction of Yeh Chien-ying) in Juichin, with over 1,000 students recruited from the soviet districts, the Reds trained about sixty theatrical troupes, according to Miss Wei. They traveled through the villages and at the front. Every troupe had long waiting lists of requests from village soviets. The peasants, always grateful for any diversion in their culture-starved lives, voluntarily arranged all transport, food, and housing for these visits.

In the South, Miss Wei had been an assistant director, but in the Northwest she had charge of the whole organization of dramatics. She made the Long March from Kiangsi, one of the very few soviet women who lived through it. Theatrical troupes were created in Soviet Shensi before the southern army reached the Northwest, but with the arrival of new talent from Kiangsi the dramatic art apparently acquired new life. There were about thirty such traveling theatrical troupes there now, Miss Wei told me, and others in Kansu. I was to meet many later on in my travels.

"Every army has its own dramatic group," Miss Wei continued, "as well as nearly every district. The actors are nearly all locally recruited. Most of our experienced players from the South have now become instructors."

I met several Young Vanguards, veterans of the Long March, still in their early teens, who had charge of organizing and training children's dramatic societies in various villages.

"Peasants come from long distances to our Red dramatics," Miss Wei proudly informed me. "Sometimes, when we are near the White borders, Kuomintang soldiers secretly send messages to ask our players to come to some market town in the border districts. When we do this, both Red soldiers and White leave their arms behind and go to this market place to watch our performance. But the higher officers of the Kuomintang never permit this, if they know about it, because once they have seen our players many of the Kuomintang soldiers will no longer fight our Red Army."

这些剧团使我奇怪的不是他们向世界提供什么有艺术价值的东西，他们显然没有，而是他们设备这么简陋，可是却能满足真正的社会需要。他们的道具和服装都很少，但就是能够用这种原始的材料演出逼真的戏剧。演员们除了伙食和衣着之外，所得生活津贴极微，但是他们像所有共产党员一样天天学习，他们相信自己是在为中国和中国人民工作。他们到哪儿就睡在哪儿，给他们吃什么就愉快地吃什么，从一个村子长途跋涉走到另一个村子。从物质享受来说，他们无疑是世界上报酬最可怜的演员，然而我没有见过比他们更愉快的演员了。

红军的剧本和歌曲都是自己写作的。有些是多才多艺的干部给他们写的，但是大多数是宣传部门的作家和艺术家写的。有些短剧是成仿吾写的，他是一个著名的文学批评家，3年前参加红军，另外一些是中国最著名的女作家丁玲最近写的，她现在也参加了红军。

在共产主义运动中，没有比红军剧社更有力的宣传武器了，也没有更巧妙的武器了。由于不断地改换节目，几乎每天变更活报剧，许多军事、政治、经济、社会上的新问题都成了演戏的材料，农民是不易轻信的，许多怀疑和问题就都用他们所容易理解的幽默方式加以解答。红军占领一个地方以后，往往是红军剧社消除了人民的疑虑，使他们对红军纲领有个基本的了解，大量传播革命思想，进行反宣传，争取人民的信任。例如，在最近[1]红军东征山西时，成百上千的农民听说随军来了红军剧社，都成群结队来看他们演出，自愿接受用农民喜闻乐见的形式的戏剧进行的宣传。

总的来说，这是把"艺术搞成宣传"到了极端的程度，很多人会说，"为什么把艺术扯了进去？"但从广义来说，这就是艺术，因为它为观众带来了生活的幻觉，如果说这是一种简单的艺术的话，那是因为它所根据的活的材料和它作为对象的活的人在对待人生的问题上也是简单的。对中国的人民大众来说，艺术和宣传是划不清界限的。唯一的不同在于：什么是人生经验中可以理解的，什么是不能理解的。

你知道在某种意义上你也可以把整个中国共产主义运动史看成是一个盛大的巡回宣传演出，与其说是为了保卫某种思想的绝对正确，不如说是为了保卫这种思想的存在权利。我现在也很难说，但是这很可能是红军最有永久价值的贡献，即使他们最终遭到失败和打垮。已有千百万年轻的农民听到了这些嘴上无毛的青年所宣传

---

1. 指1935年。

What surprised me about these dramatic "clubs" was that, equipped with so little, they were able to meet a genuine social need. They had the scantest properties and costumes, yet with these primitive materials they managed to produce the authentic illusion of drama. The players received only their food and clothing and small living allowances, but they studied every day, like all Communists, and they believed themselves to be working for China and the Chinese people. They slept anywhere, cheerfully ate what was provided for them, walked long distances from village to village. From the standpoint of material comforts they were unquestionably the most miserably rewarded thespians on earth, yet I hadn't seen any who looked happier.

The Reds wrote nearly all their own plays and songs. Some were contributed by versatile officials, but most of them were prepared by story writers and artists in the propaganda department. Several Red dramatic skits were written by Ch'eng Fang-wu, a well-known Hunanese author whose adherence to Soviet Kiangsi in 1933 had excited Shanghai. More recently Ting Ling, China's foremost woman author, had added her talent to the Red Theater.

There was no more powerful weapon of propaganda in the Communist movement than the Reds' dramatic troupes, and none more subtly manipulated. By constant shifts of program, by almost daily changes of the "Living Newspaper" scenes, new military, political, economic, and social problems became the material of drama, and doubts and questionings were answered in a humorous, understandable way for the skeptical peasantry. When the Reds occupied new areas, it was the Red Theater that calmed the fears of the people, gave them rudimentary ideas of the Red program, and dispensed great quantities of revolutionary thoughts, to win the people's confidence. During the Reds' 1935 Shansi expedition, for example, hundreds of peasants heard about the Red players with the army, and flocked to see them.

The whole thing was "propaganda in art" carried to the ultimate degree, and plenty of people would say, "Why drag art into it?" Yet in its broadest meaning it was art, for it conveyed for its spectators the illusions of life, and if it was a naive art it was because the living material with which it was made and the living men to whom it appealed were in their approach to life's problems also naive. For the masses of China there was no fine partition between art and propaganda. There was only a distinction between what was understandable in human experience and what was not.

One could think of the whole history of the Communist movement in China as a grand propaganda tour, and the defense, not so much of the absolute rightness of certain ideas, perhaps, as of their right to exist. I was not sure that they might not prove to be the most permanent service of the Reds, even if they were in the end defeated and broken. For millions of young peasants who had heard the Marxist gospel preached by those beardless

的马克思主义福音，即使这些青年已有成千上万的人如今已经牺牲了，对这些农民来说，中国古旧文化的禁忌束缚是决不会再那样有效了。不论命运使这些红军颠沛流离到什么想象不到的地方，他们都有力地要求进行深入的社会改革——对此，农民是不可能用其他方法知道的——而且他们给穷人和受压迫者带来了必须行动起来的新信念。

不论他们有时犯过多么严重的错误，不论他们的过火偏向造成了多大的悲剧，不论他们在这个问题上或那个问题上的强调或重视有多么夸大，但是他们真诚的迫切的宣传目标始终是要震撼、唤起中国农村中的亿万人民，使他们意识到自己在社会中的责任，唤起他们的人权意识，同儒道两教的胆小怕事、消极无为、静止不变的思想作斗争，教育他们，说服他们，而且没有疑问，有的时候也缠住他们，强迫他们起来为"人民当家作主"——这是中国农村中的新气象——而斗争，为共产党心目中的具有正义、平等、自由、人类尊严的生活而斗争。农民阶级经过两千年的沉睡以后在觉醒的状态下逐渐站起来，由此而产生的这种越来越大的压力，较之南京方面所通过的一切口头上十分虔诚而实际上毫无意义的决议，更加能够迫使在中国实现巨大的变化。

这种"共产主义"究竟意味着什么？从某种意义上来说，这是历史上第一次，成千上万的知识青年，由于突然得到大量的科学知识，引起了伟大的梦想，开始"回到民间去"，到他们国家的基层乡土中去，把他们新获得的知识"启示"一些给知识上贫乏的农村，给生活在黑暗中的农民，争取他们的联盟，一起来建设一种"比较富裕的生活"。一个更好的世界是能够创造的，而且只有他们才能够创造这样一个世界，在这样的信念的鼓舞下，他们把实行的方案——公社的理想——带到人民中去，征求他们的认可和支持。他们赢得的支持似乎达到了令人吃惊的程度。他们通过宣传和具体行动使亿万人民对于国家、社会和个人有了新的概念。

我置身在红军之中常常有一种奇怪的感觉，仿佛我是在一批过着暴力生活的学生中间，只是因为历史所造成的奇怪的缘故，这种暴力的生活对他们来说，较之踢足球、教科书、谈恋爱，较之其他国家中青年的主要关心的事情，似乎更加重要得多。有时我几乎不能相信，只是由于这一批坚决的青年，有了一种思想的武装之后，竟然能够对南京的千军万马进行群众性斗争达 10 年之久。这种不可置信的战斗友谊是怎么产生的呢？是用什么连结在一起的呢？它的力量来自什么地方？也许可以说，它毕竟还是没有成熟，但这是为什么？它看来基本上仍旧像是一种有力的示威，像一种青年运动，这又是为什么？

youths, thousands of whom were now dead, the old exorcisms of Chinese culture would never again be quite as effective. Wherever in their incredible migrations destiny had moved these Reds, they had vigorously demanded deep social changes—for which the peasants could have learned to hope in no other way—and they had brought new faith—in action to the poor and the oppressed.

However badly they had erred at times, however tragic had been their excesses, however exaggerated had been the emphasis here or the stress there, it had been their sincere and sharply felt propagandist aim to shake, to arouse, the millions of rural China to their responsibilities in society; to awaken them to a belief in human rights, to combat the timidity, passiveness, and static faiths of Taoism and Confucianism, to educate, to persuade, and, no doubt, at times to beleaguer and coerce them to fight for "the reign of the people"—a new vision in rural China—to fight for a life of justice, equality, freedom, and human dignity, as the Communists saw it. Far more than all the pious but meaningless resolutions passed at Nanking, this growing pressure from a peasantry gradually standing erect in a state of consciousness, after two millenniums of sleep, could force the realization of a vast mutation over the land.

What this "communism" amounted to in a way was that, for the first time in history, thousands of educated youths, stirred to great dreams themselves by a universe of scientific knowledge to which they were suddenly given access, "returned to the people," went to the deep soil-base of their country, to "reveal" some of their new-won learning to the intellectually sterile countryside, the dark-living peasantry, and sought to enlist its alliance in building a "more abundant life." Fired by the belief that a better world could be made, and that only they could make it, they carried their formula—the ideal of the commune—back to the people for sanction and support. And to a startling degree they seemed to be winning it. They had brought to millions, by propaganda and by action, a new conception of the state, society, and the individual.

I often had a queer feeling among the Reds that I was in the midst of a host of schoolboys, engaged in a life of violence because some strange design of history had made this seem infinitely more important to them than football games, textbooks, love, or the main concerns of youth in other countries. At times I could scarcely believe that it had been only this determined aggregation of youth, equipped with an idea, that had directed a mass struggle for ten years against all the armies of Nanking. How had the incredible brotherhood arisen, banded together, held together, and whence came its strength? And why had it perhaps, after all, failed to mature, why did it still seem fundamentally like a mighty demonstration, like a crusade of youth? How could one ever make it plausible to those who had seen nothing of it?

只有当你了解中国的历史在过去 1/4 的世纪中所经过的那种突出的孕育过程的时候，这个问题才能得到答复。这一孕育的合法产儿显然就是现在这支红军。几百年来，中国的文人一直要努力凌驾于人民之上，跻身于高高在上统治人民大众的一小批官僚阶级之列——所凭借的手段就是把象形文字和仅有的一些知识据为己有，以此来作为控制乡村的愚昧的武器，而不是用来启蒙。但是新的孕育却产生了一种现象——这个婴儿不但要同"愚昧的大众"共享知识，而且甚至要把大众理想化。

我在保安的时候常常暗自思量，我怎么才能够把这震撼中国胎盘的极其自然的动荡解释清楚。我怎么才能够把这缓慢的受孕、临产的胎动、产时的阵痛、产后的结果描写出来？我可以一一列举简单的历史事实；但我无法表达它对人造成的苦难剧痛。这时，毛泽东开始向我谈到他的一些个人历史，我一个晚上接着一个晚上，一边写着他的个人历史，一边开始认识到，这不仅是他的个人历史，也是共产主义——一种对中国有实际意义的适合国情的共产主义，而不是像有些作者所天真地认为的那样，不过是从国外领来的孤儿——如何成长，为什么能赢得成千上万青年男女的拥护和支持的记录。这种个人历史，我后来在红军许多其他领导人身上也会不断听到，只是细节上有很多的不同。我想读者要想知道的，就是这样的故事。下面就是这个故事。

Then Mao Tse-tung began to tell me something about his personal history, and as I wrote it down, night after night, I realized that this was not only his story but an explanation of how communism grew—a variety of it real and indigenous to China—and why it had won the adherence and support of thousands of young men and women. It was a story that I was to hear later on, with rich variations, in the life stories of many other Red leaders. It was a story people would want to read, I thought.

PART FOUR
Genesis of a Communist

第四篇
一个共产党员的由来

一、　　童年

我交给毛泽东一大串有关他个人的问题要他回答，我为我的爱追根究底感到很不好意思，几乎就像一个日本移民官员应该——然而却没有——为他的无礼唐突感到不好意思一样。对于我在不同事情上提出的五六组问题，毛泽东一谈就是十几个晚上，但很少提到他自己或者他个人在谈到的某些事件中的作用。我开始以为，要想他给我谈谈这方面的详细情况是不可能的了：他显然认为个人是不关重要的。他也像我所遇见过的其他共产党人一样，往往只谈委员会啦、组织啦、军队啦、决议案啦、战役啦、战术啦、"措施"啦等等等等，而很少谈到个人的经历。

有一段时间，我以为这种不愿详谈私事，甚至不愿谈他们同志们的个人功绩，也许是出于谦虚，或者是对我有所顾忌或怀疑，或者是考虑到其中许多人头上悬有赏格的缘故。后来我才发现，与其说是出于上述的原因，而不如说是因为他们大多数人实在不记得那些个人琐事了。当我开始搜集传记材料的时候，我一再发现，共产党人是能够说出青少年时代所发生的一切事情的，但是一旦他参加红军以后，他就把自己给忘掉在什么地方了；如果你不是一再地问他，就不会听到更多关于他自己的事情，你所听到的只是关于红军、苏维埃或党的故事——这些名词的第一个字母都是大写的。他们能够滔滔不绝地谈每次战役的日期和经过，他们进进出出别人从来没有听说过的无数地方的情况；但是这些事件对他们只有集体的意义，不是因为他们作为个人在那里创造了历史，是因为红军曾经到过那里，而在红军后面的是他们为之战斗的那个意识形态的整个有机力量。这是一个有趣的发现，却造成了报道的困难。

一天晚上，当我的其他问题都得到答复以后，毛泽东便开始回答我列为"个人历史"的问题表。他看到"你结过几次婚"这个问题的时候微笑起来。后来传出谣言说我问毛泽东有几个老婆，但是他毕竟是主张实行一夫一妻制的。不管怎样，他是不

1   CHILDHOOD

On the five or six sets of questions I had submitted on different matters, Mao had talked for a dozen nights, hardly ever referring to himself or his own role in some of the events described. I was beginning to think it was hopeless to expect him to give me such details: he obviously considered the individual of very little importance. Like other Reds I met he tended to talk only about committees, organizations, armies, resolutions, battles, tactics, "measures," and so on, and seldom of personal experience.

For a while I thought this reluctance to expand on subjective matters, or even the exploits of their comrades as individuals, might derive from modesty, or a fear or suspicion of me, or a consciousness of the price so many of these men had on their heads. Later on I discovered that that was not so much the case as it was that most of them actually did not remember personal details. As I began collecting biographies I found repeatedly that the Communist would be able to tell everything that had happened in his early youth, but once he had become identified with the Red Army he lost himself somewhere, and without repeated questioning one could hear nothing more about *him*, but only stories of the Army, or the Soviets, or the Party—capitalized. These men could talk indefinitely about dates and circumstances of battles, and movements to and from a thousand unheard-of places, but those events seemed to have had significance for them only collectively, not because they as individuals had made history there, but because the Red Army had been there, and behind it the whole organic force of an ideology for which they were fighting. It was an interesting discovery, but it made difficult reporting.

One night when all other questions had been satisfied, Mao turned to the list I had headed "Personal History." He smiled at a question, "How many times have you been married?"—and the rumor later spread that I had asked Mao how many wives he had. He was skeptical, anyway, about the necessity for supplying an autobiography. But I argued

大相信有必要提供自传的。但我力争说,在一定程度上,这比其他问题上所提供的情况更为重要。我说:"大家读了你说的话,就想知道你是怎样一个人。再说,你也应该纠正一些流行的谣言。"

我提请他注意关于他的死亡的各种传说,有些人认为他能说流利的法语,有些人则说他是一个无知的农民,有一条消息说他是一个半死的肺病患者,有的消息则强调他是一个发疯的狂热分子。他好像稍为感到意外,人们竟然会花费时间对他进行种种猜测。他同意应该纠正这类传说。于是他再一次审阅我写下的那些问题。

最后他说,"如果我索性撇开你的问题,而是把我的生平的梗概告诉你,你看怎么样?我认为这样会更容易理解些,结果也等于回答了你的全部问题。"

"我要的就是这个!"我叫道。

在以后接着几个晚上的谈话中,我们真像搞密谋的人一样,躲在那个窑洞里,伏在那张铺着红毡的桌子上,蜡烛在我们中间毕剥着火花,我奋笔疾书,一直到倦得要倒头便睡为止。吴亮平坐在我身旁,把毛泽东的柔和的南方方言译成英语,在这种方言中,"鸡"不是说成实实在在的北方话的"chi",而是说成有浪漫色彩的"ghii","湖南"不是"Hunan",而是"Funan",一碗"茶"念成一碗"ts'a",还有许多更奇怪的变音。毛泽东是凭记忆叙述一切的;他边说我边记。我在上文已经说过,我记下的笔记又重译成中文,加以改正。除了对耐心的吴先生的句法作了必要的修改以外,我并没有把它作文学上的加工,下面就是这样做的结果:

"我于1893年生在湖南省湘潭县[1]韶山冲。我父亲叫毛顺生,我母亲在娘家的名字叫文七妹。

"我父亲原是一个贫农,年轻的时候,因为负债过多而只好去当兵。他当了好多年的兵。后来,他回到我出生的村子,做小生意和别的营生,克勤克俭,攒积下一点钱,买回了他的地。

"这时我家有15亩[2]田地,成了中农,靠此每年可以收60担[3]谷。一家五口一年共吃35担——即每人7担左右——这样每年还有25担剩余。我的父亲利用这些剩

---
1. 大体与美国的县相当,是中央政府管辖的最小区划单位,由县长治理。
2. 约2.5英亩,合1公顷。
3. 1担合$133\frac{1}{3}$磅。

that in a way that was more important than information on other matters. "People want to know what sort of man you are," I said, "when they read what you say. Then you ought also to correct some of the false rumors circulated."

I reminded him of various reports of his death, how some people believed he spoke fluent French, while others said he was an ignorant peasant, how one report described him as a half-dead tubercular, while others maintained that he was a mad fanatic. He seemed mildly surprised that people should spend their time speculating about him. He agreed that such reports ought to be corrected. Then he looked over the items again, as I had written them down.

"Suppose," he said at last, "that I just disregard your questions, and instead give you a general sketch of my life? I think it will be more understandable, and in the end all of your questions will be answered just the same."

During the nightly interviews that followed—we were like conspirators indeed, huddled in that cave over the red-covered table, with sputtering candles between us—I wrote until I was ready to fall asleep. Wu Liang-p'ing sat next to me and interpreted Mao's soft southern dialect, in which a chicken, instead of being a good substantial northern *chi*, became a romantic *ghii*, and *Hunan* became *Funan*, and a bowl of *ch'a* turned into *ts'a*, and many much stranger variations occurred. Mao related everything from memory, and I put it down as he talked. It was, as I have said, retranslated and corrected, and this is the result, with no attempt to give it literary excellence, beyond some necessary corrections in the syntax of the patient Mr. Wu:

"I was born in the village of Shao Shan, in Hsiang T'an *hsien*,[1] Hunan province, in 1893. My father's name was Mao Jen-sheng [Mao Shun-sheng], and my mother's maiden name was Wen Ch'i-mei.

"My father was a poor peasant and while still young was obliged to join the army because of heavy debts. He was a soldier for many years. Later on he returned to the village where I was born, and by saving carefully and gathering together a little money through small trading and other enterprise he managed to buy back his land.

"As middle peasants then my family owned fifteen *mou*[2] of land. On this they could raise sixty *tan*[3] of rice a year. The five members of the family consumed a total of thirty-five *tan*—that is, about seven each—which left an annual surplus of twenty-five *tan*. Using

---

1. A *hsien* roughly corresponds to a U.S. county. It was the smallest territorial unit under the central government, and was ruled by a magistrate.
2. About 2.5 acres, or one hectare.
3. One *tan* is a *picul*, or 133⅓ pounds.

余,又积蓄了一点资本,后来又买了7亩地,这样我家就有'富'农的地位了。那时候我家每年可以收84担谷。

"当我10岁家中只有15亩地的时候,一家5口人是:我父亲、母亲、祖父、弟弟和我。我们又买了7亩地以后,祖父去世了,但又添了一个弟弟。可是我们每年仍然有49担谷的剩余,我的父亲就靠此渐渐富裕起来。

"我父亲还是一个中农的时候,就开始做贩运谷子的生意,赚了一些钱。他成了'富'农之后,就用大部分时间做这个生意了。他雇了一个长工,还叫孩子们和妻子都到地里干活。我6岁就开始干农活了。我父亲做生意并没有开铺子,他只是从贫苦农民那里把谷子买下来,然后运到城里卖给商人,在那里得到个高一些的价钱。在冬天碾谷的时候,他便多雇一个短工干活,那时我家就有7口人吃饭。我家吃得很俭省,不过总是够吃的。

"我8岁那年开始在本地一个小学堂读书,一直读到13岁。早晚我到地里干活。白天我读孔夫子的《论语》和'四书'。我的国文教员是主张严格对待学生的。他态度粗暴严厉,常常打学生。因为这个缘故,我10岁的时候曾经逃过学。但我又不敢回家,怕挨打,便朝县城的方向走去,以为县城就在一个山谷里。乱跑了3天之后,终于被我家里的人找到了。我这才知道我只是来回兜了几个圈子,走了那么久,离家才8里[1]路。

"可是,我回到家里以后,想不到情形有点改善。我父亲比以前稍微体谅一些了,老师态度也比较温和一些。我的抗议行动的效果,给了我深刻的印象,这次'罢课'胜利了。

"我刚识了几个字,父亲就让我开始给家里记账。他要我学珠算。既然我父亲坚持,我就在晚上记起账来。他是一个严格的监工,看不得我闲着;如果没有账要记,就叫我去做农活。他性情暴躁,常常打我和两个弟弟。他一文钱也不给我们,给我

---

[1] 合 $2\frac{2}{3}$ 英里。

this surplus, my father accumulated a little capital and in time purchased seven more *mou*, which gave the family the status of 'rich' peasants. We could then raise eighty-four *tan* of rice a year.

"When I was ten years of age and the family owned only fifteen *mou* of land, the five members of the family consisted of my father, mother, grandfather, younger brother, and myself. After we had acquired the additional seven *mou*, my grandfather died, but there came another younger brother. However, we still had a surplus of forty-nine *tan* of rice each year, and on this my father steadily prospered.

"At the time my father was a middle peasant he began to deal in grain transport and selling, by which he made a little money. After he became a 'rich' peasant, he devoted most of his time to that business. He hired a full-time farm laborer, and put his children to work on the farm, as well as his wife. I began to work at farming tasks when I was six years old. My father had no shop for his business. He simply purchased grain from the poor farmers and then transported it to the city merchants, where he got a higher price. In the winter, when the rice was being ground, he hired an extra laborer to work on the farm, so that at that time there were seven mouths to feed. My family ate frugally, but had enough always.

"I began studying in a local primary school when I was eight and remained there until I was thirteen years old. In the early morning and at night I worked on the farm. During the day I read the *Confucian Analects* and the 'Four Classics.' My Chinese teacher belonged to the stern-treatment school. He was harsh and severe, frequently beating his students. Because of that I ran away from the school when I was ten. I was afraid to return home for fear of receiving a beating there, and set out in the general direction of the city, which I believed to be in a valley somewhere. I wandered for three days before I was finally found by my family. Then I learned that I had circled round and round in my travels, and in all my walking had got only about eight *li*[1] from my home.

"After my return to the family, however, to my surprise conditions somewhat improved. My father was slightly more considerate and the teacher was more inclined to moderation. The result of my act of protest impressed me very much. It was a successful 'strike.'

"My father wanted me to begin keeping the family books as soon as I had learned a few characters. He wanted me to learn to use the abacus. As my father insisted upon this I began to work at those accounts at night. He was a severe taskmaster. He hated to see me idle, and if there were no books to be kept he put me to work at farm tasks. He was a hot-tempered man and frequently beat both me and my brothers. He gave us no

---

1. Two and two-thirds miles.

们吃的又是最差的。他每月十五对雇工们特别开恩，给他们鸡蛋下饭吃，可是从来没有肉。对于我，他不给蛋也不给肉。

"我母亲是个心地善良的妇女，为人慷慨厚道，随时愿意接济别人。她可怜穷人，他们在荒年前来讨饭的时候，她常常给他们饭吃。但是，如果我父亲在场，她就不能这样做了。我父亲是不赞成施舍的。我家为了这事多次发生过争吵。

"我家分成两'党'。一党是我父亲，是执政党。反对党由我、母亲、弟弟组成，有时连雇工也包括在内。可是在反对党的'统一战线'内部，存在着意见分歧。我母亲主张间接打击的政策。凡是明显的感情流露或者公开反抗执政党的企图，她都批评，说这不是中国人的做法。

"但我到了13岁的时候，发现了一个同我父亲辩论的有效的方法，那就是用他自己的办法，引经据典地来驳他。父亲喜欢责备我不孝和懒惰。我就引用经书上长者必须仁慈的话来回敬。他指摘我懒惰，我就反驳说，年纪大的应该比年纪小的多干活，我父亲年纪比我大两倍多，所以应该多干活。我还宣称：等我到他这样年纪的时候，我会比他勤快得多。

"老头儿继续'聚财'，这笔财产在那个小村子里已被认为是笔大财了。他不再买进土地，但他典进了许多别人的地。他的资本增加到了两三千元。[1]

"我的不满增加了。在我们家里，辩证的斗争在不断地发展着。[2] 有一件事我记得特别清楚。我大约13岁的时候，有一次父亲请了许多客人到家里；我们两人在他们面前争论了起来。父亲当众骂我懒而无用。这激怒了我。我骂了他，就离开了家。母亲追上前来，竭力劝我回去。父亲也赶来，一边骂一边命令我回去。我跑到一个池塘旁边，恫吓说如果他再走近一步，我就要跳下去。在这种情况下，双方都

---

1. 毛泽东使用的是汉语"元"，经常被译作"Chinese dollars"；3,000元现金在1900年的中国农村相当可观。
2. 毛泽东追忆这些事情的时候，幽默地笑着应用这些政治名词来说明。

money whatever, and the most meager food. On the fifteenth of every month he made a concession to his laborers and gave them eggs with their rice, but never meat. To me he gave neither eggs nor meat.

"My mother was a kind woman, generous and sympathetic, and ever ready to share what she had. She pitied the poor and often gave them rice when they came to ask for it during famines. But she could not do so when my father was present. He disapproved of charity. We had many quarrels in my home over this question.

"There were two 'parties' in the family. One was my father, the Ruling Power. The Opposition was made up of myself, my mother, my brother, and sometimes even the laborer. In the 'united front' of the Opposition, however, there was a difference of opinion. My mother advocated a policy of indirect attack. She criticized any overt display of emotion and attempts at open rebellion against the Ruling Power. She said it was not the Chinese way.

"But when I was thirteen I discovered a powerful argument of my own for debating with my father on his own ground, by quoting the Classics. My father's favorite accusations against me were of unfilial conduct and laziness. I quoted, in exchange, passages from the Classics saying that the elder must be kind and affectionate. Against his charge that I was lazy I used the rebuttal that older people should do more work than younger, that my father was over three times as old as myself, and therefore should do more work. And I declared that when I was his age I would be much more energetic.

"The old man continued to 'amass wealth,' or what was considered to be a great fortune in that little village. He did not buy more land himself, but he bought many mortgages on other people's land. His capital grew to two or three thousand Chinese dollars.[1]

"My dissatisfaction increased. The dialectical struggle in our family was constantly developing.[2] One incident I especially remember. When I was about thirteen my father invited many guests to his home, and while they were present a dispute arose between the two of us. My father denounced me before the whole group, calling me lazy and useless. This infuriated me. I cursed him and left the house. My mother ran after me and tried to persuade me to return. My father also pursued me, cursing at the same time that he commanded me to come back. I reached the edge of a pond and threatened to jump in if he came any nearer. In this situation demands and counterdemands were presented

---

1. Mao used the Chinese term *yuan*, which was often translated as "Chinese dollars"; 3,000 *yuan* in cash in 1900 was an impressive sum in rural China.
2. Mao used all these political terms humorously in his explanations, laughing as he recalled such incidents.

提出了停止内战的要求和反要求。父亲坚持要我磕头[1]认错。我表示如果他答应不打我，我可以跪一条腿磕头。战争就这样结束了。我从这件事认识到，我如果公开反抗，保卫自己的权利，我父亲就软了下来；可是如果我仍温顺驯服，他反而打骂我更厉害。

"回想起来，我认为我父亲的严厉态度到头来是自招失败。我学会了恨他，我们对他建立了真正的统一战线。同时，他的严厉态度大概对我也有好处。这使我干活非常勤快，使我仔细记账，免得他有把柄来批评我。

"我父亲读过两年书，认识一些字，足够记账之用。我母亲完全不识字。两人都是农民家庭出身。我是家里的'读书人'。我熟读经书，可是不喜欢它们。我爱看的是中国旧小说，特别是关于造反的故事。我很小的时候，尽管老师严加防范，还是读了《岳飞传》、《水浒传》、《反唐》、《三国演义》和《西游记》。这位老先生讨厌这些禁书，说它们是坏书。我常常在学堂里读这些书，老师走过来的时候就用一本正经书遮住。大多数同学也都是这样做的。许多故事，我们几乎背得出，而且反复讨论了许多次。关于这些故事，我们比村里的老人知道得还要多些。他们也喜欢这些故事，常常和我们互相讲述。我认为这些书大概对我影响很大，因为是在容易接受的年龄里读的。

"我13岁时，终于离开了小学堂，开始整天在地里帮长工干活，白天做一个全劳力的活，晚上替父亲记账。尽管这样，我还是继续读书，如饥如渴地阅读凡是我能够找到的一切书籍，经书除外。这叫我父亲很生气，他希望我熟读经书，尤其是在一次打官司时，由于对方在法庭上很恰当地引经据典，使他败诉之后，更是这样了。我常常在深夜里把我屋子的窗户遮起，好使父亲看不见灯光。就这样我读了一本叫做《盛世危言》[2]的书，这本书我非常喜欢。作者是一位老派改良主义学者，以为中国之所以弱，在于缺乏西洋的器械——铁路、电话、电报、轮船，所以想把这些

---

1. 字面含义为"撞头"。旧时认为以头触及地板或地面是儿子对父亲、臣子对皇帝效忠的表示。
2. 作者是郑观应，他倡导了许多民主改革，包括议会制政府和现代的教育和交通通讯方法。该书出版于1898年，产生了广泛的影响。同年，"百日维新"惨遭失败。

for cessation of the civil war. My father insisted that I apologize and k'ou-t'ou[1] as a sign of submission. I agreed to give a one-knee k'ou-t'ou if he would promise not to beat me. Thus the war ended, and from it I learned that when I defended my rights by open rebellion my father relented, but when I remained meek and submissive he only cursed and beat me the more.

"Reflecting on this, I think that in the end the strictness of my father defeated him. I learned to hate him, and we created a real united front against him. At the same time it probably benefited me. It made me most diligent in my work; it made me keep my books carefully, so that he should have no basis for criticizing me.

"My father had had two years of schooling and he could read enough to keep books. My mother was wholly illiterate. Both were from peasant families. I was the family 'scholar.' I knew the Classics, but disliked them. What I enjoyed were the romances of Old China, and especially stories of rebellions. I read the *Yo Fei Chuan* [the *Yo Fei Chronicles*], *Shui Hu Chuan* [*The Water Margin*], *Fan T'ang* [*Revolt Against the T'ang*], *San Kuo* [the *Three Kingdoms*] and *Hsi Yu Chi* [*Travels in the West*, the story of Hsuan Tsang's seventh-century semilegendary pilgrimage to India] while still very young, and despite the vigilance of my old teacher, who hated these outlawed books and called them wicked. I used to read them in school, covering them up with a Classic when the teacher walked past. So also did most of my schoolmates. We learned many of the stories almost by heart, and discussed and rediscussed them many times. We knew more of them than the old men of the village, who also loved them and used to exchange stories with us. I believe that perhaps I was much influenced by such books, read at an impressionable age.

"I finally left the primary school when I was thirteen and began to work long hours on the farm, helping the hired laborer, doing the full labor of a man during the day and at night keeping books for my father. Nevertheless, I succeeded in continuing my reading, devouring everything I could find except the Classics. This annoyed my father, who wanted me to master the Classics, especially after he was defeated in a lawsuit because of an apt Classical quotation used by his adversary in the Chinese court. I used to cover up the window of my room late at night so that my father would not see the light. In this way I read a book called *Sheng-shih Wei-yen* [*Words of Warning*],[2] which I liked very much. The author, one of a number of old reformist scholars, thought that the weakness of China lay in her lack of Western appliances—railways, telephones, telegraphs, and steamships—and wanted to have them introduced into the country. My father considered

---

1. Literally, to "knock head." To strike one's head to the floor or earth was expected of son to father and subject to emperor, in token of filial obedience.
2. By Chung Kuang-ying, who advocated many democratic reforms, including parliamentary government and modern methods of education and communications. His book had a wide influence when published in 1898, the year of the ill-fated Hundred Days Reform.

东西传入中国。我父亲认为读这些书是浪费时间。他要我读一些像经书那样实用的东西，可以帮助他打赢官司。

"我继续读中国旧小说和故事。有一天我忽然想到，这些小说有一件事情很特别，就是里面没有种田的农民。所有的人物都是武将、文官、书生，从来没有一个农民做主人公。对于这件事，我纳闷了两年之久，后来我就分析小说的内容。我发现它们颂扬的全都是武将，人民的统治者，而这些人是不必种田的，因为土地归他们所有和控制，显然让农民替他们种田。

"我父亲毛顺生早年和中年都不信神，可是我母亲信佛却很虔诚。她向自己的孩子灌输宗教信仰，我们都因为父亲不信佛而感到伤心。我9岁的时候，曾经同母亲认真地讨论过我父亲不信佛的问题。从那以后，我们好几次想把他转变过来，可是没有成功。他只是骂我们，在他进攻之下，我们只好退让，另想办法。但他总是不愿意和神佛打交道。

"可是，我看的书，逐渐对我产生了影响，我自己也越来越怀疑了。我母亲开始为我担忧，责备我不热心拜佛，可是我父亲却不置可否。后来，有一天，他出去收账，路上遇到一只老虎。老虎猝然遇见人，慌忙逃跑了。可是我父亲却感到更加吃惊，对于他这次脱险的奇迹，他后来想得很多。他开始觉得，是不是得罪了神佛。从此，他开始比较敬佛，有时也烧些香。然而，对于我越来越不信佛，老头儿却不加干涉。他只有处境不顺当的时候，才求神拜佛。

"《盛世危言》激起我想要恢复学业的愿望。我也逐渐讨厌田间劳动了。不消说，我父亲是反对这件事的。为此我们发生了争吵，最后我从家里跑了。我到一个失业的法科学生家里，在那里读了半年书。以后我又在一位老先生那里读了更多的经书，也读了许多时论和一些新书。

"这时，湖南发生了一件事情，影响了我的一生。在我读书的那个小学堂外边，我们学生看到许多豆商从长沙回来。我们问他们为什么都离开长沙。他们告诉我们城里闹了大乱子。

"那年发生了严重的饥荒，长沙有成千上万的人饿饭。饥民派了一个代表团到抚台衙门请求救济。但抚台傲慢地回答他们说：'为什么你们没有饭吃？城里有的是。

such books a waste of time. He wanted me to read something practical like the Classics, which could help him in winning lawsuits.

"I continued to read the old romances and tales of Chinese literature. It occurred to me one day that there was one thing peculiar about such stories, and that was the absence of peasants who tilled the land. All the characters were warriors, officials, or scholars; there was never a peasant hero. I wondered about this for two years, and then I analyzed the content of the stories. I found that they all glorified men of arms, rulers of the people, who did not have to work the land, because they owned and controlled it and evidently made the peasants work it for them.

"My father was in his early days, and in middle age, a skeptic, but my mother devoutly worshiped Buddha. She gave her children religious instruction, and we were all saddened that our father was an unbeliever. When I was nine years old I seriously discussed the problem of my father's lack of piety with my mother. We made many attempts then and later on to convert him, but without success. He only cursed us, and, overwhelmed by his attacks, we withdrew to devise new plans. But he would have nothing to do with the gods.

"My reading gradually began to influence me, however; I myself became more and more skeptical. My mother became concerned about me, and scolded me for my indifference to the requirements of the faith, but my father made no comment. Then one day he went out on the road to collect some money, and on his way he met a tiger. The tiger was surprised at the encounter and fled at once, but my father was even more astonished and afterwards reflected a good deal on his miraculous escape. He began to wonder if he had not offended the gods. From then on he showed more respect to Buddhism and burned incense now and then. Yet when my own backsliding grew worse, the old man did not interfere. He prayed to the gods only when he was in difficulties.

"*Sheng-shih Wei-yen* [*Words of Warning*] stimulated in me a desire to resume my studies. I had also become disgusted with my labor on the farm. My father naturally opposed me. We quarreled about it, and finally I ran away from home. I went to the home of an unemployed law student, and there I studied for half a year. After that I studied more of the Classics under an old Chinese scholar, and also read many contemporary articles and a few books.

"At this time an incident occurred in Hunan which influenced my whole life. Outside the little Chinese school where I was studying, we students noticed many bean merchants coming back from Changsha. We asked them why they were all leaving. They told us about a big uprising in the city.

"There had been a severe famine that year, and in Changsha thousands were without food. The starving sent a delegation to the civil governor to beg for relief, but he replied to them haughtily, 'Why haven't you food? There is plenty in the city. I always have enough.'

我就总是吃得饱饱的。'抚台的答复一传到人们的耳朵里，大家都非常愤怒。他们举行了群众大会，并且组织了一次游行示威。他们攻打清朝衙门，砍断了作为官府标志的旗杆，赶走了抚台。这以后，一个姓庄的布政使骑马出来，晓谕百姓，说官府要采取措施帮助他们。这个姓庄的说话显然是有诚意的，可是皇上不喜欢他，责他同'暴民'勾结。结果他被革职，接着来了一个新抚台，马上下令逮捕闹事的领袖，其中许多人被斩首示众，他们的头挂在旗杆上，作为对今后的'叛逆'的警告。

"这件事在我们学堂里讨论了许多天，给我留下了深刻的印象。大多数学生都同情'造反的'，但他们仅仅是从旁观者的立场出发。他们并不懂得这同他们自己的生活有什么关系。他们单纯地把它看作一件耸听的事而感兴趣。我却始终忘不掉这件事。我觉得造反的人也是些像我自己家里人那样的老百姓，对于他们受到冤屈，我深感不平。

"不久以后，在韶山，秘密会社哥老会[1]里的人同本地一个地主发生了冲突。这个地主到衙门里去控告他们。因为他有钱有势，所以很容易胜诉。哥老会里的人败诉了。但是他们并没有屈服，他们起来反抗地主和政府，撤到本地一个叫做浏山的山里，在那里建立了一个山寨。官府派兵去攻打他们，那个地主散布谣言说，哥老会举起义旗的时候，曾经杀死一个小孩祭旗。起义的领袖，是一个叫做彭磨匠的人。最后他们被镇压下去了，彭磨匠被逼逃走，后来终于被捕斩首。但是在学生眼里，他是一个英雄，因为大家都同情这次起义。

"第二年青黄不接的时候，我们乡里发生了粮荒。穷人要求富户接济，他们开始了一个叫做'吃大户'[2]的运动。我父亲是一个米商，尽管本乡缺粮，他仍然运出大批粮食到城里去。其中有一批被穷苦的村民扣留了，他怒不可遏。我不同情他，可是我又觉得村民们的方法也不对。

"这时还有一件事对我有影响，就是本地的一所小学来了一个'激进派'教师。说他是'激进派'，是因为他反对佛教，想要去除神佛。他劝人把庙宇改成学堂。大

---

1. 就是贺龙曾经加入过的秘密团体。
2. 字面含义为"我们去大户人家吃吧"，即去地主家的粮仓里吃。

When the people were told the governor's reply, they became very angry. They held mass meetings and organized a demonstration. They attacked the Manchu yamen, cut down the flagpole, the symbol of office, and drove out the governor. Following this, the Commissioner of Internal Affairs, a man named Chang, came out on his horse and told the people that the government would take measures to help them. Chang was evidently sincere in his promise, but the Emperor disliked him and accused him of having intimate connections with 'the mob.' He was removed. A new governor arrived, and at once ordered the arrest of the leaders of the uprising. Many of them were beheaded and their heads displayed on poles as a warning to future 'rebels.'

"This incident was discussed in my school for many days. It made a deep impression on me. Most of the other students sympathized with the 'insurrectionists,' but only from an observer's point of view. They did not understand that it had any relation to their own lives. They were merely interested in it as an exciting incident. I never forgot it. I felt that there with the rebels were ordinary people like my own family and I deeply resented the injustice of the treatment given to them.

"Not long afterward, in Shao Shan, there was a conflict between members of the Ke Lao Hui,[1] a secret society, and a local landlord. He sued them in court, and as he was a powerful landlord he easily bought a decision favorable to himself. The Ke Lao Hui members were defeated. But instead of submitting, they rebelled against the landlord and the government and withdrew to a local mountain called Liu Shan, where they built a stronghold. Troops were sent against them and the landlord spread a story that they had sacrificed a child when they raised the banner of revolt. The leader of the rebels was called P'ang the Millstone Maker. They were finally suppressed and P'ang was forced to flee. He was eventually captured and beheaded. In the eyes of the students, however, he was a hero, for all sympathized with the revolt.

"Next year, when the new rice was not yet harvested and the winter rice was exhausted, there was a food shortage in our district. The poor demanded help from the rich farmers and they began a movement called 'Eat Rice Without Charge.'[2] My father was a rice merchant and was exporting much grain to the city from our district, despite the shortage. One of his consignments was seized by the poor villagers and his wrath was boundless. I did not sympathize with him. At the same time I thought the villagers' method was wrong also.

"Another influence on me at this time was the presence in a local primary school of a 'radical' teacher. He was 'radical' because he was opposed to Buddhism and wanted to get rid of the gods. He urged people to convert their temples into schools. He was a widely

---

1. The same society to which Ho Lung belonged.
2. Literally "Let's eat at the Big House," that is, at the landlord's granary.

家对他议论纷纷。我钦佩他，赞成他的主张。

"这些事情接连发生，在我已有反抗意识的年轻心灵上，留下了磨灭不掉的印象。在这个时期，我也开始有了一定的政治觉悟，特别是在读了一本关于瓜分中国的小册子以后。我现在还记得这本小册子的开头一句：'呜呼，中国其将亡矣！'这本书谈到了日本占领朝鲜、台湾的经过，谈到了越南、缅甸等地的宗主权的丧失。我读了以后，对国家的前途感到沮丧，开始意识到，国家兴亡，匹夫有责。

"我父亲决定送我到湘潭一家同他有来往的米店去当学徒。起初我并不反对，觉得这也许是有意思的事。可是差不多就在这个时候，我听说有一个非常新式的学堂，于是决心不顾父亲反对，要到那里去就学。学堂设在我母亲娘家住的湘乡县。我的一个表兄就在那里上学，他向我谈了这个新学堂的情况和'新法教育'的改革。那里不那么注重经书，西方'新学'教得比较多。教学方法也是很'激进'的。

"我随表兄到那所学堂去报了名。我说我是湘乡人，以为这所学堂只收湘乡人。后来我发现这所学堂招收各地学生，我就改用湘潭的真籍贯了。我缴纳1,400个铜元，作为5个月的膳宿费和学杂费。我父亲最后也同意我进这所学堂了，因为朋友们对他说，这种'先进的'教育可以增加我赚钱的本领。这是我第一次到离家50里以外的地方去。那时我16岁。

"在这所新学堂里，我能够学到自然科学和西学的新学科。另外一件事值得一提，教员中有一个日本留学生，他戴着假辫子。很容易看出他的辫子是假的。大家都笑他，叫他'假洋鬼子'。

"我以前从没有见过这么多孩子聚在一起。他们大多数是地主子弟，穿着讲究；很少农民供得起子弟上这样的学堂。我的穿着比别人都寒酸。我只有一套像样的短衫裤。学生是不穿大褂的，只有教员才穿，而洋服只有'洋鬼子'才穿。我平常总是穿一身破旧的衫裤，许多阔学生因此看不起我。可是在他们当中我也有朋友，特别有两个是我的好同志。其中一个现在是作家，住在苏联。[1]

---

1. 即萧三。

discussed personality. I admired him and agreed with his views.

"These incidents, occurring close together, made lasting impressions on my young mind, already rebellious. In this period also I began to have a certain amount of political consciousness, especially after I read a pamphlet telling of the dismemberment of China. I remember even now that this pamphlet opened with the sentence: 'Alas, China will be subjugated!' It told of Japan's occupation of Korea and Taiwan, of the loss of suzerainty in Indochina, Burma, and elsewhere. After I read this I felt depressed about the future of my country and began to realize that it was the duty of all the people to help save it.

"My father had decided to apprentice me to a rice shop in Hsiang T'an, with which he had connections. I was not opposed to it at first, thinking it might be interesting. But about this time I heard of an unusual new school and made up my mind to go there, despite my father's opposition. This school was in Hsiang Hsiang *hsien*, where my mother's family lived. A cousin of mine was a student there and he told me of the new school and of the changing conditions in 'modern education.' There was less emphasis on the Classics, and more was taught of the 'new knowledge' of the West. The educational methods, also, were quite 'radical.'

"I went to the school with my cousin and registered. I claimed to be a Hsiang Hsiang man, because I understood that the school was open only to natives of Hsiang Hsiang. Later on I took my true status as a Hsiang T'an native when I discovered that the place was open to all. I paid 1,400 coppers here for five months' board, lodging, and all materials necessary for study. My father finally agreed to let me enter, after friends had argued to him that this 'advanced' education would increase my earning powers. This was the first time I had been as far away from home as fifty *li*. I was sixteen years old.

"In the new school I could study natural science and new subjects of Western learning. Another notable thing was that one of the teachers was a returned student from Japan, and he wore a false queue. It was quite easy to tell that his queue was false. Everyone laughed at him and called him the 'False Foreign Devil.'

"I had never before seen so many children together. Most of them were sons of landlords, wearing expensive clothes; very few peasants could afford to send their children to such a school. I was more poorly dressed than the others. I owned only one decent coat-and-trousers suit. Gowns were not worn by students, but only by the teachers, and none but 'foreign devils' wore foreign clothes. Many of the richer students despised me because usually I was wearing my ragged coat and trousers. However, among them I had friends, and two especially were my good comrades. One of those is now a writer, living in Soviet Russia.[1]

---

1. Hsiao San (Emi Siao).

"人家不喜欢我也因为我不是湘乡人。在这个学堂，是不是湘乡本地人是非常重要的，而且还要看是湘乡哪一乡来的。湘乡有上、中、下三里，而上、下两里，纯粹出于地域观念而殴斗不休，彼此势不两立。我在这场斗争中采取中立的态度，因为我根本不是本地人。结果三派都看不起我。我精神上感到很压抑。

"我在这个学堂里有了不少进步。教员都喜欢我，尤其是那些教古文的教员，因为我写得一手好古文。但是我无心读古文。当时我正在读表兄送给我的两本书，讲的是康有为的变法运动。一本是《新民丛报》，是梁启超编的。[1] 这两本书我读了又读，直到可以背出来。我崇拜康有为和梁启超，也非常感谢我的表兄，当时我以为他是很进步的，但是他后来变成了反革命，变成了一个豪绅，在1924到1927年的大革命中参加了反动派。

"许多学生因为假辫子而不喜欢那个'假洋鬼子'，可是我喜欢听他谈日本的事情。他教音乐和英文。他教的歌中有一首叫做《黄海之战》的日本歌，我还记得里面的一些动人的歌词：

> 麻雀歌唱，
> 夜莺跳舞，
> 春天里绿色的田野多可爱，
> 石榴花红，
> 杨柳叶绿，
> 展现一幅新图画。

"这首歌是歌颂日本战胜俄国的，我当时从这首歌里了解到并且感觉到日本的美，也感觉到一些日本的骄傲和强大。[2] 我没有想到还有一个野蛮的日本——我们今天所知道的日本。

---

1. 梁启超是清朝末年一个有才华的政论家，维新运动的领袖，因此被迫流亡。康有为和他两人是1911年第一次革命的"精神之父"。林语堂称梁启超是"中国新闻史上最伟大的人物"。
2. 这首歌唱的显然是在日俄战争终了、缔结《朴次茅斯条约》之后日本欢庆春节的情况。

"I was also disliked because I was not a native of Hsiang Hsiang. It was very important to be a native of Hsiang Hsiang and also important to be from a certain district of Hsiang Hsiang. There was an upper, lower, and middle district, and lower and upper were continually fighting, purely on a regional basis. Neither could become reconciled to the existence of the other. I took a neutral position in this war, because I was not a native at all. Consequently all three factions despised me. I felt spiritually very depressed.

"I made good progress at this school. The teachers liked me, especially those who taught the Classics, because I wrote good essays in the Classical manner. But my mind was not on the Classics. I was reading two books sent to me by my cousin, telling of the reform movement of K'ang Yu-wei. One was by Liang Ch'i-ch'ao,[1] editor of the *Hsin-min Ts'ung-pao* [*New People's Miscellany*]. I read and reread those books until I knew them by heart. I worshiped K'ang Yu-wei and Liang Ch'i-ch'ao, and was very grateful to my cousin, whom I then thought very progressive, but who later became a counterrevolutionary, a member of the gentry, and joined the reactionaries in the period of the Great Revolution of 1924—1927.

"Many of the students disliked the False Foreign Devil because of his inhuman queue, but I liked hearing him talk about Japan. He taught music and English. One of his songs was Japanese and was called 'The Battle on the Yellow Sea.' I still remember some charming words from it:

The sparrow sings,

The nightingale dances,

And the green fields are lovely in the spring.

The pomegranate flowers crimson,

The willows are green-leaved,

And there is a new picture.

"At that time I knew and felt the beauty of Japan, and felt something of her pride and might, in this song of her victory over Russia.[2] I did not think there was also a barbarous Japan—the Japan we know today.

---

1. Liang Ch'i-ch'ao, a talented essayist at the end of the Manchu Dynasty, was the leader of a reform movement which resulted in his exile. K'ang Yu-wei and he were the "intellectual godfathers" of the first revolution, in 1911.
2. The poem evidently referred to the spring festival and tremendous rejoicing in Japan following the *Treaty of Portsmouth* and the end of the Russo-Japanese War.

"我从假洋鬼子那里学到的就是这些。

"我还记得我是在那个时候第一次听说光绪皇帝和慈禧太后都已死去的——虽然新皇帝宣统[溥仪]已经在朝两年了。那时我还不是一个反对帝制派；说实在的，我认为皇帝像大多数官吏一样都是诚实、善良和聪明的人。他们不过需要康有为帮助他们变法罢了。中国古代帝王尧、舜、秦皇、汉武的事迹使我向往，我读了许多关于他们的书。同时我也学了一些外国历史和地理。在一篇讲美国革命的文章里，我第一次听到美国这个国家，里面有这样一句：'华盛顿经8年苦战始获胜利遂建国家。'在一部叫做《世界英杰传》的书里，我也读到了拿破仑、俄国叶卡捷琳娜女皇、彼得大帝、惠灵顿、格莱斯顿、卢梭、孟德斯鸠和林肯。"

"This is all I learned from the False Foreign Devil.

"I recall also that at about this time I first heard that the Emperor and Tzu Hsi, the Empress Dowager, were both dead, although the new Emperor, Hsuan T'ung [P'u Yi], had already been ruling for two years. I was not yet an anti-monarchist; indeed, I considered the Emperor as well as most officials to be honest, good, and clever men. They only needed the help of K'ang Yu-wei's reforms. I was fascinated by accounts of the rulers of ancient China: Yao, Shun, Ch'in Shih Huang Ti, and Han Wu Ti, and read many books about them. I also learned something of foreign history at this time, and of geography. I had first heard of America in an article which told of the American Revolution and contained a sentence like this: 'After eight years of difficult war, Washington won victory and built up his nation.' In a book called *Great Heroes of the World*, I read also of Napoleon, Catherine of Russia, Peter the Great, Wellington, Gladstone, Rousseau, Montesquieu, and Lincoln."

二、 在长沙的日子

毛泽东接着说：

"我开始向往到长沙去。长沙是一个大城市，是湖南省的省会，离我家120里。听说这个城市很大，有许许多多的人，不少的学堂，抚台衙门也在那里。总之，那是个很繁华的地方。那时我非常想到那里去，进一所专为湘乡人办的中学。那年冬天，我请我的一位高小教员介绍我去，他同意了。我步行到长沙去，极其兴奋，一面又担心不让我入学，我几乎不敢希望真能进这所有名的学堂。出乎意料，我居然没有遇到困难就入学了。但是政局迅速发生变化，我后来在那里只呆了半年。

"在长沙，我第一次看到报纸——《民立报》，那是一份民族革命的报纸，刊载着一个名叫黄兴的湖南人领导的广州反清起义和七十二烈士殉难的消息。我深受这篇报道的感动，发现《民立报》充满了激动人心的材料。这份报纸是于右任主编的，他后来成为国民党的一个有名的领导人。这个时候，我也听说了孙中山这个人和同盟会的纲领。[1] 当时全国处于第一次革命的前夜。我激动之下写了一篇文章贴在学堂的墙上。这是我第一次发表政见，思想还有些糊涂。我还没有放弃我对康有为、梁启超的钦佩。我并不清楚他们之间的差别。所以我在文章里提出，把孙中山从日本

---

1. 同盟会是孙中山创建的一个秘密革命团体，是国民党的前身。其成员大多为流亡日本的人士，他们奋力"笔伐""改良君主主义"派的领导人物梁启超和康有为。

2   Days in Changsha

Mao Tse-tung continued:

"I began to long to go to Changsha, the great city, the capital of the province, which was 120 *li* from my home. It was said that this city was very big, contained many, many people, numerous schools, and the yamen of the governor. It was a magnificent place altogether. I wanted very much to go there at this time, and enter the middle school for Hsiang Hsiang people. That winter I asked one of my teachers in the higher primary school to introduce me there. The teacher agreed, and I walked to Changsha, exceedingly excited, half fearing that I would be refused entrance, hardly daring to hope that I could actually become a student in this great school. To my astonishment, I was admitted without difficulty. But political events were moving rapidly and I was to remain there only half a year.

"In Changsha I read my first newspaper, *Min-li-pao* [*People's Strength*], a nationalist revolutionary journal which told of the Canton Uprising against the Manchu Dynasty and the death of the Seventy-two Heroes, under the leadership of a Hunanese named Huang Hsing. I was most impressed with this story and found the *Min-li-pao* full of stimulating material. It was edited by Yu Yu-jen, who later became a famous leader of the Kuomintang. I learned also of Sun Yat-sen at this time, and of the program of the T'ung Meng Hui.[1] The country was on the eve of the First Revolution. I was so agitated that I wrote an article, which I posted on the school wall. It was my first expression of a political opinion, and it was somewhat muddled. I had not yet given up my admiration of K'ang Yu-wei and Liang Ch'i-ch'ao. I did not clearly understand the differences between them. Therefore in my article I advocated that Sun Yat-sen must be called back from Japan to

---

1. The T'ung Meng Hui, a revolutionary secret society, was founded by Dr. Sun Yat-sen and was the forerunner of the Kuomintang. Most of its members were exiles in Japan, where they carried on a vigorous "brush-war" (war by writing brushes, or pens) against Liang Ch'i-ch'ao and K'ang Yu-wei, leaders of the "reformed monarchist" party.

请回来当新政府的总统，康有为当国务总理，梁启超当外交部长！ [1]

"由于修筑川汉铁路而兴起了反对外国投资的运动。立宪成为广大人民的要求。皇帝的答复只是下旨设立一个资政院。在我的学堂里，同学们越来越激动。为了发泄排满情绪，他们反对留辫子。[2] 我的一个朋友和我剪去了我们的辫子，但是，其他一些相约剪辫子的人，后来却不守信用。于是我的朋友和我就出其不意强剪他们的辫子，总共有十几个人成了我们剪刀下的牺牲品。就这样，在一个很短的时间里，我从讥笑假洋鬼子的假辫子发展到主张全部取消辫子了。政治思想是怎样能够改变一个人的观点啊！

"在剪辫子事件上，我和一个在法政学堂的朋友发生了争论，双方就这个问题提出了相反的理论。这位法政学生引经据典来论证自己的看法，说身体发肤受之父母，不可毁伤。但是，我自己和反对蓄辫子的人，站在反清的政治立场上，提出了一种相反的理论，驳得他哑口无言。

"黎元洪领导的武昌起义发生以后，[3] 湖南宣布了戒严令。政局迅速改观。有一天，一个革命党人得到校长的许可，到中学来作了一次激动人心的演讲。当场有七八个学生站起来，支持他的主张，强烈抨击清廷，号召大家行动起来，建立民国。会上人人聚精会神地听着。那个革命的演说家是黎元洪属下的一个官员，他向兴奋的学生演说的时候，会场里面鸦雀无声。

"听了这次演讲以后四五天，我决心参加黎元洪的革命军。我决定同其他几位朋友到汉口去，我们从同学那里筹到了一些钱。听说汉口的街道很湿，必须穿雨鞋，于是我到一个驻扎在城外的军队里的朋友那里去借鞋。我被防守的卫兵拦住了。那个地方显得非常紧张。士兵们第一次领到子弹，他们正拥到街上去。

---

1. 这是一个荒谬的联合政府，因为当时康梁二人为君主主义者，而孙中山为反君主主义者。
2. 此举与其说是反满，倒不如说是反孔。一些传统的儒家信徒认为人不应干涉自然，其中便包括头发和指甲的生长。
3. 1911年是推翻满清王朝的革命的开始。

become president of the new government, that K'ang Yu-wei be made premier, and Liang Ch'i-ch'ao minister of foreign affairs![1]

"The anti-foreign-capital movement began in connection with the building of the Szechuan-Hankow railway, and a popular demand for a parliament became widespread. In reply to it the Emperor decreed merely that an advisory council be created. The students in my school became more and more agitated. They demonstrated their anti-Manchu sentiments by a rebellion against the pigtail.[2] One friend and I clipped off our pigtails, but others, who had promised to do so, afterward failed to keep their word. My friend and I therefore assaulted them in secret and forcibly removed their queues, a total of more than ten falling victim to our shears. Thus in a short space of time I had progressed from ridiculing the False Foreign Devil's imitation queue to demanding the general abolition of queues. How a political idea can change a point of view!

"I got into a dispute with a friend in a law school over the pigtail episode, and we each advanced opposing theories on the subject. The law student held that the body, skin, hair, and nails are heritages from one's parents and must not be destroyed, quoting the Classics to clinch his argument. But I myself and the anti-pigtailers developed a counter-theory, on an anti-Manchu political basis, and thoroughly silenced him.

"After the Wuhan Uprising occurred,[3] led by Li Yuan-hung, martial law was declared in Hunan. The political scene rapidly altered. One day a revolutionary appeared in the middle school and made a stirring speech, with the permission of the principal. Seven or eight students arose in the assembly and supported him with vigorous denunciation of the Manchus, and calls for action to establish the Republic. Everyone listened with complete attention. Not a sound was heard as the orator of the revolution, one of the officials of Li Yuan-hung, spoke before the excited students.

"Four or five days after hearing this speech I determined to join the revolutionary army of Li Yuan-hung. I decided to go to Hankow with several other friends, and we collected some money from our classmates. Having heard that the streets of Hankow were very wet, and that it was necessary to wear rain shoes, I went to borrow some from a friend in the army, who was quartered outside the city. I was stopped by the garrison guards. The place had become very active, the soldiers had for the first time been furnished with bullets, and they were pouring into the streets.

---

1. An absurd coalition since K'ang and Liang were monarchists at that time, and Sun Yat-sen was anti-monarchist.
2. An act perhaps more anti-Confucian than anti-Manchu. Some orthodox Confucianists held that man should not interfere with nature, including growth of hair and fingernails.
3. In 1911, the start of the revolution that overthrew the Manchu Dynasty.

"起义军当时正沿着粤汉铁路逼近长沙,战斗已经打响。在长沙城外已经打了一个大仗。同时,城里面也发生起义,各个城门都被中国工人攻占了。我穿过一个城门,回到城里。进城后我就站在一个高地上观战,最后终于看到衙门上升起了'汉旗'。那是一面白色的旗子,上面写着一个'汉'字。[1] 我回到学校,发现它已经由军队守卫了。

"第二天成立了都督府,[2] 哥老会的两名首领焦达峰和陈作新被推举为都督和副都督。新政府设在省咨议局的旧址,议长谭延闿被免职了。省咨议局本身也被撤销。革命党人所发现的清廷文件中,有几份请求召开国会的请愿书。原稿是由现在的苏维埃政府教育人民委员徐特立用血书写的。当时他切断指尖,表示诚意和决心。他的请愿书是这样开头的:'为吁请召开国会,予(为本省赴京代表)断指以送。'

"新都督和副都督在职不久。他们不是坏人,而且有些革命要求。但他们很穷,代表被压迫者的利益。地主和商人都对他们不满。过了没有几天,我去拜访一个朋友的时候,看见他们已经陈尸街头了。原来代表湖南地主和军阀的谭延闿组织了一次叛乱推翻了他们。

"这时,有许多学生投军。一支学生军已经组织起来,在这些学生里面有唐生智[3]。我不喜欢这支学生军,我认为它的基础太复杂了。我决定参加正规军,为完成革命尽力。那时清帝还没有退位,还要经过一个时期的斗争。

"我的军饷是每月7元——不过,这比我现在在红军所得的要多了。在这7元之中,我每月伙食用去两元。我还得花钱买水。士兵用水必须到城外去挑,但是我是一个学生,不屑挑水,只好向挑夫买水。剩下的饷银,我都用在订报纸上,贪读不

---

1. 汉人指"汉朝人"的后裔,与绵长的汉朝(前202—公元220)有关。欧洲人从紧接汉朝之前的秦朝(Ch'in Dynasty)派生出了"China(中国)"和"Chinese(中国人;汉语)"等名词。"China"对汉人来说就是中国,即中央王国。在正式的术语中,包括非汉各族人民在内的所有中国居民都是中国人。因此满族是中国人,但不是汉人。
2. 都督即军事总督。
3. 唐生智后来在1927年担任武汉汪精卫政府的国民军司令。他对汪精卫和共产党都叛变了,在湖南展开"农民大屠杀"。

"Rebels were approaching the city along the Canton-Hankow railway, and fighting had begun. A big battle occurred outside the city walls of Changsha. There was at the same time an insurrection within the city, and the gates were stormed and taken by Chinese laborers. Through one of the gates I re-entered the city. Then I stood on a high place and watched the battle, until at last I saw the *Han*[1] flag raised over the yamen. It was a white banner with the character *Han* in it. I returned to my school, to find it under military guard.

"On the following day, a *tutu*[2] government was organized. Two prominent members of the Ke Lao Hui [Elder Brother Society] were made *tutu* and vic*e-tutu*. These were Chiao Ta-feng and Chen Tso-hsing, respectively. The new government was established in the former buildings of the provincial advisory council, whose chief had been T'an Yen-k'ai, who was dismissed. The council itself was abolished. Among the Manchu documents found by the revolutionaries were some copies of a petition begging for the opening of parliament. The original had been written in blood by Hsu T'eh-li, who is now commissioner of education in the Soviet Government. Hsu had cut off the end of his finger, as a demonstration of sincerity and determination, and his petition began, 'Begging that parliament be opened, I bid farewell [to the provincial delegates to Peking] by cutting my finger.'

"The new *tutu* and vice-*tutu* did not last long. They were not bad men, and had some revolutionary intentions, but they were poor and represented the interests of the oppressed. The landlords and merchants were dissatisfied with them. Not many days later, when I went to call on a friend, I saw their corpses lying in the street. T'an Yen-k'ai had organized a revolt against them, as representative of the Hunan landlords and militarists.

"Many students were now joining the army. A student army had been organized and among these students was T'ang Sheng-chih.[3] I did not like the student army; I considered the basis of it too confused. I decided to join the regular army instead, and help complete the revolution. The Ch'ing Emperor had not yet abdicated, and there was a period of struggle.

"My salary was seven *yuan* a month—which is more than I get in the Red Army now, however—and of this I spent two *yuan* a month on food. I also had to buy water. The soldiers had to carry water in from outside the city, but I, being a student, could not condescend to carrying, and bought it from the water peddlers. The rest of my wages were

---

1. *Han-jen* means the ethnical descendants of "men of Han," referring to the long-lived Han Dynasty (202 B.C.–220 A.D.). Europeans derived the name "China" and "Chinese" from the Ch'in Dynasty which immediately preceded the Han. China was known to *Han-jen* as Chung-kuo, the "Central Realm," also translated as "Middle Kingdom." In official terminology all its inhabitants, including non-Han peoples, were called *Chung-kuo-jen*, or "Central-Realm People." Thus the Manchu were *Chung-kuo-jen* (China-men) but not *Han-jen*.
2. A *tutu* was a military governor.
3. T'ang Sheng-chih later became commander of the Nationalist armies of the Wuhan Government of Wang Ching-wei in 1927. He betrayed both Wang and the Reds and began the "peasant massacre" of Hunan.

厌。当时鼓吹革命的报刊中有《湘江日报》，里面讨论到社会主义，我就是从那里第一次知道社会主义这个名词的。我也同其他学生和士兵讨论社会主义，其实那只是社会改良主义。我读了江亢虎写的一些关于社会主义及其原理的小册子。我热情地写信给几个同班同学，讨论这个问题，可是只有一位同学回信表示同意。

"在我那个班里，有一个湖南矿工和一个铁匠，我非常喜欢他们。其余的都是一些庸碌之辈，有一个还是流氓。我另外又劝说两个学生投了军，我同排长和大多数士兵也交上了朋友。因为我能写字，有些书本知识，他们敬佩我的'大学问'。我可以帮助他们写信或诸如此类的事情。

"革命这时还没有定局。清朝还没有完全放弃政权，而国民党内部却发生了争夺领导权的斗争。湖南有人说战事不可避免要再起。有好几支军队组织起来反对清朝，反对袁世凯[1]。湘军就是其中之一。可是，正当湘军准备采取行动的时候，孙中山和袁世凯达成了和议，预定的战争取消了，南北'统一'了，南京政府解散了。我以为革命已经结束，便退出军队，决定回到我的书本子上去。我一共当了半年兵。

"我开始注意报纸上的广告。那时候，办了许多学校，通过报纸广告招徕新生。我并没有一定的标准来判断学校的优劣，对自己究竟想做什么也没有明确主见。一则警察学堂的广告，引起我的注意，于是去报名投考。但在考试以前，我看到一所制造肥皂的'学校'的广告，不收学费，供给膳宿，还答应给些津贴。这则广告很吸引人，鼓舞人。它说制造肥皂对社会大有好处，可以富国利民。我改变了投考警校的念头决定去做一个肥皂制造家。我在这里也交了1元钱的报名费。

"这时候，我有一个朋友成了法政学生，他劝我进他的学校。我也读到了这所法政学堂的娓娓动听的广告，它许下种种好听的诺言，答应在3年内教完全部法律课

---

1. 袁世凯曾任清政府的军机大臣，1911年迫使清室退位。孙中山被称为"民国之父"，返国并在南京的一次典礼上由其追随者选举为大总统。然而，袁世凯控制着全国大部分地区的军权。为免冲突，孙中山在袁同意召开制宪会议和组建议会之后辞职。袁以军事独裁者的身份统治全国，1915年自称皇帝，失去了军阀支持者的拥护。数月后，被迫取消帝制，袁死而共和国（即便不是立宪政府）存，从此中国进入了一个地方军阀混战和国家四分五裂的时代。

spent on newspapers, of which I became an avid reader. Among journals then dealing with the revolution was the *Hsiang Chiang Jih-pao* [*Hsiang River Daily News*]. Socialism was discussed in it, and in these columns I first learned the term. I also discussed socialism, really social-reformism, with other students and soldiers. I read some pamphlets written by Kiang K'ang-hu about socialism and its principles. I wrote enthusiastically to several of my classmates on this subject, but only one of them responded in agreement.

"There was a Hunan miner in my squad, and an ironsmith, whom I liked very much. The rest were mediocre, and one was a rascal. I persuaded two more students to join the army, and came to be on friendly terms with the platoon commander and most of the soldiers. I could write, I knew something about books, and they respected my 'great learning.' I could help by writing letters for them or in other such ways.

"The outcome of the revolution was not yet decided. The Ch'ing had not wholly given up power, and there was a struggle within the Kuomintang concerning the leadership. It was said in Hunan that further war was inevitable. Several armies were organized against the Manchus and against Yuan Shih-k'ai.[1] Among these was the Hunan army. But just as the Hunanese were preparing to move into action, Sun Yat-sen and Yuan Shih-k'ai came to an agreement, the scheduled war was called off, North and South were 'unified,' and the Nanking Government was dissolved. Thinking the revolution was over, I resigned from the army and decided to return to my books. I had been a soldier for half a year.

"I began to read advertisements in the papers. Many schools were then being opened and used this medium to attract new students. I had no special standard for judging schools; I did not know exactly what I wanted to do. An advertisement for a police school caught my eye and I registered for entrance to it. Before I was examined, however, I read an advertisement of a soap-making 'school.' No tuition was required, board was furnished and a small salary was promised. It was an attractive and inspiring advertisement. It told of the great social benefits of soap making, how it would enrich the country and enrich the people. I changed my mind about the police school and decided to become a soap maker. I paid my dollar registration fee here also.

"Meanwhile a friend of mine had become a law student and he urged me to enter his school. I also read an alluring advertisement of this law school, which promised many wonderful things. It promised to teach students all about law in three years and

---

1. Yuan Shih-k'ai, army chief of staff to the Manchu rulers, forced their abdication in 1911. Sun Yat-sen, regarded as "father of the Republic," returned to China and was elected president by his followers in a ceremony at Nanking. Yuan held military control throughout most of the country, however. To avoid a conflict, Sun resigned when Yuan Shih-k'ai agreed to a constitutional convention and formation of a parliament. Yuan continued to rule as a military dictator, and in 1915 proclaimed himself emperor, whereupon his warlord supporters deserted him. The proclamation was rescinded after a few months, Yuan died, and the Republic (if not constitutional government) survived, to enter a period of provincial warlordism and national division.

程，并且保证期满之后马上可以当官。我的那位朋友不断向我称赞这个学校，最后我写信给家里，把广告上所答应的一切诺言重述一遍，要求给我寄学费来。我把将来当法官的光明图景向他们描述了一番。我向法政学堂交了 1 元钱的报名费，等候父母的回信。

"命运再一次插手进来，这一次采取的形式是一则商业学堂的广告。另外一位朋友劝告我，说国家现在处于经济战争之中，当前最需要的人才是能建设国家经济的经济学家。他的议论打动了我，我又向这个商业中学付了 1 元钱的报名费。我真的参加考试而且被录取了。可是我还继续注意广告。有一天我读到一则把一所公立高级商业学校说得天花乱坠的广告。它是政府办的，设有很多课程，而且我听说它的教员都是非常有才能的人。我决定最好能在那里学成一个商业专家，就付了 1 块钱报名，然后把我的决定写信告诉父亲。他听了很高兴。我父亲很容易理解善于经商的好处。我进了这个学校，但是只住了 1 个月。

"我发现，在这所新学校上学的困难是大多数课程都用英语讲授。我和其他学生一样，不懂得什么英语；说实在的，除了字母就不知道什么了。另外一个困难是学校没有英语教师。这种情况使我感到很讨厌，所以到月底就退学了，继续留心报上的广告。

"我下一个尝试上学的地方是省立第一中学。我花 1 块钱报了名，参加了入学考试，发榜时名列第一。这个学校很大，有许多学生，毕业生也不少。那里的一个国文教员对我帮助很大，他因为我有文学爱好而很愿接近我。这位教员借给我一部《御批通鉴辑览》，其中有乾隆[1]的上谕和御批。

"大致就在这个时候，长沙的一个政府火药库发生爆炸，引起大火。我们学生却感到很有趣。成吨的枪弹炮弹爆炸着，火药燃烧成一片烈焰，比起放爆竹来要好看得多了。过了一个月左右，谭延闿被袁世凯赶走，袁现在控制了民国的政治机器。汤芗铭接替了谭延闿，开始为袁筹备登基。

---

1. 清朝第四位皇帝，很有天赋，1736 年登基。

guaranteed that at the end of this period they would instantly become mandarins. My friend kept praising the school to me, until finally I wrote to my family, repeated all the promises of the advertisement, and asked them to send me tuition money. I painted a bright picture for them of my future as a jurist and mandarin. Then I paid a dollar to register in the law school and waited to hear from my parents.

"Fate again intervened in the form of an advertisement for a commercial school. Another friend counseled me that the country was in economic war, and that what was most needed were economists who could build up the nation's economy. His argument prevailed and I spent another dollar to register in this commercial middle school. I actually enrolled there and was accepted. Meanwhile, however, I continued to read advertisements, and one day I read one describing the charms of a higher commercial public school. It was operated by the government, it offered a wide curriculum, and I heard that its instructors were very able men. I decided it would be better to become a commercial expert there, paid my dollar and registered, then wrote my father of my decision. He was pleased. My father readily appreciated the advantages of commercial cleverness. I entered this school and remained—for one month.

"The trouble with my new school, I discovered, was that most of the courses were taught in English, and, in common with other students, I knew little English; indeed, scarcely more than the alphabet. An additional handicap was that the school provided no English teacher. Disgusted with this situation, I withdrew from the institution at the end of the month and continued my perusal of the advertisements.

"My next scholastic adventure was in the First Provincial Middle School. I registered for a dollar, took the entrance examination, and passed at the head of the list of candidates. It was a big school, with many students, and its graduates were numerous. A Chinese teacher there helped me very much; he was attracted to me because of my literary tendency. This teacher lent me a book called the *Yu-p'i T'ung-chien* [*Chronicles with Imperial Commentaries*], which contained imperial edicts and critiques by Ch'ien Lung.[1]

"About this time a government magazine exploded in Changsha. There was a huge fire, and we students found it very interesting. Tons of bullets and shells exploded, and gunpowder made an intense blaze. It was better than firecrackers. About a month later T'an Yen-k'ai was driven out by Yuan Shih-k'ai, who now had control of the political machinery of the Republic. T'ang Hsiang-ming replaced T'an Yen-k'ai and he set about making arrangements for Yuan's enthronement [in an attempted restoration of the monarchy, which speedily failed].

---

1. The gifted fourth emperor of the Manchu, or Ch'ing, Dynasty, who took the throne in 1736.

"我不喜欢第一中学。它的课程有限，校规也使人反感。我读了《御批通鉴辑览》以后，得出结论，还不如自学更好。我在校 6 个月就退学了，定了一个自修计划，每天到湖南省立图书馆去看书。我非常认真地执行，持之以恒。我这样度过的半年时间，我认为对我极有价值。每天早晨图书馆一开门我就进去。中午只停下来买两块米糕吃。这就是我每天的午饭。我天天在图书馆读到关门才出来。

"在这段自修期间，我读了许多的书，学习了世界地理和世界历史。我在那里第一次看到一幅世界地图，怀着很大的兴趣研究了它。我读了亚当·斯密的《原富》，达尔文的《物种起源》和约翰·穆勒的一部关于伦理学的书。我读了卢梭的著作，斯宾塞的《逻辑》和孟德斯鸠写的一本关于法律的书。我在认真研读俄、美、英、法等国历史地理的同时，也阅读诗歌、小说和古希腊的故事。

"我那时住在湘乡会馆里。许多士兵也住在那里，都是'退伍'或者被遣散的湘乡人。他们没有工作，也没有什么钱。住在会馆里的学生和士兵总是吵架。一天晚上，他们之间的这种敌对爆发成为武斗了。士兵袭击学生，要想杀死他们。我躲到厕所里去，直到殴斗结束以后才出来。

"那时候我没有钱，家里不肯供养我，除非我进学校读书。由于我在会馆里住不下去了，我开始寻找新的住处。同时，我也在认真地考虑自己的'前途'，我差不多已经作出结论，我最适合于教书。我又开始留意广告了。这时候湖南师范学校的一则动听的广告，引起我的注意，我津津有味地读着它的优点：不收学费。膳宿费低廉。有两个朋友也鼓励我投考。他们需要我帮助他们准备入学考试的作文。我把我的打算写信告诉家里，结果得到他们的同意。我替那两位朋友写了作文，为自己也写了一篇。三个人都录取了——因此，我实际上是考取了 3 次。那时候我并不认为我为朋友代笔是不道德的行为，这不过是朋友之间的义气。

"我在师范学校读了 5 年书，抵住了后来一切广告的引诱。最后，我居然得到了毕业文凭。我在这里——湖南省立第一师范度过的生活中发生了很多事情，我的政治思想在这个时期开始形成。我也是在这里获得社会行动的初步经验的。

"I did not like the First Middle School. Its curriculum was limited and its regulations were objectionable. After reading *Yu-p'i T'ung-chien* I had also come to the conclusion that it would be better for me to read and study alone. After six months I left the school and arranged a schedule of education of my own, which consisted of reading every day in the Hunan Provincial Library. I was very regular and conscientious about it, and the half-year I spent in this way I consider to have been extremely valuable to me. I went to the library in the morning when it opened. At noon I paused only long enough to buy and eat two rice cakes, which were my daily lunch. I stayed in the library every day reading until it closed.

"During this period of self-education I read many books, studied world geography and world history. There for the first time I saw and studied with great interest a map of the world. I read Adam Smith's *The Wealth of Nations*, and Darwin's *Origin of Species*, and a book on ethics by John Stuart Mill. I read the works of Rousseau, Spencer's *Logic*, and a book on law written by Montesquieu. I mixed poetry and romances, and the tales of ancient Greece, with serious study of history and geography of Russia, America, England, France, and other countries.

"I was then living in a guild house for natives of Hsiang Hsiang district. Many soldiers were there also 'retired' or disbanded men from the district, who had no work to do and little money. Students and soldiers were always quarreling in the guild house, and one night this hostility between them broke out in physical violence. The soldiers attacked and tried to kill the students. I escaped by fleeing to the toilet, where I hid until the fight was over.

"I had no money then, my family refusing to support me unless I entered school, and since I could no longer live in the guild house I began looking for a new place to lodge. Meanwhile, I had been thinking seriously of my 'career' and had about decided that I was best suited for teaching. I had begun reading advertisements again. An attractive announcement of the Hunan Normal School now came to my attention, and I read with interest of its advantages: no tuition required, and cheap board and cheap lodging. Two of my friends were also urging me to enter. They wanted my help in preparing entrance essays. I wrote of my intention to my family and I received their consent. I composed essays for my two friends, and wrote one of my own. All were accepted—in reality, therefore, I was accepted three times. I did not then think my act of substituting for my friends an immoral one; it was merely a matter of friendship.

"I was a student in the normal school for five years, and managed to resist the appeals of all future advertising. Finally I actually got my degree. Incidents in my life here, in the Hunan Provincial First Normal [Teachers' Training] School, were many, and during this period my political ideas began to take shape. Here also I acquired my first experiences in social action.

"这所新学校有许多校规，我赞成的极少。例如，我反对自然科学列为必修课。我想专修社会科学。我对自然科学并不特别感兴趣，我没有好好地去学，所以大多数这些课程我得到的分数很差。我尤其讨厌一门静物写生必修课。我认为这门课极端无聊。我往往想出最简单的东西来画，草草画完就离开教室。记得有一次我画了一条直线，上面加上一个半圆，表示'半壁见海日'。[1] 又有一次，在图画考试时，我画了一个椭圆形就算了事，说这是蛋。结果图画课得了 40 分，不及格。幸亏我的社会科学各课得到的分数都很高，这样就扯平了其他课程的坏分数。

"学校里有一个国文教员，学生给他起了'袁大胡子'的绰号。他嘲笑我的作文，说它是新闻记者的手笔。他看不起我视为楷模的梁启超，认为他半通不通。我只得改变文风。我钻研韩愈的文章，学会了古文文体。所以，多亏袁大胡子，今天我在必要时仍然能够写出一篇过得去的文言文。

"给我印象最深的教员是杨昌济，他是从英国回来的留学生，后来我同他的生活有密切的关系。他教授伦理学，是一个唯心主义者，一个道德高尚的人。他对自己的伦理学有强烈信仰，努力鼓励学生立志做有益于社会的正大光明的人。我在他的影响之下，读了蔡元培翻译的一本伦理学的书。我受到这本书的启发，写了一篇题为《心之力》的文章。那时我是一个唯心主义者，杨昌济老师从他的唯心主义观点出发，高度赞赏我的那篇文章。他给了我 100 分。

"一位姓唐的教员常常给我一些旧《民报》看，我读得很有兴趣。从那上面我知道了同盟会的活动和纲领[2]。有一天我读到一份《民报》，上面刊载两个中国学生旅行全国的故事，他们一直走到西藏边境的打箭炉。这件事给我很大的鼓舞。我想效法他们的榜样，可是我没有钱，所以我想应当先在湖南旅行一试。

"第二年夏天，我开始在湖南徒步旅行，游历了 5 个县。一个名叫萧瑜的学生与我同行。我们走遍了这 5 个县，没有花一个铜板。农民们给我们吃的，给我们地方睡觉；所到之处，都受到款待和欢迎。和我一同旅行的萧瑜这个家伙，后来在南京在易培基手下当国民党的官。易培基原来是湖南师范的校长，后来成了南京的大官，

---

1. 李白的一首名诗中的话。
2. 同盟会是孙逸仙博士成立的秘密革命团体，为目前在南京当政的国民党的前身。当时大多数会员流亡在日本，对"帝制维新"派领袖梁启超和康有为进行激烈的"笔战"。

"There were many regulations in the new school and I agreed with very few of them. For one thing, I was opposed to the required courses in natural science. I wanted to specialize in social sciences. Natural sciences did not especially interest me, and I did not study them, so I got poor marks in most of these courses. Most of all I hated a compulsory course in still-life drawing. I thought it extremely stupid. I used to think of the simplest subjects possible to draw, finish up quickly and leave the class. I remember once, drawing a picture of the 'half-sun, half-rock,'[1] which I represented by a straight line with a semicircle over it. Another time during an examination in drawing I contented myself with making an oval. I called it an egg. I got 40 in drawing, and failed. Fortunately my marks in social sciences were all excellent, and they balanced my poor grades in these other classes.

"A Chinese teacher here, whom the students nicknamed 'Yuan the Big Beard,' ridiculed my writing and called it the work of a journalist. He despised Liang Ch'i-ch'ao, who had been my model, and considered him half-literate. I was obliged to alter my style. I studied the writings of Han Yu, and mastered the old Classical phraseology. Thanks to Yuan the Big Beard, therefore, I can today still turn out a passable Classical essay if required.

"The teacher who made the strongest impression on me was Yang Ch'ang-chi, a returned student from England, with whose life I was later to become intimately related. He taught ethics, he was an idealist and a man of high moral character. He believed in his ethics very strongly and tried to imbue his students with the desire to become just, moral, virtuous men, useful in society. Under his influence I read a book on ethics translated by Ts'ai Yuan-p'ei and was inspired to write an essay which I entitled 'The Energy of the Mind.' I was then an idealist and my essay was highly praised by Professor Yang Ch'ang-chi, from his idealist viewpoint. He gave me a mark of 100 for it.

"A teacher named T'ang used to give me old copies of Min Pao [*People's Journal*], and I read them with keen interest. I learned from them about the activities and program of the T'ung Meng Hui. One day I read a copy of the Min Pao containing a story about two Chinese students who were traveling across China and had reached Tatsienlu, on the edge of Tibet. This inspired me very much. I wanted to follow their example; but I had no money, and thought I should first try out traveling in Hunan.

"The next summer I set out across the province by foot, and journeyed through five counties. I was accompanied by a student named Hsiao Yu. We walked through these five counties without using a single copper. The peasants fed us and gave us a place to sleep; wherever we went we were kindly treated and welcomed. This fellow, Hsiao Yu, with whom I traveled, later became a Kuomintang official in Nanking, under Yi Pei-ch'i, who was then president of Hunan Normal School. Yi Pei-ch'i became a high official at Nanking

---

1. The reference is to a line in a poem by Li T'ai-po.

他给萧瑜谋到北京故宫博物院管理的职位。萧瑜盗卖了博物院里一些最珍贵的文物，于1934年卷款潜逃。

"我这时感到心情舒畅，需要结交一些亲密的同伴，有一天我就在长沙一家报纸上登了一个广告，邀请有志于爱国工作的青年和我联系。我指明要结交能刻苦耐劳、意志坚定、随时准备为国捐躯的青年。我从这个广告得到的回答一共有三个半人。一个回答来自罗章龙，他后来参加了共产党，接着又转向了。两个回答来自后来变成极端反动的青年。'半'个回答来自一个没有明白表示意见的青年，名叫李立三[1]。李立三听了我说的话之后，没有提出任何具体建议就走了。我们的友谊始终没有发展起来。

"但是，我逐渐地团结了一批学生在我的周围，形成了一个核心，后来成为对中国的国事和命运产生广泛影响的一个学会。[2] 这是一小批态度严肃的人，他们不屑于议论身边琐事。他们的一言一行，都一定要有一个目的。他们没有时间谈情说爱，他们认为时局危急，求知的需要迫切，不允许他们去谈论女人或私人问题。我对女人不感兴趣。我14岁的时候，父母给我娶了一个20岁的女子，可是我从来没有和她一起生活过——后来也没有。我并不认为她是我的妻子，这时也没有想到她。在这个年龄的青年的生活中，议论女性的魅力通常占有重要的位置，可是我的同伴非但没有这样做，而且连日常生活的普通事情也拒绝谈论。记得有一次我在一个青年的家里，他对我说起要买些肉，当着我的面把他的佣人叫来，谈买肉的事，最后吩咐他去买一块。我生气了，以后再也不同那个家伙见面了。我的朋友和我只愿意谈论大事——人的天性，人类社会，中国，世界，宇宙！

"我们也热心于体育锻炼。在寒假当中，我们徒步穿野越林，爬山绕城，渡江过河。遇见下雨，我们就脱掉衬衣让雨淋，说这是雨浴。烈日当空，我们也脱掉衬衣，说是日光浴。春风吹来的时候，我们高声叫嚷，说这是叫做'风浴'的体育新项目。在已经下霜的日子，我们就露天睡觉，甚至到11月份，我们还在寒冷的河

---

1. 李立三后来实行有名的"李立三路线"，遭到毛泽东的激烈反对。本书下文将述及毛泽东谈到李立三与红军的斗争以及斗争的结果。
2. 新民学会。

and had Hsiao Yu appointed to the office of custodian of the Peking Palace Museum. Hsiao sold some of the most valuable treasures in the museum and absconded with the funds in 1934.

"Feeling expansive and the need for a few intimate companions, I one day inserted an advertisement in a Changsha paper inviting young men interested in patriotic work to make a contact with me. I specified youths who were hardened and determined, and ready to make sacrifices for their country. To this advertisement I received three and one half replies. One was from Lu Chiang-lung, who later was to join the Communist Party and afterwards to betray it. Two others were from young men who later were to become ultrareactionaries. The 'half' reply came from a noncommittal youth named Li Li-san. Li listened to all I had to say, and then went away without making any definite proposals himself, and our friendship never developed.[1]

"But gradually I did build up a group of students around myself, and the nucleus was formed of what later was to become a society[2] that was to have a widespread influence on the affairs and destiny of China. It was a serious-minded little group of men and they had no time to discuss trivialities. Everything they did or said must have a purpose. They had no time for love or 'romance' and considered the times too critical and the need for knowledge too urgent to discuss women or personal matters. I was not interested in women. My parents had married me when I was fourteen to a girl of twenty, but I had never lived with her—and never subsequently did. I did not consider her my wife and at this time gave little thought to her. Quite aside from the discussions of feminine charm, which usually play an important role in the lives of young men of this age, my companions even rejected talk of ordinary matters of daily life. I remember once being in the house of a youth who began to talk to me about buying some meat, and in my presence called in his servant and discussed the matter with him, then ordered him to buy a piece. I was annoyed and did not see that fellow again. My friends and I preferred to talk only of large matters—the nature of men, of human society, of China, the world, and the universe!

"We also became ardent physical culturists. In the winter holidays we tramped through the fields, up and down mountains, along city walls, and across the streams and rivers. If it rained we took off our shirts and called it a rain bath. When the sun was hot we also doffed shirts and called it a sun bath. In the spring winds we shouted that this was a new sport called 'wind bathing.' We slept in the open when frost was already falling and even

---

1. Li Li-san later became responsible for the CCP "Li Li-san line," which Mao Tse-tung bitterly opposed. Further on Mao tells of Li's struggle with the Red Army, and of its results.
2. The Hsin-min Hsueh-hui, New People's Study Society.

水里游泳。这一切都是在'体格锻炼'的名义下进行的。这对于增强我的体格大概很有帮助,我后来在华南多次往返行军中,从江西到西北的长征中,特别需要这样的体格。

"我同住在其他大小城市的许多学生和朋友建立了广泛的通信关系。我逐渐认识到有必要建立一个比较严密的组织。1917年,我和其他几位朋友一道,成立新民学会。学会有七八十名会员,其中许多人后来都成了中国共产主义和中国革命史上的有名人物。参加过新民学会的较为知名的共产党人有:罗迈,现任党的组织委员会书记;夏曦,现在在二方面军;何叔衡,中央苏区的最高法院法官,后来被蒋介石杀害;郭亮,有名的工会组织者,1928年被何键杀害;萧子暲[1],作家,现在在苏联;蔡和森,共产党中央委员会委员,1931年被蒋介石杀害;易礼容,后来当了中央委员,接着'转向'国民党,成了一个工会的组织者;萧铮,党的一个著名领导人,是在最早发起建党的文件上签名的六人之一,不久以前病逝。新民学会的大多数会员,在1927年反革命中都被杀害了。[2]

"大约就在这个时候,湖北成立了另外一个团体,叫做互助社,同新民学会性质相近。它的许多社员后来也成了共产党人。其中有它的领袖恽代英,在反革命政变中被蒋介石杀害。现在的红军大学校长林彪也是社员。还有张浩,现在负责白军工作。北京也有一个团体叫做辅社,它的一些社员后来也成了共产党员。在中国其他地方,主要是上海、杭州、汉口、天津[3],一些激进的团体由富有战斗精神的青年组织起来,开始对中国政治产生影响。

---

1. 萧三,萧瑜的弟弟。
2. 其他成员包括刘少奇、任弼时、李富春、王若飞、滕代远、李维汉、肖劲光和至少一名女性,即蔡和森之妹蔡畅。所有这些人都成了中国共产党的高级干部。毛泽东最喜欢的老师和未来的岳父杨昌济与毛在第一师范学校时的老师徐特立是该会的支持者。
3. 在天津,领导激进青年的组织是觉悟社。周恩来是创始人之一。此外还有:邓颖超(现为周恩来夫人);马骏,1927年在北京被处死;谌小岑,现在担任国民党广州市委书记。

in November swam in the cold rivers. All this went on under the title of 'body training.' Perhaps it helped much to build the physique which I was to need so badly later on in my many marches back and forth across South China, and on the Long March from Kiangsi to the Northwest.

"I built up a wide correspondence with many students and friends in other towns and cities. Gradually I began to realize the necessity for a more closely knit organization. In 1917, with some other friends, I helped to found the Hsin-min Hsueh-hui. It had from seventy to eighty members, and of these many were later to become famous names in Chinese communism and in the history of the Chinese Revolution. Among the better-known Communists who were in the Hsin-min Hsueh-hui were Lo Man (Li Wei-han), now secretary of the Party Organization Committee; Hsia Hsi, now in the Second Front Red Army; Ho Shu-heng, who became high judge of the Supreme Court in the Central Soviet regions and was later killed by Chiang Kai-shek (1935); Kuo Liang, a famous labor organizer, killed by General Ho Chien in 1928; Hsiao Chu-chang,[1] a writer now in Soviet Russia; Ts'ai Ho-sen, a member of the Central Committee of the Communist Party, killed by Chiang Kai-shek in 1931; Yeh Li-yun, who became a member of the Central Committee, and later 'betrayed' to the Kuomintang and became a capitalist trade-union organizer; and Hsiao Chen, a prominent Party leader, one of the six signers of the original agreement for the formation of the Party, who died not long ago from illness. The majority of the members of the Hsin-min Hsueh-hui were killed in the counterrevolution of 1927.[2]

"Another society that was formed about that time, and resembled the Hsin-min Hsueh-hui, was the 'Social Welfare Society' of Hupeh. Many of its members also later became Communists. Among them was Yun Tai-ying, who was killed during the counterrevolution by Chiang Kai-shek. Lin Piao, now president of the Red Army University, was a member. So was Chang Hao, now in charge of work among White troops [those taken prisoner by the Reds]. In Peking there was a society called Hu Sheh, some of whose members later became Reds. Elsewhere in China, notably in Shanghai, Hangchow, Hankow, and Tientsin,[3] radical societies were organized by the militant youth then beginning to assert an influence on Chinese politics.

---

1. Hsiao San (Emi Siao), brother of Hsiao Yu (Siao Yu).
2. Other members included Liu Shao-ch'i, Jen Pi-shih, Li Fu-ch'un, Wang Jo-fei, T'eng Tai-yuan, Li Wei-han, Hsiao Ching-kuang, and at least one woman, Ts'ai Ch'ang, the sister of Ts'ai Ho-sen. All of these achieved high rank in the CCP. Mao's favorite professor and future father-in-law, Yang Ch'ang-chi, and Hsu T'eh-li, Mao's teacher at the First Normal School, were patrons.
3. In Tientsin it was the Chueh-wu Shih, or "Awakening Society," which led in organization of radical youth. Chou En-lai was one of the founders. Others included Teng Ying-ch'ao (Mme. Chou En-lai); Ma Chun, who was executed in Peking in 1927; and Sun Hsiao-ch'ing, who later became secretary of the Canton Committee of the Kuomintang.

"这些团体的大多数，或多或少是在《新青年》影响之下组织起来的。《新青年》是有名的新文化运动的杂志，由陈独秀主编。我在师范学校学习的时候，就开始读这个杂志了。我非常钦佩胡适和陈独秀的文章。他们代替了已经被我抛弃的梁启超和康有为，一时成了我的楷模。

"在这个时候，我的思想是自由主义、民主改良主义、空想社会主义等思想的大杂烩。我憧憬'19世纪的民主'、乌托邦主义和旧式的自由主义，但是我反对军阀和反对帝国主义是明确无疑的。

"我在1912年进师范学校，1918年毕业。"

"Most of these societies were organized more or less under the influences of *Hsin Ch'ing-nien* [*New Youth*], the famous magazine of the literary renaissance, edited by Ch'en Tu-hsiu. I began to read this magazine while I was a student in the normal school and admired the articles of Hu Shih and Ch'en Tu-hsiu very much. They became for a while my models, replacing Liang Ch'i-ch'ao and K'ang Yu-wei, whom I had already discarded.

"At this time my mind was a curious mixture of ideas of liberalism, democratic reformism, and utopian socialism. I had somewhat vague passions about 'nineteenth-century democracy,' utopianism, and old-fashioned liberalism, and I was definitely anti-militarist and anti-imperialist.

"I had entered the normal school in 1912. I was graduated in 1918."

三、　革命的前奏

在毛泽东追述往事的时候，我注意到，有一个旁听者至少和我同样感兴趣，这就是他的妻子贺子珍。很明显，他谈到的有关自己和共产主义运动情况，有许多是她以前从来没有听见过的；毛泽东在保安的同志，大多数也是这样。后来，当我向红军其他领导人搜集传记材料的时候，他们的同事常常围拢来兴趣盎然地聆听他们第一次听到的故事。尽管他们已经在一起战斗了多年，他们多半不知道彼此在参加共产党以前的日子的情况，他们往往把这些日子看做一种黑暗时代，真正的生命只是在成为共产党人以后才开始的。

在另一个晚上，毛泽东盘膝而坐，背靠在两只公文箱上。他点燃了一支纸烟，接起前一天晚上中断的故事的线索说下去：

"我在长沙师范学校的几年，总共只用了 160 块钱——里面包括我许多次的报名费！在这笔钱里，想必有 1/3 花在报纸上，因为订阅费是每月 1 元。我常常在报摊买书、买杂志。我父亲责骂我浪费。他说这是把钱挥霍在废纸上。可是我养成了读报的习惯，[1] 从 1911 年到 1927 年我上井冈山为止，我从来没有中断过阅读北京、上海和湖南的日报。

"我在学校的最后一年，母亲去世了，这样我更不想回家了。那年夏天，我决定到北平去，当时叫北京。当时湖南有许多学生打算用'勤工俭学'的办法到法国去留学。法国在世界大战中曾经用这种办法招募中国青年为它工作。这些学生打算出国前先去北京学法文。我协助组织了这个运动，在一批批出国的人里面有许多湖南

---

1. 当时现代报纸在中国仍是个新鲜事物。

3   PRELUDE TO REVOLUTION

During Mao's recollections of his past I noticed that an auditor at least as interested as I was Ho Tzu-chen, his wife. Many of the facts he told about himself and the Communist movement she had evidently never heard before, and this was true of most of Mao's comrades in Pao An. Later on, when I gathered biographical notes from other Red leaders, their colleagues often crowded around interestedly to listen to the stories for the first time. Although they had all fought together for years, very often they knew nothing of each other's pre-Communist days, which they had tended to regard as a kind of Dark Ages period, one's real life beginning only when one became a Communist.

It was another night, and Mao sat cross-legged, leaning against his dispatch boxes. He lit a cigarette from a candle and took up the thread of the story where he had left off the evening before:

"During my years in normal school in Changsha I had spent, altogether, only $160—including my numerous registration fees! Of this amount I must have used a third for newspapers, because regular subscriptions cost me about a dollar a month, and I often bought books and journals on the newsstands. My father cursed me for this extravagance. He called it wasted money on wasted paper. But I had acquired the newspaper-reading habit, and from 1911 to 1927, when I climbed up Chingkangshan, I never stopped reading the daily papers of Peking, Shanghai, and Hunan.

"In my last year in school my mother died, and more than ever I lost interest in returning home. I decided, that summer, to go to Peking. Many students from Hunan were planning trips to France, to study under the 'work and learn' scheme, which France used to recruit young Chinese in her cause during the World War. Before leaving China these students planned to study French in Peking. I helped organize the movement, and in the groups who went abroad were many students from the Hunan Normal School, most of whom

师范学校的学生，其中大多数后来成了著名的激进分子。徐特立也受到这个运动的影响，他放弃了湖南师范学校的教席到法国去，这时他已经 40 多岁了。不过他到 1927 年才参加共产党。

"我陪同一些湖南学生去北京。虽然我协助组织了这个运动，而且新民学会也支持这个运动，但是我并不想去欧洲。我觉得我对自己的国家还了解得不够，我把时间花在中国会更有益处。那些决定去法国的学生从现在任中法大学校长的李石曾那里学习法文，我却没有这样做。我另有打算。

"北京对我来说开销太大。我是向朋友们借了钱来首都的，来了以后，非马上就找工作不可。我从前在师范学校的伦理学教员杨昌济，这时是国立北京大学的教授。我请他帮助我找工作，他把我介绍给北大图书馆主任。他就是李大钊，后来成了中国共产党的一位创始人，被张作霖[1]杀害。李大钊给了我图书馆助理员的工作，工资不低，每月有 8 块钱。

"我的职位低微，大家都不理我。我的工作中有一项是登记来图书馆读报的人的姓名，可是对他们大多数人来说，我这个人是不存在的。在那些来阅览的人当中，我认出了一些有名的新文化运动头面人物的名字，如傅斯年、罗家伦等等，我对他们极有兴趣。我打算去和他们攀谈政治和文化问题，可是他们都是些大忙人，没有时间听一个图书馆助理员说南方话。

"但是我并不灰心。我参加了哲学会和新闻学会，为的是能够在北大旁听。在新闻学会里，我遇到了别的学生，例如陈公博，他现在在南京当大官了；谭平山，他后来参加了共产党，之后又变成所谓'第三党'的党员；还有邵飘萍。特别是邵飘萍，对我帮助很大。他是新闻学会的讲师，是一个自由主义者，一个具有热烈理想和优良品质的人。1926 年他被张作霖杀害了。

"我在北大图书馆工作的时候，还遇到了张国焘[2]——现在的苏维埃政府副主席；康白情，他后来在美国加利福尼亚州加入了三 K 党〔！！！〕；段锡朋，现在在南京

---

1. 张当过土匪，后成为东北地区的军事独裁者。张大帅在北京掌权，后被国民党逐出。1928 年被日本人杀害。其子张学良继位，人称"少帅"。
2. 张国焘 1938 年叛党，投靠蒋介石国民党。——译注

were later to become famous radicals. Hsu T'eh-li was influenced by the movement also, and when he was over forty he left his professorship at Hunan Normal School and went to France. He did not become a Communist, however, till 1927.

"I accompanied some of the Hunanese students to Peking. However, although I had helped organize the movement, and it had the support of the Hsin-min Hsueh-hui, I did not want to go to Europe. I felt that I did not know enough about my own country, and that my time could be more profitably spent in China. Those students who had decided to go to France studied French then from Li Shi-htseng, who is now president of the Chung-fa [Sino-French] University, but I did not. I had other plans.

"Peking seemed very expensive to me. I had reached the capital by borrowing from friends, and when I arrived I had to look for work at once. Yang Ch'ang-chi, my former ethics teacher at the normal school, had become a professor at Peking National University. I appealed to him for help in finding a job, and he introduced me to the university librarian. He was Li Ta-chao, who later became a founder of the Communist Party of China, and was afterwards executed by Chang Tso-lin.[1] Li Ta-chao gave me work as assistant librarian, for which I was paid the generous sum of $8 a month.

"My office was so low that people avoided me. One of my tasks was to register the names of people who came to read newspapers, but to most of them I didn't exist as a human being. Among those who came to read I recognized the names of famous leaders of the renaissance movement, men like Fu Ssu-nien, Lo Chia-lun, and others, in whom I was intensely interested. I tried to begin conversations with them on political and cultural subjects, but they were very busy men. They had no time to listen to an assistant librarian speaking southern dialect.

"But I wasn't discouraged. I joined the Society of Philosophy, and the Journalism Society, in order to be able to attend classes in the university. In the Journalism Society I met fellow students like Ch'en Kung-po, who is now a high official at Nanking; T'an P'ing-shan, who later became a Communist and still later a member of the so-called 'Third Party'; and Shao P'iao-p'ing. Shao, especially, helped me very much. He was a lecturer in the Journalism Society, a liberal, and a man of fervent idealism and fine character. He was killed by Chang Tso-lin in 1926.

"While I was working in the library I also met Chang Kuo-t'ao, now vice-chairman of the Soviet Government; K'ang P'ei-ch'en, who later joined the Ku Klux Klan in California [!!! —E. S.]; and Tuan Hsi-p'eng, now Vice-Minister of Education in Nanking. And here

---

1. The ex-bandit who became military dictator of Manchuria. Marshal Chang held power in Peking before the arrival of the Nationalists there. He was killed by the Japanese in 1928. His son, Chang Hsueh-liang, known as the "Young Marshal," succeeded him.

当教育部次长。也是在这里,我遇见而且爱上了杨开慧。她是我以前的伦理学教员杨昌济的女儿。在我的青年时代杨昌济对我有很深的影响,后来在北京成了我的一位知心朋友。

"我对政治的兴趣继续增长,我的思想越来越激进。我已经把这种情况的背景告诉你了。可是就在这时候,我的思想还是混乱的,用我们的话来说,我正在找寻出路。我读了一些关于无政府主义的小册子,很受影响。我常常和来看我的一个名叫朱谦之[1]的学生讨论无政府主义和它在中国的前景。在那个时候,我赞同许多无政府主义的主张。

"我自己在北京的生活条件很可怜,可是在另一方面,故都的美对于我是一种丰富多彩、生动有趣的补偿。我住在一个叫做三眼井的地方,同另外7个人住在一间小屋子里。我们大家都睡到炕上的时候,挤得几乎透不过气来。每逢我要翻身,得先同两旁的人打招呼。但是,在公园里,在故宫的庭院里,我却看到了北方的早春。北海[2]上还结着坚冰的时候,我看到了洁白的梅花盛开。我看到杨柳倒垂在北海上,枝头悬挂着晶莹的冰柱,因而想起唐朝诗人岑参咏北海冬树挂珠的诗句:'千树万树梨花开'。北京数不尽的树木激起了我的惊叹和赞美。

"1919年初,我和要去法国的学生一同前往上海。我只有到天津的车票,不知道到后怎样才能再向前走。可是,像中国俗语所说的,'天无绝人之路',很幸运,一位同学从北京孔德学校弄到了一些钱,他借了10元给我,使我能够买一张到浦口的车票。在前往南京途中,我在曲阜下车,去看了孔子的墓。我看到了孔子的弟子濯足的那条小溪,看到了圣人幼年所住的小镇。在历史性的孔庙附近那棵有名的树,相传是孔子栽种的,我也看到了。我还在孔子的一个有名弟子颜回住过的河边停留了一下,并且看到了孟子的出生地。在这次旅行中,我登了山东的神岳泰山,冯玉祥将军曾在这里隐居,并且写了些爱国的对联。

"可是我到达浦口的时候又不名一文了,我也没有车票。没有人可以借钱给我;我不知道怎样才能离开浦口。可是最糟糕的是,我仅有的一双鞋子给贼偷去了。哎呀!怎么办呢?又是'天无绝人之路',我又碰到了好运气。在火车站外,我遇见了

---

1. 原文为 Chu Hsun-pei。——译注
2. 北海及其他的"海"均为先前紫禁城的人工湖。

also I met and fell in love with Yang K'ai-hui. She was the daughter of my former ethics teacher, Yang Ch'ang-chi, who had made a great impression on me in my youth, and who afterwards was a genuine friend in Peking.

"My interest in politics continued to increase, and my mind turned more and more radical. I have told you of the background for this. But just now I was still confused, looking for a road, as we say. I read some pamphlets on anarchy, and was much influenced by them. With a student named Chu Hsun-pei, who used to visit me, I often discussed anarchism and its possibilities in China. At that time I favored many of its proposals.

"My own living conditions in Peking were quite miserable, and in contrast the beauty of the old capital was a vivid and living compensation. I stayed in a place called San Yen-ching ['Three-Eyes Well'], in a little room which held seven other people. When we were all packed fast on the *k'ang* there was scarcely room enough for any of us to breathe. I used to have to warn people on each side of me when I wanted to turn over. But in the parks and the old palace grounds I saw the early northern spring, I saw the white plum blossoms flower while the ice still held solid over Pei Hai ['the North Sea'].[1] I saw the willows over Pei Hai with the ice crystals hanging from them and remembered the description of the scene by the T'ang poet Chen Chang, who wrote about Pei Hai's winter-jeweled trees looking 'like ten thousand peach trees blossoming.' The innumerable trees of Peking aroused my wonder and admiration.

"Early in 1919 I went to Shanghai with the students bound for France. I had a ticket only to Tientsin, and I did not know how I was to get any farther. But, as the Chinese proverb says, 'Heaven will not delay a traveler,' and a fortunate loan of ten *yuan* from a fellow student, who had got some money from the Auguste Comte School in Peking, enabled me to buy a ticket as far as P'u-k'ou. On the way to Nanking I stopped at Ch'u Fu and visited Confucius' grave. I saw the small stream where Confucius' disciples bathed their feet and the little town where the sage lived as a child. He is supposed to have planted a famous tree near the historic temple dedicated to him, and I saw that. I also stopped by the river where Yen Hui, one of Confucius' famous disciples, had once lived, and I saw the birthplace of Mencius. On this trip I climbed T'ai Shan, the sacred mountain of Shantung, where General Feng Yu-hsiang retired and wrote his patriotic scrolls.

"But when I reached P'u-k'ou I was again without a copper, and without a ticket. Nobody had any money to lend me; I did not know how I was to get out of town. But the worst of the tragedy happened when a thief stole my only pair of shoes! *Ai-ya!* What was I to do? But again, 'Heaven will not delay a traveler,' and I had a very good piece of luck. Outside

---

1. Pei Hai and the other "seas" were artificial lakes in the former Forbidden City.

从湖南来的一个老朋友，他成了我的'救命菩萨'。他借钱给我买了一双鞋，还足够买一张到上海去的车票。就这样，我安全地完成了我的旅程——随时留神着我的新鞋。到了上海，我了解到已经募集了大批款项，协助把学生送到法国去，还拨出一些钱帮助我回湖南。我送朋友们上轮船以后，就启程回长沙了。

"记得我在第一次到北方去的途中游历过这些地方：

"我在北海湾的冰上散步。我沿着洞庭湖环行，绕保定府城墙走了一圈。《三国演义》上有名的徐州城墙，历史上也有盛名的南京城墙，我都环绕过一次。最后，我登了泰山，看了孔墓。这些事情，我在那时看来，是可以同步行游历湖南相媲美的。

"我回到长沙以后，就更加直接地投身到政治中去。在五四运动[1]以后，我把大部分时间用在学生的政治活动上。我是《湘江评论》的主笔；这是湖南学生的报纸，对于华南学生运动有很大的影响。我在长沙帮助创办了文化书社，这是一个研究现代文化和政治趋势的团体。这个书社，特别是新民学会，都激烈地反对当时的湖南督军张敬尧，这家伙很坏。我们领导了一次学生总罢课反对张敬尧，要求撤换他，并且派遣代表团分赴北京和西南进行反张的宣传，因为那时孙中山正在西南进行活动。张敬尧查禁了《湘江评论》来报复学生的反对。

"于是我前往北京，代表新民学会，在那里组织反军阀运动。新民学会把反对张敬尧的斗争扩大成为普遍的反军阀的宣传，为了促进这个工作我担任了一个通讯社社长的职务。这个运动在湖南取得了一些成功。张敬尧被谭延闿推翻了，长沙建立了新政权。大致就在这个时候，新民学会开始分成两派——右派和左派，左派坚持进行深刻的社会、经济、政治改革的纲领。

"1919年我第二次前往上海。在那里我再次看见了陈独秀[2]。我第一次同他见面是

---

1. 被认为是"第二次革命"和现代中国民族主义的开端。
2. 陈独秀于1879年生于安徽，乃一著名学者和政论家，担任"新文化运动的摇篮"国立北京大学文学系主任多年，他本人就是新文化运动的领袖。他主编的《新青年》杂志主张采用白话代替文言，开始了这个运动。他是中国共产党的创建人和主要提倡者，后来担任国民党中央执行委员会委员。他在1933年在上海被国民党当局逮捕，举行了一次滑稽戏一样的"审判"，被判长期徒刑，现在南京狱中。他与鲁迅一起是他那个时代最重要的文学人物。陈独秀和李大钊都是马克思主义在中国的主要倡导者和中国共产党的先驱组织者。

the railway station I met an old friend from Hunan, and he proved to be my 'good angel.' He lent me money for a pair of shoes, and enough to buy a ticket to Shanghai. Thus I safely completed my journey—keeping an eye on my new shoes. At Shanghai I found that a good sum had been raised to help send the students to France, and an allowance had been provided to help me return to Hunan. I saw my friends off on the steamer and then set out for Changsha.

"During my first trip to the North, as I remember it, I made these excursions:

"I walked around the lake of T'ung T'ing, and I circled the wall of Paotingfu. I walked on the ice of the Gulf of Pei Hai. I walked around the wall of Hsuchou, famous in the *San Kuo* [*Three Kingdoms*], and around Nanking's wall, also famous in history. Finally I climbed T'ai Shan and visited Confucius' grave. These seemed to me then achievements worth adding to my adventures and walking tours in Hunan.

"When I returned to Changsha I took a more direct role in politics. After the May Fourth Movement[1] I had devoted most of my time to student political activities, and I was editor of the *Hsiang River Review*, the Hunan students' paper, which had a great influence on the student movement in South China. In Changsha I helped found the Wen-hua Shu-hui [Cultural Book Society], an association for study of modern cultural and political tendencies. This society, and more especially the Hsin-min Hsueh-hui, were violently opposed to Chang Ching-yao, then *tuchun* of Hunan, and a vicious character. We led a general student strike against Chang, demanding his removal, and sent delegations to Peking and the Southwest, where Sun Yat-sen was then active, to agitate against him. In retaliation for the students' opposition, Chang Ching-yao suppressed the *Hsiang River Review*.

"After this I went to Peking, to represent the New People's Study Society and organize an anti-militarist movement there. The society broadened its fight against Chang Ching-yao into a general anti-militarist agitation, and I became head of a news agency to promote this work. In Hunan the movement was rewarded with some success. Chang Ching-yao was overthrown by T'an Yen-k'ai, and a new regime was established in Changsha. About this time the society began to divide into two groups, a right and left wing—the left wing insisting on a program of far-reaching social and economic and political changes.

"I went to Shanghai for the second time in 1919. There once more I saw Ch'en Tu-hsiu.[2]

---

1. Considered the beginning of the "Second Revolution," and of modern Chinese nationalism.
2. Ch'en Tu-hsiu was born in Anhui, in 1879, became a noted scholar and essayist, and for years headed the department of literature at Peking National University—"cradle of the literary renaissance." His *New Youth* magazine began the movement for adoption of the *pai-hua*, or vernacular Chinese, as the national language to replace the "dead" *wen-yen*, or Classical language. With Li Ta-chao, he was a chief promoter of Marxist study in China and a pioneer organizer of the Chinese Communist Party.

在北京，那时我在国立北京大学。他对我的影响也许超过其他任何人。那时候我也遇见了胡适，我去拜访他，想争取他支持湖南学生的斗争。在上海，我和陈独秀讨论了我们组织'改造湖南联盟'的计划。接着我回到长沙着手组织联盟。我在长沙一边当教员，一边继续我在新民学会的活动。那时新民学会的纲领要争取湖南'独立'，所谓独立，实际上是指自治。我们的团体对于北洋政府感到厌恶。认为湖南如果和北京脱离关系，可以更加迅速地现代化，所以主张同北京分离。那时候，我是美国门罗主义和门户开放的坚决拥护者。

"谭延闿被一个叫做赵恒惕的军阀赶出湖南，赵利用'湖南独立'运动来达到他自己的目的。他假装拥护这个运动，主张中国联省自治。可是他一旦当权，就大力镇压民主运动了。我们的团体曾经要求实行男女平权和代议制政府，一般地赞成资产阶级民主纲领。我们在自己办的报纸《新湖南》上公开鼓吹进行这些改革。我们领导了一次对省议会的冲击，因为大多数议员都是军阀指派的地主豪绅。这次斗争的结果，我们把省议会里张挂的胡说八道和歌功颂德的对联匾额都扯了下来。

"冲击省议会这件事被看成湖南的一件大事，吓慌了统治者。但是，赵恒惕篡夺控制权以后，背叛了他支持过的一切主张，特别是他凶暴地压制一切民主要求。因此，我们的学会就把斗争矛头转向他。我记得1920年的一个插曲，那年新民学会组织了一个示威游行，庆祝俄国十月革命3周年。这次示威游行遭到警察镇压。有些示威者要想在会场上升起红旗，警察禁止这样做。示威者指出，依照宪法第12条，人民有集会、结社和言论自由的权利，但是警察听不进去。他们回答说，他们不是来上宪法课，而是来执行省长赵恒惕的命令的。从此以后，我越来越相信，只有经过群众行动取得群众政治权力，才能保证有力的改革的实现。[1]

"1920年冬天，我第一次在政治上把工人们组织起来了，在这项工作中我开始

---

1. 1920年10月，毛泽东在长沙建立了一个社会主义青年团支部，他和林伯渠开始着手组建湖南同业工会。

I had first met him in Peking, when I was at Peking National University, and he had influenced me perhaps more than anyone else. I also met Hu Shih at that time, having called on him to try to win his support for the Hunanese students struggle. In Shanghai I discussed with Ch'en Tu-hsiu our plans for a League for Reconstruction of Hunan. Then I returned to Changsha and began to organize it. I took a place as a teacher there, meanwhile continuing my activity in the New People's Study Society. The society had a program then for the 'independence' of Hunan, meaning, really, autonomy. Disgusted with the Northern Government, and believing that Hunan could modernize more rapidly if freed from connections with Peking, our group agitated for separation. I was then a strong supporter of America's Monroe Doctrine and the Open Door.

"T'an Yen-k'ai was driven out of Hunan by a militarist called Chao Heng-t'i, who utilized the 'Hunan independence' movement for his own ends. He pretended to support it, advocating the idea of a United Autonomous States of China, but as soon as he got power he suppressed the democratic movement with great energy. Our group had demanded equal rights for men and women, and representative government, and in general approval of a platform for a bourgeois democracy. We openly advocated these reforms in our paper, the *New Hunan*. We led an attack on the provincial parliament, the majority of whose members were landlords and gentry appointed by the militarists. This struggle ended in our pulling down the scrolls and banners, which were full of nonsensical and extravagant phrases.

"The attack on the parliament was considered a big incident in Hunan, and frightened the rulers. However, when Chao Heng-t'i seized control he betrayed all the ideas he had supported, and especially he violently suppressed all demands for democracy. Our society therefore turned the struggle against him. I remember an episode in 1920, when the Hsin-min Hsueh-hui organized a demonstration to celebrate the third anniversary of the Russian October Revolution. It was suppressed by the police. Some of the demonstrators had attempted to raise the Red flag at that meeting, but were prohibited from doing so by the police. The demonstrators pointed out that, according to Article 12 of the Constitution, the people had the right to assemble, organize, and speak, but the police were not impressed. They replied that they were not there to be taught the Constitution, but to carry out the orders of the governor, Chao Heng-t'i. From this time on I became more and more convinced that only mass political power, secured through mass action, could guarantee the realization of dynamic reforms.[1]

"In the winter of 1920 I organized workers politically for the first time, and began to

---

1. In October, 1920, Mao organized a Socialist Youth Corps branch in Changsha, in which he worked with Lin Tsu-han to set up craft unions in Hunan.

受到马克思主义理论和俄国革命历史的影响的指引。我第二次到北京期间,读了许多关于俄国情况的书。我热心地搜寻那时候能找到的为数不多的用中文写的共产主义书籍。有3本书特别深地铭刻在我的心中,建立起我对马克思主义的信仰。我一旦接受了马克思主义是对历史的正确解释以后,我对马克思主义的信仰就没有动摇过。这3本书是:《共产党宣言》,陈望道译,这是用中文出版的第一本马克思主义的书;《阶级斗争》,考茨基著;《社会主义史》,柯卡普著。到了1920年夏天,在理论上,而且在某种程度的行动上,我已成为一个马克思主义者了,而且从此我也认为自己是一个马克思主义者了。同年,我和杨开慧结了婚。[1]"

---

1. 毛泽东没有更多涉及他和杨开慧的生活,只是提及她的遇害。从各方面的记述来看,她是一个杰出的妇女,北京大学的一个学生,后来成了大革命中的一个青年领袖,最活跃的女共产党员之一。他们的结合被当时湖南的新青年认为是"理想的罗曼史"。他们两人显然十分忠诚。杨开慧女士后来大约是在1930年被何键杀害的。

be guided in this by the influence of Marxist theory and the history of the Russian Revolution. During my second visit to Peking I had read much about the events in Russia, and had eagerly sought out what little Communist literature was then available in Chinese. Three books especially deeply carved my mind, and built up in me a faith in Marxism, from which, once I had accepted it as the correct interpretation of history, I did not afterwards waver. These books were the *Communist Manifesto*, translated by Ch'en Wang-tao and the first Marxist book ever published in Chinese; *Class Struggle*, by Kautsky; and a *History of Socialism*, by Kirkup. By the summer of 1920 I had become, in theory and to some extent in action, a Marxist, and from this time on I considered myself a Marxist. In the same year I married Yang K'ai-hui."[1]

---

1. Mao made no further reference to his life with Yang K'ai-hui, except to mention her execution. She was a student at Peking National University and later became a youth leader during the Great Revolution, and one of the most active women Communists. Their marriage had been celebrated as an "ideal romance" among radical youths in Hunan.

四、 国民革命时期

毛泽东这时候已是一个马克思主义者,但还不是一个共产党员,这是因为当时中国还没有共产党的组织。早在 1919 年,陈独秀就同共产国际建立了联系。[1] 1920 年,第三国际的精力充沛、富有口才的代表马林[2]前来上海,安排同中国党联系。不久之后陈独秀就在上海召集了一次会议[3],几乎同一个时候,在巴黎的一批中国学生也开了会,打算在那里成立一个共产党组织。

如果我们想到中国共产党还不过是个 16 岁的少年,那么她的成就实在不能算少了。除了俄国以外,她是世界上最强大的共产党;也是除了俄国以外,唯一能够自称有一支自己的强大军队的共产党。

又是一个晚上,毛继续他的叙述:

"1921 年 5 月,我到上海去出席共产党成立大会。在这个大会的组织上,起领导作用的是陈独秀和李大钊,他们两人都是中国最有才华的知识界领袖。我在李大钊手下在国立北京大学当图书馆助理员的时候,就迅速地朝着马克思主义的方向发展。陈独秀对于我在这方面的兴趣也是很有帮助的。我第二次到上海去的时候,曾

---

1. 和李大钊一样,陈独秀也是通过在北京居住的俄国人。1920 年春,共产国际全权代表维经斯基抵达北京,陪同兼翻译为俄共党员杨明斋。他们会晤了李大钊,很可能还会见了李的马克思主义学说研究会的会员。
2. 荷兰人。
3. 此次会议组织了一个核心的共产主义小组。一些与会者(李大钊的北京小组、广州陈独秀的另一个小组、山东和湖北的小组以及毛泽东的湖南小组)成为第二年中共一大的召集人。

4   The Nationalist Period

Mao was now a Marxist but not a Communist, because as yet there did not exist in China an organized Communist Party. As early as 1919 Ch'en Tu-hsiu had established contact with the Comintern through Russians living in Peking, as had Li Ta-chao. It was not until the spring of 1920 that Gregori Voitinsky, an authorized representative of the Communist International, reached Peking, in the company of Yang Ming-chai, a member of the Russian Communist Party who acted as his interpreter. They conferred with Li Ta-chao and probably also met members of Li's Society for the Study of Marxist Theory. In the same year the energetic and persuasive Jahn Henricus Sneevliet, a Dutch agent of the Third International—Tisan Kuo-chi, in Chinese—came to Shanghai for talks with Ch'en Tu-hsiu, who was conferring with serious Chinese Marxists there. It was Ch'en who, in May, 1920, summoned a conference that organized a nuclear Communist group. Some members of it became (with Li Ta-chao's group in Peking, another group set up in Canton by Ch'en, groups in Shantung and Hupeh, and Mao's group in Hunan) conveners of a Shanghai conference the following year that (with the help of Voitinsky) summoned the first Chinese Communist Party congress.

When one remembered, in 1937, that the Chinese Communist Party was still an adolescent in years, its achievements could be regarded as not inconsiderable. It was the strongest Communist Party in the world, outside of Russia, and the only one, with the same exception, that could boast an army of its own.

Another night, and Mao carried on his narrative:

"In May of 1921 I went to Shanghai to attend the founding meeting of the Communist Party. In its organization the leading roles were played by Ch'en Tu-hsiu and Li Ta-chao, both of whom were among the most brilliant intellectual leaders of China. Under Li Ta-chao, as assistant librarian at Peking National University, I had rapidly developed toward Marxism, and Ch'en Tu-hsiu had been instrumental in my interests in that direction too.

经和陈独秀讨论我读过的马克思主义书籍。陈独秀谈他自己的信仰的那些话，在我一生中可能是关键性的这个时期，对我产生了深刻的印象。

"在上海这次有历史意义的会议上，除了我以外，只有一个湖南人[1]。其他出席会议的人有张国焘、包惠僧和周佛海。我们一共有12个人。那年10月，共产党的第一个省支部在湖南组织起来了。我是委员之一。接着其他省市也建立了党组织。在上海，党中央委员会包括陈独秀、张国焘（现在四方面军）、陈公博（现为国民党官员）、施存统（现为南京官员）、沈玄庐、李汉俊（1927年在武汉被害[2]）、李达和李森（后被害）。在湖北的党员有董必武（现任保安共产党党校校长）、许白昊和施洋（1923年被杀）。在陕西的党员有高崇裕（即高岗）和一些有名的学生领袖。在北京是李大钊（后被害）[3]、邓中夏[4]、张国焘（现红军军事委员会副主席）、罗章龙、刘仁静（现为托洛茨基派）和其他一些人。在广州是林伯渠（现任苏维埃政府财政人民委员）、彭湃（1929年被害）。王尽美和邓恩铭是山东支部的创始人。

"同时，在法国，许多勤工俭学的人也组织了中国共产党[5]，几乎是同国内的组织同时建立起来的。那里的党的创始人之中有周恩来、李立三和向警予。向警予是蔡和森的妻子，唯一的一个女创始人。罗迈（即李维汉）和蔡和森也是法国支部的创始人。在德国也组织了中国共产党，只是时间稍后一些；党员有高语罕、朱德（现任红军总司令）和张申府（现任清华大学教授）。在莫斯科，支部的创始人有瞿秋白等人。在日本是周佛海。

"到1922年5月，湖南党——我那时是书记[6]——已经在矿工、铁路工人、市政

---

1. 即何叔衡，毛泽东的老朋友和新民学会的创建者之一；1935年被国民党杀害。
2. 被害时间早于1927年的是被军阀杀害的，晚于1927年3月的是被国民党将领杀害的。
3. 1927年和其他19位北京的共产党员一同被害。
4. 1933年被蒋介石杀害。
5. 指共产主义青年团，起初为社会主义青年团。其他成员包括邓颖超、李富春及其夫人蔡畅。
6. 毛泽东同时也是该省国民党的领导成员之一。在与越飞达成两党合作的协议之后，孙中山开始秘密肃清国民党内的反共势力。在湖南，孙中山授权老同事林伯渠与毛泽东和夏曦一同重组国民党。1923年1月，他们已将湖南的国民党转化为左派的激进工具。

I had discussed with Ch'en, on my second visit to Shanghai, the Marxist books that I had read, and Ch'en's own assertions of belief had deeply impressed me at what was probably a critical period of my life.

"There was only one other Hunanese[1] at that historic meeting [the First National Congress of the Party] in Shanghai. Others present were Chang Kuo-t'ao, now vice-chairman of the Red Army military council; Pao Hui-sheng; and Chou Fu-hai. Altogether there were twelve of us. In Shanghai [those elected to] the Central Committee of the Party included Ch'en Tu-hsiu, Chang Kuo-t'ao, Ch'en Kung-po, Shih Tseng-tung (now a Nanking official), Sun Yuan-lu, Li Han-chun (killed[2] in Wuhan in 1927), Li Ta, and Li Sun (later executed). The following October the first provincial branch of the Party was organized in Hunan and I became a member of it. Organizations were also established in other provinces and cities. Members in Hupeh included Tung Pi-wu (now chairman of the Communist Party School in Pao An), Hsu Pai-hao, and Shih Yang (executed in 1923). In the Shensi Party were Kao Chung-yu (Kao Kang) and some famous student leaders. In [the Party branch of] Peking were Li Ta-chao (executed, with nineteen other Peking Communists, in 1927), Teng Chung-hsia (executed by Chiang Kai-shek in 1933), Lo Chung-lun, Liu Jen-ching (now a Trotskyite), and others. In Canton were Lin Po-chu (Lin Tsu-han), now Commissioner of Finance in the Soviet Government, and P'eng P'ai (executed in 1929). Wang Chun-mei and Teng En-ming were among the founders of the Shantung branch.

"Meanwhile, in France, a Chinese Communist Party[3] had been organized by many of the worker-students there, and its founding was almost simultaneous with the beginning of the organization in China. Among the founders of the Party [CYL] there were Chou En-lai, Li Li-san, and Hsiang Ching-wu, the wife of Ts'ai Ho-sen. Lo Man (Li Wei-han) and Ts'ai Ho-sen were also founders of the French branch. A Chinese Party was organized in Germany, but this was somewhat later; among its members were Kao Yu-han, Chu Teh (now commander-in-chief of the Red Army), and Chang Sheng-fu (now a professor at Tsinghua University). In Moscow the founders of the branch were Ch'u Ch'iu-pai and others, and in Japan there was Chou Fu-hai.

"In May, 1922, the Hunan Party, of which I was then secretary,[4] had already organized more than twenty trade unions among miners, railway workers, municipal employees,

---

1. Ho Shu-heng, Mao's old friend and co-founder of the New People's Study Society; he was executed in 1935 by the Kuomintang.
2. Those here noted as "killed" or "executed" were liquidated by warlord regimes if before 1927, and by Nationalist generals if after March, 1927.
3. Meaning the Communist Youth League, which began as the Socialist Youth Corps (Society, League). Other members included Teng Ying-ch'ao and Li Fu-ch'un and his wife, Ts'ai Ch'ang.
4. Mao was also a leading member of the provincial KMT. Following his agreement with Adolf Joffe for a two-party alliance, Sun Yat-sen had begun a secret purge of anti-Communist elements in the KMT. In Hunan, Sun authorized his old colleague Lin Tsu-han, together with Mao Tse-tung and Hsia Hsi, to reorganize the Party. By January, 1923, they had turned the Hunan KMT into a radical tool of the left.

职员、印刷工人和政府造币厂工人中组织了 20 多个工会。那年冬天，展开了蓬蓬勃勃的劳工运动。那时共产党的工作主要集中在学生和工人身上，在农民中间工作做得非常少。大部分大矿的工人都组织起来了，学生几乎全数组织了起来。在学生战线和工人战线上，进行了多次的斗争。1922 年冬天，湖南省长赵恒惕下令处决两个湖南工人——黄爱和庞人铨，这引起了广泛的反对赵恒惕的宣传运动。被杀死的两个工人之一黄爱，是右派工人运动的一个领袖，以工业学校学生为基础，是反对我们的。可是在这次事件以及其他许多斗争中，我们都是支持他们的。无政府主义者在工会当中也很有势力，这些工会那时候已经组织成为湖南全省劳工会。但是我们同无政府主义者达成妥协，并且通过协商，防止了他们许多轻率和无益的行动。

"我被派到上海去帮助组织反对赵恒惕的运动。那年（1922 年）冬天，第二次党代表大会在上海召开，我本想参加，可是忘记了开会的地点，又找不到任何同志，结果没有能出席。我回到湖南，大力推动工会的工作。第二年春天，湖南发生多次罢工，要求增加工资，改善待遇和承认工会。大部分罢工都是成功的。5 月 1 日湖南举行了总罢工，这标志着中国工人运动的力量已经达到空前的地步。

"1923 年，共产党第三次代表大会在广州举行，大会作出了有历史意义的决定：参加国民党，和它合作，建立反对北洋军阀的统一战线。我到上海去，在党中央委员会中工作。第二年（1924 年）春天，我前往广州，出席国民党第一次全国代表大会。3 月，我回到上海，在共产党执行局工作的同时，兼任国民党上海执行部的委员。其他执行委员，有（后任南京政府行政院长的）汪精卫和胡汉民。我和他们共事，协调共产党和国民党的行动。那年夏天，黄埔军官学校成立了。加林担任该校顾问，其他苏联顾问也从俄国来到。国共合作开始具有全国革命运动的规模。那年冬天我回到湖南休养——我在上海生了病。但在湖南期间，我组织了该省伟大的农民运动的核心。

printers, and workers in the government mint. A vigorous labor movement began that winter. The work of the Communist Party was then concentrated mainly on students and workers, and very little was done among the peasants. Most of the big mines were organized, and virtually all the students. There were numerous struggles on both the students' and workers' fronts. In the winter of 1922, Chao Heng-t'i, civil governor of Hunan, ordered the execution of two Hunanese workers, Huang Ai and Pang Yuan-ch'ing, and as a result a widespread agitation began against him. Huang Ai, one of the two workers killed, was a leader of the right-wing labor movement, which had its base in the industrial-school students and was opposed to us, but we supported them in this case, and in many other struggles. Anarchists were also influential in the trade unions, which were then organized into an All-Hunan Labor Syndicate. But we compromised and through negotiation prevented many hasty and useless actions by them.

"I was sent to Shanghai to help organize the movement against Chao Heng-t'i. The Second Congress of the Party was convened in Shanghai that winter [1922], and I intended to attend. However, I forgot the name of the place where it was to be held, could not find any comrades, and missed it. I returned to Hunan and vigorously pushed the work among the labor unions. That spring there were many strikes for better wages and better treatment and recognition of the labor unions. Most of these were successful. On May 1, a general strike was called in Hunan, and this marked the achievement of unprecedented strength in the labor movement of China.

The Third Congress of the Communist Party was held in Canton in [May] 1923 and the historic decision was reached to enter the Kuomintang, cooperate with it, and create a united front against the northern militarists. I went to Shanghai and worked in the Central Committee of the Party. Next spring [1924] I went to Canton and attended the First National Congress of the Kuomintang. In March, I returned to Shanghai and combined my work in the executive bureau [Central Committee] of the Communist Party with membership in the executive bureau [Central Executive Committee] of the Kuomintang of Shanghai. The other members of this bureau then were Wang Ching-wei (later premier at Nanking) and Hu Han-min, with whom I worked in coordinating the measures of the Communist Party and the Kuomintang. That summer the Whampoa Military Academy was set up. Galin became its adviser, other Soviet advisers arrived from Russia, and the Kuomintang-Communist Party entente began to assume the proportions of a nationwide revolutionary movement. The following winter I returned to Hunan for a rest—I had become ill in Shanghai—but while in Hunan I organized the nucleus of the great peasant movement of that province.

"以前我没有充分认识到农民中间的阶级斗争的程度,但是,在(1925年)'五卅'惨案[1]以后,以及在继之而起的政治活动的巨浪中,湖南农民变得非常富有战斗性。我离开了我在休养的家,发动了一个把农村组织起来的运动。在几个月之内,我们就组织了20多个农会,这引起了地主的仇恨,他们要求把我抓起来。赵恒惕派军队追捕我,于是我逃到广州。我到达那里的时候,正逢黄埔学生打败云南军阀杨希闵和广西军阀刘震寰。广州市和国民党内部弥漫着一片乐观气氛。孙中山在北京逝世之后,蒋介石被任命为第一军总司令,汪精卫任国民政府主席。

"我在广州担任《政治周报》的主编,这是国民党宣传部出版的一个刊物[2]。后来它在抨击和揭露以戴季陶为首的国民党右派时,起了非常积极的作用。我还负责训练农民运动组织人员,为此目的,开办了一个讲习所[3],参加学习的来自21个不同省份的代表。包括从内蒙来的学生。我到广州不久,便任国民党宣传部长和中央候补委员。林祖涵那时是国民党农民部长,另一个共产党员谭平山是工人部长。

"我那时文章写得越来越多,在共产党内,我特别负责农民工作。根据我的研究和我组织湖南农民的经验。我写了两本小册子,一本是《中国社会各阶级的分析》,另一本是《赵恒惕的阶级基础和我们当前的任务》。陈独秀反对第一本小册子里表示的意见,这本小册子主张在共产党领导下实行激进的土地政策和大力组织农民。陈独秀拒绝在党中央机关报刊上发表它。后来它在广州《农民月刊》和在《中国青年》杂志上刊出了。第二篇论文在湖南出了小册子。大致在这个时候,我开始不同意陈独秀的右倾机会主义政策。我们逐渐地分道扬镳了,虽然我们之间的斗争直到1927年才达到高潮。

---

1. 1925年,国共干部共同组建了第一个上海总工会,总工会领导了5月30日的示威游行,要求取消治外法权,将上海国际租界返还中国。英租界巡捕向示威群众开枪,杀害多人,激起了抵制英货的运动。示威的主要组织者有刘少奇和陈云。
2. 汪精卫当时兼任国民党宣传部长。
3. 1925年,毛泽东接替彭湃担任农民运动讲习所所长,该讲习所由后者于1924年成立于广州。他的弟弟毛泽民就是他的一名学生,学生中有很大一部分来自湖南,很可能是由毛的湖南省党委录取的。他们的刊物是《中国农民》。

"Formerly I had not fully realized the degree of class struggle among the peasantry, but after the May 30th Incident [1925],[1] and during the great wave of political activity which followed it, the Hunanese peasantry became very militant. I left my home, where I had been resting, and began a rural organizational campaign. In a few months we had formed more than twenty peasant unions, and had aroused the wrath of the landlords, who demanded my arrest. Chao Heng-t'i sent troops after me, and I fled to Canton. I reached there just at the time the Whampoa students had defeated Yang Hsi-ming, the Yunnan militarist, and Lu Tsung-wai, the Kwangsi militarist, and an air of great optimism pervaded the city and the Kuomintang. Chiang Kai-shek had been made commander of the First Army and Wang Ching-wei chairman of the government, following the death of Sun Yat-sen in Peking.

"I became editor of the *Political Weekly*, a publication of the propaganda department of the Kuomintang [headed by Wang Ching-wei]. It later played a very active role in attacking and discrediting the right wing of the Kuomintang, led by Tai Chi-t'ao. I was also put in charge of training organizers for the peasant movement [the Peasant Movement Training Institute[2]], and established a course for this purpose which was attended by representatives from twenty-one different provinces, and included students from Inner Mongolia. Not long after my arrival in Canton I became chief of the agit-prop department of the Kuomintang, and candidate for the Central Committee. Lin Tsu-han was then chief of the Peasant Department of the Kuomintang, and T'an P'ing-shan, another Communist, was chief of the workers' department.

"I was writing more and more, and assuming special responsibilities in peasant work in the Communist Party. On the basis of my study and of my work in organizing the Hunan peasants, I wrote two pamphlets, one called *Analysis of Classes in Chinese Society* and the other called *The Class Basis of Chao Heng-t'i, and the Tasks Before Us*. Ch'en Tu-hsiu opposed the opinions expressed in the first one, which advocated a radical land policy and vigorous organization of the peasantry, under the Communist Party, and he refused its publication in the Communist central organs. It was later published in *Chung-kuo Nung-min* [*The Chinese Peasant*], of Canton, and in the magazine *Chung-kuo Ch'ing-nien* [*Chinese Youth*]. The second thesis was published as a pamphlet in Hunan. I began to disagree with Ch'en's Right-opportunist policy about this time, and we gradually drew further apart, although the struggle between us did not come to a climax until 1927.

---

1. Communist and Nationalist cadres in 1925 organized the first Shanghai Federation of Trade Unions, which led to the May 30 demonstration, with demands for an end to extraterritoriality and a return of the Shanghai International Settlement to Chinese sovereignty. British Settlement police fired on the demonstrators and killed several, which provoked a boycott of British goods. Leading organizers were Liu Shao-ch'i and Ch'en Yun.
2. In 1925 Mao was director of the Peasant Movement Training Institute, succeeding P'eng P'ai, who had set it up in Canton in 1924. His brother, Mao Tse-min, was one of his students, who included a large percentage of Hunanese, probably recruited by Mao's provincial Party committee. Their publication was *Chung-kuo Nung-min* (*The Chinese Peasant*).

"我继续在广州国民党内工作,大概一直到1926年3月蒋介石在那里发动他的第一次政变的时候。在国民党左右两派达成和解,国共团结得到重申以后,我于1926年春天前往上海。同年5月国民党第二次全国代表大会在蒋介石主持下召开。[1] 我在上海指导共产党农民部的工作,接着被派到湖南去担任农民运动的视察员。[2] 同时,在国共两党结成统一战线的情况下,1926年秋天开始了具有历史意义的北伐。

"在湖南我视察了长沙、醴陵、湘潭、衡山、湘乡5个县的农民组织和政治情况,并向中央委员会作了报告,主张在农民运动中采取新的路线。第二年初春,我到达武汉的时候,各省农民联席会议正在举行。我出席会议并讨论了我的文章中提出的建议——广泛地重新分配土地。出席会议的还有彭湃、方志敏等人和约克、沃伦两个俄国共产党员,会议通过了决议,采纳我的主张并提交共产党第五次代表大会考虑。但是,中央委员会把它否决了。

"党的第五次代表大会1927年5月在武汉召开的时候,党仍然在陈独秀支配之下。尽管蒋介石已经发动反革命政变,在上海、南京开始袭击共产党,陈独秀却依旧主张对武汉的国民党妥协退让。他不顾一切反对,执行小资产阶级右倾机会主义政策。对于当时党的政策,特别是对农民运动的政策,我非常不满意。我今天认为,如果当时比较彻底地把农民运动组织起来,把农民武装起来,开展反对地主的阶级斗争,那么,苏维埃就会在全国范围早一些并且有力得多地发展起来。

"但是,陈独秀强烈反对。[3] 他不懂得农民在革命中的地位,大大低估了当时农民可能发挥的作用。结果,在大革命危机前夜举行的第五次代表大会,没有能通过一

---

1. 毛泽东出席了国民党二大,并被重选为中央执行委员会候补委员。当时国民党中央执行委员会中共产党的人数仍旧为总人数的1/3左右。
2. 自成立之日起,国民党的农民部便一直由共产党人担任部长,毛泽东是担任过此职的5人中的最后一位。毛泽东还是此间成立的中国共产党农民部的首位部长(1926年5月至10月)。
3. 斯大林也强烈反对。中共五大最后几次会议毛泽东并未出席,会议根据斯大林的指示通过了一项决议,将没收土地一项仅限于成为"人民敌人"的大地主。

"I continued to work in the Kuomintang in Canton until about the time Chiang Kai-shek attempted his first *coup d'état* there in March, 1926. After the reconciliation of left- and right-wing Kuomintang and the reaffirmation of Kuomintang-Communist solidarity, I went to Shanghai, in the spring of 1926. The Second Congress of the Kuomintang was held in May of that year, under the leadership of Chiang Kai-shek.[1] In Shanghai I directed the Peasant Department of the Communist Party, and from there was sent to Hunan, as inspector of the peasant movement [for both the Kuomintang and the Communist Party].[2] Meanwhile, under the united front of the Kuomintang and the Communist Party, the historic Northern Expedition began in the autumn of 1926.

"In Hunan I inspected peasant organization and political conditions in five *hsien*—Changsha, Li Ling, Hsiang T'an, Hung Shan and Hsiang Hsiang—and made my report [*Report on an Investigation into the Peasant Movement in Hunan*] to the Central Committee, urging the adoption of a new line in the peasant movement. Early next spring, when I reached Wuhan, an interprovincial meeting of peasants was held, and I attended it and discussed the proposals of my thesis, which carried recommendations for a widespread redistribution of land. At this meeting were P'eng P'ai, Fang Chih-min, and two Russian Communists, Jolk [York?] and Volen, among others. A resolution was passed adopting my proposal for submission to the Fifth Congress of the Communist Party. The Central Committee, however, rejected it.

"When the Fifth Congress of the Party was convened in Wuhan in May, 1927, the Party was still under the domination of Ch'en Tu-hsiu. Although Chiang Kai-shek had already led the counterrevolution and begun his attacks on the Communist Party in Shanghai and Nanking, Ch'en was still for moderation and concessions to the Wuhan Kuomintang. Overriding all opposition, he followed a Right-opportunist pettybourgeois policy. I was very dissatisfied with the Party policy then, especially toward the peasant movement. I think today that if the peasant movement had been more thoroughly organized and armed for a class struggle against the landlords, the soviets would have had an earlier and far more powerful development throughout the whole country.

"But Ch'en Tu-hsiu violently disagreed.[3] He did not understand the role of the peasantry in the revolution and greatly underestimated its possibilities at this time. Consequently the Fifth Congress, held on the eve of the crisis of the Great Revolution, failed to pass

---

1. Mao attended the Second KMT Congress and was re-elected an alternate to the CEC. Communist membership in the Kuomintang CEC at that time was still about one-third of the total.
2. Since its inception, the Peasant Department of the Kuomintang had been headed by Communists, of whom Mao was the last of five. Mao was first chief of the CCP Peasant Department (May—October, 1926), formed at this time.
3. So did Stalin. Mao was not present during the terminal sessions of the Fifth Congress, when a resolution was passed to limit land confiscation only to great landlords who were also "enemies of the people," in line with Stalin's directives.

个适当的土地政纲。我要求迅速加强农民斗争的主张，甚至没有加以讨论。因为中央委员会也在陈独秀支配之下，拒绝把我的意见提交大会考虑。大会给地主下了个定义，说'有500亩[1]以上土地的农民'为地主，就没有再讨论土地问题。以这个定义为基础来开展阶级斗争，是完全不够和不切实际的，它根本没有考虑到中国农村经济的特殊性。然而，大会以后，还是组织了全国农民协会，我是第一任会长。

"到1927年春天，尽管共产党对农民运动采取冷淡的态度，而国民党也肯定感到惊慌，湖北、江西、福建，特别是湖南的农民运动已经有了一种惊人的战斗精神。高级官员和军事将领开始要求镇压农运，他们把农会称作'痞子会'，认为农会的行动和要求都过火了。陈独秀把我调出了湖南，认为那里发生的一些情况是我造成的，激烈地反对我的意见。[2]

"4月间，反革命运动已经在南京和上海开始，在蒋介石指使下对有组织的工人的大屠杀已经发生。在广州也采取了同样的措施。5月21日，湖南发生了许克祥的叛乱，许多农民和工人被反动派杀害。不久以后，在武汉的国民党'左'派，取消了它和共产党的协议，把共产党员从国民党和政府中'开除'出去，而这个政府本身很快也就不存在了。

"许多共产党领导人这时得到党的命令，要他们离开中国，到俄国去或者到上海和其他安全的地方去。我奉命前往四川，但我说服陈独秀改派我到湖南去担任省委书记，10天以后，他又命令我立刻回去，指责我组织暴动反对当时在武汉当权的唐生智。这时，党内情况处于混乱状态。几乎人人反对陈独秀的领导和他的机会主义路线。不久之后，武汉的国共合作瓦解，陈独秀也就垮台了。"

---

1. 约合33公顷，接近于每个农民所拥有的可耕地的100倍。
2. 毛泽东支持（而且很可能提出了）湖南农民协会要求没收所有大地主的土地的决议。

an adequate land program. My opinions, which called for rapid intensification of the agrarian struggle, were not even discussed, for the Central Committee, also dominated by Ch'en Tu-hsiu, refused to bring them up for consideration. The Congress dismissed the land problem by defining a landlord as 'a peasant who owns over 500 *mou* of land'[1]— a wholly inadequate and unpractical basis on which to develop the class struggle, and quite without consideration of the special character of land economy in China. Following the Congress, however, an All-China Peasants' Union was organized and I became first president of it.

"By the spring of 1927 the peasant movement in Hupeh, Kiangsi, and Fukien, and especially in Hunan, had developed a startling militancy, despite the lukewarm attitude of the Communist Party to it, and the definite alarm of the Kuomintang. High officials and army commanders began to demand its suppression, describing the Peasants' Union as a 'vagabond union,' and its actions and demands as excessive. Ch'en Tu-hsiu had withdrawn me from Hunan, holding me responsible for certain happenings there, and violently opposing my ideas.[2]

"In April, the counterrevolutionary movement had begun in Nanking and Shanghai, and a general massacre of organized workers had taken place under Chiang Kai-shek. The same measures were carried out in Canton. On May 21, the Hsu K'o-hsiang Uprising occurred in Hunan. Scores of peasants and workers were killed by the reactionaries. Shortly afterwards the Left Kuomintang at Wuhan annulled its agreement with the Communists and 'expelled' them from the Kuomintang and from a government which quickly ceased to exist.

"Many Communist leaders were now ordered by the Party to leave the country, go to Russia or Shanghai or places of safety. I was ordered to go to Szechuan. I persuaded Ch'en Tu-hsiu to send me to Hunan instead, as secretary of the Provincial Committee, but after ten days he ordered me to return at once, accusing me of organizing an uprising against T'ang Sheng-chih, then in command at Wuhan. The affairs of the Party were now in a chaotic state. Nearly everyone was opposed to Ch'en Tu-hsiu's leadership and his opportunist line. The collapse of the entente at Wuhan soon afterwards brought about his downfall."

---

1. About thirty-three hectares, or nearly a hundred times the available cultivable land per farmer.
2. Mao supported (and probably initiated) the Hunan Peasants' Union resolutions demanding confiscation of all large land holdings.

五、　　苏维埃运动

关于1927年春天发生的引起很多争论的事件，我和毛泽东曾有一次谈话，我觉得完全有必要在这里一提。这并不是他向我口述的自传的一部分，但是，作为他个人对一个中国共产党人一生经历中的转折点的看法，在这里提一下，还是有重要意义的。

我问毛泽东，在他看来，对于1927年共产党的失败，武汉联合政府的失败，南京独裁政权的整个胜利，谁应负最大的责任。毛泽东认为陈独秀应负最大的责任，陈独秀的"动摇的机会主义，在继续妥协显然意味着灾难的时刻，使党失去了决定性的领导作用和自己的直接路线"。

他认为仅次于陈独秀，对于失败应负最大责任的是俄国首席政治顾问鲍罗廷。毛泽东解释说，鲍罗廷完全改变了他的立场，他在1926年是赞成大规模重新分配土地的，可是到了1927年又竭力反对，对于自己的摇摆没有提出任何合乎逻辑的根据。"鲍罗廷站在陈独秀右边一点点，"毛泽东说，"他随时准备尽力去讨好资产阶级，甚至于准备解除工人的武装，最后他也下令这样做了。"共产国际的印度代表罗易，"站在陈独秀和鲍罗廷两人左边一点点，可是他只是站着而已"。据毛泽东说，他"能说，而且说得太多了，却不提出任何实现的方法"。毛泽东认为，客观地来说，罗易是个蠢货，鲍罗廷是个冒失鬼，陈独秀是个不自觉的叛徒。

"陈独秀实在害怕工人，特别害怕武装起来的农民。武装起义的现实终于摆在他面前的时候，他完全失掉了他的理智。他不能再看清当时的形势。他的小资产阶级的本性使他陷于惊惶和失败。"

毛泽东说，在那个时候，陈独秀是中国党的彻头彻尾的独裁者，他甚至不同中

5   THE SOVIET MOVEMENT

A conversation I had with Mao Tse-tung concerning the much-disputed events of the spring of 1927 seemed to me of sufficient interest to mention here. It was not part of his autobiography, as he told it to me, but it was important to note as a personal reflection on what was a turning-point experience in the life of every Chinese Communist.

I asked Mao whom he considered most responsible for the failure of the Communist Party in 1927, the defeat of the Wuhan coalition government, and the whole triumph of the Nanking dictatorship. Mao placed the greatest blame on Ch'en Tu-hsiu, whose "wavering opportunism deprived the Party of decisive leadership and a direct line of its own at a moment when further compromise clearly meant catastrophe."

After Ch'en, the man he held responsible for the defeat was Mikhail Markovich Borodin, chief Russian political adviser, who was answerable directly to the Soviet Politburo. Mao explained that Borodin had completely reversed his position, favoring a radical land redistribution in 1926, but strongly opposing it in 1927, without any logical support for his vacillations. "Borodin stood just a little to the right of Ch'en Tu-hsiu," Mao said, "and was ready to do everything to please the bourgeoisie, even to the disarming of the workers, which he finally ordered." M. N. Roy, the Indian delegate to the Comintern, "stood a little to the left of both Ch'en and Borodin, but he only stood." He "could talk," according to Mao, "and he talked too much, without offering any method of realization." Mao thought that, objectively, Roy had been a fool, Borodin a blunderer, and Ch'en an unconscious traitor.

"Ch'en was really frightened of the workers and especially of the armed peasants. Confronted at last with the reality of armed insurrection, he completely lost his senses. He could no longer see clearly what was happening, and his petty-bourgeois instincts betrayed him into panic and defeat."

Mao asserted that Ch'en was at that time complete dictator of the Chinese Party, and took

央委员会商量就作出重大的决定。"他不把共产国际的命令给党的其他领导人看，"据毛泽东说，"甚至于不和我们讨论这些命令。"但是，到头来还是罗易促成了同国民党的分裂。共产国际发给鲍罗廷一个电报，指示党开始没收地主的土地。罗易得到了一个抄件，马上拿给汪精卫看。汪精卫那时是国民党左派武汉政府的主席。这种轻率的做法的结果[1]是大家都知道的。武汉政权把共产党人从国民党中开除出去，它自己的力量就垮了，不久就被蒋介石所摧毁。

看来共产国际在1927年提供给中国共产党的不是什么"意见"，而是干脆发的命令，中国共产党显然甚至无权不接受。当然，武汉的大失败，后来成了俄国国内在世界革命性质问题上的斗争的焦点。在这个阶段以后，俄国反对派被摧毁，托洛茨基的"不断革命"理论被弄臭，苏联开始认真"在一国建设社会主义"——它由此出发，今天成了世界和平砥柱的地位。

即使共产党在和国民党分裂以前采取了比较积极的政策，从工人和农民中创建了党的军队，毛泽东也并不认为反革命在1927年会被打败，"但是，苏维埃就可能在南方大规模展开，就可能有一个后来无论如何不会被消灭的根据地。"

毛泽东的自述现在已经谈到苏维埃的开端。苏维埃是从革命的废墟上兴起的，它要赤手空拳从失败中斗争出一个胜利的结果来。他接着说：

"1927年8月1日，贺龙、叶挺率领的第二十军，同朱德合作，领导了具有历史意义的南昌起义，红军的前身组织起来了。1星期以后，即8月7日，党中央委员会举行了非常会议，撤销了陈独秀的总书记职务。自从1924年广州第三次代表大会以来，我就是党的政治局委员，对于这个决定，我是积极出了力的。出席会议的其他10位委员中，有蔡和森、彭公达[2]和瞿秋白[3]。党采取了新的路线，同国民党合作的一切希望暂时是放弃了，因为国民党已经无可救药地成了帝国主义的工具，不能完成民主革命的任务了。长期的公开夺取政权的斗争现在开始了。

"我被派到长沙去组织后来被称为'秋收起义'的运动。我在那里的纲领，要求实现下面五点：（一）省的党组织同国民党完全脱离；（二）组织工农革命军；

---

1. 从国民党左派观点来看的这个事件和这个时期的一个有趣的叙述，见唐良礼（译音）著《中国革命内幕史》（1930年伦敦）。
2. 应为彭湃。张国焘也参加了此次会议。
3. 陈独秀因"右倾"辞去总书记职务后，瞿秋白当选总书记。

vital decisions without even consulting the Central Committee. "He did not show other Party leaders the orders of the Comintern," according to Mao, "or even discuss them with us." But in the end it was Roy who forced the break with the Kuomintang. The Comintern sent a message to Borodin ordering the Party to begin a limited confiscation of the landlords' land. Roy got hold of a copy of it and promptly showed it to Wang Ching-wei, then chairman of the Left Kuomintang Government at Wuhan. The result of this caprice is well known. The Communists were expelled from the Kuomintang by the Wuhan regime, which soon afterward collapsed, having lost the support of regional warlords, who now sought safety in compromises with Chiang Kai-shek. Borodin and other Comintern agents fled to Russia, and arrived there in time to see the Opposition crushed and Trotsky's "permanent revolution" discredited, while Stalin set out in earnest to "build socialism [Stalinism?] in one country."

Mao did not think that the counterrevolution would have been defeated in 1927 even if the Communist Party had carried out a more aggressive policy of land confiscation and created Communist armies from among the workers and peasants before the split with the Kuomintang. "But the soviets could have got an immense start in the South, and a base in which, afterwards, they would never have been destroyed."

In his narrative of himself Mao had now reached the beginning of the soviets, which arose from the wreckage of the revolution and struggled to build a victory out of defeat. He continued:

"On August 1, 1927, the Twentieth Army, under Ho Lung and Yeh T'ing, and in cooperation with Chu Teh, led the historic Nanchang Uprising, and the beginning of what was to become the Red Army was organized. A week later, on August 7, an extraordinary meeting [Emergency Conference] of the Central Committee of the Party deposed Ch'en Tu-hsiu as secretary. I had been a member of the political bureau of the Party since the Third Conference at Canton in 1924, and was active in this decision, and among the ten other members present at the meeting were: Ts'ai Ho-sen, P'eng P'ai, Chang Kuo t'ao and Ch'u Ch'iu-pai.[1] A new line was adopted by the Party, and all hope of cooperation with the Kuomintang was given up for the present, as it had already become hopelessly the tool of imperialism and could not carry out the responsibilities of a democratic revolution. The long, open struggle for power now began.

"I was sent to Changsha to organize the movement which later became known as the Autumn Harvest Uprising. My program there called for the realization of five points: (1) complete severance of the provincial Party from the Kuomintang, (2) organization of a

---

1. Ch'u Ch'iu-pai was here chosen general secretary of the Politburo, replacing Ch'en Tu-hsiu, who was accused of "rightism" and dropped from the Politburo.

（三）除了大地主以外也没收中、小地主的财产；（四）在湖南建立独立于国民党的共产党政权；（五）组织苏维埃。第五点当时受到共产国际的反对，后来它才把这一点作为一个口号提出来。

"9月间，我们通过湖南的农会已经成功地组织了一次广泛的起义，工农军队的第一批部队建立起来了。新战士有3个主要来源：农民本身，汉阳矿工，起义的国民党部队。这个早期的革命军事力量称为'工农第一军第一师'。第一团由汉阳矿工组成。[1] 第二团是由平江、浏阳、醴陵和湖南其他两县的部分农民赤卫队组成。第三团来自反叛了汪精卫的武汉警卫团的一部分。这支军队经湖南省委批准建立，但湖南省委和我军的总纲领，却为党中央委员会所反对，不过后者似乎只是采取观望的政策，而不是积极反对的政策。

"当我正在组织军队、奔走于汉阳矿工和农民赤卫队之间的时候，我被一些同国民党勾结的民团抓到了。那时候，国民党的恐怖达到顶点，好几百共产党嫌疑分子被枪杀。那些民团奉命把我押到民团总部去处死。但是我从一个同志那里借了几十块钱，打算贿赂押送的人释放我。普通的士兵都是雇佣兵，我遭到枪决，于他们并没有特别的好处，他们同意释放我，可是负责的队长不允许。于是我决定逃跑。但是直到离民团总部大约200码的地方，我才得到了机会。我在那地方挣脱出来，跑到田野里去。

"我跑到一个高地，下面是一个水塘，周围长了很高的草，我在那里躲到太阳落山。士兵们追捕我，还强迫一些农民帮助他们搜寻。有好多次他们走得很近，有一两次我几乎可以碰到他们。虽然有五六次我已经放弃希望，觉得我一定会再被抓到，可是我还是没有被发现。最后，天黑了，他们放弃了搜寻。我马上翻山越岭，连夜

---

1. 矿工已由毛泽东、刘少奇和陈云组织起来。在组建工农军、战士苏维埃和人民委员会方面，毛泽东脱离中央委员会独自行动，受到了批评。在他建立起第一批战士苏维埃时，中央委员会的路线已再次发生变化。1927年11月，中央委员会以"右倾"为由将毛泽东从政治局除名。当年冬天他在井冈山所做的全部工作都成了"非法"，不过他有数个月都不清楚这一点。1928年6月，毛泽东被复职。

peasant-worker revolutionary army, (3) confiscation of the property of small and middle, as well as great, landlords, (4) setting up the power of the Communist Party in Hunan, independent of the Kuomintang, and (5) organization of soviets. The fifth point at that time was opposed by the Comintern, and not till later did it advance it as a slogan.

"In September we had already succeeded in organizing a widespread uprising, through the peasant unions of Hunan, and the first units of a peasant-worker army were formed. Recruits were drawn from three principal sources—the peasantry itself, the Hanyang miners, and the insurrectionist troops of the Kuomintang. This early military force of the revolution was called the 'First Division of the First Peasants' and Workers' Army.' The first regiment was formed from the Hanyang miners.[1] A second was created among the peasant guards in P'ing Kiang, Liu Yang, Li Ling and two other *hsien* of Hunan, and a third from part of the garrison forces of Wuhan, which had revolted against Wang Ching-wei. This army was organized with the sanction of the Hunan Provincial Committee, but the general program of the Hunan Committee and of our army was opposed by the Central Committee of the Party, which seemed, however, to have adopted a policy of wait-and-see rather than of active opposition.

"While I was organizing the army and traveling between the Hanyang miners and the peasant guards, I was captured by some *min-t'uan*, working with the Kuomintang. The Kuomintang terror was then at its height and hundreds of suspected Reds were being shot. I was ordered to be taken to the *min-t'uan* headquarters, where I was to be killed. Borrowing several tens of dollars from a comrade, however, I attempted to bribe the escort to free me. The ordinary soldiers were mercenaries, with no special interest in seeing me killed, and they agreed to release me, but the subaltern in charge refused to permit it. I therefore decided to attempt to escape, but had no opportunity to do so until I was within about two hundred yards of the *min-t'uan* headquarters. At that point I broke loose and ran into the fields.

"I reached a high place, above a pond, with some tall grass surrounding it, and there I hid until sunset. The soldiers pursued me, and forced some peasants to help them search. Many times they came very near, once or twice so close that I could almost have touched them, but somehow I escaped discovery, although half a dozen times I gave up hope, feeling certain I would be recaptured. At last, when it was dusk, they abandoned the search. At once I set off across the mountains, traveling all night. I had no shoes and my

---

1. Miners who had been organized by Mao, Liu Shao-ch'i and Ch'en Yun. In forming a peasants' and workers' army, and soldiers' soviets and people's councils, Mao acted independently of the Central Committee and was reprimanded. By the time he had set up his first soldiers' soviets the CMT line had changed again. In November of 1927 the Central Committee expelled Mao from the Politburo for "rightism." All the basic work he did in Chingkangshan that winter was "illegal," although Mao was not aware of it for some months. He was reinstated in June, 1928.

赶路。我没有鞋,我的脚损伤得很厉害。路上我遇到一个农民,他同我交了朋友,给我地方住,又领我到了下一乡。我身边有7块钱,买了一双鞋、一把伞和一些吃的。当我最后安全地走到农民赤卫队那里的时候,我的口袋里只剩下两个铜板了。

"新师成立以后,我担任党的前敌委员会书记,原武汉警卫团的一个指挥员余洒度,任第一军军长。余多少是因部下的态度而被迫就任的;不久他就逃到国民党那里去了。现在他在南京给蒋介石工作。

"这支领导农民起义的小小队伍,穿过湖南向南转移。它得突破成千上万的国民党部队,进行多次战斗,经受多次挫折。当时部队的纪律差,政治训练水平低,指战员中有许多动摇分子。开小差的很多。余洒度逃跑以后,部队到达宁都时进行了改编。陈浩被任命为剩下来大约一团兵力的部队的指挥员;后来他也'叛变'了。但是,在这个最早的部队中,有许多人始终忠心耿耿,直到今天还在红军中,例如现任一军团政委的罗荣桓,现任军长的杨立三。这支小队伍最后上井冈山[1]的时候,人数总共只有1,000左右。

"由于秋收起义的纲领没有得到中央委员会批准,又由于第一军遭受严重损失,而且从城市观点来看,这个运动好像是注定要失败的,因此中央委员会这时明确地批评我。[2]我被免去政治局和党的前委的职务。湖南省委也攻击我们,说我们是'枪杆子运动'。尽管这样,我们仍然在井冈山把军队团结起来了,深信我们执行的是正确的路线。后来的事实充分地证明了这一点。部队补充了新兵,这个师人员又充实了,我担任了师长。

"从1927年冬天到1928年秋天,第一师守住了井冈山的根据地。1927年11月第一个苏维埃在湖南边界的茶陵成立了,第一个苏维埃政府选举出来了。[3]主席是杜修经。在这个苏维埃以及后来的苏维埃中,我们推行了一个民主的纲领,采取温和的政策,建筑在缓慢而不断的发展这一基础上。这样一来,井冈山就遭到党内盲动

---

1. 井冈山在湘赣边界,是个不可攻破的山寨,原来为土匪所占。史沫特莱所著《中国的红军在前进》(1933年纽约)一书对共产党攻占此山及后来在那里的情况有所记述。
2. 毛泽东3次受到中央委员会的批评,3次被除名。
3. 同月,彭湃在海陆丰也成立了一个苏维埃,但很快失败。

feet were badly bruised. On the road I met a peasant who befriended me, gave me shelter and later guided me to the next district. I had seven dollars with me, and used this to buy some shoes, an umbrella, and food. When at last I reached the peasant guards safely, I had only two coppers in my pocket.

"With the establishment of the new division, I became chairman of its Party Front Committee, and Yu Sha-t'ou, a commander of the garrison troops at Wuhan, became commander of the First Army. Yu, however, had been more or less forced to take the position by the attitude of his men; soon afterwards he deserted and joined the Kuomintang. He is now working for Chiang Kai-shek at Nanking.

"The little army, leading the peasant uprising, moved southward through Hunan. It had to break its way through thousands of Kuomintang troops and fought many battles, with many reverses. Discipline was poor, political training was at a low level, and many wavering elements were among the men and officers. There were many desertions. After Yu Sha-t'ou fled, the army was reorganized when it reached Ningtu. Ch'en Hao was made commander of the remaining troops, about one regiment; he, too, later on betrayed. But many in that first group remained loyal to the end, and are today still in the Red Army— men such as Lo Jung-huan, political commissar of the First Army Corps, and Yang Li-san, now an army commander. When the little band finally climbed up Chingkangshan they numbered in all only about one thousand.

"Because the program of the Autumn Harvest Uprising had not been sanctioned by the Central Committee, because also the First Army had suffered some severe losses, and from the angle of the cities the movement appeared doomed to failure, the Central Committee now definitely repudiated me.[1] I was dismissed from the Politburo, and also from the Party [General] Front Committee. The Hunan Provincial Committee also attacked us, calling us 'the rifle movement.' We nevertheless held our army together at Chingkangshan, feeling certain that we were following the correct line, and subsequent events were to vindicate us fully. New recruits were added and the division filled out again. I became its commander.

"From the winter of 1927 to the autumn of 1928, the First Division held its base at Chingkangshan. In November, 1927, the first soviet was set up in Tsalin [Ch'aling] on the Hunan border, and the first soviet government was elected.[2] Its chairman was Tu Chung-pin. In this soviet, and subsequently, we promoted a democratic program, with a moderate policy, based on slow but regular development. This earned Chingkangshan the recriminations of putschists in the Party, who were demanding a terrorist policy of

---

1. Mao was reprimanded three times by the Central Committee and three times expelled by it.
2. In the same month a "soviet" was established by P'eng P'ai in Hailufeng, but it was quickly destroyed.

主义者的斥责，他们要求对地主实行抢、烧、杀的恐怖政策，为了使他们丧胆。第一军前敌委员会拒绝采用这种策略，所以被头脑发热的人污蔑为'改良主义者'。我因为没有实行更加'激进的'政策，遭到他们猛烈的攻击。

"1927年冬天，两个以前在井冈山附近当土匪头子的王佐和袁文才参加了红军。这使红军的实力增加到将近3团人。王、袁都被任命为团长，我是军长。这两个人虽然过去当过土匪，可是率领队伍投身于国民革命，现在愿意向反动派作战。我在井冈山期间，他们是忠实的共产党人，是执行党的命令的。

"1928年5月，朱德来到井冈山，我们的队伍会了师。我们一同制订了一个计划[1]，要建立一个包括6个县的苏区，逐步地稳定并巩固湘赣粤边区的共产党政权，并以此为根据地，向更广大的地区发展。这个战略同党的建议是相反的，后者一味作迅速发展的空想。在军队内部，朱德和我得同两个倾向作斗争：第一个倾向是要立即进攻长沙，我们认为这是冒险主义；第二个倾向是要撤退到广东边界以南去，我们认为这是'退却主义'。根据我们当时的看法，我们的主要任务有二：分地和建立苏维埃。我们要武装群众来加速这个过程。我们的政策主张自由贸易，优待被俘敌军，以及总的来说主张民主的温和主义。

"1928年秋天，在井冈山召开了一个代表会议[2]，出席的有井冈山以北的苏区的代表。在苏区的党员中，对于上述各点仍然有一些意见分歧。在这次会议上，各种不同的意见充分地发表出来了。少数人认为在上述政策的基础上我们的前途大受限制，但是多数人相信这个政策，因此当宣告苏维埃运动将获得胜利的决议案提交表决的时候很容易就通过了。但是，党中央委员会还没有批准这个运动。直到1928年

---

1. 在第一次茅坪会议上，毛泽东和朱德与林彪、陈毅、萧克、何长工、谭震林、张文彬、夏曦及其他人联合起来，共同抵制来自由共产国际撑腰的政治局领导人李立三以及后来称为"二十八布尔什维克"的莫斯科留学生的所有压力。参见第六章。
2. 即第二次茅坪会议。

raiding, and burning and killing of landlords, in order to destroy their morale. The First Army Front Committee refused to adopt such tactics, and were therefore branded by the hotheads as 'reformists.' I was bitterly attacked by them for not carrying out a more 'radical' policy.

"Two former bandit leaders near Chingkangshan, named Wang Tso and Yuan Wen-t'sai, joined the Red Army in the winter of 1927. This increased the strength to about three regiments. Wang and Yuan were both made regimental commanders and I was army commander. These two men, although former bandits, had thrown in their forces with the Nationalist Revolution, and were now ready to fight against the reaction. While I remained on Chingkangshan they were faithful Communists, and carried out the orders of the Party. Later on, when they were left alone at Chingkangshan, they returned to their bandit habits. Subsequently they were killed by the peasants, by then organized and sovietized and able to defend themselves.

"In May of 1928, Chu Teh arrived at Chingkangshan and our forces were combined. Together we drew up a plan [at the first Maoping Conference[1]] to establish a six-*hsien* soviet area, to stabilize and consolidate gradually the Communist power in the Hunan-Kiangsi-Kwangtung border districts, and, with that as a base, to expand over greater areas. This strategy was in opposition to recommendations of the Party, which had grandiose ideas of rapid expansion. In the army itself Chu Teh and I had to fight against two tendencies: first, a desire to advance on Changsha [the capital of Hunan] at once, which we considered adventurism; second, a desire to withdraw to the south of the Kwangtung border, which we regarded as 'retreatism' [capitulationism]. Our main tasks, as we saw them then, were two: to divide the land, and to establish soviets. We wanted to arm the masses to hasten those processes. Our policy called for free trade [with the White areas], generous treatment of captured enemy troops, and, in general, democratic moderation.

"A representative meeting [the second Maoping Conference] was called at Chingkangshan in the autumn of 1928, and was attended by delegates from soviet districts north of Chingkangshan. Some division of opinion still existed among Party men in the soviet districts concerning the points mentioned above, and at this meeting differences were thoroughly aired. A minority argued that our future on this basis was narrowly limited, but the majority had faith in the policy, and when a resolution was proposed declaring that the soviet movement would be victorious, it was easily passed. The Party Central Committee, however, had not yet given the movement its sanction. This was not received

---

1. Here Mao Tse-tung and Chu Teh formed an alliance with Lin Piao, Ch'en Yi, Hsiao K'e, Ho Chang-kung, T'an Chen-lin, Chang Wen-ping, Hsia Hsi, and others, which held together against all pressure from Comintern-backed Politburo leader Li Li-san and, later on, the Moscow-educated returned students called the "Twenty-eight Bolsheviks." See Chapter 6.

冬天，中国共产党第六次代表大会在莫斯科举行的消息传到井冈山的时候，才得到批准。

"对于那次代表大会所采取的新路线，朱德和我是完全同意的。从那时起，党的领导人和农村地区苏维埃运动的领导人之间的分歧消除了，党恢复了一致。

"六大的决议总结了1925年到1927年的革命和南昌起义、广州起义、秋收起义的经验。它的结论是赞成把重点放在土地运动上。大约在这时候，红军开始在中国其他地方出现。1927年冬天，湖北西部和东部发生了暴动，为建立新苏区打下了基础。在西面的贺龙和在东面的徐海东，开始建立自己的工农军队。徐海东活动的区域成了鄂豫皖苏区的核心，后来徐向前和张国焘去了那里。1927年冬天，方志敏和邵式平在邻接福建的江西东北部边界，也开展了一个运动，后来发展成为强大的苏维埃根据地。广州起义失败以后，彭湃率领一部分忠心耿耿的部队到海陆丰去，那里成立了一个苏维埃，由于它执行盲动主义的政策，很快就被摧毁。它的一部分军队在古大存[1]指挥下从那个地区突围，同朱德和我取得了联系，后来成为红军第十一军的核心。

"1928年春天，由李文林、李韶九领导的游击队，开始在江西的兴国、乐安活跃起来。这个运动以吉安一带为根据地，这些游击队后来成为第三军的核心，而这个地区本身则成为中央苏维埃政府的根据地。在福建西部，张鼎丞[2]、邓子恢和后来变成社会民主党人的傅柏翠，建立了苏维埃。

"在井冈山'反冒险主义斗争'时期，第一军打败了白军两次攻占井冈山的企图。对于我们正在建立的那种机动部队来说，井冈山证明是绝好的根据地。它有很好的天然屏障，种的农作物足够供给一支小小的军队。它方圆有500里，纵横约80里。本地人有另外的名称，叫它大小五井；真正的井冈山是附近的一座早已荒废的山。五井这个名称是从山麓五口大井得来的，即大、小、上、下、中五井，山上的五个村就是以这五口井相称。

---

1. 参见第九篇第一章。
2. 张鼎丞招的新兵中有一位便是杨成武，1936年作者在陕北曾遇到过他。

till the winter of 1928, when the report of proceedings at the Sixth Congress of the Chinese Communist Party, held in Moscow, reached Chingkangshan.

"With the new line adopted at that Congress, Chu Teh and I were in complete agreement. From that time on, the differences between the leaders of the Party and the leaders of the soviet movement in the agrarian districts disappeared. Party harmony was re-established.

"Resolutions of the Sixth Congress summarized the experience of the 1925—1927 revolution and the Nanchang, Canton, and Autumn Harvest uprisings. It concluded with approval of the emphasis on the agrarian movement. About this time Red armies began to appear elsewhere in China. Uprisings had occurred in western and eastern Hupeh, in the winter of 1927, and these furnished the basis for new soviet districts. Ho Lung in the west and Hsu Hai-tung in the east began to form their own worker-peasant armies. The latter's area of operations became the nucleus of the Oyuwan Soviet, to which later on went Hsu Hsiang-ch'ien and Chang Kuo-t'ao. Fang Chih-min and Hsiao Shih-p'ing had also begun a movement along the northeastern frontier of Kiangsi, adjacent to Fukien, in the winter of 1927, and out of this later developed a powerful soviet base. After the failure of the Canton Uprising, P'eng P'ai had led part of the loyal troops to Hailufeng, and there formed a soviet, which, following a policy of putschism, was soon destroyed. Part of the army, however, emerged from the district under the command of Ku Ta-chen,[1] and made connections with Chu Teh and myself, later on becoming the nucleus of the Eleventh Red Army.

"In the spring of 1928, partisans became active in Hsingkuo and Tungku in Kiangsi, led by Li Wen-lung and Li Shao-tsu. This movement had its base around Kian, and these partisans later became the core of the Third Army, while the district itself became the base of the Central Soviet Government. In western Fukien soviets were established by Chang Ting-ch'eng,[2] Teng Tzu-hui, and Hu P'ei-teh, who afterwards became a Social Democrat.

"During the 'struggle v. adventurism' period at Chingkangshan, the First Army had defeated two attempts by White troops to retake the mountain. Chingkangshan proved to be an excellent base for a mobile army such as we were building. It had good natural defenses, and grew enough crops to supply a small army. It had a circuit of 500 *li* and was about 80 *li* in diameter. Locally it was known otherwise, as Ta Hsiao Wu Chin [Big-Little Five Wells], the real Chingkangshan being a nearby mountain, long deserted, and got its name from five main wells on its sides—*ta, hsiao, shang, hsia,* and *chung,* or big, small, upper, lower, and middle wells. The five villages on the mountain were named after these wells.

---

1. See Part Nine, Chapter 1.
2. One of Chang's recruits was Yang Ch'eng-wu, whom the author met in north Shensi in 1936.

"我们的队伍在井冈山会师以后,进行了改编,著名的红军第四军创立了,朱德任军长,我任党代表。1928年冬天,何键的部队发生起义和哗变以后,井冈山来了更多的军队,这样就产生了红军第五军。彭德怀任军长。除了彭德怀以外,还有长征途中在贵州遵义牺牲的邓萍;1931年在江西牺牲的黄公略;和滕代远。

　　"来了这么多军队,山上的条件变得很差了。部队没有冬衣,粮食奇缺。我们有好几个月几乎只靠吃南瓜过活,战士们喊出他们自己的口号:'打倒资本主义吃南瓜!'——在他们看来资本主义就是地主和地主的南瓜。朱德留下彭德怀守井冈山,自己突破了白军的封锁,1929年1月,我们的第一次守山就此结束。

　　"第四军这时迅速而顺利地展开了打通江西南部的战斗。我们在乐安建立了苏维埃,和当地的红军部队会合。我们接着分兵挺进永定、上杭和龙岩,在这几县成立了苏维埃。红军来到以前就存在于这些地区的战斗的群众运动,保证了我们的胜利,帮助我们能够在稳定的基础上,非常迅速地巩固苏维埃政权。通过群众性的土地运动和游击队活动,红军的影响扩大到了其他几个县,但是共产党人到后来才在那里充分掌握权力。

　　"红军在物质上和政治上的情况都有了改进,但是还存在着许多不良倾向。例如'游击主义'就是一种弱点,反映在缺乏纪律,极端民主化和组织涣散上面。另一种需要克服的倾向,是'流寇思想'——不愿意安心做建立政权的艰苦工作,喜欢流动,变换环境,喜欢新奇的经历和事件。还有军阀主义残余,个别指挥员虐待甚至殴打战士,凭个人好恶,对人有所歧视或者偏爱。

　　"1929年12月在闽西古田召开红四军第九次党代表大会以后,许多这样的弱点都被克服了。大会讨论了改进的办法,消除了许多的误解,通过了新的计划,这就为在红军中提高思想领导奠定了基础。在这以前,上面所说那些倾向是十分严重的,而且被党内和军事领导内的一个托洛茨基派别利用了来削弱运动的力量。这时开展

"After the forces of our army combined at Chingkangshan there was a reorganization, the famous Fourth Red Army was created, and Chu Teh was made commander, while I became political commissar. More troops arrived at Chingkangshan after uprisings and mutinies in Ho Chien's army, in the winter of 1928, and out of these emerged the Fifth Red Army, commanded by P'eng Teh-huai. In addition to P'eng there were Teng P'ing, killed at Tsunyi, Kweichow, during the Long March, Huang Kuo-nu, killed in Kiangsi in 1931, and T'ien Teh-yuan.

"Conditions on the mountain, with the arrival of so many troops, were becoming very bad. The troops had no winter uniforms, and food was extremely scarce. For months we lived practically on squash. The soldiers shouted a slogan of their own: 'Down with capitalism, and eat squash!'—for to them capitalism meant landlords and the landlords' squash. Leaving P'eng Teh-huai at Chingkangshan, Chu Teh broke through the blockade established by the White troops, and in January, 1929, our first sojourn on the embattled mountain ended.

"The Fourth Army now began a campaign through the south of Kiangsi which rapidly developed successfully. We established a soviet in Tungku, and there met and united with local Red troops. Dividing forces, we continued into Yungting, Shangheng, and Lung Yen, and established soviets in all those counties. The existence of militant mass movements prior to the arrival of the Red Army assured our success, and helped to consolidate soviet power on a stable basis very quickly. The influence of the Red Army now extended, through the agrarian mass movement and partisans, to several other *hsien*, but the Communists did not fully take power there until later on.

"Conditions in the Red Army began to improve, both materially and politically, but there were still many bad tendencies. 'Partisanism,' for example, was a weakness reflected in lack of discipline, exaggerated ideas of democracy, and looseness of organization. Another tendency that had to be fought was 'vagabondage'—a disinclination to settle down to the serious tasks of government, a love of movement, change, new experience and incident. There were also remnants of militarism, with some of the commanders maltreating or even beating the men, and discriminating against those they disliked personally, while showing favoritism to others.

"Many of the weaknesses were overcome after the convening of the Ninth Party Conference of the Fourth Red Army, held in west Fukien [at Ku-t'ien] in December, 1929. Ideas for improvements were discussed, many misunderstandings leveled out, and new plans were adopted, which laid the foundations for a high type of ideological leadership in the Red Army. Prior to this the tendencies already described were very serious, and were utilized by a Trotskyist faction in the Party and military leadership to undermine the strength of the movement. A vigorous struggle was now begun against them, and

了猛烈的斗争来反对他们，有些人被撤销了党内职务和军队指挥职务。刘恩康——一个军长，就是其中的一个典型。据揭发，他们阴谋在对敌作战时使红军陷入困境而消灭红军。几次作战失败后，他们的计划就暴露得非常明显了。他们恶毒地攻击我们的纲领，反对我们的一切主张。经验已经证明他们的错误，他们被撤去领导职务，在福建会议以后，他们就没有影响了。

"这次会议为在江西建立苏维埃政权铺平了道路。第二年取得了一些光辉的胜利。几乎整个江西南部都落入红军之手。中央苏区的根据地建立起来了。

"1930年2月7日，江西南部召开了一个重要的地方党会议，讨论今后苏维埃的纲领。当地党、军、政代表都出席了会议。会上详细讨论了土地政策的问题，由那些反对分配土地的人所发动的反对'机会主义'的斗争被打败了。会议决定分配土地，加速建立苏维埃，在这以前，红军只是组织地方的和乡的苏维埃，在这次会议上，决定了建立江西省苏维埃政府。对于这个新的纲领，农民报以热烈的拥护，这有助于在后来的几个月中打败国民党军队的'围剿'。"

several were deprived of their Party positions and army command. Of these Liu En-k'ang, an army commander, was typical. It was found that they intended to destroy the Red Army by leading it into difficult positions in battles with the enemy, and after several unsuccessful encounters their plans became quite evident. They bitterly attacked our program and everything we advocated. Experience having shown their errors, they were eliminated from responsible positions and after the Fukien Conference lost their influence.

"This conference prepared the way for the establishment of the soviet power in Kiangsi. The following year was marked with some brilliant successes. Nearly the whole of southern Kiangsi fell to the Red Army. The base of the central soviet regions had been established.

"On February 7, 1930, an important local Party conference was called in south Kiangsi to discuss the future program of the soviets. It was attended by local representatives from the Party, the army, and the government. Here the question of the land policy was argued at great length, and the struggle against 'opportunism,' led by those opposed to redistribution, was overcome. It was resolved to carry out land redistribution and quicken the formation of soviets. Until then the Red Army had formed only local and district soviets. At this conference it was decided to establish the Kiangsi Provincial Soviet Government. To the new program the peasants responded with a warm, enthusiastic support which helped, in the months ahead, to defeat the extermination campaigns of the Kuomintang armies."

六、　　红军的成长

毛泽东的叙述，已经开始脱离"个人历史"的范畴，有点不着痕迹地升华为一个伟大运动的事业了，虽然他在这个运动中处于支配地位，但是你看不清他作为个人的存在。所叙述的不再是"我"，而是"我们"了；不再是毛泽东，而是红军了；不再是个人经历的主观印象，而是一个关心人类集体命运的盛衰的旁观者的客观史料记载了。

他的叙述越接近结束，我越发需要询问他自己的事情。当时他在做什么？当时他担任什么职务？遇到这种或那种情况，他抱什么态度？我的提问，总的来说，使得他在这最后一章自述中有几处提到自己：

"逐渐地，红军的群众工作改进了，纪律加强了，新的组织方法也摸索出来了。各地的农民开始自愿帮助革命了。早在井冈山时期，红军就给战士规定了三条简明的纪律：行动听指挥；不拿贫农一点东西；打土豪要归公。1928年会议[1]以后，曾经作了很大努力争取农民的支持，在上述三条之外，又添了八项。这八项是：

"一、上门板[2]；

"二、捆铺草；

---

1. 指第二次茅坪会议。
2. 这条命令并不像听起来那么神秘费解。中国房子的木板门是可以轻易卸下来的，到晚上常常卸下来放在板凳上临时当床使。

6   Growth of the Red Army

Mao Tse-tung's account had begun to pass out of the category of "personal history," and to sublimate itself somehow intangibly in the career of a great movement in which, though he retained a dominant role, you could not see him clearly as a personality. It was no longer "I" but "we"; no longer Mao Tse-tung, but the Red Army; no longer a subjective impression of the experiences of a single life, but an objective record by a bystander concerned with the mutations of collective human destiny as the material of history.

As his story drew to a close it became more and more necessary for me to interrogate him about himself. What was *he* doing at that time? What office did *he* hold then? What was *his* attitude in this or that situation? And my questioning, generally, evoked such references as there are to himself in this last chapter of the narrative:

"Gradually the Red Army's work with the masses improved, discipline strengthened, and a new technique in organization developed. The peasantry everywhere began to volunteer to help the revolution. As early as Chingkangshan the Red Army had imposed three simple rules of discipline upon its fighters, and these were: prompt obedience to orders; no confiscations whatever from the poor peasantry; and prompt delivery directly to the government, for its disposal, of all goods confiscated from the landlords. After the 1928 Conference [second Maoping Conference] emphatic efforts to enlist the support of the peasantry were made, and eight rules were added to the three listed above. These were as follows:

"1. Replace all doors when you leave a house;[1]

"2. Return and roll up the straw matting on which you sleep;

---

1. This order is not so enigmatic as it sounds. The wooden doors of a Chinese house are easily detachable, and are often taken down at night, put across wooden blocks, and used for an improvised bed.

"三、对老百姓要和气，要随时帮助他们；

"四、借东西要还；

"五、损坏东西要赔；

"六、和农民买卖要公平；

"七、买东西要付钱；

"八、要讲卫生，盖厕所离住家要远。

"最后两项是林彪加的。这八项执行得越来越成功，到今天还是红军战士的纪律，他们经常背诵[1]。另外还向红军宣讲三项守则，作为主要任务：第一、对敌人要斗争到死；第二、要武装群众；第三、要筹款帮助斗争。

"早在1929年，李文林、李韶九领导的几支游击队，经过改编加入了红军第三军。第三军由黄公略指挥，陈毅任政委。在同一时期，朱培德的民团有一部分哗变，加入了红军。他们是在一个国民党指挥员罗炳辉率领下投奔共产党营垒的。他对国民党感到幻灭而愿意参加红军。现在他是红二方面军第三十二军军长。从福建的游击队和红军正规部队骨干，又创立了红军第十二军，由伍中豪指挥，谭震林是政委。后来伍中豪作战牺牲，由罗炳辉继任。

"红军一军团也是在这个时候建立的，总司令是朱德，我是政委。它由第三军、林彪指挥的第四军和罗炳辉指挥的第十二军组成。党的领导是前敌委员会，我是前委主席。那时一军团已经有1万多人，编成10个师。在这支主力之外，还有许多地方的独立团、赤卫队和游击队。

"除了这个运动的政治基础以外，红军的战术在很大程度上造成了军事上的胜利发展。我们在井冈山采取了4个口号，提纲挈领地说明了我们所采用的游击战术，而红军就是从这种游击战中成长起来的。这些口号是：

"一、敌进我退！

"二、敌驻我扰！

---

1. 红军有一个这样内容的歌曲，也是每天唱的。

"3. Be courteous and polite to the people and help them when you can;

"4. Return all borrowed articles;

"5. Replace all damaged articles;

"6. Be honest in all transactions with the peasants;

"7. Pay for all articles purchased;

"8. Be sanitary, and, especially, establish latrines a safe distance from people's houses.

"The last two rules were added by Lin Piao. These eight points were enforced with better and better success, and today are still the code of the Red soldier, memorized and frequently repeated by him.[1] Three other duties were taught to the Red Army, as its primary purpose: first, to struggle to the death against the enemy; second, to arm the masses; third, to raise money to support the struggle.

"Early in 1929 several groups of partisans under Li Wen-lung and Li Shao-tsu were reorganized into the Third Red Army, commanded by Wang Kung-lu, and with Ch'en Yi as political commissar. During the same period, part of Chu P'ei-teh's *min-t'uan* mutinied and joined the Red Army. They were led to the Communist camp by a Kuomintang commander, Lo Ping-hui, who was disillusioned about the Kuomintang and wanted to join the Red Army. He is now commander of the Thirty-second Red Army of the Second Front Army. From the Fukien partisans and nucleus of regular Red troops the Twelfth Red Army was created under the command of Wu Chung-hao, with T'an Chen-lin as political commissar. Wu was later killed in battle and replaced by Lo Ping-hui.

"It was at this time that the First Army Corps was organized, with Chu Teh as commander and myself as political commissar. It was composed of the Third Army, the Fourth Army commanded by Lin Piao, and the Twelfth Army, under Lo Ping-hui. Party leadership was vested in a Front Committee, of which I was chairman. There were already more than 10,000 men in the First Army Corps then, organized into ten divisions. Besides this main force, there were many local and independent regiments, Red Guards and partisans.

"Red tactics, apart from the political basis of the movement, explained much of the successful military development. At Chingkangshan four slogans had been adopted, and these give the clue to the methods of partisan warfare used, out of which the Red Army grew. The slogans were:

"1. When the enemy advances, we retreat!

"2. When the enemy halts and encamps, we trouble them!

---

1. They were also sung daily in a Red Army song.

"三、敌疲我打！

"四、敌退我追！

"这4个口号最初为许多有经验的军人所反对，他们不赞成我们所主张的这种战术。但是，后来许多的经验都证明这种战术是正确的。一般说来，凡是红军背离了这些口号，他们就不能打胜仗。我们的军力很小，敌人超过我们10倍到20倍；我们的资源和作战物资有限，只有把运动战术和游击战术巧妙地结合起来，我们才能有希望在反对国民党的斗争中取得胜利，因为国民党是在雄厚得多的基础上作战的。

"红军的最重要的一个战术，过去是，现在仍然是，在进攻时集中主力，在进攻后迅速分散。这意味着避免阵地战，力求在运动中歼灭敌人的有生力量。红军的机动性和神速而有力的'短促突击战'，就是在上述战术的基础上发展起来的。

"在扩大苏区时，红军一般地采取波浪式或潮水式的推进政策，而不是跳跃式的不平衡的推进，不去深入地巩固既得地区。这种政策同上面说过的战术一样，是切合实际的，是从许多年集体的军事经验和政治经验产生出来的。这些战术，遭到李立三的激烈批评，他主张把一切武器集中到红军中去，把一切游击队合并到红军中。他只要进攻，不要巩固；只要前进，不要后方；只要耸动视听地攻打大城市，伴之以暴动和极端的行动。那时候李立三路线在苏区以外的党组织中占统治地位，其声势足以强迫红军在某种程度上违反战地指挥部的判断而接受它的做法。它的一个结果，是进攻长沙；另一个结果是向南昌进军。但是在这两次冒险中，红军并没有停止游击队的活动或把后方暴露给敌人。

"1929年秋天，红军挺进江西北部，攻占了许多城市，多次打败了国民党军队。一军团在前进到离南昌很近的时候，突然转向西方，向长沙进发。在进军中，一军团同彭德怀会师了，彭德怀曾一度占领长沙，但为避免遭占极大优势的敌军所包围而被迫撤出。彭德怀在1929年4月曾不得不离开井冈山到赣南活动，结果他的部队大大地增加了。1930年4月，他在瑞金同朱德和红军主力重新会合，接着召开了会

"3. When the enemy seeks to avoid a battle, we attack!

"4. When the enemy retreats, we pursue!

"These slogans [of four characters each in Chinese] were at first opposed by many experienced military men, who did not agree with the type of tactics advocated. But much experience proved that the tactics were correct. Whenever the Red Army departed from them, in general, it did not succeed. Our forces were small, exceeded from ten to twenty times by the enemy; our resources and fighting materials were limited, and only by skillfully combining the tactics of maneuvering and guerrilla warfare could we hope to succeed in our struggle against the Kuomintang, fighting from vastly richer and superior bases.

"The most important single tactic of the Red Army was, and remains, its ability to concentrate its main forces in the attack, and swiftly divide and separate them afterwards. This implied that positional warfare was to be avoided, and every effort made to meet the living forces of the enemy while in movement, and destroy them. On the basis of these tactics the mobility and the swift, powerful 'short attack' of the Red Army was developed.

"In expanding soviet areas in general the program of the Red Army favored a wavelike or tidal development, rather than an uneven advance, gained by 'leaps' or 'jumps,' and without deep consolidation in the territories gained. The policy was pragmatic, just as were the tactics already described, and grew out of many years of collective military and political experience. These tactics were severely criticized by Li Li-san, who advocated the concentration of all weapons in the hands of the Red Army, and the absorption of all partisan groups. He wanted attacks rather than consolidation; advances without securing the rear; sensational assaults on big cities, accompanied by uprisings and extremism. The Li Li-san line dominated the Party then—outside soviet areas—and was sufficiently influential to force acceptance, to some extent, in the Red Army, against the judgment of its field command. One result of it was the attack on Changsha and another was the advance on Nanchang. But the Red Army refused to immobilize its partisan groups and open up its rear to the enemy during these adventures.

"In the autumn of 1929 the Red Army moved into northern Kiangsi, attacking and occupying many cities, and inflicting numerous defeats on Kuomintang armies. When within striking distance of Nanchang the First Army Corps turned sharply west and moved on Changsha. In this drive it met and joined forces with P'eng Teh-huai, who had already occupied Changsha once, but had been forced to withdraw to avoid being surrounded by vastly superior enemy troops. P'eng had been obliged to leave Chingkangshan in April, 1929, and had carried out operations in southern Kiangsi, resulting in greatly increasing his troops. He rejoined Chu Teh and the main forces of the Red Army at Juichin in April,

议，决定彭德怀的三军团在湘赣边界活动，朱德和我则转入福建。1930年6月，三军团和一军团再次会师，开始第二次攻打长沙。一、三军团合并为一方面军，由朱德任总司令，我任政委。在这种领导下，我们到达长沙城外。

"大致在这个时候，中国工农革命委员会成立了，我当选为主席。红军在湖南有广泛的影响，几乎和在江西一样。湖南农民都知道我的名字。因为悬了很大的赏格不论死活要缉拿我、朱德和其他红军领导人。我在湘潭的地被国民党没收了[1]。我的妻子和我的妹妹，还有我的兄弟毛泽民、毛泽覃两个人的妻子和我自己的儿子，都被何键逮捕。我的妻子和妹妹被杀害了。其余的后来得到释放。红军的威名甚至于扩展到湘潭我自己的村里，因为我听到一个故事，说当地的农民相信我不久就会回到家乡去。有一天，一架飞机从上空飞过，他们就断定飞机上坐的是我。他们警告那时种我的地的人，说我回来看我的地了，看看地里有没有树木被砍掉。他们说，如果有砍掉的，我一定会向蒋介石要求赔偿。

"但是第二次打长沙失败了。国民党派来大批援军，城内有重兵防守；9月间，又有新的军队纷纷开到湖南来攻打红军。在围城期间，只发生一次重大的战斗，红军在这次战斗中消灭了敌军两个旅。但是，它没有能占领长沙城，几星期以后就撤到江西去了。

"这次失败有助于摧毁李立三路线，并使红军不必按照李立三所要求的那样对武汉作可能招致惨败的进攻。红军当时的主要任务是补充新的兵员，在新的农村地区实行苏维埃化，尤其重要的是在苏维埃政权的坚强领导下巩固红军攻克的地区。为了这些目的，没有必要打长沙，这件事本身含有冒险的成分。然而如果第一次的占领只是一种暂时的行动，不想固守这个城市，并在那里建立政权的话，那么，它的效果也可以认为是有益处的，因为这对全国革命运动所产生的反响是非常大的。企图把长沙当作一种根据地，而不在后面巩固苏维埃政权，这在战略上和在战术上都是错误的。"

---

1. 毛泽东在大革命中曾把这些地的地租用于湖南农民运动。

1930, and after a conference it was decided that P'eng's Third Army should operate on the Kiangsi-Hunan border, while Chu Teh and I moved into Fukien. It was in June, 1930, that the Third Army and the First Army corps re-established a junction and began the second attack on Changsha. The First and Third Army corps were combined into the First Front Army, with Chu Teh as commander-in-chief and myself as political commissar. Under this leadership we arrived outside the walls of Changsha.

"The Chinese Workers' and Peasants' Revolutionary Committee was organized about this time, and I was elected chairman. The Red Army's influence in Hunan was widespread, almost as much so as in Kiangsi. My name was known among the Hunanese peasants, for big rewards were offered for my capture, dead or alive, as well as for Chu Teh and other Reds. My land[1] in Hsiang T'an was confiscated by the Kuomintang. My wife and my sister, as well as the wives of my two brothers, Mao Tse-min and Mao Tse-t'an, and my own sons were all arrested by Ho Chien [the warlord governor]. My wife (K'ai-hui) and my sister (Tse-hung) were executed. The others were later released. The prestige of the Red Army even extended to my own village, in Hsiang T'an, for I heard the tale that the local peasants believed that I would be soon returning to my native home. When one day an airplane passed overhead, they decided it was I. They warned the man who was then tilling my land that I had come back to look over my old farm, to see whether or not any trees had been cut. If so, I would surely demand compensation from Chiang Kai-shek, they said.

"But the second attack on Changsha proved to be a failure. Great reinforcements had been sent to the city and it was heavily garrisoned; besides, new troops were pouring into Hunan in September to attack the Red Army. Only one important battle occurred during the siege, and in it the Red Army eliminated two brigades of enemy troops. It could not, however, take the city of Changsha, and after a few weeks withdrew to Kiangsi.

"This failure helped to destroy the Li Li-san line and saved the Red Army from what would probably have been a catastrophic attack on Wuhan, which Li was demanding. The main tasks of the Red Army then were the recruiting of new troops, the sovietization of new rural areas, and, above all, the consolidation under thorough soviet power of such areas as already had fallen to the Red Army. For such a program the attacks on Changsha were not necessary and had an element of adventure in them. Had the first occupation been undertaken as a temporary action, however, and not with the idea of attempting to hold the city and set up a state power there, its effects might have been considered beneficial, for the reaction produced on the national revolutionary movement was very great. The error was a strategic and tactical one, in attempting to make a base of Changsha while the soviet power was still not consolidated behind it."

---

1. The rent from which Mao had used earlier for the peasant movement in Hunan.

我在这里要冒昧打断一下毛泽东的叙述，对李立三提供一些令人感到兴趣的情况。李立三是湖南人，法国留学生。他经常来往于上海、汉口之间，因为共产党在这两个地方都设"地下"总部，到1930年以后，党的中央委员会才迁到苏区去。李立三是中国共产党人中最有才华的一个人，也许也是最难以捉摸的一个人，大概也是中国所产生的最够得上成为托洛茨基的一个人。从1929到1930年，李立三统治了中国共产党，1930年他被解除了政治局的职务，派到莫斯科去"学习"，至今仍在那里。李立三也和陈独秀一样，对农村苏维埃缺乏信心，他主张对长沙、武汉、南昌那样的战略大城市采取大举进攻的策略。他主张在农村搞"恐怖"，来打掉地主豪绅的气焰；主张工人发动"强大的攻势"，举行暴动和罢工，使敌人在自己的地盘上陷于瘫痪；主张在苏联支持下从外蒙和满洲展开北面的"侧击"。也许在莫斯科心目中他的最大"罪过"是他在1930年认为中国是世界革命的"中心"，这就否认苏联的这个地位。

现在话归原处：

"但是李立三既过高估计了那时候红军的军事力量，也过高估计了全国政局的革命因素。他认为革命已经接近胜利，很快就要在全国掌握政权。当时助长他这种信心的，是蒋介石和冯玉祥之间的旷日持久、消耗力量的内战，这使李立三认为形势十分有利。但是在红军看来，敌人正准备内战一停就大举进攻苏区，这不是进行可能招致惨败的盲动和冒险的时候。这种估计后来证明是完全正确的。

"由于湖南事件、红军撤回江西、特别是占领吉安以后，'李立三主义'在军队里被克服了。而李立三本人在被证明是错误了以后，很快就丧失了党内影响。但是，在'李立三主义'被确定地埋葬以前，军内曾经历一个危急的时期。三军团的一部分人赞成执行李立三路线，要求三军团从红军中分离出来。但是，彭德怀对这种倾向进行了坚决的斗争，维持了在他的指挥下的部队的团结和他们对上级指挥部的忠诚。但是，第二十军在刘铁超领导下公开叛变，逮捕了江西苏维埃的主席，逮捕了许多指挥员和政府干部，并在李立三路线的基础上对我们进行了政治的攻击。这件事发生在富田，因此称为'富田事件'。富田在苏区的心脏吉安的附近，因此这个事件引起了一时的震动，有许多人想必认为革命的前途取决于这个斗争的结局。幸而这次叛乱很快就被镇压下去，这是由于三军团的忠诚、党和红军部队的总的团结，以及农民的支持。刘铁超被逮捕，其他叛乱分子被解除武装和消灭。我们的路线重新得到肯定，'李立三主义'确定地被镇压下去了，结果苏维埃运动随后取得了很大的进展。

To interrupt Mao's narrative for a moment: Li Li-san was a Hunanese and a returned student from France. He divided time in Shanghai and Hankow, where the Communist Party had "underground" headquarters—only after 1930 was the Central Committee transferred to the soviet districts. Li dominated the Chinese Party from 1929 to 1930, when he was removed from the Politburo and sent to Moscow. Like Ch'en Tu-hsiu, Li Li-san lacked faith in the rural soviets, and urged that strong aggressive tactics be adopted against strategic big capitals like Changsha, Wuhan, and Nanchang. He wanted a "terror" in the villages to demoralize the gentry, a "mighty offensive" by the workers, risings and strikes to paralyze the enemy in his bases, and "flank attacks" in the north, from Outer Mongolia and Manchuria, backed by the U.S.S.R.

To continue:

"But Li Li-san overestimated both the military strength of the Red Army at that time and the revolutionary factors in the national political scene. He believed that the revolution was nearing success and would shortly have power over the entire country. This belief was encouraged by the long and exhausting civil war then proceeding between Feng Yu-hsiang and Chiang Kai-shek, which made the outlook seem highly favorable to Li Li-san. But in the opinion of the Red Army the enemy was making preparations for a great drive against the soviets as soon as the civil war was concluded, and it was no time for possibly disastrous putschism and adventures. This estimate proved to be entirely correct.

"With the events in Hunan, the Red Army's return to Kiangsi, and especially after the capture of Kian, 'Lilisanism' was overcome in the army; and Li himself, proved to have been in error, soon lost his influence in the Party. There was, however, a critical period in the army before 'Lilisanism' was definitely buried. Part of the Third Corps favored following out Li's line, and demanded the separation of the Third Corps from the rest of the army. P'eng Teh-huai fought vigorously against this tendency, however, and succeeded in maintaining the unity of the forces under his command and their loyalty to the high command. But the Twentieth Army, led by Liu Teh-ch'ao, rose in open revolt, arrested the chairman of the Kiangsi Soviet, arrested many officers and officials, and attacked us politically, on the basis of the Li Li-san line. This occurred at Fu T'ien and is known as the Fu T'ien Incident. Fu T'ien being near Kian, then the heart of the soviet districts, the events produced a sensation, and to many it must have seemed that the fate of the revolution depended on the outcome of this struggle. However, the revolt was quickly suppressed, due to the loyalty of the Third Army, to the general solidarity of the Party and the Red troops, and to the support of the peasantry. Liu Teh-ch'ao was arrested, and other rebels disarmed and liquidated. Our line was reaffirmed, 'Lilisanism' was definitely suppressed, and as a result the soviet movement subsequently scored great gains.

"这时南京被江西苏区的革命潜力完全惊醒了,在1930年年底开始了对红军的第一次'围剿'[1]。敌军总数超过10万,兵分五路开始包围苏区,以鲁涤平为总指挥。当时红军能动员起来抗击敌军的部队约有4万人。我们巧妙地运用运动战术,迎击并克服了第一次'围剿',取得了巨大的胜利。我们贯彻执行了迅速集中和迅速分散的战术,以我主力各个击破敌军。我们诱敌深入苏区,集中优势兵力突然进攻孤立的国民党部队,取得主动地位,能够暂时包围他们,这样就把数量上占巨大优势的敌人所享有的总的战略优势扭转过来。

"1931年1月,第一次'围剿'完全被打败了。我认为红军如果不是在'围剿'开始时创造了三个条件,那么这次胜利是不可能的:第一,一军团和三军团在集中的指挥下统一起来了;第二,清算了李立三路线;第三,党战胜了红军内和苏区内的AB团(刘铁超)及其他现行反革命分子。

"仅仅经过4个月的喘息,南京就发动了第二次'围剿',以现任军政部长何应钦为总司令。他的兵力超过20万,分七路向苏区推进。当时红军的处境被认为非常危急。苏维埃政权管辖的区域很小,资源有限,装备缺乏,敌人的物质力量在各方面都远远超过红军。但是,红军仍然坚持迄今赖以制胜的战术来对付这次进攻。我们放敌军诸路深入苏区,然后集中主力突然攻击敌第二路,打败了好几个团,摧毁了他们的进攻力量。我们马上迅速地相继进攻第三路、第六路、第七路,逐个击败他们。第四路不战而退,第五路被部分地消灭。在14天中,红军打了6仗,走了8天路,结果得到决定性的胜利。蒋光鼐、蔡廷锴指挥的一路军,在其他六路被击溃或退却以后,没有认真打一仗就撤退了。

"1个月以后,蒋介石亲身出马统率30万军队,要'最后剿灭"赤匪"'。协助

---

1. 这次"围剿"在杨健(译音)著《中国共产党现况》(1931年南京)一书中有详尽描述,颇有趣。

"But Nanking was now thoroughly aroused to the revolutionary potentialities of the soviets in Kiangsi, and at the end of 1930 began its First Extermination Campaign[1] against the Red Army. Enemy forces totaling over 100,000 men began an encirclement of the Red areas, penetrating by five routes, under the chief command of Lu Ti-p'ing. Against these troops the Red Army was then able to mobilize a total of about 40,000 men. By skillful use of maneuvering warfare we met and overcame this First Campaign, with great victories. Following out the tactics of swift concentration and swift dispersal, we attacked each unit separately, using our main forces. Admitting the enemy troops deeply into soviet territory, we staged sudden concentrated attacks, in superior numbers, on isolated units of the Kuomintang troops, achieving positions of maneuver in which, momentarily, we could encircle them, thus reversing the general strategic advantage enjoyed by a numerically greatly superior enemy.

"By January, 1931, this First Campaign had been completely defeated. I believe that this would not have been possible except for three conditions achieved by the Red Army just before its commencement. First, the consolidation of the First and Third Army corps under a centralized command; second, the liquidation of the Li Li-san line; and third, the triumph of the Party over the anti-Bolshevik (Liu Teh-ch'ao) faction and other active counterrevolutionaries within the Red Army and in the soviet districts.

"After a respite of only four months, Nanking launched its Second Campaign, under the supreme command of Ho Ying-ch'in, now Minister of War. His forces exceeded 200,000 men, who moved into the Red areas by seven routes. The situation for the Red Army was then thought to be very critical. The area of soviet power was very small, resources were limited, equipment scanty, and enemy material strength vastly exceeded that of the Red Army in every respect. To meet this offensive, however, the Red Army still clung to the same tactics that had thus far won success. Admitting the enemy columns well into Red territory, our main forces suddenly concentrated against the Second Route of the enemy, defeated several regiments, and destroyed their offensive power. Immediately afterwards we attacked in quick succession the Third Route, the Sixth, and the Seventh, defeating each of them in turn. The Fourth Route retreated without giving battle, and the Fifth Route was partly destroyed. Within fourteen days the Red Army had fought six battles, and marched eight days, ending with a decisive victory. With the break-up or retreat of the other six routes the First Route Army, commanded by Chiang Kuang-nai and Ts'ai T'ing-k'ai, withdrew without any serious fighting.

"One month later, Chiang Kai-shek took command of an army of 300,000 men 'for the final extermination of the "Red bandits."' He was assisted by his ablest commanders:

---

1. This campaign is described in interesting detail by Yang Chien in *The Communist Situation in China* (Nanking, 1931).

他的有他最得力的将领陈铭枢、何应钦、朱绍良，每人负责一路大军。蒋介石指望用长驱直入的办法占领苏区，'荡平赤匪'。他一开始就每天进军80里，深入苏区的腹地。这恰恰给红军提供了最合适的作战条件，蒋介石的战术很快就被证明犯了严重错误。我军主力只有3万人，我们进行了一系列杰出的运动，在5天之中进攻了五路敌军。第一仗红军就俘虏了许多敌军，缴获了大批弹药、枪炮和装备。到9月间，蒋介石就承认第三次'围剿'已经失败，在10月间撤退了他的军队。

"这时候红军进入一个比较和平的成长时期。发展是非常迅速的。第一次苏维埃代表大会于1931年12月11日召开，中央苏维埃政府宣告成立，我担任主席。朱德当选为红军总司令。就在这个月，发生了宁都大起义，国民党二十八路军有两万多人反正，参加了红军。他们是由董振堂、赵博生率领的。赵博生后来在江西作战牺牲，董振堂今天仍然是红五军军长，五军团就是由宁都起义后过来的部队建立的。

"红军现在发动自己的攻势了。1932年它在福建漳州打了一个大仗，占领了这个城市。在南方，红军在南雄进攻了陈济棠，而在蒋介石的路线上，红军猛攻乐安、黎川、建宁和泰宁。它攻打了赣州，但没有占领。从1932年10月起，直到长征西北开始，我本人几乎用全部时间处理苏维埃政府工作，军事指挥工作交给了朱德和其他的人。

"1933年4月，南京开始第四次，也许是败得最惨的一次'围剿'[1]。这一次红军第一仗就把敌两个师解除了武装，俘虏了两个师长。敌第五十九师被部分消灭，第

---

1. 在许多关于"剿共"战争的报道中，对于进攻苏区的大围剿次数，众说纷纭。有的作者说"围剿"共达8次之多，但是南京所进行的这几次大动员，有些完全是防御性的。红军指挥员口中只有5次大围剿。每次直接卷入的南京军队兵力大致如下：第一次，1930年12月到1931年1月，10万人；第二次，1931年5月到6月，20万人；第三次，1931年7月到10月，30万人；第四次，1933年4月到10月，25万人；第五次，1933年10月到1934年10月，40万人（共动员了90万以上的军队进攻3个主要苏区）。1932年南京没有发动大围剿，当时蒋介石用50万左右军队在红区周围设防。但这一年却是红军发动大攻势的一年。显然南京在1932年的防御活动被许多作者误解为大围剿了，因为南京当时是把它作为"剿共"来宣传的。但红军没有这么谈论，蒋介石也没有。

Ch'en Ming-shu, Ho Ying-ch'in, and Chu Shao-liang, each of whom had charge of a main route of advance. Chiang hoped to take the Red areas by storm—a rapid 'wiping-up' of the 'Red bandits.' He began by moving his armies 80 *li* a day into the heart of soviet territory. This supplied the very conditions under which the Red Army fights best, and it soon proved the serious mistake of Chiang's tactics. With a main force of only 30,000 men, by a series of brilliant maneuvers, our army attacked five different columns in five days. In the first battle the Red Army captured many enemy troops and large amounts of ammunition, guns and equipment. By September the Third Campaign had been admitted to be a failure, and Chiang Kai-shek in October withdrew his troops.

"The Red Army now entered a period of comparative peace and growth. Expansion was very rapid. The First Soviet Congress was called on December 11, 1931, and the Central Soviet Government was established, with myself as chairman. Chu Teh was elected commander-in-chief of the Red Army. In the same month there occurred the great Ningtu Uprising, when more than 20,000 troops of the Twenty-eighth Route Army of the Kuomintang revolted and joined the Red Army. They were led by Tung Chen-t'ang and Chao Po-sheng. Chao was later killed in battle in Kiangsi, but Tung is today still commander of the Fifth Red Army—the Fifth Army Corps having been created out of the troops taken in from the Ningtu Uprising.

"The Red Army now began offensives of its own. In 1932 it fought a great battle at Changchow, in Fukien, and captured the city. In the South it attacked Ch'en Chi-t'ang at Nan Hsiang, and on Chiang Kai-shek's front it stormed Lo An, Li Chuan, Chien Ning and T'ai Ning. It attacked but did not occupy Kanchow. From October, 1932, onward, and until the beginning of the Long March to the Northwest, I myself devoted my time almost exclusively to work with the Soviet Government, leaving the military command to Chu Teh and others.

"In April, 1933, began the fourth and, for Nanking, perhaps the most disastrous of its 'extermination campaigns.'[1] In the first battle of this period two divisions were disarmed and two divisional commanders were captured. The Fifty-ninth Division was partly

---

1. There was considerable confusion, in many accounts written of the anti-Red wars, concerning the number of major expeditions sent against the soviet districts. Some writers totaled up as many as eight "extermination" or "annihilation" drives, but several of these big mobilizations by Nanking were purely defensive. Red Army commanders spoke of only five main anti-Red campaigns. These were, with the approximate number of Nanking troops directly involved in each, as follows: First, December, 1930, to January, 1931, 100,000; Second, May to June, 1931, 200,000; Third, July to October, 1931, 300,000; Fourth, April to October, 1933, 250,000; Fifth, October, 1933, to October, 1934, 400,000 (over 900,000 troops were *mobilized* against the three main soviet districts). No major expedition was launched by Nanking during 1932, when Chiang Kai-shek was using approximately 500,000 troops in defensive positions around the Red districts. It was, on the contrary, a year of big Red offensives. Evidently Nanking's defensive operations in 1932, which were, of course, propagandized as "anti-Red campaigns," were misunderstood by many writers as major expeditions.

五十二师被全部消灭。这一仗是在乐安县的大龙坪和桥汇打的，红军一举就俘虏了1.3万敌军。蒋介石最精锐的部队国民党第十一师，接着也被消灭，几乎全部被缴械，它的师长受了重伤。这几仗构成了决定性的转折点，第四次'围剿'随即结束。蒋介石当时写信给他的战地司令官陈诚，说他认为这次失败是他一生中'最大的耻辱'。陈诚是不赞成搞这种'围剿'的。他当时对人说，在他看来，同红军作战是一种'终身职业'，也是一种'无期徒刑'。这话传到蒋介石那里，他就解除了陈诚的总司令职务。

"为了他的第五次，也是最后一次'围剿'，蒋介石动员了将近100万人，而且采取了新的战术和战略。蒋介石根据德国顾问们的建议，在第四次'围剿'时就已经开始采用堡垒体系。在第五次'围剿'中，他就完全依赖这个了。

"在这个时期，我们犯了两个重大的错误。其一是在1933年福建事变中没有能同蔡廷锴的部队联合。其二是放弃了我们以前的运动战术，而采用错误的单纯防御战略。用阵地战对付占巨大优势的南京军队，是一个严重的错误，因为红军无论在技术上或者在精神上都不适合于阵地战。

"由于犯了这些错误，由于蒋介石在'围剿'中采用新的战术和战略，加上国民党军队在数量上技术上占压倒的优势，到了1934年，红军就不得不努力去改变它在江西的迅速恶化的处境了。其次，全国的政治形势也促使我们决定将主要的活动场所迁移到西北去。由于日本侵略东北和上海，苏维埃政府早在1932年2月就已经正式对日宣战。但因苏维埃中国遭到国民党军队封锁包围，宣战自然不能生效。接着，苏维埃政府又发表宣言，号召中国所有的武装力量组成统一战线，抵抗日本帝国主义。1933年初，苏维埃政府宣布愿在下列基础上同任何白军合作：停止内战，停止进攻苏区和红军；保障民众的公民自由和民主权利；武装人民进行抗日战争。

"第五次'围剿'于1933年10月开始。1934年1月，在苏维埃首都瑞金召开了第二次中华全国苏维埃代表大会，总结革命的成就。我在会上作了长篇报告，大会选举了中央苏维埃政府——就是现在的这批人员。不久以后，我们就准备长征了。

destroyed and the Fifty-second was completely destroyed. Thirteen thousand men were captured in this one battle at Ta Lung P'ing and Chiao Hui in Lo An Hsien. The Kuomintang's Eleventh Division, then Chiang Kai-shek's best, was next eliminated, being almost totally disarmed; its commander was seriously wounded. These engagements proved decisive turning points and the Fourth Campaign soon afterwards ended. Chiang Kai-shek at this time wrote to Ch'en Ch'eng, his field commander, that he considered this defeat 'the greatest humiliation' in his life. Ch'en Ch'eng did not favor pushing the campaign. He told people then that in his opinion fighting the Reds was a 'lifetime job' and a 'life sentence.' Reports of this coming to Chiang Kai-shek, he removed Ch'en Ch'eng from the high command.

"For his fifth and last campaign, Chiang Kai-shek mobilized nearly one million men and adopted new tactics and strategy. Already, in the Fourth Campaign, Chiang had, on the recommendation of his German advisers, begun the use of the blockhouse and fortifications system. In the Fifth Campaign he placed his entire reliance upon it.

"In this period we made two important errors. The first was the failure to unite with Ts'ai T'ing-k'ai's army in 1933 during the Fukien Rebellion. The second was the adoption of the erroneous strategy of simple defense, abandoning our former tactics of maneuver. It was a serious mistake to meet the vastly superior Nanking forces in positional warfare, at which the Red Army was neither technically nor spiritually at its best.

"As a result of these mistakes, and the new tactics and strategy of Chiang's campaign, combined with the overwhelming numerical and technical superiority of the Kuomintang forces, the Red Army was obliged, in 1934, to seek to change the conditions of its existence in Kiangsi, which were rapidly becoming more unfavorable. Second, the national political situation influenced the decision to move the scene of main operations to the Northwest. Following Japan's invasion of Manchuria and Shanghai, the Soviet Government had, as early as February, 1932, formally declared war on Japan. This declaration, which could not, of course, be made effective, owing to the blockade and encirclement of Soviet China by the Kuomintang troops, had been followed by the issuance of a manifesto calling for a united front of all armed forces in China to resist Japanese imperialism. Early in 1933 the Soviet Government announced that it would cooperate with any White army on the basis of cessation of civil war and attacks on the soviets and the Red Army, guarantee of civil liberties and democratic rights to the masses, and arming of the people for an anti-Japanese war.

"The Fifth Extermination Campaign began in October, 1933. In January, 1934, the Second All-China Congress of Soviets was convened in Juichin, the soviet capital, and a survey of the achievements of the revolution took place. Here I gave a long report, and here the Central Soviet Government, as its personnel exists today, was elected. Preparations soon

长征开始于 1934 年 10 月，在蒋介石发动他的最后一次'围剿'刚好 1 年以后，这一年作战和斗争几乎不断，双方的损失都很大。

"1935 年 1 月，红军主力到达贵州遵义。在随后的 4 个月，红军几乎不断地行军，并且进行了最有力的战斗。红军经历了无数艰难险阻，横渡中国最长、最深、最湍急的江河，越过一些最高、最险的山口，通过凶猛的土著居民的地区，跋涉荒无人烟的大草地，经受严寒酷暑、风霜雨雪，遭到全中国白军半数的追击——红军通过了所有这一切天然障碍物，并且打破了粤、湘、桂、黔、滇、康、川、甘、陕地方军队的堵截，终于在 1935 年 10 月到达了陕北，扩大了目前在中国的大西北的根据地。[1]

"红军的胜利行军，胜利到达甘、陕，而其有生力量依然完整无损，这首先是由于共产党的正确领导，其次是由于苏维埃人民的基本干部的伟大的才能、勇气、决心以及几乎是超人的吃苦耐劳和革命热情。中国共产党过去、现在、将来都忠于马列主义，并将继续进行斗争反对一切机会主义倾向。它之所以不可战胜，所以一定取得最后胜利，其原因之一就在于这种决心。"

---

1. 在这段叙述中，毛泽东没有提到中央委员会在遵义召开的那次重要会议，正是在这次会议上毛泽东入选中央领导机构。

afterwards were made for the Long March. It was begun in October, 1934, just a year after Chiang Kai-shek launched his last campaign—a year of almost constant fighting, struggle and enormous losses on both sides.

"By January, 1935, the main forces of the Red Army reached Tsunyi, in Kweichow. For the next four months the army was almost constantly moving and the most energetic combat and fighting took place. Through many, many difficulties, across the longest and deepest and most dangerous rivers of China, across some of its highest and most hazardous mountain passes, through the country of fierce aborigines, through the empty grasslands, through cold and through intense heat, through wind and snow and rainstorm, pursued by half the White armies of China, through all these natural barriers, and fighting its way past the local troops of Kwangtung, Hunan, Kwangsi, Kweichow, Yunnan, Sikang, Szechuan, Kansu, and Shensi, the Red Army at last reached northern Shensi in October, 1935, and enlarged its base in China's great Northwest.[1]

"The victorious march of the Red Army, and its triumphant arrival in Kansu and Shensi with its living forces still intact, was due first to the correct leadership of the Communist Party, and second to the great skill, courage, determination, and almost superhuman endurance and revolutionary ardor of the basic cadres of our soviet people. The Communist Party of China was, is, and will ever be faithful to Marxism-Leninism, and it will continue its struggles against every opportunist tendency. In this determination lies one explanation of its invincibility and the certainty of its final victory."

---

1. In this account Mao made no reference to the important meeting of the Central Committee held at Tsunyi, which elected him to the leadership.

PART FIVE
The Long March

第五篇
长征

一、 第五次"围剿"

华南苏区的6年，注定是要成为长征这部英雄史诗的前奏曲的。这6年的历史动人心魄，但是只有零星的记载。我在这里即使要概括地介绍一下也是很难做到的。毛泽东简单地谈到了苏区的有机发展和红军的诞生过程。他谈到了共产党怎样从几百个衣衫褴褛、食不果腹的年轻然而坚决的革命者建立起一支由好几万工农所组成的军队，最后到1930年时已经成了政权的争夺者，其威胁严重到使南京不得不对他们进行第一次大规模的进攻。第一次"围剿"和接着的第二次、第三次、第四次"围剿"完全以失败告终。在每次这样的战役中红军都几旅几旅地、整师整师地消灭了国民党军队，补充了自己的武器和弹药，招来了新兵，扩大了地盘。

在这期间，在红军非正规部队的这道不可逾越的防线后面，生活究竟是怎样的呢？我们这一时代的一个令人惊异的事实是，在华南苏区的全部历史中，竟没有一个"外来的"外国观察家曾经进入过红区——世界上除了苏联以外唯一的这个由共产党统治的国家。因此，外国人所写的关于华南苏区的一切材料都是第二手材料。但是，这些记载不论是友好的还是敌意的，现在可以证实几点重要事实，这些事实清楚地说明了红军所取得的人民拥护的基础是什么。土地给重新分配了，捐税给减轻了。集体企业大规模地成立了；到1933年，仅江西一地就有1,000多个苏维埃合作社。失业、鸦片、卖淫、奴婢、买卖婚姻都已绝迹，和平地区的工人和贫农生活条件大为改善。群众教育在情况稳定的苏区有了很大的进展。在有些县里，红军在三四年中扫除文盲所取得的成绩，比中国农村任何其他地方几个世纪中所取得的成绩还要大，这甚至包括晏阳初在洛克菲勒资助下在定县进行的"豪华"的群众教育试验。在共产党模范县兴国，据说80%的人口是有文化的——比那个有名的洛克菲勒资助的县份还高。

1 — THE FIFTH CAMPAIGN

Here I could not even outline the absorbing and then only fragmentarily written history of the six years of the soviets of South China—a period that was destined to be a prelude to the epic of the Long March. Mao Tse-tung had told briefly of the organic development of the soviets and of the birth of the Red Army. He had told how the Communists built up, from a few hundred ragged and half-starved but young and determined revolutionaries, an army of several tens of thousands of workers and peasants, until by 1930 they had become such serious contenders for power that Nanking had to hurl its first large-scale offensive against them. The initial "annihilation drive," and then a second, a third, and a fourth were net failures. In each of those campaigns the Reds destroyed many brigades and whole divisions of Kuomintang troops, replenished their supplies of arms and ammunition, enlisted new warriors, and expanded their territory.

Meanwhile, what sort of life went on beyond the impenetrable lines of the Red irregulars? It seemed to me one of the amazing facts of our age that during the entire history of the soviets in South China not a single "outside" foreign observer had entered Red territory—the only Communist-ruled nation in the world besides the U.S.S.R. Everything written about the southern soviets by foreigners was therefore secondary material. But a few salient points seemed now confirmable from accounts both friendly and inimical, and these clearly indicated the basis of the Red Army's support. Land was redistributed and taxes were lightened. Collective enterprise was established on a wide scale; by 1933 there were more than 1,000 soviet cooperatives in Kiangsi alone. Unemployment, opium, prostitution, child slavery, and compulsory marriage were reported to be eliminated, and the living conditions of the workers and poor peasants in the peaceful areas greatly improved. Mass education made much progress in the stabilized soviets. In some counties the Reds attained a higher degree of literacy among the populace in three or four years than had been achieved anywhere else in rural China after centuries. In Hsing Ko, the Communists' model *hsien*, the populace was said to be nearly 80 per cent literate.

许多不偏不倚的材料现在至少已经证明了这一些。但是，关于这个小小的苏维埃共和国生活的其他方面虽然越来越多地可以搞到文献材料，我们仍然只能从理论上来加以探讨，而这又不属本书的范围。比如，要是当初红军坚守住了南方的根据地，并且得到巩固，他们会有什么成就？这马上使我们进入了纯粹臆测的领域，所得结论自然受到主观因素的制约。

无论如何，关于南方苏区的猜测，现在主要是只具有学术兴趣的事了。因为到1933年10月，南京已发动了它的第五次，也是最大的一次反共战争，1年之后，红军终于被迫实行总退却。当时几乎人人都认为完了，认为这是为红军送葬出殡。他们这种估计错误到多么严重的程度，要到几乎两年以后才看得出来，因为那时将要发生一场惊人事件，使蒋介石总司令的性命掌握在共产党的手中，这样的卷土重来在历史上是很少有先例的。而在这以前，蒋介石有一阵子却真的相信了自己的吹牛——他已经"消灭了共产主义的威胁"。

对红军进行的战争到了第七个年头，要想消灭他们的尝试才取得了显著的成功。当时红军对江西的一个很大部分和福建湖南的大块地区，有实际行政控制权。在湖南、湖北、河南、安徽、四川、陕西诸省还有其他的苏区，只是与江西苏区并不连接而已。

蒋介石在第五次战役中对红军发动了大约90万军队，其中也许有40万——约360个团——实际参加了赣闽苏区的战争和对付鄂豫皖苏区的红军。但是江西是整个战役的枢纽。红军在这里能够动员一共18万正规军，包括所有后备师，它还有大约20万游击队和赤卫队，但是全部火力却只有不到10万支步枪，没有大炮，手榴弹、炮弹和弹药来源极其有限，这全部是在瑞金的红军军火厂中制造的。

蒋介石采取了新战略，充分利用他的最大有利条件——优势资源、技术装备、外面世界的无限供应（红军却同外面世界隔绝），机械化战术，一支现代化空军，可以飞航的作战飞机近400架。红军缴获了少数几架蒋介石的飞机，他们也有三四个

"Revolution," observed Mao Tse-tung, "is not a tea party." That "Red" terror methods were widely used against landlords and other class enemies—who were arrested, deprived of land, condemned in "mass trials," and often executed—was undoubtedly true, as indeed the Communists' own reports confirmed. Were such activities to be regarded as atrocities or as "mass justice" executed by the armed poor in punishment of "White" terror crimes by the rich when they held the guns? Never having seen Soviet Kiangsi, I could add little, with my testimony, to an evaluation of second-hand materials about it, or to the usefulness of this book, which is largely limited to the range of an eyewitness. For that reason I decided to omit from this volume some interview material concerning Soviet Kiangsi which the reader would be entitled to regard as self-serving, in the absence of independent corroboration. Speculation on the southern soviets in any case was now a matter chiefly of academic interest. For late in October, 1933, Nanking mobilized for the fifth and greatest of its anti-Red wars, and one year later the Reds were finally forced to carry out a general retreat. Nearly everyone then supposed it was the end, the Red Army's funeral march. How badly mistaken they were was not to become manifest for almost two years, when a remarkable comeback, seldom equaled in history, was to reach a climax with events that put into the hands of the Communists the life of the Generalissimo, who for a while really had believed his own boast—that he had "exterminated the menace of communism."

It was not until the seventh year of the fighting against the Reds that any notable success crowned the attempts to destroy them. The Reds then had actual administrative control over a great part of Kiangsi, and large areas of Fukien and Hunan. There were other soviet districts, not physically connected with the Kiangsi territory, located in the provinces of Hunan, Hupeh, Honan, Anhui, Szechuan, and Shensi.

Against the Reds, in the Fifth Campaign, Chiang Kai-shek mobilized about 900,000 troops, of whom perhaps 400,000—some 360 regiments—actively took part in the warfare in the Kiangsi-Fukien area, and against the Red Army in the Anhui-Honan-Hupeh (Oyuwan) area. But Kiangsi was the pivot of the whole campaign. Here the regular Red Army was able to mobilize a combined strength of 180,000 men, including all reserve divisions, and it had perhaps 200,000 partisans and Red Guards, but altogether could muster a firing power of somewhat less than 100,000 rifles, no heavy artillery, and a very limited supply of grenades, shells, and ammunition, all of which were being made in the Red arsenal at Juichin.

Chiang adopted a new strategy to make the fullest use of his greatest assets—superior resources, technical equipment, access to supplies from the outside world (to which the Reds had no outlet), and some mechanized equipment, including an air force that had come to comprise nearly 400 navigable war planes. The Reds had captured a few of

飞行员，但是他们缺乏汽油、炸弹、机工。过去经验证明，进犯红区，企图以优势兵力突袭攻占，结果要遭到惨败，蒋介石现在改用新的战略，把他大部分军队包围"匪军"，对他们实行严密的经济封锁。因此，这基本上是一场消耗战。

这样做代价很大。蒋介石修建了几百、几千英里的军事公路，成千上万个小碉堡，可以用机关枪火力或大炮火力连成一片。他的又攻又守的战略和战术可以减弱红军在运动战上的优势，而突出了红军兵力少、资源缺的弱点。实际上，蒋总司令在他著名的第五次"围剿"中等于对苏区修建了一条长城，逐步收拢，其最后目的是要像个铁钳似的夹住和击溃红军。

蒋介石聪明地避免在公路碉堡网以外暴露大部队。他们只有在得到大炮、装甲车、坦克和飞机滥炸的非常良好的掩护下才前进，很少进到碉堡圈几百码以外。这些碉堡圈遍布江西、福建、湖南、广东、广西诸省。红军由于被剥夺了佯攻、伏击或在公开交战中出奇制胜的机会，不得不采取新战略，他们开始把他们的主要力量放在阵地战上，这一决定的错误及其错误的理由，本书以后还要述及。

据说第五次战役主要是蒋介石的德国顾问们设计的，特别是已故的冯·泽克特将军[1]，他曾任纳粹陆军参谋长，有一个时期是蒋介石的首席顾问。新战术是彻底的，但进展缓慢，代价浩大。作战进行了几个月，但是南京对敌军主力还没有打出决定性的一击。不过，封锁的效果在红区是严重地感觉到了，特别是完全缺盐这一点。小小的红色根据地是越来越不足以击退它所受到的全部军事和经济压力了。为了要维持这次战役中所进行的一年惊人的抵抗，尽管红军否认，但我怀疑对农民想必进行了相当程度的剥削。但是同时必须记住，红军的战士大多数都是新分了土地和获得了选举权的农民。中国的农民仅仅为了土地，大多数也是愿意拼死作战的。江西的人民知道，国民党卷土重来意味着土地回到地主的手中。

南京方面当时认为它的歼灭战快要成功。"敌人"已陷入重围，无法脱身。除了在国民党收复的地区进行"清剿"以外，每天还从空中进行轰炸和扫射，消灭的农民当有千千万万。据周恩来说，红军本身在这次围困中死伤超过6万人，平民的牺牲是惊人的。整块整块的地方被清除了人口，所采取办法有时是强迫集体迁移，有时更加干脆地集体处决。国民党自己估计，在收复江西苏区的过程中，杀死或饿死的人有100万。

---

1. 应为冯·法尔肯豪森将军。

Chiang's airplanes, and they had three or four pilots, but they lacked gasoline, bombs, and mechanics. Instead of an invasion of the Red districts and an attempt to take them by storm of superior force, which had in the past proved disastrous, Chiang now used the majority of his troops to surround the "bandits" and impose on them a strict economic blockade.

And it was very costly. Chiang Kai-shek built hundreds of miles of military roads and thousands of small fortifications, which were made connectable by machine gun or artillery fire. His defensive-offensive strategy and tactics tended to diminish the Reds' superiority in maneuvering, and emphasized the disadvantages of their smaller numbers and lack of resources.

Chiang wisely avoided exposing any large body of troops beyond the fringes of his network of roads and fortifications. They advanced only when very well covered by artillery and airplanes and rarely moved more than a few hundred yards ahead of the noose of forts, which stretched through the provinces of Kiangsi, Fukien, Hunan, Kwangtung, and Kwangsi. Deprived of opportunities to decoy, ambush, or outmaneuver their enemy in open battle, the Reds began to place their main reliance on positional warfare—and the error of this decision, and the reasons for it, will be alluded to further on.

The Fifth Campaign was said to have been planned largely by Chiang Kai-shek's German advisers, notably General von Falkenhausen of the German Army, who was then the Generalissimo's chief adviser. The new tactics were thorough, but they were also very slow and expensive. Operations dragged on for months and still Nanking had not struck a decisive blow at the main forces of its enemy. The effect of the blockade, however, was seriously felt in the Red districts, and especially the total absence of salt. The little Red base was becoming inadequate to repel the combined military and economic pressure being applied against it. Considerable exploitation of the peasantry must have been necessary to maintain the astonishing year of resistance which was put up during this campaign. At the same time, it must be remembered that their fighters were peasants, owners of newly acquired land. For land alone most peasants in China would fight to the death. The Kiangsi people knew that return of the Kuomintang meant return to the landlords.

Nanking believed that its efforts at annihilation were about to succeed. The enemy was caged and could not escape. Thousands supposedly had been killed in the daily bombing and machine gunning from the air, as well as by "purgations" in districts reoccupied by the Kuomintang. The Red Army itself, according to Chou En-lai, suffered over 60,000 casualties in this one siege. Whole areas were depopulated, sometimes by forced mass migrations, sometimes by the simpler expedient of mass executions. Kuomintang press releases estimated that about 1,000,000 people were killed or starved to death in the process of recovering Soviet Kiangsi.

尽管如此，第五次战役仍没有定局。它没有能达到消灭红军的"有生力量"[1]这个预期目标。红军在瑞金举行了一次军事会议，决定撤出，把红军主力转移到一个新根据地去。这次大远征为期达整整1年，计划周密，很有效能，这种军事天才是红军在采取攻势阶段所不曾显过身手的。因为指挥胜利进军是一回事，而在如今已尽人皆知的西北长征中那样的困难条件下，胜利完成撤退计划又是另外一回事。

从江西撤出来，显然进行得极为迅速秘密，因此到红军主力——估计约9万人——已经行军好几天以后，敌人的大本营才发现他们已经撤走了。红军在赣南进行了动员，把大部分正规军从北线撤下来，由游击队换防。这种行动总是在夜间进行的。到全部红军在赣南的雩都附近集中后，才下令作大行军，这是在1934年10月16日开始的。

连续三夜，红军把部队分成西、南两个纵队。第四天晚上他们出其不意地进发了，几乎同时攻打湖南和广东的碉堡线。他们攻克了这些碉堡，敌军惊惶奔逃。红军猛攻不停，一直到占领了南线的全部碉堡工事封锁网，这就给他们打开了通向西方和南方的道路，红军的先锋部队就开始了他们轰动一时的长征。

除了红军主力以外，成千上万的红区农民也开始行军——男女老幼、党与非党的都有。兵工厂拆迁一空，工厂都卸走机器，凡是能够搬走的值钱东西都装在骡子和驴子的背上带走，组成了一支奇怪的队伍。随着征途的拉长，这些负担大部分都得在中途扔掉，据红军告诉我，成千上万支步枪和机枪，大量机器和弹药，甚至还有大量银洋都埋在他们从南方出发的长征途上。他们说，现在遭到成千上万警备部队包围的红区农民有朝一日会把它们从地下挖出来，恢复他们的苏区。他们只等着信号——抗日战争也许就是那个信号。

红军主力撤出江西后，经过了许多星期，南京的军队才终于占领红军的主要城市。因为成千上万的农民赤卫队和游击队在少数正规人员领导下[2]仍继续坚决抵抗到底。这些红军领袖不怕牺牲，自愿留下来，他们许多人的英勇事迹今天仍为红军所津津乐道。他

---

1. 红军使用的一种措辞，指主要的作战力量。
2. 留下来的红军指战员有：陈毅、粟裕、谭震林、项英、方志敏、刘晓、邓子恢、瞿秋白、何叔衡和张鼎丞。他们只有6,000身体健全的正规军，却有2万处于农民保护之下的伤员。他们中有成千上万的人被俘遇害。

Nevertheless, the Fifth Campaign proved inconclusive. It failed to destroy the "living forces"[1] of the Red Army. A Red military conference was called at Juichin, and it was decided to withdraw, transferring the main Red strength to a new base.

The retreat from Kiangsi evidently was so swiftly and secretly managed that the main forces of the Red troops, estimated at about 90,000 men, had already been marching for several days before the enemy headquarters became aware of what was taking place. They had mobilized in southern Kiangsi, withdrawing most of their regular troops from the northern front and replacing them with partisans. Those movements occurred always at night. When practically the whole Red Army was concentrated near Yutu, in southern Kiangsi, the order was given for the Great March, which began on October 16, 1934.

For three nights the Reds pressed in two columns to the west and to the south. On the fourth they advanced, totally unexpectedly, almost simultaneously attacking the Hunan and Kwangtung lines of fortifications. They took these by assault, put their astonished enemy on the run, and never stopped until they had occupied the ribbon of blockading forts and entrenchments on the southern front. This gave them roads to the south and to the west, along which their vanguard began its sensational trek.

Besides the main strength of the army, thousands of Red peasants began this march—old and young, men, women, children, Communists and non-Communists. The arsenal was stripped, the factories were dismantled, machinery was loaded onto mules and donkeys—everything that was portable and of value went with this strange cavalcade. As the march lengthened out, much of this burden had to be discarded, and the Reds told me that thousands of rifles and machine guns, much machinery, much ammunition, even much silver, lay buried on their long trail from the South. Some day in the future, they said, Red peasants, now surrounded by thousands of policing troops, would dig it up again. They awaited only the signal—and the war with Japan might prove to be that beacon.

After the main forces of the Red Army evacuated Kiangsi, it was still many weeks before Nanking troops succeeded in occupying the chief Red bases. Thousands of peasant Red Guards continued guerrilla fighting. To lead them, the Red Army left behind some of its ablest commanders: Ch'en Yi, Su Yu, T'an Chen-lin, Hsiang Ying, Fang Chih-min, Liu Hsiao, Teng Tzu-hui, Ch'u Ch'iu-pai, Ho Shu-heng, and Chang Ting-ch'eng. They had only 6,000 able-bodied regular troops, however—and 20,000 wounded, sheltered among the peasants. Many thousands of them were captured and executed, but they managed

---

1. An expression used by the Reds, meaning main combat forces.

们打了一场后卫战，使主力能够突围远去，南京来不及动员足够部队来加以追逐和消灭于行军途上。即使到 1937 年，江西、福建、贵州仍有一些地方由这些红军残部据守，而在最近政府宣布又要对福建开始进行一次"最后肃清"的反共战役。

to fight a rear-guard action which enabled the main forces to get well under way before Chiang Kai-shek could mobilize new forces to pursue and attempt to annihilate them on the march. Even in 1937 there were regions in Kiangsi, Fukien, and Kweichow held by these fragments of the Red Army, and that spring the government announced the beginning of another anti-Red campaign for a "final clean-up" in Fukien.

二、　　举国大迁移

红军成功地突破了第一道碉堡线以后，就开始走上它历时一年的划时代的征途，首先向西，然后向北。这是一次丰富多彩、可歌可泣的远征，这里只能作极简略的介绍。共产党人现在正在写一部长征的集体报告，由好几十个参加长征的人执笔，已经有了30万字，还没有完成。冒险、探索、发现、勇气和胆怯、胜利和狂喜、艰难困苦、英勇牺牲、忠心耿耿，这些千千万万青年人的经久不衰的热情、始终如一的希望、令人惊诧的革命乐观情绪，像一把烈焰，贯穿着这一切，他们不论在人力面前，或者在大自然面前，上帝面前，死亡面前都绝不承认失败——所有这一切以及还有更多的东西，都体现在现代史上无与伦比的一次远征的历史中了。

红军说到它时，一般都叫"二万五千里长征"，从福建的最远的地方开始，一直到遥远的陕西西北部道路的尽头为止，其间迂回曲折，进进退退，因此有好些部分的长征战士所走过的路程肯定有那么长，甚至比这更长。根据一军团按逐个阶段编的一张精确的旅程表[1]，长征的路线共达 18,088 公里，折合英里为 6,000 英里，大约为横贯美洲大陆的距离的两倍，这个数字大约是主力部队的最低行军长度。不要忘记，整个旅程都是步行的，有些是世界上最难通行的小道，大多数无法通行车辆轱辘，还有亚洲最高的山峰和最大的河流。从头到尾都是一场旷日持久的战斗。

有4道主要的防御工程，在钢筋混凝土机枪阵地和碉堡网的支援下，包围着中国西南[2]的苏区，红军必须先粉碎这四道防线才能到达西面的没有封锁地区。在江西的第一道防线于1934年10月21日突破；在湖南的第二道防线于11月3日占领；

---

1. 《长征记》，一军团编（1936年8月预旺堡）。
2. 为东南之误。——译注

2 A NATION EMIGRATES

Having successfully broken through the first line of fortifications, the Red Army set out on its epochal year-long trek to the west and to the north, a varicolored and many-storied expedition describable here only in briefest outline. The Communists told me that they were writing a collective account of the Long March, with contributions from dozens who made it, which already totaled about 300,000 words. Adventure, exploration, discovery, human courage and cowardice, ecstasy and triumph, suffering, sacrifice, and loyalty, and then through it all, like a flame, an undimmed ardor and undying hope and amazing revolutionary optimism of those thousands of youths who would not admit defeat by man or nature or God or death—all this and more seemed embodied in the history of an odyssey unequaled in modern times.

The Reds themselves generally spoke of it as the "25,000-li March," and with all its twists, turns and countermarches, from the farthest point in Fukien to the end of the road in far northwest Shensi, some sections of the marchers undoubtedly did that much or more. An accurate stage-by-stage itinerary prepared by the First Army Corps[1] showed that its route covered a total of 18,088 *li*, or 6,000 miles—about twice the width of the American continent—and this figure was perhaps the average march of the main forces. The journey took them across some of the world's most difficult trails, unfit for wheeled traffic, and across the high snow mountains and the great rivers of Asia. It was one long battle from beginning to end.

Four main lines of defense works, supported by strings of concrete machine gun nests and blockhouses, surrounded the soviet districts in Southwest China, and the Reds had to shatter those before they could reach the unblockaded areas to the west. The first line, in Kiangsi, was broken on October 21, 1934; the second, in Hunan, was occupied

---

1. *An Account of the Long March*, First Army Corps (Yu Wang Pao, August, 1936).

一个星期以后，在湖南的第三道防线经过血战之后陷入红军之手。广西和湖南的军队在11月29日放弃了第四道也是最后一道的防线，红军就挥师北上，深入湖南，开始直捣四川，计划进入那里的苏区，与徐向前领导下的四方面军会合。在上述的日期中间，共打了9次大仗。南京方面和地方军阀陈济棠、何键、白崇禧沿途一共动员了110个团的兵力。

在经过江西、广东、广西、湖南的征途上，红军遭到了非常惨重的损失。他们到达贵州边境时，人数已减少了1/3。这首先是由于大量运输工作所造成的障碍，当时用于这项工作的竟达5,000人之多。因此先锋部队被拖了后腿，有时敌人得以在行军途上遍设障碍。其次，从江西出发时一直不变地保持着一条西北向的路线，因此南京方面可以预计到红军的大部分动向。

这些错误所造成的严重损失，使红军在贵州采取了新的战术。他们不再直线前进，而是开始采取一系列的转移视线的运动，使南京的飞机要弄清楚主力部队逐日的具体目标越来越困难。经常有两个纵队，有时多到4个纵队，在中央纵队的两侧从事一系列的声东击西的活动，而先锋部队则采取钳形攻势。装备方面只保留了最低限度的最轻便的必要装备，运输部队由于每天遭到空袭，改为夜间行军，人数亦大为减少。

蒋介石为了防止红军过长江进入四川，把大量部队从湖北、安徽、江西撤出，匆匆西运，要想（从北方）切断红军的进军路线。每个渡口都有重兵设防，每只渡船都撤至长江北岸；所有道路都封锁起来；大批大批的地方清仓绝粮。南京还另派大批部队到贵州去增援地方军阀王家烈的烟枪部队，后者终于被红军几乎全部消灭了。另外又派了军队去云南边境，设立障碍。因此，红军在贵州遇到了一二十万的军队的迎击，后者在沿途遍设障碍。这就使得红军不得不在贵州进行了两次反方向的大行军，对省会作了大迂回。

贵州境内的作战占了红军4个月的时间。他们一共消灭了5师敌军，攻占了王家烈省主席的司令部，占领了他在遵义的洋房，招了二万新战士入伍，到了省内大

on November 3; and a week later the third, also in Hunan, fell to the Reds after bloody fighting. The Kwangsi and Hunan troops gave up the fourth and last line on November 29, and the Reds swung northward into Hunan, to begin trekking in a straight line for Szechuan, where they planned to enter the soviet districts and combine with the Fourth Front Army there, under Hsu Hsiang-ch'ien. Between the dates mentioned above, nine battles were fought. In all, a combination of 110 regiments had been mobilized in their path by Nanking and by the provincial warlords Ch'en Chi-tang, Ho Chien, and Pai Chung-hsi.

During the march through Kiangsi, Kwangtung, Kwangsi, and Hunan, the Reds suffered very heavy losses. Their numbers were reduced by about one-third by the time they reached the border of Kweichow province. This was due, first, to the impediment of a vast amount of transport, 5,000 men being engaged in that task alone. The vanguard was very much retarded, and in many cases the enemy was given time to prepare elaborate obstructions in the line of march. Second, from Kiangsi an undeviating northwesterly route was maintained, which enabled Nanking to anticipate most of the Red Army's movements.

Serious losses as a result of these errors caused the Reds to adopt new tactics in Kweichow. Instead of an arrowlike advance, they began a series of distracting maneuvers, so that it became more and more difficult for Nanking planes to identify the day-by-day objective of the main forces. Two columns, and sometimes as many as four columns, engaged in a baffling series of maneuvers on the flanks of the central column, and the vanguard developed a pincerlike front. Only the barest and lightest essentials of equipment were retained, and night marches for the greatly reduced transport corps—a daily target for the air bombing—became routine.

Anticipating an attempt to cross the Yangtze River into Szechuan, Chiang Kai-shek withdrew thousands of troops from Hupeh, Anhui, and Kiangsi and shipped them hurriedly westward, to cut off (from the north) the Red Army's route of advance. All crossings were heavily fortified; all ferries were drawn to the north bank of the river; all roads were blocked; great areas were denuded of grain. Other thousands of Nanking troops poured into Kweichow to reinforce the opium-soaked provincials of warlord Wang Chia-lieh, whose army in the end was practically immobilized by the Reds. Still others were dispatched to the Yunnan border, to set up obstacles there. In Kweichow, therefore, the Reds found a reception committee of a couple of hundred thousand troops, and obstructions thrown up everywhere in their path. This necessitated two great countermarches across the province, and a wide circular movement around the capital.

Maneuvers in Kweichow occupied the Reds for four months, during which they destroyed five enemy divisions, captured the headquarters of Governor Wang and occupied his foreign-style palace in Tsunyi, recruited about 20,000 men, and visited most of the

部分大小村镇，召开了群众大会，在青年中间培养了共产党干部。他们的损失有限，但渡江仍有问题。蒋介石在川贵边境迅速集中兵力，封锁了去长江的捷径短道。他现在把歼灭红军的主要希望寄托于防止红军渡江上面，妄图把红军进一步驱向西南，或者驱进西藏的不毛之地。他电告麾下将领和地方军阀："在长江南岸堵截红军乃党国命运所系。"

突然，在1935年5月初，红军又回师南向，进入云南，那里是中缅和中越交界的地方。他们在四天急行军后到达距省会云南府10英里处，地方军阀龙云紧急动员一切部队进行防御。与此同时，蒋介石的增援部队从贵州过来追击。蒋介石本人和他的夫人原来在云南府逗留，这时赶紧搭上法国火车到印度支那去。一大队南京轰炸机每天在红军上空下蛋，但是红军仍继续进来。不久，这场惊惶结束了，原来发现红军向云南府的进军不过是少数部队的佯攻。红军主力已西移，显然想在长江上游少数几个通航点之一龙街渡江。

长江在尽是荒山野岭的云南境内，流经深谷高峰，水深流急，有的地方高峰突起，形成峡谷，长达一二英里，两岸悬崖峭壁。少数的几个渡口早已为政府军所占领。蒋介石感到很高兴。他现在下令把所有渡船撤至北岸焚毁，然后他命自己的部队和龙云的军队开始包抄红军，希望在这条有历史意义的和险阻莫测的长江两岸一劳永逸地把红军消灭掉。

红军好像不知道自己的命运似的，仍继续向西面的龙街分三路急行军。那里的渡船已经焚毁，南京的飞行员报告，红军一支先锋部队在造一条竹桥。蒋介石更加信心百倍了，造一条桥要好几个星期时间。但是有一天晚上，有一营红军突然悄悄地倒过方向，强行军一天一夜，像奇迹一样，走了85英里，到傍晚时分到达附近其他一个唯一可以摆渡的地方——皎平渡。他们穿着缴获的国民党军服，在黄昏时分到了镇上，没有引起任何注意，悄悄地解除了驻军的武装。

渡船早已撤到北岸——但没有焚毁！（红军远在好几百里外，反正不到这里来，为什么要烧掉渡船呢？政府军可能是这样想的。）但是怎样才能弄一条船到南岸来

villages and towns of the province, calling mass meetings and organizing Communist cadres among the youth. Their losses were negligible, but they still faced the problem of crossing the Yangtze. By his swift concentration on the Kweichow-Szechuan border, Chiang Kai-shek had skillfully blocked the short, direct roads that led to the great river. He now placed his main hope of exterminating the Reds on the prevention of this crossing at any point, hoping to push them far to the southwest, or into the wastelands of Tibet. To his various commanders and the provincial warlords he telegraphed: "The fate of the nation and the party depends on bottling up the Reds south of the Yangtze."

Suddenly, early in May, 1935, the Reds turned southward and entered Yunnan, where China's frontier meets Burma and Indochina. A spectacular march in four days brought them within ten miles of the capital, Yunnanfu, and warlord Lung Yun (Dragon Cloud) frantically mobilized all available troops for defense. Chiang's reinforcements meanwhile moved in from Kweichow in hot pursuit. Chiang himself and Mme. Chiang, who had been staying in Yunnanfu, hastily repaired down the French railway toward Indochina. A big squadron of Nanking bombers kept up their daily egg-laying over the Reds, but on they came. Presently the panic ended. It was discovered that their drive on Yunnanfu had been only a diversion carried out by a few troops. The main Red forces were moving westward, obviously with the intention of crossing the river at Lengkai, one of the few navigable points of the Upper Yangtze.

Through the wild mountainous country of Yunnan, the Yangtze River flows deeply and swiftly between immense gorges, great peaks in places rising in defiles of a mile or more, with steep walls of rock lifting almost perpendicularly on either side. The few crossings had all been occupied long ago by government troops. Chiang was well pleased. He now ordered all boats drawn to the north bank of the river and burned. Then he started his own troops, and Lung Yun's, in an enveloping movement around the Red Army, hoping to finish it off forever on the banks of this historic and treacherous stream.

Seemingly unaware of their fate, the Reds continued to march rapidly westward in three columns toward Lengkai. The boats had been burned there, and Nanking pilots reported that a Red vanguard had begun building a bamboo bridge. Chiang became more confident; this bridge-building would take weeks. But one evening, quite unobtrusively, a Red battalion suddenly reversed its direction. On a phenomenal forced march it covered eighty-five miles in one night and day, and in late afternoon descended upon the only other possible ferry crossing in the vicinity, at Chou P'ing Fort. Dressed in captured Nanking uniforms, the battalion entered the town at dusk without arousing comment, and quietly disarmed the garrison.

Boats had been withdrawn to the north bank—but they had not been destroyed. (Why spoil boats, when the Reds were hundreds of *li* distant, and not coming there anyway? So the government troops may have reasoned.) But how to get one over to the south bank?

呢？到天黑后，红军押着一个村长到河边，大声喊叫对岸的哨兵，说是有政府军开到，需要一条渡船。对岸没有起疑，派了一条渡船过来。一支"南京"部队就鱼贯上了船，不久就在北岸登陆——终于到了四川境内。他们不动声色地进了守军营地，发现守军正在高枕无忧地打麻将，枪支安然无事地靠在墙边。红军叫他们"举起手来"，收了武器，他们只得张口瞪目地瞧着，过了好久才明白，自己已成了原来以为还要3天才能到达的"土匪"的俘虏。

与此同时，红军主力部队大举进行了反方向进军，到第二天中午先锋到达皎平渡。现在过河已不是难事了。6条大船昼夜不停地运了9天。全军运到四川境内，没有损失一兵一卒。渡江完成后，红军马上破坏了渡船，躺下来睡觉。两天后蒋军到达河边时，他们的敌军的殿后部队在北岸高兴地叫他们过去，说游泳很舒服。政府军不得不迂回200多英里才能到最近的渡口，因此红军把他们甩掉了。总司令一怒之下飞到了四川，在红军的进军途上部署新的部队，希望在另外一个战略要冲——大渡河——上切断他们。

After dark the Reds escorted a village official to the river and forced him to call out to the guards on the opposite side that some government troops had arrived and wanted a boat. Unsuspectingly one was sent across. Into it piled a detachment of these "Nanking" soldiers, who soon disembarked on the north shore—in Szechuan at last. Calmly entering the garrison, they surprised guards who were peacefully playing mah-jong and whose stacked weapons the Reds took over without any struggle.

Meanwhile the main forces of the Red Army had executed a wide countermarch, and by noon of the next day the vanguard reached the fort. Crossing was now a simple matter. Six big boats worked constantly for nine days. The entire army was transported into Szechuan without a life lost. Having concluded the operation, the Reds promptly destroyed the vessels and lay down to sleep. When Chiang's forces reached the river, two days later, the rear guard of their enemy called cheerily to them from the north bank to come on over, the swimming was fine. The government troops were obliged to make a detour of over 200 *li* to the nearest crossing, and the Reds thus shook them from their trail. Infuriated, the Generalissimo now flew to Szechuan, where he mobilized new forces in the path of the oncoming horde, hoping to cut them off at one more strategic river—the great Tatu.

三、　　大渡河英雄

强渡大渡河是长征中关系最重大的一个事件。如果当初红军渡河失败，就很可能遭到歼灭了。这种命运，历史上是有先例的。在遥远的大渡河两岸，三国的英豪和后来的许多战士都曾遭到失败，也就是在这个峡谷之中，太平天国的残部，翼王石达开领导的10万大军，在19世纪遭到名将曾国藩统率的清朝军队的包围，全军覆灭。蒋介石总司令现在向他在四川的盟友地方军阀刘湘和刘文辉，向进行追击的政府军将领发出电报，要他们重演一次太平天国的历史。红军在这里必然覆灭无疑。

但是红军也是知道石达开的，知道他失败的主要原因是贻误军机。石达开到达大渡河岸以后，因为生了儿子——小王爷——休息了3天，这给了他的敌人一个机会，可以集中兵力来对付他，同时在他的后方进行迅速包抄，断绝他的退路。等到石达开发觉自己的错误已经晚了，他要想突破敌人的包围，但无法在狭隘的峡谷地带用兵，终于被彻底消灭。

红军决心不要重蹈他的覆辙。他们从金沙江（长江在这一段的名字）迅速北移到四川境内，很快就进入骁勇善战的土著居民、独立的彝族[1]区的"白"彝和"黑"彝的境内。桀骜不驯的彝族从来没有被住在周围的汉人征服过，同化过，他们好几百年以来就一直占据着四川境内这片林深树密的荒山野岭，以长江在西藏东面南流的大弧线为界。蒋介石完全可以满怀信心地指望红军在这里长期滞留，遭到削弱，这样他就可以在大渡河北面集中兵力。彝族仇恨汉人历史已久，汉人军队经过他们境内很少有不遭到惨重损失或全部歼灭的。

---

1. 当时称"倮倮"。——译注

3 THE HEROES OF TATU

The crossing of the Tatu River was the most critical single incident of the Long March. Had the Red Army failed there, quite possibly it would have been exterminated. The historic precedent for such a fate already existed. On the banks of the remote Tatu the heroes of the *Three Kingdoms* and many warriors since then had met defeat, and in these same gorges the last of the T'ai-p'ing rebels, an army of 100,000 led by Prince Shih Ta-k'ai, was in the nineteenth century surrounded and completely destroyed by the Manchu forces under the famous Tseng Kuo-fan. To warlords Liu Hsiang and Liu Wen-hui, his allies in Szechuan, and to his own generals in command of the government pursuit, Generalissimo Chiang now wired an exhortation to repeat the history of the T'ai-p'ing.

But the Reds also knew about Shih Ta-k'ai, and that the main cause of his defeat had been a costly delay. Arriving at the banks of the Tatu, Prince Shih had paused for three days to honor the birth of his son—an imperial prince. Those days of rest had given his enemy the chance to concentrate against him, and to make the swift marches in his rear that blocked his line of retreat. Realizing his mistake too late, Prince Shih had tried to break the enemy encirclement, but it was impossible to maneuver in the narrow terrain of the defiles, and he was erased from the map.

The Reds determined not to repeat his error. Moving rapidly northward from the Gold Sand River (as the Yangtze there is known) into Szechuan, they soon entered the tribal country of warlike aborigines, the "White" and "Black" Lolos of Independent Lololand. Never conquered, never absorbed by the Chinese who dwelt all around them, the turbulent Lolos had for centuries occupied that densely forested and mountainous spur of Szechuan whose borders are marked by the great southward arc described by the Yangtze just east of Tibet. Chiang Kai-shek could well have confidently counted on a long delay and weakening of the Reds here which would enable him to concentrate north of the Tatu. The Lolos' hatred of the Chinese was traditional, and rarely had any Chinese army crossed their borders without heavy losses or extermination.

但是红军有办法。他们已经安全地通过了贵州和云南的土著民族苗族和傣族的地区，赢得了他们的友谊，甚至还吸收了一些部族的人参军。现在他们派使者前去同彝族谈判。他们在一路上攻占了独立的彝族区边界上的一些市镇，发现有一些彝族首领被省里的军阀当作人质监禁着。这些首领获释回去后，自然大力称颂红军。

率领红军先锋部队的是指挥员刘伯承，他曾在四川一个军阀的军队里当过军官。刘伯承熟悉这个部落民族，熟悉他们的内争和不满。他特别熟悉他们仇恨汉人，而且他能够说几句彝族话。他奉命前去谈判友好联盟，进入了彝族的境内，同彝族的首领进行谈判。他说，彝族人反对军阀刘湘、刘文辉和国民党；红军也反对他们。彝族人要保持独立；红军的政策主张中国各少数民族都自治。彝族人仇恨汉人是因为他们受到汉人的压迫，但是汉人有"白"汉和"红"汉，正如彝族人有"白"彝和"黑"彝，老是杀彝族人，压迫彝族人的是"白"汉。"红"汉和"黑"彝应该团结起来反对他们的共同敌人"白"汉。彝族人很有兴趣地听着。他们狡黠地要武器和弹药好保卫独立，帮助"红"汉打"白"汉。结果红军都给了他们，使他们感到很意外。

于是红军不仅迅速地而且安然无事地高高兴兴过了境。好几百个彝族人参加了"红"汉，一起到大渡河去打共同的敌人。这些彝族人中有一些还一直走到了西北。刘伯承在彝族的总首领面前同他一起饮了新杀的一只鸡的血，他们两人按照部落传统方式，歃血为盟，结为兄弟。红军用这种立誓方式宣布凡是违反盟约的人都像那只鸡一样懦弱胆怯。

这样，一军团的一个先锋师在林彪率领下到达了大渡河。在行军的最后一天，他们出了彝族区的森林（在枝茂叶繁的森林中，南京方面的飞行员完全失去了他们的踪迹），出其不意地猛扑河边的安顺场小镇，就像他们奇袭皎平渡一样突然。先锋部队由彝族战士带路，通过狭隘的山间羊肠小道，悄悄地到了镇上，从高处往河岸望去，又惊又喜地发现3条渡船中有一条系在大渡河的南岸！命运再一次同他们交了朋友。

But the Reds had already safely passed through the tribal districts of the Miao and the Shan peoples, aborigines of Kweichow and Yunnan, and had won their friendship and even enlisted some tribesmen in their army. Now they sent envoys ahead to parley with the Lolos. On the way they captured several towns on the borders of independent Lololand, where they found a number of Lolo chieftains who had been imprisoned as hostages by provincial Chinese warlords. Freed and sent back to their people, these men naturally praised the Reds.

In the vanguard of the Red Army was Commander Liu Po-ch'eng, who had once been an officer in a warlord army of Szechuan. Liu knew the tribal people, and their inner feuds and discontent. Especially he knew their hatred of Chinese, and he could speak something of the Lolo tongue. Assigned the task of negotiating a friendly alliance, he entered their territory and went into conference with the chieftains. The Lolos, he said, opposed warlords Liu Hsiang and Liu Wen-hui and the Kuomintang; so did the Reds. The Lolos wanted to preserve their independence; Red policies favored autonomy for all the national minorities of China. The Lolos hated the Chinese because they had been oppressed by them; but there were "White" Chinese and "Red" Chinese, just as there were "White" Lolos and "Black" Lolos, and it was the "White" Chinese who had always slain and oppressed the Lolos. Should not the "Red" Chinese and the "Black" Lolos unite against their common enemies, the "White" Chinese? The Lolos listened interestedly. Slyly they asked for arms and bullets to guard their independence and help "Red" Chinese fight the Whites. To their astonishment, the Reds gave them both.

And so it happened that not only a speedy but a politically useful passage was accomplished. Hundreds of Lolos enlisted with the "Red" Chinese to march to the Tatu River to fight the common enemy. Some of those Lolos were to trek clear to the Northwest. Liu Po-ch'eng drank the blood of a newly killed chicken before the high chieftain of the Lolos, who drank also, and they swore blood brotherhood in the tribal manner. By this vow the Reds declared that whosoever should violate the terms of their alliance would be even as weak and cowardly as the fowl.

Thus a vanguard division of the First Army Corps, led by Lin Piao, reached the Tatu Ho. On the last day of the march they emerged from the forests of Lololand (in the thick foliage of which Nanking pilots had completely lost track of them), to descend suddenly on the river town of An Jen Ch'ang, just as unheralded as they had come into Chou P'ing Fort. Guided over narrow mountain trails by the Lolos, the vanguard crept quietly up to the little town and from the heights looked down to the river bank, and saw with amazement and delight one of the three ferryboats made fast on the *south* bank of the river! Once more an act of fate had befriended them.

这怎么会发生的呢？在对岸，只有四川两个独裁者之一刘文辉将军的一团兵力。其他的四川军队和南京的增援部队一样还在不慌不忙前来大渡河的途上，当时一团兵力已经足够了。的确，由于全部渡船都停泊在北岸，一班兵力也就够了。该团团长是个本地人；他了解红军要经过什么地方，要到达河边需要多长时间。那得等好多天，他很可能这么告诉他的部下。他的老婆又是安顺场本地人，因此他得到南岸来访亲问友，同他们吃吃喝喝。因此红军奇袭安顺场时，俘获了那个团长、他的渡船，确保了北渡的通道。

先锋部队的5个连每连出了16个战士自告奋勇搭那条渡船过河把另外两条带回来，一边红军就在南岸的山边建立机枪阵地，在河上布置掩护火力网，目标集中在敌人外露阵地。时当5月，山洪暴发，水流湍急，河面甚至比长江还宽。渡船从上游启碇，需要两个小时才能到镇对岸靠岸。南岸安顺场镇上的人们屏息凝神地看着，担心他们要被消灭掉。但是别忙。他们看到渡河的人几乎就在敌人的枪口下靠了岸。现在，没有问题，他们准是要完蛋了。可是……南岸红军的机枪继续开火。看热闹的人看着那一小批人爬上了岸，急忙找个隐蔽的地方，然后慢慢地爬上一个俯瞰敌人阵地的陡峭的悬崖。他们在那里架起了自己的轻机枪，掷了一批手榴弹到河边的敌人碉堡里。

突然白军停了火，从碉堡里窜出来，退到了第二道、第三道防线。南岸的人嗡嗡地说开了，叫"好"声传过了河，到那一小批占领了渡头的人那里。这时，第一条渡船回来了，还带来了另外两条，第二次过河每条船就载过去80个人。敌人已经全部逃窜。当天的白天和晚上，第二天，第三天，安顺场的3条渡船不停地来回，最后约有1师人员运到了北岸。

但是河流越来越湍急。渡河越来越困难了。第三天渡一船人过河需要4个小时。照这样的速度，全部人马辎重过河需要好几个星期才行。还没有完成过河，他们就会受到包围。这时一军团已挤满了安顺场，后面还有侧翼纵队，辎重部队，后卫部队陆续开到。蒋介石的飞机已经发现了这个地方，大肆轰炸。敌军从东南方向疾驰而来，还有其他部队从北方赶来。林彪召开了紧急军事会议。这时朱德、毛泽东、

How had it happened? On the opposite shore there was only one regiment of the troops of General Liu Wen-hui, the co-dictator of Szechuan province. Other Szechuan troops, as well as reinforcements from Nanking, were leisurely proceeding toward the Tatu, but the single regiment meanwhile must have seemed enough. A squad should have been ample, with all boats moored to the north. But the commander of that regiment was a native of the district; he knew the country the Reds must pass through, and how long it would take them to penetrate to the river. They would be many days yet, he could have told his men. And his wife, one learned, had been a native of An Jen Ch'ang, so he must cross to the south bank to visit his relatives and his friends and to feast with them. Thus it happened that the Reds, taking the town by surprise, captured the commander, his boat, and their passage to the north.

Sixteen men from each of five companies volunteered to cross in the first boat and bring back the others, while on the south bank the Reds set up machine guns on the mountainsides and over the river spread a screen of protective fire concentrated on the enemy's exposed positions. It was May. Floods poured down the mountains, and the river was swift and even wider than the Yangtze. Starting far upstream, the ferry took two hours to cross and land just opposite the town. From the south bank the villagers of An Jen Ch'ang watched breathlessly. They would be wiped out! But wait. They saw the voyagers land almost beneath the guns of the enemy. Now, surely, they would be finished. And yet . . . from the south bank the Red machine guns barked on. The onlookers saw the little party climb ashore, hurriedly take cover, then slowly work their way up a steep cliff overhanging the enemy's positions. There they set up their own light machine guns and sent a downpour of lead and hand grenades into the enemy redoubts along the river.

Suddenly the White troops ceased firing, broke from their redoubts, and fled to a second and then a third line of defense. A great murmur went up from the south bank and shouts of "*Hao!*" drifted across the river to the little band who had captured the ferry landing. Meanwhile the first boat returned, towing two others, and on the second trip each carried eighty men. The enemy had fled. That day and night, and the next, and the next, those three ferries of An Jen Ch'ang worked back and forth, until at last nearly a division had been transferred to the northern bank.

But the river flowed faster and faster. The crossing became more and more difficult. On the third day it took four hours to shift a boatload of men from shore to shore. At this rate it would be weeks before the whole army and its animals and supplies could be moved. Long before the operation was completed they would be encircled. The First Army Corps had now crowded into An Jen Ch'ang, and behind were the flanking columns, and the transport and rear guard. Chiang Kai-shek's airplanes had found the spot, and heavily bombed it. Enemy troops were racing up from the southeast; others approached from the north. A hurried military conference was summoned by Lin Piao. Chu Teh, Mao Tse-tung,

周恩来和彭德怀都已到达河边。他们作出了一个决定，立即执行。

安顺场以西400里，峡谷高耸，河流又窄、又深、又急的地方，有条有名的铁索悬桥叫做泸定桥。[1] 这是大渡河上西藏以东的最后一个可以过河的地方。现在赤脚的红军战士就沿着峡谷间迂回曲折的小道，赤足向泸定桥出发，一路上有时要爬几千英尺高，有时又降到泛滥的河面，在齐胸的泥淖中前进。如果他们能够占领泸定桥，全军就可以进入川中，否则就得循原路折回，经过彝族区回到云南，向西杀出一条路来到西藏边境的丽江，迂回1,000多里，很少人有生还希望。

南岸主力西移时，已经过河到了北岸的一师红军也开动了。峡谷两岸有时极窄，两队红军隔河相叫可以听到。有时又极辽阔，使他们担心会从此永远见不了面，于是他们就加快步伐。他们在夜间摆开一字长蛇阵沿着两岸悬崖前进时，1万多把火炬照映在夹在中间的河面上，仿佛万箭俱发。这两批先锋部队日夜兼程，休息、吃饭顶多不超过10分钟，这时还得听精疲力竭的政治工作者向他们讲话，反复解释这次急行军的重要意义，鼓励他们要拿出最后一口气，最后一点精力来夺取在前面等着的考验的胜利。不能放松步伐，不能灰心，不能疲倦。彭德怀说，"胜利就是生命，失败就必死无疑。"

第二天，右岸的先锋部队落在后面了。四川军队沿路设了阵地，发生了接触。南岸的战士就更加咬紧牙关前进。不久，对岸出现了新的部队，红军从望远镜中看出他们是白军增援部队，赶到泸定桥去的！这两支部队隔河你追我赶，整整一天之久，红军先锋部队是全军精华，终于慢慢地把精疲力竭的敌军甩到后面去了，因为他们休息的时间久，次数多，精力消耗得快，因为他们毕竟并不太急于想为夺桥送命呀。

泸定桥建桥已有数百年的历史，同华西急流深河上的所有桥梁一样都是用铁索修成的。一共有16条长达100多码的粗大铁索横跨在河上，铁索两端埋在石块砌成

---

1. 字面含义为由泸"安定"的桥。（其实，泸定桥之名为康熙所赐，取自"泸水（大渡河旧称）"和"平定（西藏准噶尔叛乱）"之意。——编注）

Chou En-lai, and P'eng Teh-huai had by now reached the river. They took a decision and began to carry it out at once.

Some 400 *li* to the west of An Jen Ch'ang, where the gorges rise very high and the river flows narrow, deep, and swift, there was an iron-chain suspension bridge called the Liu Ting Chiao—the Bridge Fixed by Liu.[1] It was the last possible crossing of the Tatu east of Tibet. Toward this the barefoot Reds now set out along a trail that wound through the gorges, at times climbing several thousand feet, again dropping low to the level of the swollen stream itself and wallowing through waist-deep mud. If they captured the Liu Ting Chiao the whole army could enter central Szechuan. If they failed they would have to retrace their steps through Lololand, re-enter Yunnan, and fight their way westward toward Likiang, on the Tibetan border—a detour of more than a thousand *li*, which few might hope to survive.

As their main forces pushed westward along the southern bank, the Red division already on the northern bank moved also. Sometimes the gorges between them closed so narrowly that the two lines of Reds could shout to each other across the stream; sometimes that gulf between them measured their fear that the Tatu might separate them forever, and they stepped more swiftly. As they wound in long dragon files along the cliffs at night their 10,000 torches sent arrows of light slanting down the dark face of the imprisoning river. Day and night these vanguards moved at double-quick, pausing only for brief ten-minute rests and meals, when the soldiers listened to lectures by their weary political workers, who over and over again explained the importance of this one action, exhorting each to give his last breath, his last urgent strength, for victory in the test ahead of them. There could be no slackening of pace, no halfheartedness, no fatigue. "Victory was life," said P'eng Teh-huai; "defeat was certain death."

On the second day the vanguard on the right bank fell behind. Szechuan troops had set up positions in the road, and skirmishes took place. Those on the southern bank pressed on more grimly. Presently new troops appeared on the opposite bank, and through their field glasses the Reds saw that they were White reinforcements, hurrying to the Bridge Fixed by Liu. For a whole day these troops raced each other along the stream, but gradually the Red vanguard, the pick of all the Red Army, pulled away from the enemy's tired soldiers, whose rests were longer and more frequent, whose energy seemed more spent, and who were perhaps none too anxious to die for a bridge.

The Bridge Fixed by Liu was built centuries ago, and in the manner of all bridges of the deep rivers of western China. Sixteen heavy iron chains, with a span of some 100 yards or more, were stretched across the river, their ends imbedded on each side under great piles

---

1. Literally the bridge "made fast" by Liu.

的桥头堡下面，用水泥封住。铁索上面铺了厚木板做桥面，但是当红军到达时，他们发现已有一半的木板被撬走了，在他们面前到河流中心之间只有空铁索。在北岸的桥头堡有个敌军的机枪阵地面对着他们，后面是一师白军据守的阵地。当然，这条桥本来是应该炸毁的，但是四川人对他们少数几座桥感情很深；修桥很困难，代价也大。据说光是修泸定桥"就花了18省捐献的钱财"。反正谁会想到红军会在没有桥板的铁索上过桥呢，那不是发疯了吗？但是红军就是这样做的。

时不可失。必须在敌人援军到达之前把桥占领。于是再一次征求志愿人员。红军战士一个个站出来愿意冒生命危险，于是在报名的人中最后选了30个人。他们身上背了毛瑟枪和手榴弹，马上就爬到沸腾的河流上去了，紧紧地抓住了铁索一步一抓地前进。红军机枪向敌军碉堡开火，子弹都飞进在桥头堡上。敌军也以机枪回报，狙击手向着在河流上空摇晃地向他们慢慢爬行前进的红军射击。第一个战士中了弹，掉到了下面的急流中，接着又有第二个，第三个。但是别的人越来越爬近到桥中央，桥上的木板对这些敢死队起了一点保护作用，敌人的大部分子弹都迸了开去，或者落在对岸的悬崖上。

四川军队大概从来没有见过这样的战士——这些人当兵不只是为了有个饭碗，这些青年为了胜利而甘于送命。他们是人，是疯子，还是神？迷信的四川军队这样嘀咕。他们自己的斗志受到了影响；也许他们故意开乱枪不想打死他们；也许有些人暗中祈祷对方冒险成功！终于有一个红军战士爬上了桥板，拉开一个手榴弹，向敌人碉堡投去，一掷中的。军官这时急忙下令拆毁剩下的桥板，但是已经迟了。又有几个红军爬了过来。敌人把煤油倒在桥板上，开始烧了起来。但是这时已有20个左右红军匍匐向前爬了过来，把手榴弹一个接着一个投到了敌军机枪阵地。

突然，他们在南岸的同志们开始兴高采烈地高呼："红军万岁！革命万岁！大渡河三十英雄万岁！"原来白军已经仓惶后撤！进攻的红军全速前进，冒着舔人的火焰冲过了余下的桥板。纵身跳进敌人碉堡，把敌人丢弃的机枪掉过头来对准岸上。

这时便有更多的红军蜂拥爬上了铁索，赶来扑灭了火焰，铺上了新板。不久，在安顺场过了河的一师红军也出现了，对残余的敌军阵地展开侧翼进攻，这样没有

of cemented rock, beneath the stone bridgeheads. Thick boards lashed over the chains made the road of the bridge, but upon their arrival the Reds found that half this wooden flooring had been removed, and before them only the bare iron chains swung to a point midway in the stream. At the northern bridgehead an enemy machine gun nest faced them, and behind it were positions held by a regiment of White troops. The bridge should, of course, have been destroyed, but the Szechuanese were sentimental about their few bridges; it was not easy to rebuild them, and they were costly. Of Liu Ting it was said that "the wealth of the eighteen provinces contributed to building it." And who would have thought the Reds would insanely try to cross on the chains alone? But that was what they did.

No time was to be lost. The bridge must be captured before enemy reinforcements arrived. Once more volunteers were called for. One by one Red soldiers stepped forward to risk their lives, and, of those who offered themselves, thirty were chosen. Hand grenades and Mausers were strapped to their backs, and soon they were swinging out above the boiling river, moving hand over hand, clinging to the iron chains. Red machine guns barked at enemy redoubts and spattered the bridgehead with bullets. The enemy replied with machine gunning of his own, and snipers shot at the Reds tossing high above the water, working slowly toward them. The first warrior was hit, and dropped into the current below; a second fell, and then a third. But as others drew nearer the center, the bridge flooring somewhat protected these dare-to-dies, and most of the enemy bullets glanced off, or ended in the cliffs on the opposite bank.

Probably never before had the Szechuanese seen fighters like these—men for whom soldiering was not just a rice bowl, and youths ready to commit suicide to win. Were they human beings or madmen or gods? Was their own morale affected? Did they perhaps not shoot to kill? Did some of them secretly pray that these men would succeed in their attempt? At last one Red crawled up over the bridge flooring, uncapped a grenade, and tossed it with perfect aim into the enemy redoubt. Nationalist officers ordered the rest of the planking torn up. It was already too late. More Reds were crawling into sight. Paraffin was thrown on the planking, and it began to burn. By then about twenty Reds were moving forward on their hands and knees, tossing grenade after grenade into the enemy machine gun nest.

Suddenly, on the southern shore, their comrades began to shout with joy. "Long live the Red Army! Long live the Revolution! Long live the heroes of Tatu Ho!" For the enemy was withdrawing in pell-mell flight. Running full speed over the remaining planks of the bridge, through the flames licking toward them, the assailants nimbly hopped into the enemy's redoubt and turned the abandoned machine gun against the shore.

More Reds now swarmed over the chains, and arrived to help put out the fire and replace the boards. And soon afterwards the Red division that had crossed at An Jen Ch'ang came into sight, opening a flank attack on the remaining enemy positions, so that in a little

多久白军就全部窜逃——有的是窜逃，有的是同红军一起追击，因为有 100 左右的四川军队缴械投诚，参加追击。一两个小时之内，全军就兴高采烈地一边放声高唱，一边渡过了大渡河，进入了四川境内。在他们头顶上空，蒋介石的飞机无可奈何地怒吼着，红军发疯一样向他们叫喊挑战。在共军蜂拥渡河的时候，这些飞机企图炸毁铁索桥，但炸弹都掉在河里，溅起一片水花。

安顺场和泸定桥的英雄由于英勇过人得到了金星奖章，这是中国红军的最高励章。我后来在宁夏，还会碰到他们几个，对他们那样年轻感到惊讶，因为他们的年纪都不到 25 岁。

while the White troops were wholly in flight—either in flight, that is, or with the Reds, for about a hundred Szechuan soldiers here threw down their rifles and turned to join their pursuers. In an hour or two the whole army was joyously tramping and singing its way across the River Tatu into Szechuan. Far overhead angrily and impotently roared the planes of Chiang Kai-shek, and the Reds cried out in delirious challenge to them.

For their distinguished bravery the heroes of An Jen Ch'ang and Liu Ting Chiao were awarded the Gold Star, highest decoration in the Red Army of China.

四、　　过大草地

安然渡过了大渡河以后,红军进入了相对来说是自由天地的川西,因为这里的碉堡体系还没有完成,主动权基本上操在他们自己手里。但是战斗之间的困难还没有结束。他们面前还需进行两千英里的行军,沿途有7座高耸的山脉。

红军在大渡河以北爬上了1.6万英尺高的大雪山,在空气稀薄的山顶向西望去,只见一片白雪皑皑的山顶——西藏。这时已是6月了。在平原地带天气很热,可是在过大雪山时,这些衣衫单薄、气血不旺的南方战士不习惯于高原气候,冻死不少。更难的是爬荒凉的炮铜岗,他们可以说是自己铺出一条路出来的,一路砍伐长竹,在齐胸深的泥淖上铺出一条曲折的路来。毛泽东告诉我,"在这个山峰上,有一个军团死掉了2/3的驮畜。成百上千的战士倒下去就没有再起来。"

他们继续爬山。下一个是邛崃山脉,又损失了许多人马。接着他们过美丽的梦笔山、打鼓山,又损失了不少人。最后在1935年7月20日,他们进入了四川西北的富饶的毛儿盖地区。同四方面军和松潘苏区会合。他们在这里停下来作长期的休整,对损失作了估计,重整了队伍。

一、三、五、八、九军团9个月以前在江西开始长征时有大约9万武装,现在他们的镰刀锤子旗下只剩下4.5万人。并不是全部都是牺牲的、掉队的或者被俘的。作为防御战术,红军在湖南、贵州、云南的长征路上留下一小部分正规军干部在农

4   Across the Great Grasslands

Safely across the Tatu, the Reds struck off into the comparative freedom of western Szechuan, where the blockhouse system had not been completed, and where the initiative rested largely in their own hands. But hardships between battles were not over. Another 2,000 miles of marching, studded by seven great mountain ranges, still lay ahead of them.

North of the Tatu River the Reds climbed 16,000 feet over the Great Snowy Mountain, and in the rarefied air of its crest looked to the west and saw a sea of snow peaks—Tibet. It was already June, and in the lowlands very warm, but as they crossed the Ta Hsueh Shan many of those poorly clad, thin-blooded southerners, unused to the high altitudes, perished from exposure. Harder yet to ascend was the desolate Paotung Kang Mountain, up which they literally built their own road, felling long bamboos and laying them down for a track through a tortuous treacle of waist-deep mud. "On this peak," Mao Tse-tung told me, "one army corps lost two-thirds of its transport animals. Hundreds fell down and never got up."

They climbed on. The Chung Lai range next, and more lost men and animals. Then they straddled the lovely Dream Pen Mountain, and after it the Big Drum and these also took their toll of life. Finally, on July 20, 1935, they entered the rich Moukung area, in northwest Szechuan, and connected with the Fourth Front Army and the soviet regions of the Sungpan. Here they paused for a long rest, took assessment of their losses, and re-formed their ranks.

The First, Third, Fifth, Eighth, and Ninth Army corps, which had begun the journey in Kiangsi nine months earlier with about 90,000 armed men, could now muster beneath their hammer-and-sickle banners about 45,000. Not all had been lost, strayed, or captured. Behind the line of march in Hunan, Kweichow, and Yunnan the Red Army had, as part of its tactics of defense, left small cadres of regular troops to organize partisan

民中间组织游击队，在敌军侧翼进行骚扰和牵制活动。成百上千条缴获的步枪一路分发，从江西到四川给国民党军队造成了许多新的多事地区。贺龙在湖南北部仍守住他的小小的苏区，后来又有萧克的部队前去会合。许多新建的游击队都开始慢慢地向那里移动。南京要赶走贺龙还得花整整1年时间，而且那也是在红军总司令部命令他入川以后才做到的，他的入川行动在极其艰难险阻的情况下经过西康[1]才完成。

江西的红军到这时为止的经历为他们提供了许多值得反省的教训。他们交了不少新朋友，也结了不少新怨仇。他们沿途"没收"有钱人——地主、官吏、豪绅——的财物作为自己的给养。穷人则受到了保护。没收是根据苏维埃法律有计划进行的，只有财政人民委员部的没收部门才有权分配没收物资。它统一调配全军物资，所有没收物资都要用无线电向它报告，由它分配行军各部队的供给数量，他们往往迂回在山间，首尾相距足足达50英里以上。

"剩余物资"——红军运输力所不及的物资——数量很大，就分配给当地穷人。红军在云南时从有钱的火腿商那里没收了成千上万条火腿，农民们从好几里外赶来免费领一份，这是火腿史上的新鲜事儿。成吨的盐也是这样分配的。在贵州从地主官僚那里没收了许多养鸭场，红军就顿顿吃鸭，一直吃到——用他们的话来说——"吃厌为止"。他们从江西带着大量南京的钞票、银洋和自己的国家银行的银块，一路上凡是遇到贫困地区就用这些货币来付所需的物资。地契都已焚毁，捐税也取消了，贫农还发给了武装。

红军告诉我，除了在川西的经验以外，他们到处受到农民群众的欢迎。他们大军未到，名声早就已经传到，常常有被压迫农民派代表团来要求他们绕道到他们乡里去"解放"他们。当然，他们对红军的政纲是很少有什么概念的，他们只知道这是一支"穷人的军队"。这就够了。毛泽东笑着告诉我有一个这样的代表团来欢迎"苏维埃先生"[2]！但是这些乡下佬并不比福建军阀卢兴邦更无知，后者曾在他统辖的境

---

1. 旧省名，下辖今四川西部和西藏自治区东部，1928年改名西康省，1955年撤销。——编注
2. 音译Soviet的第一个汉字"苏"是个常见的中国姓氏，加上"维埃"两字，很容易被当作一个人的姓名。

groups among the peasantry, and create disturbances and diversionist activity on the enemy's flanks. Hundreds of captured rifles had been distributed along the route, and stretching clear from Kiangsi to Szechuan were new zones of trouble for the Kuomintang forces. Ho Lung still held his little soviet area, in northern Hunan, and had been joined there by the army of Hsiao K'eh. The numerous newly created partisan detachments began working slowly toward that region. Nanking was not to dislodge Ho Lung for a whole year, and then only after he had been ordered by Red Army headquarters to move into Szechuan, an operation which he would complete—via Tibet—against amazing obstacles.

The journey of the Kiangsi Reds thus far had provided them with much food for reflection. They had won many new friends and made many bitter enemies. Along their route they had provisioned themselves by "confiscating" the supplies of the rich—the landlords, officials, bureaucrats, and big gentry. Finance Commissioner Lin Tsu-han told me that such seizures were systematically carried out according to soviet laws, and that only the confiscation department of the finance commission was empowered to distribute the goods that were taken. It husbanded the army's resources, was informed by radio of all confiscations made, and assigned quantities of provisions for each section of the marchers, who often made a solid serpentine of fifty miles or more curling over the hills.

There were big "surpluses"—more than the Reds could carry—and these were distributed among the local poor. In Yunnan the Reds seized thousands of hams from rich packers there, and peasants came from miles around to receive their free portions—a new incident in the history of the ham industry, said Mao Tse-tung. Tons of salt were likewise distributed. In Kweichow many duck farms were seized from the landlords and officials and the Reds ate duck until, in the words of Wu Liang-p'ing, they were "simply disgusted with duck." From Kiangsi they had carried Nanking notes, and silver dollars and bullion from their state bank, and in poor districts in their path they used this money to pay for their needs. Land deeds were destroyed, taxes abolished, and the poor peasantry armed.

Except for their experiences in western Szechuan, the Reds told me they were welcomed everywhere by the mass of the peasantry. Their Robin Hood policies were noised ahead of them, and often the "oppressed peasantry" sent groups to urge them to detour and "liberate" their districts. They had little conception of the Red Army's political program, of course; they only knew that it was "a poor man's army," said Wu Liang-p'ing. That was enough. Mao Tse-tung told me laughingly of one such delegation which arrived to welcome "Su Wei-ai Hsien-sheng"—Mr. Soviet![1] These rustics were no more ignorant, however, than the Fukien militarist Lu Hsing-pang, who once posted a notice throughout

---

1. *Su*, the first Chinese character used in transliterating the word "soviet," is a common family name, and *wei-ai* suffixed to it, might easily seem like a given name.

内出了一张告示，悬赏"缉拿苏维埃，死活不论"。他宣称此人到处横行不法，应予歼灭！

在毛儿盖和懋功，南方来的红军休整了3个星期，在这期间，革命军事委员会、党和苏维埃政府的代表开了会讨论未来计划。读者想必记得，四方面军早在1933年就在四川占了根据地，原来是在湘鄂皖苏区组成的。它经过河南到达四川的长征是由徐向前和张国焘领导的，关于这两位老红军，下文还将述及。他们在四川的战役卓有成效——但也烧杀过甚——整个川北一度都在他们影响之下。他们在毛儿盖与南方来的布尔什维克会师时，徐向前部下约有5万人，因此1935年7月在川西集中的红军全部兵力几近10万人。

这两方面军在这里又分道扬镳了，一部分南方来的军队继续北上，余下的就同四方面军留在四川。当时对于应采取什么正确行军路线有不同的意见。张国焘是主张留在四川，在长江以南恢复共产党的势力。毛泽东、朱德和"契卡"的大部分委员决心要继续到西北。这个踌躇不决的时期由于两个因素而打断了。一个因素是蒋介石的军队从东、北两个方向调入四川，包围红军，在这两部分红军之间成功地打入了一个楔子。第二个因素是把这两部分红军隔开的那条河是四川的急流之一，这时河面突然上涨，无法相通。此外还有党内斗争的其他因素，不需在此详述。

8月间，以一军团为先锋，江西主力继续北征，把朱德[1]留下在四川指挥，和徐向前、张国焘在一起。四方面军在这里和西康要多留1年，等贺龙的二方面军来会合后，[2]才向甘肃进军，引起一时的轰动，这在下文再说。1935年8月领导红军进入川藏边界的大草地的是指挥员林彪、彭德怀、左权、陈赓、周恩来和毛泽东，江西中央政府的大部分干部和党中央多数委员。他们开始作这最后一个阶段的长征时大约有3万人。

在他们面前的那条路程最危险紧张，因为他们所选择的那条路线经过藏族人部落和川康一带好战的游牧的藏族人所居住的荒野地带。红军一进入藏族地带，就第

---

1. 还有李先念。
2. 任弼时时任贺龙的政治委员。

his fiefdom offering a reward for the "capture, dead or alive, of Su Wei-ai." Lu announced that this fellow had been doing a lot of damage everywhere, and must be exterminated.

In Maoerhkai and Moukung the southern armies rested for three weeks, while the revolutionary military council, and representatives of the Party and the Soviet Government, discussed plans for the future. It may be recalled that the Fourth Front Red Army, which had made its base in Szechuan as early as 1933, had originally been formed in the Honan-Hupeh-Anhui soviet districts. Its march across Honan to Szechuan had been led by Hsu Hsiang-ch'ien and Chang Kuo-t'ao, two veteran Reds, of whom something more is said later on. Remarkable successes—and tragic excesses—had marked their campaigns in Szechuan, the whole northern half of which had once been under their sway. At the time of its junction in Moukung with the southern Bolsheviks, Hsu Hsiang-ch'ien's army numbered about 50,000 men, so that the combined Red force concentrated in western Szechuan in July, 1935, was nearly 100,000.

Here the two armies divided, part of the southerners continuing northward while the rest remained with the Fourth Front Army in Szechuan. There was disagreement about the correct course to pursue. Chang Kuo-t'ao and Hsu Hsiang-ch'ien favored remaining in Szechuan and attempting to reassert Communist influence south of the Yangtze. Mao Tse-tung, Chu Teh, and the majority of the Politburo were determined to continue into the Northwest. The period of indecision was ended by two factors. First was an enveloping movement by Chiang Kai-shek's troops, moving into Szechuan from the east and from the north, which succeeded in driving a wedge between two sections of the Red Army. Second was the rapid rise of one of the hurried rivers of Szechuan, which then physically divided the forces, and which suddenly became impassable. There were other factors of intraparty struggle involved which need not be discussed here.

In August, with the First Army Corps as vanguard, the main forces from Kiangsi continued the northward march, leaving Chu Teh and Li Hsien-nien with Hsu Hsiang-ch'ien and Chang Kuo-t'ao. The Fourth Front Army was to remain here and in Tibet for another year, and be joined by Ho Lung's Second Front Army,[1] before making a sensational march into Kansu. Leading the Red cavalcade that in August, 1935, moved toward the Great Grasslands, on the border of Szechuan and Tibet, were Commanders Lin Piao, P'eng Teh-huai, Tso Ch'uan, Ch'en Keng, Chou En-lai, and Mao Tse-tung, most of the officials from the Kiangsi Central Government, and a majority of the members of the Central Committee of the Party. They began this last phase of the march with about 30,000 men.

The most dangerous and exciting travel lay before them, for the route they chose led through wild country inhabited by the independent Mantzu tribesmen and the nomadic Hsifan, a warring people of eastern Tibet. Passing into the Mantzu and Tibetan territories,

---

1. Jen Pi-shih was Ho Lung's political commissar.

一次遇到了团结起来敌视他们的人民，他们在这一段行军途中所吃到的苦头远远超过以前的一切。他们有钱，但是买不到吃的。他们有枪，但是敌人无影无踪。他们走进浓密的森林和跨过十几条大河的源流时，部族的人就从进军途上后退，坚壁清野，把所有吃的、牲口、家禽都带到高原去，整个地区没有了人烟。

但是沿途两旁一二百码以外就很不安全。许多红军想去找头羊来宰，就没有再回来。山区的人民躲在浓密的树丛中，向进军的"入侵者"狙击。他们爬上山去，在红军鱼贯经过又深又窄的山口只能单行前进时，就推下大石头来压死他们和他们的牲口。这里根本没有机会解释什么"红军对少数民族的政策"，没有机会结成友好的联盟！藏民的女酋长对不论哪种汉人，不分红、白，都有不共戴天的宿怨。谁帮助过路的人，她就要把他活活用开水烫死。

由于不抢就没有吃的，红军就不得不为了几头牛羊打仗。毛泽东告诉我，他们当时流行一句话叫"一条人命买头羊"。他们在藏民地里收割青稞，挖掘甜菜和萝卜等蔬菜，据毛泽东说，萝卜大得可以一个"够 15 个人吃"。[1] 他们就是靠这种微不足道的给养过大草地。毛泽东幽默地对我说，"这是我们唯一的外债，有一天我们必须向藏民偿还我们不得不从他们那里拿走的给养。"他们只有俘获了部族人以后才能找到向导引路。他们同这些向导交上了朋友，出了藏族境界之后，许多向导继续参加长征。有些人现在是陕西党校的学员，有朝一日可能回到本土去向人民解释"红"汉和"白"汉的不同。

在大草地一连走了 10 天还不见人烟。在这个沼泽地带几乎大雨连绵不断，只有沿着一条为红军当向导的本地山民才认得出的像迷宫一样的曲折足迹，才能穿过它的中心。沿途又损失了许多牲口和人员。许多人在一望无际的一些水草中失足陷入沼泽之中而没了顶，同志们无从援手。沿途没有柴火，他们只好生吃青稞和野菜。

---

1. 在西藏空气稀薄的高原地带，蔬菜作物生长期很短，个头却能长到"正常"个头的 5 至 10 倍。

the Reds for the first time faced a populace united in its hostility to them, and their sufferings on this part of the trek exceeded anything of the past. They had money but could buy no food. They had guns but their enemies were invisible. As they marched into the thick forests and jungles and across the headwaters of a dozen great rivers, the tribesmen withdrew from the vicinity of the march. They stripped their houses bare, carried off all edibles, drove their cattle and fowl to the plateaus, and simply disinhabited the whole area.

A few hundred yards on either side of the road, however, it was quite unsafe. Many a Red who ventured to forage for a sheep never returned. The mountaineers hid in the thick bush and sniped at the marching "invaders." They climbed the mountains, and when the Reds filed through the deep, narrow, rock passes, where sometimes only one or two could move abreast, the Mantzu rolled huge boulders down to crush them and their animals. Here were no chances to explain "Red policy toward national minorities," no opportunities for friendly alliance. The Mantzu Queen had an implacable traditional hatred for Chinese of any variety, and recognized no distinctions between Red and White. She threatened to boil alive anyone who helped the travelers.

Unable to get food except by capturing it, the Reds were obliged to make war for a few cattle. Mao told me that they had a saying then, "To buy one sheep costs the life of one man." From the Mantzu fields they harvested green Tibetan wheat, and vegetables such as beets and turnips—the latter of an enormous size that would "feed fifteen men," according to Mao Tse-tung.[1] On such meager supplies they equipped themselves to cross the Great Grasslands. "This is our only foreign debt," Mao said to me humorously, "and some day we must pay the Mantzu and the Tibetans for the provisions we were obliged to take from them." Only by capturing tribesmen could they find guides through the country. But of these guides they made friends, and after the Mantzu frontier was crossed many continued the journey. Some of them were now students in the Communist Party school in Shensi, and might one day return to their land to tell the people the difference between "Red" and "White" Chinese.

In the Grasslands there was no human habitation for ten days. Almost perpetual rain falls over this swampland, and it was possible to cross its center only by a maze of narrow footholds known to the native mountaineers who led the Reds. More animals were lost, and more men. Many foundered in the weird sea of wet grass and dropped from sight into the depth of the swamp, beyond reach of their comrades. There was no firewood; they were obliged to eat their wheat green and vegetables raw. There were no trees for shelter,

---

1. Vegetable crops in the rarefied air of the Tibetan highlands attain five to ten times "normal" size during the brief growing season.

没有树木遮阴，轻装的红军也没有带帐篷。到了夜里他们就蜷缩在捆扎在一起的灌木枝下面，挡不了什么雨。但是他们还是胜利地经过了这个考验，至少比追逐他们的白军强，白军迷路折回，只有少数的人生还。

红军现在到达了甘肃边境。前面仍有几场战斗，任何哪一仗如果打败，都可能是决定性的失败。在甘肃南部部署了更多的南京、东北、回民军队要拦阻他们，但是他们还是闯过了所有这些障碍，在这过程中还俘获了回民骑兵的几百匹马，原来一般都认为这些骑兵能一举把他们消灭掉。他们精疲力竭，体力已达到无法忍受的程度，终于到达了长城下的陕北。1935年10月20日，即他们离开江西一周年的日子，一方面军先锋部队同早在1933年就已在陕西建立了苏维埃政权小小根据地的二十五、二十六、二十七军会师。他们现在只剩下了2万人不到，坐下来以后方始明白他们的成就的意义。

长征的统计数字[1]是触目惊心的。几乎平均每天就有一次遭遇战，发生在路上某个地方，总共有15个整天用在打大决战上。路上一共368天，有235天用在白天行军上，18天用在夜间行军上。息下来的100天——其中有许多天打遭遇战——有56天在四川西北，因此总长5,000英里的路上只休息了44天，平均每走114英里休息一次。平均每天行军71华里，即近24英里，一支大军和它的辎重要在一个地球上最险峻的地带保持这样的平均速度，可说近乎奇迹。

红军一共爬过18座山脉，其中5座是终年盖雪的，渡过24条河流，经过12个省份，占领过62座大小城市，突破10个地方军阀军队的包围，此外还打败、躲过或胜过派来追击他们的中央军各部队。他们开进和顺利地穿过6个不同的少数民族地区，有些地方是中国军队几十年所没有去过的地方。[2]

不论你对红军有什么看法，对他们的政治立场有什么看法（在这方面有很多辩论的余地），但是不能不承认他们的长征是军事史上伟大的业绩之一。在亚洲，只有蒙古人曾经超过它，而在过去3个世纪中从来没有发生过类似的举国武装大迁移，

---

1. 《长征记》，一军团编（1936年8月预旺堡）。
2. 资料由左权将军提供。

and the lightly equipped Reds carried no tents. At night they huddled under bushes tied together, which gave but scant protection against the rain. But from this trial, too, they emerged triumphant—more so, at least, than the White troops, who pursued them, lost their way, and turned back with only a fraction of their number intact.

The Red Army now reached the Kansu border. Several battles still lay ahead, the loss of any one of which might have meant decisive defeat. More Nanking, Tungpei, and Moslem troops had been mobilized in southern Kansu to stop their march, but they managed to break through all these blockades, and in the process annexed hundreds of horses from the Moslem cavalry which people had confidently predicted would finish them once and for all. Footsore, weary, and at the limit of human endurance, they finally entered northern Shensi, just below the Great Wall. On October 20, 1935, a year after its departure from Kiangsi, the vanguard of the First Front Army connected with the Twenty-fifth, Twenty-sixth, and Twenty-seventh Red armies, which had already established a small base of soviet power in Shensi in 1933. Numbering fewer than 20,000 survivors now, they sat down to realize the significance of their achievement.

The statistical recapitulation[1] of the Long March is impressive. It shows that there was an average of almost a skirmish a day, somewhere on the line, while altogether fifteen whole days were devoted to major pitched battles. Out of a total of 368 days en route, 235 were consumed in marches by day, and 18 in marches by night. Of the 100 days of halts—many of which were devoted to skirmishes—56 days were spent in northwestern Szechuan, leaving only 44 days of rest over a distance of about 5,000 miles, or an average of one halt for every 114 miles of marching. The mean daily stage covered was 71 *li*, or nearly 24 miles—a phenomenal pace for a great army and its transport to *average* over some of the most hazardous terrain on earth.

According to data furnished to me by Commander Tso Ch'uan, the Reds crossed eighteen mountain ranges, five of which were perennially snow-capped, and they crossed twenty-four rivers. They passed through twelve different provinces, occupied sixty-two cities and towns, and broke through enveloping armies of ten different provincial warlords, besides defeating, eluding, or outmaneuvering the various forces of Central Government troops sent against them. They crossed six different aboriginal districts, and penetrated areas through which no Chinese army had gone for scores of years.

However one might feel about the Reds and what they represented politically (and there was plenty of room for argument), it was impossible to deny recognition of their Long March—the Ch'ang Cheng, as they called it—as one of the great exploits of military history. In Asia only the Mongols had surpassed it, and in the past three centuries there had been no similar armed *migration of a nation* with the exception, perhaps, of the

---

1. *An Account of the Long March* . . .

也许除了惊人的土尔扈特部的迁徙以外，对此斯文·赫定在他的著作《帝都热河》一书中曾有记述。与此相比，汉尼拔经过阿尔卑斯山的行军看上去像一场假日远足。另外一个比较有意思的比较是拿破仑从莫斯科的溃败，但当时他的大军已完全溃不成军，军心涣散。

红军的西北长征，无疑是一场战略撤退，但不能说是溃退，因为红军终于到达了目的地，其核心力量仍完整无损，其军心士气和政治意志的坚强显然一如往昔。共产党人认为，而且显然也这么相信，他们是在向抗日前线进军，而这是一个非常重要的心理因素。这帮助他们把原来可能是军心涣散的溃退变成一场精神抖擞的胜利进军。进军到战略要地西北去，无疑是他们大转移的第二个基本原因，他们正确地预见到这个地区要对中、日、苏的当前命运起决定性的作用。后来的历史证明，他们强调这个原因是完全对的。这种宣传上的巧妙手法必须看成是杰出的政治战略。在很大程度上，这是造成英勇长征得以胜利结束的原因。

在某种意义上来说，这次大规模的转移是历史上最盛大的武装巡回宣传。红军经过的省份有2亿多人民。在战斗的间隙，他们每占一个城镇，就召开群众大会，举行戏剧演出，重"征"富人，解放许多"奴隶"（其中有些参加了红军），宣传"自由、平等、民主"，没收"卖国贼"（官僚、地主、税吏）的财产，把他们的财物分配给穷人。现在有千百万的农民看到了红军，听到了他们讲话，不再感到害怕了。红军解释了土地革命的目的，他们的抗日政策。他们武装了千千万万的农民，留下干部来训练游击队，使南京军队从此疲于奔命。在漫长的艰苦的征途上，有成千上万的人倒下了，可是另外又有成千上万的人——农民、学徒、奴隶、国民党逃兵、工人、一切赤贫如洗的人们——参加进来充实了行列。

总有一天有人会把这部激动人心的远征史诗全部写下来。在此以前，我得继续写我的报道，因为我们现在已经写到红军在西北的会师。我把毛泽东主席关于这6,000英里的长征的旧体诗附在这里作为尾声，他是一个既能领导远征又能写诗的叛逆者：

红军不怕远征难，
万水千山只等闲。
五岭逶迤腾细浪，

amazing Flight of the Torgut, of which Sven Hedin told in his *Jehol, City of Emperors.* Hannibal's march over the Alps looked like a holiday excursion beside it. A more interesting comparison was Napoleon's retreat from Moscow, when the Grand Army was utterly broken and demoralized.

While the Red Army's March to the Northwest was unquestionably a strategic retreat, forced upon it by regionally decisive defeats, the army finally reached its objective with its nucleus still intact, and its morale and political will evidently as strong as ever. The Communists rationalized, and apparently believed, that they were advancing toward an anti-Japanese front, and this was a psychological factor of great importance. It helped them turn what might have been a demoralized retreat into a spirited march of victory. History has subsequently shown that they were right in emphasizing what was undoubtedly the second fundamental reason for their migration: an advance to a region which they correctly foresaw was to play a determining role in the immediate destinies of China, Japan, and Soviet Russia. This skillful propagandive maneuver must be noted as a piece of brilliant political strategy. It was to a large extent responsible for the successful conclusion of the heroic trek.

In one sense this mass migration was the biggest armed propaganda tour in history. The Reds passed through provinces populated by more than 200,000,000 people. Between battles and skirmishes, in every town occupied, they called mass meetings, gave theatrical performances, heavily "taxed" the rich, freed many "slaves" (some of whom joined the Red Army), preached "liberty, equality, democracy," confiscated the property of the "traitors" (officials, big landlords, and tax collectors) and distributed their goods among the poor. Millions of the poor had now seen the Red Army and heard it speak, and were no longer afraid of it. The Reds explained the aims of agrarian revolution and their anti-Japanese policy. They armed thousands of peasants and left cadres behind to train Red partisans who kept Nanking's troops busy. Many thousands dropped out on the long and heartbreaking march, but thousands of others—farmers, apprentices, slaves, deserters from the Kuomintang ranks, workers, all the disinherited—joined in and filled the ranks.

Some day someone will write the full epic of this exciting expedition. Meanwhile, as epilogue, I offer a free translation of a classical poem about this 6,000-mile excursion written by Chairman Mao Tse-tung—a rebel who could write verse as well as lead a crusade:

The Red Army, never fearing the challenging Long March,

Looked lightly on the many peaks and rivers.

Wu Ling's Range rose, lowered, rippled,

乌蒙磅礴走泥丸。
金沙水拍云崖暖,
大渡桥横铁索寒。
更喜岷山千里雪,
三军过后尽开颜。

And green-tiered were the rounded steps of Wu Meng.

Warm-beating the Gold Sand River's waves against the rocks,

And cold the iron-chain spans of Tatu's bridge.

A thousand joyous li of freshening snow on Min Shan,

And then, the last pass vanquished, Three Armies smiled!

PART SIX
Red Star in the Northwest

第六篇
红星在西北

一、　　陕西苏区：开创时期

在江西、福建、湖南的共产党人于 1927 年起逐步建立起他们反对南京的根据地的时候，中国其他各地到处都出现了红军。其中最大的一个地方是鄂豫皖苏区，占了长江中游这 3 个盛产大米的省份的很大一部分地区，人口有 200 多万。那里的红军开始是由徐海东指挥的，后来由徐向前来领导，徐向前是黄埔军校一期生，在国民党军队中当过上校，是广州公社的老战士。

在他们西北方向的远远的山区里，另外一个黄埔军校生刘志丹当时正在为目前陕西、甘肃、宁夏的苏区打基础。刘志丹是个现代侠盗罗宾汉，对有钱人怀有山区人民的一贯仇恨。在穷人中间，他的名字带来了希望，可是在地主和老财中间，他成了惩奸除恶的天鞭。

这个乱世的豪杰生于陕西北部群山环抱的保安，是个中农的儿子。他到榆林去上中学，榆林位于长城南面，是陕西同蒙古商队进行兴旺贸易的中心。刘志丹离开榆林以后就进了广州的黄埔军校，1926 年在那里结业，就成了一个共产党员和国民党军队的青年军官。他随军北伐到了汉口，国共分裂时他正好在那里。

1927 年南京政变后，他逃脱了"清洗"，在上海为党做秘密工作。1928 年回到故乡陕西省，恢复了同当时在冯玉祥的国民军中的以前的一些同志的联系。第二年他在陕西南部领导了一次农民起义。起义发生的地点就在最近西北事变中南京轰炸机轰炸了东北军先锋部队、造成了很大损失的华县附近。他的起义虽遭血腥镇压，陕西省的第一批游击队核心却由此产生。

1   THE SHENSI SOVIETS: BEGINNINGS

While the Communists in Kiangsi, Fukien, and Hunan from 1927 onward gradually built bases for their opposition to Nanking, Red armies appeared in other widely scattered parts of China. Of these the biggest single area was the Honan-Anhui-Hupeh Soviet, which covered a good part of those three rich provinces of the Central Yangtze Valley, and embraced a population of more than 2,000,000 people. The Red Army there began under the command of Hsu Hai-tung, and later on, to lead it came Hsu Hsiang-ch'ien, a graduate of the first class of Whampoa Academy, a former colonel in the Kuomintang Army, and a veteran of the Canton Commune.

Far in the mountains to the northwest of them, another Whampoa cadet, Liu Chih-tan, was laying the foundations for the soviet areas in Shensi, Kansu, and Ninghsia. Liu was a modern Robin Hood, with the mountaineer's hatred of rich men; among the poor he was becoming a name of promise, and among landlords and moneylenders the scourge of the gods.

This chaotic warrior was born in the hill-cradled town of Pao An, north Shensi, the son of a landlord family. He went to high school in Yulin, which stood under the shadow of the Great Wall and was the seat of Shensi's prosperous trade with the caravans of Mongolia. Leaving Yulin, Liu Chih-tan secured an appointment to the Whampoa Academy in Canton, completed his course there in 1926, and became a Communist and a young officer in the Kuomintang. With the Nationalist Expedition as far as Hankow, he was there when the split occurred in the Kuomintang-Communist alliance.

In 1927, following the Nanking *coup d'état*, he fled from the "purgation" and worked secretly for the Communist Party in Shanghai. Returning to his native province in 1928, he re-established connections with some of his former comrades, then in the Kuominchun, the "People's Army," of General Feng Yu-hsiang. Next year he led a peasant uprising in south Shensi. Although Liu's uprising was sanguinarily suppressed, out of it grew the nucleus of the first guerrilla bands of Shensi.

刘志丹在1929年到1932年的生涯仿佛一个万花筒，其间历经各种各样的失败、挫折、捣乱、冒险、死里逃生，有时还官复原职，不失体面。他率领下的小支部队几经消灭。有一次他还担任保安的民团团长，他利用职权逮捕了好几个地主老财加以处决，这出于一个民团团长之手，是很怪诞的行为。因此保安县长被撤了职，刘志丹只带领了3个部下逃到了邻县。那里的冯玉祥部下一个军官请他们赴宴，在酒酣耳热之间，刘志丹和他的朋友把他们的主人缴了械，夺了20支枪，逃到山间去，马上就纠集300个左右的追随者。

但是这支小小的部队遭到了包围，刘志丹提出议和。他的要求被接受，他担任了国民党军队的上校军官，在陕西西部驻防。他在那里又开始反对地主，于是又被"围剿"，这次遭到了逮捕。主要由于他在陕西哥老会的势力，他再次得到赦免，但他的军队改组为一个运输旅，由他任旅长。但是令人难以置信的是他第三次又故态复萌。他的驻区的一些地主向来享有免税优待（这是陕西地主的一种"传统特权"），拒绝向他付税，他马上逮捕一些人，结果豪绅们都武装反他，要求西安方面把他撤职惩办。他的军队遭到包围解散。

最后在悬赏缉拿他的首级的情况下他被迫退到保安去，但是有他自己旅里许多年轻的共产党官兵跟着他去。他终于在这里着手组织一支独立的军队，于1931年举起一面红旗，攻占了保安和中阳[1]两县，在陕北迅速展开活动。派来攻打他的政府军常常在战斗中投诚过来；有的逃兵甚至从山西渡过黄河来投奔他，这个不法之徒的大胆勇敢、轻率鲁莽很快在整个西北名闻遐迩，传开了"刀枪不入"的神话。

从我所能收集到的一切超然的证据来看，似乎没有疑问，在陕西头一两年的斗争中，对官僚、税吏、地主的杀戮是过分的。武装起来的农民长期积压的怒火一旦爆发出来，就到处打家劫舍，掳走人俘，扣在他们的山寨里勒索赎金。他们的行为很像普通的土匪。到1932年刘志丹的徒众在陕北黄土山区占领了11个县，共产党特地在榆林成立一个政治部来指导刘志丹的军队。1933年初成立了陕西的第一个苏维埃，设立了正规的政府，实行了一个与江西类似的纲领。

1934年和1935年间，陕西红军迅速扩大，提高了素质，多少稳定了他们所在地区的情况。成立了陕西省苏维埃政府，设立了一所党校，司令部设在安定。苏区

---

1. 中阳在山西省，疑为甘肃省镇原县之误。——译注

Liu Chih-tan's career from 1929 to 1932 was a kaleidoscope of defeats, failures, discouragements, escapades, adventure, and remarkable escapes from death, interspersed with periods of respectability as a reinstated officer. Several small armies under him were completely destroyed. Once he was made head of the *min-t'uan* at Pao An, and he used his office to arrest and execute several landlords and moneylenders—strange behavior for a *min-t'uan* leader. The magistrate of Pao An was dismissed, and Liu fled, with but three followers, to a neighboring *hsien*. There one of General Feng Yu-hsiang's officers invited them to a banquet, in the midst of which Liu and his friends disarmed their hosts, seized twenty guns, and made off to the hills, where they soon collected a following of about 300 men.

This little army was surrounded, however, and Liu sued for peace. His offer was accepted, and he became a colonel in the Kuomintang Army, with a garrison post in west Shensi. Again he began an anti-landlord movement and again he was outlawed, this time arrested. Owing chiefly to his influence in the Shensi Ke Lao Hui, he was pardoned once more, but his troops were reorganized into a transportation brigade, of which he was made commander. And then for the third time Liu Chih-tan repeated the error of his ways. Some landlords in his district, long accustomed to tax exemption (a more or less "hereditary right" of landlords in Shensi), refused to pay taxes. Liu promptly arrested a number of them, with the result that the gentry rose up in arms and demanded that Sian remove and punish him. His troops were surrounded and disarmed.

Finally he was driven back to Pao An with a price on his head—but followed by many young Communist officers and men from his own brigade. Here at last he set about organizing an independent army under a Red flag in 1931, took possession of Pao An and Chung Yang counties, and rapidly pushed operations in north Shensi. Government troops sent against him very often turned over to the Reds in battle; deserters even drifted across the Yellow River from Shansi to join this outlaw whose daredeviltry, courage, and impetuousness soon won him fame throughout the Northwest and created the usual legend that he was "invulnerable to bullets."

Killings of officials, tax collectors, and landlords became widespread. Unleashing long-hushed fury, the armed peasants raided, plundered, carried off captives, whom they held for ransom in their fortified areas, and conducted themselves much like ordinary bandits. By 1932 Liu Chih-tan's followers had occupied eleven counties in the loess hills of northern Shensi, and the Communist Party had organized a political department at Yulin to direct Liu's troops. Early in 1933 the first Shensi Soviet and a regular administration were established, and a program was attempted similar to that in Kiangsi.

In 1934 and 1935 these Shensi Reds expanded considerably, improved their armies, and somewhat stabilized conditions in their districts. A Shensi Provincial Soviet Government was set up, a Party training school established, and military headquarters were located

有自己的银行、邮局，开始发行粗糙的钞票、邮票。在完全苏维埃化的地区，开始实行苏维埃经济，地主的土地遭到没收，重新分配，取消了一切苛捐杂税，设立了合作社，党发出号召，为小学征求教员。

这时，刘志丹从红色根据地南进，向省会进逼。他攻占了西安府外的临潼，对西安围城数日，但没有成功。一个纵队南下陕南，在那里的好几个县里成立了苏区。在与杨虎城将军（后来成了红军的盟友）的交战中遭到了一些严重失败和挫折，但是也赢得了一些胜利。军内纪律加强，土匪成分消除后，农民就开始更加拥护红军。到1935年中，苏区在陕西和甘肃控制了22个县。现在在刘志丹指挥下有二十六、二十七军，总共5,000人，能与南方和西方的红军主力有无线电联系。在南方红军开始撤离赣闽根据地后，陕西这些山区红军却大大加强了自己，后来到1935年，蒋介石不得不派他的副总司令张学良少帅率领大军来对付他们。

1934年末，红二十五军8,000人在徐海东率领下离开河南。10月间他们到达陕西南部，同刘志丹所武装起来的该地1,000名左右红色游击队会合。徐海东在那里扎营过冬，帮助游击队建立正规军，同杨虎城将军的军队打了几次胜仗，在陕西南部5个县里武装了农民，成立了一个临时苏维埃政府，由陕西省"契卡"的一个23岁的委员郑位三任主席；李龙桂和陈先瑞为红军两个独立旅的旅长。徐海东把这个地区留给他们去保卫，自己率二十五军进入甘肃，在成千上万的政府军包围中杀出一条血路来到了苏区，一路上攻占了5个县城，把马鸿宾将军的回民军队两个团缴了械。

1935年7月25日，二十五、二十六、二十七军在陕西北部的云长整编为红十五军团，以徐海东为司令，刘志丹为副司令兼陕甘晋革命军事委员会[1]主席。1935

---

1. 李雪峰是委员之一。

at An Ting. The soviets opened their own bank and post office and began to issue crude money and stamps. In the completely sovietized areas a soviet economy was begun, landlords' land was confiscated and redistributed, all surtaxes were abolished, cooperatives were opened, and a call was sent out by the Party to enlist members to volunteer as teachers for primary schools.

Meanwhile Liu Chih-tan moved well south of the Red base toward the capital. He occupied Lintung, just outside Sianfu, and besieged the city for some days, without success. A column of Reds pushed down to southern Shensi and established soviets in several counties there. They had some bad defeats and reverses in battles with General Yang Hu-ch'eng (later to become the Reds' ally), and they won some victories. As discipline increased in the army, and bandit elements were eliminated, support for the Reds deepened among the peasantry. By the middle of 1935 the soviets controlled twenty-two counties in Shensi and Kansu. The Twenty-sixth and Twenty-seventh Red armies, with a total of over 5,000 men, were now under Liu Chih-tan's command, and could establish contact by radio with the main forces of the Red Army in the South and in the West. As the southern Reds began to withdraw from their Kiangsi-Fukien base, these hill men of Shensi greatly strengthened themselves, until in 1935 Chiang Kai-shek was forced to send his vice-commander-in-chief, Marshal Chang Hsueh-liang, to lead a big army against them.

Late in 1934 the Twenty-fifth Red Army, under Hsu Hai-tung, left Honan with some 8,000 men. By October it had reached south Shensi and connected with about 1,000 Red partisans in that area who had been armed by Liu Chih-tan. Hsu encamped for the winter there, helped the partisans to build a regular army, fought several successful battles against General Yang Hu-ch'eng's troops, and armed peasants in five counties of south Shensi. A provisional soviet government was established, with Cheng Wei-shan, a twenty-three-year-old member of the Central Committee of Shensi province, as chairman, and Li Lung-kuei and Cheng Shan-jui as commanders of two independent Red brigades. Leaving them to defend this area, Hsu Hai-tung then moved into Kansu with his Twenty-fifth Army, and fought his way into the soviet districts through thousands of government troops, capturing five county seats en route and disarming two regiments of Mohammedan troops under General Ma Hung-ping.

On July 25, 1935, the Twenty-fifth, Twenty-sixth, and Twenty-seventh armies united near Yung Ch'ang, north Shensi. Their troops were reorganized into the Fifteenth Red Army Corps, with Hsu Hai-tung as commander and Liu Chih-tan as vice-commander and chairman of the Shensi-Kansu-Shansi Revolutionary Military Committee.[1] In August,

---

1. Of which Li Hsueh-feng was a member.

年 8 月，该军团遇到了王以哲将军率领的东北军两个师，加以击败，补充了新兵和亟需的枪支弹药。

这时发生了一件奇怪的事。8 月间陕北来了一个共产党中央委员会的代表，一个名叫张敬佛[1]的胖胖的年轻人。据告诉我消息的人（他当时是刘志丹部下的参谋）说，这位张先生（外号张胖子）有权"改组"党和军队。他可以说是个钦差大臣。

张胖子开始着手收集证据，证明刘志丹没有遵循"党的路线"。他"审问"了刘志丹，命令刘志丹辞去一切职务。现在可笑的是，或者说奇怪的是，或者也可以说既可笑又奇怪的是——不过，反正这是遵守"党纪"的一个突出例子：刘志丹不但没有反诘张先生凭什么权利批评他，反而乖乖地接受了他的决定，放弃了一切实际指挥权，像阿喀琉斯[2]一样，退到保安窑洞里去发闷气了！张先生还下令逮捕和监禁了 100 多个党内军内其他"反动派"，心满意足地稳坐下来。

就是在这个奇怪的事情发生的时候，南方的红军先遣部队，即在林彪、周恩来、彭德怀、毛泽东率领下的一军团在 1935 年 10 月到达。他们对这奇怪的情况感到震惊，下令复查，发现大多数证据都是无中生有的，并且发现张敬佛不仅越权，并且本人受到了"反动派"的欺骗。他们立即恢复了刘志丹和他所有部下的原职。张胖子本人遭到逮捕，受到审判，关了一个时期以后，分配他去从事体力劳动。

这样，在 1936 年初，两支红军会合起来尝试著名的"抗日"东征，他们过了黄河，进了邻省山西，仍由刘志丹任指挥。他在那次战役中表现杰出，红军在两个月内在那个所谓"模范省"攻占了 18 个以上的县份。但是他在东征途中牺牲的消息，不像许多其他类似的消息那样不过是国民党报纸的主观幻想。他在 1936 年 3 月领导突击队袭击敌军工事时受了重伤，但红军能够渡过黄河靠他攻占那个工事。刘志丹被送回陕西，他双目凝视着他幼时漫游的心爱的群山，在他领导下走上他所坚信的革命斗争道路的山区人民中间死去。他葬在瓦窑堡，苏区把红色中国的一个县份改名志丹县[3]来纪念他。

在保安，我看到了他的遗妻和孩子，一个 6 岁的美丽的小女孩。红军为她特地裁制了一套军服；她束着军官的皮带，帽檐上有颗红星。她得到那里人人的疼爱，像个小元帅一样，对她的"土匪"父亲极感自豪。

---

1. 疑为张慕陶。
2. 荷马史诗《伊利亚特》中的英雄，因与统帅阿伽门农争吵，生气退回帐篷。——译注
3. 即保安。——译注

1935, this army corps met and defeated two divisions of Tungpei (Manchurian) troops, under General Wang Yi-che. New recruits were added, and much-needed guns and ammunition.

And now a curious thing occurred. In August there came to north Shensi a delegate of the Central Committee of the Communist Party, a stout young gentleman named Chang Ching-fu (Chang Mu-t'ao?). According to my informant, who was then a staff officer under Liu Chih-tan, this Mr. Chang (nicknamed Chang the Corpulent) was empowered to "reorganize" the Party and the army. He was a kind of superinspector.

Chang the Corpulent proceeded to collect evidence to prove that Liu Chih-tan had not followed the "Party line." He "tried" Liu, and demanded his resignation from all posts. Liu Chih-tan did not put Mr. Chang against a wall as an interloper for presuming to criticize him, but retired from all active command and went, Achilles-like, to sulk in his cave in Pao An. Mr. Chang also ordered the arrest and imprisonment of more than a hundred other "reactionaries" in the Party and the army and quietly sat back, well satisfied with himself.

It was into this queer scene that the vanguard of the southern Reds, the First Army Corps, headed by Lin Piao, Chou En-lai, P'eng Teh-huai, and Mao Tse-tung, entered in October, 1935. According to my local informants in Pao An, Mao and his Politburo called for a re-examination of evidence, found most of it baseless, discovered that Chang Ching-fu had exceeded his orders and been misled by "reactionaries" himself. They reinstated Liu and all his confederates. Chang the Corpulent was himself arrested, tried, imprisoned for a term, and later given menial tasks to perform.

Thus it happened that when, early in 1936, the combined Red armies attempted their famous "anti-Japanese" expedition, crossed the river, and invaded neighboring Shansi, Liu Chih-tan was again in command. He distinguished himself in that remarkable campaign during which the Reds occupied over eighteen counties of the so-called "model province" in two months. He was fatally wounded in March, 1936, when he led a raiding party against an enemy fortification, the capture of which enabled the Red Army to cross the Yellow River. Liu Chih-tan was carried back to Shensi and died gazing upon the hills he had roamed and loved as a boy, and among the mountain people he had led along the road he believed in, the road of revolutionary struggle. He was buried at Wa Ya Pao, and the soviets renamed a county of their Red China after him—Chih-tan *hsien*.

In Pao An I met his widow and his child, a beautiful little girl of six. The Reds had tailored her a special uniform; she wore an officer's belt, and a red star on her cap. She was the idol of everybody there. Young Liu carried herself like a field marshal and she was mightily proud of her "bandit" father.

但是，虽然西北这些苏区是围绕着刘志丹这个人物发展壮大的，但不是刘志丹，而是生活条件本身产生了他的人民这个震天撼地的运动。要了解他们所取得的任何胜利，不仅必须了解他们所为之奋斗的目标，而且要了解他们所反对的东西。

But although Liu Chih-tan was the personality around which these soviets of the Northwest grew up, it was not Liu, but the conditions of life itself, which produced this convulsive movement of his people. And to understand whatever success they had had it was necessary not so much just now to look at what these men fought for, as to examine what they fought against.

二、　　死亡和捐税

西北大灾荒曾经持续约有3年，遍及四大省份，我在1929年6月访问了蒙古边缘上的绥远省的几个旱灾区。在那些年月里究竟有多少人饿死，我不知道确切数字，大概也永远不会有人知道了；这件事现在已经被人忘怀。一般都同意300万这个保守的半官方数字，但是我并不怀疑其他高达600万的估计数字。

这场灾难在西方世界几乎没有人注意到，甚至在中国沿海城市也是如此，但是有少数几个中国国际赈灾委员会的勇气可嘉的人，为了抢救一些灾民，冒着生命的危险到这些伤寒流行的灾区去。他们中间有许多中国人，也有一些外国人如德怀特·爱德华兹[1]、O.J.托德[2]和一个杰出的老医生罗伯特·英格兰姆[3]。我有几天同他们一起，走过许多死亡的城市，跨过一度肥沃、如今变成了荒芜不毛之地的乡野，所到之处无不感到怵目惊心。

我当时23岁。我想我是到东方来寻找"东方的魅力"的。我以为自己是个冒险家，那次绥远之行就是那样开始的。但是在这里，我有生以来第一次蓦然看到了人们因为没有吃的而活活饿死。我在绥远度过的那一段噩梦般的时间里，看到了成千上万的男女老幼在我眼前活活饿死。

你有没有见到过一个人——一个辛勤劳动、"奉公守法"、于人无犯的诚实的好人——有1个多月没有吃饭了？这种景象真是令人惨不忍睹。挂在他身上快要死去的皮肉打着皱褶；你可以一清二楚地看到他身上的每一根骨头；他的眼光茫然无神；

---

1. 赈灾委员会秘书。
2. 美国工程师。
3. 教会医生，数年后遇害，杀人者是中国的土匪，但**不是**"赤匪"。

2 _____ Death and Taxes

During the great Northwest famine, which lasted roughly for three years and affected four huge provinces, I visited some of the drought-stricken areas in Suiyuan, on the edge of Mongolia, in June, 1929. How many people starved to death in those years I do not accurately know, and probably no one will ever know; it is forgotten now. A conservative semi-official figure of 3,000,000 is often accepted, but I am not inclined to doubt other estimates ranging as high as 6,000,000.

This catastrophe passed hardly noticed in the Western world, and even in the coastal cities of China, but a few courageous Chinese and foreigners attached to the American-financed China International Famine Relief Commission—including its secretary, Dwight Edwards; O. J. Todd, the American engineer; and a wonderful American missionary doctor, Robert Ingram[1]—risked their lives in those typhus-infested areas, trying to salvage some of the human wreckage. I spent some days with them, passing through cities of death, across a once-fertile countryside turned into desert wasteland, through a land of naked horror.

I was twenty-three. I had come to the East looking for the "glamor of the Orient," searching for adventure. This excursion to Suiyuan had begun as something like that. But here for the first time in my life I came abruptly upon men who were dying because they had nothing to eat. In those hours of nightmare I spent in Suiyuan I saw thousands of men, women, and children starving to death before my eyes.

Have you ever seen a man—a good honest man who has worked hard, a "law-abiding citizen," doing no serious harm to anyone—when he has had no food for more than a month? It is a most agonizing sight. His dying flesh hangs from him in wrinkled folds; you can clearly see every bone in his body; his eyes stare out unseeing; and even if he is a youth of twenty he

---

1. Dr. Ingram was killed a few years later by Chinese bandits, but *not* Red bandits.

他即使是个 20 岁的青年，行动起来也像个干瘪的老太婆，一步一迈，走不动路。他早已卖了妻鬻了女，那还算是他的运气。他把什么都已卖了——房上的木梁，身上的衣服，有时甚至卖了最后的一块遮羞布。他在烈日下摇摇晃晃，睾丸软软地挂在那里像干瘪的橄榄核儿——这是最后一个严峻的嘲弄，提醒你他原来曾经是一个人！

儿童们甚至更加可怜，他们的小骷髅弯曲变形，关节突出，骨瘦如柴，鼓鼓的肚皮由于塞满了树皮锯末像生了肿瘤一样。女人们躺在角落里等死，屁股上没有肉，瘦骨嶙峋，乳房干瘪下垂，像空麻袋一样。但是，女人和姑娘毕竟不多，大多数不是死了就是给卖了。

我并不想要危言耸听。这些现象都是我亲眼看到而且永远不会忘记的。在灾荒中，千百万的人就这样死了，今天还有成千上万的人在中国这样死去。我在沙拉子街上看到过新尸，在农村里，我看到过万人冢里一层层埋着几十个这种灾荒和时疫的受害者。但是这毕竟还不是最叫人吃惊的。叫人吃惊的事情是，在许多这种城市里，仍有许多有钱人，囤积大米小麦的商人、地主老财，他们有武装警卫保护着他们在大发其财。叫人吃惊的事情是，在城市里，做官的和歌妓舞女跳舞打麻将，那里有的是粮食谷物，而且好几个月一直都有；在北京、天津等地，有千千万万吨的麦子小米，那是赈灾委员会收集的（大部分来自国外的捐献），可是却不能运去救济灾民。为什么？因为在西北，有些军阀要扣留他们的全部铁路车皮，一节也不准东驶，而在东部，其他国民党将领也不肯让车皮西去——哪怕去救济灾民——因为怕被对方扣留。

在灾情最甚的时候，赈灾委员会决定（用美国经费）修一条大渠灌溉一些缺水的土地。官员们欣然合作——立刻开始以几分钱 1 亩的低价收购了灌溉区的所有土地。一群贪心的兀鹰飞降这个黑暗的国家，以欠租或几个铜板大批收购饥饿农民手中的土地，然后等待有雨情后出租给佃户。

然而那些饿死的人大多数是在不作任何抗议的情况下死去的。

"他们为什么不造反？"我这样问自己，"为什么他们不联成一股大军，攻打那些向他们征收苛捐杂税却不能让他们吃饱、强占他们土地却不能修复灌溉渠的恶棍坏蛋？为什么他们不打进大城市里去抢那些把他们妻女买去，那些继续摆 36 道菜的筵席而让诚实的人挨饿的流氓无赖？为什么？"

moves like an ancient crone, dragging himself from spot to spot. If he has been lucky he has long ago sold his wife and daughters. He has also sold everything he owns—the timber of his house itself, and most of his clothes. Sometimes he has, indeed, even sold the last rag of decency, and he sways there in the scorching sun, his testicles dangling from him like withered olive seeds—the last grim jest to remind you that this was once a man.

Children are even more pitiable, with their little skeletons bent over and misshapen, their crooked bones, their little arms like twigs, and their purpling bellies, filled with bark and sawdust, protruding like tumors. Women lie slumped in corners, waiting for death, their black blade-like buttocks protruding, their breasts hanging like collapsed sacks. But there are, after all, not many women and girls. Most of them have died or been sold.

Those were things I myself had seen and would never forget. Millions of people died that way in famine, and thousands more still died in China like that. I had seen fresh corpses on the streets of Saratsi, and in the villages I had seen shallow graves where victims of famine and disease were laid by the dozens. But these were not the most shocking things after all. The shocking thing was that in many of those towns there were still rich men, rice hoarders, wheat hoarders, moneylenders, and landlords, with armed guards to defend them, while they profiteered enormously. The shocking thing was that in the cities—where officials danced or played with sing-song girls—there were grain and food, and had been for months; that in Peking and Tientsin and elsewhere were thousands of tons of wheat and millet, collected (mostly by contributions from abroad) by the Famine Commission, but which could not be shipped to the starving. Why not? Because in the Northwest there were some militarists who wanted to hold all of their railroad rolling stock and would release none of it toward the east, while in the east there were other Kuomintang generals who would send no rolling stock westward—even to starving people—because they feared it would be seized by their rivals.

While famine raged the Commission decided to build a big canal (with American funds) to help flood some of the lands baked by drought. The officials gave them every cooperation—and promptly began to buy for a few cents an acre all the lands to be irrigated. A flock of vultures descended upon this benighted country and purchased from the starving farmers thousands of acres for the taxes in arrears, or for a few coppers, and held it to await tenants and rainy days.

Yet the great majority of those people who died did so without any act of protest.

"Why don't they revolt?" I asked myself. "Why don't they march in a great army and attack the scoundrels who can tax them but cannot feed them, who can seize their lands but cannot repair an irrigation canal? Or why don't they sweep into the great cities and plunder the wealth of the rascals who buy their daughters and wives, the men who continue to gorge on thirty-six-course banquets while honest men starve? Why not?"

他们的消极无为使我深为迷惑不解。我有一段时间认为，没有什么事情会使一个中国人起来斗争。

我错了。中国农民不是消极的；中国农民不是胆小鬼。只要有方法，有组织，有领导，有可行的纲领，有希望——**而且有武器**，他们是会斗争的。中国共产主义运动的发展证明了这一点。因此，在上述这种背景下，我们得悉共产党人在西北特别受人民欢迎，是不应该感到奇怪的，因为那里的情况对于农民群众来说同中国其他地方一样，都没有根本的改善。

这方面的事实已经得到你万万没有想到的一个人士的生动的证实，我在这里指的是斯坦普尔博士[1]所提出的精彩报告，他是国际联盟派赴南京政府担任顾问的著名卫生专家。他的材料是这方面最精彩的材料。斯坦普尔博士最近在陕西和甘肃省的国民党统辖区进行了考察，他的报告所根据的材料除了是向他提供的官方材料以外也有他本人的观察。

他指出在"公元前240年据说有一个名叫郑国的工程师"，在中华民族的摇篮、历史上有名的陕西渭水流域"修筑了一个能灌溉近100万英亩土地的灌溉网，但是后来年久失修，水坝崩塌，虽然经常修筑了新的工程，到清朝末年（1912年），灌溉面积只有2万亩不到"——约3,300英亩！他弄到的数字证明，在大灾荒期间，陕西有一个县，死的就有62%的人口；另一县死的有75%；如此等等。据官方估计，单在甘肃一省就饿死200万人——约占人口总数的20%。要是官厅禁止囤积粮食，交战的军阀没有干扰赈济物资的运输的话，这些人有许多是可以不死的。

这里引述一段这位日内瓦来的调查人员关于红军到达以前在西北见到的情况的话：

> 在1930年灾荒中，3天口粮可以买到20英亩的土地。该省［陕西］有钱阶级利用这个机会购置了大批地产，自耕农人数锐减。中国国际赈灾委员会的芬德莱·安德鲁先生1930年报告中的下述一段话充分说明了该年的情况：
> "……该省外表情况比去年大有改善。为什么？因为在甘肃省内我们工作的那一地区，饥饿、疾病、兵燹在过去两年中夺去了大量人口，因此对粮食的需求

---

1. 见斯坦普尔博士著《西北各省与其发展前途》，由国家经济委员会非公开出版（1934年7月南京）。不幸，像斯坦普尔博士和国联其他调查华南和华中的专家的许多说明问题的报告一样，这本书没有公开发行。

I was profoundly puzzled by their passivity. For a while I thought nothing would make a Chinese fight.

I was mistaken. The Chinese peasant was not passive; he was not a coward. He would fight when given a method, an organization, leadership, a workable program, hope—*and arms*. The development of "communism" in China had proved that. Against the above background, therefore, it should not surprise us to learn that Communists were popular in the Northwest, for conditions there had been no better for the mass of the peasantry than elsewhere in China.

Evidence to that effect had been vividly documented by Dr. A. Stampar,[1] the distinguished health expert sent by the League of Nations as adviser to the Nanking Government. It was the best thing available on the subject. Dr. Stampar had toured the Kuomintang areas of Shensi and Kansu, and his reports were based on his own observations as well as official data opened for him.

He pointed out that "in the year 240 B.C. an engineer called Cheng Kuo is said to have constructed a system for irrigating nearly a million acres" in the historic Wei Valley of Shensi, cradle of the Chinese race, but that "this system was neglected; the dams collapsed, and, though new works were from time to time carried out, the amount of territory irrigated at the end of the Manchu Dynasty (1912) was less than 20,000 *mou*" — about 3,300 acres. Figures he obtained showed that during the great famine 62 per cent of the population died outright in one county of Shensi; in another, 75 per cent; and so on. Official estimates revealed that 2,000,000 people starved in Kansu alone—about 20 per cent of the population.

To quote from this Geneva investigator on conditions in the Northwest before the Reds arrived:

In the famine of 1930 twenty acres of land could be purchased for three days' food supply. Making use of this opportunity, the wealthy classes of the province [Shensi] built up large estates, and the number of owner-cultivators diminished. The following extract from the report for 1930 of Mr. Findlay Andrew of the China International Famine Relief Commission conveys a good impression of the situation in that year:

". . . The external appearances of the Province have much improved on those of last year. Why? Because in this particular section of Kansu with which our work deals, death from starvation, pestilence, and sword have doomed during the past two years

---

1. Dr. A. Stampar, *The Northwestern Provinces and Their Possibilities of Development*, published privately by the National Economic Council (Nanking, July, 1934).

已大为缓和。"

许多土地荒芜,许多土地集中在地主官僚手中。特别是甘肃,有"数量大得惊人"的可耕而未耕的大批土地。"1928 到 1930 年灾荒期间,地主极其廉价地收购了土地,他们从那时候起就靠修筑渭北灌溉工程[1]而发了财。"

在陕西,不付土地税被认为是件体面的事,因此有钱的地主一般都免税……特别可恶的一件事是征收在灾荒期间外出逃荒的农民在此期间积欠的税款,在欠税付清之前,他们被剥夺了土地所有权。

斯坦普尔博士发现,陕西的农民(显然不包括地主,因为他们"一般免税")所付土地税和附加税达收入 45% 左右,其他捐税"又占 20%";"不仅捐税如此繁重惊人,而且估税方式也似乎很随便,至于征收方式则浪费、残暴,在许多情况下贪污腐败。"

至于甘肃,斯坦普尔博士说:

在过去 5 年内甘肃税收平均超过 800 万……比中国最富饶的、也是收税最重的省份之一浙江还重。也可以看到,这种税收的来源,特别是在甘肃,不止一两种主要的捐税,而是名目繁多的许多杂税,每种收集一笔小款,几乎没有一种货物、没有一种生产或商业活动不收税的。人民实际所付税款要比公布数字还高。首先,收税的可以从所收税款中保留一份——有时极大的一份。其次,除了省政府、县政府所收税款以外,还有军方领导人所征的税,官方估计这在甘肃省约 1,000 多万[2]。

---

1. 赈灾委员会出资扶持的一项赈灾措施。
2. 这是个保守的估计,因为它没有提到甘肃和陕西两省军方主要的非法税收——多年以来一直是鸦片税。西安府给我的数字表明,冯玉祥将军控制这一带时,每年可从这一来源得到 8,000 万元。从那时以后,此数无疑已大为减少,那是由于南京鸦片专卖的竞争,但仍每年有好几百万。

such large numbers of the population that the very demand for food has considerably lessened."

Much land had become waste, much had been concentrated in the hands of landlords and officials. Kansu especially had "surprisingly large" areas of cultivable but uncultivated land. "Land during the famine of 1928—1930 was bought at extremely cheap rates by landowners who, since that period, have realized fortunes by the execution of the Wei Pei Irrigation project" (a famine-relief measure financed by the Commission).

In Shensi it is considered a mark of honor to pay no land tax, and wealthy landowners are therefore as a rule exempted . . . . A practice which is particularly undesirable is to claim arrears of taxes, for the period during which they were absent, from the farmers who abandoned their land during famines, the farmers being forbidden to resume possession until their arrears are paid.

Dr. Stampar found that Shensi farmers (evidently excluding the landlords, who were "as a rule exempted") had to pay land taxes and surtaxes amounting to about 45 per cent of their income, while other taxes "represent a further 20 per cent"; and "not only is taxation thus fantastically heavy, but its assessment appears to be haphazard and its manner of collection wasteful, brutal, and in many cases corrupt."

As for Kansu, Dr. Stampar said:

The revenues of Kansu have during the last five years averaged over eight millions . . . heavier taxation than in Chekiang, one of the richest and most heavily taxed provinces in China. It will be seen also that this revenue, especially in Kansu, is not drawn from one or two major sources, but from a multitude of taxes each yielding a small sum, scarcely any commodity or productive or commercial activity going untaxed. The amount which the population pays is even higher than is shown by the published figures. In the first place, the tax collectors are able to retain a share—in some cases a very large share—of the amounts collected. In the second place, to the taxes levied by the provincial or hsien governments must be added those imposed by military leaders, which in Kansu province are officially estimated at more than ten millions.[1]

---

1. This was a conservative estimate, since it included no mention of the chief illegal military taxation in both Kansu and Shensi, for many years the opium revenue.

造成人民负担的另一个原因是地方民团，这本来是为了防范土匪而组织的，在许多情况下已堕落成为鱼肉乡里的匪帮。

斯坦普尔博士引证的数字表明，民团的维持费达地方政府总预算的30%到40%，当然，在维持大规模正规军的负担之外，再加上这一笔负担是很可观的。据斯坦普尔博士说，正规军的维持费占去了甘肃陕西两省收入的60%以上。

我在陕西遇到的一个外国传教士告诉我，他有一次曾经跟着一头猪从养猪人到消费者那里，在整个过程中，看到了征六种不同的税。甘肃的另外一个传教士谈到，他看见农民把家里的木梁拆下来（在西北木料很值钱）运到市场上去卖掉来付税。他说，甚至是有些"富"农，虽然在红军到达之初态度并不友好，但也是无所谓的，而且认为"随便什么政府都不会比原来那个更坏"。

但是从经济上来说，西北绝不是个没有希望的地方。它的人口不多，许多土地都很肥沃，要生产大大超过消费，是轻而易举的事，只要改进灌溉系统，它的一些地方很可能成为"中国的乌克兰"。陕西和甘肃有丰富的煤矿。陕西还有一点石油。斯坦普尔博士预言，"陕西，特别是西安附近的平原，很可能成为一个工业中心，其重要性仅次于长江流域，只需把煤田用来为自己服务就行了。"甘肃、青海、新疆的矿藏据说非常丰富，很少开发。斯坦普尔说，单是黄金，"这一地带很可能成为第二个克朗代克。[1]"

这里，肯定地说，存在着早已成熟的实行变革的条件。这里，肯定地说，存在着人们要起来反对的东西，即使他们还没有斗争的**目标**！因此，当红星在西北出现时，无怪有千千万万的人起来欢迎它，把它当作希望和自由的象征。

但是红军究竟是不是好一些呢？

---

1. 在加拿大西北边境，上世纪末曾发现金矿。——译注

> *A further cause of expense to the population is the local militia [min-t'uan], which, formed originally for defense against the bandits, has in many instances degenerated into a gang living at the cost of the countryside.*

Dr. Stampar quoted figures showing that the cost of supporting the *min-t'uan* ranged from 30 to 40 per cent of the total local government budget—this quite in addition, of course, to the burden of maintaining the big regular armies. These latter, according to Dr. Stampar, had absorbed over 60 per cent of the provincial revenues in both Kansu and Shensi.

A foreign missionary I met in Shensi told me that he had once personally followed a pig from owner to consumer, and in the process saw six different taxes being paid. Another missionary, of Kansu, described seeing peasants knock down the wooden walls of their houses (wood being expensive in the Northwest) and cart it to market to sell in order to pay tax collectors. He said that the attitude of even some of the "rich" peasants, while not friendly when the Reds first arrived, was one of indifference, and a belief that "no government could be worse than the old."

And yet the Northwest was by no means a hopeless country economically. It was not overpopulated; much of its land was very rich; it could easily produce far more than it could consume; and with an improved irrigation system parts of it might become a "Chinese Ukraine." Shensi and Kansu had abundant coal deposits. Shensi had oil. Dr. Stampar prophesied that "Shensi, especially the plain in the neighborhood of Sian, may itself become an industrial center of an importance second only to the Yangtze Valley, and needing for its service its own coal fields." Mineral deposits of Kansu, Chinghai, and Sinkiang, said to be very rich, were scarcely touched. In gold alone, said Stampar, "the region may turn out to be a second Klondike."

Here, surely, were conditions which seemed overripe for change. Here, surely, were things for men to fight against, even if they had nothing to fight *for.* And no wonder, when the Red Star appeared in the Northwest, thousands of men arose to welcome it as a symbol of hope and freedom.

But did the Reds, after all, prove any better?

三、　　苏维埃社会

不论中国共产主义运动在南方的情况如何，就我在西北所看到的而论，如果称之为农村平均主义，较之马克思作为自己的模范产儿而认为合适的任何名称，也许更加确切一些。这在经济上尤其显著。在有组织的苏区的社会、政治、文化生活中，虽然有一种马克思主义的简单指导，但是物质条件的局限性到处是显而易见的。

前已强调指出西北没有任何有重要意义的机器工业，这个地区比中国东部一些地区受到的工业化影响要少得多，它主要是农业和畜牧区，好几个世纪以来，文化趋于停滞状态，虽然现在存在的许多经济上的弊端无疑是半工业化城市中经济情况变化的反映。但是红军本身就是"工业化"对中国的影响的显著产物，它对这里化石般的文化所带来的思想震荡确确实实是革命性质的。

但是，客观条件不允许共产党有可能组织大大地超过社会主义经济初生时期的政治体制，对此他们自然只能从未来角度来加以考虑，以期有朝一日他们有可能在大城市中取得政权，那时他们可以把外国租界中的工业基地接过手来，从而为一个真正的社会主义社会奠定基础。在此以前，他们在农村地区的活动主要集中在解决农民的当前问题——土地和租税。这听起来可能有点像俄国以前的民粹派反动纲领，但是，其根本不同之处在于这个事实：中国共产党人从来只把分配土地看成是建设群众基础的一个阶段，使他们能够发展革命斗争，以夺取政权和最后实现彻底的社会主义改革的一种策略。届时集体化就势所难免。中华全国苏维埃第一次代表大会1931年就在《中华苏维埃共和国的基本法律》[1]中详细地提出了中国共产党的"最高纲领"——

---

1. 毛泽东等。

3   SOVIET SOCIETY

Whatever it may have been in the South, Chinese communism as I found it in the Northwest might more accurately be called rural equalitarianism than anything Marx would have found acceptable as a model child of his own. This was manifestly true economically, and although in the social, political, and cultural life of the organized soviets there was a crude Marxist guidance, limitations of material conditions were everywhere obvious.

There was no machine industry of any importance in the Northwest. It was farming and grazing country primarily, the culture of which had been for centuries in stagnation, though many of the economic abuses prevalent no doubt reflected the changing economy in the semi-industrialized cities. Yet the Red Army itself was an outstanding product of the impact of "industrialization" on China, and the shock of the ideas it had brought into the fossilized culture here was in a true sense revolutionary.

Objective conditions, however, denied the Reds the possibility of organizing much more than the political framework for the beginnings of a modern economy, of which naturally they could think only in terms of a future which might give them power in the great cities, where they could take over the industrial bases from the foreign concessions and thus lay the foundations for a Socialist society. Meanwhile, in the rural areas their activity centered chiefly on the solution of the immediate problems of the peasants—land and taxes. But Chinese Communists never regarded land distribution as anything more than a phase in the building of a mass base, a stage enabling them to develop the revolutionary struggle toward the conquest of power and the ultimate realization of thoroughgoing Socialist changes. In *Fundamental Laws of the Chinese Soviet Republic*,[1] the First All-China Soviet Congress in 1931 had set forth in detail the "maximum program" of the Communist Party of China—and reference to it showed clearly that the ultimate aim of

---

1. Mao Tse-tung *et al.*

提到"最高纲领"的话清楚地表明，中国共产党人的最终目的是按照马克思列宁主义理论建设一个真正的完全的社会主义国家。但是，在此以前，必须记住，红区的社会、政治、经济组织一直不过是一种非常临时性的过渡。甚至在江西，也完全是如此。由于苏区从一开始起就得为生存而战，他们的主要任务一直是建设一个军事政治根据地，以便在更广泛、更深刻的规模上扩大革命，而不是"在中国试行共产主义"，而有不少人却以为这就是共产党在他们小小的被封锁的地区中在尝试的事情。

共产党在西北所以受到群众拥护，其当前的基础显然不是"各尽所能，各取所需"，而是有点像孙逸仙博士的主张："耕者有其田"。共产党可以自居有功的一些经济改革措施中，对农民最有重要意义的显然有这四项：重新分配土地，取消高利贷，取消苛捐杂税，消灭特权阶级。

从理论上来说，苏维埃固然是一种"工农"政府，但在实际执行中，全部选民中不论从成分上来说，还是从职业上来说，农民占压倒多数，因此政权得与此适应。为了要制约农民的势力，抵消这种势力，把农村人口划分为这几个阶层：大地主、中小地主、富农、中农、贫农、佃农、雇农、手工业者、流氓无产阶级和自由职业者，即专业工作者，包括教员、医生、技术人员、"农村知识分子"。这种划分不仅是经济上的划分，也是政治上的划分，在苏区选举中，佃农、雇农、手工业者等比其他阶层的代表的名额比例大得多，其目的显然是要造成"农村无产阶级"的某种民主专政。但是，很难看到这些类别之中有什么重要的根本阶级区别在起作用，因为他们都是直接依附于农业经济的。

在这些限度内，凡是政权稳定的地方，苏维埃似乎工作得很顺利。代议制政府结构是从最小的单位村苏维埃开始建立的，上面是乡苏维埃、县苏维埃、省苏维埃，最后是中央苏维埃。每村各选代表若干人参加上级苏维埃，依此类推，一直到苏维埃代表大会的代表。凡年满16岁的，普遍都有选举权，但选举权不是平等的，理由已如上述。

每一乡苏维埃下设各种委员会。权力最大的委员会是革命委员会，那往往是红军占领一个乡以后经过一阵紧张的宣传运动再举行群众大会选出来的。它有决定选举或改选权，同共产党合作紧密。乡苏维埃下面设教育、合作社、军训、政训、土地、卫生、游击队训练、革命防御、扩大红军、农业互助、红军耕田等等委员会，由乡苏维埃指派。苏维埃的每一分支机构中都有这种委员会，一直到负责统一各项政策和作出全国性决策的中央政府。

Chinese Communists was a Socialist State of the Marxist-Leninist conception. Meanwhile, however, the social, political, and economic organization of the Red districts had all along been a very provisional affair. Even in Kiangsi it was little more than that. Because the soviets had to fight for an existence from their beginning, their main task was always to build a military and political base for the extension of the revolution on a wider and deeper scale, rather than to "try out communism in China," which is what some people thought the Reds were attempting in their little blockaded areas.

The immediate basis of support for the Reds in the Northwest was obviously not so much the idea of "from each according to his ability, to each according to his needs" as it was something like the promise of Dr. Sun Yat-sen: "Land to those who till it."

While theoretically the soviets were a "workers' and peasants'" government, in actual practice the whole constituency was overwhelmingly peasant in character and occupation, and the regime had to shape itself accordingly. An attempt was made to balance peasant influence, and offset it, by classifying the rural population into these categories: great landlords, middle and small landlords, rich peasants, middle peasants, poor peasants, tenant peasants, rural workers, handicraft workers, *lumpen* proletariat, and a division called *tzu-yu chihi-yeh chieh*, or professional workers which included teachers, doctors, and technicians, the "rural intelligentsia." These divisions were political as well as economic, and in the soviet elections the tenant peasants, rural workers, handicraft workers, and so on were given a very much greater representation than the other categories—the aim apparently being to create some kind of democratic dictatorship of the "rural proletariat."

Within these limitations the soviets seemed to work very well in areas where the regime was stabilized. The structure of representative government was built up from the village soviet, as the smallest unit: above it were the district soviet, the county soviet, and the provincial and central soviets. Each village elected its delegates to the higher soviets clear up to the delegates elected for the Soviet Congress. Suffrage was universal over the age of sixteen, but it was not equal, for reasons mentioned above.

Various committees were established under each of the district soviets. An all-powerful committee, usually elected in a mass meeting shortly after the occupation of a district by the Red Army, and preceded by an intensified propaganda campaign, was the revolutionary committee. It called for elections or re-elections, and closely cooperated with the Communist Party. Under the district soviet, and appointed by it, were committees for education, cooperatives, military training, political training, land, public health, partisan training, revolutionary defense, enlargement of the Red Army, agrarian mutual aid, Red Army land tilling, and others. Such committees were found in every branch organ of the soviets, right up to the Central Government, where policies were coordinated and state decisions made.

组织工作并不是到政府机构为止。共产党在工农、城乡中有大量的党员。此外，还有共青团，团之下又有两个组织，把大部分青年都组织起来。这两个组织是少年先锋队和儿童团。共产党把妇女们也组织到共青团、抗日协会、幼儿园、纺纱班、耕种队中去。成年的农民组织在贫民会、抗日协会中。甚至哥老会这个古老的秘密会社，也让它参加到苏维埃生活中来，从事公开合法的活动。农卫队和游击队也属于组织严密的农村政治社会结构的一部分。

这些组织和它们各个委员会的工作都是由中央苏维埃政府、共产党、红军来领导的。我们在这里不需要引用详尽的统计数字或令人厌烦的图表来说明这些机构的组织联系，但是总的可以说它们都是巧妙地结合在一起的，都是在一个共产党员的直接领导下，尽管每个组织似乎是由农民自己用民主方式作出决定、吸收成员、进行工作的。苏维埃组织的目的显然是使得每一个男女老幼都是某个组织的成员，有一定的工作分派他去完成。

苏维埃这种紧张频繁的活动具有典型性的一个例子，是他们为了要增加产量、利用大片荒地而采取的方法。我弄到了土地委员会发给各个分支机构，指导他们组织农民从事耕种和在这方面进行宣传的许多命令，范围之广和内容之实际，使人相当惊讶。例如，我在土地委员会一个办事处看到的一项命令，对于春耕工作发出了具体的指示，土地委员会要求工作人员"进行广泛的宣传，争取农民自愿参加，不要有任何强迫命令"。对于如何在耕种季节完成4项主要的要求，提出了具体的意见。这4项要求根据去年冬天苏维埃的决定是：更加充分地利用荒地和扩大红军耕地；增加作物产量；扩大作物品种，特别重视新品种的瓜菜；扩大棉花种植面积。

这项命令[1]为了扩大劳动力，特别是争取妇女直接参加农业生产（尤其是在那些

---

1. 土地委员会的指示。1936年1月28日（陕西瓦窑堡）。

Organization did not stop with the government itself. The Communist Party had an extensive membership among farmers and workers, in the towns and in the villages. In addition there were the Young Communists, and under them two organizations which embraced in their membership most of the youth. These were called the Shao-Nien Hsien-Feng Tui and the Erh-T'ung T'uan—the Young Vanguards and the Children's Brigades. The Communist Party organized the women also into Communist Youth Leagues, anti-Japanese societies, nursing schools, weaving schools, and tilling brigades. Adult farmers were organized into the P'in-Min Hui, or Poor People's Society, and into anti-Japanese societies. Even the Elder Brother Society was brought into soviet life and given open and legal work to do. The Nung-min Tui, or Peasant Guards, and the Yu Chi Tui, or Partisan (Roving) Brigades, were also part of the intensely organized rural political and social structure.

The work of all these organizations and their various committees was coordinated by the Central Soviet Government, the Communist Party, and the Red Army. Here we need not enter into statistical detail to explain the organic connections of these groups, but it can be said in general that they were all skillfully interwoven, and each directly under the guidance of some Communist, though decisions of organization, membership, and work seemed to be carried out in a democratic way by the peasants themselves. The aim of soviet organization obviously was to make every man, woman, and child a member of something, with definite work assigned to him to perform.

Rather typical of the intensity of soviet efforts were the methods used to increase production and utilize great areas of wasteland. I procured copies of many orders, quite astonishing in their scope and common-sense practicality, issued by the Land Commission to its various branches to guide them in organizing and propagandizing the peasants in the tasks of cultivation. To illustrate: in one of these orders that I picked up in a branch land office, instructions were given concerning spring cultivation, the commission urging its workers to "make widespread propaganda to induce the masses to participate voluntarily, without involving any form of compulsory command." Detailed advice was offered on how to achieve the four main demands of this planting period, which the previous winter had been recognized by the soviets to be: more extensive utilization of wasteland, and expansion of Red Army land; increased crop yields; greater diversity of crops, with special emphasis on new varieties of melons and vegetables; and expansion of cotton acreage.

Among the devices recommended by this order[1] to expand labor power, and especially to bring women directly into agricultural production (particularly in districts where the

---

1. *Order of Instruction*, Land Commission (Wa Ya Pao, Shensi), January 28, 1936.

由于参加红军而男性人口减少的地方）所提出的方法中，下面这个绝妙的指示说明红军利用现有材料极有效果：

> 要动员妇女、儿童、老人参加春播春耕，各人按其能力在劳动生产过程中担任主要的或辅助的工作。例如，应动员大脚妇女和年轻妇女组织生产训练队，从事从清地到农业生产主要任务等工作。小脚妇女、儿童、老人应动员起来帮助除草、积肥等其他辅助劳动。

但是农民的反应怎样？中国农民一般不愿受组织、纪律的约束，不愿从事超过自己家庭范围以外的任何社会活动。共产党听到这话就大笑。他们说，中国农民如果是为自己工作而不是为民团——地主和税吏，他们没有不喜欢组织或社会活动的。我不得不承认，我所接触到的农民，大多数似乎是拥护苏维埃和红军的。他们有许多人意见批评一大堆，但是问到他们是否愿意过现在的生活而不愿过以前的生活，答复几乎总是有力地肯定的。我也注意到他们大多数人谈到苏维埃时用的是"我们的政府"，这使我觉得，在中国农村，这是一种新现象。

有一件事可以说明共产党在人民群众中有基础，那就是在所有老苏区里，警卫工作几乎全部由农民自己组织起来担任的。苏区很少有红军的驻防部队，因为所有战斗力量都在前线。地方的保卫工作是由村革命保卫队、农卫队、游击队分担的。这个事实可以说明红军在农民中间得到拥护的一部分原因，因为红军很少像其他军队那样是强加在他们身上的压迫和剥削工具，而一般是在前线，在那里为自己的口粮作战，应付敌人进攻。另一方面，把农民严密地组织起来，红军便有了后卫和基地，可以放手进行极其机动的作战，而这正是它的特点。

但是要真正了解农民对共产主义运动的拥护，必须记住它的经济基础。我已经谈到过西北农民在旧政权下所承受的沉重负担。现在，红军不论到哪里，他们都毫

male population had declined as a result of enlistments in the Red Army), the following ingenious instruction suggested the efficiency with which the Reds went about utilizing their available materials:

To mobilize women, boys, and old men to participate in spring planting and cultivation, each according to his ability to carry on either a principal or an auxiliary task in the labor processes of production. For example, 'large feet' [natural feet] and young women should be mobilized to organize production-teaching corps, with tasks varying from land clearance up to the main tasks of agricultural production itself. 'Small feet' [bound feet], young boys, and old men must be mobilized to help in weed-pulling, collecting dung, and for other auxiliary tasks.

But how did the peasants feel about this? The Chinese peasant was supposed to hate organization, discipline, and any social activity beyond his own family. The Reds laughed when that was mentioned. They said that no Chinese peasant disliked organization or social activity if he was working for himself and not the *min-t'uan*—the landlord or the tax collector. And I had to admit that most of the peasants to whom I talked seemed to support soviets and the Red Army. Many of them were very free in their criticisms and complaints, but when asked whether they preferred it to the old days, the answer was nearly always an emphatic yes. I noticed also that most of them talked about the soviets as *wo-menti chengfu*—"our government" —and this struck me as something new in rural China.

One thing which suggested that the Reds had their "base" in the mass of the population was that in all the older soviet districts the policing and guarding was done almost entirely by the peasant organizations alone. There were few actual Red Army garrisons in the soviet districts, all the fighting strength of the army being kept at the front. Local defense was shared by the village revolutionary defense corps, peasant guards, and partisans. This fact could explain some of the apparent popularity of the Red Army with the (poor) peasantry, for it was rarely planted down on them as an instrument of oppression and exploitation, like other armies, but was generally at the front, fighting for its food there, and engaged in meeting enemy attacks. On the other hand, the intensive organization of the peasantry created a rear guard and base which freed the Red Army to operate with the extreme mobility for which it was noted.

To understand peasant support for the Communist movement it was necessary to keep in mind the burden borne by the peasantry in the Northwest under the former regime. Now, wherever the Reds went there was no doubt that they radically changed the situation for

无疑问地根本改变了佃农、贫农、中农以及所有"贫苦"成分的处境。在新区中第一年就取消了**一切**租税，使农民们有透口气的机会，在老区里，只保留一种单一的累进土地税和一种单一的小额营业税（5%到10%）。其次，他们把土地分给缺地农民，大片大片地开"荒"——多数是在外或在逃地主的土地。第三，他们没收有钱阶级的土地和牲口，分配给穷人。

重新分配土地是共产党政策中的一个根本要素。这是怎样进行的？后来，为了全国性的政治策略上的考虑，苏维埃土地政策作了大踏步的后退，但是我在西北访问期间所实行的土地法（由西北苏维埃政府在1935年12月颁布）规定要没收所有地主的土地，没收富农不是由自己耕种的所有土地。不过不论地主或富农都有一份自己有能力耕种的土地。在不缺地的乡里——那样的乡在西北有不少——在乡地主和富农的土地实际上一点也没有没收，分配的只是荒地和在外地主的土地，有时还把最好的土地重新分配，好地给贫农，同样数量的劣地给地主。

什么人算地主？根据共产党的（大大简化了的）定义，凡是大部分收入来自出租给别人种的土地而自己不劳动的人都是地主。根据这个定义，高利贷者和土豪[1]与地主属于同类，因此受到同样对待。据斯坦普尔博士说，高利贷的利率在西北原来高达60%，在困难时期还要高得多。虽然在甘肃、陕西、宁夏的许多地方，土地很便宜，一个雇工或者佃户，如果没有资金，几乎不可能积钱为自己家庭买足够的田的。我在红区遇到过许多农民，他们以前是从来不可能拥有土地的，虽然有些地方地价低到只有两三元银洋1英亩。[2]

除了上述以外的阶级都不受没收的影响，因此土地重新分配使很大比例的农民得到眼前利益。贫农、佃农、雇农都得到了足以维持生计的土地。看来并没有想起

---

1. 土豪是红军称呼那些其收入中一大部分来自放债和抵押品买卖的地主。
2. 家畜的价格远远高于土地。参见第七篇第二章。

the tenant farmer, the poor farmer, the middle farmer, and all the "have-not" elements. *All* forms of taxation were abolished in the new districts for the first year, to give the farmers a breathing space, and in the old districts only a progressive single tax on land was collected, and a small single tax (from 5 to 10 per cent) on business. Second, the Reds gave land to the land-hungry peasants, and began the reclamation of great areas of "wasteland"—mostly the land of absentee or fleeing landlords. Third, they took land and livestock from the wealthy classes and redistributed them among the poor.

Redistribution of land was a fundamental of Red policy. How was it carried out? Later on, for reasons of national political maneuver, there was to be a drastic retreat in the soviet land policy, but when I traveled in the Northwest the land laws in force (promulgated by the Northwest Soviet Government in December, 1935) provided for the confiscation of all landlords' land and the confiscation of all land of rich peasants that was not cultivated by the owners themselves. However, both the landlord and the rich peasant were allowed as much land as they could till with their own labor. In districts where there was no land scarcity—and there were many such districts in the Northwest—the lands of resident landlords and rich peasants were in practice not confiscated at all, but the wasteland and land of absentee owners was distributed, and sometimes there was a redivision of best-quality land, poor peasants being given better soil, and landlords being allotted the same amount of poorer land.

What was a landlord? According to the Communists definition (greatly simplified), any farmer who collected the greater part of his income from land rented out to others, and not from his own labor, was a landlord. By this definition the usurers and *t'u-hao*[1] were put in about the same category as landlords, and similarly treated. Usury rates, according to Dr. Stampar, had formerly ranged as high as 60 per cent in the Northwest, or very much higher in times of stress. Although land was very cheap in many parts of Kansu, Shensi, and Ninghsia, cash was unbelievably scarce. In practice it was nearly impossible for a farm worker or tenant with no capital to accumulate enough to buy sufficient land for his family. I met farmers in the Red districts who formerly had never been able to own any land, although rates in some places were as low as two or three dollars (in silver) an acre.[2]

Classes other than those mentioned above were not subject to confiscatory action, so a big percentage of the farmers stood to benefit immediately by the redistribution. The poorest farmers, tenants, and farm laborers were all provided with land enough

---

1. *T'u-hao*, which actually means "local rascals," was the Reds' term for landowners who also derived a large part of their income from lending money and buying and selling mortgages.
2. Domestic animals were far more costly than land. See Part Seven, Chapter 2.

把土地所有权"平均化"。据王观澜（29岁的俄国留学生，西北三省的土地人民委员）向我解释，苏维埃土地法的主要目的是为每个人提供足够的土地，保证他和他的一家人能够过足够温饱的生活，他们认为这是农民的最"迫切要求"。

土地问题——没收和分配土地问题——在西北由于大地产多半是属于官僚、税吏、在外地主而简单化了。在没收以后，多数情况是贫农的当前要求得到了满足，不怎么干扰在乡小地主或富农。因此红军不仅由于给贫农和无地农民土地而得到他们拥护的经济基础，而且在有些情况下也由于取消捐税剥削而赢得了中农的感激，在少数情况下由于同样原因或者通过抗日运动的爱国宣传而争取到了小地主的支持。陕西好几个著名的共产党员出身于地主家庭。

对于贫农还采用低利或无利放款形式给予额外的帮助。高利贷完全取缔，但私人借款年息最高不超过10%仍属许可。政府放款年息一般为5%。红军兵工厂里制造的好几千简易农具和成千上万磅种子供应无地农民开荒。还开办了一所简单的农业学校，据说还要开办一所畜牧学校，只等这方面的一个专家从上海来到。

合作化运动在大力推广，其活动已超过生产和分配合作社，而扩大到像集体使用牲口和农具——特别是耕种公共土地和红军土地——这样新奇（对中国来说）形式方面的合作，和组织劳动互助组方面的合作。用后一种方法，大片土地可以很快地集体耕种、集体收获，个别农民一时农闲现象就不再出现。共产党做到每个人都不是白白得到土地的！在农忙季节里，采用了"星期六突击队"的办法，不仅所有的儿童组织，而且所有的苏维埃干部、游击队员、赤卫队员、妇女组织的会员、驻在附近的红军部队都动员起来，每个星期至少要有一天到田里劳动。甚至毛泽东也参加了这种劳动。

这里，共产党在播下集体劳动这一根本革命化的思想的种子——为将来实现集体化做初步的教育工作。同时，一种比较广阔的社会生活观念开始慢慢地渗入到农

for a livelihood. There did not seem to be an attempt to "equalize" land ownership. The primary purpose of the soviet land laws, as explained to me by Wang Kuan-lan (the twenty-nine-year-old Russian-returned student who was land commissioner for the three Red provinces of the Northwest), was to provide for every person sufficient land to guarantee him and his family a decent livelihood—which was claimed to be the most "urgent demand" of the peasantry.

The land problem—confiscation and redistribution—was greatly simplified in the Northwest by the fact that big estates were formerly owned by officials, tax collectors, and absentee landlords. With the confiscation of these, in many cases the immediate demands of the poor peasantry were satisfied, without much interference with either the resident small landlords or the rich peasants. Thus the Reds not only created the economic base for support in the poor and landless peasantry by giving them farms, but in some cases won the gratitude of middle peasants by abolishing tax exploitation, and in a few instances enlisted the aid of small landlords on the same basis or through the patriotic appeals of the anti-Japanese movement. Several prominent Shensi Communists came from landlord families.

Additional help was given to the poor farmers in the form of loans at very low rates of interest or no interest at all. Usury was entirely abolished, but private lending, at rates fixed at a maximum of 10 percent annually, was permitted. The ordinary government lending rate was 5 per cent. Several thousand simple agricultural implements made in the Red arsenals, and thousands of pounds of seed grain, were supplied to landless peasants breaking wasteland. A primitive agricultural school had been established, and I was told it was planned to open an animal-husbandry school as soon as an expert in this field, expected from Shanghai, had arrived.

A cooperative movement was being vigorously pushed. These activities extended beyond production and distribution cooperatives, branching out to include cooperation in such novel (for China) forms as the collective use of farm animals and implements—especially in tilling public lands and Red Army lands—and in the organization of labor mutual-aid societies. By the latter device great areas could be quickly planted and harvested collectively, and periods of idleness by individual farmers eliminated. The Reds saw to it that a man earned his new land! In busy periods the system of "Saturday Brigades" was used, when not only all the children's organizations but every soviet official, Red partisan, Red Guard, women's organization member, and any Red Army detachment that happened to be nearby, were mobilized to work at least one day a week at farming tasks. Even Mao Tse-tung took part in this work.

Here the Reds were introducing the germs of the drastically revolutionary idea of collective effort—and doing primary education work for some future period when collectivization might become practicable. At the same time, into the dark recesses of

民意识的深处去。因为在农民中间建立起来的各种组织,是共产党称为经济、政治、文化三结合的东西。

共产党在这些人们中间所取得的文化上的成就,按西方先进标准来衡量,的确是微不足道的。但是在陕西北部的二十几个苏维埃化已久的县里,中国大部分地方常见的某些明显的弊端肯定是被消灭了,而且在新区的居民中间也在进行大力的宣传,要在那里进行同样的基本改革。陕北已经彻底消灭了鸦片,这是个杰出的成就。事实上,我一进苏区以后就没有看到过什么罂粟的影子。贪官污吏几乎是从来没有听到过。乞丐和失业的确像共产党所说的那样被"消灭"了。我在红区旅行期间没有看到过一个乞丐。缠足和溺婴是犯法的,奴婢和卖淫已经绝迹,一妻多夫或一夫多妻都遭到禁止。

关于"共妻"和"妇女国有化"的谣言,一望而知是荒谬可笑的,不屑一驳。但在结婚、离婚、遗产等方面的改革,按照中国其他地方的半封建法律和习惯来看,本身就是很激进彻底的。婚姻法[1]里有这样有趣的规定:禁止婆婆虐待媳妇、买卖妻妾以及"包办婚姻"的习惯。婚姻必须取得双方同意,婚龄提高到男子20岁,女子18岁,禁止彩礼,到县、市、村苏维埃登记结婚的,发给一份结婚证书,不取任何费用。男女同居的,不论是否登过记,都算是合法结过婚,——这似乎排除了乱交——而且他们的子女都是合法的。不承认有私生子。

如果夫妻双方有任何一方"坚决要求"就可以到苏维埃登记处离婚,不需任何费用,但红军的妻子须得男方同意才可离婚。离婚双方财产均分,双方都有法律义务抚养子女,但债务却由男方单独负担(!),他并有义务提供子女2/3的生活费。

从理论上来说,教育"免费普及",但父母有义务供给子女吃穿。实际上,还没有做到"免费普及",虽然教育人民委员徐特立向我吹嘘,如果他们在西北能有几年

---

1. 《中华苏维埃共和国婚姻法》(1936年7月保安重印)。

peasant mentality there was slowly penetrating the concept of a broader realm of social life. For the organizations created among the peasantry were what the Reds called three-in-one: economic, political, and cultural in their utility.

What cultural progress the Reds had made among these people was by advanced Western standards negligible indeed. But certain outstanding evils common in most parts of China had definitely been eliminated in the score of long-sovietized counties in north Shensi, and a crusade of propaganda was being conducted among inhabitants of newer areas to spread the same elementary reforms there. As an outstanding achievement, opium had been completely eliminated in north Shensi, and in fact I did not see any sign of poppies after I entered the soviet districts. Official corruption was almost unheard-of. Beggary and unemployment did seem to have been, as the Reds claimed, "liquidated." I did not see a beggar during all my travels in the Red areas. Foot binding and infanticide were criminal offenses, child slavery and prostitution had disappeared, and polyandry and polygamy were prohibited.

The myths of "communized wives" and "nationalization of women" are too patently absurd to be denied, but changes in marriage, divorce, and inheritance were in themselves extremely radical against the background of semifeudal law and practice elsewhere in China. Marriage regulations[1] included interesting provisions against mother-in-law tyranny, the buying and selling of women as wives and concubines, and the custom of "arranged matches." Marriage was by mutual consent, the legal age had been moved up sharply to twenty for men and eighteen for women, dowries were prohibited, and any couple registering as man and wife before a county, municipal, or village soviet was given a marriage certificate without cost. Men and women actually cohabiting were considered legally married, whether registered or not—which seemed to rule out "free love." All children were legitimate under soviet law.

Divorce could also be secured from the registration bureau of the soviet, free of charge, on the "insistent demand" of either party to the marriage contract, but wives of Red Army men were required to have their husbands' consent before a divorce was granted. Property was divided equally between the divorcees, and both were legally obliged to care for their children, but responsibility for debts was shouldered by the male alone (!), who was also obliged to supply two-thirds of the children's living expenses.

Education, in theory, was "free and universal," but parents were obliged to supply their children with food and clothing. In practice, nothing like "free and universal" education had yet been achieved, although old Hsu T'eh-li, the commissioner of education, boasted to me that if they were given a few years of peace in the Northwest they would astound

---

1. *The Marriage Law of the Chinese Soviet Republic* (reprinted in Pao An, July, 1936).

和平，他们在教育方面的成就将会使全国震惊。我以后再来更加详细地谈谈共产党人在这一地区消灭文盲所取得的成就和希望做到什么程度，但是首先使人感到兴趣的还是弄清楚政府用什么经费来不仅维持这样的教育计划，而且维持我称之为苏维埃社会的这个表面看来很简单但实际上却极其复杂的有机体。

the rest of China with the educational progress they would make. Further on I was to learn in more detail what the Communists had done and hoped to do to liquidate the appalling illiteracy of this region, but first it was interesting to know how the government was financing not only the educational program, such as it was, but this whole seemingly simple and yet in its way vastly complex organism which I have called soviet society.

四、　　货币解剖

苏维埃经济至少有两个基本任务必须完成：供养和装备红军，为贫苦农民济燃眉之急。这两个任务有一项没有完成，苏维埃的基础就马上要崩溃。为了保证这两项任务的完成，共产党甚至在苏区初创之日起就必须开始从事某种经济建设。

西北苏区的经济是私人资本主义、国家资本主义、原始社会主义的奇怪混合。私人企业和工业得到许可和受到鼓励，土地和土地产品的私人交易也得到允许，但有限制。同时，国家拥有和开发像油井、盐井、煤矿等企业，也从事牛羊、皮革、食盐、羊毛、棉花、纸张等其他原料的贸易。但国家在这些物品方面没有垄断专卖，私人企业是能够在所有这些方面进行竞争的，而且在一定程度上也的确进行了竞争。

第三种方式的经济是合作社，政府和群众合伙参加经营，不仅同私人资本主义进行竞争，而且同国家资本主义进行竞争！但这都是在一种非常小而原始的规模上进行的。因此，虽然在这样一种安排中，基本矛盾很明显，如果在经济上比较发达的地区，会招致破坏性的后果，但是在红区这里，它们却起着互相补充的作用。

苏区合作社运动的趋向显然是社会主义性质的。共产党认为合作社是"抵制私人资本主义和发展新的经济制度的工具"，他们规定它的5项主要任务如下："制止商人对群众的剥削；克服敌人的封锁；发展苏区国民经济；提高群众经济政治水平；为社会主义建设准备条件"——在这个阶段内，"在无产阶级领导下的中国资产阶级民主革命，可以创造有利的条件使这一革命过渡到社会主义。"[1]

---

1. 《合作社发展规划》，国民经济部（1935年11月陕西瓦窑堡）第4页。

4   ANATOMY OF MONEY

It was imperative for soviet economy to fulfill at least two elementary functions: to feed and equip the Red Army, and to bring immediate relief to the poor peasantry. Failing in either, the soviet base would soon collapse. To guarantee success at these tasks it was necessary for the Reds, even from the earliest days, to begin some kind of economic construction.

Soviet economy in the Northwest was a curious mixture of private capitalism, state capitalism, and primitive socialism. Private enterprise and industry were permitted and encouraged, and private transaction in the land and its products was allowed, with restrictions. At the same time the state owned and exploited enterprises such as oil wells, salt wells, and coal mines, and it traded in cattle, hides, salt, wool, cotton, paper, and other raw materials. But it did not establish a monopoly in these articles, and in all of them private enterprises could, and to some extent did, compete.

A third kind of economy was created by the establishment of cooperatives, in which the government and the masses participated as partners, competing not only with private capitalism, but also with state capitalism! But it was all conducted on a very small and primitive scale. Thus although the fundamental antagonisms in such an arrangement were obvious, and in an economically more highly developed area would have been ruinous, here in the Red regions they somehow supplemented each other.

The Reds defined the cooperative as "an instrument to resist private capitalism and develop a new economic system," and they listed its five main functions as follows: "to combat the exploitation of the masses by the merchants; to combat the enemy's blockade; to develop the national economy of the soviet districts; to raise the economic-political level of the masses; and to prepare the conditions for Socialist construction"—a period in which "the democratic revolution of the Chinese bourgeoisie, under the leadership of the proletariat, may create energetic conditions enabling the transition of this revolution into socialism."[1]

---

1. *Outline for Cooperative Development*, Department of National Economy (Wa Ya Pao, Shensi, November, 1935), p. 4.

上面这些说起来很动听的任务中头两项实际不过是，合作社帮助群众组织自己的偷运队，作为政府的偷运活动的辅助。南京禁止红白两区之间进行贸易，但共产党利用山间小道，贿赂边境哨兵，有时能够进行相当活跃的出境贸易。为国家贸易局或合作社服务的运输队从苏区运原料出境，换成国民党货币或者换购急需的工业制成品。

村、乡、县、省各级都组织消费、销售、生产、信用合作社。它们的上面则是合作社总局，属财政人民委员和一个国民经济部门领导。这些合作社的组成方式的确是为了鼓励社会的最底层参加。消费者入社每股低到5角，有时甚至只有2角，参加后的组织义务则非常广泛，使得每一入股的人都要参加合作社的经济或政治生活。虽然对于每一入股的人购买股票数目没有加以任何限制，但每一入股的人不管有多少股票，只有一票的权利。合作社在总局指导下选举自己的管理委员会和监察委员会，总局另外还为他们培养工作人员和组织人员。每个合作社还设有营业、宣传、组织、调查、统计等部门。

对于经营得法的给予各种奖励，并且对农民进行了关于合作社运动好处的普遍宣传和教育。政府除了提供技术援助以外也提供了财政上的援助，政府在分红的基础上参加经营，像普通社员一样。在陕西和甘肃两省的合作社里，政府已投下了约7万元的无息贷款。

除了边境各县也通用白区纸币以外，一律只流通苏区纸币。共产党在江西、安徽、四川的苏区中曾铸造了银圆和作为辅币的铜币，有的还是银币，其中很多已运到了西北。但在1935年11月南京发表命令收回中国全部银币以后，银价飞涨，共产党也收回了银币，把它当作发行纸币的储备。今天全国还有少数藏银没有落入国民党手中，其中就有一部分是他们的。

南方印的纸币印刷十分讲究，用的是钞票纸，上面印着"中国工农苏维埃政府国家银行"的印记。在西北，由于技术上的困难，纸币就粗糙得多，纸质低劣，有时用布。所有的钞票上都印有他们的口号。陕西印的钞票上有这样的口号："停止内战！""联合抗日！""中国革命万岁！"

The first two of those high-sounding functions in practice meant simply that the cooperative could help the masses organize their own blockade-running corps, as auxiliaries to the blockade-running activity of the government. Trade between Red and White districts was prohibited by Nanking, but by using small mountain roads, and by oiling the palms of border guards, the Reds at times managed to carry on a fairly lively export business. Taking out raw materials from the soviet districts, the transport corps in the service of the state trade bureau or the cooperatives exchanged them for Kuomintang money and needed manufactures.

Consumption, sales, production, and credit cooperatives were organized in the village, district, county, and province. Above them was a central bureau of cooperatives, under the finance commissioner and a department of national economy. These cooperatives were really constructed to encourage the participation of the lowest strata of society. Shares entitling the purchaser to membership were priced as low as fifty cents, or even twenty cents, and organizational duties were so extensive as to bring nearly every shareholder into the economic or political life of the cooperative. While there was no restriction on the number of shares an individual member could buy, each member was entitled to but one vote, regardless of how many shares he held. Cooperatives elected their own managing committees and supervisory committees, with the assistance of the central bureau, which also furnished trained workers and organizers. Each cooperative had departments for business, propaganda, organization, survey, and statistics.

Various prizes were offered for efficient management, and widespread propaganda stimulated and educated the peasants concerning the usefulness of the movement. Financial as well as technical help was furnished by the government, which participated in the enterprises on a profit-sharing basis, like the members. Some $70,000 in non-interest-bearing loans had been invested by the government in the cooperatives of Shensi and Kansu.

Only soviet paper was in use, except in the border counties, where White paper was also accepted. In their soviets in Kiangsi, Anhui, and Szechuan the Reds minted silver dollars, and subsidiary coins in copper, and some also in silver, and much of this metal was transported to the Northwest. But after the decree of November, 1935, when Nanking began the confiscation of all silver in China, and its price soared, the Reds withdrew their silver and held it as reserve for their note issue.

Paper currency in the South, bearing the signature of the "Chinese Workers' and Peasants' Soviet Government State Bank," was excellently printed, on good bank paper. In the Northwest, technical deficiencies resulted in a much cruder issue on poor paper, and sometimes on cloth. Their slogans appeared on all money. Notes issued in Shensi bore such exhortations as: "Stop civil war!" "Unite to resist Japan!" "Long live the Chinese revolution!"

但是，商人们把货物从白区运来，出售之后所得是一种在苏区以外无交换价值的货币，这有什么用呢？这个困难由国库来解决，它规定苏区货币与国民党货币的兑换率为 1.21 元对 1 元。条例规定：

> 凡是从白区进境的一切货物如直接售给国家贸易局就以外（国民党）币偿付；必需品进口后如不直接卖给国家贸易局，而是通过合作社或私商出售者，必须先向国家贸易局登记，其所售收入可兑换白区货币；其他凡证明必要者亦可兑换。[1]

实际上这当然等于是说所有"外国"进口货必须付以"外"汇。但是由于进口制成品（够少的了）的价值大大地超过苏区出口货的价值（主要是原料，而且是作为走私货削价出售的），便总存在着支付极其不平衡的趋向。换句话说，破产。这如何克服？

这没有完全克服。就我所能发现的来看，这个问题主要是靠白发苍苍、神态庄严的财政人民委员林祖涵的才智来解决的。林祖涵的任务是使红军入够敷出，收支两抵。这位令人感到兴趣的老财神一度担任过国民党的司库，他的经历令人惊叹，我这里只能简单一述。

林祖涵是湖南一个教员的儿子，生于 1882 年，自幼学习经史，在常德府入师范，后留学东京。他在日本时遇见被清廷放逐的孙逸仙，就参加了他的秘密组织同盟会。孙逸仙把同盟会与其他革命团体合并组成国民党后，林祖涵就成了创始党员。他后来遇见陈独秀，受到后者很大影响，就在 1922 年参加了共产党。但是他仍在孙逸仙手下工作，孙逸仙吸收共产党员参加国民党，林祖涵先后担任国民党司库和总务部长。孙逸仙逝世时他在身边。

国民革命开始时，林祖涵是国民党中央执行委员会中年资高过蒋介石的几个元老之一。他在广州担任农民部长，北伐时任程潜将军指挥的第六军政委，程潜后来

---

1. 《关于苏区货币政策》，载《党的工作》第 12 期（1936 年保安）。

But how could merchants sell articles imported from the White regions for currency which had no exchange value outside the soviet districts? This difficulty was met by the state treasury, which had fixed an exchange rate of soviet $1.21 to Kuomintang $1. Regulations provided that "all goods imported from the White districts, and sold directly to the State Trade Bureau, will be paid for in foreign [Kuomintang] currency; imports of necessities, when not sold directly to the State Trade Bureau, but through cooperatives or by private merchants, shall first be registered with the State Trade Bureau, and proceeds of their sale for soviet currency may be exchanged for White paper, other exchange will be given when its necessity is established."[1]

In practice this of course meant that all "foreign" imports had to be paid for in "foreign" exchange. But as the value of imported manufactures (meager enough) greatly exceeded the value of soviet exports (which were chiefly raw materials, and were all sold in a depressed market as smuggled goods), there was always a tendency toward a heavy unfavorable balance of payments. In other words, bankruptcy. How was it overcome?

It was not, entirely. As far as I could discover, the problem was met principally by the ingenuity of Lin Tsu-han, the dignified white-haired Commissioner of Finance, whose task was to make Red ends meet. This interesting old custodian of the exchequer had once been treasurer of the Kuomintang, and behind him lay an amazing story.

Son of a Hunanese schoolteacher, Lin Tsu-han was born in 1882, educated in the Classics, attended normal college at Changtehfu, and later studied in Tokyo. While in Japan he met Sun Yat-sen, then exiled from China by the Manchus, and joined his secret revolutionary society, the T'ung Meng Hui. When Sun merged his T'ung Meng Hui with other revolutionary groups to found the Kuomintang, Lin became a charter member. Later on he met Ch'en Tu-hsiu, was much influenced by him, and in 1922 joined the Communist Party. He continued to work closely with Dr. Sun Yat-sen, however, who admitted Communists to his party, and Lin was in turn treasurer and chairman of the General Affairs Department of the Kuomintang. He was with Sun Yat-sen when he died.

At the beginning of the Nationalist Revolution, Lin was one of the several elders in the Central Executive Committee of the Kuomintang who held seniority over Chiang Kai-shek. In Canton he was chairman of the Peasant Department and during the Northern Expedition he became political commissar of the Sixth Army, commanded by General

---

1. "Concerning Soviet Monetary Policy," *Tangti Kungtso* [*Party Work*], No. 12 (Pao An, 1936).

任南京的参谋总长。蒋介石在 1927 年开始镇压共产党时，林祖涵反对他，逃到了香港，然后去了苏俄，在共产主义大学学习了 4 年。他回国后乘"地下火车"，安全抵达江西，任财政人民委员。林祖涵现在丧偶，自从 1927 年后没有见过已经长大的子女。他在 45 岁那年放弃了他的名誉地位，不惜把自己的命运同年轻的共产党人结合在一起。

一天早上，这位 55 岁的长征老战士来到了我在外交部的房间，满面春风，身上穿着一套褪色的制服，红星帽的帽檐软垂，慈蔼的眼睛上戴着一副眼镜，一只腿架已经断了，是用一根绳子系在耳朵上的。这就是财政人民委员！他在炕边坐下，我们就开始谈论税收来源。我了解，政府是简直不收税的；工业收入肯定微不足道；那么我就想知道，钱是从哪里来的？

林祖涵开始解释："我们说我们对群众不收税，这话不错。但是我们对剥削阶级是狠狠地收税的，没收他们的剩余现款和物资。因此我们所有的税都是直接税。这与国民党的做法正好相反，他们到头来由工人和贫农负担大部分税款。我们这里只对 10% 人口征税，那就是地主和高利贷者。我们对少数大商人也征收很少的一部分税，但对小商人不征税。以后我们可能对农民征小额的累进税，但在目前，群众的税全部都取消了。

"另外一个收入来源是人民的自愿捐献。在战争还在进行的地方，革命爱国热情很高，人民认识到他们有可能丧失苏区，因此他们志愿大量捐献粮食、金钱、布匹给红军。我们也从国家贸易，从红军的土地，从自己的工业，从合作社，从银行贷款得到一些收入。但是当然，我们最大的收入是没收。"

"你说没收，"我打断他的话说，"指的是一般所说的抢劫吧？"

林祖涵笑了几声。"国民党叫抢劫。好吧，如果说对剥削群众的人征税是抢劫，国民党对群众征税也是抢劫。但是红军不做白军抢劫那样的事。没收只有在负责人士的财政人民委员部指导下进行。每一项都要上报政府，只用于对社会有普遍好处的事。私自抢劫要受到严惩的。你去问一问人民吧，红军战士有没有不付钱而拿走任何东西的。

Ch'eng Ch'ien—the late chief of staff at Nanking. When Chiang Kai-shek began the extermination of the Communists in 1927, Lin denounced him, fled to Hongkong, and then to Soviet Russia, where he studied for four years in the Communist academy. On his return to China he took passage on the "underground railway" and safely reached Kiangsi. Now a widower, Lin had not seen his grown-up daughter and son since 1927. At the age of forty-five he had abandoned the comfortable assets of his position and staked his destiny with the young Communists.

Into my room in the Foreign Office one morning came this fifty-five-year-old veteran of the Long March, wearing a cheerful smile, a faded uniform, a redstarred cap with a broken peak, and in front of his kindly eyes a pair of spectacles one side of which was trussed up over his ear with a piece of string. The Commissioner of Finance! He sat down on the edge of the *k'ang* and we began to talk about sources of revenue. The government, I understood, collected practically no taxes; its industrial income must be negligible; then where, I wanted to know, did it get its money?

Lin began to explain: "We say we do not tax the masses, and this is true. But we do heavily tax the exploiting classes, confiscating their surplus cash and goods. Thus all our taxation is direct. This is just the opposite of the Kuomintang practice, under which ultimately the workers and the poor peasants have to carry most of the tax burden. Here we tax less than 10 per cent of the population—the landlords and usurers. We also levy a small tax on a few big merchants, but none on small merchants. Later on we may impose a small progressive tax on the peasantry, but at the present moment all mass taxes have been completely abolished.

"Another source of income is from voluntary contributions of the people. Revolutionary patriotic feeling runs very high where war is on and the people realize that they may lose their soviets. They make big voluntary contributions of food, money, and clothing to the Red Army. We derive some income also from state trade, from Red Army lands, from our own industries, from the cooperatives, and from bank loans. But of course our biggest revenue is from confiscations."

"By confiscation," I interrupted, "you mean what is commonly described as loot?"

Lin laughed shortly. "The Kuomintang calls it loot. Well, if taxation of the exploiters of the masses is loot, so is the Kuomintang's taxation of the masses. But the Red Army does no looting in the sense that White armies loot. Confiscations are made only by authorized persons, under the direction of the Finance Commission. Every item must be reported by inventory to the government, and is utilized only for the general benefit of society. Private looting is heavily punished. Just ask the people if Red soldiers take anything without paying for it."

"你这话不错,但这个问题的答案自然取决于你是向地主还是向农民提这个问题。"

"如果我们不用不断地打仗,"林祖涵继续说,"我们在这里很容易建设自给自足的经济。我们的预算定得很仔细,尽力节约。因为苏维埃人员每个人都既是爱国者又是革命家,我们不要工资,我们只靠一点点粮食生活,我们预算之小可能令你吃惊。这整个地区[1],我们目前的开支每月只有32万元。不论从货币还是货物的价值计算都是这样。此数中有40%到50%来自没收,15%到20%自愿捐献,包括党在白区支持者中间募得的款项。[2] 其余的收入来自贸易、经济建设、红军的土地、银行给政府的贷款。"

共产党自称发明了一种能防止舞弊的预算方法、收支方法。我读了林祖涵所著《预算制定大纲》的一部分,该书详尽地介绍了这个方法和它的一切防范措施。它的有效性似乎主要依靠集体控制收支。从最高机构一直到村,各级会计在收支方面要受一个委员会的监督,因此,为个人利益篡改账目是极为困难的。

林委员对他的方法很得意,他说,采用这个方法,任何舞弊都是办不到的。这话可能确实不假。反正,在红区中真正的问题显然不是传统意义上的舞弊问题,而是如何勉力维持的问题。尽管林祖涵很乐观,访问后我记的日记是这样写的:

> 不论林祖涵的数字的确切含义如何,这完全是中国式的一个奇迹,因为我们记得,游击队在这一带进进退退已经打了5年,经济居然能够维持下来,没有发生饥荒,整个来说,农民似乎接受苏区货币,相信它。事实上,这不是能仅仅用财政的角度来解释的,只有在社会和政治基础上才能理解。
>
> 尽管如此,十分清楚,哪怕是对一个像红军那样靠小本经营来维持的组织,情况也极为严重。在苏区经济中,不久一定会发生以下3种变化之一:(一)为了

---

1. 当时约有奥地利那么大。
2. 当时这个苏区很可能很少或者根本就没有得到俄国的资金援助,它们在地理上并不接壤。

"Well, you are quite right. The answer to that naturally would depend on whether you asked a landlord or a peasant."

"If we did not have to conduct incessant war," Lin continued, "we could easily build a self-supporting economy here. Our budget is carefully made, and every possible economy is practiced. Because every soviet official is also a patriot and a revolutionary, we demand no wages, and we can exist on but little food. It will probably surprise you to know how small our budget is. For this whole area[1] our present expenditure is only about $320,000 per month. This represents goods value as well as money value. Of this sum, from 40 to 50 per cent comes from confiscations, and 15 or 20 per cent comes from voluntary contributions, including cash raised by the Party among our supporters in the White districts.[2] The rest of our revenue is derived from trade, economic construction, Red Army lands, and bank loans to the government."

The Reds claimed to have devised a squeeze-proof machinery of budgeting, of receipts and disbursements. I read part of Lin Tsu-han's *Outline for Budget Compilation*, which gave a detailed description of the system and all its safeguards. Its integrity seemed to be based primarily on collective control of receipts and disbursements. From the highest organ down to the village, the treasurer was accountable, for both payments and collections, to a supervising committee, so that juggling of figures for individual profit was extremely difficult.

Commissioner Lin was very proud of his system, and asserted that under it any kind of squeeze was effectively impossible. It may have been true. Anyway, it was obvious that in the Red districts the real problem as yet was not one of squeeze, in the traditional sense, but of squeezing through. Despite Lin's cheerful optimism, this was what I wrote in my diary after that interview:

> *Whatever Lin's figures may mean exactly, it is simply a Chinese miracle, when one remembers that partisans have been fighting back and forth across this territory for five years, that the economy maintains itself at all, that there is no famine, and that the peasants on the whole seem to accept soviet currency, with faith in it. In fact this cannot be explained in terms of finance alone, but is only understandable on a social and political basis.*
>
> *Nevertheless, it is perfectly clear that the situation is extremely grave, even for an organization that exists on such shoestrings as the Reds feed upon, and one of three changes must shortly occur in soviet economy: (1) some form of machine*

---

1. Then about the size of Austria.
2. At that time this soviet area was probably receiving little or no financial aid from Russia, with which it had no direct geographical connection.

供应市场所需的制成品,实行某种形式的机器工业化;(二)同外界某个现代化经济基地建立良好关系,或者攻占比目前的经济基地水平高一些的某个经济基地(例如西安或兰州);或者(三)红区同现在在白军控制下的这样一个基地实际合并。

但是共产党并不同意我的悲观看法。"出路是一定能够找到的。"几个月后果然找到了!这个"出路"以一种"实际合并"的形式出现。

附带说一句,林祖涵本人在经济方面似乎并没有很"得发"。他作为财政人民委员的"补贴"是5元钱一月——红区的钱。

industrialization, to supply the market with needed manufactures; (2) the establishment of a good connection with some modern economic base in the outside world, or the capture of some economic base on a higher level than the present one (Sian or Lanchow, for example); or (3) the actual coalescence of such a base, now under White control, with the Red districts.

The Reds did not share my pessimism. "A way out is sure to be found." And in a few months it was. The "way out" appeared in the form of an "actual coalescence."

Lin didn't seem to be "getting ahead" financially very fast himself, by the way. His "allowance" as Commissioner of Finance was five dollars a month—Red money.

五、　人生五十始！

我叫他老徐，因为苏区人人都是这样叫他——教书先生老徐——因为，虽然在东方其他地方，61岁不过是政府最高级官员的平均年龄，可是在红色中国，同别人相比，他似乎是个白发老翁。然而他并不是老朽昏聩的标本。像他的60老翁的同辈谢觉哉（你可以常常看到这一对白发土匪在携手同行，好像中学生一样）一样，他步履矫健，双目炯炯，他的一双健腿在长征途上曾经帮他渡过大河，爬过高山。

徐特立原来是一个极受敬重的教授，但是到了50岁那一年，他突然放弃家庭、4个儿女、长沙一所师范校长的职位，投身到共产党中来。他于1877年生于长沙附近一个贫农家庭，与彭德怀诞生的地方相去不远。他是第四个儿子。他的父母省吃俭用，供他上了6年学，完了以后在清朝当个塾师，一直到29岁那一年上长沙师范，毕业后留校教数学[1]。

毛泽东是他在长沙师范的学生（徐特立说他数学很糟！），他的学生中还有许多青年后来成了共产党。徐特立本人在毛泽东能分辨共和派和保皇派之前很早就参与了政治。他身上仍留着帝制时代与封建政治作斗争的标志，那是他为了要表示他上书请愿实行宪政的诚意割去的小指尖。在第一次革命后，湖南一度有个省议会，老徐是议员之一。

战后他随湖南省的勤工俭学学生去法国，在里昂学习1年，在一家铁工厂打杂

---

1. 数学是徐特立自学的。

5   LIFE BEGINS AT FIFTY!

I called him "Old Hsu" because that was what everyone in the soviet districts called him—Lao Hsu, the Educator—for, although sixty-one was only just an average age for most high government officials elsewhere in the Orient, in Red China he seemed a sort of hoary grandfather by contrast with others. Yet he was no specimen of decrepitude. Like his sexagenarian crony, Hsieh Chueh-tsai (and you could often see this pair of white-haired bandits walking along arm-in-arm like middle-school lads), he had an erect and vigorous step, bright and merry eyes, and a pair of muscular legs that had carried him across the greatest rivers and mountain ranges of China on the Long March.

Hsu T'eh-li had been a highly respected professor until at the age of fifty he amazingly gave up his home, four children, and the presidency of a normal school in Changsha to stake his future with the Communists. Born in 1877 near Changsha, not far from P'eng Teh-huai's birthplace, he was the fourth son in a poor peasant family. By various sacrifices his parents gave him six years of schooling, at the end of which he became a schoolteacher under the Manchu regime. There he remained till he was twenty-nine, when he entered the Changsha Normal College, graduated, and became an instructor in mathematics—a discipline in which he was self-taught.

Mao Tse-tung was one of his students in the normal school (Hsu said he was terrible in math), and so were many youths who later became Reds. Hsu himself had a role in politics long before Mao knew a republican from a monarchist. He still bore that mark of combat from feudal politics in days of the empire, when he cut off the tip of his little finger to demonstrate his sincerity in begging by petition that a parliament be granted to the people. After the first revolution, when for a while Hunan had a provincial parliament, Old Hsu was a member of it.

He accompanied the Hunanese delegation of "worker-students" to France after the war, and he studied a year at Lyons, where he paid his way by odd-time work in a metal factory.

做工维持生活。后来他在巴黎大学当了3年学生，靠为中国学生补习数学筹措自己学费。1923年回湖南后，协助在长沙办了两个新式的师范学校，境况顺遂，有4年之久。他到1927年才成了共产党员，资产阶级社会的叛逆者。

在国民革命期间，徐特立在国民党省党部很活跃，但是他同情共产党。他向学生公开宣传马克思主义。"清洗"期间，他遭到追捕，不得不销声匿迹。由于与共产党没有关系，他不得不自找避难的地方。"我早想当共产党，"他怀念地告诉我，"但是没有人要求我参加。我年已50，我想共产党大概认为我太老了。"但是有一天，一个共产党员到他避难的地方来找他，请他入党。这个老家伙高兴之极，他告诉我，他当时想到他对建设新世界仍有一些用处不禁哭了。

党把他派去俄国，他在那里学习两年。回国后，他闯破封锁，到了江西，不久就在瞿秋白下面担任副教育人民委员，瞿秋白遭难后，执行委员会任命徐特立继任。从此以后，他就以教书先生老徐著称。没有疑问，他的丰富多样的经验——在帝制、资本主义、共产主义形式的社会中的生活和教书的经验——使他能够胜任他所面临的任务。他当然需要所有这些经验，而且还需要更多的经验，因为这些任务十分艰巨，要是西方的教育家，谁都会感到气馁。但是老徐正当壮年，是不会感到气馁的。

一天，我们正在谈话的时候，他开始幽默地一一列举他的一些困难。"同我们所估计的几乎一样，"他说，"在西北，在我们到达以前，除了少数地主、官吏、商人以外几乎没有人识字。文盲几乎达95%左右。在文化上，这是地球上最黑暗的一个角落。你知道吗，陕北和甘肃的人竟相信水对他们是有害的！这里的人平均一生只洗两次澡——一次在出生的时候，一次在结婚的时候。他们不愿洗脚、洗手、洗脸，不愿剪指甲、剃头发。这里留辫子的人比中国任何其他地方都多。

"但是所有这一切，还有许多其他偏见，都是由于无知愚昧所造成的，我的任务就是改变他们的这种思想状态。这样的人民，同江西相比，的确非常落后。江西的文盲占90%，但是文化水平高得多，我们在那里工作的物质条件也较好，合格教师也多得多。在我们的模范县兴国，我们有300多所小学，约800名教师——这与我们这里全部红区的小学和教师数目相等。我们从兴国撤出时，文盲已减低到全部人口20%以下！

Later he was a student for three years at the University of Paris, earning his tuition then by tutoring Chinese students in mathematics. Returning to Hunan in 1923, he helped establish two modern normal schools in the capital, and for four years enjoyed some prosperity. Not till 1927 did he become a Communist and an outcast from bourgeois society.

During the Nationalist Revolution, Hsu T'eh-li was active in the provincial Kuomintang, but he sympathized with the Communists. He openly preached Marxism to his students. When the "purgation" period began he was a marked man; he had to do the disappearing act, and, having no connection with the Communist Party, he had to find a haven on his own. "I had wanted to be a Communist," he told me rather wistfully, "but nobody ever asked me to join. I was already fifty, and I concluded that the Communists considered me too old." But one day a Communist sought out Hsu in his hiding place and asked him to enter the Party. He told me he wept then to think that he was still of some use in building a new world.

The Party sent him to Russia, where he studied for two years. On his return he ran the blockade to Kiangsi; soon afterwards he became assistant commissioner of education, under Ch'u Ch'iu-pai, and after Ch'u was killed, the Executive Committee appointed Hsu in his place. Since then he had been Lao Hsu, the Educator. And surely his varied experience—life and teaching under monarchist, capitalist, and Communist, forms of society—seemed to qualify him for the tasks that faced him. He certainly needed all that experience, and more, for those tasks were so great that any Western educator would have despaired. But Old Hsu was too young to be discouraged.

One day when we were talking he began humorously to enumerate some of his difficulties. "As nearly as we can estimate," he asserted, "virtually nobody but a few landlords, officials, and merchants could read in the Northwest before we arrived. The illiteracy seemed to be about 95 per cent. This is culturally one of the darkest places on earth. Do you know the people in north Shensi and Kansu believe that water is harmful to them? The average man here has a bath all over only twice in his life—once when he is born, the second time when he is married. They hate to wash their feet, hands, or faces, or cut their nails or their hair. There are more pigtails left in this part of China than anywhere else.

"But all this and many other prejudices are due to ignorance, and it's my job to change their mentality. Such a population, compared with Kiangsi, is very backward indeed. There the illiteracy was about 90 percent, but the cultural level was very much higher, we had better material conditions to work in, and many more trained teachers. In our model *hsien*, Hsing Ko, we had over three hundred primary schools and about eight hundred schoolteachers—which is as many as we have of both in all the Red districts here. When we withdrew from Hsing Ko, illiteracy had been reduced to less than 20 per cent of the population.

"这里的工作的进展要慢得多。我们一切都得从头开始。我们的物质资源非常有限。甚至我们的印刷机也被破坏了,我们现在什么东西都只能用油印和石刻来印刷。由于封锁,我们不能进口足够的纸张。我们已开始自己造纸,但质量太差。但是别去管这些困难吧。我们已经能够取得一些成就。如果有时间,我们在这里能够做到使全中国震惊的事情。我们现在从群众中间正在训练几十名教师,党也在培养。他们之中有许多人要担任群众文化学校的义务教员。我们的成绩表明,这里的农民只要给他们机会是极愿意学习的。

"而且他们也不笨。他们学得很快,只要把道理对他们说清楚,他们就改变了习惯。在这里的老苏区,你看不到姑娘缠足,你会看到许多年轻妇女剪短发。男人现在慢慢地剪掉辫子了,许多人在共青团和少先队那里学读书写字。"

应该说明:在紧急状态下,苏区教育制度分3个部分:学校、军队、社会。第一部分多少都是苏维埃办的,第二部分是红军办的,第三部分是共产党各组织办的。重点都主要在政治方面——甚至最小的儿童初识字时也是通过简单的革命口号来学的。接着读红军和国民党、地主和农民、资本家和工人等等冲突的故事,尽是共青团员和红军战士的英勇事迹和将来苏维埃政权下人间乐园的描绘。

在学校教育方面,共产党自称已经办了约200所小学,为小学教师办了1所师范,还办了1所农业学校、1所纺织学校、1所5个年级的工会学校、1所有400名学员的党校。所有技术学校的课程为期都只有6个月。

重点当然放在军事教育上面,两年来在这方面取得了很大成就,尽管这个遭到四面包围的小国有种种困难。有红军大学、骑兵学校、步兵学校,上文已提到。还有一所无线电学校、一所医科学校,后者实际上只训练护士。有一所工程学校,学员所受的实际上是当学徒工的基本训练。像整个苏维埃组织一样,一切都是十分临时性的,主要是当作一种加强红军后方的活动,为红军供应干部。许多教员连中学毕业生都不是。令人感到有趣的是,他们把什么知识都共同分享。这些学校是地地

"Here the work is very much slower. We have to start everything from the beginning. Our material resources are very limited. Even our printing machinery has been destroyed, and now we have to print everything by mimeograph and stone-block lithograph. The blockade prevents us from importing enough paper. We have begun to make paper of our own, but the quality is terrible. But never mind these difficulties. We have already been able to accomplish something. If we are given time we can do things here that will astonish the rest of China. We are training scores of teachers from the masses now, and the Party is training others. Many of them will become voluntary teachers for the mass-education schools. Our results show that the peasants here are eager to learn when given the chance.

"And they are not stupid. They learn very quickly, and they change their habits when they are given good reasons for doing so. In the older soviet districts here you won't see any girl children with bound feet and you will see many young women with bobbed hair. The men are gradually cutting off their queues now and a lot of them are learning to read and write from the Young Communists and the Vanguards."

Hsu explained that under the emergency soviet educational system there were three sections: institutional, military, and social. The first was run more or less by the soviets, the second by the Red Army, the third by Communist organizations. Emphasis in all of them was primarily political—even the smallest children learned their first characters in the shape of simple revolutionary slogans, and then worked forward into stories of conflict between the Reds and the Kuomintang, landlords and peasants, capitalists and workers, and so on, with plenty of heroics about the Young Communists and the Red Army, and promises of an earthly paradise in the soviet future.

Under institutional education the Reds already claimed to have established about two hundred primary schools, and they had one normal school for primary teachers, one agricultural school, a textile school, a trade-union school of five grades, and a Party school with some four hundred students. Courses in all the technical schools lasted only about six months.

Greatest emphasis naturally was on military education, and here much had been achieved in two years, despite all the handicaps of the beleaguered little state. There were the Red Army University, the cavalry and infantry schools, and two Party training schools, already described. There was a radio school, and a medical school, which was really for training nurses. There was an engineering school, where students received the rudimentary training of apprentices. Like the whole soviet organization itself, everything was very provisional and designed primarily as a kind of rear-line activity to strengthen the Red Army and provide it with new cadres. Many of the teachers were not even middle-school graduates. What was interesting was the collective use of whatever knowledge they had.

道道共产主义的，不仅在意识形态方面是如此，而且在利用他们所能搜刮的技术知识，"提高文化水平"方面也是如此。

甚至在社会教育方面，苏区的目标也主要是政治方面的。根本没有时间或者机会教授农民欣赏文学或者花卉布置。共产党是讲实际的人。他们向列宁俱乐部、共青团、游击队、村苏维埃送插图简单粗糙的识字课本，帮助群众团体组织自学小组，以一个共产党员或者识字的人担任组长。年轻人，有时甚至是上了年纪的农民一开始朗读短句，就在认字的同时吸收了其中的思想。例如，你一进到山区这种小"社会教育站"，你就会听到这些人在这样高声问答：

"这是什么？"

"这是红旗。"

"这是谁？"

"这是一个穷人。"

"什么是红旗？"

"红旗是红军的旗。"

"什么是红军？"

"红军是穷人的军队！"

如此等等，一直到如果这个青年走在别人前面，第一个学会五六百字，就可以得奖，不是红旗，就是铅笔，或者别的奖品。当然，这是粗糙的宣传。但是农民和他们的子女读完这本书以后，他们不但有生以来第一次能读书识字，而且知道是谁教给他们的和为什么教他们。他们掌握了中国共产主义的基本战斗思想。

而且，反正，我认为这比教人们用学"这是一只猫，那是一只老鼠，猫在干什么，猫在捉老鼠"来识字的方法有趣。为什么要教现实主义者学寓言呢？

为了要有一个更快地在群众中间扫除文盲的手段，共产党开始在有限范围内使用汉语拉丁化拼音。他们用28个字母，据说可以发出几乎所有的汉语语音，并且编了一本袖珍小字典，把最常见的汉语词句译成多音节的容易认读的词汇。《红色中华》有一部分篇幅是用拉丁化拼音出版的，老徐在保安挑选了一班学生在进行试验。

These schools were really Communist, not only in ideology but in the utilization of every scrap of technical experience they could mobilize, to "raise the cultural level."

Even in social education the soviet aims were primarily political. There was no time or occasion to be teaching farmers literature or flower arrangement. The Reds were practical people. To the Lenin clubs, the Communist Youth Leagues, the Partisans, and the village soviets they sent simple, crudely illustrated *Shih-tzu* ("Know Characters") texts, and helped mass organizations form self-study groups of their own, with some Communist or literate among them as a leader. When the youths, or sometimes even aged peasants, began droning off the short sentences, they found themselves absorbing ideas along with their ideographs. Thus, entering one of these little "social education centers" in the mountains, you might hear these people catechizing themselves aloud:

"What is this?"

"This is the Red Flag."

"What is this?"

"This is a poor man."

"What is the Red Flag?"

"The Red Flag is the flag of the Red Army."

"What is the Red Army?"

"The Red Army is the army of the poor men!"

And so on, right up to the point where, if he knew the whole five or six hundred characters before anyone else, the youth could collect the red tassel or pencil or whatever was promised. When farmers and farmers' sons and daughters finished the book they could not only read for the first time in their lives, but they knew who had taught them, and why. They had grasped the basic fighting ideas of Chinese communism.

In an effort to find a quicker medium for bringing literacy to the masses, the Communists had begun a limited use of Latinized Chinese. They had worked out an alphabet of twenty-eight letters by which they claimed to be able to reproduce nearly all Chinese phonetics, and had written and published a little pocket dictionary with the commonest phrases of Chinese rendered into polysyllabic, easily readable words. Part of the paper *Hung Ssu Chung Hua* (*Red China*) was published in *Latin-hua*, and Old Hsu was experimenting with it on a class of youngsters he had picked up in Pao An. He believed

他相信繁复的汉字将来在大规模教育中终究要放弃不用,他对他的这个方法已做了多年工作,提出许多赞成的理由。

迄今为止,他还没有吹嘘他的拉丁化或其他教育工作上的成绩,他说,"这里的文化水平实在低得不能再低,所以我们自然获得了一些成绩。"至于将来,他只需要时间。同时他要求我把重点放在研究红军中的教育方法,他认为在那方面可以看到真正革命化的教学。

that the complicated Chinese characters would eventually have to be abandoned in education on a mass scale, and he had many arguments in favor of his system, on which he had been working for years.

Thus far he wasn't boasting about results, either with his *Latin-hua* or his other educational efforts. "The cultural level was so low here it couldn't be made worse, so naturally we've made some progress," he said. As for the future, he only wanted time. Meanwhile he urged me to concentrate on studying educational methods in the Red Army, where he claimed real revolutionary teaching could be seen.

PART SEVEN
En Route to the Front

第七篇
去前线的路上

一、 同红色农民谈话

我到保安以西的甘肃边境和前线去的时候,一路上借宿农民的茅屋,睡在他们的土炕上(在弄不到门板那样的奢侈品的时候),吃他们的饭,同他们谈话。他们都是穷人,心地善良,殷勤好客。他们有些人听说我是个"外国客人"便拒绝收我的钱。我记得一个农村小脚老太太,自己有五六个孩子吃饭,却坚持要把她养的五六只鸡杀一只招待我。

"咱们可不能让一个洋鬼子告诉外面的人说咱们红军不懂规矩,"我听到她同我的一个同伴说。我知道她这么说并不是有意无礼。她除了"洋鬼子"以外实在不知道该用什么称呼来叫我。

我当时是同傅锦魁一起旅行,他是一个年轻的共产党员,由外交部派来陪我上前线。像在后方的所有共产党一样,傅因有机会到前线的部队里去而很高兴,把我看成是天赐给他的良机。同时,他直率地把我看成是个帝国主义分子,对我整个旅行公开抱怀疑态度。但是,在一切方面,他总是乐意帮忙的,因此后来没有等到旅行结束,我们就成了很要好的朋友。

一天夜里在陕北接近甘肃边境的一个叫周家的村子里,傅和我在一个住了五六户农民的院子里找到了住处。有15个小孩不断地在跑来跑去,其中6个孩子的父亲是一个年约45岁的农民,他很客气地慨然同意接待我们。他给了我们一间干净的屋子,炕上铺了一张新毡子,给我们的牲口喂玉米和干草。他卖了一只鸡和几个鸡蛋给我们,那只鸡只收2角钱,但是那间屋子,他坚决不收钱。他到过延安,以前看到过外国人,但其他的男女老幼都没有见过外国人,他们现在都怯生生地来偷偷看一眼。一个小孩子看到这副奇怪的容貌吓得哇地大哭起来。

1   Conversation with Red Peasants

As I traveled beyond Pao An, toward the Kansu border and the front, I stayed in the rude huts of peasants, slept on their mud *k'ang* (when the luxury of wooden doors was not available), ate their food, and enjoyed their talk. They were all poor people, kind and hospitable. Some of them refused any money from me when they heard I was a "foreign guest." I remember one old bound-footed peasant woman, with five or six youngsters to feed, who insisted upon killing one of her half-dozen chickens for me.

"We can't have a foreign devil telling people in the outer world that we Reds don't know etiquette," I overheard her say to one of my companions. I am sure she did not mean to be impolite. She simply knew no other words but "foreign devil" to describe the situation.

I was traveling then with Fu Chin-kuei, a young Communist who had been delegated by the Red Foreign Office to accompany me to the front. Like all the Reds in the rear, Fu was delighted at the prospect of a chance to be with the army, and he looked upon me as a godsend. At the same time he regarded me frankly as an imperialist, and viewed my whole trip with open skepticism. He was unfailingly helpful in every way, however, and before the trip was over we were to become very good friends.

One night at Chou Chia, a village of north Shensi near the Kansu border, Fu and I found quarters in a compound where five or six peasant families lived. A farmer of about forty-five, responsible for six of the fifteen little children who scampered back and forth incessantly, agreed to accommodate us, with ready courtesy. He gave us a clean room with new felt on the *k'ang*, and provided our animals with corn and straw. He sold us a chicken for twenty cents, and some eggs, but for the room would take nothing. He had been to Yenan and he had seen foreigners before, but none of the other men, women, or children had seen one, and they all now came round diffidently to have a peek. One of the young children burst into frightened tears at the astonishing sight.

晚饭后，有一些农民到我们屋里来，给我烟叶，开始聊天。他们想知道我们美国种什么庄稼，我们有没有玉米、小米、牛马，我们用不用羊粪做肥料（一个农民问我们美国有没有鸡，我的房东对此嗤之以鼻。他说，"哪儿有人就有鸡！"）。我们美国有没有富人和穷人？有没有共产党和红军？我的关于为什么有共产党却没有红军的答复，恐怕使他们很费解。

我回答了他们好多问题以后，也问了他们一些问题。他们对红军怎么看？他们马上开始抱怨骑兵的马吃得过多的习惯。情况似乎是，红军大学最近在迁移骑兵学校的校址时，曾在这个村子里暂憩几天，结果使该村的玉米和干草储备大为减少。

"他们买东西不付钱吗？"傅锦魁问。

"付的，付的，他们付钱，问题不在这里。我们存底不多，你知道，只有这几担玉米、小米、干草。我们只够自己吃的，也许还有一些剩余，但是我们还要过冬呢。明年1月合作社肯卖粮食给我们吗？我们不知道。苏区的钱能买什么？连鸦片都不能买！"

这话是个衣服破烂的老头说的，他仍留着辫子，不高兴地低垂双眼，看着自己的皱鼻和两英尺长的竹子旱烟筒。他说话的时候，年轻的人都笑。傅锦魁承认他们不能买到鸦片，但是他们不论要什么其他东西都可以到合作社里去买。

"能买到吗？"我们的房东问，"我们可以买到这样的碗吗，哎？"他拣起我从西安带来的一只廉价的红色赛璐珞碗（我想大概是日本货）。傅承认合作社没有红色的碗，但是说，他们有不少粮食、布匹、煤油、蜡烛、针、火柴、盐——他们还要什么？

"我听说每人只能买6尺布；有没有这回事？"一个农民问道。

傅不清楚。他认为布有的是。他于是求助于抗日的论点。"我们的生活同你们一样苦，"他说，"红军是在为你们，为农民工人打仗，保护你们抵抗日本和国民党。就算你们不是总能买到你要的那么多的布，买不到鸦片吧，但是你们也不用付税，这是不是事实？你们不欠地主的债，不会失掉房屋土地，是不是？那么，大哥，你是不是喜欢白军，不喜欢我们？请你回答这个问题。白军收了你的庄稼付给你什么，哎？"

一听到这话，一切抱怨似乎都烟消云散了，意见是一致的。"当然不，老傅，当

After dinner a number of the peasants came into our room, offered me tobacco, and began to talk. They wanted to know what we grew in my country, whether we had corn and millet, horses and cows, and whether we used goat dung for fertilizer. (One peasant asked whether we had chickens, and at this our host sniffed contemptuously. "Where there are men, there must be chickens," he observed.) Were there rich and poor in my country? Was there a Communist Party and a Red Army?

In return for answering their numerous questions, I asked a few of my own. What did they think of the Red Army? They promptly began to complain about the excessive eating habits of the cavalry's horses. It seemed that when the Red Army University recently moved its cavalry school it had paused in this village for several days, with the result that a big depression had been made in the corn and straw reserves.

"Didn't they pay you for what they bought?" demanded Fu Chin-kuei.

"Yes, yes, they paid all right; that isn't the question. We haven't a great amount, you know, only so many *tan* of corn and millet and straw. We have only enough for ourselves and maybe a little more, and we have the winter ahead of us. Will the cooperatives sell us grain next January? That's what we wonder. What can we buy with soviet money? We can't even buy opium!"

This came from a ragged old man who still wore a queue and looked sourly down his wrinkled nose and along the two-foot stem of his bamboo pipe. The younger men grinned when he spoke. Fu admitted they couldn't buy opium, but he said they could buy in the cooperatives anything else they needed.

"Can we now?" demanded our host. "Can we buy a bowl like this one, eh?" And he picked up the cheap red celluloid bowl (Japanese-made, I suspect) which I had brought with me from Sian. Fu confessed that the cooperatives had no red bowls, but said they had plenty of grain, cloth, paraffin, candles, needles, matches, salt—what did they want?

"I hear you can't get more than six feet of cloth per man; now, isn't it so?" demanded one farmer.

Fu wasn't sure; he thought there was plenty of cloth. He resorted to the anti-Japanese argument. "Life is as bitter for us as for you," he said. "The Red Army is fighting for you, the farmers and workers, to protect you from the Japanese and the Kuomintang. Suppose you can't always buy all the cloth you want, and you can't get opium, it's a fact you don't pay taxes, isn't it? You don't go in debt to the landlords and lose your house and land, do you? Well, old brother, do you like the White Army better than us, or not? —just answer that question. What does the White Army give you for your crops, eh?"

At this, all complaints appeared to melt away, and opinion was unanimous. "Certainly not,

然不！"我们的房东点头道。"如果让我们选择，我们当然要红军。我的一个儿子就在红军里，是我自己把他送去的。谁能说不是？"

我问他们为什么宁可要红军。

那个对合作社没有鸦片卖表示不满的老头儿在回答时说了一席热烈的话。

"白军来了怎么样？"他问道，"他们要多少多少粮食，从来不说一句付钱的话。如果我们不给，就把我们当共产党逮起来。如果我们给他们，就没有钱缴税。反正不论怎么样，我们都没有力量缴税。那么怎么办呢？他们就拿我们的牲口去卖。去年，红军不在这里，白军回来了，他们拿走了我的两头骡子，四头猪。骡子每头值30元钱，猪长足了值2元钱，他们给了我什么？

"哎呀，哎呀！他们说我欠了80元的税和地租，我的牲口折价40元，他们还要我40元。我到哪里去弄这笔钱？我没有别的东西给他们偷了。他们要我卖闺女，这是真的！我们有的人只好这样！没有牲口没有闺女的只好到保安去坐牢，许多人给冻死了……"

我问这个老头，他有多少地。

"地？"他哑着声说，"那就是我的地。"他指着一个种着玉米、小米、蔬菜的山顶。隔着一条小溪，就在我们院子的对岸。

"那块地值多少钱？"

"这里的地不值钱，除非是河谷地。"他说，"这样的一座山，我们花25元钱就能买到。值钱的是骡子、羊、猪、鸡、房子、农具。"

"那么，打比方来说，你的地值多少？"

他仍旧不愿说他的地值多少钱。"你花100元钱可以把我房子、牲口、农具都买去——再算进那座山。"他最后这么估计。

"那你得缴多少税和地租呢？"

"40元一年！"

"那是在红军来这里以前？"

Old Fu, certainly not!" Our host nodded. "If we have to choose, we take the Red Army. A son of mine is in the Red Army, and I sent him there. Does anyone deny that?"

I asked why they preferred the Red Army.

In answer the old man who had sneered at the cooperatives for having no opium gave a heated discourse.

"What happens when the Whites come?" he asked. "They demand such and such amounts of food, and never a word about payment. If we refuse, we are arrested as Communists. If we give it to them we cannot pay the taxes. *In any case* we cannot pay the taxes! What happens then? They take our animals to sell. Last year, when the Red Army was not here and the Whites returned, they took my two mules and my four pigs. These mules were worth $30 each, and the pigs were full grown, worth $2 each. What did they give me?

"*Ai-ya, ai-ya!* They said I owed $80 in taxes and rent, and they allowed me $40 for my stock. They demanded $40 more. Could I get it? I had nothing else for them to steal. They wanted me to sell my daughter; it's a fact! Some of us here had to do that. Those who had no cattle and no daughters went to jail in Pao An, and plenty died from the cold. . . ."

I asked this old man how much land he had.

"Land?" he croaked. "There is my land," and he pointed to a hilltop patched with corn and millet and vegetables. It lay just across the stream from our courtyard.

"How much is it worth?"

"Land here isn't worth anything unless it's valley land," he said. "We can buy a mountain like that for $25. What costs money are mules, goats, pigs, chickens, houses, and tools."

"Well, how much is your farm worth, for example?"

He still refused to count his land worth anything at all. "You can have the house, my animals and tools for $100—with the mountain thrown in," he finally estimated.

"And on that you had to pay how much in taxes and rent?"

"Forty dollars a year!"

"That was before the Red Army came?"

"是的，现在我们不缴税。但是谁知道明年又怎样？红军一走，白军就来。一年红军，一年白军。白军来了，他们叫我们'赤匪'。红军来了，他们逮反革命分子。"

"但是有着不同，"一个青年农民插嘴说，"如果我们的街坊说我们没有帮助白军，红军就相信了。但是碰上白军，我们即使有100个好人为我们担保，而没有一个地主，仍把我们当'赤匪'。可不是这样？"

那个老头点点头。他说上次白军来时，把山那一头的村子里一家贫农统统杀了。为什么？因为白军问红军藏在哪里，那家子人不肯告诉他们。"从那以后，我们全都逃了，把牲口带走。我们后来同红军一起回来。"

"要是下次白军来了，你走吗？"

"哎呀！"一个头发很长，长得一口好牙的老头叫道。"这次我们当然走！他们会杀死我们的！"

他开始一一说村子里的人的罪名。他们参加了贫民会，他们投票选举乡苏维埃，他们把白军动向报告给红军，他们有两家的儿子在红军里，另一家有两个女儿在护士学校。这不是罪名吗？他向我保证，随便哪一个罪名就可以把他们枪决。

这时一个赤脚的十几岁少年站了起来，他一心注意讨论，忘记了有洋鬼子。"老大爷，你说这是罪名？这是爱国行为！我们为什么这样做？难道不是因为红军是穷人的军队，为咱们的权利在打仗？"

他热烈地继续说："咱们国家以前有过免费学校吗？红军把无线电带来以前咱们听到过世界新闻吗？世界是怎么样的，有谁告诉过咱们？你说合作社没有布，但是咱们以前有过合作社吗？还有你的地，从前不是押给了王地主吗？我的姐姐3年前饿死了，但是自从红军来了以后，咱们不是有足够的粮食吃吗？你说这苦，但是如果咱们年轻人能学会识字，这就不算苦！咱们少先队学会开枪打汉奸和日本，这就不算苦！"

凡是知道中国普通农民对日本侵略或任何其他民族问题都是无知的（不是冷漠的）人听来，这样不断提到日本和汉奸可能觉得是不可能的。但是我发现这种情况不断发生，不仅在共产党人的嘴里，而且也在农民的嘴里，像这些农民那样。共产党的宣传已造成普遍的影响，这些落后的山民相信他们马上有受到"日本矮子"奴

"Yes. Now we pay no taxes. But who knows about next year? When the Reds leave, the Whites come back. One year Red, the next White. When the Whites come they call us Red bandits. When the Reds come they look for counterrevolutionaries."

"But there is this difference," a young farmer interposed. "If our neighbors say we have not helped the Whites that satisfies the Reds. But if we have a hundred names of honest men, but no landlord's name, we are still Red bandits to the Whites! Isn't that a fact?"

The old man nodded. He said the last time the White Army was here it had killed a whole family of poor farmers in a village just over the hill. Why? Because the Whites had asked where the Reds were hiding, and this family refused to tell them. "After that we all fled from here, and took our cattle with us. We came back with the Reds."

"Will you leave next time, if the Whites return?"

"*Ai-ya!*" exclaimed an elder with long hair and fine teeth. "This time we will leave, certainly! They will kill us!"

He began to tell of the villagers' crimes. They had joined the Poor People's League, they had voted for the district soviets, they had given information to the Red Army about the White Army's movements, two had sons in the Red Army, and another had two daughters in a nursing school. Were these crimes or not? They could be shot for any one of them, I was assured.

But now a barefoot youth in his teens stepped up, engrossed in the discussion and forgetful of the foreign devil. "You call these things crimes, grandfather? These are patriotic acts! Why do we do them? Isn't it because our Red Army is a poor people's army and fights for our rights?"

He continued enthusiastically: "Did we have a free school in Chou Chia before? Did we ever get news of the world before the Reds brought us wireless electricity? Who told us what the world is like? You say the cooperative has no cloth, but did we ever even have a cooperative before? And how about your farm, wasn't there a big mortgage on it to landlord Wang? My sister starved to death three years ago, but haven't we had plenty to eat since the Reds came? You say it's bitter, but it isn't bitter for us young people if we can learn to read! It isn't bitter for us Young Vanguards when we learn to use a rifle and fight the traitors and Japan!"

This constant reference to Japan and the "traitors" may sound improbable to people who know the ignorance (not indifference) of the mass of the ordinary Chinese peasants concerning Japanese invasions or any other national problems. But I found it constantly recurring, not only in the speech of the Communists but among peasants like these. Red propaganda had made such a wide impression that many of these backward mountaineers believed themselves in imminent danger of being enslaved by the "Japanese

役的危险，而他们大多数人除了在共产党招贴和漫画中以外还没有见过这样的人种。

那个青年一口气说完以后不响了。我看了一眼傅锦魁，看到他脸上露出满意的笑容。几个别的农民也连声称是，他们大多数人都面露笑容。

谈话一直快到9点，早已过了上床时间。使我感到兴趣的是，这次谈话是在傅锦魁面前进行的，农民们似乎并不怕他是个共产党"官员"。他们似乎把他看成是自己人——而且，看成是一个农民的儿子，他确实也是农民的儿子。

最后一个离开我们的是那个留着辫子和牢骚最多的老头。他走到门旁时转过身来，再次低声向傅说："老同志，"他央求道，"保安有鸦片吗？现在，那里有吗？"

他走后，傅厌恶地对我说："你相信吗？那个他妈的[1]老头是这里的贫民会主席，但他仍要鸦片！这个村子需要加强教育工作。"

---

1. "他妈的"是中国最常见的骂人话之一，大致译为 defile-mother。鲁迅曾就此写过一篇轻松的讽刺短文。参见埃德加·斯诺著的《活的中国》(1935年纽约)。

dwarfs"—a specimen of which most of them had yet to see outside Red posters and cartoons.

The youth subsided, out of breath. I looked at Fu Chin-kuei and saw a pleased smirk on his face. Several others present called out in approval, and most of them smiled.

The dialogue went on until nearly nine o'clock, long past bedtime. It interested me chiefly because it took place before Fu Chin-kuei, whom the farmers appeared to hold in no awe as a Red "official." They seemed to look upon him as one of themselves—and indeed, as a peasant's son, he was.

The last one to leave us was the old man with the queue and most of the complaints. As he went out the door he leaned over and whispered once more to Fu. "Old comrade," he implored, "is there any opium at Pao An; now, is there any?"

When he had left, Fu turned to me in disgust. "Would you believe it?" he demanded. "That old defile-mother[1] is chairman of the Poor People's Society here, and still he wants opium. This village needs more educational work."

---

1. Approximate translation of *T'a ma-ti*, one of the commonest oaths in China. Lu Hsun wrote a delightful satirical essay on this subject. See Edgar Snow, *Living China* (New York, 1935).

二、　　苏区工业

我在去前线的途上，离保安向西北方向走了几天的路程以后，停下来在吴起镇访问了一下。吴起镇是陕西苏区的一个"工业中心"，它之所以突出，读者不久就会知道，并不是由于在工艺学方面有什么成就使底特律或曼彻斯特不能等闲视之，而是因为居然有它的存在。

因为在它方圆数百英里之内都是半牧区，人民住在窑洞里，完全同几千年以前他们的祖先一模一样，许多农民仍留着辫子，盘在头上，马、驴、骆驼是最新式的交通工具。这里用菜油点灯，蜡烛是奢侈品，电灯闻所未闻，外国人像爱斯基摩人在非洲一样罕见。

在这个中世纪的世界里，突然看到了苏区的工厂，看到了机器在运转，看到了一批工人在忙碌地生产红色中国的商品和农具，确实使人感到意想不到。

我知道在江西的时候，尽管由于缺乏海港和敌人封锁造成的障碍，切断了共产党同现代化大工业基地的联系，他们还是建立了好些繁荣的工业。例如，他们所经营的钨矿是中国最丰富的，每年生产100多万磅这种珍贵的矿物，秘密地卖给陈济棠将军在广东的钨垄断企业。在吉安的中央苏区印刷厂有800名工人，印刷许多书籍、杂志，还有一家"全国性"报纸——《红色中华》……

在江西还有纺纱厂、织布厂、机器车间。这些小型工业生产足够的工业制成品可供简单的需要。共产党自称1933年"对外出口贸易"超过1,200万元，其中大部分是通过南方敢于冒险的商人进行的，他们闯破国民党封锁大获其利。但是大部分制造业是手工艺和家庭工业，产品通过生产合作社出售。

2 _____ SOVIET INDUSTRIES

A few days northwest of Pao An, on my way to the front, I stopped to visit Wu Ch'i Chen, a soviet "industrial center" of Shensi. Wu Ch'i Chen was remarkable, not for any achievements in industrial science of which Detroit or Manchester need take note, but because it was there at all.

For hundreds of miles around there was only semipastoral country, the people lived in cave houses exactly as their ancestors did millenniums ago, many of the farmers still wore queues braided around their heads, and the horse, the ass, and the camel were the latest thing in communications. Rape oil was used for lighting here, candles were a luxury, electricity was unknown, and foreigners were as rare as Eskimos in Africa.

In this medieval world it was astonishing suddenly to come upon soviet factories, and find machines turning, and a colony of workers busily producing the goods and tools of a Red China.

In Kiangsi the Communists had, despite the lack of a seaport and the handicap of an enemy blockade which cut them off from contact with any big modern industrial base, built up several prosperous industries. They operated China's richest tungsten mines, for example, annually turning out over one million pounds of this precious ore—secretly selling it to General Ch'en Chi-t'ang's Kwangtung tungsten monopoly. In the central soviet printing plant at Kian with its eight hundred workers, many books, magazines, and a "national" paper—the *Red China Daily News* were published...

In Kiangsi also were weaving plants, textile mills and machine shops. Small industries produced sufficient manufactured goods to supply their simple needs. The Reds claimed to have had a "foreign export trade" of over $12,000,000 in 1933, most of which was carried on through adventurous southern merchants, who made extraordinary profits by running the Kuomintang blockade. The bulk of manufacturing, however, was by handicraft and home industry, the products of which were sold through production cooperatives.

据毛泽东说，到1933年9月，江西苏区共有1,423个"产销"合作社，都是为人民所有，由人民管理的[1]。国联调查人员的报告使人没有怀疑，共产党搞这种集体企业是成功的，哪怕是在他们为了生存仍在打仗的时候。国民党事实上在南方有些地方模仿共产党的办法，但至今为止所取得的结果证明，要在纯粹的自由资本主义制度下经营这种合作社极为困难，即使不是不可能的。

但是在西北，我并没有想到会有什么工业。共产党在这里遇到的困难要比在南方大得多，因为在成立苏维埃之前，甚至连一个小规模的机器工业都几乎完全不存在。在整个西北，在陕西、甘肃、青海、宁夏、绥远，这些面积总和几乎与俄国除外的整个欧洲相当的省份里，机器工业总投资额肯定大大低于——打个比方来说——福特汽车公司某一大装配线上的一个工厂。

西安和兰州有少数几家工厂，但这两个地方主要依靠华东的大工业中心。只有从外界引进技术和机器，西北的庞大工业潜力才有可能得到大规模的发展。如果说这话适用于西北的这两个大城市西安和兰州，那么共产党所占的地方是甘肃、陕西、宁夏一些更加落后的地方，他们所面对的困难就可想而知了。

当然，封锁切断了苏维埃政府的机器进口和技术人员的"进口"。但是关于后者，共产党说目前他们的来源不绝。机器和原料是更严重的问题。为了弄几台车床、纺织机、发动机或者一点废铁，红军不惜作战。在我访问期间，他们所有的属于机器项目的一切东西几乎都是"缴获"的！例如，在他们1936年远征山西时，他们缴获了机器、工具、原料后就用骡子一路跨山越岭运回陕西，到他们令人难以想象的窑洞工厂里。

南方的红军到西北时激起了一阵"工业繁荣"。他们带来了（经过6,000英里世界上最难通过的路线）许多车床、旋床、冲床、铸模等。他们带来了数十台胜家缝纫机，配备了他们的被服厂。他们从四川红色矿井里带来了金银。他们还带来了制版机和轻型印刷机。怪不得红军尊重爱惜马骡，特别是那些把重负从南方驮来的力壮的牲口！

在我访问红色中国的时候，苏区工业都是手工业[2]，有保安和河连湾（甘肃）的织布厂、被服厂、制鞋厂、造纸厂，定边（在长城上）的制毯厂，永平的煤矿，所产的煤是中国最便宜的[3]，还有其他几县的毛纺厂和纺纱厂——所有这些工厂都计划

---

1. 《红色中国：毛泽东主席……》，第26页。
2. 没有电力。
3. 红区行情是1银元800斤——约半吨。见毛泽民著《甘陕苏区的经济建设》，载《斗争》，1936年4月24日，陕西保安。

According to Mao Tse-tung, in September, 1933, the soviets had 1,423 "production and distribution" cooperatives in Kiangsi, all owned and run by the people.[1] Testimony by League of Nations investigators left little doubt that the Reds were succeeding with this type of collective enterprise—even while they were still fighting for their existence. The Kuomintang was attempting to copy the Red system in parts of the South, but results thus far suggested that it was extremely difficult, if not impossible, to operate such cooperatives under a strictly *laissez-faire* capitalism.

But in the Northwest I had not expected to find any industry at all. Much greater handicaps faced the Reds here than in the South, for even a small machine industry was almost entirely absent before the soviets were set up. In the whole Northwest, in Shensi, Kansu, Chinghai, Ninghsia and Suiyuan, provinces in area nearly the size of all Europe excluding Russia, the combined machine-industry investment certainly must have been far less than the plant of one big assembly branch of, for instance, the Ford Motor Company.

Sian and Lanchow had a few factories, but for the most part were dependent upon industrial centers farther east. Any major development of the tremendous industrial possibilities of the Northwest could take place only by borrowing technique and machinery from the outside. And if this were true in Sian and Lanchow, the two great cities of the region, the difficulties which confronted the Reds, occupying the even more backward areas of Kansu, Shensi, and Ninghsia, were manifest.

The blockade cut off the Soviet Government from imports of machinery, and from "imports" of technicians. Of the latter, however, the Reds said their supply was ample. Machinery and raw materials were more serious problems. Battles were fought by the Red Army just to get a few lathes, weaving machines, engines, or a little scrap iron. Nearly everything they had in the category of machinery while I was there had been "captured." During their expedition to Shansi province in 1936, for example, they seized machines, tools, and raw materials, which were carried by mule all the way across the mountains of Shensi, to their fantastic cliff-dwelling factories.

Soviet industries, when I visited Red China, were all handicraft; there was no electric power. They included clothing, uniform, shoe, and paper factories at Pao An and Holienwan (Kansu), rug factories at Tingpien (on the Great Wall), mines at Yung P'ing which produced the cheapest coal[2] in China, and woolen and cotton-spinning factories in seven *hsien*—all of which had plans to produce enough goods to stock the 400

---

1. Mao Tse-tung, *Red China*..., p. 26.
2. The price quoted in the Red districts was 800 catties—about half a ton—for $1 silver. See Mao Tse-min, "Economic Construction in the Kansu and Shensi Soviet Districts," *Tou Tsung* [*Struggle*] (Pao An, Shensi), April 24, 1936.

生产足够的商品供红色陕西和甘肃的 400 家合作社销售。据经济人民委员毛泽民说，这个"工业计划"的目标是要使红色中国"在经济上自足"——也就是，如果南京拒绝接受共产党提出的结成统一战线和停止内战的建议，能够有不怕国民党封锁而维持下去的能力。

苏区国营企业中最大最重要的是宁夏边境长城上的盐池的制盐工业和永平、延长的油井，那里生产汽油、煤油、凡士林、蜡、蜡烛和其他副产品。盐池的盐是中国最好的，所产的盐色白如晶，产量很大。因此苏区的盐比国民党中国又便宜又多，盐在国民党中国是政府的主要收入来源，对农民不利。红军攻占盐池以后，同意把一部分产品给长城以北的蒙古人，废除了国民党的全部产品专卖政策，因此获得了蒙古人的好感。

陕北的油井是中国仅有的一些油井，以前的产品卖给一家美国公司，该公司对该地的其他油藏拥有租让权。红军占领永平后，开凿了两口新油井，生产据说比以前永平和延长在"非匪徒"手中任何一个时期都增长了 40%。这里面包括所统计的 3 个月内增加的"2,000 担石油，2.5 万担头等油，1.35 万担二等油"[1]。

在清除了罂粟的地方正在努力发展植棉，共产党在安定办了一所纺织学校，收了 100 名女学生。每天上 3 小时文化课，5 小时纺织训练。学完 3 个月后就派到各地去办手工纺织厂。"预计在两年内陕北能够生产全部所需的布匹。"[2]

但是吴起镇是红区工厂工人最"集中"的地方，作为红军的主要兵工厂所在地，也很重要。它位于甘肃的贸易要道，附近两个古代碉堡的废墟说明了它以前的战略重要性。镇址是在一条湍急的河流的陡峭河岸上，一半是"洋房"——陕西人把有四道墙、一个屋顶的建筑都叫洋房———一半是窑洞。

---

1. 毛泽民上引文。
2. 毛泽民上引文。

cooperatives in Red Shensi and Kansu. The aim of this "industrial program," according to Mao Tse-min, brother of Mao Tse-tung and Commissioner of People's Economy, was to make Red China "economically self-sufficient"—strong enough to survive despite the Kuomintang blockade if Nanking refused to accept the Communists' offers for a united front and a cessation of civil war.

The most important soviet state enterprises were the salt-refining plants at Yen Ch'ih, the salt lakes on the Ninghsia border, along the Great Wall, and the oil wells at Yung P'ing and Yen Ch'ang, which produced gasoline, paraffin, and vaseline, wax, candles, and other by-products on a very small scale. Salt deposits at Yen Ch'ih were the finest in China and yielded beautiful rock-crystal salt in large quantities. Consequently salt was cheaper and more plentiful in the soviet districts than in Kuomintang China, where it was a principal source of government income. After the capture of Yen Ch'ih the Reds won the sympathy of the Mongols north of the Wall by agreeing to turn over part of the production to them, revoking the Kuomintang's practice of monopolizing the entire output.

North Shensi's oil wells were the only ones in China, and their output had formerly been sold to an American company which had leases on other reserves in the district. After they had seized Yung P'ing the Reds sank two new wells, and claimed increased production, by about 40 per cent over any previous period, when Yung P'ing and Yen Ch'ang were in "non-bandit" hands. This included increases of "2,000 catties of petrol, 25,000 catties of first-class oil, and 13,500 catties of second-class oil" during a three-month period reported upon. (A few barrels at best.)[1]

Efforts were being made to develop cotton growing in areas cleared of poppies, and the Reds had established a spinning school at An Ting, with a hundred women students. The workers were given three hours' general education daily and five hours' instruction in spinning and weaving. Upon completion of their course, after three months, students were sent to various districts to open handicraft textile factories. "It is expected that in two years north Shensi will be able to produce its entire supply of cloth."[2]

But Wu Ch'i Chen had the largest "concentration" of factory workers in the Red districts, and was important also as the location of the Reds' main arsenal. It commanded an important trade route leading to Kansu, and the ruins of two ancient forts nearby testified to its former strategic importance. The town was built high up on the steep clay banks of a rapid stream, and was made up half of *yang-fang*, or "foreign houses"—as the Shensi natives still called anything with four sides and a roof—and half of *yao-fang*, or cave dwellings.

---

1. *Ibid.*
2. *Ibid.*

我是深夜到达的，感到很累。前线部队给养委员听说我要来，骑马出来相迎。他"把我安排"在工人列宁俱乐部里——是个墙壁刷得很白的窑洞，在不朽的伊里奇画像的四周挂着彩纸条。

马上给我送来了热水，干净的毛巾——上面印着蒋介石新生活运动的口号！——和肥皂。然后是一顿丰盛的晚饭，有很好的烘制的面包。我开始觉得好过一些。我把被褥在乒乓球桌上摊开，点了一支烟。但是，人是很难满足的动物。这一切奢侈和照顾只有使我更加想喝一杯我最爱喝的饮料。

这时，给养委员居然从天晓得的什么地方端出褐色的浓咖啡和白糖来！吴起镇赢得了我的欢心。

"我们五年计划的产品！"给养委员笑道。

"你是说，你们征用没收部的产品，"我纠正说。我想这一定是来路不正的，因为它有违禁品的一切魅力。

I arrived late at night and I was very tired. The head of the supply commissariat for the front armies had received word of my coming, and he rode out to meet me. He "put me up" at a workers' Lenin Club—an earthen-floored *yao-fang* with clean whitewashed walls strung with festoons of colored paper chains encircling a portrait of the immortal Ilyitch.

Hot water, clean towels—stamped with slogans of Chiang Kai-shek's New Life movement!—and soap soon appeared. They were followed by an ample dinner, with good *baked* bread. I began to feel better. I unrolled my bedding on the table-tennis court and lighted a cigarette. But man is a difficult animal to satisfy. All this luxury and attention only made me yearn for my favorite beverage.

And then, of all things, this commissar suddenly produced, from heaven knows where, some rich brown coffee and sugar! Wu Ch'i Chen had won my heart.

"Products of our five-year plan!" the commissar laughed.

"Products of your confiscation department, you mean," I amended.

三、 "他们唱得太多了"

我在吴起镇呆了3天，在工厂里访问工人，"考察"他们的工作条件，观看他们的演出，出席他们的政治集会，阅读他们的墙报、他们的识字课本，同他们谈话——还参加了锻炼。因为我参加了在吴起镇3个球场之一举行的篮球赛。我们临时由外交部代表傅锦魁、在政治部工作的一个能说英语的年轻大学生、一个红军医生、一个战士和我本人组成了一个球队。兵工厂篮球队接受了我们的挑战，把我们打得稀烂。至少在我个人身上来说是名副其实地打得稀烂。

兵工厂的这些工人不但能投篮也能造枪炮。我在他们这不同一般的工厂里逗留了一天，在他们的列宁俱乐部吃了午饭。

兵工厂像红军大学一样设在山边一排大窑洞里。里面很凉快，又通风，用斜插在墙上的烛台扦取明，主要的好处是完全不怕轰炸。我在这里看到有100多个工人在制造手榴弹、迫击炮弹、火药、手枪、小炮弹和枪弹，还有少数农具。修理车间则在修复成排的步枪、机枪、自动步枪、轻机关枪。不过兵工厂的产品粗糙，大部分用来装备游击队，红军正规部队几乎完全是靠从敌军缴获的枪炮弹药为供应的！

兵工厂厂长何锡阳带我参观了好几个窑洞，介绍他的工人，把他们和他本人的一些情况告诉我。他36岁，未婚，在日本侵华前原来在著名的沈阳兵工厂当技术员。1931年9月18日以后，他去了上海，在那里参加了共产党，后来就设法来了西北，进入红区。这里大多数机工也都是"外地"人。其中有许多人曾在中国最大的日资汉阳铁厂工作，少数人曾在国民党的兵工厂工作过。我见到了两个上海机工师傅，和一个钳工能手，他们给我看了著名的英美商行如怡和洋行、慎昌洋行、上

3   "They Sing Too Much"

I stayed three days at Wu Ch'i Chen, visiting workers in the factories, "inspecting" their working conditions, attending their theater and their political meetings, reading their wall newspapers and their character books, talking—and getting athletic. I took part in a basketball game on one of Wu Ch'i's three courts. We made up a scratch team composed of the Foreign Office emissary, Fu Chin-kuei; a young English-speaking college student working in the political department; a Red doctor; a soldier; and myself. The arsenal basketball team accepted our challenge and beat us to a pulp.

The arsenal, like the Red University, was housed in a big series of vaulted rooms built into a mountainside. They were cool, well ventilated, and lighted by a series of shafts sunk at angles in the walls, and had the major advantage of being completely bombproof. Here I found over a hundred workers making hand grenades, trench mortars, gunpowder, pistols, small shells and bullets, and a few farming tools. A repair department was engaged in rehabilitating stacks of broken rifles, machine guns, automatic rifles and submachine guns. But the arsenal's output was crude work, and most of its products equipped the Red partisans, the regular Red forces being supplied almost entirely with guns and munitions captured from enemy troops.

Ho Hsi-yang, director of the arsenal, took me through its various chambers, introduced his workers, and told me something about them and himself. He was thirty-six, unmarried, and had formerly been a technician in the famous Mukden arsenal, before the Japanese invasion. After September 18, 1931, he went to Shanghai, and there he joined the Communist Party, later on making his way to the Northwest, and into Red areas. Most of the machinists here were also "outside" men. Many had been employed at Hanyang, China's greatest iron works (Japanese-owned), and a few had worked in Kuomintang arsenals. I met two young Shanghai master mechanics, and an expert fitter, who showed me excellent letters of recommendation from the noted British and American firms of Jardine, Matheson & Co., Anderson Meyer & Co., and the Shanghai Power Company.

海电力公司的很出色的介绍信。另外一个工人曾在上海一家机器工厂当过工头。还有从天津、广州、北平来的机工,有些还同红军一起经过长征。

我了解到兵工厂的114名机工和学徒中,只有20人结了婚。他们的妻子同他们一起在吴起镇,有的当工人,有的当党的干部。兵工厂的工会会员是红区技术最熟练的工人,党员百分比很大,有80%是党团员。

除了兵工厂,吴起镇还有几家被服厂、1家鞋厂、1家袜厂、1家制药厂、1家药房,有1个医生看门诊。他是个刚从山西医校毕业的青年,他的年轻漂亮的妻子在他身旁做护士。他们两人都是前一年冬天红军东征山西时参加红军的。附近还有1所医院,有3个军医,住的大多数是伤兵。还有1个电台、1所简陋的实验室、1个合作社和兵站。

除了兵工厂和军服厂以外,大多数工人是18岁到25岁或30岁的年轻妇女。有的已同上了前线的红军战士结了婚,几乎全部都是甘肃、陕西、山西人,都剪了短发。中国苏区的一个口号是"同工同酬",对妇女据说没有工资上的歧视。在苏区的工人似乎比别人在经济上都得到优待。后者包括红军指挥员,他们没有正规薪饷,只有少额生活津贴,根据财政负担情况而有不同。

吴起镇是漂亮的刘群仙女士的总部所在地。她29岁,曾在无锡和上海纱厂做过工,雷娜·普罗姆的朋友,莫斯科中山大学留学生[1],现在是红色工会妇女部长。刘女士向我介绍了工作条件。工厂工人每月工资10到15元,膳宿由国家供给。工人可得免费医疗,公伤可以得到补偿。女工怀孕生产期间有4个月假期,不扣工资,还为工人的子女设了一个简陋的托儿所,但是他们大多数人一到学会走路就变成野孩子了。做母亲的可以得到她们的一部分"社会保险",那是由从工资额中扣除10%加上政府同额津贴所得的一笔基金。政府并捐助相当于工资总额的2%的款项供工人作文娱费用,这些基金都由工会和工人组织的工厂委员会共同管理。每星期工作6天,

---

1. 刘在莫斯科中山大学结识并嫁给了博古(即秦邦宪)。在莫斯科期间,她深情地铭记着文森特·希恩在《个人历史》中刻画的那位非凡的美国红发反叛女神——雷娜·普罗姆。

Another had been foreman in a Shanghai machine shop. There were also machinists from Tientsin, Canton, and Peking, and some had made the Long March with the Red Army.

I learned that of the arsenal's 114 machinists and apprentices only 20 were married. These had their wives with them in Wu Ch'i Chen, either as factory workers or as party functionaries. In the arsenal trade union, which represented the most highly skilled labor in the Red districts, more than 80 per cent of the members belonged to the Communist Party or to the Communist Youth League.

Besides the arsenal, in Wu Ch'i Chen there were cloth and uniform factories, a shoe factory, a stocking factory, and a pharmacy and drug dispensary, with a doctor in attendance. He was a youth just out of medical training school in Shansi and his young and pretty wife was with him working as a nurse. Both of them had joined the Reds during the Shansi expedition the winter before. Nearby was a hospital, with three army doctors in attendance and filled mostly with wounded soldiers, and there was a radio station, a crude laboratory, a cooperative, and the army supply base.

Except in the arsenal and the uniform factory, most of the workers were young women from age eighteen to twenty-five or thirty. Some of them were married to Red soldiers then at the front; nearly all were Kansu, Shensi, or Shansi women; and all had bobbed hair. "Equal pay for equal labor" was a slogan of the Chinese soviets, and there was supposed to be no wage discrimination against women. Workers appeared to get preferential financial treatment over everybody else in the soviet districts. This included Red commanders, who received no regular salary, but only a small living allowance, which varied according to the weight of the treasury.

Wu Ch'i Chen was headquarters for Miss Liu Ch'un-hsien, aged twenty-nine. A former mill worker from Wusih and Shanghai, she was a student in Moscow's Sun Yat-sen University when she met and married Po Ku (Ch'in Pang-hsien). From her Moscow days she warmly remembered Rhena Prohm, the improbable red-haired American rebel goddess enshrined in Vincent Sheean's *Personal History.* Now Miss Liu was director of the women's department of the Red trade unions. She said that factory workers were paid $10 to $15 monthly, with board and room furnished by the state. Workers were guaranteed free medical attention (such as it was) and compensation for injuries. Women were given four months of rest with pay during and after pregnancy, and there was a crude "nursery" for workers' children—but most of them seemed to run wild as soon as they could walk. Mothers could collect part of their "social insurance," which was provided from a fund created by deducting 10 per cent of the workers' salaries, to which the government added an equal amount. The government also contributed the equivalent of 2 per cent of the wage output for workers' education and recreation, funds managed jointly by the trade unions and the workers' factory committees. There was an eight-hour day and a six-day

每天 8 小时。我访问的时候,那些工厂都一天开工 24 小时,分三班倒——也许是中国最忙的工厂!

这一切规定似乎都很进步,当然与共产主义理想来说也许还有很大距离。但是苏区为求生存还忙不过来,居然能实现这种情况,这一点是的确令人感到兴趣的。至于实现的情况是多么**原始**,那是另外一回事!他们有俱乐部、学校、宽敞的宿舍——这一切都是肯定的——但是这都是在窑洞里,下面是土地,没有淋浴设备,没有电影院,没有电灯。他们有伙食供应,但吃的是小米、蔬菜,偶尔有羊肉,没有任何美味。他们领到苏区货币发的工资和社会保险金,这一点也没有问题,但是能买的东西严格地限于必需品——而且也不多!

"无法忍受"!一个普通美国工人或英国工人会这样说。但是对这些人来说并不是如此。你得把他们的生活同中国其他地方的制度作一对比,才能了解是什么原因,例如,我记得上海的工厂里,小小的男女童工一天坐在那里或站在那里要干十二三小时的活,下了班精疲力竭地就躺倒在他们的床——机器下面铺的脏被子——上睡着了。我也记得缫丝厂的小姑娘和棉纺厂的脸色苍白的年轻妇女——她们同上海大多数工厂的包身工一样——实际上卖身为奴,为期四五年,给工厂做工,未经许可不得擅离门警森严、高墙厚壁的厂址。我还记得 1935 年在上海的街头和河浜里收殓的 2.9 万具尸体,这都是赤贫的穷人的尸体,他们无力喂养的孩子饿死的尸体和溺婴的尸体。

对吴起镇这些工人来说,不论他们的生活是多么原始简单,但至少这是一种健康的生活,有运动、新鲜的山间空气、自由、尊严、希望,这一切都有充分发展的余地。他们知道没有人在靠他们发财,我觉得他们是意识到他们是在为自己和为中国做工,而且他们说他们是**革命者**!因此,我了解为什么他们对每天两小时的读书写字、政治课、剧团非常重视,为什么他们认真地参加在运动、文化、卫生、墙报、提高效率方面举行的个人或团体的比赛,尽管奖品很可怜。所有这一切东西,对他们来说都是**实际的**东西,是他们以前所从来没有享受到的东西,也是中国任何其他工厂中从来没有过的东西。对于他们面前所打开的生活的大门,他们似乎是心满意足的。

要我这样一个中国通相信这一点是很困难的,而且我对它的最终意义仍感到不明白。但是我不能否认我看到的证据。这里篇幅不许可我把这种证据详细提出来,我需要把我接触到的一些工人告诉我的十多个故事一一介绍;引用他们在墙报上的文章和批评——是刚学会文化的人用稚气笔迹书写的,其中有不少由我在那个大学生的帮助下译成了英文;也需要报道我参加过的政治集会,这些工人所创作和演出

week. When I visited them the factories were running twenty-four hours a day, with three shifts working.

All this seemed progressive, though perhaps far from a Communistic utopia. That such conditions were actually being realized in the midst of the soviets' impoverishment was really interesting. How *primitively* they were being realized was quite another matter. They had clubs, schools, ample dormitories—all these, certainly—but in cave houses with earthen floors, no shower baths, no movies, no electricity. They were furnished food; but meals consisted of millet, vegetables, and sometimes mutton, with no delicacies whatever. They collected their wages and social insurance all right in soviet currency, but the articles they could buy were strictly limited to necessities—and none too much of those.

"Unbearable," the average American or English worker would say. But I remembered Shanghai factories where little boy and girl slave workers sat or stood at their tasks twelve or thirteen hours a day, and then dropped, in exhausted sleep, to the dirty cotton quilt, their bed, directly beneath their machines. I remembered little girls in silk filatures, and the pale young women in cotton factories sold into jobs as virtual slaves for four or five years, unable to leave the heavily guarded, high-walled premises day or night without special permission. And I remembered that during 1935 more than 29,000 bodies were picked up from the streets and rivers and canals of Shanghai—bodies of the destitute poor, of the starved or drowned babies or children they could not feed.

For these workers in Wu Ch'i Chen, however primitive it might be, here seemed to be a life at least of good health, exercise, clean mountain air, freedom, dignity, and hope, in which there was room for growth. They knew that nobody was making money out of them, I think they felt they were working for themselves and for China, and they said they were *revolutionaries!* They took very seriously their two hours of daily reading and writing, their political lectures, and their dramatic groups, and they keenly contested for the miserable prizes offered in competitions between groups and individuals in sport, literacy, public health, wall newspapers, and "factory efficiency." All these things were *real* to them, things they had never known before, could never possibly know in any other factory of China, and they seemed grateful for the doors of life opened up for them.

It was hard for an old China hand like me to believe, and I was confused about its ultimate significance, but I could not deny the evidence I saw. To present that evidence in detail I would have had to tell dozen stories of workers to whom I talked; quote from their essays and criticisms in the wall newspapers—written in the childish scrawl of the newly literate—many of which I translated, with the aid of the college student; tell of the political meetings I attended; and of the plays created and dramatized by these workers;

的戏,以及许许多多构成一个总"印象"的小事情。

但是我在执笔写本书时正好记得这样的一件"小事情"。我在吴起镇遇到一个电气工程师,一个名叫朱作其的很有才能但严肃认真的共产党员。他的英语和德语都很好,是个电力专家,所写的工程教科书在中国普遍采用。他曾在上海电力公司工作过,后来在慎昌洋行。最近以前,他在南方担任顾问工程师,他是个很能干的人,一年收入可达1万元。但他放弃了这样的收入,丢下家庭,到陕西的这些荒山中来,尽义务为共产党贡献他的力量。这简直是不可相信的!这个现象的背景要追溯到他敬爱的祖父,宁波的一个著名慈善家,他临死时对他年轻的孙儿的遗言是要"把一生贡献给提高人民大众的文化水平"。朱作其于是断定最快的方法是共产党的方法。

朱作其这样做是有点戏剧性的,是本着一种殉道者和热心家的精神。对他来说,这是一件严肃的事,意味着早死,他以为别人也这么想。我相信,当他看到周围居然嬉嬉闹闹,大家都高高兴兴的,他一定感到有点意外。当我问他有什么感想时,他严肃地说,他只有一个意见。"这些人花在**唱歌**的时间实在太多了!"他抱怨说。"现在不是唱歌的时候!"

我认为这一句话概括了陕西苏区这个奇特的"工业中心"的年轻气氛。他们即使缺乏社会主义工业的物质,却有社会主义工业的精神!

and of the many little things that go to make up an "impression."

As one example, I met an electrical engineer in Wu Ch'i Chen, a man named Chu Tso-chih. He knew English and German very well, he was a power expert, and he had written an engineering textbook widely used in China. He had once been with the Shanghai Power Company, and later with Anderson Meyer & Co. Until recently he had had a practice of $10,000 a year in South China, where he was a consulting engineer and efficiency man, and had given it up and left his family to come up to these wild dark hills of Shensi and offer his services to the Reds for nothing. Incredible! The background of this phenomenon traced to a beloved grandfather, a famous philanthropist of Ningpo, whose deathbed injunction to young Chu had been to "devote his life to raising the cultural standard of the masses." And Chu had decided the quickest method was the Communist one.

Chu had come into the thing somewhat melodramatically, in the spirit of the martyr and zealot. It was a solemn thing for him; he thought it meant an early death, and he expected everyone else to feel that way. I believe he was a little shocked when he found so much that he considered horseplay going on, and everybody apparently happy. When I asked him how he liked it, he replied gravely that he had but one serious criticism. "These people spend entirely too much time *singing*!" he complained. "This is no time to be singing!"

Part Eight
With the Red Army

第八篇
同红军在一起

一、　　"真正的"红军

在甘肃和宁夏的山间和平原上骑马和步行了两个星期以后,我终于来到预旺堡,那是宁夏南部一个很大的有城墙的市镇,那时候是红军一方面军[1]和司令员彭德怀的司令部所在地。

虽然在严格的军事意义上来说,所有的红军战士都可以称为"非正规军"(而且有些人会说是"高度非正规军"),但红军自己对于他们的方面军、独立军、游击队和农民赤卫队是作了明确的区分的。我在陕西初期的短暂旅行中,没有看见过任何"正规的"红军,因为它的主力部队那时候正在离保安将近 200 英里的西部活动。我原打算到前线去,但蒋介石正在南线准备发动另一次大攻势的消息传来,使我想到兵力较强的一边去,趁还来得及越过战线去写我的报道的时候,及早离开这里。

有一天,我对吴亮平表示了这些犹豫的考虑。吴亮平是在我同毛泽东的长时间正式谈话中充当翻译的一位年轻的苏维埃官员。吴亮平虽然只是个脸色红润的 26 岁青年,但已写了两本关于辩证法的书。我发现他为人很讨人喜欢,除了对辩证法以外,对什么事情都有幽默感,因此我把他当作朋友看待,坦率地向他表示了我的担心。

他听了我说的话,惊讶得发呆。"你现在有机会到前线去,你却不知道该不该要这个机会?可不要犯这样的错误!蒋介石企图消灭我们已有 10 年了,这次他也不会成功的。你没有看到**真正**的红军就回去,那可不行!"他提出了证据说明我不应当这么做。最使我感动的是,光是提到要到前线去,就在他这个久经锻炼的老布尔什维克和长征老战士身上引起那样大的热情。我想大概总有什么东西值得一看,因此决定作此长途旅行,安然无事地到达了吴亮平的真正的红军作战的地点。

---

1. 斯诺原文可能有误,叶剑英时任一方面军参谋长;萧华时任红一方面军第二师政委。——编注

1 The "Real" Red Army

After two weeks of hacking and walking over the hills and plains of Kansu and Ninghsia I came to Yu Wang Pao, a walled town in southern Ninghsia, which was then the headquarters of the First Front Red Army[1]—and of its commander-in-chief, P'eng Teh-huai.

Although in a strict military sense all Red warriors might be called "irregulars" (and some people would say "highly irregulars"), the Reds themselves made a sharp, distinction between their front armies, independent armies, partisans, and peasant guards. During my first brief travels in Shensi I had not seen any of the "regular" Red Army, for its main forces were then moving in the west, nearly two hundred miles from Pao An. I had planned a trip to the front, but news that Chiang Kai-shek was preparing to launch another major offensive from the south had inclined me toward the better part of valor and an early departure while I could still get past the lines to write my story.

One day I had expressed these doubts to Wu Liang-p'ing, the young soviet official who had acted as interpreter in my long official interviews with Mao Tse-tung. He had been dumbfounded. "You have a chance to go to the front, and you wonder whether you should take it? Don't make such a mistake! Chiang Kai-shek has been trying to destroy us for ten years, and he is not going to succeed now. You can't go back without seeing the *real* Red Army!" He had produced evidence to show why I shouldn't, and it was well that I took his advice.

---

1. Of which Nieh Ho-t'ing was chief of staff and Hsiao Hua was deputy political commissar of the army's Second Division.

我幸亏接受了他的劝告。我要是没有接受他的劝告，我在离开保安时就仍旧不明白红军不可战胜的声誉从何而来，仍旧不相信正规红军的年轻、精神、训练、纪律、出色的装备、特别是高度的政治觉悟，仍旧不了解红军是中国唯一的一支从政治上来说是铁打的军队。

要了解这些所谓的土匪，最好方法也许是用统计数字。因为我发现红军对全部正规人员都有完整的数据。下面的事实，我觉得极有兴趣和意义，是一方面军政治部主任、能说俄语的29岁的杨尚昆从他的档案中找出来的。除了少数例外，这个统计材料限于我有机会进行观察核实的一些问题。

首先，许多人以为红军是一批顽强的亡命之徒和不满分子。我自己也有一些这样的模糊观念。不久，我就发现自己完全错了。红军的大部分是青年农民和工人，他们认为自己是为家庭、土地和国家而战斗。

据杨尚昆说，普通士兵的平均年龄是19岁。这很容易相信。虽然许多红军士兵已经作战七八年甚至10年，但大量还只是十多岁的青年。甚至大多数"老布尔什维克"，那些身经百战的老战士，现在也只有20刚出头。他们大多数是作为少年先锋队员参加红军的，或者是在15岁或16岁时入伍。

在一方面军中，共有38%的士兵，不是来自农业无产阶级（包括手工业者、赶骡的、学徒、长工等）就是来自工业无产阶级，但58%是来自农民。只有4%来自小资产阶级——商人、知识分子、小地主等的子弟。在一方面军中，包括指挥员在内的50%以上的人，都是共产党员或共青团员。

60%到70%的士兵是有文化的——这就是说，他们能够写简单的信件、文章、标语、传单等。这比白区中普通军队的平均数高得多了，比西北农民中的平均数更高。红军士兵从入伍的第一天起，就开始学习专门为他们编写的红色课本。进步快的领到奖品（廉价笔记簿、铅笔、锦旗等，士兵们很重视这些东西），此外，还作出巨大的努力来激励他们的上进心和竞赛精神。

像他们的指挥员一样，红军士兵是没有正规薪饷的。但每一个士兵有权取得一份土地和这块土地上的一些收入。他不在的时候，由他的家属或当地苏维埃耕种。然而，如果他不是苏区本地人，则从"公田"（从大地主那里没收而来）的作物收益中取出一份作报酬，公田的收益也用于红军的给养。公田由当地苏区的村民耕种。公田上的无偿劳动是义务的，但在土地重新分配中得到好处的农民，大多数是愿意合作来保卫改善了他们的生活的制度的。

Perhaps the best way to approach an understanding of these so-called bandits was—statistical. The facts assembled below were furnished from his files by Yang Shang-k'un, the Russian-speaking, twenty-nine-year-old chairman of the political department of the First Front Red Army. With a few exceptions, this statistical report is confined to matters which I had some opportunity to verify by observation.

First of all, many people supposed the Reds to be a hard-bitten lot of outlaws and malcontents. I vaguely had some such notion myself. I soon discovered that the great mass of the Red soldiery was made up of young peasants and workers who believed themselves to be fighting for their homes, their land, and their country.

According to Yang, the average age of the rank and file was nineteen. Although many men with the Reds had fought for seven or eight or even ten years, they were balanced by a vast number of youths still in their middle teens. And even most of the "old Bolsheviks," veterans of many battles, were only now in their early twenties. The majority had joined the Reds as Young Vanguards, or enlisted at the age of fifteen or sixteen.

In the First Front Army a total of 38 per cent of the men came from either the agrarian working class (including craftsmen, muleteers, apprentices, farm laborers, etc.) or from the industrial working class, while 58 per cent came from the peasantry. Only 4 per cent were from the petty bourgeoisie—sons of merchants, intellectuals, small landlords, and such. In this army over 50 per cent of the troops, including commanders, were members of the Communist Party or the Communist Youth League.

Between 60 and 70 per cent of the soldiers were literate—that is, they could write simple letters and texts, posters, handbills, etc. This was much higher than the average among ordinary troops in the White districts, and it was very much higher than the average in the peasantry of the Northwest. Red soldiers began to study characters in Red texts specially prepared for them, from the day of their enlistment. Prizes were offered (cheap notebooks, pencils, tassels, etc., much valued by the soldiers) for rapid progress and a great effort was made to stimulate the spirit of ambition and competition.

Red soldiers, like their commanders, received no regular salaries. But every enlisted man was entitled to his portion of land, and some income from it. This was tilled in his absence either by his family or by his local soviet. If he was not a native of the soviet districts, however, his remuneration came from a share in the proceeds of crops from "public lands" (confiscated from the "great" landlords), which also helped provision the Red Army. Public lands were tilled by villagers in the local soviets. Such free labor was obligatory, but the majority of the peasants, having benefited in the land redistribution, may have cooperated willingly enough to defend a system that had bettered their livelihood.

红军中军官的平均年龄是 24 岁。这包括从班长直到军长的全部军官，尽管这些人很年轻，平均都有 8 年的作战经验。所有的连长以上的军官都有文化，虽然我遇见过几位军官，他们参加红军以前还不能认字写字。红军指挥员约有 1/3 以前是国民党军人。在红军指挥员中，有许多是黄埔军校毕业生、莫斯科红军大学毕业生、张学良的"东北军"的前军官、保定军官学校的学生、前国民军（"基督将军"冯玉祥的军队）的军人，以及若干从法国、苏联、德国和英国回来的留学生。我只见到过一个美国留学生。红军不叫"兵"（在中国这是一个很遭反感的字），而称自己为"战士"。

红军的士兵和军官大多数未婚。他们当中许多人"离了婚"——这就是说他们丢下了妻子和家人。在有几个人身上，我真的怀疑，这种离婚的愿望事实上可能同他们参加红军有些关系，但这也许说得太刻薄了。

从在路上和在前线的许多交谈中，我所得的印象是这些"红军战士"大多数依然是童男。在前线和军队在一起的女人很少，她们本人几乎全都是苏维埃干部或同苏维埃干部结了婚的。

就我所能看到或知道的，红军都以尊重的态度对待农村妇女和姑娘，农民对红军的道德似乎都有很好的评价。我没有听到过强奸或污辱农村妇女的事件，虽然我从一些南方士兵那里了解到丢在家乡的"爱人"的事情。[1] 红军很少有人吸烟喝酒；烟酒不沾是红军"八项注意"之一，虽然对这两种坏习惯没有规定特别的处罚，但我在墙报上的"黑栏"上看了好几宗对有吸烟恶习的人提出严厉的批评。喝酒不禁止，但也不鼓励。喝得酩酊大醉的事情，就我的见闻来说，却没有听到过。

彭德怀司令员曾任国民党将军，他告诉我说，红军极其年轻，说明它为什么能够吃苦耐劳，这是很可信的。这也使得女伴问题不太严重。彭德怀本人在 1928 年率领国民党军队起义参加红军后，就没有见过自己的妻子。

---

1. 这里没有禁止私通的法律，但是一旦红军士兵与某位姑娘有恋情，就应该娶她为妻。由于男子的人数远远多于女子，所以这样的机会很少。我没有看到过任何乱交行为。在性自由问题上，红军抱着禁欲的观点，高强度的日常训练使这支年轻的军队无暇他顾。

The average age of the officers in the Red Army was twenty-four. This included squad leaders and all officers up to army commanders, but despite their youth these men had behind them an average of eight years' fighting experience. All company commanders or higher were literate, though I met several who had not learned to read and write till after they had entered the Red Army. About a third of the Red commanders were former Kuomintang soldiers. Among Red commanders were many graduates of Whampoa Academy, graduates of the Red Army Academy in Moscow, former officers of Chang Hsueh-liang's "Northeastern Army," cadets of the Paoting Military Academy, former Kuominchun ("Christian General" Feng Yu-hsiang's army) men, and a number of returned students from France, Soviet Russia, Germany, and England. I met only one returned student from America. The Reds did not call themselves *ping*, or "soldiers"—a word to which much odium was attached in China—but *chan-shih*, which means "fighters" or "warriors."

The majority of the soldiers as well as officers of the Red Army were unmarried. Many of them were "divorced"—that is, they had left their wives and families behind them. In several cases I had serious suspicions that the desire for this kind of divorce, in fact, might have had something to do with their joining the army, but this may be a cynical opinion.

My impression, from scores of conversations on the road and at the front, was that most of these "Red fighters" were still virgins. There were few Communist women at the front with the army, and they were nearly all soviet functionaries in their own right or married to soviet officials.

As far as I could see or learn, the Reds treated the peasant women and girls with respect, and the peasantry seemed to have a good opinion of Red Army morality. I heard of no cases of rape or abuse of the peasant women, though I heard from some of the southern soldiers of "sweet-hearts" left behind them. There was no law against fornication, but any Red Army man who got into difficulties with a girl was expected to marry her. As men far outnumbered women here, the opportunities were few. I saw nothing going on that looked like promiscuity. The Red Army was puritanical in its views on sexual license, and a vigorous daily routine kept the young troops occupied. Very few of the Reds smoked or drank: abstention was one of the "eight disciplines" of the Red Army, and although no special punishment was provided for either vice, I read in the "black column" of wall newspapers several grave criticisms of habitual smokers. Drinking was not forbidden, but drunkenness was unheard of.

Commander P'eng Teh-huai, who had been a Kuomintang general, told me that the extreme youth of the Red Army explained much of its capacity to withstand hardship, and that was quite believable. It also made the problem of feminine companionship less poignant. P'eng himself had not seen his own wife since 1928, when he led an uprising of Kuomintang troops and joined the Reds.

红军指挥员中的伤亡率很高。他们向来都同士兵并肩作战，团长以下都是这样。一位外国武官曾经说，单单是一件事情就可以说明红军同拥有极大优势的敌人作战的能力了。这就是红军军官习惯说的："弟兄们，跟我来！"而不是说："弟兄们，向前冲！"在南京发动的第一次和第二次"最后清剿"中，红军军官的伤亡率往往高达50%。但红军不能经受这样的牺牲，因此后来采取了多少要减少有经验的指挥员的生命危险的战术。虽然这样，但在第五次江西战役中，红军指挥员的伤亡率还是平均在23%左右。关于这一点，在红区中，人们可以看到许多证据。通常可以看到，20刚出头的青年就丢了一只胳膊或一条腿，或者是手指被打掉了，或者是头上或身上留有难看的伤痕——但他们对于革命依然是高高兴兴的乐观主义者！

在红军的各支队伍里，几乎中国各省的人都有。在这个意义上，红军或许是中国唯一的真正**全国性**军队了。它也是"征途最辽阔"的军队！老兵们走过18个省份。他们也许比其他任何军队更加熟悉中国的地理。在长征途上，他们发现大多数的旧中国地图了无用处，于是红军制图员重新绘制了许许多多英里的区域地图，特别是在土著居民地区和西部边疆地区。

一方面军约有3万人，南方人占的百分率很高，约有1/3来自江西、福建、湖南或贵州。将近40%来自西部的四川、陕西和甘肃等省。一方面军包括一些土著居民（苗族和彝族），此外还有一支新组织起来的回民红军。在独立部队中，当地人的百分率还更高，平均占总数的3/4。

从最高级指挥员到普通士兵，吃的穿的都是一样。但是，营长以上可以骑马或骡子。我注意到，他们弄到美味食物甚至大家平分——在我和军队在一起时，这主要表现在西瓜和李子上。指挥员和士兵的住处，差别很少，他们自由地往来，不拘形式。

有一件事情使我感到迷惑。共产党人是怎样给他们的军队提供吃的、穿的和装备呢？像其他许多人一样，我原以为他们一定是完全靠劫掠来维持生活。我已经说过，我发现这种臆想是错误的，因为我看到，他们每占领一个地方，就着手建设他们自己的自给经济，单单是这件事实，就能够使他们守住一个根据地而不怕敌人的封锁。此外，对于中国无产阶级军队能够靠几乎不能相信的极少经费活下去，我也是没有认识的。

Casualties among Red Army commanders were very high. They customarily went into battle side by side with their men, from regimental commanders down. Joseph Stilwell once said to me that one thing alone might explain the fighting power of the Reds against an enemy with vastly superior resources. That was the Red officers' habit of saying, "Come on, boys!" instead of, "Go on, boys!" During Nanking's first and second "final annihilation" campaigns, casualties among Red officers were often as high as 50 per cent. But the Red Army could not stand these sacrifices, and later adopted tactics tending somewhat to reduce the risk of life by experienced commanders. Nevertheless, in the Fifth Kiangsi Campaign, Red commanders' casualties averaged about 23 per cent of the total officer personnel. One could see plenty of evidence of this in the Red districts. Common sights were youths still in their early twenties with an arm or a leg missing, or fingers shot away, or with ugly wounds, on the head or anatomy—but still cheerful optimists about their revolution.

Nearly every province in China was represented in the various armies. In this sense the Red Army was probably the only *national* army in China. It was also the "most widely traveled." Veteran cadres had crossed parts of eighteen provinces. They probably knew more about Chinese geography than any other army. On their Long March they had found most of the old Chinese maps quite useless, and Red cartographers remapped many hundreds of miles of territory, especially in aboriginal country and on the western frontiers.

In the First Front Army, consisting of about 30,000 men, there was a high percentage of southerners, about one-third coming from Kiangsi, Fukien, Hunan, or Kweichow. Nearly 40 per cent were from the western provinces of Szechuan, Shensi, and Kansu. The First Front Army included some aborigines—Miaos and Lolos—and also attached to it was a newly organized Mohammedan Red Army. In the independent armies the percentage of natives was much higher, averaging three-fourths of the total.

From the highest commander down to the rank and file these men ate and dressed alike. Battalion commanders and higher, however, were entitled to the use of a horse or a mule. I noticed there was even an equal sharing of the delicacies available—expressed, while I was with the Red Army, chiefly in terms of watermelons and plums. There was very little difference in living quarters of commanders and men, and they passed freely back and forth without any formality.

One thing had puzzled me. How did the Reds manage to feed, clothe, and equip their armies? Like many others, I had assumed that they must live entirely on loot. This I discovered to be wrong, as I have already shown, for I saw that they started to construct a self-supplying economy of their own as soon as they occupied a district, and this single fact made it possible for them to hold a base despite enemy blockade. I had also failed to realize on what almost unbelievably modest sums it was possible for a Chinese proletarian army to exist.

红军声称他们80%以上的枪械和70%以上的弹药是从敌军那里夺来的。如果说这是难以相信的话,我可以作证,我所看到的正规军基本上是用英国、捷克斯洛伐克、德国和美国的机关枪、步枪、自动步枪、毛瑟枪和山炮装备起来,这些武器都是大量地卖给南京政府的。[1]

我看见红军使用的唯一俄国制步枪,是1917年造的产品。我直接从几个前马鸿逵将军的士兵口中听到,这些步枪是从马的军队那里夺来的。而国民党手中的宁夏省残余部分的省主席马将军又是从冯玉祥将军那里把这些步枪接过手来的。冯将军在1924年统治过这个地区,曾从外蒙古得到一些武器。红军正规军不屑使用这些老武器,我看见只有游击队的手中才有这种武器。

我在苏区时,要想同俄国的武器来源发生任何接触,客观上是不可能的。红军为总数将近40万的各种敌军所包围,而且敌人控制着每一条通向外蒙古、新疆或苏联的道路。别人老是指责他们从俄国那里得到武器,我想,要是有一些这样的武器居然从天而降,他们是乐意得到的。但是,只要看一看地图就十分明白,在中国共产党人往北方和西方扩大更多的面积以前,莫斯科没法供应任何定货,姑且假定莫斯科有意这样做,但那是大可怀疑的。

第二,共产党没有高薪的和贪污的官员和将军,这是事实,而在其他的中国军队中,这些人侵吞了大部分军费。在军队和苏区中厉行节约。实际上,军队给人民造成的唯一负担,是必须供给他们吃穿。

实际上,我已经说过,西北苏区占地面积相当于英国,它的全部预算当时每月只有32万美元!这个惊人的数目中将近60%是用来维持武装部队的。财政人民委员林祖涵老先生为此感到很抱歉,但是说"在革命获得巩固以前,这是不可避免的"。当时武装部队为数(不包括农民辅助部队)约4万人。这是在二方面军和四方面军到达甘肃以前的事情,此后红色区域大大扩大,西北的红军主力不久就接近9万人的总数了。

---

1. "当被问及红军的弹药来源时,蒋总司令承认大多数都是从战败的政府军那里缴获的。"(蒋于1934年10月9日接受《字林西报》采访时的访谈摘录)

The Reds had a very limited output of armaments; their enemy was really their main source of supply. For years the Reds had called the Kuomintang troops their "ammunition carriers," and they claimed to capture more than 80 per cent of their guns and more than 70 per cent of their ammunition from enemy troops. The regular troops (as distinct from local partisans) I saw were equipped mainly with British, Czechoslovakian, German, and American machine guns, rifles, automatic rifles, Mausers, and mountain cannon, such as had been sold in large quantities to the Nanking Government.[1]

The only Russian-made rifles I saw with the Reds were the vintage of 1917. These had been captured from the troops of General Ma Hung-kuei, as I heard directly from some of Ma's ex-soldiers themselves. General Ma, governor of what remained of Kuomintang Ninghsia, had inherited those rifles from General Feng Yu-hsiang, who ruled this region in 1924 and got some arms from Outer Mongolia. Red regulars disdained to use these ancient weapons, which I saw only in the hands of the partisans.

While I was in the soviet districts any contact with a Russian source of arms was physically impossible. The Reds were surrounded by various enemy troops totaling nearly 400,000 men, and the enemy controlled every road to Outer Mongolia, Sinkiang, or the U.S.S.R. I gathered that they would be glad to get some of the manna they were frequently accused of receiving by some miracle from Russia. But it was quite obvious from a glance at the map that, until the Chinese Reds possessed much more territory to the north and to the west, Moscow would be unable to fill any orders, assuming Moscow to be so inclined, which was open to serious doubts.

Second, it was a fact that the Reds had no highly paid and squeezing officials and generals, who in other Chinese armies absorbed most of the military funds. Great frugality was practiced in both the army and the soviets. In effect, about the only burden of the army upon the people was the necessity of feeding and clothing it.

Actually, as I have already said, the entire budget of the Northwest soviets was then only $320,000 a month. Nearly 60 per cent went to the maintenance of the armed forces. Old Lin Tsu-han, the finance commissioner, was apologetic about that, but said that it was "inevitable until the revolution has been consolidated." The armed forces then numbered (not including peasant auxiliaries) about 40,000 men. This was before the arrival in Kansu of the Second and Fourth Front armies, after which Red territory greatly expanded, and the main Red forces in the Northwest soon approached a total of 90,000 men.

---

1. "Questioned as to the source of the Reds' munitions, Generalissimo Chiang admitted that most of them had been taken from defeated government troops" (in an interview with the *North China Daily News*, October 9, 1934).

统计数字就说到这里。但是要了解中国红军为什么能在这几年中维持下来，必须对他们的内在的精神、士气斗志、训练方法有所了解。而且，也许更重要的是，对他们的政治和军事领导要有所了解。

例如，南京悬赏要取红军司令员彭德怀的首级，为数之大足以维持他领导下的全军（如果财政人民委员林祖涵的数字是正确的）1个多月，他究竟是怎样一个人？

So much for statistics. But to understand why the Chinese Reds had survived all these years it was necessary to get a glimpse of their inner spirit, their morale and fighting will, and their methods of training. And, perhaps still more important, their political and military leadership.

For example, what sort of man was P'eng Teh-huai, for whose head Nanking once offered a reward sufficient to maintain his whole army (if Finance Commissioner Lin's figures were correct) for more than a month?

二、 彭德怀印象

我在八、九两月访问前线的时候，一、二、四方面军统一指挥的工作还没有开始。一方面军有8个"师"当时驻守从宁夏的长城到宁夏的固原和甘肃平凉一线。一军团派出一支先遣部队向南向西移动，为当时领导二、四方面军从西康和四川北上，在甘肃南部突破南京部队纵深封锁的朱德开辟一条道路。预旺堡是位于宁夏东南部的一个古老的回民城池，现在成了一方面军司令部的驻地，我在这里找到了该军的参谋部和司令员彭德怀。[1]

彭德怀的"赤匪"生涯是快10年前开始的，他当时在多妻的军阀省主席何键将军的国民党军队中领导了一次起义。彭德怀是行伍出身，先在湖南，后在南昌进过军校，毕业后，他因才能出众，迅获提升，1927年年方28岁就已任旅长，在湘军中以"自由派"军官著称，因为他办事真的同士兵委员会商量。

彭德怀当时在国民党左派中、在军队中、在湖南军校中的影响，使何键极为头痛。何键将军在1927年冬天开始大举清洗他的军队中的左派分子，发动了有名的湖南"农民大屠杀"，把成千上万的激进农民和工人当作共产党惨杀。但是因为彭德怀极孚众望，他不敢贸然下手。这一迟疑，给他带来了很大损失。1928年7月彭德怀

---

1. 此时黄华（即王汝梅）赶来和我结伴，他是燕京大学的学生，我要他来协助我。

2   Impression of P'eng Teh-huai

The consolidation of command of the First, Second, and Fourth Front Red armies had not yet occurred when I visited the front in August and September. Eight "divisions" of the First Front Red Army were then holding a line from the Great Wall in Ninghsia down to Kuyuan and Pingliang in Kansu. A vanguard of the First Army Corps was moving southward and westward, to clear a road for Chu Teh, who was leading the Second and Fourth Front armies up from Sikang and Szechuan, breaking through a deep cordon of Nanking troops in southern Kansu. Yu Wang Pao, an ancient Mohammedan walled city in southeast Ninghsia, was headquarters of the First Front Army, and here I found its staff and Commander P'eng Teh-huai.[1]

P'eng's career as a "Red bandit" had begun almost a decade before, when he led an uprising in the Kuomintang army of the polygamous warlord-governor, General Ho Chien. P'eng had risen from the ranks and won admission to a military school in Hunan and later on to another school at Nanchang. After graduation he had quickly distinguished himself and secured rapid promotions. By 1927, when he was twenty-eight years old, he was already a brigade commander, and noted throughout the Hunanese army as the "liberal" officer who actually consulted his soldiers' committee.

P'eng's influence in the then left-wing Kuomintang, in the army, and in the Hunan military school were serious problems for Ho Chien. In the winter of 1927 General Ho began a drastic purgation of leftists in his troops and launched the notorious Hunan "Peasant Massacre," in which thousands of radical farmers and workers were killed as "Communists." He hesitated to act against P'eng, however, because of his widespread popularity. It was a costly delay. In July, 1928, with his own famous First Regiment as

---

1. At this point in my travels I was joined by Huang Hua (Wang Ju-mei), a Yenching University student whom I had asked to come to assist me.

以他自己的著名第一团为核心，联合二、三团部分官兵和军校学生，举行平江起义，又同起义的农民会合，成立了湖南的第一苏维埃政府。

两年以后，彭德怀积聚了一支约有8,000个兄弟的"铁军"，这就是红军五军团。他以这支部队攻占了湖南省会长沙这个大城市，把何键的6万军队赶跑——他们大多数都是鸦片鬼。红军守城10日，抵御宁湘联军的反攻，最后因受到日、英、美炮舰的轰击，才被迫撤出。

不久之后，蒋介石就开始对"赤匪"进行第一次大"围剿"。这些"围剿"经过，前文已有概述。南方红军长征时，彭德怀是打先锋的一军团司令员。他突破了几万敌军的层层防线，在进军途上一路攻克战略要冲，为主力部队保证交通，最后胜利进入陕西，在西北苏区根据地找到了栖身之地。他的部下告诉我说，6,000英里的长征，大部分他是步行过来的，常常把他的马让给走累了的或受了伤的同志骑。

彭德怀过去即有这样一种斗争历史，我原来以为他是个疲惫的、板着脸的狂热领袖，身体也许已经垮了。结果我却发现彭德怀是个愉快爱笑的人，身体极为健康，只是肚子不好，这是在长征途上有一个星期硬着头皮吃没有煮过的麦粒和野草，又吃带有毒性的食物和几天颗粒不进的结果。他身经百战，只受过一次伤，而且只是表面的。

我住在彭德怀设在预旺堡的司令部的院子里，因此我在前线常常看到他。附带说一句，司令部——当时指挥3万多军队——不过是一间简单的屋子，内设一张桌子和一条板凳、两只铁制的文件箱、红军自绘的地图、一台野战电话、一条毛巾、一只脸盆和铺了他的毯子的炕。他同部下一样，只有两套制服，他们都不佩军衔领章。他有一件个人衣服，孩子气地感到很得意，那是在长征途上击下敌机后用缴获的降落伞做的背心。

我们在一起吃过好几顿饭。他吃得很少很简单，伙食同部下一样，一般是白菜、面条、豆、羊肉，有时有馒头。宁夏产瓜，种类很多，彭德怀很爱吃。可是，好吃惯了的作者却发现彭德怀在吃瓜方面并不是什么对手，但是在彭德怀参谋部里的一位医生前面只好低头认输，他的吃瓜能力已为他博得了"韩吃瓜的"这样一个美名。

我必须承认彭德怀给我的印象很深。他的谈话举止里有一种开门见山、直截了当、不转弯抹角的作风很使我喜欢，这是中国人中不可多得的品质。他动作和说话都很敏捷，喜欢说说笑笑，很有才智，善于驰骋，又能吃苦耐劳，是个很活泼的人。这也许一

nucleus, and joined by parts of the Second and Third regiments and the cadets of the military school, P'eng Teh-huai directed the P'ing Kiang Insurrection, which united with a peasant uprising and established the first Hunan Soviet Government.

Two years later P'eng had accumulated an "iron brotherhood" of about 8,000 followers, and this was the Fifth Red Army Corps. With this force he attacked and captured the great walled city of Changsha, capital of Hunan, and put to rout Ho Chien's army of 60,000 men—then mostly opium smokers. The Red Army held this city for ten days against counterattacks by combined Nanking-Hunan troops, but was finally forced to evacuate by greatly superior forces, including bombardment by foreign gunboats.

It was shortly afterwards that Chiang Kai-shek began his first "grand annihilation campaign" against the Red bandits. On the Long March of the southern Reds, P'eng Teh-huai was commander of the vanguard First Army Corps. He broke through lines of tens of thousands of enemy troops, captured vital points on the route of advance, and secured communications for the main forces, at last winning his way to Shensi and a refuge in the base of the Northwest soviets. Men in his army told me that he walked most of the 6,000 miles of the Long March, frequently giving his horse to a tired or wounded comrade.

I found P'eng a gay, laughter-loving man, in excellent health except for a delicate stomach—the result of a week's forced diet of uncooked wheat grains and grass during the Long March, and of semipoisonous food, and of a few days of no food at all. A veteran of scores of battles, he had been wounded but once, and then only superficially.

I stayed in the compound where P'eng had his headquarters in Yu Wang Pao, and so I saw a great deal of him at the front. This headquarters, by the way—then in command of over 30,000 troops—was a simple room furnished with a table and wooden bench, two iron dispatch boxes, maps made by the Red Army, a field telephone, a towel and washbasin, and the *k'ang* on which his blankets were spread. He had only a couple of uniforms, like the rest of his men, and they bore no insignia of rank. One personal article of attire, of which he was childishly proud, was a vest made from a parachute captured from an enemy airplane shot down during the Long March.

We shared many meals together. He ate sparingly and simply, of the same food his men were given—consisting usually of cabbage, noodles, beans, mutton, and sometimes bread. Ninghsia grew beautiful melons of all kinds, and P'eng was very fond of these. Your pampered investigator, however, found P'eng poor competition in the business of melon eating, but had to bow before the greater talents of one of the doctors on P'eng's staff, whose capacity had won him the nickname of Han Ch'ih-kua-ti (Han the Melon Eater).

Open, forthright, and undeviating in his manner and speech, quick in his movements, full of laughter and wit, P'eng was physically very active, an excellent rider, and a man of

半是由于他不吸烟、也不喝酒的缘故。有一天红二师进行演习，我正好同他在一起，要爬一座很陡峭的小山。"冲到顶上去！"彭德怀突然向他气喘吁吁的部下和我叫道。他像兔子一般蹿了出去，在我们之前到达山顶。又有一次，我们在骑马的时候，他又这样叫了一声，提出挑战。从这一点和其他方面可以看出他精力过人。

彭德怀迟睡早起，不像毛泽东那样迟睡也迟起。就我所知，彭德怀每天晚上平均只睡四五小时。他从来都是不急不忙的，但总是很忙碌。我记得那天早上一军团接到命令要前进 200 里到敌区的海原，我多么吃惊：彭德怀在早饭以前发完了一切必要的命令后，下来同我一起吃饭，饭后他就马上上路，好像是到乡下去郊游一样，带着他的参谋人员走过预旺堡的大街，停下来同出来向他道别的穆斯林阿訇说话。大军似乎是自己管理自己的。

附带说一句，虽然政府军飞机常常在红军前线扔传单，悬赏 5 万到 10 万元要缉拿彭德怀，不论死擒活捉，但是他的司令部门外只有一个哨兵站岗，他在街上走时也不带警卫。我在那里的时候，看到有成千上万张传单空投下来要悬赏缉拿他、徐海东、毛泽东。彭德怀下令要保存这些传单。这些传单都是单面印的，当时红军缺纸，就用空白的一面来印红军的宣传品。

我注意到，彭德怀很喜欢孩子，他的身后常常有一群孩子跟着。许多孩子充当勤务员、通信员、号兵、马夫，作为红军正规部队组织起来，叫做少年先锋队。我常常见到彭德怀和两三个"红小鬼"坐在一起，认真地向他们讲政治和他们的个人问题。他很尊重他们。

一天我同彭德怀和他一部分参谋人员到前线去参观一所小兵工厂，视察工人的文娱室，也就是他们的列宁室即列宁俱乐部。在屋子里的一道墙上有工人画的一幅大漫画，上面是一个穿和服的日本人双脚踩着满洲、热河、河北，举起一把沾满鲜血的刀，向其余的中国劈去。漫画中的日本人鼻子很大。

"那是谁？"彭德怀问一个负责管理列宁俱乐部的少先队员。

"那是日本帝国主义者！"那个孩子回答。

endurance. Perhaps this was partly because he was a nonsmoker and a teetotaler. I was with him one day during maneuvers of the Red Second Division when we had to climb a very steep hill. "Run to the top!" P'eng suddenly called out to his panting staff and me. He bounded off like a rabbit, and beat us all to the summit. Another time, when we were riding, he yelled out a similar challenge. In this way and others he gave the impression of great unspent energy.

P'eng retired late and arose early, unlike Mao Tse-tung, who retired late and also got up late. As far as I could learn, P'eng slept an average of only four or five hours a night. He never seemed rushed, but he was always busy. I remember the morning of the day the First Army Corps received orders to advance 200 *li* to Haiyuan, in enemy territory: P'eng issued all the commands necessary before breakfast and came down to eat with me; immediately afterwards he started off on the road, as if for an excursion to the countryside, walking along the main street of Yu Wang Pao with his staff, stopping to speak to the Moslem priests who had assembled to bid him good-by. The big army seemed to run itself.

Government airplanes frequently dropped leaflets over Red lines offering from $50,000 to $100,000 for P'eng, dead or alive, but he had only one sentry on duty before his headquarters, and he sauntered down the streets of the city without any bodyguard. While I was there, when thousands of handbills had been dropped offering rewards for himself, Hsu Hai-tung, and Mao Tse-tung, P'eng Teh-huai ordered that they be preserved. They were printed on only one side, and there was a paper shortage in the Red Army. The blank side of these handbills was used later for printing Red Army propaganda.

P'eng was very fond of children, I noticed, and he was often followed by a group of them. Many youngsters, who acted as mess boys, buglers, orderlies, and grooms, were organized as regular units of the Red Army, in the groups called Shao-nien Hsien-feng-tui, or Young Vanguards. I often saw P'eng seated with two or three "little Red devils," talking seriously to them about politics or their personal troubles. He treated them with great dignity.

One day I went with P'eng and part of his staff to visit a small arsenal near the front, and to inspect the workers' recreation room, their own Lieh-ning T'ang, or Lenin Club. There was a big cartoon, drawn by the workers, on one side of the room. It showed a kimonoed Japanese with his feet on Manchuria, Jehol, and Hopei, and an upraised sword, dripping with blood, poised over the rest of China. The caricatured Japanese had an enormous nose.

"Who is *that*?" P'eng asked a Young Vanguard whose duty it was to look after the Lenin Club.

"That," replied the lad, "is a Japanese imperialist!"

"你怎么知道的？"彭德怀问。

"你瞧那个大鼻子就行了！"

彭德怀听了大笑，看看我。"好吧，"他指着我说，"这里有个洋鬼子，他是帝国主义者吗？"

"他是个洋鬼子，那没问题，"那个少先队员说，"但不是日本帝国主义者。他有个大鼻子，但要做日本帝国主义者还不够大！"

彭德怀高兴地大笑，后来就开玩笑地叫我大鼻子。事实上，我的鼻子在西方人的社会中是正常的，并不惹眼，但在中国人看来，外国人都是大鼻子。我向彭德怀指出，当红军真的与日本人接触后，发现日本人的鼻子同他们自己的鼻子一般大时，这种漫画可能使他们感到极其失望。他们可能认不出敌人，而不愿打仗。

"不用担心！"司令员说，"我们会认出日本人来的，不管他有没有鼻子。"

有一次我同彭德怀一起去看一军团抗日剧团的演出，我们同其他战士一起在临时搭成的舞台前面的草地上坐下来。他似乎很欣赏那些演出，带头要求唱一个喜欢听的歌。天黑后天气开始凉起来，虽然还只8月底。我把棉袄裹紧。在演出中途，我突然奇怪地发现彭德怀却已脱了棉衣。这时我才看到他已把棉衣披在坐在他身旁的一个小号手身上。

我后来了解彭德怀为什么喜欢这些"小鬼"，那是他向我的再三要求让步，把他自己的童年的一些情况告诉了我的时候。他在自己的童年所受的苦，可能使西方人听来感到惊奇，但是却是够典型的背景材料，可以说明为什么许多中国青年像他那样投奔红军。

"How do you know?" P'eng demanded.

"Just look at his big nose!" was the response.

P'eng laughed and looked at me. "Well," he said, indicating me, "here is a *yang kuei-tzu* [foreign devil], is he an imperialist?"

"He is a foreign devil all right," the Vanguard replied, "but not a Japanese imperialist. He has a big nose, but it isn't big enough for a Japanese imperialist!"

I pointed out to P'eng that such cartoons might result in serious disillusionment when the Reds actually came into contact with the Japanese and found Japanese noses quite as reasonable as their own. They might not recognize the enemy and might refuse to fight.

"Don't worry!" said the commander. "We will know a Japanese, whether he has a nose or not."

Once I went to a performance of the First Army Corps' Anti-Japanese Theater with P'eng, and we sat down with the other soldiers on the turf below the improvised stage. He seemed to enjoy the plays immensely, and he led a demand for a favorite song. It grew quite chilly, after dark, although it was still late August. I wrapped my padded coat closer to me. In the middle of the performance I suddenly noticed with surprise that P'eng had removed his own coat. Then I saw that he had put it around a little bugler sitting next to him.

I understood P'eng's affection for these "little devils" later on, when he yielded to persuasion one night and told me something of his childhood. The trials of his own youth might amaze an Occidental ear, but they were typical enough of background events which explained many of the young Chinese who, like him, "saw Red."

三、　　为什么当红军？

彭德怀生于湘潭县的一个农村，离长沙约 90 里地，靠湘江的蓝色江水旁边的一个富裕的农村里。湘潭是湖南风景最好的一个地方，深深的稻田和茂密的竹林绣成一片绿色的田野。人口稠密，一县就有 100 多万人。湘潭土地虽然肥沃，大多数农民却穷得可怜，没有文化。据彭德怀说，"比农奴好不了多少"。那里的地主权力极大，拥有最好的地，租税高得吓人，因为他们许多人也是做官的。

湘潭有些大地主一年收入有四五万担[1]谷子，湖南省有些最富有的米商就住在那里。

彭德怀自己的家庭是富农。他 6 岁那年死了母亲，他的父亲续弦后，后母憎嫌彭德怀，因为他使她想起了她的前任。她送他到一所老式私塾去念书，在那里常常挨老师打。彭德怀显然很有能力照顾自己：有一次挨打时，他举起一条板凳，揍了老师一下，就逃之夭夭。老师在本地法院告他，他的后母把他赶了出来。

他的父亲对这次吵架并不怎么在意，但是为了迁就妻子，把这个摔凳子的年轻人送去同他喜欢的一个婶母那里去住。这位婶母把他送进了所谓新学堂。他在那里遇到了一个"激进派"教师，是不信孝敬父母的。有一天彭德怀在公园里玩耍的时候，那个教师过来，坐下来同他谈话。彭德怀问他孝敬不孝敬父母，问他是否认为彭德怀应该孝敬父母？那位教师说，从他本人来说，他不相信这种胡说八道。孩子们是在他们父母作乐的时候诞生到这个世界上来的，正如彭德怀在公园里作乐一样。

---

1. 约合 2,600 至 3,300 吨。

3   WHY IS A RED?

P'eng Teh-huai was born in a village of Hsiang T'an *hsien*, near the native place of Mao Tse-tung. It was a wealthy farming community beside the blue-flowing Hsiang River, about 90 *li* from Changsha. Hsiang T'an was one of the prettiest parts of Hunan—a green countryside quilted with deep rice lands and thickets of tall bamboo. More than a million people lived in this one county. Though the soil of Hsiang T'an was rich, the majority of the peasants were miserably poor, illiterate, and "little better than serfs," according to P'eng. Landlords were all-powerful there, owned the finest lands, and charged exorbitant rents and taxes, for they were in many cases also the officials—the gentry.

Several great landlords in Hsiang T'an had incomes of from forty to fifty thousand *tan*[1] of rice annually, and some of the wealthiest grain merchants in the province lived there.

P'eng's own family were rich peasants. His mother died when he was six, his father remarried, and this second wife hated P'eng because he was a constant reminder of her predecessor. She sent him to an old-style Chinese school, where the teacher frequently beat him. P'eng was apparently quite capable of looking after his own interests: in the midst of one of these beatings he picked up a stool, scored a hit, and fled. The teacher brought a lawsuit against him in the local courts, and his stepmother denounced him.

His father was rather indifferent in this quarrel, but to keep peace with his wife he sent the young stool tosser off to live with an aunt, whom he liked. She put the boy into a so-called modern school. There he met a "radical" teacher, who did not believe in filial worship. One day, when Teh-huai was playing in the park, this teacher came along and sat down to talk with him. P'eng asked whether he worshiped his parents, and whether he thought P'eng should worship his. As for himself, said the teacher, he did not believe in such nonsense. Children were brought into the world while their parents were playing, just as Teh-huai had been playing in this park.

---

1. About 2,600 to 3,300 tons.

"我很赞成这种看法，"彭德怀说，"我回家后便向婶母说了。她吓了一大跳。第二天就不让我去上学，受这种可恶的'外国影响'。"他的祖母——看来是个残酷的专制魔王——听到他反对孝敬父母的话以后，"每逢初一月半、逢年过节、或者刮风下雨的日子"就跪下来祷告，祈求天雷打死这个不孝孽子。

接着发生了一件惊人的事，这最好用彭德怀自己的话来说：

"我的祖母把我们统统看做是她的奴隶。她抽鸦片烟很凶。我不喜欢闻鸦片烟，有一天晚上我再也忍受不住了，起身把她的烟盘从炉子上踢了下来。她大发脾气，把全族都叫来开了会，正式要求把我溺死，因为我是不孝的孩子。她对我提出了一大串罪状。

"当时族人已准备执行她的要求。我的继母赞成把我溺死，我的父亲说，既然这是一家的意见，他也不反对。这时我的舅舅站了出来，狠狠地责备我的父母没有把我教养好。他说这是他们的过失，因此孩子没有责任。

"我的命就得了救，但是我得离家。我当时才9岁，10月里天气很冷，我除了一身衣裤外身无长物。我的继母还想把我身上的衣裤留下，但我证明这不是她的，这是我生身的母亲给我做的。"

这就是彭德怀闯世界的生活的开始。他起先当放牛娃，后来又做矿工，一天拉14小时风箱。工作时间这么长使他吃不消，于是他就离开煤矿，去当鞋匠学徒，一天只工作12小时，这已是个大改善了。他没有工资，过了8个月他又逃跑了，这次去到烧碱矿做工。矿井歇业后，他再一次地去找工作。身上除了一身破烂以外仍一无长物。他去修水渠，终于有了个"好差使"，拿到了工资。二年攒了1,500文——大约12元钱！但换了军阀后，原来的纸币成了废纸，他又一文不名。灰心丧气之下，他决定回家乡。

彭德怀现在16岁，他去找一个有钱的舅舅，就是那个救了他一命的舅舅。那人自己的儿子刚死，他过去一直很喜欢彭德怀，就欢迎他去，留他在家。彭德怀爱上了自己的表妹，舅舅对婚事也颇赞同。他们请一个古文先生上课，在一起嬉戏，计划将来的共同生活。

但是这些计划被彭德怀的无法抑制的暴躁脾气所打断了。第二年，湖南发生大饥荒，成千上万的农民赤贫无依。彭德怀的舅舅救了许多农民，但是最大的一些米

"I liked this notion," said P'eng, "and I mentioned it to my aunt when I went home. She was horrified, and the very next day had me withdrawn from the evil 'foreign influence.'" Hearing something of the young man's objection to filial worship, his grandmother began to pray regularly "on the first and fifteenth of each month, and at festivals, or when it stormed," for heaven to strike this unfilial child and destroy him.

In P'eng's own words:

"My grandmother regarded us all as her slaves. She was a heavy smoker of opium. I hated the smell of it, and one night, when I could stand it no longer, I got up and kicked a pan of her opium from the stove. She was furious. She called a meeting of the whole clan and formally demanded my death by drowning, because I was an unfilial child. She made a long list of charges against me.

"The clan was about ready to carry out her demand. My stepmother agreed that I should die, and my father said that since it was the family will, he would not object. Then an uncle, my own mother's brother, stepped forward and bitterly attacked my parents for their failure to educate me properly. He said that it was their fault and that in this case no child could be held responsible.

"My life was spared, but I had to leave home. I was nine years old, it was cold October, and I owned nothing but my coat and trousers. My stepmother tried to take those from me, but I proved that they did not belong to her, but had been given to me by my own mother."

Such was the beginning of P'eng Teh-huai's life in the great world. He got a job first as a cowherd, and next as a coal miner, where he pulled a bellows for fourteen hours a day. Weary of these long hours, he fled from the mine to become a shoemaker's apprentice, working only twelve hours a day. He received no salary, and after eight months he ran away again, this time to work in a sodium mine. The mine closed; he was forced to seek work once more. Still owning nothing but the rags on his back, he became a dike-builder. Here he had a "good job," actually received wages, and in two years had saved 1,500 *cash*— about $12! But he "lost everything" when a change of warlords rendered the currency worthless. Very depressed, he decided to return to his native district.

Now sixteen, P'eng went to call on a rich uncle, the uncle who had saved his life. This man's own son had just died; he had always liked Teh-huai, and he welcomed him and offered him a home. Here P'eng fell in love with his own cousin, and the uncle was favorably disposed to a betrothal. They studied under a Chinese tutor, played together, and planned their future.

These plans were interrupted by P'eng's irrepressible impetuosity. Next year there was a big rice famine in Hunan, and thousands of peasants were destitute. P'eng's uncle helped many, but the biggest stores of rice were held by a great landlord-merchant who

店是一个大地主开的，靠此大发横财。有一天 200 多个农民拥到他家中，要求他把大米平价卖给他们——这是在饥荒之年一向要大善士做的事。但这个有钱人拒绝讨论，把人们赶走，闩上了大门。

彭德怀继续说："我正好走过他家，便停下来看示威。我看到有许多人都已饿得半死，我知道那个人的米仓里有 1 万担大米，可是他却一点也不肯帮穷人的忙。我生气起来，便带领农民攻打他的家，他们把他的存粮都运走了。我事后想起来也不知自己为什么这样做。我只知道，他应该把米卖给穷人，要是不卖，他们把米拿走是应该的。"

彭德怀又得逃命，这次他已够年岁可以当兵。他的军人生涯由此开始。不久之后他就成了一个革命家。

他 18 岁当了排长，参加了推翻当时统治该省的一个姓胡的督军的密谋。彭德怀当时受到军中一个学生领袖的很大影响，这个人遭到了督军的杀害。彭德怀负了刺杀督军的任务来到长沙，等他有一天上街时扔炸弹过去。这颗炸弹却是虎头蛇尾的，像中国小说中的情况一样：它没有爆炸，彭德怀逃走了。

不久之后，孙逸仙博士担任西南联军的大元帅，打败了胡督军，但后来又被北洋军阀赶出湖南。彭德怀同孙逸仙的军队一起南逃。后来他奉孙逸仙的一个将领程潜[1] 的命令从事谍报活动，到了长沙以后被叛徒出卖，遭到逮捕。当时湖南当权的军阀是张敬尧。彭德怀对他这段经历是这么叙述的：

"我每天受各种各样刑罚约 1 小时。有一天晚上我被手足反绑，在手腕上缚一根绳子吊在梁上。狱卒们在我背上堆上一块块大石头，站在周围踢我，要我招供——因为他们至今仍没有弄到我的证据。我昏过去了好几次。

"这样的刑罚继续了 1 个月。每次受刑后我常常想，下一次得招供了，因为我实在受不了这种刑罚。但每次我又决定不屈服，坚持到第二天再说。最后他们从我口中得不到什么东西，出乎意料地释放了我。我一生中最惬意的一件事是几年以后我们攻占长沙时把这个用刑室拆毁了。我们放了关在那里的好几百名政治犯——其中许多人由于挨打、虐待、挨饿已奄奄一息。"

---

1. 林伯渠当时在程潜军中当参谋长。

profiteered fabulously. One day a crowd of over two hundred peasants gathered at his house, demanding that the merchant sell them rice without profit—traditionally expected of a virtuous man in time of famine. The rich man refused to discuss it, had the people driven away, and barred his gates.

P'eng went on: "I was passing his place, and paused to watch the demonstration. I saw that many of the men were half starved, and I knew this man had over 10,000 *tan* of rice in his bins, and that he had refused to help the starving at all. I became infuriated, and led the peasants to attack and invade his house. They carted off most of his stores. Thinking of it afterwards, I did not know exactly why I had done that. I only knew that he should have sold rice to the poor, and that it was right for them to take it from him if he did not."

P'eng had to flee once more for his life, and this time he was old enough to join the army. His career as a soldier began. Not long afterwards he was to become a revolutionary.

At eighteen he was made a platoon commander and was involved in a plot to overthrow the ruling governor—*Tuchun* Hu. P'eng had been deeply influenced by a student leader in his army, whom the *tuchun* had killed. Entrusted with the task of assassinating Hu, he entered Changsha, waited for him to pass down the street one day, and threw a bomb at him. The bomb failed to explode. P'eng escaped.

Not long afterwards Dr. Sun Yat-sen became Generalissimo of the allied armies of the Southwest, and succeeded in defeating *Tuchun* Hu, but was subsequently driven out of Hunan again by the northern militarists. P'eng fled with Sun's army. Sent upon a mission of espionage by Ch'eng Ch'ien, one of Sun's commanders, P'eng returned to Changsha, was betrayed and arrested. Chang Ching-yao was then in power in Hunan. P'eng described his experiences:

"I was tortured every day for about an hour in many different ways. One night my feet were bound and my hands were tied behind my back. I was hung from the roof with a rope around my wrists. Then big stones were piled on my back, while the jailers stood around kicking me and demanding that I confess—for they still had no evidence against me. Many times I fainted.

"This torture went on for about a month. I used to think after every torture that next time I would confess, as I could not stand it. But each time I decided that I would not give up till the next day. In the end they got nothing from me, and to my surprise I was finally released. One of the deep satisfactions of my life came some years later when we [the Red Army] captured Changsha and destroyed that old torture chamber. We released several hundred political prisoners there—many of them half-dead from beatings, fiendish treatment, and starvation."

彭德怀重获自由以后就回到他舅舅家去看他的表妹，他想同她结婚，因为他认为自己仍有婚约。他发现她已死了。他于是又去当兵，不久就第一次任军官，派到湖南军校学习。毕业后他在鲁涤平部下第二师当营长，到家乡驻防。

"我的舅舅死了，我听到消息以后就请假回去奔丧。路上我要经过童年时代的家。我的老祖母还活着，80多了，身体还很健旺，她听说我回来，走了10里路来迎我，请我不要计较过去。她的态度非常谦恭。我对这一转变感到很奇怪。是什么原因呢？我马上想到这不是因为她个人感情有了什么转变，而是因为我在外面发了迹，从一个无业游民变成为一个月挣200元大洋军饷的军官。我给老太太一些钱，她以后就在家里赞扬我是个模范'孝子'！"

我问彭德怀受到什么书籍的影响。他说，他年轻的时候读过司马光[1]的《资治通鉴》，第一次开始对军人应对社会负有什么责任有了一些认真的考虑。"司马光笔下的战争都是完全没有意义的，只给人民带来痛苦——很像我自己的时代里中国军阀之间的混战。为了要使我们的斗争有一些意义，为了实现长期的变革，我们能够做些什么？"

彭德怀读了梁启超、康有为以及其他许多对毛泽东也发生过影响的作家的著作。有一个时期，他对无政府主义也有一些信仰。陈独秀的《新青年》使他对社会主义发生了兴趣，从此开始研究马克思主义。国民革命正在酝酿中，他当时任团长，觉得有必要用一种政治学说来激励他的部下的士气。孙逸仙的三民主义"比起梁启超来是个进步"，但彭德怀感到"太含糊混乱"，虽然当时他已是国民党员。布哈林的《共产主义入门》使他觉得是"第一次提出了一个实际合理形式的社会和政府的一本书"。

到1926年彭德怀已读了《共产党宣言》、《资本论》简介、《新社会》（一个著名中国共产党员著）、考茨基的《阶级斗争》以及许多对中国革命作了唯物主义解释的文章和小册子。彭德怀说，"以前我只是对社会不满，看不到有什么进行根本改革的希望。在读了《共产党宣言》以后，我不再悲观，开始怀着社会是可以改造的新信念而工作。"

---

1. 司马光（1019—1086），杰出的史学家。

When P'eng regained his freedom he went back to his uncle's home to visit his cousin. He intended to marry her, as he still considered himself betrothed. He found that she had died. Re-enlisting in the army, he soon afterwards received his first commission and was sent to the Hunan military school. Following his graduation he became a battalion commander in the Second Division, under Lu Ti-p'ing, and was assigned to duty in his native district.

"My uncle died and, hearing of it, I arranged to return to attend the funeral. On the way there I had to pass my childhood home. My old grandmother was alive, now past eighty, and still very active. Learning that I was returning, she walked down the road ten *li* to meet me, and begged my forgiveness for the past. She was very humble and very respectful. I was quite surprised by this change. What could be the cause of it? Then I reflected that it was not due to any change in her personal feeling, but to my rise in the world from a social outcast to an army officer with a salary of $200 a month. I gave the old lady a little money, and she sang my praises in the family as a model 'filial son'!"

I asked P'eng what reading had influenced him. He said that when as a youth he read Ssu-ma Kuang's[1] *Sze Chih Chien* (*History of Governing*), he began for the first time to have some serious thoughts concerning the responsibility of a soldier to society. "The battles described by Ssu-ma Kuang were completely pointless, and only caused suffering to the people—very much like those that were being fought between the militarists in China in my own time. What could we do to give purpose to our struggles, and bring about a permanent change?"

P'eng read Liang Ch'i-ch'ao and K'ang Yu-wei and many of the writers who had influenced Mao Tse-tung. For a time he had some interest in anarchism. In Ch'en Tu-hsiu's *New Youth* he learned of socialism, and from that point he began to study Marxism. The Nationalist Revolution was forming, he was a regimental commander, and he felt the necessity of a political doctrine to give morale to his troops. Sun Yat-sen's *San Min Chu I* (*Three Principles of the People*) "was an improvement over Liang Ch'i-ch'ao," but P'eng felt that it was "too vague and confused," although he was by then a member of the Kuomintang. Bukharin's *ABC of Communism* seemed to him "for the first time a book that presented a practicable and reasonable form of society and government."

By 1926 P'eng had read the *Communist Manifesto*, an outline of *Capital*, *A New Conception of Society* (by a leading Chinese Communist), Kautsky's *Class Struggle*, and many articles and pamphlets giving a materialist interpretation of the Chinese Revolution. "Formerly," said P'eng, "I had been merely dissatisfied with society, but saw little chance of making any fundamental improvement. After reading the *Communist Manifesto* I dropped my pessimism and began working with a new conviction that society could be changed."

---

1. Ssu-ma Kuang was an outstanding historian (1019–1086).

虽然彭德怀到 1927 年才参加共产党，他在自己的部队里吸收相信共产主义的青年，办马克思主义的政治训练班，成立士兵委员会。1926 年，他同一个中学女生结了婚，她是社会主义青年团团员，但在革命期间，他们分了手。1928 年以后彭德怀就没有见到过她。就是在那一年 7 月，彭德怀举行起义，占领了平江，开始了他的叛逆或土匪——看你怎么叫——的生涯。

他在把这些青年时代和斗争的情况告诉我时，他手里执着一个用蒙古马鬃做的苍蝇拂，为了强调语气，漫不经心地随手挥舞着，一边在屋子里踱来踱去，说说笑笑。这时有个通讯员送来了一束电报，他开始看电报时又突然成了一个严肃的司令员了。

"反正，要说的就是这么一些，"他最后说，"这可以说明一个人怎么变成'赤匪'的！"

Although P'eng did not join the Communist Party until 1927, he enlisted Communist youths in his troops, began Marxist courses of political training, and organized soldiers' committees. In 1926 he married a middle-school girl who was a member of the Socialist Youth, but during the revolution they became separated. P'eng had not seen her since 1928. It was in July of that year that P'eng revolted, seized Ping Kiang, and began his long career as a rebel, or bandit—as you prefer.

He had been pacing back and forth, grinning and joking as he told me these incidents of his youth and struggle, carrying in his hand a Mongolian horsehair fly swatter, which he brandished absent-mindedly for emphasis. A messenger now brought in a sheaf of radiograms, and he suddenly looked the serious commander again as he turned to read them.

"Well, that's about all, anyway," he concluded. "That explains something about how a man becomes a 'Red bandit'!"

四、　游击战术

这里我要报道一下我访问彭德怀，了解红军怎样成长和为什么成长的一次极为有兴趣的谈话。我记得我们是坐在预旺堡前县长的公馆里，这是一所两层楼的房子，有栏杆围着的阳台。坐在阳台上，你可以越过宁夏平原眺望蒙古。

在预旺堡高高的结实的城墙上，红军的一队号兵在练习吹军号，这个堡垒一样的城中有一角落飘着一面猩红的大旗，上面的黄色锤子和镰刀在微风中时隐时现，好像后面有一只手在抚弄一样。我们从一边望下去，可以看到一个清洁的院子，回族妇女在舂米做饭，另一边晾着衣服。远处一个空地里，红军战士在练爬墙、跳远、掷手榴弹。

彭德怀和毛泽东虽是湖南同乡，在成立红军以前却没有见过面。彭德怀说话南方口音很重，快得像连珠炮。只有他慢条斯理地讲得很简单的时候我才能听懂，但他总是很不耐烦慢条斯理地说话。在这次谈话里，黄华做我的翻译，他的英语很好。我希望他仍活着，总有一天会读到我在这里对他表示的最深切的感谢。

"中国采用游击战的主要原因，"彭德怀开始说，"是因为经济破产，特别是农村破产。帝国主义、封建主义、军阀混战加在一起，破坏了农村经济的基础，不消灭它的主要敌人是不能恢复的。苛捐杂税，加上日本侵略，军事上和经济上的侵略，在地主的帮助下加速了农民破产的速度。农村中的豪绅的滥用权力使大多数农民无法生活下去。农村中失业现象普遍。穷人阶级愿意为改变处境而斗争。

"其次，游击战得到了发展是因为内地的落后。缺乏交通、道路、铁路、桥梁，使得人民可以武装起来，组织起来。

4   TACTICS OF PARTISAN WARFARE

We sat in the house of a former magistrate, in Yu Wang Pao, in a two-story edifice with a balustraded porch—a porch from which you could look out toward Mongolia, across the plains of Ninghsia.

On the high, stout walls of Yu Wang Pao a squad of Red buglers was practicing, and from a corner of the fortlike city flew a big scarlet flag, its yellow hammer and sickle cracking out in the breeze now and then as though a fist were behind it. We could look down on one side to a clean courtyard, where Mohammedan women were hulling rice and baking. Washing hung from a line on another side. In a distant square some Red soldiers were practicing wall scaling, broad jumping, and grenade throwing.

Although P'eng Teh-huai and Mao Tse-tung were *t'ung-hsien-ti*, or natives of the same county, they had not met until the Red Army was formed. P'eng spoke with a pronounced southern accent, and machine gun rapidity. I could understand him clearly only when he spoke slowly and simply, which he was generally too impatient to do. For this interview Huang Hua, whose English was excellent, acted as my interpreter.

"The main reason for partisan warfare in China," P'eng began, "is economic bankruptcy, and especially rural bankruptcy. Imperialism, landlordism, and militaristic wars have combined to destroy the basis of rural economy, and it cannot be restored without eliminating its chief enemies. Enormous taxes, together with Japanese invasion, both military and economic, have accelerated the rate of this peasant bankruptcy, aided by the landlords. The gentry's exploitation of power in the villages makes life difficult for the majority of the peasants. There is widespread unemployment in the villages. There is a readiness among the poor classes to fight for a change.

"Second, partisan warfare has developed because of the backwardness of the hinterland. Lack of communications, roads, railways, and bridges makes it possible for the people to arm and organize.

"第三，虽然中国的战略中心多少都控制在帝国主义者手中，这种控制是不平衡的，不统一的。在帝国主义的势力范围之间，有很多空隙，可以迅速发展游击战。

"第四，大革命（1924—1927）在许多人的心中播下了革命的思想，甚至在1927年发生反革命，城市里进行了大屠杀以后，许多革命者拒绝屈服，寻求反对的方法。由于大城市里帝国主义和买办[1]联合控制的特殊制度，由于在开始的时候缺乏一支武装力量，不可能在城市地区找到一个根据地，因此许多革命工人、知识分子、农民回到农村地区去领导农民起义。无法容忍的社会经济条件造成了革命的条件：所需要的只是为这一农村群众运动提供领导、方式和目标。

"所有这些因素都有助于革命游击战的发展和成功。当然，这些道理说得很简单，没有谈到其中更深刻的问题。

"除了这些理由以外，游击战所以能够成功，游击队所以能够战无不胜，还因为群众同作战部队打成一片。红色游击队不仅是战士，他们同时也是政治宣传员和组织者。他们到哪儿就把革命的思想带到哪儿，向农民群众耐心解释红军的真正使命，使他们了解只有通过革命才能满足他们的需要，为什么共产党是唯一能够领导他们的政党。

"但是至于游击战的具体任务，你问到为什么在有些地方发展很快，成了强大的政治力量，而在别的地方却很容易遭到迅速的镇压。这是一个很有意思的问题。

"首先，中国的游击战只有在共产党的革命领导下才能取胜，因为只有共产党有决心、有能力满足农民的要求，了解在农民中间进行深入、广泛、经常的政治和组织工作的必要性，能够实现它宣传的诺言。

"其次，游击队的实际战地领导必须坚决果断、勇敢无畏。没有这些领导品质，游击战不但不能发展，而且在反动派的进攻下一定会衰亡。

"因为群众只关心他们生计问题的实际解决，因此只有**立即**满足他们最迫切的要

---

1. 买办是充当西方和本国商人的中间人的中国人。

"Third, although the strategic centers of China are all more or less dominated by the imperialists, this control is uneven and not unified. Between the imperialist spheres of influence there are wide gaps, and in these partisan warfare can quickly develop.

"Fourth, the Great Revolution of 1924—1927 fixed the revolutionary idea in the minds of many, and even after the counterrevolution in 1927 and the killings in the cities, many revolutionaries refused to submit, and sought a method of opposition. Owing to the special system of joint imperialist-comprador[1] control in the big cities, and the lack of an armed force in the beginning, it was impossible to find a base in urban areas, so many revolutionary workers, intellectuals, and peasants returned to the rural districts to lead the peasant insurrections. Intolerable social and economic conditions had created the demand for revolution: it was only necessary to give leadership, form, and objectives to this rural mass movement.

"All these factors contributed to the growth and success of revolutionary partisan warfare. They are, of course, quite simply stated, and do not go into the deeper problems behind them.

"Besides these reasons, partisan warfare has succeeded and partisan detachments have developed their invincibility because of the identity of the masses with the fighting forces. Red partisans are not only warriors; they are at the same time political propagandists and organizers. Wherever they go they carry the message of the revolution, patiently explain to the mass of the peasantry the real missions of the Red Army, and make them understand that only through revolution can their needs be realized, and why the Communist Party is the only party which can lead them.

"But as regards the specific tasks of partisan warfare, you have asked why in some places it developed very rapidly and became a strong political power, while in others it was easily and quickly suppressed. This is an interesting question.

"First of all, partisan warfare in China can only succeed under the revolutionary leadership of the Communist Party, because only the Communist Party wants to and can satisfy the demands of the peasantry, understands the necessity for deep, broad, constant political and organizational work among the peasantry, and can fulfill its promises.

"Second, the active field leadership of partisan units must be determined, fearless, and courageous. Without these qualities in the leadership, partisan warfare not only cannot grow, but it must wither and die under the reactionary offensive.

"Because the masses are interested only in the practical solution of their problems of livelihood, it is possible to develop partisan warfare only by the *immediate* satisfaction

---

1. Compradors were Chinese who served as middlemen between Western and native businessmen.

求才能发展游击战。这意味着必须迅速解除剥削阶级的武装。

"游击队决不能静止不动,这样就会招致毁灭。他们必须不断扩充,在周围不断建立新的外围团体。每个斗争阶段都要有政治训练的配合,从每一个新参加革命的队伍中必须培养当地的领导人。在一定程度内可以从外面吸收领导人,但是如果游击运动不能鼓舞、唤醒,不能经常地从本地群众中培养新的领导人,就不可能有持久的成功。"

这些话使人感到很有兴趣,而且无疑也很重要。但是如果可能的话,我想知道红军的军事指导原则,因为这些原则使得他们成为装备比他们强大好几倍的南京军队的劲敌。凡是读到过一些关于劳伦斯上校[1]及其战役的人,无不把红军的战术同这个英国运动战伟大天才的战术相比。像阿拉伯人一样,红军在少数几次大规模阵地战中战绩平庸,但在运动战中却不可战胜。

张学良少帅所以开始尊重红军(这是他被派来摧毁的敌人)的主要原因之一是,他对他们这种作战方法的熟练掌握有很深刻的印象,他终于相信,这种方法是可以用来打日本的。他同红军达成休战协议后,就邀请红军教官到他在陕西为东北军办的军官训练班讲课,共产党在那里的影响就迅速扩大。张学良和他的大部分军官坚决抗日,他们相信,在对日战争中,中国最后必须依靠优势的机动和运动能力。他们迫切地想要知道红军在十年内战的经验中所学到的关于运动战的战略战术的所有知识。

关于这几点,我原来问过彭德怀,是否可以归纳一下"红色游击战术的原则"?他答应过给我总结一下,并且写了一些笔记,现在他念给我听。至于这个问题的详尽论述,他叫我去看毛泽东写的一本小册子,是在苏区出版的,但是我无法弄到。[2]

彭德怀说:"如果新发展的游击队要成功的话,有些战术原则必须遵守。这是我们从长期经验中学习到的,虽然视具体情况而异。我认为背离这些原则一般都会造成灭亡。主要原则可以归纳为下列 10 点:

"第一,游击队不能打打不赢的仗。除非有很大的胜利把握,否则不同敌人交战。

---

1. T.E. 劳伦斯(1888—1935),英帝国主义冒险家,第一次欧战时在阿拉伯策划反土耳其叛乱,有"阿拉伯的劳伦斯"之称。——译注
2. 毛泽东的《游击战争》1935 年在陕西瓦窑堡出版,已绝版。

of their most urgent demands. This means that the exploiting class must be promptly disarmed.

"Partisans can never remain stationary; to do so is to invite destruction. They must constantly expand, building around themselves ever new peripheral and protective groups. Political training must accompany every phase of the struggle, and local leaders must be developed from every new group added to the revolution. Leaders from the outside can be introduced to a limited extent, but no lasting success can be achieved if the movement fails to inspire, awaken, and constantly create new leaders from the local mass."

One of the chief reasons why Marshal Chang Hsueh-liang began to respect the Reds (the enemy he had been sent to destroy) was that he had been impressed with their skill at this type of combat, and had come to believe they could be utilized in fighting Japan. After he had reached a kind of truce with them he invited Red instructors to teach in the new officers' training school opened for his Manchurian army in Shensi, and there the Communist influence rapidly developed. Marshal Chang and most of his officers, bitterly anti-Japanese, had become convinced that it was superior mobility and maneuvering ability on which China would ultimately have to depend in a war with Japan. They were anxious to know all that the Reds had learned about the tactics and strategy of maneuvering warfare during ten years of fighting experience.

Was it possible, I had asked P'eng Teh-huai, to summarize the "principles of Red partisan warfare"? He had promised to do so and had written down a few notes from which he now read. For a fuller discussion of the subject he referred me to a small book written by Mao Tse-tung and published in the soviet districts; but this I was unable to get.[1]

"There are certain rules of tactics which must be followed," P'eng explained, "if the newly developing partisan army is to be successful. These we have learned from our long experience, and though they are variable according to conditions, I believe that departures from them generally lead to extinction. The main principles can be summarized under ten points, like this:

"First, partisans must not fight any losing battles. Unless there are strong indications of success, they should refuse any engagement.

---

1. Mao's *Yu-chi Chan-cheng* (*Guerrilla Warfare*), published in Wayapao, Shensi, in 1935, was out of print.

"第二，游击队如果领导得好，所采用的主要进攻战术就是奇袭。必须避免打阵地战。游击队没有辅助部队，没有后方，没有供应线和交通线，而敌人却有。因此在长期的阵地战中敌人具有一切有利条件，总的来说，游击队获胜的可能与作战时间长短成反比例。

"第三，在交战之前，不论主动或是被动，必须制订出缜密的详细的进攻计划，特别是撤退计划。任何进攻，事先如不充分准备好预防措施，游击队就有遭到敌人出奇制胜的危险。游击队的极大有利条件就是优势运动能力，在运用这种能力方面如有错误就意味着灭亡。

"第四，在发展游击战中必须注意民团[1]，这是地主豪绅的第一道，也是最后一道的最坚决的防线。从军事上来说，民团必须予以消灭。但从政治上来说，如有可能，就必须把它争取到群众一边来。一乡的民团不解除武装，群众是发动不起来的。

"第五，在与敌军正常交战时，游击队的人数必须超过敌人。但是如果遇到敌人正规军在移动、休整、或防范不严的时候，可以用一支小得多的部队，对敌人战线上的要害进行侧翼奇袭，行动要迅速坚决。红军的许多'短促突击'都是用几百个人的兵力对成千上万的敌军进行的。这种突然进攻要完全成功必须要突然、迅速、勇敢、果断、计划周密，挑选的是敌人最薄弱的又是最重要的环节。只有高度有经验的游击队才能取胜。

"第六，在实际战斗中，游击战线必须具有最大的弹性。一旦看出他们对敌人兵力或准备或火力的估计如有错误，游击队员应该能够像发动进攻那样迅速地脱离接触而后撤。每一单位必须有可靠的干部，充分能够代替在战斗中伤亡的指挥员。在游击战中必须大大依靠下级的随机应变。

"第七，必须掌握牵制佯攻、骚扰伏击等分散注意的战术。在中文中，这种战术叫做'声东击西的原则'。

---

1. 彭德怀估计民团为数至少 300 万人（中国的庞大正规军有 200 万人）。

"Second, surprise is the main offensive tactic of the well-led partisan group. Static warfare must be avoided. The partisan brigade has no auxiliary force, no rear, no line of supplies and communications except that of the enemy. In a lengthy positional war the enemy has every advantage, and in general the chances of partisan success diminish in proportion to the duration of the battle.

"Third, a careful and detailed plan of attack, and especially of retreat, must be worked out before any engagement is offered or accepted. Any attack undertaken without full knowledge of the particular situation opens the partisans to outmaneuver by the enemy. Superior maneuvering ability is a great advantage of the partisans, and errors in its manipulation mean extinction.

"Fourth, in the development of partisan warfare the greatest attention must be paid to the *min-t'uan*,[1] the first, last, and most determined line of resistance of the landlords and gentry. The *min-t'uan* must be destroyed militarily, but must, if at all possible, be won over politically on the side of the masses. Unless the *min-t'uan* in a district is disarmed it is impossible to mobilize the masses.

"Fifth, in a regular engagement with enemy troops the partisans must exceed the enemy in numbers. But if the enemy's regular troops are moving, resting, or poorly guarded, a swift, determined, surprise flank attack on an organically vital spot of the enemy's line can be made by a much smaller group. Many a Red 'short attack' has been carried out with only a few hundred men against an enemy of thousands. Surprise, speed, courage, unwavering decision, flawlessly planned maneuver, and the selection of the most vulnerable and vital spot in the enemy's 'anatomy' are absolutely essential to the complete victory of this kind of attack. Only a highly experienced partisan army can succeed at it.

"Sixth, in actual combat the partisan line must have the greatest elasticity. Once it becomes obvious that their calculation of enemy strength or preparedness or fighting power is in error, the partisans should be able to disengage and withdraw with the same speed as they began the attack. Reliable cadres must be developed in every unit, fully capable of replacing any commander eliminated in battle. Resourcefulness of subalterns must be greatly relied upon in partisan warfare.

"Seventh, the tactics of distraction, decoy, diversion, ambush, feint, and irritation must be mastered. In Chinese these tactics are called 'the principle of pretending to attack the east while attacking the west.'

---

1. P'eng Teh-huai estimated that the *min-t'uan* numbered at least 3,000,000 men (in addition to China's huge regular army of 2,000,000 men).

"第八，游击队要避免同敌军主力交战，要集中在最薄弱的或最致命的环节。

"第九，必须提防敌人找到游击队主力。为此，游击队员在敌人前进时应避免集中在一个地方，应该在进攻之前经常变换位置——一天或一晚上两三次。游击队行动神出鬼没是要取得成功所绝对必备的条件。进攻后迅速分散的周密计划同实际集中力量应付敌人进攻的计划一样重要。

"第十，除了优势机动以外，游击队由于同地方群众不可分离，在优势情报方面具有有利条件，必须充分利用这一条件。理想的情况是，每个农民都是游击队的情报员，这样敌人每走一步，游击队就无不事先知道。应努力保护敌情渠道，并建立好几道辅助情报网。"

据彭德怀司令员说，这就是红军力量所系的主要原则，每次扩大红区都要运用这些原则。他最后说：

"因此你可以看到游击战要成功，需要这些基本条件：无畏、迅速、计划周密、机动、保密、行动神出鬼没和坚决果断。缺一项，游击队就不能取胜。如果在战斗开始时，他们没有决断，战斗就要拖延时日。他们必须迅速，否则敌人就能得到增援。他们必须机动灵活，否则就会失掉运动的有利条件。

"最后，游击队绝对必须得到农民群众的拥护和参加。如果没有武装农民运动，事实上就没有游击队根据地，军队就不可能存在。只有深深扎根于人民的心中，只有实现群众的要求，只有巩固农村苏维埃中的根据地，只有掩护在群众之中，游击战才能带来革命的胜利。"

彭德怀在阳台上踱来踱去，每次走到我伏案疾书的桌子边上时就提出一个论点。现在他突然停下来，沉思地回想。

"但是没有任何东西，绝对没有任何东西，"他说，"比这一点更重要——那就是红军是人民的军队，它所以壮大是因为人民帮助我们。

"我记得1928年的冬天，我的部队在湖南只剩下2,000多人，还受到包围。国

"Eighth, partisans must avoid engagements with the main force of the enemy, concentrating on the weakest link, or the most vital.

"Ninth, every precaution must be taken to prevent the enemy from locating the partisans' main forces. For this reason, partisans should avoid concentrating in one place when the enemy is advancing, and should change their position frequently—two or three times in one day or night, just before an attack. Secrecy in the movements of the partisans is absolutely essential to success. Well-worked-out plans for dispersal after an attack are as important as plans for the actual concentration to meet an enemy advance.

"Tenth, besides superior mobility, the partisans, being inseparable from the local masses, have the advantage of superior intelligence, and the greatest use must be made of this. Ideally, every peasant should be on the partisans' intelligence staff, so that it is impossible for the enemy to take a step without the partisans knowing of it. Great care should be taken to protect the channels of information about the enemy, and several auxiliary lines of intelligence should always be established."

These were the main principles, according to Commander P'eng, on which the Red Army had built up its strength, and it was necessary to employ them in every enlargement of Red territory. He finished up:

"So you see that successful partisan warfare demands these fundamentals: fearlessness, swiftness, intelligent planning, mobility, secrecy, and suddenness and determination in action. Lacking any of these, it is difficult for partisans to win victories. If in the beginning of a battle they lack quick decision, the battle will lengthen. They must be swift, otherwise the enemy will be reinforced. They must be mobile and elastic, otherwise they will lose their advantages of maneuver.

"Finally, it is absolutely necessary for the partisans to win the support and participation of the peasant masses. If there is no movement of the armed peasantry, there is in fact no partisan base, and the army cannot exist. Only by implanting itself deeply in the hearts of the people, only by fulfilling the demands of the masses, only by consolidating a base in the peasant soviets, and only by sheltering in the shadow of the masses, can partisan warfare bring revolutionary victory."

P'eng had been pacing up and down the balcony, delivering one of his points each time he returned to the table where I sat writing. Now he suddenly stopped and stood thoughtfully reflecting.

"But nothing, absolutely nothing," he said, "is more important than this—that the Red Army is a people's army, and has grown because the people helped us.

"I remember the winter of 1928, when my forces in Hunan had dwindled to a little over two thousand men, and we were encircled. The Kuomintang troops burned down all the

民党军队把方圆 300 里内的所有房子都烧掉了,抢去了所有粮食,然后对我们进行封锁。我们没有布,就用树皮做短衫,把裤腿剪下来做鞋子。头发长了没法剃,没有住的地方,没有灯,没有盐。我们病的病,饿的饿。农民们也好不了多少,他们剩下的也不多,我们不愿碰他们的一点点东西。

"但是农民鼓励我们。他们从地下挖出他们藏起来不让白军知道的粮食给我们吃,他们自己吃芋头和野菜。他们痛恨白军烧了他们的房子,抢了他们的粮食。甚至在我们到达之前他们就在同地主老财作斗争了,因此他们欢迎我们。许多人参加了我们的队伍,几乎所有的人都用某种方式帮助我们。他们希望我们取胜!因此我们继续战斗,冲破了封锁。"

他向我转过身来,简单地结束道。"战术很重要,但是如果人民的大多数不支持我们,我们就无法生存。我们不过是人民打击压迫者的拳头!"

houses in a surrounding area of about 300 *li*, seized all the food there, and then blockaded us. We had no cloth, we used bark to make short tunics, and we cut up the legs of our trousers to make shoes. Our hair grew long, we had no quarters, no lights, no salt. We were sick and half-starved. The peasants were no better off, and we would not touch what little they had.

"But the peasants encouraged us. They dug up from the ground the grain which they had hidden from the White troops and gave it to us, and they ate potatoes and wild roots. They hated the Whites for burning their homes and stealing their food. Even before we arrived they had fought the landlords and tax collectors, so they welcomed us. Many joined us, and nearly all helped us in some way. They wanted us to win! And because of that we fought on and broke through the blockade."

He turned to me and ended simply. "Tactics are important, but we could not exist if the majority of the people did not support us. We are nothing but the fist of the people beating their oppressors!"

五、　　红军战士的生活

在国外，中国士兵的名声很差。许多人认为他们的枪主要是装饰品，他们唯一打的仗是用鸦片烟枪打的；如果有步枪交火，都是事先商定，朝天开枪；战局用银洋决定胜负，士兵用鸦片发饷。对过去的大部分军队来说，这种说法有一部分确是如此，可是现在装备良好的第一流中国士兵（红白两军都是如此），不再是滑稽戏中的笑话了。这在不久就会让全世界看到。中国未能击退日本的进攻并不是判断的标准：除了上海曾经进行过后来受到破坏的抵抗以外，迄今没有进行认真的抵抗。

中国依然有着很多滑稽戏式的军队，但近年来，已经出现了一种新型中国战士，他们不久就会取代那些旧式的战士。内战，特别是红军和白军之间的阶级战争，付出的代价一直很高，打得往往很猛烈凶狠，双方都没有宽恕或妥协的余地。中国这十年的内争，如果说别无成就，那至少已建立了对运用现代技术和战术有经验的一支战斗力量和军事头脑的核心，这不久就会建立一支强有力的军队，不再能够被看做是银样镴枪头了。

问题从来不在于人才本身。我在1932年的淞沪战役中就知道，中国人同任何别国的人一样能打仗。撇开技术上的局限性不谈，问题完全是统帅部自己没有能力训练麾下的这种人才，赋予军事纪律、政治信念和**致胜意志**。红军的优越性就在这里——它往往是在战斗中相信自己是为一定目而作战的唯一一方。红军在建军的教育工作方面的成功，使他们能够抵抗得住敌人在技术上和数量上的巨大优势。

中国农民占红军的大部分，他们坚忍卓绝，任劳任怨，是无法打败的。这在长征中已经表现了出来，这也在红军日常生活的严格要求上表现出来。可能也有外国的军队能够吃得消这种同样的风吹雨打、食物粗粝、住所简陋、长期艰苦的生活，但我

5   Life of the Red Warrior

The Chinese soldier had had a poor reputation abroad. Many people thought his gun was chiefly ornamental, that he did his only fighting with an opium pipe, that any rifle shots exchanged were by mutual agreement and in the air, that battles were fought with silver and the soldier was paid in opium. Some of that had been true enough of most armies in the past, but the well-equipped first-class Chinese soldier (White as well as Red) was now no longer a vaudeville joke.

There were still plenty of comic-opera armies in China, but in recent years there had arisen a new type of Chinese warrior, who would soon supplant the old. Civil war, especially the class war between Reds and Whites, had been very costly, and often heavily and brutally fought, with no quarter or umbrella truces given by either side. Those ten years of strife in China had, if nothing else, created the nucleus of a fighting force and military brains experienced in the use of modern technique and tactics, which would before long build a powerful army that could no longer be dismissed as a tin-soldier affair.

The trouble had never been with the human material itself. The Chinese could fight as well as any people, as I had learned during the Shanghai War in 1932. Technical limitations disregarded, the trouble had been the inability of the command to train that human material at its disposal and give to it military discipline, political morale, and the *will* to *victory*. Therein lay the superiority of the Red Army—it was so often the only side in a battle that believed it was fighting for something. It was the Reds' greater success at the educative tasks in the building of an army that enabled them to withstand the tremendous technical and numerical superiority of their enemy.

For sheer dogged endurance, and ability to stand hardship without complaint, the Chinese peasants, who composed the greater part of the Red Army, were unbeatable. This was shown by the Long March, in which the Reds took a terrific pummeling from all sides, slept in the open and lived on unhulled wheat for many days, but still held together and

没有见过。我对美、英、法、日、意、德的军队都比较熟悉，但是我相信只有最优秀的军队才能吃得消红军战士这样紧张艰苦的日常条件。

我在宁夏和甘肃所看到的红军部队，住在窑洞里，富有地主原来的马厩里，用泥土和木料草率建成的营房里，以前的官吏或驻军丢弃的场地和房子里。他们睡在硬炕上，甚至没有草垫，每人只有一条棉毯——然而这些房间却相当清洁整齐，虽则地板、墙壁和天花板都是刷了白粉的泥土。他们难得有桌子或书桌，把砖头或石头堆起来就当椅子用，因为大部分家具在敌人撤退以前就给毁坏或运走了。

每一个连都有自己的炊事员和后勤部门。红军的饮食极为简单。咖啡、茶、蛋糕、各种糖果或新鲜蔬菜，几乎是闻所未闻的东西，他们也不想。咖啡罐头比咖啡更有价值；没有谁喜欢咖啡，它的味道像药一样，但是一个好罐头却可以做成一个耐用的饭盒！热开水几乎是唯一的饮料，喝冷水受到特别禁止。

红色士兵不作战时，一天到晚都很忙，实际上，在西北，像在南方一样，经常长时期没有活动，因为占领了一个新地方后，红军就要休整一两个月时间，成立苏维埃或者进行其他的"巩固"，只派少数人去前哨值勤。敌人除了定期发动大"围剿"以外，几乎总是处于守势。但是在红军和敌人各自的攻势之间往往有很长间隙的闲暇。

红军士兵不作战或不值勤时，每星期休息一天。他们5点钟起床，晚上9点钟吹熄灯号睡觉。每天的时间表包括：起床后即进行一小时的早操；早餐；两小时的军事训练；两小时的政治课和讨论；午餐；一小时的休息；两小时的识字课；两小时的运动；晚餐；唱歌和开小组会；熄灯号。

跳远、跳高、赛跑、爬墙、盘绳、跳绳、掷手榴弹和射击方面的激烈竞赛，受到鼓励。看了红军跳墙、跳杆和盘绳，就不难明白为什么中国报纸因他们行动敏捷和爬山迅速而给他们起了"人猿"的绰号。由班到团，在运动、军事训练、政治常识、识字和公共卫生等方面的集体竞赛中，都颁发奖旗。我在获得这类荣誉的部队的列宁室里，看见这些奖旗陈列在那里。

每一个连和每一个团都有列宁室，这里是一切社会和"文化"生活的中心。团的列宁室是部队营房中最好的，但这话说明不了什么；我所看到的总是很简陋，临

emerged as a potent military force. It was also demonstrated by the rigors and impositions of daily life in the Red Army.

The Red troops I saw in Ninghsia and Kansu were quartered in caves, former stables of wealthy landlords, hastily erected barracks of clay and wood, and in compounds and houses abandoned by former officials or garrison troops. They slept on hard *k'ang*, without mattresses and with only a cotton blanket each—yet these rooms were fairly neat, clean and orderly, although their floors, walls, and ceilings were of whitewashed clay. They seldom had tables or desks, and piles of bricks or rocks served as chairs, most of the furniture having been destroyed or carted off by the enemy before his retreat.

Every company had its own cook and commissariat. The Reds' diet was extremely simple: millet and cabbage, with a little mutton and sometimes pork, were an average meal, but they seemed to thrive on it. Coffee, tea, cake, sweets of any kind, or fresh vegetables were almost unknown, but also unmissed. Coffee tins were more valued than their contents; nobody liked coffee, it tasted like medicine, but a good tin could be made into a serviceable canteen. Hot water was almost the only beverage consumed, and the drinking of cold water (very often contaminated) was specifically forbidden.

The Red soldier, when not fighting, had a full and busy day. In the Northwest, as in the South, he had long periods of military inactivity, for when a new district was occupied, the Red Army settled down for a month or two to establish soviets and otherwise "consolidate," and only put a small force on outpost duty. The enemy was nearly always on the defensive, except when one of the periodic big annihilation drives was launched.

When not in the trenches or on outpost duty, the Red soldier observed a six-day week. He arose at five and retired to a "Taps" sounded at nine. The schedule of the day included: an hour's exercise immediately after rising; breakfast; two hours of military drill; two hours of political lectures and discussion; lunch; an hour of rest; two hours of character study; two hours of games and sports; dinner, songs and group meetings; and "Taps."

Keen competition was encouraged in broad jumping, high jumping, running, wall scaling, rope climbing, rope skipping, grenade throwing, and marksmanship. Watching the leaps of the Reds over walls, bars, and ropes, you could easily understand why the Chinese press had nicknamed them "human monkeys," for their swift movement and agile feats of mountain climbing. Pennants were given in group competitions, from the squad up to the regiment, in sports, military drill, political knowledge, literacy, and public health. I saw these banners displayed in the Lenin clubs of units that had won such distinctions.

There was a Lenin Club for every company and for every regiment, and here all social and "cultural" life had its center. The regimental Lenin rooms were the best in the unit's quarters, but that said little; such as I saw were always crude, makeshift affairs,

时凑合成的，它们使人注意的是室内的人的活动，而不是室内的设备。它们全都悬挂了马克思和列宁像，那是由连团中有才能的人画的。像中国的一些基督像一样，这些马克思和列宁像一般都带有鲜明的东方人的外貌，眼睛细得像条线，前额高大，像孔子的形象，或者全然没有前额。红军士兵给马克思起了"马大胡子"的绰号。他们对他似乎又敬又爱。回民战士特别是这样，中国人喜欢大胡子而且能够留大胡子的，似乎也只有他们。

列宁室的另一个特点，是室中有专为研究军事战术而设的一角，有土制模型。微型城镇、山岳、要塞、河流、湖泊和桥梁，都建在这些角落里，学员在研究一些战术问题时，玩具军队就在这些模型上来回作战。例如，在有些地方，可以看到中日淞沪战争的重演，在另外地方，又可以看到长城战役，但大多数模型当然是表现红军和国民党之间过去的战争的。此外，它们也用来说明军队驻扎地区的地理特点，表现一场假设战役的战术，或只是用来引起红军士兵对地理和政治课的兴趣，他们上这些课是军事训练的一部分。在一个卫生连的列宁室里，我看到人体各部分的泥塑模型，说明某些疾病的影响、人体的卫生等等。

室的另一角是用来学识字的，这里可以看到每个战士的笔记簿都挂在墙壁上指定的木钉上。有3个识字班：识字不到100个的一班；识字100到300个的一班；能读写的字超过300个的又是一班。红军为每班出版了自己的课本（以政治宣传作为学习材料）。除了政治训练以外，每个连、营、团和军的政治部都负责群众教育。他们告诉我，在一军团中，只有20%左右的人依然在"瞎子"班，这是中国人对完全不识字的人的称呼。

"列宁室的原则，"第二师那位22岁的政治部主任萧华对我说，"十分简单。它们的全部生活和活动，必须同战士的日常工作和发展联系起来。必须由战士自己去进行活动。必须简单和容易了解。必须把娱乐同关于军队当前任务的实际教育结合起来。"

一般列宁室的"藏书"要及时得多，后者主要是标准的中国红军教科书和讲义、俄国革命史、各种从白区偷运进来或夺取而来的杂志以及中国苏维埃出版物，如《红色中华》《党的工作》《斗争》等等。

and what interest they aroused derived from the human activity in them rather than from their furnishings. They all had pictures of Marx and Lenin, drawn by company or regimental talent. Like some of the Chinese pictures of Christ, they generally bore a distinctly Oriental appearance, with eyes like stitches, and either a bulbous forehead like an image of Confucius, or no forehead at all. Marx, whose Chinese moniker is Ma K'e-ssu, was nicknamed by the Red soldiers Ma Ta Hu-tzu, or Ma the Big Beard. They seemed to have an affectionate awe for him. That was especially true of the Mohammedans, who appeared to be the only people in China capable of growing luxuriant beards as well as appreciating them.

Another feature of the Lenin Club was a corner devoted to the study of military tactics, in models of clay. Miniature towns, mountains, forts, rivers, lakes, and bridges were constructed in these corners, and toy armies battled back and forth, while the class studied some tactical problem. Thus in some places you saw the Sino-Japanese battles of Shanghai refought, in another the battles on the Great Wall, but most of the models were devoted to past battles between the Reds and the Kuomintang. They were also used to explain the geographical features of the district in which the army was stationed, to dramatize the tactics of a hypothetical campaign, or merely to animate the geography and political lessons which Red soldiers got as part of their military training. In a hospital company's Lenin room I saw displays of clay models of various parts of the anatomy, showing the effects of certain diseases, illustrating body hygiene, and so on.

Another corner of the club was devoted to character study, and here one saw the notebook of each warrior hanging on its appointed peg on the wall. There were three character-study groups: those who knew fewer than 100 characters; those who knew from 100 to 300; and those who could read and write more than 300 characters. The Reds had printed their own textbooks (using political propaganda as materials of study) for each of these groups. The political department of each company, battalion, regiment, and army was responsible for mass education, as well as political training. Only about 20 per cent of the First Army Corps, I was told, was still *hsia-tzu*, or "blind men," as the Chinese call total illiterates.

"The principles of the Lenin Club," it was explained to me by Hsiao Hua, the twenty-two-year-old political director of the Second Division, "are quite simple. All the life and activity in them must be connected with the daily work and development of the men. It must be done by the men themselves. It must be simple and easy to understand. It must combine recreational value with practical education about the immediate tasks of the army."

The "library" of the average Lenin Club consisted chiefly of standard Chinese Red Army textbooks and lectures, a history of the Russian Revolution, miscellaneous magazines which might have been smuggled in or captured from the White areas, and files of Chinese soviet publications like the *Red China Daily News*, *Party Work*, *Struggle*, and others.

每个室也都有墙报，由战士组成的委员会负责定期出版。列宁室的墙报可以使人相当深入地了解士兵的问题和他们的发展情况。我把许多墙报详细记下来，翻译成英文。预旺堡二师三团二连列宁室的9月1日的一张墙报是有代表性的。它的内容包括：共产党和共青团每天和每星期的通告；两篇新识字的人写的粗糙稿件，主要是革命的勉励和口号；红军在甘肃南部获得胜利的无线电新闻简报；要学唱的新歌；白区的政治新闻；最使人感到兴趣的也许是分别用来进行表扬和批评的红栏和黑栏了。

"表扬"的内容是称赞个人或集体的勇气、无私、勤劳和其他美德。在黑栏里，同志们互相进行严厉的批评，并批评他们的军官（指名道姓的），例如说没有把步枪擦干净、学习马虎、丢掉一颗手榴弹或一把刺刀、值勤时抽烟、"政治落后"、"个人主义"、"反动习气"等等。在有一个黑栏上，我看到一个炊事员因把小米煮得"半生不熟"而受到批评；在另一个黑栏里，一位炊事员揭发一个人"老是抱怨"他烧的饭不好吃。

许多人听到红军爱好英国的乒乓球，觉得很有意思。这的确有点奇怪，可是每一个列宁室屋子中间都有一张大乒乓球桌，通常两用，又做饭桌。吃饭的时候，列宁室变成了饭堂，但总有四五个"共匪"拿着乒乓球拍、乒乓球和球网站在旁边，催促同志们快些吃；他们要打乒乓球。每一个连都有个乒乓球选手，我简直不是他们的对手。

有些列宁室有留声机，那是从以前官员的家里或白军军官那里没收来的。一天晚上，他们开了美国维克特罗拉留声机招待我，说是高桂滋将军送来的"礼物"，当时，他在陕绥交界地区指挥国民党军队打红军。高将军的唱片，除了两张是法国的以外，全是中国的。法国唱片其中一张灌了《马赛曲》和《蒂珀拉赖》。另一张是一首法国滑稽歌曲。这张唱片引起惊愕的听众纵声大笑，虽然一句话也不懂。

红军有他们自己的许多游戏，而且不断地在创造新的游戏。有一种叫做"识字牌"，是帮助不识字的人学习他们的基本汉字的比赛。另一种游戏有点像扑克牌，但高分牌上分别写的是"打倒日本帝国主义！""打倒地主！""革命万岁！"和"苏维埃万岁！"低分牌上写上的口号，根据政治和军事目的而不同。此外，还有许多

There was also a wall newspaper in every club, and a committee of soldiers was responsible for keeping it up to date. The wall newspaper gave considerable insight into the soldier's problems and a measure of his development. I took down full notes, in translation, of many of these papers. A typical one was in the Lenin Club, Second Company, Third Regiment, Second Division, in Yu Wang Pao, for September 1. Its contents included daily and weekly notices of the Communist Party and the Communist Youth League; a couple of columns of crude contributions by the newly literate, mostly revolutionary exhortations and slogans; radio bulletins of Red Army victories in south Kansu; new songs to be learned; political news from the White areas; and, perhaps most interesting of all, two sections called the red and black columns, devoted respectively to praise and criticism.

"Praise" consisted of tributes to the courage, bravery, unselfishness, diligence, or other virtues of individuals or groups. In the black column comrades lashed into each other and their officers (by name) for such things as failure to keep a rifle clean, slackness in study, losing a hand grenade or bayonet, smoking on duty, "political backwardness," "individualism," "reactionary habits," etc. On one black column I saw a cook criticized for his "half-done" millet; in another a cook denounced a man for "always complaining" about his productions.

Many people had been amused to hear about the Reds' passion for the English game of table tennis. It was bizarre, somehow, but every Lenin Club had in its center a big ping-pong table, usually serving double duty as dining table. The Lenin clubs were turned into mess halls at chow time, but there were always four or five "bandits," armed with bats, balls, and the net, urging the comrades to hurry it up; they wanted to get on with their game. Each company boasted a ping-pong champion, and I was no match for them.

Some of the Lenin clubs had record players confiscated from the homes of former officials or White officers. One night I was entertained with a concert on a captured American Victrola, described as a "gift" from General Kao Kuei-tzu, who was then in command of a Kuomintang army fighting the Reds on the Shensi-Suiyuan border. General Kao's records were all Chinese, with two exceptions, both French. One had on it "The Marseillaise" and "Tipperary." The other was a French comic song. Both brought on storms of laughter from the astonished listeners, who understood not a word.

The Reds had many games of their own, and were constantly inventing new ones. One, called *Shih-tzu P'ai*, or "Know Characters Cards," was a contest that helped illiterates learn their basic hieroglyphics. Another game was somewhat like poker, but the high cards were marked "Down with Japanese Imperialism," "Down with the Landlords," "Long Live the Revolution," and "Long Live the Soviets." Minor cards carried slogans that changed according to the political and military objectives. There were many group games. The

集体游戏。共青团员负责列宁室的节目，每天也领着大家唱歌。其中许多歌曲是配着基督教赞美诗的调子唱的！

所有这些活动，使士兵们十分忙碌而又十分健康。我没有看见过随营商人或随营娼妓和红军部队在一起。吸鸦片烟是禁止的。不论在我与红军同行的路上，或者在我参观过的营房里，我都没有看见过鸦片烟或烟枪。除值班外，并不禁止吸香烟，但是有反对吸烟的宣传，吸香烟的红军士兵似乎很少。我请他们吸烟时，他们多数谢绝。

这就是后方正规红军战士的有组织的生活。也许并不是十分有刺激性，但跟宣传捏造大为不同，而根据这些宣传捏造，你很可能以为红军的生活是纵酒宴乐，由裸体舞女助兴，饭前饭后都大肆劫掠。这纯粹是胡说八道——其实也谈不上纯粹。事实是，任何地方的革命军队总是有过于禁欲的危险，而不是相反。

红军的有些办法，现在已为蒋介石的精锐"新军"和他的"新生活运动"所仿效——有好得多的条件来实现。但是红军说，有一样东西是白军没法仿效的，就是他们的"革命觉悟"，那是他们维系斗志的主要支柱。要知道这种革命觉悟究竟是怎么一回事，最好是看一看红军的政治课——那里你可以听到深印在这些青年的脑际，使他们为之战斗和牺牲的简单的信条。

Communist Youth League members were responsible for the programs of the Lenin clubs, and likewise led mass singing every day. Many of the songs were sung to Christian hymn tunes.

All these activities kept the mass of the soldiers fairly busy and fairly healthy. There were no camp followers or prostitutes with the Red troops I saw. Opium smoking was prohibited. I saw no opium or opium pipes with the Reds on the road, nor in any barracks I visited. Cigarette smoking was not forbidden except while on duty, but there was propaganda against it, and few Red soldiers seemed to smoke.

Such was the organized life of the regular Red soldiers behind the front. Not so very exciting, perhaps, but rather different from the propagandists' tales, from which one might have gathered that the Reds' life consisted of wild orgies, entertainment by naked dancers, and rapine before and after meals. The truth seemed to be that a revolutionary army anywhere was always in danger of becoming too puritanical, rather than the contrary.

Some of the Reds' ideas had now been copied—with much better facilities for realizing them—by Chiang Kai-shek's crack "new army" and his New Life Movement. But one thing the White armies could not copy, the Reds claimed, was their "revolutionary consciousness." What this was like could best be seen at a political session of Red troops—where one could hear the firmly implanted credos that these youths fought and died for.

六、　　政治课

一天下午无事，我就去找红军政治部的刘晓，他的办公室在预旺堡城墙上的一个碉堡里。

我见到的指挥员和党的领导人已经不少了，但是士兵群众却不够。到现在已经很明显地可以看出，红军指挥员们都是忠诚的马克思主义者，都是通过共产党派在部队每一单位的政治部中的代表有效地受到共产党的领导。当然，托洛茨基先生可能会争论，他们究竟是好马克思主义者还是坏马克思主义者，但我在这里却不想作这样微妙的区分。重要的是，按他们自己的方式，他们是社会主义的自觉战士；他们知道自己要的是什么，相信自己是一个世界性运动的一部分。

我对刘晓说，"我已见了不少指挥员，但士兵却见得不够。普通战士究竟怎么样？这些反帝和阶级斗争的玩意儿，他到底相信几分？我要去参加他们的政治课，希望你同我一起去。他们的方言太多，我一个人去不能全听懂。"

刘晓是我在红军中遇到的思想最一本正经、工作最刻苦努力的青年之一。他是个极其认真的25岁的青年，面容清秀、聪明，态度极其温和谦恭、彬彬有礼。我感觉到他内心中对自己同红军的关系极为自豪。他对共产主义有一种宗教式狂热的纯粹感情。我相信，他如接到命令是会毫不犹豫地开枪打死不管多少的"反革命分子"和"叛徒"的。

我没有权利闯到他那里去打扰他的工作，但是我知道他奉到命令要尽一切可能协助我。他有好几次充当我的翻译，因此我就充分利用这个条件。我也认为，他厌恶外国人，后来他向我谈了他的简短自传以后，我就不怪他了。他在自己的国土上曾两次遭到外国警察的逮捕和囚禁！

6   Session in Politics

Finding myself with an idle afternoon, I went around to call on Liu Hsiao, a member of the Red Army political department, with offices in a guard-house on the city wall of Yu Wang Pao.

By now it was obvious that the Red commanders were loyal Marxists, and were effectively under the guidance of the Communist Party, through its representatives in the political department of every unit of the army. Of course, Mr. Trotsky might have disputed whether they were good Marxists or bad Marxists, but the point was that they were conscious fighters for socialism, in their fashion; they knew what they wanted, and believed themselves to be part of a world movement.

Liu Hsiao was one of the most serious-minded young men I had met among the Reds, and one of the hardest-working. An intensely earnest youth of twenty-five, with an esthetic, intellectual face, he was extremely courteous, gentle, and inoffensive. I sensed an immense inner spiritual pride in him about his connection with the Red Army. He had a pure feeling of religious absolutism about communism, and I believed he would not have hesitated, on command, to shoot any number of "counterrevolutionaries" or "traitors."

I had no right to break in on his day, but I knew he had orders to assist me in any way possible—he had several times acted as my interpreter—so I made the most of it. I think also that he disliked foreigners, and when later on he gave me a brief biography of himself, I could not blame him. He had been twice arrested and imprisoned by foreign police in his own country.

刘晓以前是湖南辰州府一所美国教会学校东景书院的学生。他在1926年和大革命以前本来是个虔诚的原教旨派基督教徒。热心基督教青年会工作。一天他领导一次学生罢课，被学校开除，家庭与他断绝关系。他对在中国的"教会的帝国主义基础"有了认识以后，就去了上海，积极参加那里的学生运动，加入了共产党，被法租界警察逮捕。1929年获释后，又找到了同志们，在共产党地下省委领导下工作，又被英国警察逮捕，关在有名的华德路监狱，受电刑拷打，要他招供，后来移交给中国当局，又关监牢，到1931年才重获自由。当时他才20岁。不久之后，他就由共产党的"地下交通"送到福建苏区，从此就一直在红军里。

刘晓同意陪我一起到一个列宁室去参观上政治课。这是一军团二师二团的一个连在开会，有62人参加。这是该连的"先进小组"；另外还有一个"第二小组"。红军中的政治教育是通过3个大组进行的，每个大组分为上述两个小组。每一小组选出自己的士兵委员会，同上级军官商量办事，派代表参加苏维埃。这3个大组中，一个是由连长以上军官组成；一个是由班长和士兵组成；一个是后勤部队——炊事员、马夫、骡夫、通讯员和少先队。

屋子里装饰着绿色的松柏树枝，大门上钉着一颗纸制的大红星。里面是必备的马克思和列宁的画像，另一面墙上是淞沪战争英雄蔡廷锴将军和蒋光鼐将军的照片。[1] 有一张俄国红军在红场集合庆祝十月革命的巨幅照片——那是从上海一家杂志上剪下来的。最后，还有一幅冯玉祥将军的巨幅石版印刷像，下面的口号是"还我山河"！这是中国一句古话，现在由于抗日运动而复活了。

战士们坐在他们自己带来的砖块上（常常可以看到士兵们上学去时，一手拿着笔记本，一手带着一块砖头），带领他们的是连长和政治委员，两人都是党员。据我了解，题目是"抗日运动的发展"。一个身材颀长、面容瘦削的青年在讲课，他似乎

---

1. 淞沪战争爆发于1932年1月。展示这些非共产党的抗日将领的照片反映了中国共产党于1935年采取的统一战线政策。

Liu was an ex-student of Eastview Academy, an American missionary school in Shengchoufu, Hunan. He had been a devout Christian, a fundamentalist, and a good Y.M.C.A. man until 1926 and the Great Revolution. One day he led a student strike, was expelled, and was disowned by his family. Awakened to the "imperialistic basis of missionary institutions" in China, he went to Shanghai, became active in the student movement there, joined the Communist Party, and was imprisoned by police in the French Concession. Released in 1929, he rejoined his comrades, worked under the provincial committee of the Communist Party, was arrested by British police, put in the notorious Ward Road Jail, tortured by electricity to extort a confession, handed over to the Chinese authorities, jailed again, and did not get his freedom till 1931. He was then just twenty years old. Shortly afterwards he was sent by the Reds' "underground railway" to the Fukien Soviet district, and had ever since been with the Red Army.

Liu agreed to accompany me, and together we found our way to a Lenin Club where there was a political class in session. It was a meeting of a company in the Second Regiment of the Second Division, First Army Corps, and sixty-two were present. This was the "advanced section" of the company; there was also a "second section." Political education in the Red Army is conducted through three main groups, each of which is divided into the two sections mentioned. Each elects its soldiers' committee, to consult with its superior officers and send delegates to the soviets. The three groups are for company commanders and higher; squad commanders and the rank and file; and the service corps—cooks, grooms, muleteers, carriers, sweepers, and Young Vanguards.

Green boughs decorated the room, and a big red paper star was fixed over the doorway. Inside were the usual pictures of Marx and Lenin, and on another wall were photographs of Generals Ts'ai T'ing-k'ai and Chiang Kuang-nai, heroes of the Shanghai War.[1] There was a big picture of the Russian Red Army massed in Red Square in an October anniversary demonstration—a photograph torn from a Shanghai magazine. Finally, there was a large lithograph of General Feng Yu-hsiang, with a slogan under it, "*Huan Wo Shan Ho*"—"Give back our mountains and rivers!" —an old Classical phrase, now revived by the anti-Japanese movement.

The men sat on brick seats, which they had brought with them (one often saw soldier students going to school with notebooks in one hand and a brick in the other), and the class was led by the company commander and the political commissar, both members of the Communist Party. The subject, I gathered, was "Progress in the Anti-Japanese Movement." A lanky, gaunt-faced youth was speaking. He seemed to be summarizing five

---

1. The Shanghai War, or "Incident," occurred in January, 1932. Display of photographs of these non-Communist but anti-Japanese generals reflected the united-front policy of the CCP adopted in 1935.

是在总结5年来的中日"不宣之战",提高嗓门在喊叫。他谈到日本侵略满洲,他自己在那里的经历,他当时是张学良少帅的军队中的一个士兵。他谴责南京下令"不抵抗"。然后他介绍了日本对上海、热河、河北、察哈尔和绥远的侵略。他说每次侵略中"国民狗党"都不战而退。他们"把我国1/4的领土奉送给了日本强盗"。

"为什么?"他问道,非常激动,声音有点哽咽。"为什么我们中国军队不打仗救中国?是因为他们不愿打吗?不是!东北军战士几乎天天要求我们的军官率领我们上前线,打回老家去。每个中国人都不愿当亡国奴!但是中国的军队因为我们的卖国政府而不能打仗。"

"但是如果我们红军领导他们,人民就会打仗……"他最后总结了抗日运动在共产党领导下的西北的发展。

另一个人站了起来,立正地站着,双手贴着身子的两边。刘晓悄悄地告诉我,他是班长——一个上士——参加过长征。"不要打日本的只是卖国贼。只是有钱人,军阀,税吏,地主,银行家,他们开展'与日本合作'运动,提出'联合反共'的口号。他们只是一小撮,他们不是中国人。

"我们的农民和工人,我们每一个人都要抗战救国。只要向他们指出一条道路……我怎么知道的?在我们江西苏区,我们人口只有300万,但是我们招了50万人志愿参加的游击队!我们忠诚的苏区在我们反对卖国白军的战争中热情支援我们。红军在全国胜利后,我们就会有1,000多万的游击队。那时看日本人敢不敢抢我们!"

还有许多这样的发言,他们一个接着一个站起来痛斥日本,有时强调、有时不同意以前一个发言者的话,有时对组织讨论的人提出的问题作出答复,或者对"扩大抗日运动"提出建议,等等。

有一个青年谈到去年红军抗日东征山西时人民的反应。他叫道,"老百姓欢迎我们!他们几百几百地来参加我们红军。他们在我们行军的路上送茶水和饼来。有许多人从田里出来参加我们,向我们欢呼……他们十分清楚地明白,谁是卖国的,谁是爱国的——谁要抗日,谁要把中国出卖给日本。我们的问题是要唤起全国人民,像我们唤起山西人民一样……"

years of Sino-Japanese "undeclared war," and he was shouting at the top of his lungs. He told of the Japanese invasion of Manchuria, and his own experiences there, as a former soldier in the army of Marshal Chang Hsueh-liang. He condemned Nanking for ordering "nonresistance." Then he described the Japanese invasion of Shanghai, Jehol, Hopei, Chahar, and Suiyuan. In each case, he maintained, the "Kuomintang dog-party" had retreated without fighting. They had "given the Japanese bandits a fourth of our country."

"Why?" he demanded, intensely excited, his voice breaking a little. "Why don't our Chinese armies fight to save China? Because they don't want to? No! We Tungpei men asked our officers nearly every day to lead us to the front, to fight back to our homeland. Every Chinese hates to become a Japanese slave! But China's armies cannot fight because of our *mai-kuo cheng-fu* (literally, 'sell-country government')."

"But the people will fight if our Red Army leads...." He ended up with a summary of the growth of the anti-Japanese movement in the Northwest, under the Communists.

Another arose, stood at rigid attention, his hands pressed closely to his sides. Liu Hsiao whispered to me that he was a squad leader—a corporal—who had made the Long March. "It is only the traitors who do not want to fight Japan. It is only the rich men, the militarists, the tax collectors, the landlords and the bankers, who start the 'cooperate-with-Japan' movement, and the 'joint-war-against-communism' slogan. They are only a handful, they are not Chinese.

"Our peasants and workers, every one, want to fight to save the country. They only need to be shown a road.... Why do I know this? In our Kiangsi soviets we had a population of only 3,000,000, yet we recruited volunteer partisan armies of 500,000 men! Our loyal soviets enthusiastically supported us in the war against the traitorous White troops. When the Red Army is victorious over the whole country our partisans will number over ten millions. Let Japan dare to try to rob us then!"

And much more of it. One after another they stood up to utter their hatred against Japan, sometimes emphasizing, sometimes disagreeing with a previous speaker's remark, sometimes giving their answers to questions from the discussion leaders, making suggestions for "broadening the anti-Japanese movement," and so on.

One youth told of the response of the people to the Red Army's anti-Japanese Shansi expedition last year. "The *lao-pai-hsing* [the people] welcomed us," he shouted. "They came by the hundreds to join us. They brought us tea and cakes on the road as we marched. Many left their fields to come to join us, or cheer us.... They understood quite clearly who were the traitors and who the patriots—who want to fight Japan, and who want to sell China to Japan. Our problem is to awaken the whole country as we awakened the people of Shansi...."

有一个发言者谈到白区的抗日学生运动，另一个谈到西南的抗日运动，一个东北人谈到张学良少帅的东北军为什么不愿再打红军的原因。"中国人不打中国人，我们大家都要团结起来反对日本帝国主义，我们必须收复失地！"他慷慨激昂地结束他的发言。第四个人谈到东北抗日义勇军，另一个谈到中国各地日本纱厂中的中国工人的罢工。

讨论历时1个多小时。指挥员和政治委员有时插言总结一下刚才的发言，发挥其中的一个论点，或者补充一些新的情况，纠正刚才发言中的某一点。战士们都用小本子吃力地记了简单的笔记，他们的诚实的农民的脸上露出了认真思索的神色。整个讨论是很生硬地带有宣传性的，他们一点也不在乎夸大事实。这甚至有点传教的味道，所选的材料都是为了证明一个论点。但它的效果很大，这一点是很明显的。在这些年轻的没有什么训练的头脑中逐渐形成了简单然而强烈的信念，从形式上来说是很符合逻辑的信念，也是任何一支十字大军为了要加强精神团结、勇气、为事业而牺牲——我们称之为士气的那种精神——都认为是必要的信条。

最后我打断了他们的发言，提出一些问题。他们都举手抢着回答。我发现在场的62个人中，有9个来自城市工人阶级家庭，其余都是直接来自农村。21个以前在白军当过兵，6个前东北军。只有8个已婚，21个来自红军家庭——也就是在苏区得到土改好处的贫农家庭。34个不满20岁，24个在20到25岁之间，只有4个在30岁以上。

我问道，"红军在哪个方面比中国其他军队好？"这个问题有6个人立即站起来回答。我当时记下的答复，有一部分简述如下：

"红军是革命的军队。"

"红军是抗日的。"

"红军帮助农民。"

"红军中的生活条件同白军生活完全不同。我们在这里人人平等；在白军中，士兵群众受到压迫。我们为自己和群众打仗。白军为地主豪绅打仗。红军官兵生活一样。白军士兵受奴隶待遇。"

One talked about the anti-Japanese student movement in the White districts, another about the anti-Japanese movement in the Southwest, and a Tungpei man told of the reasons why Marshal Chang Hsueh-liang's Manchurian soldiers refused to fight the Reds any more. "Chinese must not fight Chinese, we must all unite to oppose Japanese imperialism, we must win back our lost homeland!" he concluded with terse eloquence. A fourth spoke of the Manchurian anti-Japanese volunteers, and another of the strikes of Chinese workers in the Japanese mills of China.

The discussion continued for more than an hour. Occasionally the commander or political commissar interrupted to sum up what had been said, to elaborate a point, or to add new information, occasionally to correct something that had been said. The men took brief laborious notes in their little notebooks, and the serious task of thought furrowed their honest peasant faces. The whole session was crudely propagandist, and exaggeration of fact did not bother them in the least. It was self-proselytizing in a way, with materials selected to prove a single thesis. But that it was potent in its effects was manifest. Simple but powerful convictions, logical in shape, were forming in these young, little-tutored minds—credos such as every great crusading army has found necessary in order to stiffen itself with that spiritual unity, that courage, and that readiness to die in a cause, which we call morale.

I interrupted to ask some questions. They were answered by a show of hands. I discovered that of the sixty-two present, nine were from urban working-class families, while the rest were straight from the land. Twenty-one were former White soldiers and six were from the old Manchurian Army. Only eight of this group were married, and twenty-one were from Red families—that is, from families of poor peasants who had shared in the land redistribution under some soviet. Thirty-four of the group were under twenty years of age, twenty-four were between twenty and twenty-five, four were over thirty.

"In what way," I asked, "is the Red Army better than other armies of China?" This brought half a dozen men to their feet at once.

"The Red Army is a revolutionary army."

"The Red Army is anti-Japanese."

"The Red Army helps the peasants."

"Living conditions in the Red Army are entirely different from the White Army life. Here we are all equals; in the White Army the soldier masses are oppressed. Here we fight for ourselves and the masses. The White Army fights for the gentry and the landlords. Officers and men live the same in the Red Army. In the White Army the soldiers are treated like slaves."

"红军军官来自战士行列，完全靠表现得到提拔。但白军军官是靠钱买的，或者用政治影响。"

"红军战士是志愿当兵的，白军是强征来的。"

"资本家的军队是要维护资产阶级。红军为无产阶级打仗。"

"军阀的军队的任务是收税和压榨人民的血。红军为解放人民打仗。"

"群众恨白军，他们爱红军。"

我再一次打断他们，"但是你怎么知道农民是真的爱红军的呢？"这时又有好几个人跳起来回答。政治委员指了一个。

"我们到新区去的时候，"他说，"农民们总是自动出来帮助我们做急救工作。他们把我们的受伤的战士从前线抬回医院。"

另一个："我们长征过四川时，农民给我们送来了他们自己做的草鞋，一路上给我们送来了茶和热水。"

第三个："我在刘志丹的二十六军里在定边作战的时候，我们的小分队保卫一个孤立的岗哨，抵抗国民党将领高桂滋的进攻。农民们给我们带来了吃的和喝的。我们不用派人去搞给养，人民会帮助我们。高桂滋的军队打败了。我们俘虏了几个，他们告诉我们，他们有两天没水喝了。农民们在井里放了毒逃走了。"

一个甘肃农民出身的战士："人民在各方面帮助我们。在作战的时候，他们常常把小股敌军缴了械，切断他们的电话电报线，把白军调动的消息告诉我们。但是他们从来不会切断我们的电话线，他们帮我们拉电话线！"

另一个："最近一架敌机在陕西一个山上坠毁时，只有几个农民看到。他们只有红缨枪和铁锹武装，但是还是袭击了那架飞机，把两个飞行员缴了械，捉了起来，送到瓦窑堡我们这里！"

还有一个："去年4月在延长，有5个村子成立苏维埃，我正好驻扎在那里。后来我们受到汤恩伯的进攻，不得不后撤。民团回来后捉了村里18个人，砍了他们的脑袋。这时我们进行了反攻。村里的人领我们从山上一条秘密小道袭击民团。他们没有防备，我们进攻后缴了3排敌军的械。"

"Officers of the Red Army come from our own ranks, and win their appointments by merit alone. White officers buy their jobs, or use political influence."

"Red soldiers are volunteers; White soldiers are conscripted."

"Capitalist armies are for preserving the capitalist class. The Red Army fights for the proletariat."

"The militarists' armies' work is to collect taxes and squeeze the blood of the people. The Red Army fights to free the people."

"The masses hate the White Army; they love the Red Army."

"But how," I interrupted once more, "do you know the peasants really like the Red Army?" Again several jumped up to answer. The political commissar recognized one.

"When we go into a new district," he said, "the peasants always volunteer to help our hospital service. They carry our wounded back to our hospitals from the front."

Another: "On our Long March through Szechuan the peasants brought us grass shoes, made by themselves, and they brought us tea and hot water along the road."

A third: "When I fought in Liu Chih-tan's Twenty-sixth Army, in Tingpien, we were a small detachment defending a lonely outpost against the Kuomintang general, Kao Kuei-tzu. The peasants brought us food and water. We did not have to use our men to bring supplies, the people helped us. Kao Kuei-tzu's men were defeated. We captured some and they told us they had had no water for almost two days. The peasants had poisoned the wells and run away."

A Kansu peasant soldier: "The people help us in many ways. During battles they often disarm small parties of the enemy, cut their telephone and telegraph wires, and send us news about the movements of the White troops. But they never cut our telephone lines; they help us put them up!"

Another: "When an enemy airplane crashed against a mountain in Shensi recently, nobody saw it but a few farmers. They were armed only with spears and spades, but they attacked the airplane, disarmed the two aviators, arrested them, and brought them to us in Wa Ya Pao!"

Still another: "Last April, in Yen Ch'ang, five villages formed soviets, where I was stationed. Afterwards we were attacked by T'ang En-p'o, and had to retreat. The *min-t'uan* returned, arrested eighteen villagers, and cut off their heads. Then we counterattacked. The villagers led us by a secret mountain path to attack the *min-t'uan*. We took them by surprise, and we attacked and disarmed three platoons."

这时，一个脸上长了一条长疤的青年站了起来，讲了长征路上的经历。他说，"红军过贵州时，我和几个同志在遵义附近受了伤。当时部队得前进，不能带我们走。医生给我们包扎好后，把我们留给一些农民，要他们照顾我们。他们给我们饭吃，待我们很好，白军到那个村子来时，他们把我们藏了起来。几个星期以后，我们就康复了。后来红军回到这一带来，第二次攻克了遵义。我们回到了部队，村子里有几个青年和我们一起走了。"

另一个："有一次我们在（陕西北部的）安定的一个村子里，我们只有十多个人和十多支枪。农民给我们做豆腐吃，给了我们一头羊。我们大吃了一顿就睡了，只留一个人站岗。他也睡着了。但在半夜里，有一个农村孩子跑了来把我们叫醒。他从山上跑了10里路来告诉我们，民团在那里打算包围我们。1个小时后民团果然来进攻了，但我们已有准备，把他们打退。"

一个眼光明亮的少年，嘴上还没有长毛，他站起来宣布："我只有一句话要说。白军到甘肃的一个村子中来时，没有人帮助他，没有人给他吃的，没有人要参加。但是红军来时，农民们组织起来，成立委员会来帮助我们，青年人都志愿参军。我们红军就是人民，我要说的就是这一点！"

那里的每一个青年似乎都有个人的经历可以说出来证明"农民爱我们"。对于那个问题，我记下了17个不同的答复。这样一问一答很受人欢迎，结果又过去了1个小时，我才发现这些战士早已过了晚饭时间。我向他们道歉，准备走时，该连的一个"小鬼"站起来说，"不要客气。我们红军打仗的时候顾不上吃饭，我们向我们的外国朋友介绍红军时也不在乎过了吃饭时间。"

One youth with a long scar on his cheek got up and told of some experiences on the Long March. "When the Red Army was passing through Kweichow," he said, "I was wounded with some other comrades, near Tsunyi. The army had to move on; it could not take us along. The doctors bandaged us and left us with some peasants, asking them to look after us. They fed us and treated us well, and when the White troops came to that village they hid us. In a few weeks we recovered. Later on the Red Army returned to that district and captured Tsunyi a second time. We rejoined the army, and some of the young men of the villages went with us."

Another: "Once we were staying in a village of An Ting [north Shensi] and we were only a dozen men and rifles. The peasants there made bean curd for us, and gave us a sheep. We had a feast and we ate too much and went to sleep, leaving only one sentry on guard. He went to sleep too. But in the middle of the night a peasant boy arrived and woke us up. He had run ten *li* from [some mountain] to warn us that *min-t'uan* were there and intended to surround us. The *min-t'uan* did attack us about an hour later, but we were ready for them and drove them off."

A bright-eyed lad without a shadow of whisker on his face arose and declared: "I have only this to say. When the White Army comes to a village in Kansu, nobody helps it, nobody gives it any food, and nobody wants to join. When the Red Army comes, the peasants organize, and form committees to help us, and young men volunteer to join. Our Red Army *is* the people, and this is what I have to say!"

Every youth there seemed to have a personal experience to relate to prove that "the peasants like us." I wrote down seventeen different answers to that question. It proved so popular that another hour had passed before I realized that these warriors had been delayed long past their dinner call. I apologized and prepared to leave, but one "small devil" attached to the company stood up and said: "Don't worry about ceremony. We Reds don't care about going without food when we are fighting, and we don't care about missing our food when we can tell a foreign friend about our Red Army."

Part Nine
With the Red Army (Continued)

第九篇
同红军在一起(续)

一、　　红色窑工徐海东

一天早上我到彭德怀的司令部去，发现他有好几个部下在那里，正好开完会。他们请我进去，开了一只西瓜。我们围桌而坐，淘气地在炕上吐起瓜子来。我注意到有一个我以前没有见过的年轻指挥员。

彭德怀看见我瞧着他，便开玩笑说，"那边这个人是著名的'赤匪'。你认出他来了吗？"新来的那个人马上面露笑容，脸涨得通红，嘴里露出掉了两个门牙的大窟窿，使他有了一种顽皮的孩子相，大家不由得都笑了。

"他就是你一直要想见的人，"彭德怀又补充说。"他要你去访问他的部队。他叫徐海东。"

中国共产党的军事领导人中，恐怕没有人能比徐海东更加"大名鼎鼎"的了，也肯定没有人能比他更加神秘的了。除了他曾经在湖北一个窑场做过工，外界对他很少了解。蒋介石把他称为文明的一大害。最近，南京的飞机飞到红军前线的上空，散发了传单，除了其他诱惑（红军战士携枪投奔国民党，每人可获100元奖金）以外，还有下列保证：

　　凡击毙彭德怀或徐海东，投诚我军，当赏洋10万。
　　凡击毙其他匪酋，当予适当奖励。

可是就在这里，羞怯地长在一对宽阔的孩子气肩膀上的，却是南京的悬赏不下于彭德怀的脑袋。

1   Hsu Hai-tung, the Red Potter

One morning I went to P'eng Teh-huai's headquarters and found several members of his staff there, just finishing up a conference. They invited me in and opened a watermelon. As we sat around tables, spitting out seeds on the *k'ang*, I noticed a young commander I had not seen before.

P'eng Teh-huai saw me looking at him, and he said banteringly, "That's a famous Red bandit over there. Do you recognize him?" The new arrival promptly grinned, blushed crimson, and in a most disarming way exposed a big cavern where two front teeth should have been. It gave him a childish and impish appearance, and everybody smiled.

"He is the man you have been eager to meet," supplied P'eng. "He wants you to visit his army. His name is Hsu Hai-tung."

Of all the Red military leaders of China, probably none was more "notorious," and certainly none was more of a mystery than Hsu Hai-tung. Scarcely anything was known of him to the outside world except that he had once worked in a Hupeh pottery and that Chiang Kai-shek had branded him a scourge of civilization. Recently Nanking airplanes had visited the Red lines to drop leaflets containing, among other inducements to deserters (including $100 to every Red soldier who brought his rifle with him to the Kuomintang), the following promise:

> *Kill P'eng Teh-huai or Hsu Hai-tung and we will give you $100,000 when you join our army. Kill any other bandit leader and we will reward you accordingly.*

And here, poised shyly over a pair of square boyish shoulders, sat that head which Nanking apparently valued no less than P'eng Teh-huai's.

我表示感到很荣幸，心里在想，有一条命对你部下值这么多的钱，不知有何感觉，因此问徐海东，他请我去访问他的部队是不是当真的。他是红军十五军团司令，司令部设在西北80里外的预旺堡。

"我在鼓楼已为你准备好了一间屋子，"他答道。"你什么时候想来就告诉我好了，我派人来接你。"

我们当场就谈妥了。

因此几天之后，我带了一支借来的自动步枪（这是我自己从一个红军军官那里"没收"来的），在10名带着步枪和毛瑟枪的红军骑兵护卫下前往预旺堡，因为在有些地方，我们的路线离前线红军阵地只有很短的距离。与陕西和甘肃的无穷无尽的山沟沟相比，我们走的那条路——通向长城和那历史性的内蒙草原的一条路——穿过的地方却是高高的平原，到处有长条的葱绿草地，点缀着一丛丛高耸的野草和圆圆的山丘，上面有大群的山羊和绵羊在放牧啃草。兀鹰和秃鹰有时在头上回翔。有一次，有一群野羚羊走近了我们，在空气中嗅闻了一阵，然后又纵跳飞跑躲到山后去了，速度惊人，姿态优美。

5小时后，我们到达了预旺堡城，这是一个古老的回民城市，居民约有四五百户，城墙用砖石砌成，颇为雄伟。城外有个清真寺，有自己的围墙，釉砖精美，丝毫无损。但是其他的房子却有红军攻克以前围城的痕迹。县政府的两层楼房已毁了一半，正面墙上弹痕累累。他们告诉我，这所房子和城外的其他房子都是红军开始围城时马鸿逵将军的守军毁坏的。敌人从城外房子撤出时都纵火焚毁，以免红军占领后作为攻城的阵地。

"县城攻克时，"徐海东后来告诉我，"实际上只打了一场小仗。我们包围封锁预旺堡10天。里面有马鸿逵的1旅骑兵和大约1,000民团。我们根本没有进攻，到第10天晚上天黑后，我们在城墙上放了云梯，有1连人爬了上去，这时敌人岗哨才发现。1架机枪守住云梯后，我们又有1团人爬了上去。

"没有发生什么战斗。天亮以前我们就把所有民团缴了械，包围了骑兵旅。我们的人只死了1个，伤了7个。我们给民团每人发1元银洋，遣返他们回家，给马鸿

I acknowledged the pleasure, wondering what it felt like to have a life worth that much to any one of your subordinates, and asked Hsu whether he was really serious about the invitation to visit his army. He was commander of the Fifteenth Red Army Corps, with headquarters then located about 80 *li* to the northwest, in Yu Wang *hsien*.

"I already have a room arranged for you in the bell tower," he responded. "Just let me know when you want to come, and I'll send an escort for you."

We made it a bargain on the spot.

And so a few days later, carrying a borrowed automatic (a "confiscation" of my own from a Red officer), I set out for Yu Wang, accompanied by ten Red troopers armed with rifles and Mausers—for in places our road skirted Red positions only a short distance behind the front lines. In contrast with the eternal hills and valleys of Shensi and Kansu, the road we followed—a road that led to the Great Wall and the lonely, beautiful grasslands of Inner Mongolia—crossed high tablelands, striped with long green meadows and dotted with tall bunch grass and softly rounded hills, on which great herds of sheep and goats grazed. Eagles and buzzards sometimes flew overhead. Once a herd of wild gazelles came near us, sniffed the air, and then swooped off with incredible speed and grace around a protecting mountainside.

In five hours we reached the center of Yu Wang, an ancient Mohammedan city of four or five hundred families, with a magnificent wall of stone and brick. Outside the city was a Mohammedan temple, with its own walls of beautiful glazed brick unscarred. But other buildings showed signs of the siege this city had undergone before it was taken by the Reds. A two-story building that had been the magistrate's headquarters was partly ruined, and its façade was pitted with bullet holes. I was told that this and other buildings on the outskirts had been destroyed by the defending troops of General Ma Hung-kuei when the Red siege had first begun. The enemy had withdrawn from all extramural buildings, after setting fire to them, to prevent the Reds' occupying them as positions of attack against the city walls.

"When the city fell," Hsu Hai-tung told me, "there was only a very minor battle. We surrounded and blockaded Yu Wang for ten days. Inside there was one brigade of Ma Hung-kuei's cavalry and about 1,000 *min-t'uan*. We made no attack at all until the tenth night. It was very dark. We put a ladder on the wall, a company scaled it before the enemy guards discovered it, and then they defended the ladder with a machine gun, while a regiment of our troops mounted the wall.

"There was little fighting. Before dawn we had disarmed all the *min-t'uan* and surrounded the brigade of cavalry. Only one of our men was killed, and only seven were wounded. We gave the *min-t'uan* a dollar apiece and sent them back to their farms, and we gave

遂的部下每人两元。他们有好几百人不愿走，参加了我军。县长和旅长在他们部下缴械时爬东墙逃走了。"

我在十五军团呆了5天，发现时时刻刻全都是极为有意思的。[1] 而对于我这个"红区调查员"——他们在预旺堡是这样叫我的——来说，所有这些事情，没有比徐海东本人的故事是更好的材料了。每天晚上他完成工作以后，我就同他谈话。我骑了马同他一起去七十三师前线，我同他一起去红军剧社看演出。他第一次告诉我关于鄂豫皖苏维埃共和国的历史，这在以前还从来没有为外人充分知道过。那个苏区在面积上仅次于江西中央苏区，作为这个广大地区的第一支游击队的组织者，徐海东对它的发展详情，几乎无不了若指掌。

徐海东给我的印象是我所遇到的共产党领袖中"阶级意识"最强的一个人——不论在态度上、外表上、谈吐上和背景上都是如此，事实上，除了贺龙以外，他大概是指挥员中唯一的"纯无产阶级"。虽然红军中的大多数下级军官出身于无产阶级，有许多高级指挥员出身于中产阶级或中农家庭，甚至出身于知识分子。

徐海东是个明显的例外。他对自己的无产阶级出身很为自豪，他常常笑着称自己是个"苦力"。你可以看出来，他真心真意地认为，中国的穷人，农民和工人，都是好人——善良、勇敢、无私、诚实——而有钱人则什么坏事都干尽了。我觉得，他就是认为问题是那么简单：他要为消灭这一切坏事而奋斗。这种绝对的信念使他对自己的大胆无畏，对他的部队的优势所说的自豪的话，听起来不至于使人有狂妄自大的感觉。他说，"1个红军抵得上5个白军，"你可以看出，在他看来，他这话不过是说明一个无可辩驳的事实。

他的自豪的热情未免有点幼稚天真，但是极其真诚，他的部下对他的拥戴的秘密也许就在这里。他对自己的部队极感自豪——不论他们是作为个人，还是作为战士、骑兵、革命者的能力。他对他们的列宁俱乐部，他们的艺术化的招贴——的确很好——都感到很自豪。他对他的几个师长——其中两个"像我一样是苦力"出身，一个只有21岁，当红军却有6年了——也很感到自豪。

徐海东很重视能够表现身体强壮的事，他打仗10年，负伤8次，因此行动稍有不便，使他感到很遗憾。他烟酒不沾，身材仍很修长，四肢灵活，全身肌肉发达。

---

1. 在这里十五军团政治部主任王首道跟我讲了他的身世。

Ma's men two dollars each. Several hundred of them stayed and enlisted with us. The magistrate and the brigade commander escaped over the east wall while their troops were being disarmed."

I spent five days with the Fifteenth Army Corps, and found every waking hour intensely interesting.[1] And of it all nothing was better material, for an "investigator of the soviet regions," as I was labeled in Yu Wang, than the story of Hsu Hai-tung himself. I talked with him every night when his duties were finished. I rode with him to the front lines of the Seventy-third Division, and I went to the Red theater with him. He told me for the first time the history of the Honan-Anhui-Hupeh Soviet Republic, which had never been fully known. As organizer of the first partisan army of that great Red area, which was second in size only to the Central Soviets of Kiangsi, Hsu Hai-tung knew nearly every detail of its development.

Hsu struck me as the most strongly "class-conscious" man—in manner, appearance, conversation, and background—of all the Red leaders I met. While the majority of the subordinate officers were from the poor peasantry, many of the higher commanders were from middle-class or middle-peasant families or from the intelligentsia.

Hsu was a very obvious exception. He was proud of his proletarian origin, and he often referred to himself, with a grin, as a "coolie." One could tell he sincerely believed that the poor of China, the peasants and the workers, were the good people—kind, brave, unselfish, honest—while the rich had a monopoly of all the vices. It was as simple as that for him, I thought: he was fighting to get rid of the vices. The absolutism of faith kept his cocky comments about his own daredeviltry and his army's superiority from sounding like vanity and conceit. When he said, "One Red is worth five Whites," it was to him a statement of irrefutable fact.

He was immensely proud of his army—the men as individuals, their skill as soldiers, as horsemen, and as revolutionaries. He was proud of their Lenin clubs and their artistically made posters—which were really very good. And he was proud of his division commanders, two of whom were "coolies like myself" and one of whom—a Red for six years—was only twenty-one years old.

Hsu valued very highly any act of physical prowess, and it was his regret that eight wounds he had collected in ten years of fighting now slightly handicapped him. He did not smoke or drink, and he still had a slender, straight-limbed body, every inch of which

---

1. Here Wang Shuo-tao, chief of the political department of the Fifteenth Army Corps, told me something of his personal history.

他的每条腿、每条胳膊、他的胸口、肩膀、屁股都受过伤。有一颗子弹从他眼下穿过他的脑袋又从耳后穿出。但他仍给你一个农村青年的印象，好像刚从水稻田里上来，放下卷起的裤腿，参加了一队路过的"志愿参加"的战士的队伍。

我也打听清楚了门牙是怎么掉的。那是在骑马失事时碰掉的。有一天他骑马在路上驰骋，马蹄碰了一个战士，徐海东拉紧缰绳想看看那个战士有没有受伤。马一受惊，把他撞在一棵树上。两个星期后他苏醒过来时，发现他的门牙已嵌在那棵树上了。

"你不怕有一天会受伤吗？"我问他。

"不怎么怕，"他笑道。"我从小就挨打，现在已经习惯了。"

事实上，他的童年生活足以说明他今天为什么成了一个革命者。我向他问到他的生平，要套出他的回答来很费力，因为像所有的红军一样，他只肯谈打仗。我从记下的几百字的笔记中，选出少数一些重要事实在这里。

徐海东于1900年生于汉口附近的黄陂县。他的家庭世世代代都是做窑工的，祖父一代曾经置过地，但由于旱灾、水灾、捐税，后来就赤贫化了。他的父亲和5个哥哥在黄陂的一个窑里做工，仅可糊口。他们都是文盲，但因海东聪明，又是幼子，所以凑钱送他上了学校。

"我的同学几乎全是地主或商人的子弟，"徐海东告诉我说，"因为穷人的孩子很少有上学的。我同他们一起在一张桌子上念书，但是他们很多人都讨厌我，因为我很少有鞋穿，衣服又破烂。他们骂我时我忍不住要同他们打架。如果我跑到先生那里告状，他总是打我。但是如果地主的子弟打输了，他们去先生那里告状，打的又是我！

"我上学第4年。也就是11岁那年，参加了一场'富人打穷人'的吵架，一群'富家子弟'把我逼到墙角里。我们当时扔着棍棒和石头，我扔出去的一块石头打破了一个姓黄的孩子的脑袋，他是个有钱地主的儿子。那孩子哭着走了，不久又带着他家里的人回来。他老子说我'忘了生辰八字'，对我拳打脚踢。先生又打了我一顿。我就逃学不肯再去。这件事对我印象很深。我从此相信，穷人的孩子是得不到公平的。"

seemed to be hard muscle. He had been wounded in each leg, in each arm, in the chest, a shoulder, and a hip. One bullet had entered his head just below the eye and emerged behind his ear. And yet he still gave the impression of a peasant youth who had but recently stepped out of the rice fields, rolled down his trouser legs, and joined a passing "free company" of warriors.

I found out also about the missing teeth. They had been lost during a riding accident. Galloping along the road one day, his horse's hoof struck a soldier, and Hsu turned in the saddle to see whether he had been hurt. The horse shied and knocked Hsu into a tree. When he regained consciousness two weeks later, it was to discover that his upper incisors had been left with the tree.

"Aren't you afraid you'll be hurt some day?" I asked him.

"Not much," he laughed. "I've been taking beatings since I was a child, and I'm used to it by now."

Like most other combat Reds, he spoke mainly about battles, but his few references to his childhood seemed to me significant.

Hsu Hai-tung was born in 1900 in Huangpi *hsien*—Yellow Slope county-near Hankow. His family had for generations been potters, and in his grandfather's day had owned land, but since then, through drought, flood, and taxation, had been proletarianized. His father and five brothers had worked in a kiln at Huangpi and made enough to live. They were all illiterate, but ambitious for Hai-tung, a bright child and the youngest son, and they scraped together the money necessary to send him to school.

"My fellow students," Hsu told me, "were nearly all the sons of landlords or merchants, as few poor boys ever got to school. I studied at the same desks with them, but many hated me because I seldom had any shoes and my clothes were poor and ragged. I could not avoid fighting with them when they cursed me. If I ran to the teacher for help, I was invariably beaten by him. But if the landlords' sons got the worst of it and went to the teacher, I was also beaten.

"In my fourth year in school, when I was eleven, I got involved in a 'rich-against-poor' quarrel and was driven to a corner by a crowd of 'rich sons.' We were throwing sticks and stones, and one I threw cut the head of a child named Huang, son of a wealthy landlord. This boy went off crying, and in a short time returned with his family. The elder Huang said that I had 'forgotten my birth,' and he kicked and beat me. The teacher then gave me a second beating. After that I ran away from school and refused to return. The incident made a deep impression on me. I believed from then on that it was impossible for a poor boy to get justice."

徐海东就到窑厂去当学徒，在"谢师的几年"里没有工资。他16岁满师，在300个工人中工资最高。他微笑着吹嘘说，"我做窑坯又快又好，全中国没有人能赶得上，因此革命胜利后，我仍是个有用的公民！"

他回忆起一件事件，使他更恨地主豪绅："一个戏班子到我们附近来唱戏，工人们都去看戏了。豪绅官僚的太太也在那里看戏。工人们自然很好奇，要想看看这些阔老的足不出户的老婆到底是什么模样，因此就盯着包厢瞧。阔老们就命令民团把他们赶出戏园子，结果就打了起来。后来我们厂主不得不设宴请得罪的'贵人'吃饭，放鞭炮为那些被人偷看过的女人'清白受玷'赔礼道歉。厂主想从我们工资中扣钱来办酒席，我们表示要罢工反对，他这才作罢。这是我第一次体会到组织起来的力量是穷人自己的武器。"

徐海东21岁的时候因家庭纠纷一怒离家出走。他步行到了汉口，接着又到了江西，做了一年窑工，攒了钱，打算回黄陂。但是他得了霍乱，等养好身体，积蓄也花光了。空手回家不好看，他就参加了军队，他们答应他每月10元军饷，得到的就只是"挨打"。这时国民革命在南方开始，共产党在徐海东所属军队中进行宣传。他们有好几个给砍了头，却使他关心起来。他对军阀的军队感到厌恶，和一个军官一起开了小差，逃到广州，参加了张发奎将军的国民党第四军，一直呆到1927年。他当了排长。

1927年春，国民党军队分成左翼和右翼两派，这个冲突在张发奎的部队里特别尖锐，这时这支部队已到了长江流域。徐海东站在激进派一边，不得不逃亡，他偷偷地回到了黄陂。这时他在一些学生的宣传影响下已成了共产党员，他在黄陂就立即开始建立党支部。

1927年4月发生右派政变，共产党被迫转入地下。但徐海东却没有，他单独得出结论，觉得采取独立行动的时机已经成熟。他把窑厂的工人几乎都组织了起来，还有一些当地农民。从这些人中他组织起湖北省的第一支"工农军队"。他们开始时只有17个人，1支手枪，8发子弹——那都是徐海东自己的。

这就是后来发展成为有6万人的红四方面军的核心，到1932年在它的控制下的苏区有爱尔兰那么大。它有自己的邮局、信贷系统、铸币厂、合作社、纺织厂，还

Hsu became an apprentice in a pottery, where he received no wages during his "thanking-the-master years." At sixteen he was a full journey-man, and the highest-paid potter among three hundred workers. "I can turn out a good piece of pottery as fast as anyone in China," Hsu smilingly boasted, "so when the revolution is over I'll still be a useful citizen!"

He recalled an incident that did not increase his love for the gentry: "A traveling theatrical troupe came to our neighborhood, and the workers went to see it. Wives of the gentry and officials were also there. Naturally the workers were curious to see what these closely guarded wives of the great ones looked like, and they kept staring into the boxes. At this the gentry ordered the *min-t'uan* to drive them out of the theater, and there was a fight. Later on our factory master had to give a banquet for the offended 'nobility,' and shoot off some firecrackers, to compensate for the 'spoiled purity' of those women who had been gazed upon by the people. The master tried to take the money for this banquet from our wages, but we threatened to strike and he changed his mind. This was my first experience of the power of organization as a weapon of defense for the poor."

When he was twenty-one, angered by a domestic quarrel, Hsu left home. He walked to Hankow, then made his way to Kiangsi, where he worked for a year as a potter, saved his money, and planned to return to Huangpi. But he caught cholera and exhausted his savings while recovering. Ashamed to return empty-handed, he joined the army, where he was promised $10 a month. He received "only beatings." Meanwhile the Nationalist Revolution was beginning in the South, and Communists were propagandizing in Hsu's army. Several of them were beheaded. Disgusted with the warlord army, he deserted with one of the officers, fled to Canton, and joined the Fourth Kuomintang Army under Chang Fa-kuei. There he remained till 1927. He had become a platoon commander.

In the spring of 1927 the Nationalist forces were breaking into left-wing and right-wing groups, and this conflict was especially sharp in Chang Fa-kuei's army, which had reached the Yangtze River. Siding with the radicals, Hsu was forced to flee, and secretly he returned to Yellow Slope. By now he had become a Communist, having been much influenced by some student propagandists, and in Huangpi he at once began building up a local branch of the Party.

The Right *coup d'état* occurred in April, 1927, and communism was driven underground. But not Hsu Hai-tung. He organized most of the workers' in the potteries, and some local peasants. From these he now recruited the first "workers' and peasants' army" of Hupeh. They numbered in the beginning only seventeen men, and they had one revolver and eight bullets—Hsu's own.

This was the nucleus of what later became the Fourth Front Red Army of 60,000 men, which in 1932 had under its control a sovietized territory the size of Ireland. It had its own post office, credit system, mints, cooperatives, textile factories, and in general a

有总的来说组织得相当完善的农村经济，在一个民选的政府领导之下。黄埔军校毕业生、前国民党军官徐向前成了四方面军司令。莫斯科回来的留学生、1917年中国新文化运动的伟大领袖之一张国焘任政府主席。

像江西一样，这个鄂豫皖红色共和国经受住了南京方面的头四次"围剿"，在这个过程中反而加强了自己。也像江西一样，在第五次"围剿"中，同样的战略和战术迫使四方面军主力最后作"战略后撤"，先到四川，后来又到了西北。

除了经济封锁、每天空袭，并且在鄂豫皖苏区周围建筑好几千个碉堡网以外，南京的将领们显然执行一种把红区老百姓几乎完全消灭的政策。他们最后终于认识到红军的唯一真正基础是在农民群众中间，因此着手有步骤地消灭老百姓。在第五次"围剿"中，湖北和安徽的反共部队共约30万人，由蒋介石派了在南昌和南京的军校中经一年反共宣传思想灌输的、受到法西斯训练的军官来加强。其结果是一场激烈程度不下于法西斯对西班牙的侵略的内战。

统治阶级的政权一旦受到威胁，它所进行的报复似乎到处都是采取同样野蛮的方式，不论种族或肤色。但是有些手法上的不同，却颇有启发意义，这里不妨花一些篇幅来说明一下这在中国是怎样进行的。

fairly well-organized rural economy. Hsu Hsiang-ch'ien, a Whampoa graduate and former Kuomintang officer, became commander-in-chief of the Fourth Army. His political leader was Chang Kuo-t'ao (a founder of the Communist Party who was later to challenge Mao for control of the Central Committee). Together they set up a Chinese type of soviet government in the border areas of three provinces: Hupeh, Anhui, and Honan. The ancient names of those provinces were O, Yu, and Wan. Combining them, the Reds named their interprovincial regime the Oyuwan Soviet and affiliated it with the All-China Soviet Government headed by Mao Tse-tung south of the Yangtze.

Oyuwan withstood several "surroundings" and expanded its territory until October, 1932. By then the Nationalists had succeeded in penetrating far into the richest base area. To avoid encirclement, Chang Kuo-t'ao and Hsu Hsiang-ch'ien withdrew their main forces westward. Hsu Hai-tung was ordered to remain behind, with his Twenty-fifth Army, to regroup scattered partisan units and make a new stand, while the main Nationalist forces pursued the Hsu Hsiang-ch'ien command. Unexpectedly, Hsu Hai-tung's guerrillas won important victories and once more the Nationalists were forced out of Oyuwan. In 1933 they returned to the offensive and in 1934, coincident with his Fifth Annihilation Campaign in the South, the Generalissimo strangled the little republic to death. At the end of 1934 Hsu Hai-tung led a band of no more than 2,000 men in a breakthrough to the west, finally uniting with Mao Tse-tung's forces in northern Shensi in 1935.

Besides the economic blockade, daily air bombing, and the construction of a network of thousands of small forts around the Oyuwan area, the Nanking generals evidently pursued a policy of systematic removal or annihilation of the civilian population. During the Fifth Campaign the anti-Red forces in Hupeh and Anhui, then numbering about 300,000, were stiffened with officers whom Chiang Kai-shek had spent a year indoctrinating with anti-Red propaganda in his Nanchang and Nanking military academies. The result was civil war with the intensity of religious wars.

二、　　中国的阶级战争

有 3 天之久，每天下午和晚上好几个钟头，我一直在向徐海东和他的部下提出关于他们的个人历史、他们的军队、前鄂豫皖苏区——共产党叫做鄂豫皖苏维埃共和国[1]——的斗争、他们目前在西北的情况等等的问题。后来我问了一个问题："你家里的人现在哪里？"徐海东若无其事地回答："我家的人全都给杀了，只留下一个哥哥，他现在在四方面军。"

"你是说在打仗的时候打死的？"

"哦，不是！我的哥哥只有 3 个是红军。其余的都是汤恩伯和夏斗寅将军枪决的。国民党军官一共杀死了徐家 66 个人。"

"66 个人！"我几乎不相信自己的耳朵。

"是的，被杀的有我 27 个近亲，39 个远亲——黄陂县的人都姓徐。老老少少，男男女女，甚至婴孩都给杀了。姓徐的都给杀光了，除了我的妻子和 3 个在红军中的哥哥，还有我自己。后来两个哥哥又在作战时牺牲了。"

"你的妻子呢？"

"我不知道她的下落。1931 年白军占领黄陂县时她被俘。后来我听说她被卖给汉口附近的一个商人做小老婆。这是我逃出来的哥哥告诉我的，还有其他人被杀的事。在第五次'围剿'中，徐家有 13 个人逃出黄陂，到了礼山县。但是在那里都被逮捕了。男的被砍了头，女人小孩被枪决。"

---

1. 鄂、豫、皖是湖北、河南、安徽的古名。共产党把这 3 个名字连在一起称呼他们在这三省边区的地方苏维埃。

2   CLASS WAR IN CHINA

For three days, several hours every afternoon and evening, I had been asking Hsu Hai-tung and his staff questions about their personal histories, about their troops, about the fate of the Oyuwan Soviet Republic, and about their present situation in the Northwest. Then, in answer to my question, "Where is your family now?" Hsu Hai-tung replied matter-of-factly, "All of my clan have been killed except one brother, who is with the Fourth Front Army."

"You mean killed in fighting?"

"Oh, no; only three of my brothers were Reds. The rest of the clan were executed by Generals T'ang En-p'o and Hsia Tou-yin. Altogether the Kuomintang officers killed sixty-six members of the Hsu clan."

"Sixty-six!"

"Yes, twenty-seven of my near relatives were executed and thirty-nine distant relatives—everyone in Huangpi *hsien* named Hsu. Old and young men, women, children, and even babies were killed. The Hsu clan was wiped out, except my wife and three brothers in the Red Army, and myself. Two of my brothers were killed in battle later on."

"And your wife?"

"I don't know what happened to her. She was captured when the White troops occupied Huangpi in 1931. Afterwards I heard that she had been sold as a concubine to a merchant near Hankow. My brothers who escaped told me about that, and about the other killings. During the Fifth Campaign, thirteen of the Hsu clan escaped from Huangpi and fled to Lihsiang *hsien*, but were all arrested there. The men were beheaded; the women and children were shot."

徐海东看到我脸上吃惊的脸色，就惨然一笑。"这并没有什么特别的地方，"他说。"许多红军指挥员家里都发生了这样的事，只是我家损失最大而已。蒋介石下了命令。我的家乡被占领时，姓徐的一个也不能留下。"

我们就是这样开始谈阶级报复的。我在这里必须承认，要是能够把这个问题完全略而不谈，我只有更加乐意，因为不论在什么地方，搜集暴行故事都不是愉快的事。但是为了对红军表示公正起见，对于他们的敌人所采取的毁灭他们的方法，应该说几句话。10年来国民党一直对红区保持全面的新闻封锁，在全国到处散布"恐怖"宣传，把它自己的飞机和重炮所造成的生命与财产的破坏大都归咎于"共匪"，但事实上红军是根本没有这种武器的。因此偶尔有一次听一下共产党对国民党有什么说的，不是无益的事。

我一页又一页地写了许多同徐海东及其同志们的谈话的笔记，其中有国民党军队在鄂豫皖对老百姓所犯罪行的日期、地点以及详细情况。但是我无法重述我所听到的最残暴的罪行。这些罪行不仅无法形诸笔墨，而且（像西班牙每天发生的事件一样），在那些不知阶级战争中阶级仇恨的可怕深度的天真怀疑派听来，很可能是不可信的。

我们必须记住，现在大家都已知道，在第5次反共"围剿"中，国民党将领在许多地方下令要杀光全部老百姓。这被认为是军事上的必需，因为蒋总司令在一次演讲中谈到，凡是苏维埃政权久已确立的地方，"是分不清'赤匪'和老百姓的"。这种杀光的办法在鄂豫皖共和国执行得特别凶残，主要是因为有些负责"剿共"的国民党将领是本地人，是被共产党没收了土地的地主的儿子，因此报仇心切。在第五次"围剿"结束时，苏区人口减少了60万。

共产党在鄂豫皖的战术是在广大地区实行机动作战，每次"围剿"开始，他们的主力就撤出苏区，到敌人境内与敌交战。他们没有什么重要的战略根据地要防守，很容易从一个地方转移到另一个地方，试探、佯攻、分散敌人兵力，以及用其他方法取得战术上的有利条件。不过，这使得他们的"人力基地"完全暴露在外，但是在过去，国民党军队遇到他们占领下的苏区里和平营生的农民和市民，他们是不杀的。

在第五次"围剿"中，像在江西一样，采用了新的战术。南京军队不再在战场上与红军交战，而是集中兵力挺进，构筑碉堡，逐步深入红区，把红区边界内外的整块整块地方的全部人口，不是消灭殆尽，就是迁移一空。他们要把这样的地方化为阒无人烟的荒地，如果后来红军再度占领也再无法取得补给。南京终于充分懂得，

Hsu noticed the shocked look on my face and grinned mirthlessly. "That was nothing unusual," he said. "That happened to the clans of many Red officers, though mine had the biggest losses. Chiang Kai-shek had given an order that when my district was captured no one named Hsu should be left alive."

I wrote many pages of notes of conversations with Hsu and his comrades, notes of dates, places, and detailed accounts of outrages allegedly inflicted on civilians by Nationalist troops in Oyuwan. It would be pointless to repeat the details of the more horrendous crimes reported; like the tragic events in Spain of the same period, they would seem incredible to skeptics who read of them from afar. For the person who has not actually witnessed atrocities, all remains hearsay and suspect; to accept the degradation of any man by man injures our self-esteem. And even if the stories were true, were not the Reds themselves engaged in violence differing only in the choice of class victims? The Kuomintang press, however, had for years been telling only their side of the class-war story. To help fill in the picture for history it should not be unedifying to know what the leaders of this fundamentally "peasant revolution" (as Mao Tse-tung insisted it was) said of their fellow man and saw themselves as fighting against.

During the Fifth Anti-Red Campaign, as already noted, Nationalist officers gave orders in many areas to exterminate the civilian population. This was held to be militarily necessary because, as the Generalissimo remarked in one of his speeches, where the soviets had been long established "it was impossible to tell a Red bandit from a good citizen." The method appears to have been applied with singular savagery in the Oyuwan Republic, chiefly because some of the leading Kuomintang generals in charge of anti-Red operations were natives of that region, sons of landlords who had lost their land to the Reds, and hence had an insatiable desire for revenge. The population in the soviets had decreased by about 600,000 at the end of the Fifth Campaign.

Red tactics in Oyuwan had depended upon mobility over a wide territory, and at the beginning of every annihilation drive their main forces had moved out of the Red districts, to engage the enemy on its own ground. They had no important strategic bases to defend, and readily moved from place to place, to decoy, divert, distract, and otherwise gain maneuvering advantages. This left the periphery of their "human base" very much exposed, but in the past Kuomintang troops had not killed the farmers and townsmen whom they found peacefully pursuing their tasks in soviet areas they occupied.

In the Fifth Campaign, as in Kiangsi, new tactics were adopted. Instead of engaging the Red Army in the open field, the Nanking troops advanced in heavily concentrated units, behind extensive fortifications, bit by bit penetrating into Red territory, systematically either annihilating or transporting the entire population in wide areas inside and outside the Red borders. They sought to make of such districts a desolate, uninhabited wasteland,

农民才是红军的基地，这种基地必须毁灭。

成千上万的儿童被抓了起来，送到汉口和其他城市，卖去做"学徒"。成千上万的年轻姑娘和妇女被带去卖到工厂里去做包身工或者做妓女。她们在城市里被当作"灾区难民"或者"红军杀害的人家的孤儿"卖掉。我记得在1934年有成百上千的这样的人到了大工业城市，结果生意兴隆，中间商人都从国民党军官那里收购儿童和妇女。有一个时期，获利很大，几有影响部队军纪之势。外国教士纷纷议论此事，笃信基督教的将军蒋介石不得不严令禁止这样"纳贿"，凡从事这种交易的军人，一经发现，严惩不贷。

"到1933年12月，"徐海东说，"整个鄂豫皖有一半已成一片荒地。在这一度富饶的地方，留下房子极少，牛都被赶走，土地荒芜，白军占领的村子无不尸积成山。湖北有4个县，安徽有5个县，河南有3个县都几乎完全破坏。东西400里，南北300里之内，全部人口不是被杀光就是给迁空了。

"在那一年的战斗中，我们从白军手里夺回了一些这样的地方，但我们回来时发现原来是肥沃的大地现在几乎成了沙漠。只有少数老头儿、老太婆留下，他们说的情况叫我们大吃一惊。我们不能相信中国人对中国人会犯下这种罪行。

"我们在1933年11月撤出天台山和老君山，这两个苏区当时有6万人。两个月后我们回来时，我们发现这些农民已被没收土地，房屋被烧掉或炸坏了，整个地区只有不到300名老人和少数病儿。我们从他们那儿了解到了当时发生了什么情况。

"白军一开到，军官们就开始把妇女和姑娘分开。凡是剪短发或放脚的都当共产党枪决，剩下的由高级军官挑选好看的给自己留下，接着由下级军官挑选。剩下的就交给士兵当妓女。他们告诉士兵，这些都是'土匪家属'，因此可以爱怎么样就怎么样。

"这些地方许多青年都已参加了红军，但凡是有留下来未走的，都想杀死白军军官报仇，甚至一些老人也是这样。但是谁有抗议表示，谁就被当作共产党枪决。没死的人告诉我们，白军中间为了分女人发生争吵，打了起来的也不少。这些妇女

incapable of supporting the Red troops if they should later recapture it.

Thousands of children were taken prisoner and driven to Hankow and other cities, where they were sold into "apprenticeships." Thousands of young girls and women were transported and sold into the factories as slave girls and as prostitutes. In the cities they were palmed off as "famine refugees," or "orphans of people killed by the Reds." I remembered that hundreds of them reportedly reached the big industrial centers in 1934. A considerable trade grew up, with middlemen buying the boys and women from Kuomintang officers. It became a very profitable business for a while, but threatened to corrupt the ranks of the army. Missionaries began talking about it, and Chiang Kai-shek was obliged to issue a stern order forbidding this "bribetaking" and ordering strict punishment for officers engaged in the traffic.

"By December, 1933," said Hsu Hai-tung, "about half of Oyuwan had become a vast wasteland. Over a once rich country there were very few houses left standing, cattle had all been driven away, the fields were unkept, and there were piles of bodies in nearly every village that had been occupied by the White troops. Four counties in Hupeh, five in Anhui, and three in Honan were almost completely ruined. In an area some 400 *li* from east to west and about 300 *li* from north to south the whole population was being killed or removed.

"During the year's fighting we recaptured some of these districts from the White troops, but when we returned we found fertile lands had become semideserts. Only a few old men and women remained, and they would tell tales that horrified us. We could not believe such crimes had been committed by Chinese against Chinese.

"In November, 1933, we retreated from T'ien Tai Shan and Lao Chun Shan, soviet districts where there were then about 60,000 people. When we returned, two months later, we found that these peasants had been driven from their land, their houses had been burned or destroyed by bombing, and there were not more than three hundred old men and a few sickly children in all that region. From them we learned what had happened.

"As soon as the White troops arrived the officers had begun dividing the women and girls. Those with bobbed hair or natural feet had been shot as Communists. Higher officers had looked over the others and picked out pretty ones for their own, and then the lower officers had been given their choice. The rest had been turned over to the soldiers to use as prostitutes. They had been told that these women were 'bandit wives,' and therefore they could do what they liked with them.

"Many of the young men in those districts had joined the Red Army, but many of those who remained behind, and even some of the old men, tried to kill the White officers for these crimes. Those who protested were all shot as Communists. The survivors told us that many fights had occurred among the Whites, who had quarreled among themselves

和姑娘在遭到奸污后就送到城市里去卖掉，那些军官只留了少数长得好看的当小老婆。"

"你是说这都是国民政府的军队？"我问道。

"是的，他们是汤恩伯将军的十三集团军和王均将军的第三集团军。夏斗寅、梁冠英、孙殿才[1]将军也有责任。"

徐海东谈到另外一个县，湖北省的黄冈县，红军在1933年7月从王均将军手中收复："在句容集[2]镇上，原来一条街上苏维埃合作社生意兴隆、人民安居乐业，现在成了一片废墟，只有几个老人没死。他们领我们到一条山沟里，只见有17具年轻妇女的尸体，赤条条地在阳光中躺在那里。她们是在遭到强奸后被杀死的。白军显然是很匆忙；他们只有时间剥下一个姑娘的一条裤腿。那天我们开了一个大会，全军在那里举行了一次追悼大会，我们大家都哭了。

"不久之后，在麻城，我们到了我们以前的一个运动场。在一个埋得很浅的坟地里，我们找到了12个被杀同志的尸体。他们身上的皮给剥掉了，眼珠被挖了出来，耳朵、鼻子都给割掉。看到这个惨象，我们都气得哭了出来。

"同一个月，也在黄冈，我们的红二十五军到了欧公集。这本来是个兴旺的地方，现在却荒无人烟。我们在镇外走，看到一个农民的茅屋在冒烟，那是在山边上，我们就有几个人爬了上去，但是发现里面只有一个老人，他显然已经疯了。我们再走到山下，终于看到了长长的一堆男女尸体。一共有400多个，他们显然是刚被杀不久。有些地方血有几寸厚。有些妇女尸体旁边还有紧紧抱着她们的孩子。许多尸体都是摞在一起的。

"我突然看到有一具尸体还在动，过去一看，是个还活着的男人。后来我们发现有好几个还活着，一共有十多个。我们把他们抬了回来，包扎了他们的伤口，他们把发生的事情告诉了我们。这些人是从镇上逃出来躲到山沟里来的，在空地里露宿。后来白军军官带部队来，在山边上架起机关枪，对下面的人开火。他们开了几小时的枪，以为都打死了，便看也不下来看一眼又开走了。"

---

1. 经查证，"孙殿才"疑为"宋天才"。——编注
2. 经查证，"句容集"疑为"紫云寨"。——编注

about the distribution of women. After they had been despoiled, these women and girls were sent to the towns and cities, where they were sold, only the officers keeping a few pretty ones for concubines."

"Do you mean to say these were the troops of the National Government?" I asked.

"Yes, they were the Thirteenth Army Corps of General T'ang En-p'o, and the Third Army Corps of General Wang Chun. Generals Hsia Tou-yin, Liang Kuan-yin, and Sung T'ien-tsai were also responsible."

Hsu told of another district, Huangan *hsien*, in Hupeh, which the Reds recovered from General Wang Chun in July, 1933: "In the town of Tsu Yun Chai, where there was once a street of flourishing soviet cooperatives and a happy people, everything was in ruins and only a few old men were alive. They led us out to a valley and showed us the scattered bodies of seventeen young women lying half-naked in the sun. They had all been raped and killed. The White troops had evidently been in a great hurry; they had taken the time to pull off only one leg of a girl's trousers. That day we called a meeting, the army held a memorial service there, and we all wept.

"Not long afterwards, in Ma Cheng, we came to one of our former athletic fields. There in a shallow grave we found the bodies of twelve comrades who had been killed. Their skin had been stripped from them, their eyes gouged out, and their ears and noses cut off. We all broke into tears of rage at this barbaric sight.

"In the same month, also in Huangan, our Twenty-fifth Red Army reached Ao Kung Chai. This had once been a lively place, but it was now deserted. We walked outside the town and saw a peasant's hut with smoke coming from it, on a hillside, and some of us climbed up to it, but the only occupant was an old man who had apparently gone insane. We walked down into the valley again until we came upon a long pile of dead men and women. There were more than 400 bodies lying there, and they had evidently been killed only a short time before. In some places the blood was several inches deep. Some women were lying with their children still clutched to them. Many bodies were lying one on top of another.

"Suddenly I noticed one of the bodies move, and, going over to it, found that it was a man still alive. We found several more alive after that, altogether more than ten. We carried them back with us and treated their wounds, and they told us what had happened. These people had fled from the town to hide in this valley, and had encamped in the open. Afterwards the White officers had led their troops to the spot, ordered them to put up their machine guns on the mountainsides, and had them opened fire on the people below. They had kept firing for several hours until they thought everybody was dead. Then they had marched away again without even coming down to look at them."

徐海东说，第二天他带全军到山沟里，给他们看看死难的人，其中有些战士认出是他们认识的农民，这些男女有的曾经给他们找过住的地方，卖过瓜给他们，或者在合作社作过交易。他们看了极其难受。徐海东说，这次经历加强了他的部队的士气，使他们决心要死战到底，在这最后一次大"围剿"剩下的12个月当中，二十五军没有一个人开过小差。

"到第五次'围剿'结束时，"他继续说，"几乎家家户户都有死人。我们曾经进了一个村子，看上去似乎是空无一人，我们到烧毁的房子里一看，就会在门口、地上、炕上发现尸体，或者藏在什么地方。许多村里连狗都逃走了。在那些日子里，我们不需要情报员注意敌人动向。我们可以根据烧掉的村镇在天空里飘起来的烟，很容易地跟随他们。"

我从徐海东和别人那里所听到的事情，这不过是其中很小很小的部分。这些人在那可怕的一年中战斗过来，最后终于西撤，不是因为他们的军队，而是因为他们的人力"基地"被破坏了，青年人的尸积如山，血流成河，整个地方失去了活力。后来我又同许多鄂豫皖来的战士谈了话，他们告诉我的故事比这还惨。他们不愿再谈他们看到的惨景；他们只有在我追问的时候才说，很显然，他们的经历在他们的思想深处永远地留下了一生之中不可磨灭的阶级仇恨。

我们不免又要问，这是不是说共产党自己是清白的，没有干下什么暴行或阶级报复的事？我想不是。不错，在我同他们在一起的4个月中，我进行了不受限制的调查，就我由此所了解的情况而言，他们只杀了两个老百姓。我也没有看到过有一个村庄或市镇被他们焚毁，或者从我问到的许多农民那里听说红军喜欢纵火。但是我个人的经验从开始到结束只限于在西北同他们在一起的几个月，在其他地方可能干过什么"烧杀"的事，我可无法证实也无法否认。同时这些年来在国民党和外国报纸上发表的反共宣传，90%纯属胡说八道，如果对此不加怀疑，那就不免过于天真了，因为至少其中大部分是未经可靠证实的。

确切地说，上面提到的那两个倒霉的"反革命分子"，其中之一并不是共产党杀的，而是宁夏的一些回民，他们恨死了收税的。关于他怎么会不得好死，以后再说，这里先来看看，这些回民是怎样治理的，也许由此可以明白为什么要处决他的经济学上的原因了。

Hsu said that the next day he led his whole army out to that valley and showed them the dead, among whom some of the soldiers recognized peasants they had known, men and women who must have given them shelter at one time, or sold them melons, or traded at the cooperatives. They were deeply moved. Hsu said that this experience steeled his troops with a stubborn morale and a determination to die fighting, and that throughout the entire twelve months of the last great annihilation drive not a single man had deserted from the Twenty-fifth Army.

"Toward the end of the Fifth Campaign," he continued, "nearly every house had dead in it. We used to enter a village that seemed empty until we looked into the ruined houses. Then we would find corpses in the doorways, on the floor, or on the *k'ang*, or hidden away somewhere. Even the dogs had fled from many villages. In those days we did not need spies to watch the enemy's movements. We could follow them quite easily by the skies filled with smoke from burning towns and hamlets."

This was a very small part of what I heard from Hsu Hai-tung and others who fought through the terrible year, and finally trekked westward, not their army but its human "base" destroyed, its hills and valleys stained with the blood of its youth, the living heart of it torn out. Later on I talked to many warriors from Oyuwan, and they told tales more pitiful still. They did not like to talk of what they had seen; they did so only under questioning, and it was clear their experiences had permanently marked the matrix of their minds with a class hatred ineradicable for life.

Again one asked whether that meant that the Reds were innocent of atrocity and class revenge themselves. I thought not. It was true that during my four months with them, as far as I could learn from unrestricted but limited inquiry, they had executed but two civilians. It was also true that I did not see a single village or town burned by them, or hear, from the many farmers I questioned, that the Reds were addicted to arson. But my personal experience started and ended with the few months spent with them in the Northwest: what "killing and burning" might have been done elsewhere I could not affirm or deny.

One of the two ill-fated "counterrevolutionaries" mentioned above was not killed by the Reds, but by some Ninghsia Moslems with a strong distaste for tax collectors. Further on it will be told in what manner he met his demise, but first let us see how these Moslems had been ruled.

三、 四大马

我们可以说，青海、宁夏和甘肃北部就是斯威夫特[1]那部幻想小说的雏形，那个胡乙姆[2]的国土，因为这些省份就是作为中国名闻遐迩的四大马的封疆来统治的。在上述这个地区里，权力由一家姓马的回民将领家庭分享——马鸿逵、马鸿宾、马步芳、马步青，或者应该说是在共产党开始把"胡乙姆"挤出他们大块领域之前曾由他们分享。

马鸿逵是宁夏省省主席，他的堂兄弟马鸿宾原来是该省省主席，现在割据甘肃北部一块地盘不稳的地方。他们同马步芳是远亲，后者是著名回族领袖马克勤[3]的儿子，有妻妾多人。马步芳承继他父亲的衣钵，1937年南京任命他为该省绥靖公署主任，他的兄弟马步青则占青海，此外还统治着夹在宁夏和青海之间的甘肃西部的一个狭长地带。10年来，这个边远之地就由马家像一个中世纪的苏丹国一样统治着，从他们自己的阿拉真主那里得到一些帮助。

以马鸿逵为例，他大概是四大马中最有钱有势的一个。他有许多妻妾，据说宁夏城里60%的财产是他的，并且在鸦片、盐、皮毛、捐税、自印纸币方面发了一笔大财。但是，在一个意义上来说，他还是够新派的，那就是他最近选他有名的"照片新娘"的时候。他从上海雇来一个秘书，叫他收集受过教育的合格美女照片，从中选美。价格定在5万元。老马选定了以后就包了一架飞机，在北国的尘土中起飞，到苏州接了后宫新欢，一个基督教的东吴大学毕业生，然后又飞回宁夏，像阿拉丁在他的飞行地毯上一样，引起一时轰动。

---

1. 英国作家（1667—1745），《格利佛游记》作者。——译注
2. 《格利佛游记》中的有人性的马国，"胡乙姆"取英语"马嘶"（Whinny）一词的谐音。——译注
3. 经查证，"马克勤"疑为"马阁臣"。——编注

3   Four Great Horses

One might say that Chinghai, Ninghsia, and northern Kansu were the prototype of that fantasia of Swift's, the land of the Houyhnhnms, for they were ruled as the satrapy of Four Great Horses whose fame was widespread in China. Over the areas mentioned power was divided (before the Reds began edging the Houyhnhnms out of considerable portions of their domain) by a family of Mohammedan generals named Ma—the Messrs. Ma Hung-kuei, Ma Hung-ping, Ma Pu-fang, and Ma Pu-ch'ing. And this particular *Ma* means *horse*.

Ma Hung-kuei was governor of Ninghsia, and his cousin, Ma Hung-ping, former governor of the same province, was now ruler of a shifting fiefdom in northern Kansu. They were distantly related to Ma Pu-fang, many-wived son of the famous Mohammedan leader Ma Keh-chin. Ma Pu-fang inherited his father's toga and in 1937 became the Nanking-appointed Pacification Commissioner of that province, while his brother, Ma Pu-ch'ing, helped out in Chinghai and in addition ruled the great Kansu panhandle which in the west separated Chinghai from Ninghsia. For a decade this distant country had been run like a medieval sultanate by the Ma family, with some assistance from an Allah of their own.

Take Ma Hung-kuei, probably the richest and strongest of the quartet. He had numerous wives, was said to own about 60 per cent of the property of Ninghsia city, and had made a fortune in millions from opium, salt, furs, taxes, and his own paper currency. Still, he proved himself modern enough in one sense when he chose his famous "picture bride." Importing a secretary from Shanghai, he had him gather photographs of eligible educated beauties and made his choice. The price was fixed at $50,000. Old Ma hired an airplane, flew out of the northern dust clouds to Soochow, where he swooped up the latest addition to his harem—a graduate of Soochow Christian University—and then swept back again to Ninghsia like an Aladdin on his carpet, amid a blaze of publicity. That news was well reported by the Kuomintang press at the time, as were some of the "death and taxes" data mentioned below.

对一个西方人来说，这也许是很吸引人的。但是马鸿逵的农民或者士兵是否能够充分欣赏这件事的浪漫情调，则很可怀疑，因为农民们知道这5万元从何而来，士兵们也觉得奇怪，既然大马能够出巨资买个基督教徒做新娘，为什么开不出他们的军饷。不到几个月后红军向西挺进，打入宁夏南部和甘肃北部马鸿逵的地盘时，马都很少抵抗，尽管他吹嘘他们要歼灭"匪军"，这就一点也不奇怪了。这是完全有道理的。

这里我不想开列统计表格，但宁夏发表一项政府公报，其中一篇有意义的文章[1]值得一提，它开列了马将军在该省要征收的捐税：销售税、家畜税、骆驼税、运盐税、用盐税、烟灯税、养羊税、商人税、脚夫税、养鸽税、土地税、捐客税、粮食税、特别粮食税、附加土地税、木材税、采煤税、皮税、屠宰税、船税、灌溉税、磨石税、房屋税、磨面税、秤税、礼仪税、烟税、酒税、印花税、婚税、蔬菜税。这张单子还没有囊括所有的苛捐杂税，但足以说明，对比之下人民对共产党是没有什么可以害怕的。

马鸿逵的食盐专运专销办法可谓举世无双。盐不仅专卖，而且规定每人每月必须买半磅，不管用得了用不了。买了不能转卖；私自买卖食盐要处以鞭笞，或者甚至处死。其他措施使人民不满的还有出售牛、羊、骡要征30%的税，养羊1头要征25%的税，杀猪1头征税1元，卖麦子1石征税4角。

但是最令人强烈不满的措施，也许是马将军的征兵了。他共有军队4万（加上马鸿宾的），还有数目不限的守城门的"门卫"。这些人几乎都是强征而来。每个人家凡有儿子的都要当兵，否则就雇人代替，价格已上涨到150元。穷人可以到当铺去借钱，年息40%到60%，而这些当铺都是四马之一开的。当兵的不仅没有军饷，而且得自供衣食。显然马鸿逵除了在新娘身上以外，什么地方都不乱花钱的。

苛捐杂税和欠债累累迫使许多农民卖牛卖田。大批大批的土地被官僚、税吏、债主以廉价收购，但大部分都弃置荒废，因为捐税和地租太重，找不到佃户耕种。土地、牲畜、资本加速集中，雇农人数猛增。在一个县进行了调查[2]后发现，70%的农民欠债，60%的农民靠借粮糊口。在同一县内，据说5%的人有地100到200亩，骆驼20到50头，牛20到40头，马5到10头，大车5到10辆，贸易资金1,000到2,000元，而60%的人口有地不到15亩，除一两头毛驴外没有别的牲口，平均

---

1. 《宁夏公报》（1934年12月宁夏市）。
2. 刘晓：《预旺县调查》，刊《党的工作》（1936年8月3日保安）。这项调查是由共产党人进行的，当然不会没有偏见，但是大体情况在斯坦普尔提交给国联的调查报告中还是得到了印证，该报告在前文中有所提及。

A government bulletin published in Ninghsia listed the following taxes collected in that province by General Ma: sales, domestic animals, camels, salt carrying, salt consumption, opium lamps, sheep, merchants, porters, pigeons, land, middlemen, food, special food, additional land, wood, coal, skins, slaughter, boats, irrigation, millstones, houses, milling, scales, ceremonies, tobacco, wine, stamp, marriage, and vegetables.[1] While this did not exhaust the inventory of petty taxes collected, it was enough to suggest that people had relatively little to fear from the Reds.

Ma Hung-kuei's method of salt distribution was unique. Salt was not only a monopoly, every person was required to buy half a pound per month, whether he could use it or not. He was not allowed to resell; private trade in salt was punishable by whipping or (according to Mohammedan Reds) even death. Other measures against which the inhabitants protested were the collection of a 30-per-cent tax on the sale of a sheep, cow, or mule, a 25-cent tax on the ownership of a sheep, a dollar tax for the slaughter of a pig, and a 40-cent tax on the sale of a bushel of wheat.

Excessive taxation and indebtedness had forced many farmers to sell all their cattle and abandon their lands. Great areas had been bought up by officials, tax collectors, and lenders at very cheap rates, but much of it remained wasteland because no tenants could be found to work under the tax burden and rents imposed. The concentration of land, cattle, and capital was accelerating and there was a big increase in hired farm laborers. In one district investigated it was found that over 70 per cent of the farmers were in debt, and about 60 per cent were living on food bought on credit.[2] In the same district 5 per cent of the people reportedly owned from 100 to 200 *mou* of land, twenty to fifty camels, twenty to forty cows, five to ten horses, five to ten carts, and had from $1,000 to $2,000 in trading capital, while at the same time about 60 per cent of the population had less than 15 *mou* of land, no livestock other than one or two donkeys, and an average

---

1. *Ninghsia Kung Pao* (Ninghsia city, December, 1934).
2. Liu Hsiao, "A Survey of Yu Wang Hsien," *Tang-ti Kung-Tso* (Pao An), August 3, 1936. This was a Communist and certainly not disinterested source, but the picture in general was supported by studies included in the Stampar report for the League of Nations, to which earlier reference was made.

欠债35元和366磅粮食——比他们的土地价值高得多。

最后，马鸿逵有阴谋争取日本支持反共的嫌疑。宁夏城里已有日本军事代表团，马鸿逵将军允许他们在城北修一个机场，那是在蒙古族的阿拉善旗境内。[1] 有些回民和蒙民担心日本真的武装进驻。

要是红军到达时情况不是这样，他们在回民中间是否能打开局面也是可以怀疑的。但是马鸿逵的军队根本不想打仗，抵抗起来只有5%的人才有什么好处。但是共产党仍需克服回民不愿与汉人合作的心理，向他们提出一个合适的纲领。对此，共产党在进行艰巨努力，因为回民地区的战略重要性是显而易见的。西北的这个宽阔地带控制着通向新疆和外蒙古的大道——也控制着同苏俄发生直接联系的大道。按共产党自己的看法：

> 西北有1,000多万回民，具有极为重要的地位。我们目前的任务和责任是要保卫西北，在这五省内建立抗日根据地，使得我们能够更加有力地领导全国的抗日运动，为争取立即与日本作战而努力。同时，随着形势的发展，我们可以与苏联和外蒙取得联系。但是如果我们不能把回民争取到我们的势力范围和抗日统一战线上来，我们的任务就不可能实现。[2]

共产党在好几年以前就在西北对回民进行工作了。早在1936年，红军经过宁夏和甘肃向黄河挺进，年轻的回民先遣人员就已在宁夏部队中进行宣传，鼓动推翻"国民党走狗"和"伊斯兰教叛徒"马鸿逵——他们有几个人为此而掉了脑袋。共产党向他们提出的诺言是：

取消一切苛捐杂税。

协助成立回民自治政府。

取缔征兵。

---

1. 日本后来被迫放弃其代表团和机场。1937年，马氏兄弟宣誓效忠中央政府。
2. 《连队讨论材料》：《回民问题》，第2页，一军团政治部，1936年6月2日。

indebtedness of $35 and 366 pounds of grain—much more than the average value of their land.

According to the Communist press, Ma Hung-kuei was suspected of intriguing for Japanese support against the Reds. A Japanese military mission had been established in Ninghsia city, and General Ma had given them permission to build an airfield north of the city, in the Alashan Mongol territory.[1] Some of the Moslems and Mongols feared an actual armed Japanese invasion.

Such was the picture, as the Reds saw it, which encouraged them to believe that they could "stir up a great wind" that could bring the Ma brothers' empire toppling in ruins. Ma's troops might have had little interest in fighting, but it still remained for the Communists to overcome the Moslems' aversion to cooperating with Chinese, and to offer them a suitable program. This the Reds were trying hard to do, for the strategic significance of the Mohammedan areas was manifest. They occupied a wide belt in the Northwest which dominated the roads to Sinkiang and Outer Mongolia—and direct contact with Soviet Russia. As the Communists themselves saw it:

> *There are more than ten million Mohammedans in the Northwest occupying an extremely important position. Our present mission and responsibility is to defend the Northwest and to create an anti-Japanese base in these five provinces, so that we can more powerfully lead the anti-Japanese movement of the whole country and work for an immediate war against Japan. At the same time, in the development of our situation we can get into connection with the Soviet Union and Outer Mongolia. However, it would be impossible to carry out our mission if we failed to win over the Mohammedans to our sphere and to the anti-Japanese front.[2]*

Communist work among the Mohammedans had begun several years before in the Northwest. Early in 1936, when the Red Army moved across Ninghsia and Kansu toward the Yellow River, vanguards of young Moslems were already propagandizing among the Ninghsia troops, urging the overthrow of the "Kuomintang running-dog" and "traitor to Mohammedanism," Ma Hung-kuei—and some had lost their heads for it. These were the main promises the Reds made to them:

To abolish all surtaxes.

To help form an autonomous Mohammedan government.

To prohibit conscription.

---

1. The Japanese were later forced to abandon both their mission and their airfield. In 1937 the Mas pledged their loyalty to the Central Government.
2. *Company Discussion Materials*: "The Mohammedan Problem," p. 2, First Army Corps, Pol. Dept., June 2, 1936.

取消欠债。

保护回族文化。

保证各派宗教自由。

协助创建和武装回民抗日军。

这对几乎每一个回民大概都是有一些吸引力的。甚至有些阿訇也认为这是除掉马鸿逵的一个机会（因为他放火烧掉了老教和新教的清真寺）。到 5 月份，共产党说他们已经完成了怀疑派认为办不到的事。他们自称已经创立了中国回民红军的核心。

To cancel old debts and loans.

To protect Mohammedan culture.

To guarantee religious freedom of all sects.

To help create and arm an anti-Japanese Mohammedan army.

To help unite the Mohammedans of China, Outer Mongolia, Sinkiang, and Soviet Russia.

Here, presumably, was something to appeal to nearly every Moslem. Even some of the *ahuns* reportedly saw in it an opportunity to get rid of Ma Hung-kuei (punishing him for burning the mosques of the Old and New schools), and also a chance to realize an old aspiration—to re-establish direct contact with Turkey through Central Asia. By May, the Communists were claiming that they had achieved what skeptics had said was impossible. They boasted that they had created the nucleus of a Chinese Moslem Red Army.

四、　　穆斯林和马克思主义者

　　一天早上，我同徐海东参谋部里一个能说英语的参谋人员去访问十五军团所属的回民教导团。该团驻扎在一个回民商人和做官的家里，这是一所墙头很厚的房子，摩尔式的窗户的外面是一条铺着石块的街道，驴、马、骆驼、行人络绎不绝。

　　房子里面很凉快、整洁。每间屋子里砖地中央是个水池，下通排水沟，供洗澡之用。虔诚的回民一天要洗5次澡，但是，这些战士虽然仍信伊斯兰教，显然只是偶尔使用这些水池。我想他们大概不相信把一件好事做过头。但是他们仍是我在中国看到的习惯最清洁的士兵，没有随地吐痰的恶习。

　　共产党在前线组织了两个回民教导团，基本上都是从前马鸿逵和马鸿宾的部队中来的。他们比汉人身材高大、结实、胡须深、肤色黑，有的人长得很英俊，明显地有突厥人的外表，杏眼又黑又大，高加索人种的特点很突出。他们都带着西北的大刀，熟练地给我表演了几下，能够一举手就砍下敌人的脑袋。

　　他们的营房里墙上贴满了漫画、招贴、地图、标语。"打倒马鸿逵！""废除马鸿逵的国民党政府！""反对日本造机场，绘地图，侵略宁夏！""建立回民独立政府！""建设自己的回民抗日红军！"共产党的一些回民拥护者就是靠这些主张招来的，回民战士在关于他们为什么参加红军问题上给我的答复也以此为他们的中心问题。

　　由此可见，马鸿逵将军部下士兵对他是有不满的（无疑有些被共产党夸大了），宁夏的农民似乎也是如此。我记得有一天早晨在路上向一个回民老乡买瓜，他种了一

4   MOSLEM AND MARXIST

One morning I went with an English-speaking member of Hsu Hai-tung's staff to visit the Moslem training regiment attached to the Fifteenth Army Corps. It was quartered in the compound of a Moslem merchant and official—a thick-walled edifice with Moorish windows looking down on a cobbled street through which filed donkeys, horses, camels, and men.

Inside, the place was cool and neatly kept. Every room had in the center of its brick floor a place for a cistern, connected to a subterranean drain, to be used for bathing. Properly orthodox Moslems showered themselves five times daily, but although these soldiers were still loyal to their faith and obviously made use of the cistern occasionally, I gathered that they did not believe in carrying a good thing to extremes. Still, they easily had the cleanest habits of any soldiers I had seen in China, and carefully refrained from the national gesture of spitting on the floor.

The Reds had organized two training regiments of Mohammedans at the front, both recruited largely from former troops of Ma Hung-kuei and Ma Hung-ping. They were taller and more strongly built than the Chinese, heavier of beard, and darker-skinned, with large black almond-shaped eyes and strong, sharp Caucasian features. They all carried the big sword of the Northwest, and gave a skillful demonstration of various strokes by which you can remove your enemy's head at one swift blow.

Cartoons, posters, maps, and slogans covered the walls of their barracks. "Down with Ma Hung-kuei!" "Abolish Ma Hung-kuei's Kuomintang Government!" "Oppose Japan's building of airfields, map making, and invasion of Ninghsia!" "Realize the Independent Government of the Mohammedan people!" "Build your own anti-Japanese Mohammedan Red Army!"

From this it may be gathered that there was some dissatisfaction with General Ma Hung-kuei among his soldiers, and this seemed to be shared by the Ninghsia peasants. I stopped on the road one morning to buy a melon from a Moslem farmer who had a whole hillside

山坡的瓜，是个态度和蔼的乡下佬，满面笑容，脾气随和，还有一个长得实在美丽的女儿——在这些地方这是十分不可多见的，因此我迟迟不走，买了3个瓜。我问他，马鸿逵手下做官的是不是真的像共产党所说的那么坏。他滑稽地举起双手表示气愤，一边嘴里吐着西瓜子。"哎呀！哎呀！哎呀！"他叫道。"马鸿逵，马鸿逵！征的税叫我们活不了，还抢我们的儿子，又烧又杀！妈的马鸿逵！"最后一句话的意思是你可以奸污马鸿逵的母亲，这还便宜了他。院子里的人看到这老头儿这么激动都笑了。

参加红军的回民战士原来都是在马鸿逵军队中进行颠覆宣传所争取过来的，也是他们投到红军阵营以后听的政治课所争取过来的。我问一个指挥员他为什么参加红军。

"为了打马鸿逵，"他说，"在马鸿逵统治下，我们回民的生活太苦了。没有一家是安全的。如果一家有两个儿子，一个儿子必须到他那里去当兵。如果有3个儿子，两个儿子必须去当兵。没有出路——除非你有钱，可以买替身。哪个穷人出得起？不仅如此，每个人还需自己带衣服，家里给他付粮食、柴火、灯油钱。一年要花好几十元钱。"

这两团回民红军组织起来才不到半年，看来已经有了相当的"阶级觉悟"。他们读了，或者听人家读了《共产党宣言》，《阶级斗争》的简单介绍，每天关于回民当前问题的马克思主义观点的政治课。这些课不是汉人给他们上的，而是共产党中回民党员给他们上的，后者上过共产党的党校。马鸿逵部队90%是文盲，参加红军的回民在刚来时一字不识。现在他们每人已识几百个字，能够学发给他们的简单的课本。共产党希望这两团人中能培养出一支大规模的回民红军的干部，来保卫他们梦寐以求要想在西北建立的回民自治共和国。这些回民中已有将近25%的人参加了共产党。

关于自治的口号，回民自然是会同意的；因为那是他们多年来的要求。但是他们之中大多数人是不是认为共产党说话是算数的，那就是另一回事了。我对此是怀疑的。中国军阀的多年压迫和汉回之间的仇恨，使他们对一切汉人的动机都理所当

covered with them. He was an engaging old rustic with a jolly face, a humorous manner, and a truly beautiful daughter—so rare an apparition in those parts that I stayed and bought three melons. I asked him if Ma Hung-kuei's officials were really as bad as the Reds claimed. He threw up his hands comically in indignation, spluttering watermelon seeds between his gums. "*Ai-ya! Ai-ya! Ai-ya!*" he cried. "Ma Hung-kuei, Ma Hung-kuei! Taxing us to death, stealing our sons, burning and killing! *Ma-ti Ma Hung-kuei!*" By which last expression he meant you could defile Ma's mother and it would be too good for him. Everyone in the courtyard laughed. On the other hand, the occasion was hardly appropriate for the old gentleman to offer testimony to Allah in praise of Ma Hung-kuei—if he had been so inclined.

The Moslem soldiers with the Reds ostensibly had been won over by subversive propaganda conducted among Ma's troops, and by political lectures when they reached the Red camp. I asked one commander why he had joined.

"To fight Ma Hung-kuei," he said. "Life is too bitter for us *Hui-min* under Ma Hung-kuei. No family is secure. If a family has two sons, one of them must join his army. If it has three sons, two must join. There is no escape—unless you are rich and can pay the tax for a substitute. What poor man can afford it? Not only that, but every man must bring his own clothes, and his family must pay for his food, fires, and lighting. This costs several tens of dollars a year."

Although these Red Moslem regiments had been organized less than half a year, they had already achieved considerable "class consciousness," it seemed. They had read, or heard read, the *Communist Manifesto*, brief lessons from *Class Struggle*, and daily political lectures, à la Marxism, on the immediate problems of the Mohammedan people. This instruction was given to them, not by Chinese, but by Mohammedan members of the Communist Party—men who had been through the Reds' Party school. I was told that more than 90 per cent of Ma Hung-kuei's troops were illiterate, and that most of the Moslem recruits to the Red Army had been unable to read at all when they joined. Now they were said to know a few hundred characters each, and to be able to study the simple lessons given to them. Out of their two training regiments the Communists hoped to develop cadres for a big Moslem Red Army, to defend the autonomous Moslem republic they dreamed of seeing established in the Northwest. Already nearly 25 per cent of these Moslems had joined the Communist Party.

With the autonomy slogan the Moslem population could be expected to agree; that had been their demand for many years. Whether the majority of them believed the Reds were sincere in their promises was quite another matter. I doubted it. Years of maltreatment by the Chinese militarists, and racial hatreds between Han and Hui (Chinese and Moslem), had left among them a deep and justified distrust of the motives of all Chinese, and it was

然地深为怀疑，共产党能在这么短的时间内消除回民的这种怀疑，令人难以置信。

这种回民与共产党合作，也许有他们自己的理由。如果汉人愿意帮助他们赶走国民党，帮助他们创建和武装一支自己的军队，帮助他们实现自治，帮助他们剥夺有钱人（他们无疑是这样对自己说的），他们就准备利用这个机会——如果后来共产党食言，他们就再把那支军队用于自己的用途。但是从农民的友善态度和他们在共产党领导下愿意组织起来这两点来看，共产党的纲领有明显吸引人的地方，他们小心翼翼地尊重伊斯兰教风俗习惯的政策即使在最多疑的农民和阿訇中间也留下了印象。

在战士中间，有些历史上的民族宿怨看来已经克服，或者说正在逐步蜕化为阶级仇恨。例如，我问到一些回民战士，他们是否认为回汉两族人民能够在苏维埃政体下合作，其中一个回答说：

"汉人和回民是兄弟；我们回民中间也有汉人的血统；我们都属于大中国，因此我们为什么要打来打去？我们的共同敌人是地主、资本家、放高利贷的、压迫我们的统治者、日本人。我们的共同目标是革命。"

"但是如果革命干涉到你们的宗教呢？"

"没有干涉。红军不干涉伊斯兰教礼拜。"

"我是说这样的情况。有些阿訇是有钱的地主和放高利贷的，是不是？要是他们反对红军，那么样？你怎样对待他们？"

"我们要说服他们参加革命。但大多数阿訇不是有钱人。他们同情我们。我们的一个连长原来是阿訇。"

"但是，如果有些阿訇说服不过来，而参加了国民党来反对你们，那怎么办？"

"我们就要惩罚他们。他们是坏阿訇，人民会要求惩罚他们。"

同时，在整个一军团和十五军团都在进行紧张的训练，教育战士了解共产党对回民的政策和建立"回汉统一战线"的努力。我参加了几次政治讨论会，战士们在会上讨论"回民革命"，这些讨论会很有意思。在一次会上，发生了长时间的辩论，特别是关于土地问题。有的认为，红军应该没收回民大地主的土地；有的反对。接

unbelievable that the Communists had been able to break down this Moslem skepticism in so short a time.

Such Moslems as cooperated with the Reds probably had reasons of their own. If Chinese offered to help them drive out the Kuomintang, help them create and equip an army of their own, help them get self-government, and help them despoil the rich (they no doubt said to themselves), they were prepared to take the opportunity—and later on turn that army to uses of their own, if the Reds failed to keep their bargain. But it seemed, from the friendliness of the farmers, and their readiness to organize under the Reds, that their program had some attraction, and that their careful policy of respecting Moslem institutions had made an impression.

Among the soldiers themselves it appeared that some of the historic racial animosity was being overcome, or gradually metamorphosed into class antagonism. Thus when I asked some Moslem soldiers whether they thought the Hui and Han peoples could cooperate under a soviet form of government, one replied:

"The Chinese and the Moslems are brothers; we Moslems also have Chinese blood in us; we all belong to Ta Chung Kuo [China], and therefore why should we fight each other? Our common enemies are the landlords, the capitalists, the moneylenders, our oppressive rulers, and the Japanese. Our common aim is revolution."

"But what if the revolution interferes with your religion?"

"There is no interference. The Red Army does not interfere with Mohammedan worship."

"Well, I mean something like this. Some of the *ahuns* are wealthy landlords and moneylenders, are they not? What if they oppose the Red Army? How would you treat them?"

"We would persuade them to join the revolution. But most *ahuns* are not rich men. They sympathize with us. One of our company commanders was an *ahun*."

"Still, suppose some *ahuns* can't be persuaded, but join with the Kuomintang to oppose you?"

"We would punish them. They would be bad *ahuns*, and the people would demand their punishment."

Meanwhile intensive instruction was going on throughout the First and Fifteenth Army corps to educate the soldiers to an understanding of the Communist policy toward Moslems and their effort to create a "Hui-Han United Front." I attended several political sessions in which soldiers were discussing the "Mohammedan revolution," and they were quite interesting. At one session there were long debates, especially about the land question. Some argued that the Red Army should confiscate the land of great

着政委把党的立场作了简洁的介绍，说明为什么应该由回民自己来进行他们的土地革命，由他们自己的、在回民群众中有基础的坚强革命组织来领导。

另外一个连讨论了回汉两族人民交往的简史，另外一个连讨论了发给驻在回民地区全体战士行为守则必须严格遵守的理由。这个守则规定红军战士不许：未经房主同意进入回民家中；以任何方式侵犯清真寺或教职人员；在回民前面骂"猪"或"狗"；问他们为什么不吃猪肉；叫回民是"小教"，叫汉人是"大教"。

这都是争取把全军有意识地团结在共产党的回民政策周围，除了这些努力以外，在农民中间也在不断地进行工作。这方面的宣传由那两个回民教导团来带头进行，但是红军各连也派宣传队去挨家挨户宣传共产党的政策，鼓励农民组织起来；部队的剧团到各村子里去巡回演出，表演回民戏，那是以当地情况和历史事件为根据的，目的是要"鼓动"人民；分发用汉文和阿拉伯文写的传单、报纸、招贴；常常举行群众大会，成立革命委员会和村苏维埃。农民们不论汉回，要避免一定程度的这种灌输，是很困难的。到7月间，宁夏好几十个农村成立了村苏维埃，派代表到预旺堡来与那里的回民共产党开会。

4个月后，四方面军就要渡过黄河，再向西推进200英里，到达肃州，那是马步芳的辖地，正好在通新疆的大路上。他们有此迅速进展在很大程度上是由于现在同回民建立了良好关系。我在宁夏的时候就碰到了建立这种关系的一件极有意义的事。早在9月间，宁夏已有了足够的进展，可以召开一个大会，有300名回民代表从红军当时占领下的各村苏维埃选出，还有一些阿訇、教师、商人、两三个地主参加，但大多数是贫农，因为有钱一些的阶级早已在"汉匪"到达时逃出了。代表会议选出了一位主席和一个回民苏维埃临时政府委员会。他们通过决议，要同红军合作，接受它的帮助建立回民抗日军队的建议，并且立即开始组织汉回团结同盟、贫民会以及群众性的抗日团体。

这个历史性的小小代表会议所处理的最后一项议程——但我认为对那里的农民来说是最重要的议程——是处理一个国民党税吏。此人显然在红军到达以前已民怨沸腾，红军到达后他逃到了附近山间农村中一个叫张家寨的地方，在那里继续收税。

Mohammedan landlords; others opposed it. The political commissar then gave a concise statement of the Party's position, explaining why it was necessary for the Mohammedans themselves to carry on their own land revolution, led by a strong revolutionary organization of their own, with a base in the Moslem masses.

Another company reviewed a brief history of relationships between the Moslems and Chinese, and another discussed the necessity for strict observance of the rules of conduct which had been issued to all soldiers stationed in Mohammedan districts. These latter decreed that Red soldiers must not: enter the home of a Moslem without his consent; molest a mosque or a priest in any way; say "pig" or "dog" before Moslems; or ask them why they don't eat pork; or call the Moslems "small faith" and the Chinese "big faith."

Besides these efforts to unite the whole army intelligently behind the Moslem policy of the Reds, there was incessant work with the peasantry. The two Moslem training regiments led in this propaganda, but companies in the Red Army also sent their propaganda corps from house to house, explaining Communist policies and urging the farmers to organize; army dramatic clubs toured the villages, giving Mohammedan plays, based on local situations and incidents of history, and designed to "agitate" the population; leaflets, newspapers, and posters were distributed, written in Chinese and Arabic; and mass meetings were frequently called to form revolutionary committees and village soviets. The peasants, Chinese or Moslem, had a hard squeeze of it to avoid indoctrination to at least some degree. By July several dozen Mohammedan communities in Ninghsia had elected village soviets, and were sending delegates to Yu Wang Pao to confer with Moslem Communists there.

Four months later the Fourth Front Red Army was to cross the Yellow River, move over two hundred miles farther west, and reach Hsuchow, in Ma Pu-fang's territory, astride the main road to Sinkiang. Early in September enough progress had been made in Ninghsia to convene a meeting of over 300 Moslem delegates from soviet committees elected by the villages then under the Red Army. A number of *ahuns*, teachers, merchants, and two or three small landlords were among them, but mostly they were poor farmers, members of the wealthier class having fled with the arrival of the "Han bandits." The meeting of delegates elected a chairman and a provisional Moslem Soviet Government Committee. They passed resolutions to cooperate with the Red Army and accept its offer to help create an anti-Japanese Mohammedan army, and to begin at once the organization of a Chinese-Moslem unity league, a poor people's league, and a mass anti-Japanese society.

The last item of business attended to by this historic little convention—and I suspect the most important to the peasants there—was the disposal of a Kuomintang tax collector. This man had evidently earned himself considerable enmity before the Reds arrived, and after that he had fled into the neighboring hill villages, to a place called Changchia Cha,

据说他还增加税率1倍，宣布这是他自称代表共产党政府的新规定！但回民农民了解到共产党并没有派收税的，于是他们出动了六七个人把这个坏蛋捉了起来送到预旺堡公审。我个人对这件事的反应是，在这样的时候，在这样的地方，有这样的胆略，敢冒充这样的角色，这种人才不可多得，应该保护下来。但是回民们却不那么想。全体代表一致通过把他枪决。

就我所知，他是我在预旺堡两个星期中被枪决的唯一平民。

and there continued to collect his taxes. It was alleged that he had doubled his levies—and had announced that this was due to the regulations of the new Red government which he claimed to represent! But the Mohammedan farmers learned that the Reds appointed no tax collectors, and half a dozen of them captured this miscreant and brought him into Yu Wang Pao for a mass trial. My personal reaction to the story was that any man who had sufficient nerve to act as an imposter in such a role at such a time had talents that should be preserved. The Moslems thought otherwise. There was no dissenting vote when the delegates took the decision to execute him.

As far as I could learn, he was the only civilian shot during the two weeks I spent in Yu Wang Pao.

Part Ten
War and Peace

第十篇
战争与和平

一、　　再谈马

8月29日我骑马到红城子去，那是在韦州县的一个风景幽美的小镇，以盛产梨、苹果、葡萄的美丽果园著称，这些果园都是用灌溉渠里的晶莹泉水灌溉的。七十三师一部分驻扎在这里。不远有一个碉堡扼守的山隘和一条临时的战线，没有战壕，却有一系列小地洞似的机枪阵地和圆圆的山顶碉堡——泥土堆成的矮矮的防御工事——红军就在这里同敌人对垒，后者一般都已后撤到5英里到10英里以外的城里去了。这条战线好几个星期没有发生战事了，红军趁此机会进行了休整和"巩固"新区。

回到预旺堡以后，我发现部队在吃西瓜庆祝甘肃南部传来的无线电消息，马鸿逵将军的国军有一整师向朱德的四方面军投诚。国民党的该师师长李宗义原来奉令去截堵朱德北上。但是他部下的年轻军官——其中有秘密共产党员——举行起义，带了3,000名左右官兵，包括一个骑兵营，在陇西附近参加红军。这对蒋介石总司令在南线的防御是个很大打击，加速了南方两支大军的北上。

两天以后，徐海东十五军团的3个师中有两个师准备转移，一支南下，为朱德开道，一支向西到黄河流域。大清早3点钟军号就吹响了，到6点钟部队已经出发。我本人于那天早上同两个红军军官回预旺堡，他们是去向彭德怀汇报的，我与徐海东及其参谋部人员从南门离城，跟在那大队人马的末尾，这队人马像一条灰色的长龙，蜿蜒经过一望无际的大草原，看过去没有一个尽头。

1 MORE ABOUT HORSES

On August 29 I rode out to Hung Ch'eng Shui (Red City Waters), a pretty little town in Weichow county, famous for its beautiful fruit gardens of pears, apples, and grapes, irrigated by crystal springs that bubbled through the canals. Here part of the Seventy-third Division was encamped. Not far away was a fortified pass, and a temporary line with no trenches but with a series of small molelike machine gun nests and round hilltop forts—low-walled earthwork defenses—from which the Reds faced an enemy that had generally withdrawn from five to ten miles to the walled towns. There had been no movement on this front for several weeks, while the Reds rested and "consolidated" the new territory.

Back in Yu Wang again, I found the troops celebrating with a melon feast the radio news from south Kansu that a whole division of Ma Hung-kuei's Chinese troops had turned over to Chu Teh's Fourth Front Red Army. Li Tsung-yi, the commander of this Kuomintang division, had been sent to impede Chu Teh's march to the North. His younger officers, among whom were secret Communists, led an uprising and took some 3,000 troops, including a battalion of cavalry, to join the Reds near Lung Hsi. It was a big blow to the Generalissimo's defenses in the South, and hastened the northward advance of the two southern armies.

Two days later two of the three divisions of Hsu Hai-tung's Fifteenth Army Corps were prepared to move again, one column toward the South, to break open a path for Chu Teh, and the other to the West, and the valley of the Yellow River. Bugles began sounding at about three in the morning, and by six o'clock the troops were already marching. I was myself returning to Yu Wang Pao that morning with two Red officers who were reporting to P'eng Teh-huai, and I left the city by the south gate with Hsu Hai-tung and his staff, marching toward the end of the long column of troops and animals that wound like a gray dragon across the interminable grasslands, as far as you could see.

大军离城秩序井然，除了不停的军号，悄然无声，给人一个指挥若定的印象。他们告诉我，进军计划好几天以前就准备好了，路上一切情况都已经过研究，红军自己绘制的地图上仔细地标出了敌军集中的地方，警卫人员拦住了越过战线的一切过往旅客（为了鼓励贸易，红军平时是允许越境的，但在战时或行军时除外），现在他们在国民党军队毫不知情的情况下向前挺进，后来奇袭敌军岗哨，证明此点不假。

我在这支军队中没有看到随营的人，除了三十几头甘肃猎狗，它们紧紧地挨在一起，在平原上前窜后跳，追逐偶然在远处出现的野羚羊或野猪。它们高兴地狂吠着，东嗅西闻，蹦蹦跳跳，显然很乐意到战场上去。许多战士带着他们喂养的动物一起走。有的绳子挂着小猴子，有一个战士肩上停着一只蓝灰色的鸽子；有的带着白色的小耗子，有的带着兔子。这是一支军队吗？从战士的年轻和长长的队伍中传来的歌声来看，这倒更像是中学生的假期远足。

出城没有几里路，突然下达了一个防空演习的命令。一班的战士离开了大路，躲到了高高的野草丛中去，戴上了他们用草做的伪装帽，草披肩。在大路边上多草的小土墩上支起了机枪（他们没有高射炮），准备瞄准低飞的目标。几分钟之内，整条长龙就在草原上销声匿迹了，你分不清究竟是人还是无数的草丛。路上只有骡子、骆驼、马匹仍看得见，飞行员很可能把它们当作是普通的商队的牲口。不过骑兵（当时在打先锋，我看不到）得首当其冲，因为他们唯一的预防措施是就地寻找掩护，找不到就只好尽可能分散开来，但是不能下马。空袭中无人驾驭，这些蒙古马就无法控制，全团人马就会陷入一片混乱。在听到飞机嗡嗡声时给骑兵的第一道命令就是"上马！"

演习令人满意，我们继续前进。

李长林说的不错。红军的好马都在前线。他们的骑兵师是全军的骄傲，人人都希望提拔到骑兵师去。他们骑在3,000匹左右的漂亮宁夏马上，从体格上来说是全军最优秀的。这些快骑比华北的蒙古马高大强壮，毛滑膘肥。大多数是从马鸿逵和马鸿宾那里俘获来的，但是有三足营的马是将近一年前与国民党骑兵第一军司令何

The big army left the city quietly, except for the bark of bugles that never ceased, and gave an impression of efficient command. Plans for the march had been completed days earlier, I was told; every detail of the road had been examined, the enemy's concentrations were all carefully charted on maps prepared by the Reds themselves, and guards had stopped all travelers from moving across the lines (which the Reds permitted, to encourage trade, except during battles or troop movements), and now they went ahead unknown to the Kuomintang troops, as later surprise captures of enemy outposts were to prove.

With this army I saw no camp followers except thirty or more wild Kansu greyhounds who ran in a closed pack, ranging back and forth across the plain in chase of an occasional distant gazelle or a prairie hog. They barked joyously and scrapped in excellent humor and evidently liked going to war. Many of the soldiers carried their pets along with them. Several had little monks on leashes of string; one had a slate-colored pet pigeon perched on his shoulder; some had little white mice; and some had rabbits. Was this an army? From the youth of the warriors, and the bursts of song that rang down the long line, it seemed more like a prep school on a holiday excursion.

A few *li* beyond the city an order was suddenly given for a practice air-raid defense. Squads of soldiers left the road and melted into the tall grass, donning their big wide camouflage hats made of grass, and their grass shoulder capes. Machine guns (they had no antiaircraft) were pitched at angles on grassy knolls beside the road in hopeful anticipation of a low-flying target. In a few moments that whole dragon had simply been swallowed up in the landscape, and you could not distinguish men from the numerous clumps of bunch grass. Only the mules, camels, and horses remained visible on the road, and aviators might have taken these for ordinary commercial caravans. The cavalry (which was then in the vanguard, out of sight) had to take it in the neck, however, their only possible precautionary measure being to seek cover if it was available, otherwise merely to scatter as widely as possible, but always remaining mounted. Unmounted during an air raid, these Mongolian ponies were impossible to manage, and a whole regiment could be thrown into complete disorder. The first command to a cavalry unit at the drone of airplanes was "*Shang ma!*" ("Mount horse!")

The maneuver having been pronounced satisfactory, we marched on.

Li Chiang-lin had been right. The Reds' good horses were all at the front. Their cavalry division was the pride of the army, and every man aspired to promotion to it. They were physically the pick of the army, mounted on about 3,000 beautiful Ninghsia ponies, fine fleet animals taller and stronger than the Mongolian ponies of North China, with sleek flanks and well-filled buttocks. Most of them had been captured from Ma Hung-kuei and Ma Hung-ping, but three whole battalions of horses had been taken in a battle nearly a year before with General Ho Chu-kuo, commander of Nanking's First Cavalry Army,

柱国将军作战时夺取过来的，其中一营的马全白，一营全黑。这是红军第一骑兵师的核心。

我在甘肃随红军骑兵骑了几天马，或者精确地说，随红军骑兵走了几天路。他们借给我一匹好马，配有俘获的西式鞍子，但是每天行军结束时，我觉得不是马在侍候我，而是我侍候马。这是因为我们的营长不想让他四条腿的宝贝过累了，要我们两条腿的每骑一里路就要下马牵着走三四里路。他对待马好像对待狄翁尼家的四胞胎[1]一样，我的结论是，任何人要当这个人的骑兵得首先是个护士，而不是马夫，甚至最好是个步行的，不是骑马的。我对他爱护牲口表示应有的敬意——这在中国不是常见的现象——但是我很高兴终于能够脱身出来，恢复自由行动，这样反而有的时候真的骑上了一匹马。

我对徐海东有点抱怨这件事，我怀疑他后来要对我开一开玩笑。我要回预旺堡时，他借给我一匹宁夏好马，壮得像头公牛，我一生骑马就数这次最野了。我在草原中一个大碉堡附近同十五军团分手。我向徐海东和他的参谋人员告别。不久之后我就上了借来的坐骑，一上去之后，就如脱缰一般，看我们俩谁能活着到达预旺堡了。

问题出在中国式的木鞍上，这种木鞍很窄，我无法坐下，只能双腿夹着木鞍，走了全程，而又短又沉的铁镫子又使我伸不直腿，麻木得像块木头。我只想歇下来睡觉，却没有达到目的。

这条道路50多里，经过平原，一路平坦。这中间我们只下来走过一次，最后5里是不停地快步奔驰的，到达终点时飞跑过预旺堡大街，把我的同伴甩在远远的后面。在彭德怀的司令部门前我纵身下马，检查了一下我的坐骑，以为它一定要力竭晕倒了。可是它只轻轻地喘着气，身上只有几滴汗珠，但除此以外，这畜牲纹丝不动，若无其事。

---

1. 当时加拿大一妇女一胎生了4个婴孩，轰动了全世界。——译注

including one battalion of all-white animals and one of all-black. They were the nucleus of the First Red Cavalry.

I rode with the Red cavalry several days in Kansu—or more precisely, I walked with it. They lent me a fine horse with a captured Western saddle, but at the end of each day I felt that I had been giving the horse a good time instead of the contrary. This was because our battalion commander was so anxious not to tire his four-legged charges that we two-legged ones had to lead horse three or four *li* for every one we rode. I concluded that anyone who qualified for this man's cavalry had to be a nurse, not a *mafoo*, and an even better walker than rider. I paid them due respect for kindness to animals—no common phenomenon in China—but I was glad to disengage myself and get back to freelance movement of my own, in which occasionally I could actually ride a horse.

I had been grumbling mildly about this to Hsu Hai-tung, and I suspect he decided to play a joke on me. To return to Yu Wang Pao he lent me a splendid Ninghsia pony, strong as a bull, that gave me one of the wildest rides of my life. My road parted with the Fifteenth Army Corps near a big fort in the grassland. There I bade Hsu and his staff good-by. Shortly afterwards I got on my borrowed steed, and from then on it was touch and go to see which of us reached Yu Wang Pao alive.

The trouble with that ride was the wooden Chinese saddle, so narrow that I could not sit in the seat, but had to ride on my inner thighs the whole distance, while the short, heavy iron stirrups cramped my legs.

The road lay level across the plain far over 50 *li*. In that whole distance we got down to a walk just once. We raced at a steady gallop for the last five miles, and at the finish swept up the main street of Yu Wang Pao with my companions trailing far behind. Before P'eng's headquarters I slithered off and examined my mount, expecting him to topple over in a faint. He was puffing very slightly and had a few beads of sweat on him, but was otherwise quite unruffled, the beast.

二、 "红小鬼"

一天早上,我登上预旺堡又宽又厚的黄色城墙,从上面往下看,一眼就望得到 30 英尺下的地面上在进行着许多不同的、却又单调和熟悉的工作。这仿佛把这个城市的盖子揭开了一样。城墙有一大段正在拆毁,这是红军干的唯一破坏行动。对红军那样的游击战士来说,城墙是一种障碍物,他们尽量在开阔的地方同敌人交锋,如果打败了,就不固守城池消耗兵力,因为在那里有被封锁或歼灭的危险,而要马上撤退,让敌人去处于这种境地。一旦他们有充分强大的兵力可以夺回那个城池时,城墙拆了就容易一些。

在开了枪眼的雉堞上刚兜了一半,我就遇见一队号手——这时总算在休息,这叫我感到高兴,因为他们的响亮号声已接连不断地响了好多天了。他们都是少年先锋队员,不过是小孩子,因此我停下来对其中一个号手谈话时就采取了一种多少是父辈的态度。他穿着网球鞋、灰色短裤,戴着一顶褪了色的灰色帽子,上面有一颗模模糊糊的红星。但是,帽子下面那个号手可一点也不是褪色的:红彤彤的脸,闪闪发光的明亮眼睛,这样的一个孩子你一看到心就软了下来,就像遇到一个需要友情和安慰的流浪儿一样。我想,他一定是非常想家的吧。可是很快我就发现自己估计错了。他可不是妈妈的小宝贝,而已经是一位老红军了。他告诉我,他今年 15 岁,4 年前在南方参加了红军。

"4 年!"我不信地叫道,"那么你参加红军时准是才 11 岁啰?你还参加了长征?"

"不错,"他得意洋洋有点滑稽地回答说,"我已经当了 4 年红军了。"

"你为什么参加红军?"我问道。

2 _____ "LITTLE RED DEVILS"

One morning I climbed the wide, thick, yellow wall of Yu Wang Pao, from the top of which you could look down thirty feet and see at a glance a score of different and somehow incongruously prosaic and intimate tasks being pursued below. It was as if you had pried off the lid of the city. A big section of the wall was being demolished. Walls were impediments to guerrilla warriors like the Reds, who endeavored to come to battle with an enemy in open country and, if they failed there, not to waste men in an exhausting defense of a walled city, where they could be endangered by blockade or annihilation, but to withdraw and let the enemy put himself in that position. The broken wall simplified their work if and when they were strong enough to attempt a reoccupation of the city.

Halfway around the crenellated battlement I came upon a squad of buglers—at rest for once, I was glad to observe, for their plangent calls had been ringing incessantly for days. They were all Young Vanguards, mere children, and I assumed a somewhat fatherly air toward one to whom I stopped and talked. He wore tennis shoes, gray shorts, and a faded gray cap with a dim red star on it. But there was nothing faded about the bugler under the cap: he was rosy-faced and had bright shining eyes. How homesick he must be, I thought. I was soon disillusioned. He was no mama's boy, but already a veteran Red. He told me that he was fifteen, and had joined the Reds in the South four years ago.

"Four years!" I exclaimed incredulously. "Then you must have been only eleven when you became a Red? And you made the Long March?"

"Right," he responded with comical swagger. "I have been a *hungchun* for four years."

"Why did you join?" I asked.

"我的家在福建漳州附近。我平时上山砍柴，冬天就采集树皮。我常常听村里的人讲起红军。他们说红军帮助穷人，这叫我喜欢。我们的家很穷。一家6口，我的父母和3个哥哥。我们没有地。收成一半以上拿来交租，所以我们老是不够吃。冬天，我们烧树皮汤喝，把粮食省下来作来春的种子。我总是挨饿。

"有一年，红军来到漳州附近。我翻过山头，去请他们帮助我们的家，因为我们很穷。他们待我很好。他们暂时把我送到学校去读书，我吃得很饱。几个月以后，红军占领了漳州，来到我们村子上。地主、放债的和做官的都给赶跑了。我家分到了地，用不着再缴税缴租了。家里的人很高兴，都称赞我。我的两个哥哥参加了红军。"

"他们现在在哪里？"

"现在？我不知道。我离开江西时，他们在福建的红军里；他们和方志敏在一起。现在我可不知道了。"

"农民喜欢红军吗？"

"喜欢红军？他们当然喜欢。红军分地给他们，赶走了地主、收税的和剥削者。"（这些"红小鬼"都有他们的马克思主义词汇！）

"但是说实在的，你怎么**知道**他们喜欢红军呢？"

"他们亲手替我们做了一千双、一万双鞋子。妇女给我们做军服，男子侦察敌人。每户人家都送子弟参加我们红军。老百姓就是这样待我们的！"

不用问他是不是喜欢他的同志；13岁的孩子是不会跟着他所痛恨的军队走上6,000英里的。

红军里有许多像他一样的少年。少年先锋队是由共产主义青年团组织的，据共产主义青年团书记冯文彬说，在西北苏区一共有少年先锋队员约4万名。单单在红军里谅必有好几百名：在每一个红军驻地都有一个少年先锋队"模范连"。他们都是12岁至17岁（照外国算法实际是11岁至16岁[1]）之间的少年，他们来自中国各地。他们当中有许多人像这个小号手一样，熬过了从南方出发的长征的艰苦。有许多人是出征山西期间加入了红军。

---

1. 传统上，中国年龄的算法从怀孕开始算，新年那天每个人都增加1岁。

"My family lived near Changchow, in Fukien. I used to cut wood in the mountains, and in the winter I went there to collect bark. I often heard the villagers talk about the Red Army. They said it helped the poor people, and I liked that. Our house was very poor. We were six people, my parents and three brothers, older than I. We owned no land. Rent ate more than half our crop, so we never had enough. In the winter we cooked bark for soup and saved our grain for planting in the spring. I was always hungry.

"One year the Reds came very close to Changchow. I climbed over the mountains and went to ask them to help our house because we were very poor. They were good to me. They sent me to school for a while, and I had plenty to eat. After a few months the Red Army captured Changchow, and went to my village. All the landlords and moneylenders and officials were driven out. My family was given land and did not have to pay the tax collectors and landlords any more. They were happy and they were proud of me. Two of my brothers joined the Red Army."

"Where are they now?"

"Now? I don't know. When we left Kiangsi they were with the Red Army in Fukien; they were with Fang Chih-min. Now I don't know."

"Did the peasants like the Red Army?"

"Like the Red Army, eh? Of course they liked it. The Red Army gave them land and drove away the landlords, the tax collectors, and the exploiters." (These "little devils" all had their Marxist vocabulary.)

"But really, how do you *know* they liked the Reds?"

"They made us a thousand, ten thousand shoes, with their own hands. The women made uniforms for us, and the men spied on the enemy. Every home sent sons to our Red Army. That is how the *lao-pai-hsing* treated us."

Scores of youngsters like him were with the Reds. The Young Vanguards were organized by the Communist Youth League, and altogether, according to the claims of Fang Wen-ping, secretary of the CYL, there were then some 40,000 in the Northwest soviet districts. There must have been several hundred with the Red Army alone: a "model company" of them was in every Red encampment. They were youths between twelve and seventeen (really eleven to sixteen by foreign count[1]), and they came from all over China. Many of them, like this little bugler, had survived the hardships of the march from the South. Many had joined the Red Army during its expedition to Shansi.

---

1. Traditionally, Chinese age count begins at conception, and everyone becomes one year older on New Year's Day.

少年先锋队员在红军里当通讯员、勤务员、号手、侦察员、无线电报务员、挑水员、宣传员、演员、马夫、护士、秘书甚至教员！有一次，我看见这样的一个少年在一张大地图前，向一班新兵讲解世界地理。我生平所见到的两个最优美的儿童舞蹈家，是一军团剧社的少年先锋队员，他们是从江西长征过来的。

你可能会想，他们怎样能经受这样的生活。已经死掉或者被杀的，一定有不少。在西安府污秽的监狱里，关着200多名这样的少年，他们是在做侦察或宣传工作时被捕的，或者是行军时赶不上队伍而被抓的。但是他们的刚毅坚忍精神令人叹服，他们对红军的忠贞不贰、坚定如一，只有很年轻的人才能做到。

他们大多数人穿的军服都太肥大，袖子垂到膝部，上衣几乎拖到地面。他们说，他们每天洗手、洗脸3次，可是他们总是脏，经常流着鼻涕，他们常常用袖子揩，露着牙齿笑。虽然这样，但世界是他们的：他们吃得饱，每人有一条毯子，当头头的甚至有手枪，他们有红领章，戴着大一号甚至大两号的帽子，帽檐软垂，但上面缀着红星。他们的来历往往弄不清楚：许多人记不清自己的父母是谁，许多人是逃出来的学徒，有些曾经做过奴婢，[1]大多数是从人口多、生活困难的人家来的，他们全都是自己做主参加红军的。有时，有成群的少年逃去当红军。

他们的英勇的故事流传很多。他们并没有得到或者要求作为小孩照顾，许多人实际参加了作战。据说在江西，红军主力撤离以后，许许多多少年先锋队员和共产主义青年团员同成年游击队员并肩作战，并且甚至跟敌人拼刺刀——因此白军士兵笑着说，他们能够抓住他们的刺刀，把他们拖下壕沟，他们实在太小太轻了。在蒋介石的江西"共匪"感化院里，许多被俘的"红军"是10岁至15岁的少年。

少先队员喜欢红军，大概是因为在红军中，他们生平第一次受到人的待遇。他们吃住都像人；他们似乎每样事情都参加；他们认为自己跟任何人都是平等的。我从来没有看见他们当中有谁挨过打或受欺侮。他们做通信员和勤务员当然"受到剥削"（许多命令从上而下最后传到一些少先队员，这是使人惊奇的事情），但他们也有自己的活动自由，有自己的组织保护他们。他们学会了体育运动，他们受到初步

---

1. 儿童奴隶已被国民党法律禁止，但是该法令即便是在为人所知的地区也很少实施；在其他地方儿童奴隶仍然很普遍。

The Young Vanguards worked as orderlies, messboys, buglers, spies, radio operators, water carriers, propagandists, actors, *mafoos*, nurses, secretaries, and even teachers. I once saw such a youngster, before a big map, lecturing a class of new recruits on world geography. Two of the most graceful child dancers I had ever seen were Young Vanguards in the dramatic society of the First Army Corps, and had marched from Kiangsi.

One might wonder how they stood such a life. Hundreds must have died or been killed. In the filthy jail in Sianfu there were over 200 of them, captured doing espionage or propaganda, or as stragglers unable to keep up with the army on its march. But their fortitude was amazing, and their loyalty to the Red Army was the intense and unquestioning loyalty of the very young.

Most of them wore uniforms too big for them, with sleeves dangling to their knees and coats dragging nearly to the ground. They washed their hands and faces three times a day, they claimed, but they were always dirty, their noses were usually running, and they were often wiping them with a sleeve, and grinning. The world nevertheless was theirs: they had enough to eat, they had a blanket each, the leaders even had pistols, and they wore red bars, and broken-peaked caps a size or more too large, but with the red star. They were often of uncertain origin: many could not remember their parents, many were escaped apprentices, some had been slaves,[1] most of them were runaways from huts with too many mouths to feed, and all of them had made their own decisions to join. Sometimes a whole group of youngsters had run off to the Reds together.

Many stories of courage were told of them. They gave and asked no quarter as children, and many had actually participated in battles. It was said that in Kiangsi, after the main Red Army left, hundreds of Young Vanguards and Young Communists fought beside adult partisans, and even made bayonet charges—so that the White soldiers laughingly said they could grab their bayonets and pull them into their trenches, they were so small and light. Many of the captured "Reds" in Chiang's reform schools for bandits in Kiangsi were youths from ten to fifteen years old.

Perhaps the Vanguards liked the Reds because among them they were treated like human beings probably for the first time. They ate and lived like men; they seemed to take part in everything; they considered themselves any man's equal. I never saw one of them struck or bullied. They were certainly "exploited" as orderlies and messboys (and it was surprising how many orders starting at the top were eventually passed on to some Young Vanguards), but they had their own freedom of activity, too, and their own organization to protect them. They learned games and sports, they were given a crude schooling, and they

---

1. Child slavery had been abolished by Kuomintang law, but the mandate was seldom enforced even in areas where the law was known; elsewhere child slavery was still common.

的教育，而且他们对简单的马克思主义口号有了一种信仰——在大多数情况下，这些口号对他们来说只是意味着帮助他们开枪打地主和师傅。显然，这比在师傅的工作台旁边一天工作14个小时，侍候师傅吃饭，倒他"妈的"夜壶要好。

我记得在甘肃碰到的这样一个逃跑的学徒，他的绰号叫山西娃娃。他被卖给山西洪洞县附近一个镇上的一家店铺，红军到来时，他同另外3个学徒偷偷地爬过城墙，参加了红军。他是怎样认为自己属于红军一边的，我可不知道，但显而易见，阎锡山的一切反共宣传，他的长辈的一切警告，已产生了同他们的原意相反的效果。他是一个圆滚滚的胖孩子，长着一张娃娃脸，只有12岁，但已经很能照顾自己，这在他越过晋陕边境进入甘肃的行军中得到了证明。我问他为什么当红军，他回答说："红军替穷人打仗。红军是抗日的。为什么不要当红军呢？"

又有一次，我碰到一个15岁的瘦少年，他是在甘肃河连湾附近的一所医院里工作的少年先锋队和共青团的头头。他的家在兴国，那是红军在江西的模范县，他说他有一个兄弟还在那里的游击队里，他的姐姐是护士。他不晓得他家里的人怎么样了。是的，他们都喜欢红军。为什么？因为他们"都懂得红军是我们自己的军队——为无产阶级作战"。我不知道向西北的长途跋涉在他年轻的脑海里留下什么印象，但是我没有能够弄清楚。对这个一本正经的少年来说，这整个事情是一件小事，只是徒步走过两倍于美国宽度的距离的小事情。

"很苦吧，嗯？"我试着问道。

"不苦，不苦。有同志们和你在一起，行军是不苦的。我们革命青年不能想到事情是不是困难或辛苦；我们只能想到我们面前的任务。如果要走1万里，我们就走1万里，如果要走2万里，我们就走2万里！"

"那么你喜欢甘肃吗？它比江西好还是比江西坏？南方的生活是不是好一些？"

"江西好。甘肃也好。有革命的地方就是好地方。我们吃什么，睡在哪里，都不重要。重要的是革命。"

千篇一律的回答，我心里想，这个年轻人从某个红军宣传员那里把答话学得很好。第二天，在红军士兵的一个大规模集会上，我十分惊奇地发现他是主要讲话的人之一，他自己就是个"宣传员"。他们告诉我，他是军队里最好的演说家之一，而在这次大会上，他对当前的政治形势，以及红军要停止内战并同一切抗日军队成立

acquired a faith in simple Marxist slogans—which in most cases meant to them simply helping to shoot a gun against the landlords and masters of apprentices. Obviously it was better than working fourteen hours a day at the master's bench, and feeding him, and emptying his "defile-mother's" night-bowl.

I remember one such escaped apprentice I met in Kansu who was nicknamed the Shansi Wa-wa—the Shansi Baby. He had been sold to a shop in a town near Hung T'ung, in Shansi, and when the Red Army came he had stolen over the city wall, with three other apprentices, to join it. How he had decided that he belonged with the Reds I did not know, but evidently all of Yen Hsi-shan's anti-Communist propaganda, all the warnings of his elders, had produced exactly the opposite effect from that intended. He was a fat rolypoly lad with the face of a baby, and only twelve, but he was quite able to take care of himself, as he had proved during the march across Shansi and Shensi and into Kansu. When I asked him why he had become a Red he said: "The Red Army fights for the poor. The Red Army is anti-Japanese. Why should any man not want to become a Red soldier?"

Another time I met a bony youngster of fifteen, who was head of the Young Vanguards and Young Communists working in the hospital near Holienwan, Kansu. His home had been in Hsing Ko, the Reds' model *hsien* in Kiangsi, and he said that one of his brothers was still in a partisan army there, and that his sister had been a nurse. He did not know what had become of his family. Yes, they all liked the Reds. Why? Because they "all understood that the Red Army was our army—fighting for the *wu-ch'an chieh-chi*"—the proletariat. I wondered what impressions the great trek to the Northwest had left upon his young mind, but I was not to find out. The whole thing was a minor event to this serious-minded boy, this little matter of a hike over a distance twice the width of America.

"It was pretty bitter going, eh?" I ventured.

"Not bitter, not bitter. No march is bitter if your comrades are with you. We revolutionary youths can't think about whether a thing is hard or bitter, we can only think of the task before us. If it is to walk 10,000 *li*, we walk it, or if it is to walk 20,000 *li*, we walk it!"

"How do you like Kansu, then? Is it better or worse than Kiangsi? Was life better in the South?"

"Kiangsi was good. Kansu is also good. Wherever the revolution is, that place is good. What we eat and where we sleep is not important. What is important is the revolution."

Copybook replies, I thought. Here was one lad who had learned his answers well from some Red propagandist. Next day I was quite surprised when at a mass meeting of Red soldiers I saw that he was one of the principal speakers, and a "propagandist" in his own right. He was one of the best speakers in the army, I was told, and in that meeting he gave a simple but competent explanation of the present political situation, and the reasons

"统一战线"的理由，作了一番很简单而又充分的说明。

我遇见一个 14 岁的少年，他曾经是上海一家机器厂的学徒，他同三位同伴历尽各种危险，到了西北。我见到他时，他是保安无线电学校的学生。我问他是否惦记上海，可是他说不惦记，他在上海没有什么牵挂，而他在那里有过的唯一乐趣是望着商店橱窗里的美味食品——这他当然买不起。

但我最喜欢的是保安一个当外交部交通处处长李克农通讯员的"小鬼"。他是一个约十三四岁的山西少年，我不晓得他是怎样参加红军的。他是少年先锋队中的"花花公子"，对于自己的那个角色，态度极其认真。他不知从哪里弄到一条军官皮带，穿着一套整洁合身的小军服，帽檐什么时候发软了，总是衬上新的硬板纸。在他的洗得很干净的上衣领口里面，总是衬着一条白布，露出一点。他无疑是全城最漂亮整齐的士兵。毛泽东在他旁边也显得像一个江湖流浪汉。

由于他父母缺少考虑，这个娃娃的名字恰巧叫做向季邦（译音）。这个名字本来没有什么不对，只是"季邦"听起来十分像"鸡巴"，因此别人就老是叫他"鸡巴"，这给他带来无尽的耻辱。有一天，季邦到外交部我的小房间来，带着他一贯的庄重神色，喀嚓一声立正，向我行了一个我在红区所看到的最普鲁士式的敬礼，称我为"斯诺同志"。接着，他吐露了他小小心灵里的一些不安来。他是要向我说清楚，他的名字不是"鸡巴"，而是"季邦"，两者是完全不同的。他在一张纸上细心地写下他的名字，把它放在我面前。

我惊奇之下极其严肃地回答他，说我只叫他"季邦"，从来没有叫过他别的名字，而且也不想叫他别的名字。我以为他要我选择军刀还是手枪来进行决斗呢。但是他谢了我，庄重地鞠了一个躬，又向我行了那个十分可笑的敬礼。"我希望得到保证，"他说，"你替外国报纸写到我时，可不能写错我的名字。要是外国同志以为有一个红军士兵名叫'鸡巴'，那是会给他们留下一个坏印象的！"在那个时候以前，我根本没有想把季邦写进这部不平常的书里来的，但经他这样一说，我在这件事情上就别无选择，他就走了进来同蒋总司令并排站立在一起了，尽管有失历史的尊严。

在苏区，少年先锋队员的任务之一，是在后方检查过路旅客，看他们有没有路条。他们十分坚决地执行这项任务，把没有路条的旅客带到当地苏维埃去盘问。彭

why the Red Army wanted to stop civil war and form a "united front" with all anti-Japanese armies.

I met a youth of fourteen who had been an apprentice in a Shanghai machine shop, and with three companions had found his way, through various adventures, to the Northwest. He was a student in the radio school in Pao An when I saw him. I asked whether he missed Shanghai, but he said no, he had left nothing in Shanghai, and that the only fun he had ever had there was looking into the shop windows at good things to eat—which he could not buy.

One "little devil" in Pao An served as orderly to Li K'e-nung, chief of the communications department of the Foreign Office. He was a Shansi lad of about thirteen or fourteen, and he had joined the Reds I knew not how. The Beau Brummell of the Vanguards, he took his role with utmost gravity. He had inherited a Sam Browne belt from somebody, he had a neat little uniform tailored to a good fit, and a cap whose peak he regularly refilled with new cardboard whenever it broke. Underneath the collar of his well-brushed coat he always managed to have a strip of white linen showing. He was easily the snappiest-looking soldier in town. Beside him Mao Tse-tung looked a tramp.

This *wa-wa's* name happened by some thoughtlessness of his parents to be Shang Chi-pang. There is nothing wrong with that, except that Chi-pang sounds very much like *chi-pa*, and so, to his unending mortification, he was often called *chi-pa*, which simply means "penis." One day Chi-pang came into my little room in the Foreign Office with his usual quota of dignity, clicked his heels together, gave me the most Prussian-like salute I had seen in the Red districts, and addressed me as "Comrade Snow." He then proceeded to unburden his small heart of certain apprehensions. What he wanted to do was to make it perfectly clear to me that his name was not Chi-pa, but Chi-pang, and that between these two there was all the difference in the world. He had his name carefully scrawled down on a scrap of paper, and this he deposited before me.

Astonished, I responded in all seriousness that I had never called him anything but Chi-pang, and had no thought of doing otherwise. He thanked me, made a grave bow, and once more gave that preposterous salute. "I wanted to be sure," he said, "that when you write about me for the foreign papers you won't make a mistake in my name. It would give a bad impression to the foreign comrades if they thought a Red soldier was named Chi-pa!" Until then I had had no intention of introducing Chi-pang into this strange book, but with that remark I had no choice in the matter, and he walked into it right beside the Generalissimo.

One of the duties of the Young Vanguards in the soviets was to examine travelers on roads behind the front, and see that they had their road passes. They executed this duty quite determinedly, and marched anyone without his papers to the local soviet for

德怀告诉我，有一次被几个少先队员喝令站住，要看他的路条，否则就要逮捕他。

"但是我就是彭德怀，"他说，"这些路条都是我开的。"

"你是朱总司令我们也不管，"小鬼们不信说，"你得有个路条。"他们叫人来增援，于是有几个孩子从田里跑来。

彭德怀只好写了路条，签了字，交给他们，才能够继续上路。

总的说来，红色中国中有一件事情，是很难找出有什么不对的，那就是"小鬼"。他们精神极好。我觉得，大人看到了他们，就往往会忘掉自己的悲观情绪，想到自己正是为这些少年的将来而战斗，就会感到鼓舞。他们总是愉快而乐观，不管整天行军的疲乏，一碰到人问他们好不好就回答"好！"他们耐心、勤劳、聪明、努力学习，因此看到他们，就会使你感到中国不是没有希望的，就会感到任何国家有了青少年就不会没有希望。在少年先锋队员身上寄托着中国的将来，只要这些少年能够得到解放，得到发展，得到启发，在建设新世界中得到起应有的作用的机会。我这样说听起来大概好像是在说教，但是看到这些英勇的年轻人，没有人能不感到中国的人并不是生来腐败的，而是在品格上有着无限的发展前途。

examination. P'eng Teh-huai told me of being stopped once and being asked for his *lu-t'iao* by some Young Vanguards, who threatened to arrest him.

"But I am P'eng Teh-huai," he said. "I write those passes myself."

"We don't care if you are Commander Chu Teh," said the young skeptics: "you must have a road pass." They signaled for assistance, and several boys came running from the fields to reinforce them.

P'eng had to write out his *lu-t'iao* and sign it himself before they allowed him to proceed.

Altogether, the "little devils" were one thing in Red China with which it was hard to find anything seriously wrong. Their spirit was superb. I suspected that more than once an older man, looking at them, forgot his pessimism and was heartened to think that he was fighting for the future of lads like those. They were invariably cheerful and optimistic, and they had a ready "*hao!*" for every how-are-you, regardless of the weariness of the day's march. They were patient, hardworking, bright, and eager to learn, and seeing them made you feel that China was not hopeless, that no nation was more hopeless than its youth. Here in the Vanguards was the future of China, if only this youth could be freed, shaped, made aware, and given a role to perform in the building of a new world. It sounds somewhat evangelical, I suppose, but nobody could see these heroic young lives without feeling that man in China is not born rotten, but with infinite possibilities of personality.

三、　　实践中的统一战线

1936年9月初我在宁夏、甘肃前线的时候，彭德怀部下的军队开始一边向黄河西移，一边向西安—兰州公路南移，以便同北上的朱德的部队建立联系，这一行动后来在10月底出色完成，会师后的两支大军占领了西安—兰州公路以北的甘肃北部几乎全部地方。

但是红军现在既然为了"迫使"国民党抗日，决心要同国民党觅求妥协办法，因此日益变成了一支政治宣传队，而不是一支一心要想用武力夺取政权的军队了。党下发了新的指示，要求部队在今后行动中遵守"统一战线策略"。什么是"统一战线策略"？也许在这个期间军队活动的逐日的记载可以很好地回答这个问题：

包头水（译音）**9月1日**。离一方面军司令部预旺堡，步行约40里，指挥员彭德怀一边与骡夫说笑话，一边和大家闹着玩。所到之处颇多山。彭德怀司令部在此小村中一个回民老乡家中过夜。

墙上马上挂起地图，电台开始工作。电报来了。彭德怀休息的时候，请回民老乡进来，向他们解释红军的政策。一个老太太坐着同他几乎聊了两小时，数说自己的苦处。这时红军的一支收获队走过，去收割逃亡地主的庄稼。由于他逃走，他的土地就被当作"汉奸"的没收充公。另一队人给派去守护和打扫本地的清真寺。同

3   United Front in Action

In the beginning of September, 1936, while I was at the front in Ninghsia and Kansu, the army under P'eng Teh-huai commenced moving westward toward the Yellow River, and southward toward the Sian-Lanchow highway, to establish connections with Chu Teh's troops coming up from the South—a maneuver which was to be brilliantly concluded at the end of October, when the combined Red Armies occupied nearly all north Kansu above the Sian-Lanchow highway.

But having now decided to seek a compromise with the Kuomintang in an attempt to "coerce" the latter into resistance against Japan, the Reds were becoming every day more of a force of political propagandists and less of an army intent on seizing power by conquest. New instructions from the Party ordered the troops to observe "united-front tactics" in their future movements. And what were "united-front tactics"? Perhaps a day-by-day diary account of the maneuvers of the army at this time could best answer that question:

Pao Tou Shui, September 1. Leaving Yu Wang Pao, the headquarters of the First Front Army, walked for about 40 *li*, Commander P'eng Teh-huai joking with the muleteers and generally having a lark. Most of the region traveled was hilly and mountainous. P'eng made his headquarters for the night in a Mohammedan peasant's home in this little village.

Maps immediately were put up on the wall and the radio began functioning. Messages came in. While P'eng was resting, he called in the Mohammedan peasants and explained the Red Army's policies to them. An old lady sat and talked with him for nearly two hours, pointing out her troubles. Meanwhile a Red Army harvesting brigade passed by, on its way to reap the crop of a runaway landlord. Since he was a "traitor" his land was subject to confiscation. Another squad of men has been appointed to guard and keep clean the premises of the local mosque. Relations with the peasants seem good. A week

农民关系似乎很好。本县在共产党统治下已有好几个月，不用缴税，一星期前本县农民派了一个代表团向彭德怀送来了 6 大车的粮食和辎重，对免税表示感谢。昨天有几个农民送了彭德怀一张漂亮的木床，使他感到很高兴。他把它转送给了本地的阿訇。

李周沟（译音）**9 月 2 日**。清晨 4 时上路。彭德怀早已起身。遇到 10 个农民，他们是随军从预旺堡来帮助抬伤兵回医院的。他们自告奋勇这样做，是为了要打马鸿逵，他们痛恨他，因为他强征他们儿子去当兵。一架南京轰炸机在头上飞过，侦见我们，我们四散找掩护，全军都躲了起来。飞机绕了两圈，扔了一个炸弹——照红军说是"扔了一个铁蛋"，或者"掉了一些鸟粪"——然后扫射马匹，又飞到前面去轰炸先锋部队了。有个战士找掩护慢了，大腿受了伤——一处轻伤——经包扎后继续上路，不用搀扶。

我们要在这个小村过夜，从这里望去，什么都看不见。有一团敌军守在附近一个堡垒里，十五军团派了部队去攻打。

从预旺堡发来的无线电消息说，今晨有敌机空袭该城，扔了 10 颗炸弹，死伤农民若干，战士无伤。

碉堡子（译音）**9 月 3 日**。离李周沟，一路上许多农民出来，给战士送来白茶——即热水，这是这一带最爱喝的饮料。伊斯兰教老师来向彭德怀告别，感谢他保护学校。走近碉堡子（现在已到预旺堡以西 100 里的地方）的时候，马鸿逵的一些骑兵从一个孤立的阵地撤出来，冲进我们的后方，距离只有几百码。聂参谋长[1]派司令部的一队骑兵去追逐，他们疾驰而去，扬起一阵尘土。红军一队驮兽遭到袭击，又派一队人去夺回骡子和物资，运输队完整无损地回来了。

今天晚上布告牌上贴了一些有趣的消息。李旺堡已被围，在那里附近的一个碉堡，一颗迫击炮弹落了下来，几乎命中徐海东的司令部。死了 1 名少先队员，伤了 3 名战士。在附近另一地方，1 名白军排长在侦察红军阵地时被突击队活捉。他受了轻伤，被送到司令部来。彭德怀在无线电里大发脾气，因为让他受了伤。"不是统一战

---

1. 邓小平是他的政委。

ago the peasants in this *hsien*, who have now lived under the Reds for several months without paying taxes, came in a delegation to present P'eng with six cartloads of grain and provisions as an expression of gratitude for the relief. Yesterday some peasants presented P'eng with a handsome wooden bed—which amused him very much. He turned it over to the local *ahun*.

Li Chou K'ou, September 2. On the road at four A. M. P'eng up long before. Met ten peasants, who had come with the army from Yu Wang Pao to help carry the wounded back to the hospital. They voluntarily asked to do this in order to fight Ma Hung-kuei, hated because he'd forced their sons to join the army. A Nanking bomber flew overhead, spotted us, and we scattered for cover. The whole army melted into the landscape. The plane circled twice and dropped one bomb—"laid an iron egg," or "dropped some bird dung," as the Reds say—then strafed the horses and flew on to bomb our vanguard. One soldier, slow in taking cover, was wounded in the leg—a slight injury—and after it was dressed he walked without assistance.

From this village, where we are spending the night, very little can be seen. One regiment of the enemy is holding a fort near here, a Fifteenth Army Corps detachment attacking.

From Yu Wang Pao comes a radio message reporting the visit of enemy bombers, which attacked the city and dropped ten bombs this morning. Some peasants were killed and wounded; no soldiers hit.

Tiao Pao Tzu, September 3. Left Li Chou K'ou, and on the way many peasants came out and brought the soldiers *pai ch'a* (white tea)—i.e., hot water, the favorite beverage in these parts. Mohammedan schoolteachers came over to bid P'eng good-by and thank him for protecting the school. As we neared Tiao Pao Tzu (now over 100 *li* west of Yu Wang Pao) some of Ma Hung-kuei's cavalry, withdrawing from an isolated position, ran into our rear. They were only a few hundred yards from us. Nieh Jung-chen,[1] chief of staff of the First Army Corps, sent a detachment of headquarters cavalry to chase them, and they galloped off in a whirl of dust. A Red pack train was attacked, and another detachment of soldiers was sent to recover the mules and loads. The caravan returned intact.

Tonight some interesting items of news were posted on the bulletin board. Li Wang Pao is now surrounded, and in a fort near there a trench-mortar shell fell almost directly on Hsu Hai-tung's headquarters. One Young Vanguard was killed and three soldiers were wounded. In another place nearby, a White platoon commander, reconnoitering the Reds' position, was captured by a surprise attack party. The Reds slightly wounded him and sent him back to headquarters. P'eng raised hell over the radio because he was wounded. "Not

---

1. Teng Hsiao-P'ing was his deputy political commissar.

线的策略，"他说。"一个口号抵得上10颗子弹。"他向参谋人员讲了一通统一战线和如何付诸实践的道理。

农民们在路上卖水果和西瓜，红军买东西都付钱。一个年轻战士同一个农民讨价还价半天，最后把一只心爱的兔子换了3只西瓜。吃了西瓜以后，他很不高兴，要农民把兔子还给他！

彭德怀开了一只大西瓜庆祝今天的好消息。这里的西瓜又便宜又好吃。

碉堡子9月4—5日。（政治部的）刘晓现在李旺堡附近的回民中工作。今天他发回一份那里最近情况的报告。马鸿逵部有一个团要求红军回民团派个回民去同他们谈话。马鸿逵的团长不愿见红军代表，但同意他同他的部下谈话。

王（红军回民代表）回来后报告说，他在部队营房里到处看到共产党的传单。他说他同他们谈了几小时后，他们越发有兴趣了，最后团长也来听，但是又怕了起来，想把他捉起来。战士们提出了抗议，这才派人把他送回红军方面来。该团写了一封信，答复王从刘晓那里带去的信。他们说，他们不会后撤，因为他们奉命守卫这个地方，因此必须守住；他们愿意合作抗日，但红军必须同他们师长谈判；如果红军不打他们，他们也不打红军；又说红军送去的信和小册子都在战士中间散发了。

今天有两架飞机轰炸了这里附近的一队红军骑兵。人畜无伤，但有一颗炸弹炸掉了村中清真寺一角，死了3个照顾寺院的老回民。这不会增加本地人对南京的爱戴。

碉堡子9月6日。今天休整。一军团的指挥员们全在彭德怀司令部吃西瓜，战士们休息，自己打球吃西瓜。彭德怀开了连以上指挥员会议，这是一堂政治报告。他们让我参加。彭德怀讲话摘要如下：

"我们调到这些地方的原因，首先是扩大和发展我们的苏区；第二是配合二、四方面军（在甘南）的调动和前进；第三是消除马鸿逵和马鸿宾在这些地方的影响，同他们的部队直接形成统一战线。

"我们必须扩大这里的统一战线基础。我们必须对现在表示同情的白军指挥员发生决定性的影响，坚决地把他们争取到我们这边来。我们现在同他们许多人都有了

good united-front tactics," he commented. "One slogan is worth ten bullets." He lectured the staff on the united front and how to work it out in practice.

Peasants sold fruit and melons on the road, the Reds paying for everything they bought. One young soldier traded his pet rabbit for three melons in a long transaction with a peasant. After he'd eaten the melons he was very dour, wanting his rabbit back.

Today's news was celebrated by P'eng Teh-huai with a large water-melon feast: the melons here are cheap and excellent.

Tiao Pao Tzu, September 4—5. Liu Hsiao (of the political department) is now working among the Mohammedans near Li Wang Pao. Today he sent a report of some recent developments there. One of Ma's regiments asked to have a Mohammedan sent from the Red Moslem regiment to talk to them. Ma's regimental commander refused to meet the Red delegate, but permitted him to talk to his men.

Wang (this Red Moslem delegate) returned and reported that he had seen Red handbills all over the troops' quarters. He said that after he had talked to the troops for a few hours they became more and more interested, and finally the commander listened in too but, getting worried, decided to have him arrested. The men protested, and he was safely escorted back to the Red lines. The regiment sent a letter in reply to the one which Wang had carried to them from Liu Hsiao. They said they would not retreat because they had been ordered to hold this district, and must do so; that they were ready to make an agreement to fight Japan, but the Reds should negotiate with their division commander; that if the Reds would not fight them, they would not fight the Reds; and that letters and pamphlets sent by the Reds had been distributed among the men.

Two planes bombed a Red cavalry detachment near here today. No men nor horses were hit, but one bomb struck a corner of a village mosque and three old Moslem attendants were killed. This doesn't increase local affection for Nanking.

Tiao Pao Tzu, September 6. A day of rest and recreation. All commanders of the First Army Corps met at P'eng's headquarters for a melon feast, while the soldiers rested and had sports and a melon feast of their own. P'eng called a meeting of all company commanders and higher, and there was a political session. They permitted me to attend. A summary of P'eng's speech follows:

"Reasons for our movement to these districts are first to enlarge and develop our soviet districts; second, to cooperate with movement and advance of the Second and Fourth Front armies (in south Kansu); third, to liquidate the influence of Ma Hung-kuei and Ma Hung-ping in these regions and form a united front directly with their troops.

"We must enlarge the basis of the united front here. We must decisively influence those White commanders who are now sympathetic and win them over definitely to our side.

很好的联系；我们必须继续工作，通过写信，通过报纸，通过派代表，通过秘密会社，等等。

"我们必须尽快解放这里的回民群众，把他们组织起来后马上就武装他们，让他们组织自己的代议制政府，这样及早组成一支回民抗日军。

"我们必须加强自己部队的教育工作。最近有好几个例子说明我们的人违反统一战线政策，对我们允许撤退的军队开火。还有一些例子是我们的战士不愿交还缴获的步枪，说了几次才交出来。这不是违反纪律问题，而是不服从指挥员的命令，说明这些战士不充分了解这样做的原因，有些战士甚至攻击他们的领导发出'反革命命令'。有个连长收到白军指挥员一封信，看也不看就撕掉了，还说什么'这些白军都一样'。这说明我们必须更加深入地教育战士。我们第一次讲话没有把我们的立场向他们说清楚。我们要请他们提意见，在经过彻底讨论和解释后根据他们认为必要的那样改正我们的政策。我们必须使他们感到，统一战线政策不是骗白军的诡计，而是一种根本方针，符合党的决定。

"在东征（山西）以后，我们有许多同志到甘肃、宁夏这里来，他们感到失望，因为对比之下，我们在那里受到很大欢迎。他们感到灰心，因为这里农村很穷，人民政治热情很低。别灰心丧气！努力工作！这些人民也是兄弟，会像别人一样有反应的。我们一个机会也不能错过，要说服白军和回族农民。我们工作还不够努力。"

"至于群众，我们必须鼓励他们带头参加一切革命行动。我们自己不要去碰回民地主，但是要让人民知道，他们有权那样做，我们要保护他们那样做的群众团体，这是他们的革命权利，这是他们的劳动果实，理应归他们所有。我们必须加紧努力提高群众政治觉悟。要记住，他们至今为止除了民族仇恨以外没有别的政治觉悟。我们必须唤起他们的爱国心。我们必须加强在哥老会和其他秘密会社中的工作，使他们成为抗日统一战线的积极盟友，不只是消极盟友。我们必须加强同阿訇的良好关系，鼓励他们在抗日运动中起领导作用。我们必须把每个回民青年都组织起来，加强革命政权的基础。"

彭德怀发言以后，一军团和十五军团的两个政委作了长篇的批评发言。他们两人都检查了在"统一战线教育工作"方面的情况，提出了改进的意见。所有的指挥员都做了大量笔记，后来又举行了长时间的辩论，争论一直到吃晚饭的时候。彭德

We have good contacts with many of them now; we must continue our work, by letter, in our press, through delegates, through the secret societies, etc.

"We must intensify our educational work among our own troops. In several recent instances our men have violated the united-front policy by firing on troops that we had agreed to permit to withdraw. In other instances men were reluctant to return captured rifles and had to be ordered several times to do so. This is not a breach of discipline, but a lack of confidence in their commanders' orders, showing that the men do not fully understand the reasons for such actions, some men actually accusing their leaders of 'counterrevolutionary orders.' One company commander received a letter from a White commander and did not even read it, but tore it up, saying, 'They are all the same, these Whites.' This shows that we must more deeply instruct the rank and file; our first lectures have not made our position clear to them. We must ask for their criticism and make such modifications in our policy as they think necessary after thorough discussion and explanation. We must impress upon them that the united-front policy is no trick to fool the Whites, but that it is a basic policy and in line with the decisions of our Party.

"After the East Attack [into Shansi] many of our comrades, coming here to Kansu and Ninghsia, felt discouraged because the contrast was so great compared with the response we received there. They felt depressed because of the poverty of the country here and the low level of political enthusiasm among the people. Don't be discouraged! Work harder! These people are also brothers, and will respond to the same treatment as other human beings. We must not miss a single opportunity to convince a White soldier or a Mohammedan peasant. We are not working hard enough.

"As for the masses, we must urge them to take the lead in every revolutionary action. We must not touch any Mohammedan landlord ourselves, but we must show the people clearly that they have the freedom to do so, that we will protect their mass organizations that do so, that this is their revolutionary right, that it is the produce of their labor and belongs to them. We must intensify our efforts to raise the political consciousness of the masses. Remember that they have heretofore had no political consciousness except racial hatred. We must awaken a patriotic consciousness in them. We must deepen our work in the Ke Lao Hui and other secret societies and make them active, not merely passive, allies on the anti-Japanese front. We must consolidate our good relations with the *ahuns* and urge them to take places of leadership in the anti-Japanese movement. We must strengthen the basis of revolutionary power by organizing every Mohammedan youth."

P'eng's statement was followed by long critical comments from the political commissars of the First and Fifteenth Army corps. Both of them reviewed their efforts in "united-front educational work" and suggested improvements. All commanders took copious notes, and afterwards there was a session of long debate and argument which lasted till dinner. P'eng

怀最后建议两个军团各扩充500新兵，这得到附议后，一致通过。

晚饭后一军团剧社演出新戏，以上星期经验为素材。它用发噱的方式表现了指战员们在执行新政策过程中所犯的错误。有一场戏是一个指挥员和一个战士发生了争论；另一场戏是两个指挥员之间的争论；还有一场是一个连指挥员把白军的信撕掉了。

第二幕戏中，大多数错误都改正过来，红军和抗日回民军队并肩前进，一同歌唱，一同对日本人和国民党作战。文娱部门的配合工作快得出奇。

有一个消息传来说，（国民党军队驻守的）李旺堡遭到南京飞机的猛轰。显然飞行员以为他们的军队已经撤走，因为四周到处是红军。轰炸时回民战士逃出来躲在山上的窑洞里，但红军没有对他们开枪。彭德怀说，在江西也常常发生这种现象，有时整个市镇，整批民团或南京军队被蒋介石自己的飞机炸光，飞行员还以为是在炸红军。

先锋部队还没有到海原，但在继续挺进之前已清除了几个敌军阵地。这些阵地在李旺堡和马良湖。整个固原山谷和固原以西先要苏维埃化。现在红军进入一个完全是回民的区域，要到靖远的黄河流域后才再进入汉民聚居的区域。

明天我要回保安了。

在后来的一个月中，中国每个共产党员的注意力都要焦急地集中到一系列的军事调动上面，这是苏区历史上的第一次，红军全部主力最后终于在一个广大的地区中会师和集中起来。我们在这里就有必要介绍一下这次从南方来的第二次大行军的领导——介绍一下"中华全国"红军总司令朱德，他在西藏的冰天雪地中度过了一个严冬以后，现在终于率领二、四方面军倾师进入西北，其气势之猛和成功之大是大家所意想不到的。

moved that the two army corps be enlarged by five hundred new enlistments each, and this was seconded and passed unanimously.

After dinner there was a new play by the dramatic club of the First Army Corps, based on experiences of the past week. It portrayed in an amusing way the mistakes of the commanders and men in carrying out the new policy. One scene showed an argument between a commander and a warrior; another between two commanders; a third showed a company commander tearing up a letter he had received from the Whites.

In the second act most of these mistakes were shown corrected and the Red Army and anti-Japanese Moslem Army were marching together, and singing and fighting side by side against the Japanese and the Kuomintang. Seemed magically quick work by the education-through-entertainment department.

During the next month the attention of every Red in China was to be focused anxiously upon the series of maneuvers by which, for the first time in the history of the soviets, all the main forces of the Red Army were eventually united and concentrated in a single great area. And here some illumination should be shed upon the leadership of this second great trek from the South—upon Chu Teh, commander-in-chief of the "All China" Red Army, who, after a heartbreaking winter spent on the frozen marches of Tibet, was now pouring the Second and Fourth Front armies into the Northwest.

四、关于朱德[1]

李长林告诉我：

朱德年轻时做事鲁莽，敢做敢为，勇敢无畏，热衷于自己民族的各种传奇，喜欢《水浒传》中豪侠义士的故事传说，崇拜《三国演义》中英雄豪杰的光辉事迹，《三国演义》中的好汉们曾经在朱德的故乡四川的田野和山间战斗过。他天性尚武。借助家族的政治影响，他进入了新式的云南陆军讲武堂，成了中国第一批接受现代军事训练的军官学校学生中的一员。从云南陆军讲武堂毕业后，朱德被任命为陆军中尉，加入了中国人所谓的"洋军"——所谓"洋"是因为采用了西洋的训练方法和战术，因为作战时没有了中国乐师锣鼓号角的伴奏，因为在武器方面使用的是"洋矛子"——装有刺刀的来复枪。

在1911年推翻清朝的战斗中，这支现代的滇军扮演了重要的角色，当时统帅着1连勇士的朱德迅速成为了民国的一位杰出的勇士。到了1916年，袁世凯企图复辟帝制，朱德时任旅长，在名将蔡锷率领下的滇军率先举起讨袁义旗，注定了袁世凯的皇帝梦的覆灭。正是此时朱德的名字首次响彻南方诸省，成为蔡锷的"四员猛将"之一。

威望由此树立之后，朱德在政治上迅速平步青云。他成了云南府警察厅厅长，后任云南省财政厅厅长。云南和四川两省的人对官员有两点共识：一是官员都贪污腐化，二是他们都抽大烟。在朱德所成长的地区，抽大烟就如同喝茶一样普遍，父母习惯把大烟涂抹在甘蔗上来抚慰嗷嗷待哺的婴儿，所以他也不可避免地抽上了大

---

[1] 本章内容与朱德本人的自述（见尾注"关于朱德"）出入较大，为尊重原著，未做删改。——编注

4   Concerning Chu Teh

Li Chiang-lin told me:

As a youth Chu Teh was reckless, adventurous, and courageous, moved by the legends of his people, by the tales of "free companions" of the *Shui Hu Chuan*, and by the exploits of the heroes of the *Romance of Three Kingdoms*, who had fought over the fields and mountains of his native Szechuan. He gravitated naturally toward military life. Helped by his family's political influence, he was accepted in the new Yunnan Military Academy, and he was among the first cadets in China to be given modern military training. Upon graduation from the Yunnan Academy he was commissioned a lieutenant, and entered what the Chinese referred to as the "foreign army"—"foreign" because it used Western methods of drill and tactics, because it did not go into battle accompanied by Chinese musicians, and because for arms it used "foreign spears"—rifles with fixed bayonets on them.

In the overthrow of the Manchu Dynasty in 1912 this modern army of Yunnan played a prominent role, and Chu Teh, leading a battalion of braves, soon distinguished himself as a warrior of the republic. By 1916, when Yuan Shih-k'ai attempted to restore the monarchy, he was a brigadier general, and his Yunnanese troops under the celebrated Ts'ai O were the first to raise the banner of revolt, which doomed Yuan's imperial ambitions to defeat. At this time Chu Teh first became known throughout the southern provinces as one of the "four fierce generals" of Ts'ai O.

With his prestige thus established, Chu Teh's political fortunes pyramided rapidly. He became director of the Bureau of Public Safety in Yunnanfu, and then Provincial Commissioner of Finance. People of Yunnan and Szechuan agreed that there were two things certain about officials: one was that they were corrupt, the other that they were opium smokers. Reared in a region where opium was as commonly smoked as tea was drunk, and where parents customarily spread the drug on sugarcane to soothe their bellowing infants, Chu Teh had inevitably become a smoker. And given office by a

烟。而给予了他官位的官僚体制，则不仅将劫掠公共资金视为一种权利，更大程度上视为一种对家庭的义务。朱德也效仿自己的上司们利用当官的种种特权来为自己和子嗣谋取福利。

他先后结过几次婚。据说他娶过好几个妻子，并为她们及子女在云南的省会建造了富丽堂皇的宅第。人们也许会以为他已经得到了自己想要的一切：财富、权力、爱情、子嗣、尘世的浮华、显赫的声望以及可以宣扬儒家仁义道德的安适未来。实际上，他只有一个真正的坏习惯，但是正是这个坏习惯导致了他的衰落。他喜欢读书。

虽然一直到现在他都是一个纯粹的现实主义者，但是他的性格中肯定潜藏着一丝理想主义和真正的革命热情。受到读书的影响，同时也受到偶尔进入云南这个偏远地区的一些留学生的影响，朱德逐渐明白了1911年的辛亥革命对人民大众来说毫无意义；它只不过是专制官僚体制的更迭。而且，他似乎为此感到担忧——就像任何一个生活在有着4万奴婢的云南府的有感情的人都很可能会有的感觉一样。他显然被一种羞耻感困扰着，同时又胸怀壮志要效仿西方民间的英雄豪杰，渴望使中国走向"现代化"。书读得越多，他越发认识到自己的无知和祖国的落后。他想学习，想要游历。

1922年，朱德离开了自己的妻子，在云南府给她们发放养老金后遣散了。对于了解中国的保守主义，尤其是云南的封建禁忌的人来说，这种背离传统的行为是令人难以置信的，这本身就显示出一种特立独行的性格和非凡的决心。他离开云南，前往上海。在上海他遇到了许多年轻革命者，他们来自自己加入过的国民党。在这里他也渐渐与左翼激进分子建立了联系，不过这些激进分子往往鄙视他，认为他是个旧式的军阀。一个来自封建的云南的腐化官员，有家室的将军，还抽大烟——这也能成革命者吗？

此行之前，朱德下定决心要戒掉毒瘾。这并不容易：他吸食鸦片由来已久。但是这个汉子有着身边的熟人所想象不到的意志力。一连数日他在与毒瘾的斗争中几乎不省人事；接着，带上一种治疗药物，他搭乘一艘英国轮船沿江而下，前往上海。船上不能买卖鸦片，他在沿江东下的数周里，在甲板上踱来踱去，从来都不上岸，进行着这场他一生中最艰苦的战斗。但是，1个月后他下船时，已是双目炯炯，脸颊红润，脚步中透出一种全新的自信。在上海经过了最后的住院治疗之后，他热切地过上了新生活。他的副官李长林如是说。

bureaucracy which looked upon plunder of public funds as not so much a right but a duty to one's family, he followed the example of superiors and manipulated the privileges of office to enrich himself and his heirs.

He went in for a harem, too. He was said to have acquired several wives and concubines, and he built for them and his progeny a palatial home in the capital of Yunnan. One might have thought he had everything he desired: wealth, power, love, descendants, poppy dreams, eminent respectability, and a comfortable future in which to preach the proprieties of Confucianism. He had, in fact, only one really bad habit, but it was to prove his downfall. He liked to read books.

Pure realist though he had been till now, there must have been a strain of idealism and genuine revolutionary ardor latent in his character. Influenced by reading, influenced also by a few returned students who occasionally drifted into the backwash of Yunnan, Chu Teh gradually understood that the revolution of 1911 had been for the mass of the people a complete cipher; that it had merely replaced one despotic bureaucracy of exploitation with another. What was more, he seemed to have worried about it—as anyone of feeling, living in Yunnanfu, a city of 40,000 slave girls and boys, might well have done. He was apparently possessed by a sense of shame and simultaneously with an ambition to emulate the popular heroes of the West, and a desire to "modernize" China. The more books he read the more he realized his own ignorance and China's backwardness. He wanted to study and he wanted to travel.

By 1922 Chu Teh had unburdened himself of his wives and concubines, pensioning them off in Yunnanfu. To one who knew the conservatism of China, and especially the feudal taboos of Yunnan, this act of repudiation of tradition was hardly believable, and indicated in itself a personality of unusual independence and resolution. Leaving Yunnan, he went to Shanghai, where he met many young revolutionaries of the Kuomintang, which he had joined. Here also he came into contact with left-wing radicals, who tended to look upon him condescendingly as an old-fashioned militarist. A corrupt official from feudal Yunnan, a many-wived general, an opium addict—could this also be a revolutionary?

Before this trip Chu Teh had determined to break himself of the drug habit. It was not easy: he had been using opium for a long time. But this man had more steel in his will than his acquaintances supposed. For days he lay almost unconscious as he fought his noxious craving; then, taking a medicine cure along, he boarded a British steamer on the Yangtze and took passage for Shanghai. No opium could be bought or sold on board, and for weeks he sailed down the river, pacing the deck, never going ashore, fighting this hardest battle of his life. But after a month on board he left the ship with clear eyes, a ruddy glow on his cheeks, and a new confidence in his step. After a final hospital cure in Shanghai, he began a new life in earnest. So said his aide, Li Chiang-lin.

朱德当时已年近不惑，但是身强体壮，一心迫切地追寻新知识。他和一些中国学生结伴去了德国，在汉诺威附近住了一段时间。他在那里遇到了许多共产党人，此时他似乎已经开始严肃认真地学习马克思主义了，迷恋上了社会主义革命学说所呈现的各种新观点。在学习马克思主义的过程中，他的导师主要是年轻得足以做他的儿子的中国学生——因为他从未学过法语，对德语也只是略知皮毛，而且还缺乏语言天赋。他在德国的一位学生老师告诉我他是多么地认真，多么地有耐心，学习非常吃力，但倔强地不言放弃，他在一个全新的思想世界所带来的冲突混乱中挣扎，努力探求其中的基本真理和基本含义，他又是以怎样非凡的理性使自己彻底与他所接受的中国传统教育的一切偏见和局限决裂。

就是以这样的方式他读了一些关于第一次世界大战的历史，熟悉了欧洲政治。一天他的一位学生朋友[1]来看他，兴奋地谈到了一本名为《国家与革命》的书。朱德要他帮自己读一下，就这样他开始对马克思主义和俄国革命产生了兴趣。他先是读了布哈林的《共产主义入门》及其关于辩证唯物主义的著作，然后更多地阅读列宁的著作。适逢德国革命运动风起云涌，排山倒海的革命浪潮使他和数百名中国学生一起涌入了世界革命的斗争洪流之中。他加入了成立于德国的共产党中国支部。

"朱德经验丰富，训练有素，作风务实，"一位在德国认识他的同志告诉我。"他这个人非常朴实、谦虚，不摆架子。他总是乐于接受批评；他对别人的批评百听不厌。在德国时他过着战士那样的朴素生活。朱德最初对共产主义的兴趣发自他对穷苦百姓的同情，这种同情也让他加入过国民党。有一段时间他对孙逸仙坚信不疑，因为孙逸仙主张耕者有其田，限制私人资本。但是他一旦开始理解了马克思主义，便认识到了孙逸仙的治国方略的不足。"

朱德在巴黎也住过一段时间，他在那里进入了一所专门为中国学生开办的学校。学校的创建者吴稚晖是国民党的一位国民革命元老。在法国和德国期间，朱德受教于年轻的德国、法国以及中国导师。他谦恭地听讲，心平气和地询问、辩论，力求弄清弄懂。"要做现代人，要理解革命的意义，"他年轻的导师反复重申，"你就必须去俄国。在那里你能看到未来。"朱德再次听从了他们的建议。在莫斯科，他进入了

---

1. 即周恩来。

Chu Teh was then nearing forty, but he was in excellent health and his mind was eagerly reaching out for new knowledge. Accompanying some Chinese students, he went to Germany, where he lived for a while near Hannover. There he met many Communists, and at this time seems to have seriously taken up the study of Marxism and become enamored of new perspectives opened up by the theory of social revolution. In this study he was chiefly tutored by Chinese students young enough to be his own sons—for he never learned French, he knew only a smattering of German, and he was a poor linguist. One of his student teachers in Germany told me how deadly in earnest he had been; how patiently, ploddingly, stubbornly, he struggled amid the confusion of an impact of a whole new world of ideas to integrate the basic truths and meanings, how great had been the intellectual effort with which he divested himself of all the prejudices and limitations of his traditional Chinese training.

In this way he read some histories of the Great War, and familiarized himself with the politics of Europe. One day a student friend of his[1] came to see him, talking excitedly about a book called *State and Revolution*. Chu Teh asked him to help him read it, and thus he became interested in Marxism and the Russian Revolution. He read Bukharin's *ABC of Communism*, and his works on dialectical materialism, and then he read more of Lenin. The powerful revolutionary movement then active in Germany swept him, with hundreds of Chinese students, into the struggle for world revolution. He joined the Chinese branch of the Communist Party founded in Germany.

"Chu Teh had an experienced, disciplined, practical mind," a comrade who knew him in Germany told me. "He was an extremely simple man, modest and unassuming. He always invited criticism; he had an insatiable appetite for criticism. In Germany he lived the simple life of a soldier. Chu Teh's original interest in communism sprang from his sympathy for the poor, which had also brought him into the Kuomintang. He believed strongly in Sun Yat-sen for a while, because of Sun's principles advocating land for the tillers, and the limitation of private capital. But not until he began to understand Marxism did he realize the inadequacy of Sun Yat-sen's program."

Chu Teh also lived for some time in Paris, where he entered a school for Chinese students which had been established by Wu Tze-hui, a veteran national revolutionary of the Kuomintang. In France and in Germany he sat at the feet of his young German, French, and Chinese instructors, and he humbly listened, quietly interrogated, debated, sought clarity and understanding. "To be modern, to understand the meaning of the revolution," his youthful tutors kept repeating, "you must go to Russia. There you can see the future." And again Chu Teh followed their advice. In Moscow he entered the Eastern Toilers'

---

1. Chou En-lai.

东方劳动大学，在中国老师的指导下学习马克思主义。1925年底，朱德返回上海，自此开始在共产党的指引下进行工作，并于不久之后将自己的财产捐给了党。

朱德再次加盟自己的老上司云南同乡朱培德将军的旗下，朱培德当时在国民党军中的权力仅次于蒋介石。1927年，朱培德将军的军队占领了江南数省，他任命朱德担任江西首府南昌市的公安局长。在南昌，他还掌管着一个军官学员训练团，并与驻守在江西更南部的国民党第九军建立了联系。第九军中有数个分队过去在云南时曾是他的部下，这样便为八一南昌起义奠定了基础。在南昌起义中，共产党军队第一次开始公开与国民党展开了漫长的权力斗争。

1927年8月1日对朱德来说是一个进行重大抉择的日子。朱德接到总司令朱培德的命令，要求镇压起义军，但是朱德（起义的组织者之一）却倒戈加入了起义军，彻底断绝了自己与过去藕断丝连的关系。贺龙失败之后，朱德率领自己的警察部队和训练团同起义军一同南下，身后关闭的城门成了他与少壮时的安逸和荣华富贵作最后决裂的标志。他的前面是多年的不懈斗争。

第九军也有一部分跟随了朱德，这支阵容不整的革命军一路打到汕头，先是攻克了汕头又被赶出了汕头，后来再次撤回到了江西和湖南。当时朱德的得力干将中有3个黄埔军校学员：王尔琢（后来在战斗中牺牲）、陈毅和后来成了红军大学校长的林彪。[1] 他们尚未自称红军，只是改号称国民革命军。撤出福建之后，朱德的军队由于开小差和伤亡，减员至900人，火力配备仅有500支步枪和1挺机关枪，每人仅剩数发子弹。

在这种形势下，朱德接受了与另一位云南将领范石生联合的提议。当时范石生的大军驻扎在湖南南部，他虽然不是共产党人，但是对自己军中的共产党人还是比较宽容，他希望利用他们在政治上与蒋介石抗衡。作为云南人，他也乐于为自己的同乡提供庇护。朱德的军队被改编为一四〇团，他担任第十六军的总参议。正是在这里他经历了一生中最惊心动魄的虎口脱险。

---

1. 李先念当时也追随朱德。（与史实有出入。——编注）

University, where he studied Marxism under Chinese teachers. Late in 1925 he returned to Shanghai, and from that time on he worked under the direction of the Communist Party, to which he soon gave his fortune.

Chu Teh rejoined his former superior and fellow Yunnanese, General Chu P'ei-teh, whose power in the Kuomintang Army was second only to that of Chiang Kai-shek. In 1927, when General Chu P'ei-teh's forces occupied several provinces south of the Yangtze, he made Chu Teh chief of the Bureau of Public Safety in Nanchang, capital of Kiangsi. There also he took command of a training regiment of cadets, and there he made contact with the Ninth Kuomintang Army, stationed farther south in Kiangsi. In the Ninth Army were detachments that had formerly been under his personal command in Yunnan. Thus the stage was prepared for the August Uprising in Nanchang, in which Communist troops first began the long open struggle for power against the Kuomintang.

August 1, 1927, was a day of great decision for Chu Teh. Ordered by his commander-in-chief, Chu P'ei-teh, to suppress the insurrection, Chu Teh (who had helped organize it) instead joined with the rebels, renouncing the remaining connections with his past. When, after the defeat of Ho Lung, he headed his police and his training regiment southward with the rebels, the city gates which closed behind him were symbolic of the final break with the security and success of his youth. Ahead of him lay years of unceasing struggle.

Part of the Ninth Army went with Chu Teh also, as the straggling band of revolutionaries swept down to Swatow, captured it, were driven out, and then withdrew again to Kiangsi and Hunan. Among Chu Teh's chief lieutenants at that time were three Whampoa cadets: Wang Erh-tso (later killed in battle); Ch'en Yi; and Lin Piao, who became president of the Red University.[1] They did not yet call themselves a Red Army, but renamed themselves only the National Revolutionary Army. After the retreat from Fukien, Chu Teh's forces were reduced, by desertions and casualties, to 900 men, with a fire power of only 500 rifles, one machine gun, and a few rounds of ammunition each.

In this situation Chu Teh accepted an offer to connect with General Fan Shih-sheng, another Yunnan commander whose big army was then stationed in southern Hunan, and who, though not a Communist, tolerated Communists in his army, hoping to use them politically against Chiang Kai-shek. As a Yunnanese he was also inclined to give haven to his fellow provincials. Here Chu Teh's troops were incorporated as the 140th Regiment, and he became chief political adviser to the Sixteenth Army. And here he had the narrowest escape of his life.

---

1. Li Hsien-nien was then also with Chu Teh.

共产主义势力在范石生的军中迅速壮大，不久一个反布尔什维克的小集团便秘密与蒋介石取得了联系，阴谋针对朱德发起一场军事政变。一天夜里，朱德只带了40名部下正在一家小酒馆里吃饭，突然遭到了以胡之龙（译音）为首的政变军人的袭击。枪战顷刻开始，但是由于天黑，刺杀者看不真切。当其中的几个人用手枪瞄准了朱德的头部时，他慌忙地大喊道，"别开枪，我只是个厨师。别杀一个能为你们做饭的人！"士兵们动摇了，犹豫起来，于是朱德便被带出接受仔细盘查。胡之龙的一个表弟认出了他，大喊道："他是朱德！杀了他！"但是朱德拽出了自己藏在身上的武器，打死了他，突破他的卫兵逃跑了。随他一同脱险的只有5个人。

这一事件解释了朱德自此在红军中的绰号的来由——"伙夫头"。

回到团中之后，朱德通知范石生自己准备退出，据称范石生于是赠给了朱德5万元以表示自己的善意，因为反蒋事宜尚未明确下来，像年轻的共产党人这样无隶属关系的盟友在范石生的官兵中间有着相当大的影响，是不能轻易抛弃的。但是在接下来的几个月里，事实表明这笔钱是不够的。这支小队伍现在紧密地团结在一起，所依赖的几乎单纯就是对朱德及其手下为数不多的军官的忠诚。党派问题非常混乱，还没有明确的"路线"，军事战略也悬而未决。朱德的军队仍然穿着国民党的军服，但是他们衣衫褴褛；许多人都没有鞋子穿；伙食很差，常常根本就没有食物，导致逃兵不断增加。但是广州公社的消息产生了一些鼓舞作用，为他们指出了一条明确的行动路线。朱德将自己的军队重编为3个支队，称为"农民纵队"，开往湘赣粤边界地区，并与由一名激进学生领导的一些土匪联合，开始施行一项废除赋税、重分田地和没收富人财产的计划。经过一场血战，他们占领了宜章县城，将其作为自己的根据地，这支年轻的队伍依靠南瓜勉强在政治辩论中挨过了冬天。

与此同时，毛泽东的农民军艰难地穿过了湖南，最后来到了位于湘赣南部边界的井冈山安身。在土匪首领王佐和袁文才的帮助下，他们占领了周边的两个县，在山中建立起了一个几乎固若金汤的根据地。毛泽东的这支"工农红军"派毛泽东的弟弟毛泽覃作为代表前往相距不远的朱德的军中。毛泽覃带来了党要求联合各种武装的指示和开展游击战争、进行土地革命以及建立苏维埃的明确计划。1928年5月，

Communist influence in Fan Shih-sheng's army rapidly increased, and soon an anti-Bolshevik faction, secretly connected with Chiang Kai-shek, planned a coup against Chu Teh. One night he was staying in an inn with only forty of his followers, when he was attacked by a force under Hu Chi-lung, leader of the coup. Shooting began at once, but it was dark and the assassins could not see clearly. When several of them aimed revolvers at Chu Teh's head he cried out excitedly, "Don't shoot me, I'm only the cook. Don't shoot a man who can cook for you!" The soldiers, touched to the stomach, hesitated, and Chu Teh was led outside for closer inspection. There he was recognized by a cousin of Hu Chi-lung, who shouted, "Here is Chu Teh! Kill him!" But Chu Teh pulled out a concealed weapon of his own, shot the man, overcame his guard, and fled. Only five of his men escaped with him.

This incident explained the nickname by which Chu Teh had ever since been known in the Red Army—"Chief of the Cooks."

Rejoining his regiment, Chu Teh notified Fan Shih-sheng that he was withdrawing, whereupon Fan was said to have presented him with a gift of $50,000 to keep his good will, for the issue against Chiang Kai-shek was still not clearly decided, and free-lance allies like the young Communists, who had considerable influence on many of Fan's officers and men, were not to be lightly spurned. But in the months ahead the money was to prove inadequate. The little army was now held together almost solely by loyalty to Chu Teh and a few of his commanders. Party affairs were in great confusion, no definite "line" had been established, and military strategy was undecided. Chu's troops still wore Kuomintang uniforms, but they were in rags; many of them had no shoes; and poor food, or often no food at all, caused steady desertions. But some encouragement had been provided by the news of the Canton Commune, which had suggested a clear line of action. Chu Teh re-formed his army into three sections, calling it the "Peasant Column Army," and moved to the Hunan-Kiangsi-Kwangtung border, where he united with some bandits led by a radical student, and began a program of tax abolition, redistribution of land, and confiscation of the property of the rich. Yih Chang *hsien* was occupied as a base, after a bloody struggle, and the young army eked out the winter on squash and political debates.

Meanwhile Mao Tse-tung's peasant army had marched ingloriously through Hunan, to come at last to sanctuary at Chingkangshan, on the southern Kiangsi-Hunan border, where, with the help of the bandit leaders Wang Tso and Yuan Wen-t'sai, they had occupied two surrounding counties and built up in the mountains a nearly impregnable base. To Chu Teh, not far away, the "Peasants' and Workers' Red Army" of Mao Tse-tung sent as delegate his brother, Mao Tse-min. He brought instructions from the Party to unite forces, and news of a definite program of partisan warfare, agrarian revolution, and the building of soviets. When in May, 1928, the two armies combined at Chingkangshan,

两支队伍在井冈山会师时,他们手中控制着 5 个县,拥有约 5 万名追随者。其中约 4,000 人拥有步枪,约 1 万人只有长矛、大刀和锄头作为武器;剩下的都是手无寸铁的党务工作者、宣传人员或者战士家属,其中有许多儿童。

自此便形成了将在此后 6 年内在华南创造历史的著名的朱毛组合。同苏维埃一样,朱德上升为一名令人敬畏的军事领导人也走过了同样的发展轨迹。

1931 年,在第一次苏维埃大会上,朱德以全票当选红军总司令。两年内已经组建了 4 个军团,火力配备为约 5 万支步枪和数百挺机关枪,大多数是从敌军手中缴获的,苏维埃共和国控制了赣南的广大地区和湘、闽的部分地区。红军已经开始进行强化的政治培训,建立了一座军火库,整个苏区开始实施初步的社会革命性质的经济和政治改革,红军军服在夜以继日地赶制以装备新加入的游击队员,革命士气日渐高涨。又过了两年后,红军兵力已经增加了 1 倍。

在南方的这些年里,朱德担任红军总司令经历了数百次小型战斗、几十次大型战斗和 5 次惨烈的大型剿灭战役。在最后的一次剿灭战役中,他面对的敌军拥有的技术进攻能力(包括重炮、飞机和机械化部队)大约多出自己 8 至 9 倍,物资多出自己许多倍。然而,无论怎样去评判他成功或失败的程度,都必须承认的是,就战术灵活性、惊人的机动性和足智多谋而言,他无疑已经在游击战中为革命化的中国军队培养起了令人生畏的作战能力。红军在南方犯下的重大错误是战略性的,对于这些错误政治领导层必须负主要责任。

朱德对部下的爱护是众所周知的。自从担任红军总司令以后,他在生活和穿着上就与普通战士一模一样,同甘共苦,早期常常没有鞋子穿,整整一个冬天靠南瓜充饥,另外一个冬天则靠牦牛肉度过,从来没有怨言,很少生病。他们说,他喜欢在营里转,与战士们坐在一起讲故事,或与他们一起打球。他乒乓球打得很好,对篮球也特别"上瘾"。军中的士兵不管谁都能直接将自己的不满告诉总司令。朱德向战士们讲话时总是摘下帽子。在长征途中,他曾经将自己的马让给疲惫的同志,徒步走过了大部分路途,却没有疲惫的意思。

they were in control of five counties, and had some 50,000 followers. Of these about 4,000 were armed with rifles, some 10,000 being equipped only with spears, swords, and hoes; while the rest were unarmed Party workers, propagandists, or families of the warriors, including a large number of children.

Thus began the famous Chu-Mao combination which was to make history in South China for the next six years. Chu Teh's ascension as a formidable military leader followed the same curve of growth as the soviets.

At the First Soviet Congress, in 1931, Chu Teh was unanimously elected commander-in-chief of the Red Army. Within two years four army corps had been built up, with a firing power of some 50,000 rifles and hundreds of machine guns, mostly captured from enemy troops, and the soviets controlled vast areas of southern Kiangsi and parts of Hunan and Fukien. Intensified political training had begun, an arsenal had been erected, elementary social-revolutionary economic and political reforms were being realized throughout the soviets, Red Army uniforms were being turned out day and night to equip new partisans, and revolutionary morale was strengthening. In two years more the Red forces had been doubled.

During these years in the South, Chu Teh was in overall military command of combined Red Armies in hundreds of skirmishes, through scores of major battles, and through the brunt of five great annihilation campaigns, in the last of which he faced an enemy with technical offensive power (including heavy artillery, aviation, and mechanized units) estimated at from eight to nine times greater than his own, and resources many, many times exceeding anything at his disposal. However his degree of success or failure is to be measured, it must be admitted that for tactical ingenuity, spectacular mobility, and richness of versatility in maneuver, he established beyond any doubt the formidable fighting power of revolutionized Chinese troops in partisan warfare. The great mistakes of the Red Army in the South were strategic, and for those the political leadership must be held chiefly responsible.

Chu Teh's devotion to his men was proverbial. Since assuming command of the army he had lived and dressed like the rank and file, had shared all their hardships, often going without shoes in the early days, living one whole winter on squash, another on yak meat, never complaining, rarely sick. He liked to wander through the camp, they said, sitting with the men and telling stories, or playing games with them. He played a good game of table tennis, and a "wistful" game of basketball. Any soldier in the army could bring his complaints directly to the commander-in-chief. Chu Teh took his hat off when he addressed his men. On the Long March he lent his horse to tired comrades, walking much of the way, seemingly tireless.

军中流传的关于朱德的各种神话为他增添了不可思议的力量：能够向四面八方看 100 里，能上天飞翔，精通道教法术，比如在敌人面前制造尘云，或者激起一阵狂风来对付他们。迷信的人相信他刀枪不入，不是有成千上万发子弹和炮弹都没有打倒他吗？也有人说他有死而复生的能力，国民党不是一再宣布他已经死亡，常常还有板有眼地描述他断气时的样子吗？在中国，数以百万计的人都知道朱德这个名字，有的把他看成是一种威胁，有的把他看成是一颗明亮的希望之星，这要看每个人在生活中的地位，但是对所有人来说这都是一个在十年史册上不可磨灭的名字。

Popular myths about Chu Teh were said to credit him with miraculous powers: the ability to see 100 *li* on all sides, the power to fly, and the mastery of Taoist magic, such as creating dust clouds before an enemy, or stirring a wind against them. Superstitious folk believed him invulnerable, for had not thousands of bullets and shells failed to destroy him? Others said he had the power of resurrection, for had not the Kuomintang repeatedly declared him dead, often giving minute details of the manner in which he expired? Millions knew the name Chu Teh in China, and to each it was a menace or a bright star of hope, according to his status in life, but to all it was a name imprinted on the pages of a decade of history.

PART ELEVEN
Back to Pao An

第十一篇
回到保安

一、　　路上的邂逅

我从宁夏又南下到甘肃。四五天后我回到了河连湾，又见到了蔡畅和她的丈夫李富春，同他们一起又吃了一顿法国式烹调的饭，遇见了一军团政治委员聂荣臻的年轻漂亮的妻子。她最近从白色世界溜进苏区，刚去看了她的 5 年不见的丈夫回来。

我在河连湾后勤部呆了 3 天，后勤部设在原来属于一个回民粮商的大院子里。从建筑上来说，这群房子很有意思，基本上具有中亚细亚的外表：厚厚的平屋顶，深深地嵌在至少有 4 英尺厚的墙上的阿拉伯式窗户。我牵着马到那个宽敞的马厩里去时，一个高大的白胡子老人，身穿一套褪色的灰布制服，腰上系着一条长可及地的皮围裙，走上前来，举手敬礼，他戴着一顶红星军帽，太阳晒得黧黑的脸，露出了没有牙的笑容。他把马鸿逵——我的马——牵了过去。

我心中纳闷，这个老爷爷怎么闯到我们童子军的营房里来了？我于是停了下来问他，从他嘴里套出一个故事来。他是山西人，在红军东征时参了军。他姓李，64 岁，自称是年纪最大的一个红军"战士"。他很歉然地解释，他当时不在前线是："因为杨指挥员认为我在这里看马更有用，因此我就留下来了。"

李在参加红军之前在山西省洪洞县卖肉，他痛斥"模范省主席"阎锡山和地方官吏以及他们的苛捐杂税。"你在洪洞没法做买卖，"他说，"他们连你拉的屎也要征税。"老李听说红军来了，就决定参加红军。他的妻子已死，两个女儿都已出嫁，他

1   Casuals of the Road

From Ninghsia I turned southward again into Kansu. In four or five days I was back in Holienwan, where I again saw Ts'ai Ch'ang and her husband, Li Fu-ch'un, and had another meal of French cooking with them, and met the young and pretty wife of Nieh Jung-chen, political commissar of the First Army Corps. She had but recently slipped into the soviet districts from the White world, and had now just returned from a visit to her husband, whom she had not seen for five years.

I stayed three days in Holienwan with the supply commissariat, which was quartered in a big compound formerly owned by a Mohammedan grain merchant. Architecturally it was an interesting group of buildings of a generally Central Asian appearance, with flat heavy roofs, and deep Arabic windows set into walls at least four feet thick. As I led my horse into its spacious stables a tall white-bearded man, wearing a faded gray uniform, with a long leather apron that reached to the ground, stepped up and saluted his red-starred cap, while his sunburned face wreathed a toothless smile. He took charge of Ma Hung-kuei, my horse.

How, I wondered, had this grandfather wandered into our boyscout encampment? I stopped to ask, and forced a story from him. He was from Shansi, and had joined the Red Army during its expedition there. His name was Li, he was sixty-four; and he claimed the distinction of being the oldest Red warrior. Rather apologetically he explained that he was not at the front just then "because Commander Yang thinks I am more useful here at this horse work, and so I stay."

Li had been a pork seller in the town of Hung T'ung, Shansi, before he became a Red, and he roundly cursed "Model Governor" Yen Hsi-shan and the local officials and their ruinous taxes. "You can't do business in Hung T'ung," he said; "they tax a man's excrement." When old Li heard the Reds were coming he had decided to join them. His wife was dead, and his two daughters were both married; he had no sons; he had no ties

没有儿子,在洪洞县除了课税很重的卖肉生意以外一无牵挂;而且反正洪洞县是个"死人"呆的地方。他想生活得有生气一些,所以这个冒险分子就偷偷地出了城,投到红军这边来了。

"我要求参军时,他们对我说,'你年岁大了。红军生活很艰苦。'我怎么说?我说,'不错,我这身子已64岁,可是我走路像个20岁的小伙子。我会开枪。别人能干的我都能干。你们要的是人,我也能当兵。'因此他们说你就来吧,我同红军一起行军过了山西,同红军一起渡了黄河,现在就到了甘肃。"

我微笑着问他,这比卖肉是不是强一些。他喜欢吗?

"哦!卖肉是龟子干的事!这里的工作值得干。穷人的军队在为被压迫者打仗,你说是不是?我当然喜欢。"那老头儿在胸口袋里摸索了一会,掏出来一个脏布包,他小心翼翼地打开来,里面是一个旧笔记本。"你瞧,"他说,"我已经认识了200多个字。红军每天教我认4个。我在山西活了64年,可没有人教我写自己的名字。你说红军好还是不好?"他很得意地指着他写的歪歪斜斜的字,好像是带着污泥的鸡爪子在干净的地席上留下的脚印,他还期期艾艾地念着刚写上去的几句话。接着,好像戏剧的高潮一样,他拿出一支铅笔头,龙飞凤舞地给我写了他的名字。

"我想你也在考虑再娶媳妇吧,"我对他开玩笑说。他严肃地摇摇头,说他妈的这些马一匹接着一匹,他没有工夫考虑女人问题,说完他就慢慢儿地去照顾他的牲口去了。

第二天晚上,我走过院子后面的果园里的时候,遇见了另外一个山西人,他比老李年轻20岁,但一样使人感到有趣。我听见一个小鬼在叫,"礼拜堂!礼拜堂!"觉得很奇怪,就四处张望他叫"礼拜堂"[1]的那个人是谁。在一座小山上,我看见有个理发师在给一个青年理发,把他的脑袋剃得像个鸡蛋一样光光的。我询问之下发现他的真实姓名叫贾河忠,原来在山西平阳一家美国教会医院的药房里工作。小鬼们叫他这个绰号,是因为他是个基督教徒,每天仍做祷告。

贾河忠拉起他的裤腿,给我看他腿上的一块伤口,他至今仍有些跛,他又拉起上衣给我看肚子上的一个伤口,他说这都是打仗的纪念品,因此他没有上前线。理发并不是他的工作:他又是药剂师,又是红军战士。

---

1. 字面含义为"星期日教堂"。

at all in Hung T'ung except his overtaxed pork business; and Hung T'ung was a "dead-man" sort of place, anyway. He wanted something livelier, and so the adventurer had crept out of the city to offer himself to the Reds.

"When I wanted to enlist they said to me, 'You are old. In the Red Army life is hard.' And what did I say? I said, 'Yes, this body is sixty-four years old, it's true, but I can walk like a boy of twenty, I can shoot a gun, I can do the work of any man. If it's men you need, I can also serve.' So they told me to come along, and I marched through Shansi with the Red Army, and I crossed the Yellow River with the Red Army, and here I am in Kansu."

I smiled and asked him whether it was any better than pork selling. Did he like it?

"Oh-ho! Pork selling is a turtle man's sort of business! Here is work worth doing. A poor man's army fighting for the oppressed, isn't it? Certainly I like it." The old man fumbled in his breast pocket and brought forth a soiled cloth, which he carefully unwrapped to reveal a worn little notebook. "See here," he said. "I already recognize over 200 characters. Every day the Red Army teaches me four more. In Shansi I lived for sixty-four years and yet nobody ever taught me to write my name. Is the Red Army good or isn't it?" He pointed with intense pride to the crude scrawl of his characters that resembled the blots of muddy hen's feet on clean matting, and falteringly he read off some newly inscribed phrases. And then, as a sort of climax, he produced a stub of pencil and with an elaborate flourish he wrote his name for me.

"I suppose you're thinking of marrying again," I joked with him. He shook his head gravely and said no, what with one defile-mother horse after another he had no time to think about the woman problem, and with that he ambled away to look after his beasts.

Next evening, as I was walking through an orchard behind the courtyard, I met another Shansi man, twenty years Li's junior, but just as interesting. I heard a *hsiao-kuei* calling out, "Li Pai T'ang! Li Pai T'ang!" and looked in curiosity to see whom he was addressing as the "House-of-Christian-Worship."[1] There upon a little hill I found a barber shaving a youth's head clean as an egg. Upon inquiry I discovered that his real name was Chia Ho-chung, and that he had formerly worked in the pharmacy of an American missionary hospital in P'ing Yang, Shansi. The "little devils" had given him this nickname because he was a Christian, and still said his prayers daily.

Chia pulled up his trousers and showed me a bad wound on his leg, from which he still limped, and he yanked up his coat to display a wound on his belly, where he had also been hit. These, he explained, were souvenirs of battles, and that was why he was not at the front. This hair cutting wasn't his real job at all: he was either a pharmacist or a Red warrior.

---

1. Literally, "Sunday Temple."

贾河忠说，那家基督教医院里有另外两个工作人员同他一起参加了红军。他们临走以前同医院里的中国名字叫李仁的美国医生讨论了他们的打算。李仁医生是个"好人，他给穷人治病不收钱，从来不压迫人。"当贾河忠和他的同伴征求他的意见时，他说，"去吧。我听说红军是正直的好人，不像别的军队，你们能同他们一起打仗，应该很高兴。"因此他们就去当了红色的罗宾汉。

"也许李仁医生只是要把你们打发掉。"我这样说。

那个理发师愤然否认。他说他同李仁的关系一直很好，李仁是个很好的人。他叫我去告诉这个李仁——如果我有机会见到——他仍活着，过得很好，很愉快，革命一结束，他就回药房去做原来的工作。我很恋恋不舍地离开了"礼拜堂"。他是个好红军，好理发师，真正的基督教徒。

附带地说一句，我在红军中间遇到过好几个基督教徒和前基督教徒。许多共产党领导人——周恩来是个突出的例子——曾在外国教会学校受教育，其中有些人一度是笃信的基督教徒。红军军医队长纳尔逊·傅医生[1]原来是江西一家美以美教会医院的医生。他虽然志愿参加红军工作，热情拥护他们，但仍笃信他的宗教，因此没有参加共产党。

在江西苏区进行了普遍的"反神"宣传。所有寺庙、教堂、教会产业都被没收为国家财产，和尚、尼姑、神父、牧师、外国传教士都被剥夺了公民权利，但是在西北实行了容忍宗教的政策。事实上，做礼拜自由是个基本的保证。所有外国教会的财产受到了保护，外逃传教士被请回去到他们的教民那里去工作。共产党保留了进行自己的反宗教宣传的权利，认为"反对做礼拜的自由"同做礼拜的自由一样是一种民主权利。

共产党这种对教会的新政策，加以利用的唯一外国人是一些比利时教士，他们是绥远的一些大地主。他们有一处的地产有两万亩，另一处有5,000亩左右，在长城上的定边附近。红军占领定边以后，比利时人的产业一边同苏区相邻，一边是白军。红军没有想没收比利时人的地产，但是订了一个条约，他们保证保护教会财产，但教士们必须允许他们在这天主教大庄园里种田的佃户中间组织抗日团体。这个奇怪的协定还有一个规定是，比利时人为中国苏维埃政府拍一份电报给法国的勃鲁姆总理，祝贺人民阵线的胜利。

---

1. 即傅连暲。——译注

Chia said that two other attendants in that Christian hospital had joined the Reds with him. Before leaving, they had discussed their intention with the American doctor in the hospital, whose Chinese name was Li Jen. Dr. Li Jen was "a good man, who healed the poor without charge and never oppressed people," and when Chia and his companions asked his advice he had said, "Go ahead. I have heard that the Reds are good and honest men and not like the other armies, and you should be glad to fight with them." So off they had gone to become red, red Robin Hoods.

"Maybe Dr. Li Jen just wanted to get rid of you," I suggested.

The barber indignantly denied it. He said he had always got along very well with Li Jen, who was an excellent man. He asked me to tell this Li Jen, if I ever saw him, that he was still alive, well, and happy, and that as soon as the revolution was over he was coming back to take his old job in the pharmacy. I left House-of-Worship with much reluctance. He was a fine Red, a good barber, and a real Christian.

Incidentally, I met several Christians and ex-Christians among the Reds. Many Communists had once been active Christians. Dr. Nelson Fu, head of the Red Army Medical Corps, was formerly a doctor in a Methodist hospital in Kiangsi. Although he volunteered to work with the Reds, and enthusiastically supported them, he still adhered to his faith, and hence had not joined the Communist Party.

In Kiangsi the soviets carried on extensive "anti-God" propaganda. All temples, churches, and church estates were converted into state property, and monks, nuns, priests, preachers, and foreign missionaries were deprived of the rights of citizenship; but in the Northwest a policy of religious toleration was practiced. Freedom of worship was a primary guarantee, in fact. All foreign mission property was protected, and refugee missionaries were invited to return to their flocks. The Communists reserved the right to preach anti-religious propaganda of their own, holding the "freedom to oppose worship" to be a corollary of the democratic privilege of the freedom to worship.

The only foreigners who took advantage of the new Communist policy toward religious institutions were some Belgian missionaries who were among the great landlords of Suiyuan. They owned one vast estate of 20,000 *mou*, and another of some 5,000 *mou* of land near Tingpien, on the Great Wall. After the Red Army occupied Tingpien, one side of the Belgians' property lay adjacent to soviet territory and the other side was held by White troops. The Reds did not attempt to expropriate the Belgians' land, but made a "treaty" in which they guaranteed to protect the church property, provided the priests permitted them to organize anti-Japanese societies among the tenants who tilled the land of this big Catholic missionary fiefdom. Another stipulation of the curious agreement provided that the Belgians would dispatch a message from the Chinese Soviet Government to Premier Blum of France, congratulating him on the triumph of the People's Front.

在河连湾附近发生过一系列民团的袭击,距此很近的一个村庄在我到达前两天曾遭洗劫。一队民团在天亮以前偷偷到了那里,杀死了哨兵,把一堆柴火放在十几个红军战士睡觉的房子外面就纵起了火。红军战士逃出来时,由于烟熏睁不开眼,被民团开枪打死,抢去了枪支。然后这批人就参加了另外一帮400人左右的民团,从北方下来进行袭击,烧村劫寨,他们大多数人都是国民党将领高桂滋所武装的。二十八军派了一营人去搜索他们,我离河连湾那天,这些年轻的战士刚追击成功归来。

战斗是在河连湾不远几里路的地方发生的,白匪据说正在准备攻打河连湾。有些农民在山里发现了民团的巢穴,红军据此情报,兵分三路,中路与匪徒正面交锋。在红军左右两翼包抄合拢时,战斗就有了定局。民团死40个左右,红军死16名,双方都有不少人受伤。民团被全部缴了械,两个匪酋被活捉。

我们骑马回陕西时遇到了该营带着俘虏回来。各村都准备大事欢迎,农民们在道路两旁向凯旋的部队欢呼。农卫队举着红缨枪肃立致敬,少先队向他们唱红军歌曲,姑娘们和妇女们送来了点心、茶水、水果、热水——这是她们仅有的礼物,但是使疲惫的战士的脸上现出了笑容。他们都很年轻,比前线正规军年轻得多,我觉得许多头缠带血绷带的人才只十四五岁。我看见马上一个少年,处于半昏迷状态,两边都有一个战友扶着,他的头上也缠着绷带,正中间有一块圆形的血迹。

这一队少年带的步枪几乎有他们身子一般高。在他们的行列中间走着的是两个匪首。一个是满脸胡须的中年农民,我不知道,他被这些年轻得可以做他儿子的战士带着,是不是感到难为情。但是他毫不畏惧的神态,确是使人感到惊异,我想他很可能同别人一样也是一个贫农,也许在打仗时自己也有什么信仰,遗憾的是他就要被枪毙了。我问傅锦魁时,他摇摇头。

"我们不杀俘虏的民团。我们教育他们,给他们悔过的机会,他们许多人后来成了很好的红军战士。"

There had been a series of raids by *min-t'uan* near Holienwan, and one village only a short distance away had been sacked two nights before I arrived. A band had crept up to the place just before dawn, overpowered and killed the lone sentry, and had then brought up bunches of dry brushwood and set fire to the huts in which about a dozen Red soldiers were sleeping. As the Reds ran out, blinded by the smoke, the *min-t'uan* had shot them down and seized their guns. Then they had joined with a gang of some 400, most of them armed by the Kuomintang general, Kao Kuei-tzu, who were raiding down from the North and burning farms and villages. The Twenty-eighth Army had sent a battalion out to attempt to round them up, and the day I left Holienwan these young warriors came back after a successful chase.

The battle had occurred only a few *li* from Holienwan, which the White bandits were said to be preparing to attack. Some peasants had discovered the *min-t'uan* lair in the inner mountains and, acting on this information, the Reds had divided into three columns, the center one meeting the bandits in a frontal clash. The issue was decided when the two flanking columns of Reds closed in and surrounded the enemy. Some forty *min-t'uan* were killed, and sixteen Reds, while many on both sides were wounded. The *min-t'uan* were entirely disarmed, and their two chieftains taken captive.

We passed the battalion returning with their captives as we rode back toward Shensi. A big welcome had been organized in the villages, and the peasants lined the road to cheer the victorious troops. Peasant Guards stood holding their long red-tasseled spears in salute, and the Young Vanguards sang Red songs to them, while girls and women brought refreshments, tea and fruit and hot water—all they had, but it creased the faces of the weary soldiers with smiles. They were very young, much younger than the front-line regulars, and it seemed to me that many who wore bloodstained bandages were no more than fourteen or fifteen. I saw one youth on a horse, half-conscious and held up by a comrade on each side, who had a white bandage around his forehead, in the exact center of which was a round red stain.

There in the midst of this column of youngsters, who carried rifles almost as big as themselves, marched the two bandit chieftains. One of them was a grizzled middle-aged peasant, and one wondered whether he felt ashamed, being led by these warriors all young enough to be his sons. Yet there was something rather splendid about his fearless bearing, and I thought that he was, after all, possibly a poor peasant like the rest, perhaps one who had also believed in something when he fought them, and it was regrettable that he was to be killed. Fu Chin-kuei shook his head when I asked him.

"We don't kill captured *min-t'uan*. We educate them and give them a chance to repent, and many of them later become good Red partisans."

红军清除了这批匪徒是件幸事，因为这为我们回保安扫清了道路。我们从甘肃边界回去走了5天，第5天走了100多里，虽然一路上见闻不少，却没有发生什么大事，我回去时没有带什么战利品，只有路上买的几只甜瓜和西瓜。

It was fortunate that the Reds had erased this group of bandits, for it cleared our road back to Pao An. We made the trip from the Kansu border in five days, doing more than 100 *li* on the fifth, but though there was plenty of incident there was no event, and I returned with no trophies except cantaloupes and melons I had bought along the road.

二、 保安的生活

回保安以后，我又在外交部安顿下来，从9月底一直住到10月半。我收集了足够的传记材料可以编一本《红色中国名人录》，每天早上都有一个新的指挥员或苏维埃官员来供我访问。但是我对如何离开问题越来越感不安：南京军队大批开入甘肃和陕西，凡是东北军与红军对垒的地方都逐步代替了东北军，因为蒋介石已做了一切准备要从南方和西方发动一次新的"围剿"。除非我马上出去，否则就可能走不了：封锁线上的最后一道隙缝可能给堵上了。我焦灼地等待着他们给我做好动身的安排。

在这段时间里，保安的生活仍过得很平静，你不会感到这些人是觉察到他们就要被"剿灭"的。在我住处不远的地方驻有一个新兵教导团。他们一天到晚在操练开步走，打球唱歌。有些晚上还演戏，每天晚上整个城里都歌声嘹亮，住在营房或窑洞里的各个部队的战士都朝着山脚下大声高唱。在红军大学，学员们一天学习10个小时，异常努力。城里又开始了一个新的群众教育运动，甚至外交部里的小鬼也每天要上文化课、政治课、地理课。

至于我自己，我过着假日生活，骑马，游泳，打网球。一共有两个球场，一个在红军大学附近的一个草地上，绵羊、山羊把草啃得短短的，另外一个在西北苏维埃政府主席、身材瘦长的博古家隔壁，是个硬地球场。我在这里每天早晨太阳刚在

2 _____ LIFE IN PAO AN

Back in Pao An again, I settled down once more in the Waichiaopu— the Foreign Office— where I stayed through late September and half of October. I collected enough biographies to fill a *Who's Who in Red China*, and every morning turned up a new commander or soviet official to be interviewed. But I was becoming increasingly uneasy about departure: Nanking troops were pouring into Kansu and Shensi, and were gradually replacing the Tungpei troops everywhere they held a front with the Reds, as Chiang Kai-shek made all preparations for a new annihilation drive from the South and the West. Someone else could write that story. I wished to publish the one I already had. But I wouldn't be able to do that unless I got out alive, and it took time for my hosts to guarantee a secure passage back over the lines. Unless I got out soon it might prove impossible: the last fissure in the blockade might be closed.

Meanwhile life in Pao An went on tranquilly enough and you would not have supposed that these people were aware of their imminent "annihilation." Not far from me a training regiment of new recruits was quartered. They spent their time marching and countermarching all day, playing games and singing songs. Some nights there were dramatics, and every night the whole town rang with song, as different groups gathered in barracks or in cave grottoes, yodeling down the valley. In the Red Army University the cadets were hard at work on a ten-hour day of study. A new mass-education drive was beginning in the town, even the "little devils" in the Waichiaopu being subjected to daily lessons in reading, politics, and geography.

As for myself, I lived a holiday life, riding, bathing, and playing tennis. There were two courts, one set up on the grassy meadow, clipped close by the goats and sheep, near the Red University, the other a clay court next door to the cottage of Po Ku, the gangling former Party general secretary, now chairman of the Northwest Branch Soviet Government. Here, every morning, as soon as the sun rose above the hills, I played

山上升起就同红军大学3个教员打网球：德国人李德、政委蔡树藩和政委伍修权。球场里尽是石子，救急球是很危险的，但是球还是打得很激烈。蔡树藩和伍修权同讲不了几句中文的李德讲俄文，我同李德讲英文，同蔡伍两人讲中文，所以这又是一场三国语言比赛。

我对当地的人的一个更加腐化的影响是我的赌博俱乐部。我带了一副扑克牌，到了以后没有用过，有一天我拿出来教蔡树藩打"勒美"[1]。蔡树藩在战斗中失掉一臂，但不论打球或打牌对他都没有什么妨碍。他学会打"勒美"后，很容易地就用一只手打败了我。有一阵子，打"勒美"非常流行。甚至妇女们也悄悄地到外交部赌博俱乐部来。我的土炕成了保安上层人物的聚会场所，晚上你环顾四周烛光下的脸孔，就可以看到周恩来夫人、博古夫人、凯丰夫人、邓发夫人，甚至毛夫人。这就引起了旁人说闲话。

但是，对苏区道德的真正威胁是在保安学会了打扑克以后才出现的。我们打网球的四个人先开始，每天晚上轮流在李德家和我在外交部的罪恶渊薮打。我们把博古、李克农、凯丰、洛甫那样的体面人士都拖进了这个罪恶的泥淖。赌注越来越大。最后独臂将军蔡树藩一个晚上就从博古主席那里赢去了12万元，看来博古的唯一出路是盗用公款了。这个问题我们用仲裁的办法来解决，规定博古可以从国库中提出12万元钱来交给蔡树藩，但是蔡树藩必须把钱用来为还不存在的苏维埃空军购买飞机。反正筹码都是火柴梗，而且，遗憾的是，蔡树藩买的飞机也是火柴梗。

独臂将军蔡树藩是个很有趣、很可爱、很英俊的青年，头脑机灵，容易冲动，善于辞令，妙趣横生。他当共产党已有10年，在湖南当铁路工人时就参加了，后来到莫斯科去学习了两三年，还腾出时间来爱上了一个俄国同志，同她结了婚。有时候他很不高兴地看着他的空袖子，不知他妻子看到他失去一条胳膊时会不会同他离婚。"别担心这样的小事，"伍修权教授这样安慰他。伍本人也是俄国留学生。"你再见到她时没有让你的传宗接代的东西给打掉算你的运气。"但是，蔡树藩还是再三地要求我回到白色世界后给他寄一条假臂。

我接到不少这样办不到的要求，要我寄东西进去，这不过是其中之一，陆定一要我把出售共产党照片所得的收入为他们购买一队飞机，外加武器装备和人员配备。徐海东要一对假牙补上他的缺牙：因为他陷入了情网。人人的牙齿都有毛病，他们

---

1. 一种看谁把牌脱手快的游戏，像"争上游"。——译注

tennis with three faculty members of the Red University: the German Li Teh, Commissar Ts'ai Shu-fan, and Commissar Wu Hsiu-ch'uan. The court was full of stones, it was fatal to run after a fast ball, but the games were nevertheless hotly contested. Ts'ai and Wu both spoke Russian to Li Teh, while I talked to Li Teh in English and to Ts'ai and Wu in Chinese, so that we thus had a trilingual game.

A more corrupting influence I had on the community was my gambling club. I had a pack of cards, unused since my arrival, and one day I got these out and taught Commissar Ts'ai to play rummy. Ts'ai had lost an arm in battle, but it handicapped him very little at either tennis or cards. After he had learned rummy he easily beat me with one hand. For a while rummy was the rage. Even the women began sneaking up to the Waichiaopu gambling club. My mud *k'ang* became the rendezvous of Pao An's elite, and you could look around at the candlelit faces there at night and recognize Mrs. Chou En-lai (Teng Ying-ch'ao), Mrs. Po Ku (Liu Ch'un-hsien), Mrs. K'ai Feng, Mrs. Teng Fa, and even Mrs. Mao (Ho Tzu-chen). It set tongues wagging.

But the real menace to soviet morals didn't appear till Pao An took up poker. Our tennis quartet started this, alternating nights at Li Teh's hut and my own base of iniquity in the Foreign Office. Into this sinful mire we dragged such respectable citizens as Po Ku, Li K'e-nung, K'ai Feng, Lo Fu, and others. Stakes rose higher and higher. One-armed Ts'ai Shu-fan finally cleaned up $120,000 from Chairman Po Ku in a single evening, and it looked as if Po Ku's only way out was embezzlement of state funds. We settled the matter by ruling that Po Ku would be allowed to draw $120,000 on the treasury to pay Ts'ai, provided Ts'ai would use the money to buy airplanes for the nonexistent soviet air force. It was all in matches, anyway—and, unfortunately, so were the airplanes Ts'ai bought.

One-armed Ts'ai was quick-witted, excitable, full of repartee and badinage. He had been a Red for a decade, having joined while he was a railway worker in Hunan. Later on he had gone to Moscow and studied there for two or three years, and found time to fall in love with, and marry, a Russian. Sometimes he looked ruefully at his empty sleeve and wondered whether his wife wouldn't divorce him when she saw his missing arm. "Don't worry about a little thing like that," Professor Wu, who was also a returned Russian student, would comfort him. "If you haven't had your posterity shot off when you see her again you'll be lucky." Nevertheless, Ts'ai kept urging me to send him an artificial arm when I got back to the White world.

This was only one of the impossible requests I had for things to be sent in. Lu Ting-yi wanted me to buy, equip, and man an air fleet for them from the proceeds of the sale of my pictures of the Reds. Hsu Hai-tung wanted a couple of false teeth to fill in the gap in his gums: he had fallen in love. Everybody had something wrong with his teeth;

都多年没有看过牙医了。但是他们的坚韧不拔精神令人钦佩；你从来没有听到有人诉过苦，尽管他们大多数人都有某种疾病，很多人患胃溃疡和其他肠胃病，这是多年吃了乱七八糟的东西所造成的。

从我个人来说，吃这种伙食反而长胖了，增加了体重。我每天看到千篇一律的伙食就生厌，但这并不妨碍我狼吞虎咽，食量之大使我有点不好意思。他们对我作了让步，用保麸面粉做馒头给我吃，这种馒头烤着吃还不错，有时我也吃到猪肉和烤羊肉串。除此之外，我就以吃小米为主——轮流吃煮的、炒的、烤的，或者倒过来又吃烤的、炒的、煮的。白菜很多，还有辣椒、葱头、青豆。我极想咖啡、黄油、白糖、牛奶、鸡蛋等等许多东西，可是我只能继续吃小米。

一天图书馆来了一批《字林西报》，我读到了一个十分简单的巧克力蛋糕烘制法。我知道博古家里还藏着一罐可可。我想用一些可可粉，再用一些猪油代替黄油，可以做个那样的蛋糕。因此我请李克农为我写一份正式的申请书，要求中华苏维埃共和国西北区政府主席，给我2两可可。经过了几天的耽搁，嗯嗯呃呃，甚至我做蛋糕的本领遭到怀疑和诽谤，许许多多繁复手续和对官僚主义进行斗争以后，我们终于从博古手里逼出了这2两可可，并且从粮食合作社搞到了其他材料。我还没有把作料掺和起来，我的警卫员就进来了解情况，这个可怜虫一不小心把我的可可打翻在地。又经过了一番公文手续，我最后又设法弄到了需要的材料，开始了伟大的试验。结果是不用说的。无论哪一个有头脑的主妇都可以预见到发生了什么。我的临时凑合的烘箱工作不正常，蛋糕没有发起来，我把它从火上移开时，它的底层是两英寸厚的焦炭，顶上仍是黏糊糊的。不过外交部好奇的旁观者还是津津有味地把它吃了：因为里面的好作料太多，浪费可惜。我大大地丢了面子，从此之后就乖乖地吃我的小米。

李德请我去同他一起吃一顿"西餐"作为补偿。他有的时候有办法弄到大米和鸡蛋，而且又是德国人，他非得自己做德国香肠吃。你可以在保安大街他家门口看到挂着成串成串的德国香肠。他正在准备过冬的存货。他也给自己砌了一个炉灶，教给他中国妻子———一个从江西同他一起来的姑娘——怎么烘烤。他给我看，马马虎虎做顿饭，材料倒是齐全的。只是粮食合作社（我们的伙食是包在那里的）不知道怎么做。红军指挥员罗炳辉的夫人（长征中的一位唯一小脚女人）是合作社的大师傅，我想李德的妻子同她有交情，他的鸡蛋和白糖大概是这样搞到的。

they hadn't seen a dentist for years. Most of the older leaders suffered from some kind of ailment, especially from ulcers and other stomach trouble, as a result of years on a dubious diet. But I never heard anybody complaining.

Personally I thrived on the food and put on weight, and my disgust at facing the unvaried menu every day did not prevent me from swallowing embarrassing quantities of it. They made me the concession of steamed bread made from whole-wheat flour, which when toasted was not bad, and occasionally I had pork or mutton shaslik. Besides that I lived on millet—boiled millet, fried millet, baked millet, and vice versa. Cabbage was plentiful, and peppers, onions, and beans. I missed coffee, butter, sugar, milk, eggs, and a lot of things, but I went right on eating millet.

A batch of copies of the *North China Daily News* arrived for the library one day and I read a recipe for what seemed to be a very simple chocolate sponge cake. I knew Po Ku was hoarding a tin of cocoa in his hut, and I schemed that with some of this, and by substituting pig's fat for butter, I could make that cake. Accordingly I got Li K'e-nung to write out a formal application to the chairman of the Northwest Branch Soviet Government of the Chinese Soviet Republic to supply me with two ounces of chocolate. After several days of delay, and hemming and hawing, and doubts and aspersions cast upon my ability to bake a cake anyway, and a lot of unraveling of red tape, and conflicts with the bureaucracy in general, we finally forced those two ounces of cocoa out of Po Ku, and got other materials from the food cooperative. Before I could mix up the batter my bodyguard came in to investigate, and the wretch knocked the cocoa on the ground. Followed more red tape, but finally I got the order refilled and began the great experiment. Why labor the result? Any intelligent *hausfrau* can foresee what happened. My improvised oven failed to function properly, the cake did not rise, and when I took it off the fire it was a two-inch layer of charcoal on the bottom, and a top still in a state of slimy fluidity. However, it was eaten by the interested onlookers in the Waichiaopu with great relish: there were too many good materials in it to be wasted. I lost immense face and thereafter docilely consumed my millet.

Li Teh compensated by asking me to a "foreign meal" with him. He had a way of getting rice and eggs sometimes, and, being German, he made his own sausages. You could see them swinging in strings, drying outside his door near the main street of Pao An. He was getting ready his winter's supply. He had also built himself a fireplace and taught his Chinese wife, a girl who had come with him from Kiangsi, how to bake. He showed me that the materials were there for tolerable cooking. It was only that the food cooperative (where our meals were cooked in common) didn't know how it should be done. Mrs. Lo Ping-hui, wife of a Red Army commander (and the only lily-footed woman who made the Long March), was chief chef of the cooperative, and I think Li Teh's wife had a pull with her, and that is how he garnered his eggs and sugar.

但是李德当然不仅仅是个好厨子,打扑克的能手。中国苏区这个神秘人物是何许人?国民党将领罗卓英读了在江西发现的李德一些著作后称他为共产党的"智囊",这有没有夸大了他的重要性?他同苏俄有什么关系?俄国对红色中国的事务事实上究竟起多大影响?

But Li Teh was more than a good cook and a good poker player. Who was this mystery man of the Chinese soviet district? Had his importance been exaggerated by the Kuomintang General Lo Chou-ying, who, after reading some of Li Teh's writings found in Kiangsi, described him as the "brain trust" of the Reds? What was his connection with Soviet Russia? How much influence, in fact, did Russia exercise over the affairs of Red China?

三、　　俄国的影响

考察中国共产党与俄国共产党、或共产国际、或整个苏联之间的关系，不属本书的主要目的。要完成这样一个任务，这里没有足够的背景材料。但是如果不谈一谈这种有机的联系和这种联系对中国革命史的更为重要的影响，本书就不免有所欠缺。

在过去十多年中，在中国人关于他们国家的社会、政治、经济、文化问题的想法上，俄国肯定地而且明显地起着支配性的影响，特别是在知识青年中间，它是唯一的支配性的外来影响。这在苏区固然是一个供认不讳、引以为荣的事实，在国民党地区也几乎同样是如此，尽管没有得到公开承认。在中国任何地方，凡是抱有具体政治信念的青年身上，马克思主义的意识形态的影响都很明显，不仅是作为一种哲学，而且是作为宗教的一种代替品。在这种中国青年中间，列宁几乎受到崇拜，斯大林是最受爱戴的外国领导人，社会主义被视为理所当然是中国未来的社会形式，俄罗斯文学读者最多——例如，高尔基的作品比任何本国作家的作品销路还要好，只有鲁迅除外，他本人就是一个伟大的社会革命家。

这一切都是很值得注意的，特别是为了一个原因。美国、英国、法国、德国、日本、意大利以及其他资本主义或帝国主义国家曾经派了成千上万名的政治、文化、经济或教会工作者到中国去，积极向中国群众宣传他们本国的信条。然而多年以来，俄国人在中国却没有设立一所学校、教堂、甚至辩论会，可以合法地宣传马克思列宁主义理论。除了在苏区之外，他们的影响基本上是间接的。此外，国民党到处还

3   The Russian Influence

This volume does not have as one of its primary purposes an examination of relations between the Communist Party of China and the Communist Party of Russia, or the Comintern, or the Soviet Union as a whole. No adequate background has been provided here for such a task. But the book would be incomplete without some discussion of these organic connections and their more significant effects on the revolutionary history of China.

Certainly and obviously Russia had for the past dozen or more years been a dominating influence—and particularly among educated youth it had been *the* dominating external influence—on Chinese thought about the social, political, economic, and cultural problems of the country. This had been almost as true, though unacknowledged, in the Kuomintang areas as it had been an openly glorified fact in the soviet districts. Everywhere in China that youth had any fervent revolutionary beliefs the impact of Marxist ideology was apparent, both as a philosophy and as a kind of substitute for religion. Among such young Chinese, Lenin was almost worshiped, Stalin was the most popular foreign leader, socialism was taken for granted as the future form of Chinese society, and Russian literature had the largest following—Maxim Gorky's works, for example, outselling all native writers except Lu Hsun, who was himself a great social revolutionary although not a Communist.

And all that was quite remarkable for one reason especially. America, England, France, Germany, Japan, Italy, and other capitalist or imperialist powers had sent thousands of political, cultural, economic, or missionary workers into China, actively to propagandize the Chinese masses with credos of their own states. Yet for many years the Russians had not had a single school, church, or even a debating society in China where Marxist-Leninist doctrines could legally be preached. Their influence, except in the soviet districts, had been largely indirect. Moreover, it had been aggressively opposed everywhere

积极加以抵制。然而在这十年中到过中国、并对他们所生活的社会有所了解的人，很少会否认，马克思主义、俄国革命、苏联的成就对中国人民产生的精神影响大概比所有基督教资产阶级的影响加起来还要深刻。

同许多念念不忘共产国际魔怪的人的看法相反，即使在红区里，俄国的影响大概也是精神上的和思想上的影响大于直接参与中国苏维埃运动的发展。我们必须记住，中共参加共产国际和与苏联团结一致一向是完全出于自愿的，任何时候都可以由中国人自己从内部加以撤销。在他们看来，苏联的作用最有力量的地方是作为一种活榜样，一种产生希望和信念的理想。这成了在中国人中间帮助锻炼钢铁般英勇性格的烈火和熔炉，而在以前许多人都认为中国人是不具备那种性格的。中国共产党人坚定地认为，中国革命不是孤立的，不仅在俄国，而且在全世界，亿万工人都在关心地注视着他们，到时候就会仿效他们的榜样，就像他们自己仿效俄罗斯同志的榜样一样。在马克思和恩格斯时代，说"工人无祖国"可能是正确的，但是今天这些中国共产党人认为，除了他们自己的无产阶级统治的小小根据地以外，他们还有苏联这样一个强大的祖国。这种保证，对他们来说，是巨大的革命鼓舞和营养的来源。

中华全国苏维埃第一次代表大会通过的宪法说，"中华苏维埃政府，宣布它愿意与国际无产阶级和一切被压迫民族结成革命统一战线，**宣布无产阶级专政的国家苏联是它的忠实盟友。**"中国的苏区事实上在绝大部分时候不论在地理上、经济上和政治上都完全与世隔绝，上面所引的那句用着重体排印的话，对中国苏区究竟有多大意义，西方人如果从来不认识一个中国共产党人，是很难理解的。

可是我却是耳闻目睹，而且深有体会。这个背后有这样一个强大盟友的思想——虽然越来越没有得到苏联表示积极支援的证实——对中共士气具有头等重要意义，使他们的斗争有了一种宗教事业的普天同归的性质，他们对此深为珍视。他们高呼的"世界革命万岁！"和"全世界无产者，联合起来！"的口号是贯彻于他们所有教导和信念中的思想，在这个口号中重申他们对社会主义世界大同的理想忠贞不贰。

我觉得这种思想已经显示出，它们能够改变中国人的行为作风。在共产党对我的态度中，我从来没有遇到过任何"排外主义"。他们当然是反对帝国主义的，一个美国的或者欧洲的资本家置身于他们之间可能会感到不自在，但是也不比一个中国地主或上海买办更甚。种族歧视似乎已彻底升华为不问国界的阶级对抗。甚至他们的抗日宣传也不是在种族基础上反对日本人的。共产党在他们的宣传中不断强调，他们只反对日本军阀，资本家和其他"法西斯压迫者"，日本人民是他们的潜在盟友。的确，他们

by the Kuomintang. Yet few who had been in China during that decade, and conscious of the society in which they lived, would dispute the contention that Marxism, the Russian Revolution, and the new society of the Soviet Union had probably made more profound impressions on the Chinese people than all Christian missionary influences combined.

One had to remember that the Chinese Communists' adherence to the Comintern, and unity with the U.S.S.R., were voluntary, and could have been liquidated at any time by the Chinese from within. The role of the Soviet Union for them had been most potent as a living example that bred hope and faith. The Chinese Reds stoutly believed that the Chinese revolution was not isolated, and that hundreds of millions of workers, not only in Russia but throughout the world, were anxiously watching them, and when the time came would emulate them, even as they themselves had emulated the comrades in Russia. In the day of Marx and Engels it might have been correct to say that "the workers have no country," but the Chinese Communists believed that, besides their own little bases of power, they had a mighty fatherland in the Soviet Union.

"The Soviet Government in China," read the Constitution adopted at the first All-China Soviet Congress, "declares its readiness to form a revolutionary united front with the world proletariat and all oppressed nations, and *proclaims the Soviet Union, the land of proletarian dictatorship, to be its loyal ally.*" How much the words italicized meant to the Chinese soviets, which in truth most of the time were completely isolated geographically, economically, and politically, was hard to understand for any Westerner who had never known a Chinese Communist.

This idea of having behind them a great ally—even though it was less and less validated by demonstrations of positive support from the Soviet Union—was of primary importance to the morale of the Chinese Reds. It imparted to their struggle the universality of a religious cause, and they deeply cherished it. When they shouted, "Long Live the World Revolution!" and "Proletarians of All Lands, Unite!" it was an idea that permeated all their teaching and faith, and in it they reaffirmed their allegiance to the dream of a Socialist world brotherhood.

It seemed to me that these concepts had already shown that they could change Chinese behavior. I never suffered from any "anti-foreignism" in the Reds' attitude toward me. They were certainly anti-imperialist, but racial prejudice seemed to have been sublimated in class antagonism that knew no national boundaries. Even their anti-Japanese agitation was not directed against the Japanese on a racial basis. In their propaganda the Reds constantly emphasized that they opposed only the Japanese militarists, capitalists, and other "Fascist oppressors," and that the Japanese masses were their potential allies.

从这种看法中得到很大的鼓励。这种从民族偏见上升到更高水平的对抗在很大程度上无疑地可以溯源于许多中共领导人在俄国所受的教育，他们上过中山大学，或东方劳动大学，或红军学院、或一些培养国际共产主义运动干部的其他学校，回国以后成了本国人民的导师。

说明他们的国际主义精神的一个例子是，他们对西班牙内战的发展极其关心。报上发表的公报张贴在村苏维埃的会议室，也向前线部队宣读。政治部对西班牙战争的起因和意义作了专门报告，把西班牙的"人民阵线"同中国的"统一战线"作了对比。另外还举行了群众大会，进行了示威，鼓励大家进行讨论。有时甚至在穷山僻壤之间，你也能发现红色农民也知道一些像意大利征服阿比西尼亚和德、意"侵略"西班牙这样的基本事实，说这两个国家是他们敌人日本的"法西斯盟国"！这不免相当令人惊异。尽管地理上处于与世隔绝状态，但是这些乡下佬由于无线电消息、墙报和共产党的报告和宣传，对世界政治的那一方面情况，现在比中国任何其他地方的农村居民了解的都要多得多。

共产党所采用的方法和组织都讲严格的纪律——这是共产主义思想本身所固有的一种纪律，在中国的马克思主义者中间，这似乎已经产生了某种类型的合作和对个人主义的压制，一般的"中国通"，或者通商口岸的死硬派，或者自以为"了解中国人心理"的外国传教士，如果不是亲眼看到，是很难相信的。在中国的马克思主义者的政治生活中，个人的存在是在社会整体、即群众之中的沧海一粟，必须服从于后者的意志，如果是担任领导，就要自觉地做到这一点，如果是作为物质创造者，则是不自觉地做到这一点。当然共产党人之间发生过争论和内讧，但都没有严重到使党或军队受到致命伤害的程度。这种现象，这种"非中国式的"团结一致，是把社会当作各种阶级力量争夺支配地位的斗争场所这种新观念的结果，在这场斗争中，只有团结最一致、目标最坚定、精力最充沛的力量才能取得最后胜利。这种团结一致如果不能说明他们的胜利的话，在很大程度上说明了共产党人为什么能够免遭消灭。

不论在什么时候，要是南京能够把他们的军事或政治力量分裂成为相互对立的、永远相互打内战的派系，像它对其他所有反对派那样，像蒋介石对他自己在国民党内的夺权对手那样，那么"剿共"的任务就可能会获得最后的胜利。但是南京的尝试都失败了。例如，几年以前，南京曾经希望利用国际上斯大林与托洛茨基之争来分化中共，但是，尽管出现了所谓中国"托洛茨基派"，他们却只博得了特务和叛徒的臭名，因为其中有许多人由于他们的立场所决定而参加了蓝衣社，把以前的同志出卖给警方，而

Indeed, they derived great encouragement from that conviction. This changing of national prejudice from racism to class antagonism was no doubt traceable to the education in Russia of scores of the Chinese Red leaders, who had attended Sun Yat-sen University, or the Red Academy, or some other school for international cadres of communism, and had returned as teachers to their own people.

One example of their internationalism was the intense interest with which the Reds followed the events of the Spanish Civil War. Bulletins were issued in the press, were pasted up in the meeting rooms of village soviets, were announced to the armies at the front. Special lectures were given by the political department on the cause and significance of the Spanish war, and the "people's front" in Spain was contrasted with the "united front" in China. Mass meetings of the populace were summoned, demonstrations were held, and public discussions were encouraged. It was quite surprising sometimes to find, even far back in the mountains, Red farmers who knew a few rudimentary facts about such things as the Italian conquest of Abyssinia and the German-Italian "invasion" of Spain, and spoke of these powers as the "Fascist allies" of their enemy, Japan. Despite their geographical isolation, these rustics now knew much more about that aspect of world politics, thanks to radio news and wall newspapers and Communist lecturers and propagandists, than the rural population anywhere else in China.

The strict discipline of Communist method and organization had seemingly produced among Chinese Marxists a type of cooperation and a suppression of individualism which the average "Old China Hand," or treaty-port merchant, or missionary who "knew Chinese psychology" would have found impossible to believe without witnessing for himself. In their political life the existence of the individual was an atomic pulse in the social whole, the mass, and must bend to its will, either consciously in the role of leadership, or unconsciously as part of the material demiurge. There had been disputes and internecine struggles among the Communists, but none severe enough to deal a fatal injury to either the army or the Party.

Had Nanking been able at any time to split their military and political strength into contradictory and permanently warring factions, as it did with all other Opposition groups—as Chiang Kai-shek did with his own rivals for power within the Kuomintang—the task of Communist suppression might have been rewarded with final success. But its attempts were failures. For example, a few years before, Nanking had hoped to utilize the worldwide Stalin-Trotsky controversy to divide the Chinese Communists, but although

且他们在群众中间从来没有什么重大的影响和很多的追随者，始终只是一批悲剧性的、失意的、孤立的知识分子的乌合之众。他们对共产党的领导不能形成任何严重的破坏威胁。

共产党基本上抛弃了所谓中国礼节这种封建糟粕，他们的心理和性格与中国人的传统观念极为不同。爱丽丝·蒂斯达尔·荷巴特是永远写不出一本关于他们的书的，《王宝钏》的中国作者[1]也是如此。他们直截了当、坦率简单、不转弯抹角、有科学头脑。一度是所谓中国文明的基础的中国旧哲学，他们几乎全都摒弃，而且，最重要的也许是，他们也是中国传统家庭观念的不共戴天的敌人。[2]我与他们在一起的大部分时候感到非常自在，好像同我自己的一些同胞在一起一样。附带说一句，在某种意义上，我的出现对他们很有重要意义。因为他们可以把我，而且也把我到苏区来的好奇心，当作他们的运动具有"国际主义性质"的具体证据。他们把我当作一种给怀疑派看的头号展品来加以利用。

由于他们热烈地崇拜苏联，因此难免有不少抄袭和模仿外国思想、制度、方法、组织的地方。中国红军是按俄国军事方针建立的，它的大部分战术知识来自俄国经验。社会组织总的来说按照俄国布尔什维主义规定的形式。共产党的许多的歌用俄国的音乐，在苏区很流行。有许多词汇直接从俄语音译为中文，苏维埃三字只不过是其中之一。

但在他们借用的过程中也有不少改动，俄国的思想或制度很少有不经大加改动以适应具体环境而仍存在下来的。10年的实际经验消灭了不分青红皂白一概进口的做法，结果也造成苏维埃制度中带有完全是中国式的特点。当然，在中国的资产阶级世界里，模仿和采用西方的过程也正在进行，因为甚至古老的封建遗产中的诗——斯宾格勒[3]称之为"伟大历史的废料"的东西——也很少有什么东西，不论对于建设一个资产阶级的，还是社会主义的能够应付国家今天千头万绪的新需要的现代化社会，有很多价值。在旧中国这个子宫中同时孕育了两个卵细胞，而且都是从国外受精的。因此，有意义的是，举个例来说，共产党在组织青年的方法方面取法于俄国的固然很多，而蒋介石总司令则不仅利用意大利轰炸机来毁灭他们，而且也效法基督教青年会来组织他的反共的"新生活运动"。

---

1. 指留英中国学者熊式一。——译注
2. 这里我不是指全体农民群众，而是指共产主义的先锋队。但是即便是在苏维埃化的农民中间，态度也与像亚瑟·H.史密斯在《中国人的性格》（1894年纽约）中所描述的那种截然相反。
3. 奥斯瓦德·斯宾格勒（1880—1936）德国哲学家，著有《西方的衰亡》。——译注

so-called Chinese "Trotskyites" did appear, they never developed any important mass influence or following.

The Reds had generally discarded much of the ceremony of traditional Chinese etiquette, and their psychology and character were quite different from our old conceptions of Chinese. They were direct, frank, simple, undevious, and scientific-minded. They were also implacable enemies of the old Chinese familism.[1]

With their zealous adoration of the Soviet Union there had naturally been a lot of copying and imitating of foreign ideas, institutions, methods, and organizations. The Chinese Red Army was constructed on Russian military lines, and much of its tactical knowledge derived from Russian experience. Social organizations in general followed the pattern laid down by Russian Bolshevism. Many Red songs were put to Russian music and widely sung in the soviet districts. *Su wei-ai*—Chinese for "soviet"—was only one example of many words transliterated directly from Russian into Chinese.

But in their borrowing there was much adaptation; few Russian ideas or institutions survived without drastic changes to suit the milieu in which they operated. The empirical process of a decade eliminated indiscriminate wholesale importations, and also resulted in the introduction of peculiarly Chinese features. A process of imitation and adaptation of the West had, of course, been going on in the bourgeois world of China, too—for there was very little left even of poetry of the ancient feudal heritage, that "scrap material of a great history" as Spengler calls it which the Chinese were able to use in building either a modern bourgeois or a Socialist society capable of grappling with the vast new demands of the country. While the Reds leaned heavily on Russia for organizational methods with youth, Generalissimo Chiang Kai-shek not only used Italian bombing planes to destroy them, but also borrowed from the Y.M.C.A. in building his anti-Communist New Life Movement.

---

1. Here I do not speak of the peasant masses as a whole, but of a Communist vanguard. But even among the sovietized peasantry, attitudes were in striking contrast with those described, for example, in Arthur H. Smith's *Chinese Characteristics* (N.Y., 1894).

最后，当然，中国共产党的政治思想、策略路线、理论领导都是在共产国际的密切指导之下，如果说不是积极具体指挥之下，而共产国际在过去 10 年中实际上已经成了俄国共产党的一个分局。说到最后，这意味着，不论是好是坏，中国共产党像每一个其他国家的共产党一样，他们的政策必须符合，而且往往是必须从属于斯大林独裁统治下苏俄的广泛战略需要。这一些至少是够明显的了。由于分享俄国革命的集体经验，由于共产国际的领导，中共无疑地得到了很大好处。但同样确实的是，中国共产党人在其生长发育的痛苦过程中遭到严重的挫折，也可以归因于共产国际。

And finally, of course, the political ideology, tactical line, and theoretical leadership of the Chinese Communists had been under the close guidance, if not positive direction, of the Communist International. Great benefits undoubtedly accrued to the Chinese Reds from sharing the collective experience of the Russian Revolution, and from the leadership of the Comintern. But it was also true that the Comintern could be held responsible for serious reverses suffered by the Chinese Communists in the anguish of their growth.

四、　　中国共产主义运动和共产国际

1923年到1937年的中俄关系史大致可以分为3个时期。第一个时期从1923年到1927年，是苏联和国民革命派之间的一个事实上的同盟时期。后者是由在国民党和共产党的旗帜下联合起来的同床异梦的合作者组成的，他们的目的是要用革命来推翻当时的中国政府，实现中国的独立，摆脱外国帝国主义。这项振奋人心的事业以右翼国民党的胜利，成立南京政府，同帝国主义达成妥协，中俄关系破裂而告终。

从1927年到1933年是俄国孤立于中国和南京完全绝缘于俄国影响时期。这一时期到1933年底莫斯科恢复与南京的外交关系而宣告结束。第三个时期以南京莫斯科温吞水的修好开始，由于南京不断同中共进行激烈内战而弄得很尴尬，后来到1937年初戏剧性地结束，当时共产党和国民党实行了部分和解，为中俄合作开辟了新的可能性。但我在红军的时候，对共产党的情歌，国民党仍充耳不听，这个新的时期以后在恰当场合再谈。

上面提到的中俄关系三阶段也确切地反映了共产国际近年来性质的变化，以及它从一个国际煽动组织转变为苏联国家政策的一个工具的几个过渡阶段。苏联和共产国际这种变化的国内和国际上的极为复杂原因的辩证关系，要在本书加以详述是不可能的，但是考察一下这些变化对中国革命基本上发生了什么影响，又受到中国革命什么影响，却很适宜。

凡是对这个问题有所研究的人都知道，中国革命在1927年遇到的危机与俄国内部和共产国际内部所发生的危机正好发生巧合，后者表现为托洛茨基主义和斯大林主义争夺世界革命力量的理论控制权和实际控制权的斗争。要是斯大林没有等到

4 — Chinese Communism and the Comintern

It is possible to divide the history of Sino-Russian relations from 1923 to 1937 roughly into three periods. The first, from 1923 to 1927, was a period of triple alliance between the Soviet Union and the Nationalist revolutionaries, consisting of strange bedfellows aligned under the banners of the Kuomintang and the Communist parties, and aiming at the overthrow by revolution of the then extant government of China, and the restoration of China's complete sovereignty. That enterprise ended with the triumph of the right-wing Kuomintang, the founding of the National Government at Nanking, the latter's compromise with the colonial power, and the severance of Sino-Russian relations.

From 1927 to 1933 there was a period of isolation of Russia from (Nationalist) China, and its complete insulation against Russian influence. This era closed when Moscow resumed diplomatic relations with Nanking late in 1933. The third period began with a lukewarm Nanking-Moscow *rapprochement*, embarrassed considerably by the continued heavy civil war between Nanking and the Chinese Communists. It was to end dramatically early in 1937, when a partial reconciliation was effected between the Communists and the Kuomintang, with new possibilities opened up for Sino-Russia cooperation.

The three periods of Sino-Russian relationship mentioned above, accurately reflected also the changes in the character of the Comintern and its stages of transition. It is impossible here to enter into the complex causes, domestic and international, which brought about those changes, both in the Soviet Union and in the Comintern, but it is pertinent to see how in the main they had affected, and were affected by, the Chinese Revolution.

The 1927 crisis of the Chinese Revolution coincided with a crisis in Russia, and in the Comintern, expressed in the struggle between Trotskyism and Stalinism for theoretical and practical control of Russia. Had Stalin been able to advance his slogan, "socialism in

1924年才提出他的"在一国建设社会主义"的口号，要是这个问题在这以前早就有了定论而且他又能够支配共产国际，那就很有可能，对中国的"干涉"就根本不会发生。不过无论如何，现在再进行这样的推测是毫无意义的事了。斯大林在进行他的斗争时，在中国的路线早已决定了。

在1926年以前，对中国国民革命在军事上、政治上、财政上、文化上给予积极合作的工作，主要是在季诺维也夫的指导下进行的，他当时是共产国际主席，并且这工作也受到托洛茨基的很大影响。在这以前，斯大林派还没有彻底击败托洛茨基的"不断革命"的理论。但是从1926年初开始，苏联共产党和共产国际的事务和政策主要由斯大林负责，他从此加紧了对这两个组织的控制，这一点是没有不同看法的。

因此，共产国际在1926年，接着在1927年春天发生灾难期间给予中国共产党策略路线和"指示"的时候，是由斯大林领导的。在这些瞬息万变的几个月里，当中国共产党人头上的灾祸像强劲的台风一样袭来的时候，斯大林的路线遭到托洛茨基、季诺维也夫、加米涅夫所领导的反对派的不断攻击。季诺维也夫在当共产国际主席时，充分支持共产党与国民党合作的路线，但是现在他却激烈反对斯大林执行同一路线。特别是在蒋介石第一次"叛变"，1926年在广州进行一次未遂政变后，季诺维也夫预言必然会发生反革命，民族资产阶级会与帝国主义妥协，出卖群众。

在蒋介石第二次政变成功之前至少一年，季诺维也夫就开始要求共产党人脱离国民党这个民族资产阶级政党，他现在认为国民党不能完成革命的两项主要目标，即反帝——推翻外国在中国的统治——和反封建——推翻地主豪绅在中国农村的统治。托洛茨基也这样早就开始鼓吹成立苏维埃和一支独立的中国红军。总的来说，反对派预言如果斯大林的路线继续下去，"资产阶级民主"革命——他们在这一阶段的希望顶多就是这个——就会失败。当然，这个预言是说中了。

斯大林在大失败以后为自己辩护时，嘲笑托洛茨基认为共产国际的策略路线是招致失败的主要原因这一论点，认为这是非马克思主义的：

one country" much earlier than 1924, had the issue been fought out and had he been able to dominate the Comintern before then, quite possibly the "intervention" in China might never have begun. Such a speculation in any case was idle now. When Stalin did develop his fight, the line in China had already been cast.

The active military, political, financial, and intellectual collaboration given to the Chinese Nationalist Revolution was until 1926 under the direction chiefly of Zinoviev, who was chairman of the Communist International. Then from early 1926 onward Stalin became chiefly responsible for the affairs and policies of the Comintern as well as the Communist Party of the Soviet Union, and it was nowhere disputed that he had tightened his grasp on both organizations ever since.

Thus it was Stalin who led the Comintern that gave the Chinese Communists their tactical line and "directives" in 1926 and during the catastrophe of the spring of 1927. During those fateful months, in which disaster gathered above the heads of the Chinese Communists, Stalin's line was subjected to continuous bombardment from the Opposition, dominated by Trotsky, Zinoviev, and Kamenev. While he was Comintern chairman, Zinoviev had fully supported the line of Communist cooperation with the Kuomintang, but he violently attacked this same line as carried out by Stalin. Particularly after Chiang Kai-shek's first "treachery"—the abortive attempt at a *coup d'état* in Canton in 1926—Zinoviev predicted an inevitable counterrevolution in which the national bourgeoisie would compromise with imperialism and "betray the masses."

At least a year before Chiang Kai-shek's second and successful *coup d'état*, Zinoviev began demanding the separation of the Communists from the Kuomintang, "the party of the national bourgeoisie," which he now considered incapable of carrying out the two main tasks of the revolution—anti-imperialism, i.e. the overthrow of foreign domination of China, and "anti-feudalism," or the destruction of the landlord-gentry rule in rural China. Just as early, Trotsky began urging the formation of soviets and an independent Chinese Red Army. The Opposition in general foretold the failure of the "bourgeois-democratic" revolution—all they hoped for in this period—if Stalin's line was continued.

Stalin defended himself, after the debacle, by ridiculing as non-Marxist the Trotskyist contentions that the tactical line of the Comintern had been the main cause of the

加米涅夫同志说，共产国际的政策是造成中国革命失败的原因，说我们"在中国孕育了卡芬雅克们"……怎么能够说一个政党的策略可以取消或改变阶级力量的对比呢？对于那些忘掉革命时期阶级力量对比的人，那些要想用一个政党的策略来解释一切的人，我们能说什么呢？对于这种人只能说一句话——他们抛弃了马克思主义。[1]

事实上，凡是研究这一整个时期情况的公正的人，很难能逃避这样的结论：托洛茨基派过于夸大了共产国际错误的重要性，同时又低估了客观形势的极其不利的因素。他们对于利用共产国际的错误来作为攻击斯大林的新炮弹，显然比对中国的当前命运更感到有兴趣。反正，他们的攻击并没有成功。整个来说，党仍不信斯大林是无能的。由于中国革命的失败，加上在此以前巴伐利亚和匈牙利共产党政权遭到摧毁，以及共产国际在东方各国的希望遭到普遍破灭，党已对在国外进行冒险发生厌倦，倾向于转而进行国内建设。斯大林胜利了。托洛茨基遭到了流放——而且，如果我们竟然相信莫斯科审判时提出的证据的话，干起破坏铁路的事来。

斯大林取得了胜利，通过了五年计划，对拖拉机产生了狂热，共产国际在这以后所发生的重要变化是，暂时搁置了积极促进当前世界革命的计划，苏联的革命热情集中用在从事社会主义建设的伟大攻势上。共产国际不再成为支配力量，而是变成了苏联的一个机关，逐渐变成了为一国建设社会主义的平凡单调劳动进行美化宣传的广告社。它的主要任务已从用暴力，或者用积极干涉来制造革命，改变为用榜样来促进革命。由于"世界革命根据地"苏联需要和平，共产国际便成了在全世界进行和平宣传的有力机构。

这里毋庸进一步赘述斯大林和托洛茨基的论争。

重要的是，斯大林取得了胜利，他的政策支配了共产国际在中国的未来活动。1927年以后，有一段时期，这种活动几乎等于零。俄国在中国的机构封闭了，俄国共产党人不是被杀就是被驱逐出中国，俄国来的财政、军事、政治援助陷于停顿。中国共产党陷入了大混乱，有一个时期，同共产国际失去了联系。但是**苏维埃运动和中国红军却在纯粹中国人自己的领导下自发开始**，事实上，他们并没有得到俄国的什么赞同，一直到第六次代表大会，共产国际才给予出生后的认可。

自此以后，共产国际在中国革命中的作用被大大夸大了。不错，有些机构偷偷地恢复了；还派了代表到少数几个大城市中去找中国共产党人；中国学生继续在俄国留学，然后秘密回来

---

1. 参阅斯大林著《论反对派》第518—519页（1972年人民出版社版）。——译注

failure. "Comrade Kamenev," declared Stalin, "said that the policy of the Communist International was responsible for the defeat of the Chinese Revolution, and that we 'bred Cavaignacs in China.'. . . How can it be asserted that the tactics of a party can abolish or reverse the relation of class forces? What are we to say of people who forget the relation of class forces in time of revolution, and who try to explain everything by the tactics of a party? Only one thing can be said of such people—that they have abandoned Marxism."

Trotsky required no help from me in framing appropriate replies to Stalin's self-exculpations, but as his wit had not prevented the earlier destruction of Communist regimes in Hungary and Bavaria, nor the general defeat of the Comintern's hopes throughout the East, so it did not save the Chinese Communists from a catastrophe which all but destroyed the Party. Only Stalin won—that is, he drove Trotsky from the temple—and consequently Stalin dominated future activities of the Comintern in China—which for a time were practically nil. Russian organs in China were closed, Russian Communists were killed or driven from the country, the flow of financial, military, and political help from Russia dwindled. The Chinese Communist Party was thrown into great confusion, and for a time its interior leadership lost contact with the Comintern. *The rural soviet movement and (Mao's) Chinese Red Army began spontaneously,* and they did not, in fact, get much applause from Russia till after the Sixth Congress, when the Communist International gave its postnatal sanction.

搞革命工作；而且还有一点点钱送进来。但是俄国完全没有办法同中国红色区域发生任何直接的有形联系，因为中国红色区域没有海口，完全受到敌军的重重包围。在过去，中国曾经有过好几百个共产国际的工作人员，现在却只剩下两三个，常常几乎与整个社会隔绝，很少有能冒险逗留几个月以上的。以前曾经有好几百万元钱输送到蒋介石的国民党手中，现在流到共产党手中的一次只有一两千元涓涓细流。以前整个苏联都支持1924年到1927年的大革命，现在援助中国共产主义运动的那个共产国际已不能动用"世界革命根据地"的庞大资源，只能像一个可怜的继子那样走一步看一步，如果行为稍有不当，就很可能给正式取消继承权。

在这10年之中，莫斯科和共产国际给予中共的实际财政援助，看来是少得惊人。当牛兰夫妇1932年在上海被捕，后在南京作为共产国际远东首席代理人而判刑时，警方的完整证据表明，对整个东方（不仅仅中国）的总支出最多不超过每月1.5万美元。这与大量流入中国进行基督教宣传（这基本上是资本主义宣传），或者进行亲日宣传和纳粹法西斯宣传的款项相比，可谓微乎其微。这同美国在1933年给予南京的5,000万美元小麦贷款相比，也是少得可怜。据外国军事武官的报告，后一笔贷款的收入对蒋介石反共内战有决定性的价值。

美国、英国、德国、意大利卖了大量飞机、坦克、大炮、弹药给南京，以便摧毁中国苏区，当然没有卖任何东西给共产党。美国军队出借许多军官为中国训练空军，结果炸毁了红色中国的许多城镇，意大利和德国军事教官实际上亲自领导了几次破坏性最大的轰炸，像他们在西班牙所做的那样。纳粹德国派最能干的将领冯·泽克特将军[1]去援助蒋介石，并派一大批普鲁士军官改进南京的"围剿"技术。鉴于这些众所周知的事实，再说什么俄国支撑中共，我觉得完全是胡说八道了。相反，很明显，蒋介石在近10年内却得到了外国给他而不肯给共产党的重要援助的支撑。

也许可以断言，而且我相信任何一个外国军事情报专家都无法不同意，中国共产党打仗时所得到的外国物质援助比中国近代史上任何一支军队得到的都要少。

---

1. 后来又派了冯·法尔肯豪森。

After 1927 it became impossible for Russia to have any direct physical connection with the Chinese Red areas, which had no seaport and were entirely surrounded by a ring of hostile troops. Whereas in the past there had been scores of Comintern workers in China, there were now two or three, often almost isolated from society as a whole, seldom able to risk a stay of more than a few months. Whereas a large flow of Russian gold and arms had formerly gone to Chiang Kai-shek's Nationalists, now a trickle reached the Reds. And whereas the whole Soviet Union had backed the Great Revolution of 1924—1927, the Chinese Communist movement was now aided only by a Comintern which could no longer command the vast resources of the "base of the world revolution," but had to limp along as a kind of poor stepchild which might be officially disinherited whenever it did anything malaprop.

Actual financial help given to the Chinese Reds by Moscow or the Comintern during this decade seemed to have been amazingly small. When Mr. and Mrs. Hilaire Noulens were arrested in Shanghai in 1932 and convicted in Nanking as chief Far Eastern agents of the Comintern, police evidence showed that total outpayments for the whole Orient (not just China) had not at most exceeded the equivalent of about U.S. $15,000 per month. That was a trifle compared with the vast sums poured into China to support Japanese and Nazi-Fascist propaganda. It was rather pitiful also in contrast, for example, with America's $50,000,000 Wheat Loan to Nanking in 1933—the proceeds of which were of decisive value to Chiang Kai-shek's civil war against the Reds, according to reports of foreign military observers.

America, England, Germany, and Italy sold Nanking great quantities of airplanes, tanks, guns, and munitions, but of course sold none to the Reds. The American Army released officers to train the Chinese air force, which demolished towns in Red China, and Italian and German instructors actually led some of the most destructive bombing expeditions themselves—as happened on a larger scale in Spain. To Chiang Kai-shek's aid Germany sent Von Seeckt, and after him Von Falkenhausen, with a staff of Prussian officers who improved Nanking's technique of annihilation. It seemed that Chiang Kai-shek was propped up for nearly ten years by more important aid than any foreign power gave to the Reds.

Probably the Chinese Reds fought with less material foreign help than any army in modern Chinese history.

五、　　那个外国智囊

在中国红军创立后的头5年里，并没有一个外国顾问在那里，而就在这几年里，红军建立了苏区，开创了一个有纪律的革命运动，涣散了敌人斗志和解除了敌人武装，由此增强了自己的力量。这是事实。到1933年唯一曾与中国红军在一起作过战的外国人德国顾问李德才在苏区出现，在政治上和军事上占据高位。

李德躲在一条内河小船的草席下，经过6天6夜的惊险旅行，才从广州偷渡到红军前线，到了江西苏区首都瑞金。在他到达瑞金之前，除了不定期的信使以外，共产党同共产国际的唯一联系是通过无线电交通。在上海有个顾问委员会受共产国际的指导，这对共产党获知敌人方面的重要政治军事动向有很大价值。它的活动显然比蒋介石所能在苏区建立的任何间谍组织效率高得多。

但是对于江西红色共和国末期所犯的两个大错误，这个顾问委员会，同李德一起，都是被认为有责任的。第一个错误，据毛泽东指出，是十九路军在1933年秋天起义反宁时，红军没有同他们联合起来。

由蔡廷锴、蒋光鼐指挥的十九路军在1932年英勇保卫上海抵抗日本进攻，[1] 毫无疑义地表现出它强烈的抗日革命性质。它被调到福建后，由于蒋介石和何应钦同日本谈判了丧权辱国的《塘沽协定》，开始反宁抗日，展开了要求成立民主共和国和摧毁蒋介石的军事独裁的运动。它不仅向红军提出休战（十九路军在南京破坏它抗日后被派到福建去打中共），而且也提出在抗日战线的基础上结盟。

苏维埃政府和红军的大多数领导人也十分赞成这些建议。他们准备把主力调入福建，从

---

1. 指挥十九路军的还有陈铭枢将军。

5   THAT FOREIGN BRAIN TRUST

There had not been a single foreign adviser with China's Red Army during the first five years of its existence. Not until 1933 did Li Teh appear in the Kiangsi soviet districts as a German representative of the Comintern, to take a high position both politically and militarily.

Yet despite the numerical insignificance of this "foreign influence," several responsible Communists in the Northwest apparently felt that Li Teh's advice had been to a great extent responsible for two costly mistakes in the Kiangsi Red republic. The first, as Mao Tse-tung pointed out, was the failure of the Red Army to unite with the Nineteenth Route Army, when the latter arose in revolt against Nanking in the autumn of 1933.

The Nineteenth Route Army, commanded by Generals Ch'en Ming-hsiu, Ts'ai T'ing-k'ai, and Chiang Kuang-nai, had made an impressive defense of Shanghai against the Japanese attack in 1932, and had demonstrated its strong national-revolutionary character. Transferred to Fukien after the Shanghai Truce, it gradually became a center of political opposition to Nanking's "nonresistance" policy. Following Nanking's negotiation of the humiliating *Tangku Truce* with Japan, the Nineteenth Route Army leaders set up an independent government in Fukien province and started a movement for a democratic republic and the destruction of Chiang Kai-shek's regime.

侧翼猛攻南京部队，同福建叛军组成联合政府，对十九路军在军事上和政治上都给予充分的支持。但是共产国际不知为什么缘故，通过它设在上海的顾问委员会反对这一主张。当时俄国正开始恢复同南京勾搭，莫斯科刚刚才承认国民党政权，托洛茨基派的论点是，共产国际采取这一路线的主要原因是：莫斯科反对扩大大规模内战，仍希望红军和南京联合抗日，不希望担上在这个时候煽动叛乱的罪名，特别是不希望发生这样的一种局面，那就是万一红军控制了福建的一个海港就必然会指望俄国提供物资。但是这样的看法却缺少根据。

反正不管怎样，后来发生的事实是，红军不但没有与十九路军合作，反而把主力**后撤**到江西西部，使得蒋介石无后顾之忧。于是总司令就可以不受掣肘地猛扑邻省福建，迅速镇压叛军，红军就此失掉了最强大的潜在盟友。毫无疑问，拥护革命的十九路军的歼灭，大大便利了摧毁南方苏区的任务，蒋介石就立即满怀信心地来从事这项任务。

第二个严重错误是在南京第五次"围剿"中的战术防御计划。在以前几次"围剿"中，红军依靠他们在运动战中的优势以及他们能迅速集中强大兵力和进行奇袭、从蒋介石手中夺取主动权的能力。在他们的作战中，阵地战和正规战一直只起次要的作用。但在第五次战役中，李德坚持改变战术。他拟定了一个以阵地战为中心的大规模防御计划，把游击战术降为从属的任务，尽管共产党军事委员会上"一致"反对，他还是强行通过了他的计划。

今天来看就很明显，李德大大地过高估计了苏区的资源、红军在非机动作战中的战斗力、敌军的士气涣散，另一方面他又不可原谅地低估了南京新建的空军和机械化部队改进了的进攻力量，严重地错误估计了政治形势中的重要因素，他以为政治局势的发展对共产党会比实际情况有利得多。

但问题是，李德这个孤零零的一个外国人，怎么会有足够的影响，可以把他的意志强加在整个军事委员会、政府和党的判断之上呢？这委实是件十分独断独行的事。李德无疑是个具有过人才能的军事战略家和战术家。在世界大战中，他在德国军队中就大露头角；后来他任俄国红军的师长，曾在莫斯科红军大学毕业。作为一个德国人，共产党也尊重他对冯·泽克特将军向蒋总司令提出的战术的分析（这件事也真有戏剧意味，两个德国将领，其中一个是彻头彻尾的法西斯，另一个是布尔什维克，却通过这两支中国军队互相厮杀！），而且事实证明，他们的信任是正确的。南京的将领们看到李德的一些分析他们战术的著作时，颇为钦佩地承认，想不到李德准确地预计到了这次巨大攻势的每一个步骤。

The Nineteenth Route Army was one of the few Kuomintang military units never defeated by the Reds, and they had great respect for its fighting ability. Composed mostly of Cantonese, it really reflected in its political character a loosely organized left-wing opposition movement. It was the main military support of several factions on the periphery of the Kuomintang, led by the She-hui Min-chu T'ang, the Chinese Social Democrats.

Sent to Fukien to participate in Communist suppression late in 1932, the Nineteenth Route Army leaders instead quickly built up a base of their own from which to oppose Chiang Kai-shek. They entered into a nonaggression agreement with the Reds and proposed an anti-Nanking, anti-Japanese alliance along much the same lines that were later on evolved in the Northwest between the Manchurian, the Northwestern, and the Communist armies.

But instead of cooperating with the Nineteenth Route Army the Reds *withdrew* their main forces from the Fukien border to western Kiangsi. That left Chiang Kai-shek free to descend from Chekiang into neighboring Fukien with little impediment. The Generalissimo struck before the Nineteenth Route Army was prepared militarily or politically, and quickly quashed the insurgents. The Reds consequently lost their strongest potential allies. There is no doubt that elimination of the Nineteenth Route Army very much facilitated the task of destroying the southern soviets, to which Chiang Kai-shek at once turned with a new confidence early in 1934.

The Reds' second serious mistake was made in the planning of strategy and tactics to meet Chiang's new offensive—the Fifth Campaign. In previous campaigns the Reds had relied on superiority in maneuvering warfare, and their ability to take the initiative from Chiang Kai-shek in strong swift concentrations and surprise attacks. Positional warfare and regular fighting had always played minor roles in their operations. But in the Fifth Campaign, according to Red commanders to whom I talked, Li Teh insisted upon a strategy of positional warfare, relegating partisan and guerrilla tactics to auxiliary tasks, and somehow won acceptance for his scheme against (so I was told) "unanimous" opposition of the Red military council.

But whatever errors of judgment Li Teh may have made, there was little question that his long experience with Chinese fighting methods, and on Chinese terrain, made him one of the best qualified Occidental military authorities on China. And the personal courage of a man who had endured the severe hardships of the Long March commanded admiration and remained a challenge to armchair revolutionaries all over the world. For Li Teh, an outsize foreigner, the Long March had presented some special hardships. He had stomach complaints, and was badly in need of a dentist, but his first problem was to keep supplied with shoes large enough for his enormous number elevens. There did not seem to be any shoes that big in China. For three years he had lived without any contact with Europeans, most of the time without books to read. When I was in Pao An he was delighted to have got hold of a copy of the huge *China Year Book*, which he carefully digested from cover

李德是个心灰意冷、饱经沧桑的前普鲁士军官，在他骑上马同红军一起出发长征时，也是个变得聪明了一些的布尔什维克。他在保安向我承认，西方的作战方法在中国不一定总是行得通的。他说，"必须由中国人的心理和传统，由中国军事经验的特点来决定在一定的情况下采取什么主要战术。中国同志比我们更了解在他们本国打革命战争的正确战术。"当时他的地位已降到极其次要的地位——但是他们都已埋葬了过去的不愉快感情。

但是，应该为李德说句公道话，他在江西应负的责任的实际程度可能被夸大了。实际上，他成了共产党为自己吃了大亏进行辩解的一个重要借口。他成了一个骄横跋扈的外国人，害群之马，替罪羊；能够把大部分责任归咎于他，总是使人感到宽心的事。但是实际上几乎无法相信，不论由哪个天才来指挥，红军在遇到了他们在第五次"围剿"那一年所遇到的不可逾越的障碍之后，仍能胜利归来。无论如何，这次经历是一个很好的教训，整个世界共产主义运动都可以从中受益。把全面指挥一支革命军队的战术的大权交给一个外国人，这样的错误，以后大概是决不会再重犯了。

江西的情况就谈到这里为止。在以后的两年中，红军几乎与自己在中国沿海城市中的党员都完全断绝了联系，共产国际的活动主要只限于在《国际通讯》[1]中刊登中国驻共产国际的代表王明的令人吃惊的报道。一天到了几期《国际通讯》时我正好在保安，我看到党中央委员会那位美国留学的书记洛甫来不及打开来看。他随口提到他几乎有3年没有读到《国际通讯》了！

一直到1936年9月我还在红军的时候，共产国际第七次代表大会会议情况的详尽报道最后才传到中国的红色首都，那是在整整1年以前举行的。就是这些报道第一次给中国共产党人带来了国际反法西斯统一战线策略得到充分发挥的论述，在以后几个月令人兴奋的时间里，西北即将发生普遍的反叛，震撼整个东方，就是这种策略对他们的政策将起指导的作用。共产国际就要再一次在中国的事务中发挥它自己的意志，深刻地影响革命的发展。

不过我又得在北平从侧面来观察这一事件。

1.《国际通讯》是第三国际的机关期刊，于莫斯科出版。

to cover, including its innumerable tables of statistics—a feat constituting one of the few things he could boast in common with the *Year Book* editor, H. G. W. Woodhead, C.B.E. This blue-eyed, fair-haired Aryan had not spoken a word of Chinese when he first immersed himself alone with his Oriental comrades, and he still had to conduct all his serious conversations through interpreters or in German, Russian, or French.

It was almost impossible to believe that under any genius of command, the Reds could have emerged victorious against the odds that faced them throughout the year of the Fifth Campaign. It was not the phenomenon of foreign support on the side of the Reds, but its presence in a major degree on the side of the Kuomingtang, that characterized the last struggle of the Kiangsi Soviet Republic. Quite clearly the Chinese Red Army was not "officered by Russian Bolsheviks," "mercenaries of Moscow rubles," or "puppet troops of Stalin." Chinese and foreign newspapers during the anti-Red wars used regularly to report how many "corpses of Russian officers" were found on the battlefield after a Kuomintang atttack on the Reds. No foreign corpses were ever produced, yet so effective was this propaganda that many non-Communist Chinese really thought of the Red Army as some kind of foreign invasion.

So much for Kiangsi. During the next two years of the Long March the Reds were almost entirely cut off from contact even with their own Party members in the coastal cities of China, and the Comintern only infrequently got into direct communication with the Red Army. Wang Ming (Ch'en Shao-yu), the Chinese Party's chief delegate in Moscow, must have found it very difficult at times to get accurate information even on the location of the main forces of the Red Army for his reports to the Comintern, and some of his articles in *Inprecorr*[1] seemed to reflect that. I happened to be in Pao An one day when some copies of *Inprecorr* arrived, and I saw Lo Fu, the American-educated secretary of the Central Committee of the Party, eagerly devouring them. He mentioned casually that he had not seen an *Inprecorr* for nearly three years.

And not until September, 1936, while I was still with the Reds, did the detailed account of the proceedings of the Seventh Congress of the Communist International, held just a year previously, finally reach the Red capital of China. It was these reports which brought to the Chinese Communists for the first time the fully developed thesis of the international anti-Fascist united-front tactics which were to guide them in their policy during the months ahead, when revolt was to spread throughout the Northwest, and to shake the entire Orient. And once more the Comintern and Stalin were to assert their will in the affairs of China, in a manner that would sharply affect the development of the revolution.

I was to view that episode from the sidelines again in Peking.

---

1. *International Press Correspondence*, organ of the Third, or Communist, International (Comintern), published in Moscow.

六、　　别了，红色中国

在我离开保安之前发生了两件很有意思的事。10月9日甘肃来的无线电消息告诉我们，四方面军先遣部队在会宁同一军团的陈赓领导的第一师胜利会师。几天以后，陈赓和一方面军所有重要的将领都在甘肃同二、四方面军的领导人，其中包括朱德、徐向前、贺龙、张国焘、萧克等许多其他人，高兴地碰了头。甘肃的东北部分全部落入红军之手，四方面军有一个纵队渡过黄河到了甘肃西北的狭长地带，政府军的反抗已暂时被压下去了。

现在所有正规红军都集中在西北，建立了良好的通讯联系。冬服的订单如雪片一样飞来保安和吴起镇的被服厂。三支大军据说总共有八九万久经沙场、装备良好的战士。保安和整个苏区都举行了庆祝。甘肃南部作战期间的长期悬虑不安的气氛已经结束。现在人人都对将来充满了新的信心。中国最优秀的红军现在全部集中在一大块新的地区里，旁边还有同情他们的十万东北军可以充当盟友，共产党现在认为，南京方面会比较有兴趣来听他们的统一战线的建议了。

第二件事情是我在离开以前对毛泽东进行的一次访问，他第一次表示共产党欢迎同国民党讲和与进行合作抗日的具体条件。这些条件之中，有一些已由共产党在8月间发表的宣言中公布。我在访问时请毛泽东解释一下他提出新政策的原因。

"首先是，"他开始说，"日本侵略的严重：日本日益加紧侵略，它的威胁已经严重到中国一切力量都必须团结起来的程度。除了共产党以外，中国还有其他的政党和力量，其中最强大的是国民党。没有国民党的合作，我们目前的力量是不足以在战争中抵抗日本的。南京必须参加。国民党和共产党是中国两大政治力量，如果他们现在继续打内战，结果就会对抗日运动不利。

6   FAREWELL TO RED CHINA

Two interesting things happened before I left Pao An. On October 9, radio messages from Kansu reached us telling of the successful junction at Huining of the vanguard of the Fourth Red Army with Ch'en Keng's First Divison of the First Army Corps.

All the regular Red Army forces were now concentrated in Northwest China with good lines of communications established. Orders for winter uniforms poured into the factories of Pao An and Wu Ch'i Chen. The combined forces of the three armies reportedly numbered between 80,000 and 90,000 seasoned, well-equipped warriors. Celebrations and rejoicing were held in Pao An and throughout the soviet districts. The long period of suspense during the fighting in south Kansu was ended. Everyone now felt a new confidence in the future. With the whole of the best Red troops in China concentrated in a large new territory, and near-by another 100,000 sympathetic troops of the Tungpei Army, whom they had come to think of as allies, the Reds now believed that their proposals for a united front would be heard with keener interest at Nanking.

The second important event was an interview I had with Mao Tse-tung just before I left, in which, for the first time, he indicated concrete terms on the basis of which the Communists would welcome peace with the Kuomintang and cooperation to resist Japan. Some of these terms had already been announced in a manifesto issued by the Communist Party in August. In my conversation with Mao I asked him to explain the reasons for his new policy.

"First of all," he began, "the seriousness of Japanese aggression: it is becoming more intensified every day, and is so formidable a menace that before it all the forces of China must unite. Besides the Communist Party there are other parties and forces in China, and the strongest of these is the Kuomintang. Without its cooperation our strength at present is insufficient to resist Japan in war. Nanking must participate. The Kuomintang and the Communist Party are the two main political forces in China, and if they continue to fight now in civil war the effect will be unfavorable for the anti-Japanese movement.

"其次，自从1935年8月起，共产党就发宣言，呼吁中国各党派联合起来抵抗日本，全国人民热烈响应这个纲领，尽管国民党继续进攻我们。

"第三点是，甚至在国民党里的许多爱国分子现在也赞成同共产党联合。甚至在南京政府里的抗日分子和南京自己的军队，今天都为了我国民族存亡而准备联合起来。

"这就是中国目前形势的主要特点，因此我们不得不重新详细考虑在民族解放运动中实现这种合作的具体方案。我们坚持的团结的基本原则是抗日民族解放的原则。为了要实现这一原则，我们认为必须建立一个国防民主政府。这个政府的主要任务必须是抵抗外国侵略者，给予人民群众公民权利，加强国家的经济发展。

"因此我们拥护议会形式的代议制政府，抗日救国政府，保护和支持一切人民爱国团体的政府。如果成立了这样一个共和国，中国的各苏区就成为其中的一部分。我们将在自己的地区内采取措施建立议会形式的民主政府。"

"这是不是说，"我问道，"这样一个（民主的）政府的法律也会在苏区实施？"

毛泽东对此作了肯定的回答。他说，这样一个政府应该恢复并再次实现孙逸仙的遗嘱，和他在大革命时期提出的3个"基本原则"，即联合苏联和世界上以平等待我之民族；联合中国共产党；保护中国工人阶级的基本利益。

"如果国民党里开展了这样一个运动，"他继续说，"我们准备同它合作并且支持它，组成反帝统一战线，像1925到1927年那样。我们深信，这是拯救我国的唯一出路。"

"提出新建议有没有**当前**的原因？"我问道，"这肯定地必须认为是你们党近10年历史中最重要的决定。"

"当前的原因，"毛泽东解释道，"是日本提出了严重的新要求，[1] 屈服于这种要

---
1. 日本外相广田对南京政府提出的"三点"要求，即侵华"三原则"。

"Second, since August, 1935, the Communist Party has been urging, by manifesto, a union of all parties in China for the purpose of resisting Japan, and to this program the entire populace has responded with sympathy, notwithstanding the fact that the Kuomintang has continued its attacks upon us.

"The third point is that many patriotic elements even in the Kuomintang now favor a reunion with the Communist Party. Anti-Japanese elements even in the Nanking Government, and Nanking's own armies, are today ready to unite because of the peril to our national existence.

"These are the main characteristics of the present situation in China, and because of them we are obliged to reconsider in detail the concrete formula under which such cooperation in the national liberation movement can become possible. The fundamental point of unity which we insist upon is the national-liberation anti-Japanese principle. In order to realize it we believe there must be established a national defense democratic government. Its main tasks must be to resist the foreign invader, to grant popular rights to the masses of the people and to intensify the development of the country's economy.

"We will therefore support a parliamentary form of representative government, an anti-Japanese salvation government, a government which protects and supports all popular patriotic groups. If such a republic is established, the Chinese soviets will become a part of it. We will realize in our areas measures for a democratic parliamentary form of government."

"Does that mean," I asked, "that the laws of such a [democratic] government would also apply in soviet districts?"

Mao replied in the affirmative. He said that such a government should restore and once more realize Sun Yat-sen's final will, and his three "basic principles" during the Great Revolution, which were: alliance with the U.S.S.R. and those countries which treat China as an equal; union with the Chinese Communist Party; and fundamental protection of the interests of the Chinese working class.

"If such a movement develops in the Kuomintang," he continued, "we are prepared to cooperate with and support it, and to form a united front against imperialism such as existed in 1925—1927. We are convinced that this is the only way left to save our nation."

"Is there any *immediate* cause for the new proposals?" I inquired. "They must certainly be regarded as the most important decision in your Party's history in a decade."

"The immediate causes," Mao explained, "are the severe new demands of Japan,[1] capitulation

---

1. Foreign Minister Hirota's "Three-Point" demands, served on the Nanking Government.

求必然会大大妨碍将来的抵抗，同时人民对日本侵略的日益严重威胁的反响采取了伟大的人民爱国运动的形式。这两个条件反过来也在南京的某些分子的身上造成了态度的转变。在这样的情况下，现在就可以希望实现我们所建议的这种政策。如果在一年以前或早一些时候，用这形式提出来，不论是全国还是国民党就不会有思想准备。

"目前正在进行谈判。虽然共产党对于劝说南京抗日并不存多大希望，但是可能性还是有的。只要有可能性，共产党就愿意在一切必要措施方面合作。如果蒋介石要想继续打内战，红军也奉陪到底。"

事实上，这是毛泽东正式宣布共产党、苏维埃政府、红军愿意停止内战和不再企图用武力推翻南京政府，服从代议制中央政府的最高指挥，条件是创立政治体制，使得除了国民党以外的其他政党能够进行合作。毛泽东在这时也表示——虽然不是作为正式谈话——共产党愿意在名称方面也作一些改变，以利于"合作"，但在根本上并不影响红军和共产党的独立地位。例如，如果有必要，红军愿意改名为国民革命军，放弃"苏维埃"的名称，在抗日备战期间修改土地政策。在这以后的几个兴奋紧张的星期中，毛泽东的这一谈话对时局将发生重要的影响[1]。在这个谈话刊出之前，共产党自己的几个宣言都遭到封锁，南京方面少数几个看到这些宣言的领导人对之也抱深为怀疑的态度。但在一个外国记者访问共产党领袖本人的谈话普遍发表以后，有些有影响的集团就会更加相信共产党的诚意了。又有不少人开始拥护两党"复婚"的要求，因为要求停止代价浩大的内战和实现和平团结来抵抗日本征服的威胁这一建议，对不论什么阶级都是有号召力的。

1936年10月中，我在红军中间呆了将近4个月以后，回白色世界的安排工作终于完成了。这可不容易。张学良的东北友军几乎已从所有战线上撤出，由南京的军队或其他敌意部队换防。当时只有一个出口，那是由东北军一个师在洛川附近与红军毗邻的一条战线，洛川在西安以北，只有一天的汽车路程。

我最后一次走过保安的大街，越是走近城门，越是感到恋恋不舍。人们从办公室伸出脑袋来向我道别。我的扑克俱乐部成员全体出动来送行，有些"小鬼"陪我走到保安城墙根。我停下来给老徐和老谢拍照，他们像小学生那样互相搭着肩膀。只有毛泽东没有出现，他仍在睡觉。

---

1. 访问记全文刊《密勒氏评论报》，1936年11月14日和21日上海。

to which must enormously handicap any attempts at resistance in the future, and the popular response to this deepening threat of Japanese invasion in the form of a great people's patriotic movement. These conditions have in turn produced a change in attitude among certain elements in Nanking. Under the circumstances it is now possible to hope for the realization of such a policy as we propose. Had it been offered in this form a year ago, or earlier, neither the country nor the Kuomintang would have been prepared for it.

"At present, negotiations are being conducted. While the Communist Party has no great positive hopes of persuading Nanking to resist Japan, it is nevertheless possible. As long as it is, the Communist Party will be ready to cooperate in all necessary measures. If Chiang Kai-shek prefers to continue the civil war, the Red Army will also receive him."

In effect, Mao made a formal declaration of the readiness of the Communist Party, the Soviet Government, and the Red Army, to cease civil war and further attempts to overthrow Nanking by force, and to submit to the high command of a representative central government, provided there was created the political framework in which the cooperation of other parties besides the Kuomintang would be possible. At this time also, though not as part of the formal interview, Mao indicated that the Communists would be prepared to make such changes in nomenclature as would facilitate "cooperation," without fundamentally affecting the independent role of the Red Army and the Communist Party. Thus, if it were necessary, the Red Army would change its name to National Revolutionary Army, the name "soviets" would be abandoned, and the agrarian policy would be modified during the period of preparation for war against Japan. During the turbulent weeks that lay ahead, Mao's statement was to have an important influence on events.[1]

In the middle of October, 1936, after I had been with the Reds nearly four months, arrangements were finally completed for my return to the White world. It had not been easy. Chang Hsueh-liang's friendly Tungpei troops had been withdrawn from nearly every front and replaced by Nanking or other hostile forces. There was only one outlet then, through a Tungpei division which still had a front with the Reds near Lochuan, a walled city a day's motor trip north of Sian.

I walked down the main street of Defended Peace for the last time, and the farther I got toward the gate, the more reluctantly I moved. People popped their heads out of offices to shout last remarks. My poker club turned out *en masse* to bid the *maestro* good-by, and some "little devils" trudged with me to the walls of Pao An. I stopped to take a picture of Old Hsu and Old Hsieh, their arms thrown around each other's shoulders. Only Mao Tse-tung failed to appear; he was still asleep.

---

1. The full text of this interview appeared in *The China Weekly Review* (Shanghai), November 14 and 21, 1936.

"别忘了我的假臂！"蔡树藩叫道。

"别忘了我的照片！"陆定一提醒我。

"我们等着你的航空队！"杨尚昆笑道。

"给我送个老婆来！"李克农要求。

"把4两可可送回来！"博古责怪道。

我走过红军大学的时候，红军大学全体学员都露天坐在一棵大树下听洛甫作报告。他们都走了过来，向我握手，我嘴里喃喃地说了几句话。然后我转身蹚过溪流，向他们挥手告别，很快骑上马跟着我的小旅队走了。我当时心里想，也许我是看到他们活着的最后一个外国人了。我心里感到很难过。我觉得我不是在回家，而是在离家。

5天后，我们到了南部边界，我在那里等了3天，住在一个小村子里，吃黑豆和野猪肉。这个地方风景很美，树木成林，野味很多，我在这几天里就同一些农民和红军战士打野猪和鹿。树丛中间尽是大野鸡，有一天，我们看到两只老虎在秋天一片紫金色的山谷中蹿过一片空地，可惜是在射程以外。前线一片宁静，红军在这里只驻了一营兵力。

20日那天我安全地经过了无人地带，到了东北军防线的后面，第二天借了一匹马，进了洛川，那里有一辆卡车在等待着我。一天以后我就到了西安府。到鼓楼时我就从司机座旁下了车，请一名红军战士（他穿着东北军制服）把我的包扔给我。找了半天没有找到，接着又找了半天，这时我疑惧交加。果然没有疑问。我的包不在那里。在那个包里，有我十几本日记和笔记，30卷胶卷——是第一次拍到的中国红军的照片和影片——还有好几磅重的共产党杂志、报纸和文件。必须把它找到！

在鼓楼下面激动了半天，交通警在不远的地方好奇地看着我们。于是进行了轻声的商量。最后终于弄清楚了怎么回事。那辆卡车用麻袋装着东北军要修理的枪械，我的那个包为了怕受到搜查也塞在那样的一个麻袋里，一起卸在我们旅程后面20英里渭河以北的咸阳了！司机懊丧地瞪着卡车。"他妈的"，他只好这样安慰我。

天已黑了，司机表示他等到明天早晨再回去找。明天早晨！我下意识中感到明天早晨太迟了。我坚持我的意见，终于说服了他。卡车转过头来又回去了，我在西

"Don't forget my artificial arm!" called Ts'ai.

"Don't forget my films!" urged Lu Ting-yi.

"We'll be waiting for the air fleet!" laughed Yang Shang-k'un.

"Send me in a wife!" demanded Li K'e-nung.

"And send back those four ounces of cocoa," chided Po Ku.

The whole Red University was seated out in the open, under a great tree, listening to a lecture by Lo Fu, when I went past. They all came over, and we shook hands, and I mumbled a few words. Then I turned and forded the stream, waved them a farewell, and rode up quickly with my little caravan. I might be the last foreigner to see any of them alive, I thought. It was very depressing. I felt that I was not going home, but leaving it.

In five days we reached the southern frontier, and I waited there for three days, staying in a tiny village and eating black beans and wild pig. It was a beautiful wooded country, alive with game, and I spent the days in the hills with some farmers and Red soldiers, hunting pigs and deer. The bush was crowded with huge pheasants, and one day we even saw, far out of range, two tigers streaking across a clearing in a valley drenched with the purple-gold of autumn. The front was absolutely peaceful, and the Reds had only one battalion stationed here.

On the 20th I got through no man's land safely and behind the Tungpei lines, and on a borrowed horse next day I rode into Lochuan, where a truck was waiting for me. A day later I was in Sianfu. At the Drum Tower I jumped down from beside the driver and asked one of the Reds (who were wearing Tungpei uniforms) to toss me my bag. A long search, and then a longer search, while my fears increased. Finally there was no doubt about it. My bag was not there. In that bag were a dozen diaries and notebooks, thirty rolls of film—the first still and moving pictures ever taken of the Chinese Red Army—and several pounds of Red magazines, newspapers, and documents. It had to be found.

Excitement under the Drum Tower, while traffic policemen curiously gazed from a short distance away. Whispered consultations. Finally it was realized what had happened. The truck had been loaded with gunnysacks full of broken Tungpei rifles and guns being sent for repairs, and my bag, in case of any search, had been stuffed into such a sack also. Back at Hsienyang, on the opposite shore of the Wei River, twenty miles behind us, the missing object had been thrown off with the other loads. The driver stared ruefully at the truck. "*T'a ma-ti*," he offered in consolation.

It was already dusk, and the driver suggested that he wait till morning to go back and hunt for it. Morning! Something warned me that morning would be too late. I insisted, and I finally won the argument. The truck reversed and returned, and I stayed awake all

安府一个朋友家里整宵没有合眼，不知道我能不能再见到无价之宝的那个包。要是那个包在咸阳打了开来，不仅我的一切东西都永远丢失了，而且那辆"东北军"卡车和它所有的乘客都要完了。咸阳驻有南京的宪兵。

　　幸而，你从本书的照片可以看出，那只包找到了。可是我急着要把它找回来的直觉是绝对正确的，因为第二天一早，街上停止一切交通，城门口的所有道路都遍布宪兵和军队的岗哨。沿路农民都被赶出了家。有些不雅观的破屋就干脆拆除，不致使人觉得难看。原来是蒋介石总司令突然光临西安府。那时我们的卡车要再沿原路回渭河就不可能了，因为这条道路经过重兵把守的机场。

　　总司令的驾到同我记忆犹新的场面——毛泽东、徐海东、林彪、彭德怀毫不在乎地走在红色中国的一条街上——截然不同，令人难忘。而且总司令并没有人悬赏要他首级。这生动地说明谁真的害怕人民，谁信任人民。但是即使西安府所采取的全部保护总司令生命的措施后来也证明是不充分的。就在保卫他的军队中间，他的敌人也太多了。

night in a friend's house in Sianfu wondering whether I would ever see that priceless bag again. If it were opened at Hsienyang, not only would all my things be lost forever, but that "Tungpei" truck and all its occupants would be *huai-la*—finished. There were Nationalist gendarmes at Hsienyang.

The bag was found. But my hunch about the urgency of the search had been absolutely correct, for early next morning all traffic was completely swept from the streets, and all roads leading into the city were lined with gendarmes and troops. Peasants were cleared out of their homes along the road. Some of the more unsightly huts were simply demolished, so that there would be nothing offensive to the eye. Generalissimo Chiang Kai-shek was paying a sudden call on Sianfu. It would have been impossible then for our truck to return over that road to the Wei River, for it skirted the heavily guarded airfield.

This arrival of the Generalissimo made an unforgettable contrast with the scenes still fresh in my mind—of Mao Tse-tung, or Hsu Hai-tung, or Lin Piao, or P'eng Teh-huai nonchalantly strolling down a street in Red China. And the Generalissimo did not have a price on his head. But the precautions taken to protect him in Sian were to prove inadequate. He had too many enemies among the very troops who were guarding him.

PART TWELVE
White World Again

第十二篇
又是白色世界

一、　　兵变前奏

我从红色中国出来后，发现张学良少帅的东北军与蒋介石总司令之间的紧张关系越来越尖锐了。蒋介石现在不仅是中国武装部队的总司令，而且还是行政院院长——相当于总理的职位。

我在上文[1]已经介绍过，东北军原来是被派到五六个省份里去打红军的雇佣兵，后来却在军事上和政治上逐步改造成为一支受到它的敌人的抗日民族革命口号的感染，相信继续打内战没有意义，一心一意只想"打回老家去"的军队。只有一个主张能打动他们，他们也只效忠于一个中心思想，那就是日本人把他们赶出老家东北，凌辱和杀害他们的家人，他们就要从日本人那里收复东北。这些想法同南京当时的打算是截然相反的，因此东北军对抗日的红军越来越感到同志的友情，是很自然的事。

在我4个月的旅行期间，发生了一些重要事情，加深了这种分歧。在西南，白崇禧和李宗仁将军领导反宁，他们的主要政治要求是以反对南京政府的"亲日"不抵抗政策为基础的。在经过几星期在战争边缘上徘徊以后，终于达成妥协，但这个事件对全国抗日运动起很大刺激作用。内地有几个地方的愤怒群众打死了三四个日本人，日本向南京政府提出强硬抗议，要求道歉、赔款、新的政治让步。看来很有可能再次发生一场中日"事变"，继之以日本侵略。

---

1. 特别见第一篇第三章，《汉代青铜》。

1   A Preface to Mutiny

I emerged from Red China to find a sharpening tension between the Tungpei troops of Young Marshal Chang Hsueh-liang and Generalissimo Chiang Kai-shek, who was now not only commander-in-chief of China's armed forces, but also chairman of the Executive Yuan—a position comparable to that of premier.

I have described[1] how the Tungpei troops were gradually being transformed, militarily and politically, from mercenaries who had been shipped to half a dozen different provinces to fight the Reds into an army infected by the national patriotic anti-Japanese slogans of its enemy, convinced of the futility of continued civil war, stirred by only one exhortation, loyal to but one central idea—the hope of "fighting back to the old homeland," of recovering Manchuria from the Japanese who had driven them from their homes and abused and murdered their families. These notions being directly opposed to the maxims then held by Nanking, the Tungpei troops had found themselves with a growing fellow feeling for the anti-Japanese Red Army.

The estrangement had been widened by important occurrences during the four months of my travels. In the Southwest a revolt against Nanking had been led by Generals Pai Chung-hsi and Li Tsung-jen, whose chief political demands were based on opposition to the Nationalist Government's nonresistance policies. After weeks of near-war, a compromise settlement had finally been reached, but the interim had provided a tremendous stimulus to the anti-Japanese movement throughout China. Three or four Japanese had been killed by angry mobs in various parts of the interior, and Japan had presented to Nanking strong demands for apologies, compensations, and new political concessions. Another Sino-Japanese "incident," followed by a Japanese invasion, seemed a possibility.

---

1. See especially Part One, Chapter 3.

与此同时，在左翼的救国会领导下的抗日运动，尽管政府采取了严峻的镇压措施，在全国各地风起云涌，南京间接地受到很大的群众压力，要它采取强硬态度。10月间日本指使蒙伪军在日本控制下的热河和察哈尔装备训练后进犯绥远北部（内蒙古），这样的压力就开始倍增。尽管群众普遍要求把这看做是"最后限度"和全国"抗战"的信号，但并没有得到重视。没有发布动员令。南京的一成不变的答复仍是：先"安内"——即消灭共产党。许多爱国人士开始要求南京接受共产党的停止内战和在"志愿统一"的基础上建立民族阵线的建议，以便集中全国人民的力量抵抗日本这一共同的敌人。但提倡这种主张的人马上作为"卖国贼"逮捕起来。

全国情绪之激烈以西北为最。当时很少人认识到东北军的抗日情绪同停止"剿共"战争的决心有多么密切的联系。对中国大通商口岸的外国人来说，西安固然是个遥远的地方，对大多数中国人来说也似乎是如此，很少新闻记者去那里采访。近几个月来没有一个外国记者到过西安，对于那里即要发生的事件，谁都没有任何可靠的背景材料——只有一个例外。那就是美国作家尼姆·韦尔斯女士，她在10月间到了西安，访问了少帅。韦尔斯女士确切地报道了西北越来越加速的脉搏：

在中国的西京西安府，张学良少帅驻在这里"剿共"的、激烈抗日的东北军行伍中间出现了一个严重的局面。这些军队原来在1931年有25万人，如今只剩13万人，都成了"亡国奴"，想家，厌恶内战，对南京政府对日本继续采取不抵抗政策越来越愤慨。下层官兵中间的态度完全可以说是就要谋反了。这种感情甚至传染到了高级军官。这种情况引起谣传说，甚至张学良以前同蒋介石的良好个人关系现在也紧张起来，他打算与红军结盟，组成抗日统一战线，由一个国防政府领导。

中国抗日运动的严重并不表现在从北到南的许多"事件"，而是表现在这里西安府的东北流亡者身上——从逻辑上来说，可以说这是理所当然的。抗日运动在全国其他地方虽然遭到了镇压，在西安府却在张学良帅的公开热情的领导之下，他在这方面采取行动是受到他的部队的热烈拥护的，如果说不是受着他们逼迫的话。[1]

韦尔斯女士回顾她访问少帅的意义时说：

---

1. 大约是1936年10月25日为《纽约太阳报》写。

Meanwhile the anti-Japanese movement, led by the left-wing National Salvation Association, was, despite stern measures of suppression, rising in strength everywhere, and considerable mass pressure was being indirectly exerted on Nanking to stiffen its attitude. Such pressure multiplied when, in October, Japanese-led Mongol and Chinese puppet troops, equipped and trained in Japan's conquered Jehol and Chahar, began an invasion of northern Suiyuan (Inner Mongolia). But the widespread popular demand that this be considered "the last extremity," and the signal for a "war of resistance" on a national scale, was ignored. No mobilization orders were forthcoming. Nanking's standing reply remained. "Internal unification"—i.e., extermination of the Reds—must come first. Many patriotic quarters began to urge that the Communists' proposals for an end to civil war, and the creation of a national front on the basis of "voluntary unification," be accepted by Nanking, in order to concentrate the entire energies of the people to oppose the common peril of Japan. Proponents of such opinions were arrested as "traitors."

The highest degree of emotional excitement centered in the Northwest. Few people realized then how closely the anti-Japanese sentiment of the Tungpei Army was connected with the determination to stop the war against the Reds. Sian seemed a long way off to most Chinese as well as to foreigners in the big treaty ports of China, and it was little visited by journalists. An exception was Miss Nym Wales, an American writer, who in October journeyed to Sian and interviewed the Young Marshal. Miss Wales reported:

> *The serious anti-Japanese movement in China is formulating itself not in the various "incidents" ranging from North to South, but here in Sianfu among the Northeastern exiles from Manchuria—as one might expect that it logically should. While the movement is being suppressed in other parts of China, in Sianfu it is under the open and enthusiastic leadership of Young Marshal Chang Hsueh-liang—ardently supported by his troops, if not compelled by them to act in this direction.*[1]

Reflecting on the significance of her interview with the Young Marshal, Miss Wales wrote:

---

1. Written for the *New York Sun, circa* October 25, 1936.

事实上，从这个背景来看，这次谈话可能被认为是企图影响蒋介石积极领导抗战……包含着（在他的发言中）一种威胁："只有抵抗外国侵略（即不是内战）才能表示中国的真正统一"，"如果政府不从民意，就站不住脚。"最有意义的是，这位副总司令（仅次于蒋介石）说，"如果共产党能够真诚合作抵抗共同的外国侵略者，这个问题也许有可能和平解决。"……

真是谋反的话！但是蒋介石显然低估了这个警告的严重性。10月间他派他的最精锐部队第一军去进攻甘肃的红军，他到西安府，是为了要完成第六次"围剿"的初步计划。西安和兰州已做好准备容纳100多架轰炸机。成吨的炸弹已经运到，据报道还准备使用毒气。蒋介石所以奇怪地吹嘘说，他"在两星期内，至多在1个月内即可消灭'赤匪'残部。"[1]这似乎是唯一的解释。

蒋介石在10月间到西安一行以后，有一点他是一定了解的。那就是，在反共战争中，东北军已越来越派不上用场。总司令在与东北军将领谈话中可以察觉到大家对他的新攻势毫无兴趣。张学良的一个幕僚后来告诉我说，这次少帅正式向总司令提出了成立民族阵线、停止内战、联俄抗日的纲领。蒋介石回答说，"在杀尽中国红军、捉尽'共匪'之前，我决不谈此事。只有到那时候才可以同俄国合作"。

总司令回到了他在洛阳的大本营，监督这次新战役的准备工作。如有必要，要向西北派20师兵力。到11月底，陕西古老的关隘潼关附近已经集中了十多个满员师。一列车一列车的弹药和供应品运进了西安。坦克、装甲车、摩托运输队也准备随之而来。

但是对于这一切准备在大规模基础上加强内战的计划，公众都还蒙在鼓里，只有西北是例外。关于西北的情况，报上很少透露。官方的说法是，红军已被正式"剿灭"，少数"残部"也在被驱散之中。与此同时，绥远（内蒙古）的防务交给了地方军队，他们倒打了一场硬仗。对于每天轰炸中国军队战线的日本飞机，南京飞机没有一架起飞迎战。但是他们却进行了频繁的宣传，造成一种假象，好像是南京军队在领导防御；同时东京和南京却相互保证，绥远的"局部冲突"决不允许扩大。少数中央政府军——至多两个师——已开入了绥远，但在部署上却使得地方部队不能把"抵抗"这件事搞得太认真了。当时担心地方部队可能真的进攻日本在察哈尔和热河所占据的领土。有些南京军队也部署在绥远军队与红军之间，因为蒋介石认为红军很

---

1. 见蒋介石日记。

> *In effect, and read in relation to its background, this interview may be interpreted as an attempt to influence Chiang Kai-shek to lead active resistance . . . implying a threat (in his statement) that "only by resistance to foreign aggression [i. e., not by civil war] can the real unification of China be manifested," and that "if the Government does not obey the will of the people it cannot stand." Most significant, this Deputy Commander-in-Chief (second only to Chiang Kai-shek) said that "if the Communists can sincerely cooperate to resist the common foreign invader, perhaps it is possible that this problem can be settled peacefully.". . .*

But Chiang Kai-shek plainly underestimated the seriousness of the warning. In October he sent the First Army—his best—to attack the Reds in Kansu, and when he arrived in Sianfu it was for the purpose of completing preliminary plans for his sixth general offensive against the Reds. In Sian and Lanchow arrangements were made to accommodate more than 100 bombers. Tons of bombs arrived. It was reported that poison gas was to be used. This was seemingly the only explanation of Chiang's queer boast that he would "destroy the remnant Red bandits in a couple of weeks, or at most a month."[1]

One thing Chiang must have understood after his October visit to Sian. That was that the Tungpei troops were becoming useless in the war against the Communists. In interviews with Tungpei commanders the Generalissimo could now discern a profound lack of interest in his new offensive. One of Chang Hsueh-liang's staff told me later that at this time the Young Marshal formally presented to the Generalissimo the program for a national front, cessation of civil war, alliance with Russia, and resistance to Japan. Chiang Kai-shek replied, "I will never talk about this until every Red soldier in China is exterminated, and every Communist is in prison. Only then would it be possible to cooperate with Russia." A little before this the Generalissimo had rejected a Russian offer of a mutual-defense pact through his then foreign minister, Wang Ching-wei.

Now the Generalissimo went back to his headquarters in Loyang and supervised preparations for his new campaign. Twenty divisions of troops were to be brought into the Northwest if necessary. By late November over ten full war-strength divisions had already been concentrated near Tungkuan, outside the historic pass at the gateway to Shensi. Trainloads of shells and supplies poured into Sian. Tanks, armored cars, motor transports were prepared to move after them.

---

1. See Chiang's diary.

可能从陕西开入绥远，企图带头真的进攻日本军队。

这时全国民族情绪激昂，日本要求镇压救国会，认为抗日宣传是它鼓动起来的。南京遵命办事。救国会的7位最著名领导人被捕。他们都是有地位的资产阶级人士，其中有一名著名银行家，一名律师，还有教育家和作家。与此同时，政府一下子封闭了14家畅销全国的杂志。上海日商纱厂的工人因为抗议日本侵略绥远等原因而举行的罢工，遭到日本人在国民党合作下的暴力镇压。青岛发生其他爱国罢工时，日本人派海军陆战队登陆，逮捕罢工工人，占领了全市。在蒋介石实际上同意取缔将来青岛日商纱厂一切罢工后，海军陆战队才撤退。

所有这一切事件都进一步在西北产生了反响。11月间，张学良在自己部下官兵的压力下，发出了他著名的呼吁，要求派往绥远前线。呼吁最后说：

> 为了要控制我们的军队，我们要信守诺言，一有机会就要让他们实现打敌人的愿望。否则他们就不仅把我本人，并将把钧座视为骗子，此后不再服从我们的命令。因此恳请下令至少动员东北军一部立即开赴绥远前线，增援在那里完成其抵抗日本帝国主义神圣使命的军队。我本人和我部下10万余人愿追随钧座到底。

这封信[1]口气恳切，要求报仇雪耻之心，希望恢复东北军声誉之情，溢于言表。但是蒋介石断然拒绝这个要求。他仍要东北军打共产党。

少帅并不气馁，他不久之后又坐飞机到洛阳去亲自提出这个要求。同时他也为被捕的救国会领袖说项。后来，在扣留了总司令之后，张学良记述那次谈话如下：

---

1. 1937年1月2日由西北军事委员会在西安府公布。

A flame of strong nationalist feeling swept through the country, and the Japanese demanded the suppression of the National Salvation movement, which they held responsible for the anti-Japanese agitation. Nanking obliged. Seven of the most prominent leaders of the organization, all respectable citizens, including a prominent banker, a lawyer, educators, and writers, were arrested. At the same time the government suppressed fourteen nationally popular magazines. Strikes in the Japanese mills of Shanghai, partly in patriotic protest against the Japanese invasion of Suiyuan, were also broken up with considerable violence by the Japanese, in cooperation with the Kuomintang. When other patriotic strikes occurred in Tsingtao, the Japanese landed their own marines, arrested the strikers, occupied the city. The marines were withdrawn only after Chiang had agreed virtually to prohibit all strikes in Japanese mills of Tsingtao in the future.

All those happenings had further repercussions in the Northwest. In November, under pressure from his own officers, Chang Hsueh-liang dispatched his famous appeal to be sent to the Suiyuan front.

"In order to control our troops," this missive concluded, "we should keep our promise to them that whenever the chance comes they will be allowed to carry out their desire of fighting the enemy. Otherwise they will regard not only myself, but also Your Excellency, as a cheat, and thus will no longer obey us. Please give us the order to mobilize at least a part, if not the whole, of the Tungpei Army, to march immediately to Suiyuan as reinforcements to those who are fulfilling their sacred mission of fighting Japanese imperialism there. If so, I, as well as my troops, of more than 100,000, shall follow Your Excellency's leadership to the end."

The earnest tone of this whole letter,[1] the hope of restoring an army's lost prestige, were overwhelmingly evident. But Chiang rejected the suggestion. He still wanted the Tungpei Army to fight the Reds.

Not long afterwards, importunate, the Marshal flew his plane to Loyang to repeat the request in person. At this time also he interceded for the arrested leaders of the National Salvation Association. Later on, after the arrest of the Generalissimo, Chang Hsueh-liang recounted that conversation:[2]

---

1. Published in Sianfu, January 2, 1937, by the Northwest Military Council.
2. A speech reported by the *Hsiking Min Pao* (Sianfu), December 17, 1936.

最近蒋总司令逮捕监禁了上海救国会七领袖。我请他释放这些领袖。这些救国会领袖与我非亲非友，他们多数人我连认识也不认识。但我对他们被捕一事提出抗议，因为他们信奉的原则与我相同。我要求把他们释放，但遭到拒绝。我于是向蒋说："你对待人民爱国运动的残酷，与袁世凯、张宗昌[1]并无二致。"

蒋总司令回答说："这只是你的看法。我就是政府。我的行动是革命者的行动。"

"同胞们，你们相信这话吗？"

全场数千人齐声怒喊作答。[2]

但是张学良在这个时候飞去洛阳有一个积极结果。总司令同意，他下次来西安时，他要向东北军的师以上将领详细说明他的计划和战略。少帅就回去急切地等候他的上级的第二次驾到。但是在蒋介石来到以前，发生了两件事，进一步激怒了西北。

第一件事就是签订德日反共协定和意大利的非正式参加。意大利本来已经默认日本霸占东北，作为交换条件，日本承认意大利控制阿比西尼亚。意大利与满洲国建交激怒了少帅，他一度与齐亚诺伯爵颇为友善。他接到这个消息以后就怒斥齐亚诺和墨索里尼，势必要摧毁意大利在中国的影响。他在向军校学生发表讲话时说，"这肯定是法西斯运动在中国的末日！"现在东北军的不满又增加了一项。德意军事顾问当时正在训练蒋介石的军队和他的空军去轰炸中共。他们是不是也在把他们所能弄到的关于中国的军事情报提供给日本呢？难道德日条约事先没有通知蒋介石并征得他的同意吗？有谣言说他是同意的。

接着，也是在11月里，传来了胡宗南著名的第一军失利的消息，该军21日在红军手中吃了大败仗。胡宗南将军是南京方面最能干的战术家，好几个星期以来就一直几乎毫无阻碍地向甘肃北部挺进。红军慢慢后撤，除了小规模遭遇战外，避免交锋。但是他们通过不同方式向南京军队宣传"统一战线"，设法说服他们停止进攻，发表宣言声称红军不打抗日的军队，要求敌军参加他们共同抗日。"中国人不打中国人！"这种宣传后来证明极为有效。

---

1. 20年前屈服于日本要求的军阀。
2. 1936年12月17日西安府《西京民报》所载的一篇讲话。

Recently Generalissimo Chiang arrested and imprisoned seven of our National Salvation leaders in Shanghai. I asked him to release those leaders. Now, none of the National Salvation leaders are my friends or relatives, and I do not even know most of them. But I protested at their arrest because their principles are the same as mine. My request that they be released was rejected. To Chiang I then said: "Your cruelty in dealing with the patriotic movement of the people is exactly the same as that of Yuan Shih-k'ai or Chang Tsung-chang."[1]

Generalissimo Chiang replied: "That is merely your viewpoint. I am the Government. My action was that of a revolutionary."

"Fellow countrymen, do you believe this?"

The question was answered by an angry roar from the assembled thousands.

But Chang Hsueh-liang's flight to Loyang at that time had one positive result. The Generalissimo agreed that when he next came to Sian he would explain his plans and strategy to the Tungpei division generals in detail. The Young Marshal returned to await impatiently his superior's second visit. Before Chiang arrived, however, two occurrences intervened which further antagonized the Northwest.

The first of these was the signing of the German-Japanese anti-Communist agreement, and Italy's unofficial adherence thereto. Italy had already tacitly recognized Japan's conquest of Manchuria, in return for which Japan had acknowledged Italy's control of Abyssinia. The opening of Italian relations with Manchukuo had infuriated the Young Marshal, who had once been pals with Count Ciano. With receipt of this news he denounced both Ciano and Mussolini, and swore to destroy Italian influence in his country. "This is absolutely the end of the Fascist movement in China!" he exclaimed in a speech before his cadets.

Then, in November also, came news of the disaster to Hu Tsung-nan's famed First Army, which on the 21st suffered a severe defeat from the Reds. General Hu, ablest of Nanking's tacticians, had for weeks been moving almost unimpeded into northern Kansu. The Reds had slowly withdrawn, refusing battle except in minor skirmishes. But in various ways they propagandized the Nanking troops about the "united front," trying to persuade them to halt, issuing declarations that the Red Army would attack no anti-Japanese troops, urging the enemy to join them in resisting Japan. "Chinese must not fight Chinese!" The propaganda was to prove highly effective.

---

1. Warlords who had capitulated to Japanese demands two decades earlier.

但是胡将军认为红军已经完蛋了——软弱、害怕、没有斗志。他轻率地继续推进。红军继续后撤,几乎撤到了河连湾。这时他们决定不再后撤;需要给敌军一个教训。[1]需要给他们看到统一战线也是有牙齿的。他们突然掉转方向,巧妙地把胡宗南将军的军队诱入一个黄土山谷,到黄昏时,空袭停止,他们就加以包围,入夜后发动正面奇袭,左右两翼并有刺刀冲锋。气温低达零度,红军没戴手套的手指都冻僵了,拔不掉手榴弹的雷管。他们许多人就把木柄手榴弹当作棍棒挥舞攻入敌军阵线。一军团带头进行猛攻,结果全歼敌军两个步兵旅、一个骑兵团,缴获大批步枪、机枪,政府军有一整团投诚参加红军。胡宗南将军慌忙后撤,在几天之内就把过去几个星期中"收复"的地方全部丢失了。他坐下来等待总司令的增援。

东北军一定在窃窃暗笑。这不是就像他们所说的那样吗?红军不是比以前更有力量了?这次新"围剿"旗开失利不是说明"围剿"将是一件十分困难的事?一年,两年,三年,他们在哪里?仍在打红军。那么日本呢?占领更多更大块的中国领土。但是顽固的总司令因为最精锐的部队蒙此大辱,羞怒之下申斥了胡宗南将军,只有更加坚决地要摧毁他的十年宿敌。

蒋介石1936年12月7日在西安飞机场从座机上下来时,所踏上的就是这样一个时局舞台。

与此同时,在这个舞台上的左右两侧都发生了重要的事情。东北军将领已经商量好要联合提出停止内战和抵抗日本的要求。陕西绥靖公署主任杨虎城将军的将领也参与其事。杨将军的军队大约有4万人,对继续打红军,比东北军更没有劲。他们认为这是南京的战争,他们看不出有什么理由要拼自己的命去打红军,红军许多人跟自己一样是陕西人。在他们看来,这场战争也很丢人,因为这时日本正在侵略邻省绥远。杨将军的部队叫西北军,几个月前已与东北军结成紧密的联盟,秘密参加了同红军休战的协议。

---

1. 根据马海德医生写给我的一封详述了这场战斗的信件。他当时和红军在一起。

General Hu pushed on. The Reds continued to withdraw until they had almost reached Holienwan. Then they decided to retreat no farther; the enemy needed a lesson.[1] It needed to be shown that the united front also had teeth in it. Suddenly turning, they skillfully maneuvered General Hu's troops into a valley of loessland, surrounded them at dusk, when the air bombardment had ceased, and at night staged a surprise frontal attack supported by bayonet charges from both flanks. It was zero weather, and the Reds' bare hands were so cold they could not pull the caps from their hand grenades. Hundreds of them went into the enemy lines using their potato-masher grenades for clubs. The fierce onslaught, led by the First Army Corps, resulted in the complete destruction and disarming of two infantry brigades and a regiment of cavalry, while thousands of rifles and machine guns were captured, and one government regiment turned over intact to join the Reds. General Hu beat a hasty retreat, giving up in a few days all the territory which he had "recovered" over a period of weeks.

The Tungpei generals must have been amused. Was it not just as they had said? Did not the Reds have more punch in them than ever? Did not this inauspicious beginning of the new campaign show how difficult the process of annihilation was going to be? A year, two years, three, and where would they be? Still fighting the Reds. And Japan? In occupation of new and greater areas of Chinese territory. But the obstinate Generalissimo, angered by the humiliation of his best army, censured General Hu and only became more determined to destroy his ten-year enemy.

Into this main theater of events Chiang Kai-shek stepped from his airplane onto the flying field of Sian on December 7, 1936.

Meanwhile, important things had happened on both the right and left wings of the stage. Among the Tungpei commanders an agreement had been reached to present a common request for cancellation of civil war, and resistance to Japan. Into this agreement had come the officers of the army of General Yang Hu-ch'eng, the Pacification Commissioner of Shensi. General Yang's army, of about 40,000 men, had even less interest in continuing the war against the Reds than the Tungpei troops. To them it was Nanking's war, and they saw no good reason for wrecking themselves against the Reds, many of whom were Shensi people like themselves. It was to them also a disgraceful war, when Japan was invading the neighboring province of Suiyuan. General Yang's troops, known as the Hsipei Chun, or Northwest Army, had some months previously formed a close solidarity with the Tungpei troops, and secretly joined in the truce with the Reds.

---

1. According to a letter reporting details of the battle written to me by Dr. Ma Hai-teh. He was then with the Red Army.

这一切情况，行政院长兼总司令肯定已经知道一二。他在西安虽没有正规军，但在几个月以前宪兵三团——即蓝衣社的所谓特务团——的1,500名人员在他的侄子蒋孝先将军的指挥下开到了西安，后者曾经诱捕、监禁、杀害激进分子成百上千。他们在全省设立了特务网，开始逮捕、绑架所谓共产党学生、政工人员和士兵。省城警察是南京任命的省主席邵力子掌管的。由于少帅和杨虎城在城里只有随身警卫人员，没有驻防军队，总司令在那里实际控制大局。

这种情况也促成了另外一个事件。蒋介石到达后两天，12月9日，好几千学生举行抗日示威，游行队伍向临潼进发，去向总司令递请愿书。邵主席下令驱散队伍。警察在蒋介石的一些宪兵协助下殴打了学生，一度还开了枪。两个学生受伤，正好是一个东北军军官的孩子，这次枪击事件就闹大了。张学良出面干涉，制止了殴打，劝说学生回城里去，答应把他们的请愿书交给总司令。蒋介石盛怒之下，申斥张学良"不忠"，企图"脚踏两头船"。蒋介石后来认为，他们两人之间的这一事件是后来发生反叛的近因。

总司令的整个参谋部和他的个人警卫这时全都在西安府同他一起。蒋介石拒绝东北军和西北军将领一起会见的要求，只是分别接见了他们，用各种办法诱使他们分裂。他的这个企图归于失败。他们都承认他是总司令，但一个个都表示对新"围剿"不满，都要求派他们到绥远抗日前线去。但是蒋介石对他们全体只有一个命令："摧毁红军。"蒋介石在他的日记里写道，"我告诉他们，'剿匪'已到只需最后5分钟就可实现最后胜利的阶段。"

这样，总司令不顾一切反对和警告，在10日召开了大本营会议，正式通过了发动第六次"围剿"计划。准备对已在甘肃和陕西的西北军、东北军、南京军队以及在潼关待命的南京军队颁发总动员令。当时宣布在12日公布动员令。并且公开声言，如果张少帅拒绝服从命令，他的部队将由南京军队予以缴械，本人将予撤职[1]。同时张、杨又接到消息，说明蓝衣社同警察一起已准备好一份他们部队中同情共产党分子的"黑名单"，一俟总动员令颁发就立即加以逮捕。

这样，作为这一连串复杂的历史性事件的高潮，张学良在12月11日晚上10点召开了东北军和西北军的师以上将领联席会议。前一天已经秘密发出命令，调一师东北军和一团杨虎城的军队到西安府近郊。现在作出了决定，要用这些部队"逮捕"总司令和他的僚属。17万军队的兵变已成事实。

---

1. 蒋鼎文将军已被任命接替张学良任"剿匪"总部司令。

The substance of all that surely must have been known to the Premier-Generalissimo. Although he had no regular troops in Sian, a few months earlier some 1,500 of the Third Gendarmes, a so-called "special service" regiment of the Blueshirts, commanded by his nephew, General Chiang Hsiao-hsien, who was credited with the abduction, imprisonment, and killing of hundreds of radicals, had arrived in the city. They had established espionage headquarters throughout the province, and had begun to arrest and kidnap alleged Communist students, political workers, and soldiers. Shao Li-tzu, the Nanking-appointed governor of Shensi, was in control of the police force of the capital. As neither the Young Marshal nor Yang Hu-ch'eng had any troops but bodyguards in the city, the Generalissimo had practical command there.

This situation helped to provoke a further incident. On the 9th, two days after Chiang's arrival, several thousand students held an anti-Japanese demonstration and started to march to Lintung, to present a petition to the Generalissimo. Governor Shao ordered it to be dispersed. The police, assisted by some of Chiang Kai-shek's gendarmes, handled the students roughly, and at one stage opened fire on them. Two students were wounded, and as they happened to be children of a Tungpei officer the shooting was especially inflammatory. Chang Hsueh-liang intervened, stopped the fight, persuaded the students to return to the city, and agreed to present their petition to the Generalissimo. Infuriated, Chiang Kai-shek reprimanded Chang for his "disloyalty" in trying "to represent *both sides.*" Chiang Kai-shek himself wrote that he considered this incident between them the immediate cause of the revolt.

So, despite all the objections and warnings, the Generalissimo summoned a General Staff Congress on the 10th, when final plans were formally adopted to push ahead with the Sixth Campaign. A general mobilization order was prepared for the Hsipei, Tungpei, and Nanking troops already in Kansu and Shensi, together with the Nanking troops waiting at Tungkuan. It was announced that the order would be published on the 12th. It was openly stated that if Marshal Chang refused these orders his troops would be disarmed by Nanking forces, and he himself would be dismissed from his command. General Chiang Ting-wen had already been appointed to replace Chang Hsueh-liang as head of the Bandit Suppression Commission. At the same time reports reached both Chang and Yang that the Blueshirts, together with the police, had prepared a "black list" of Communist sympathizers in their armies, who were to be arrested immediately after publication of the mobilization order.

Thus it was as the culmination of this complicated chain of events that Chang Hsueh-liang called a joint meeting of the division commanders of the Tungpei and Hsipei armies at ten o'clock on the night of December 11. Orders had been secretly given on the previous day for a division of Tungpei troops and a regiment of Yang Hu-ch'eng's army to move into the environs of Sianfu. The decision was now taken to use these forces to "arrest" the Generalissimo and his staff. The mutiny of 170,000 troops had become a fact.

二、　　总司令被逮

对于西安演出的这场惊险好戏的动机或政治背景，我们怎么说都行，但是有一点必须承认，它所选择的时机和执行的经过，可谓高明至极。它比蒋介石在南京或上海发动的政变，或者共产党占据广州的情况，其流血和笨拙程度都不知要低多少。起事计划事先一点也没有泄露给敌方。到12月12日早晨6点钟，整个事件就已经结束了。东北军和西北军控制了西安。蓝衣社特务在睡梦中惊起，被缴了械，逮捕起来；几乎整个参谋总部的人员都在西安宾馆的住处遭到包围，关了起来；邵力子省主席和警察局长也成了阶下囚；西安市警察向兵变部队投降；南京方面的50架轰炸机和飞行员在机场被扣。

但是逮捕总司令却流了血，蒋介石下榻在10英里外著名温泉胜地临潼，把所有其他客人都驱赶一空。张少帅的卫队长、26岁的孙铭九上尉午夜前往临潼，他在半路上带上200名东北军，清晨3点钟开车到临潼郊外。他们在那里等到5点钟，第一辆卡车载着15个人开到宾馆门口，被岗哨喝止，就开起火来。东北军这批先遣人员的增援部队马上开到，孙上尉率部进攻总司令住处。警卫人员猝不及防，没有久战，不过有足够时间让吃惊的总司令逃跑。孙上尉到蒋介石的寝室时，他已经逃跑了。孙率部搜索，爬上了宾馆后面的白雪掩盖、岩石嶙峋的小山。他们马上就发现了总司令的贴身仆人，接着不久就找到了总司令本人。他只穿着睡衣睡裤，外面披着一件长袍，赤裸的手脚在急急忙忙爬上山时给划破了，嘴里也没有假牙，身子索索地在寒冷中哆嗦着，躲在一块大岩石旁的小洞里——这块大岩石是长城建造者秦始皇陵寝所在地的标志。

2   THE GENERALISSIMO IS ARRESTED

Whatever we may say against its motives, or the political energies behind them, it must be admitted that the *coup de théatre* enacted at Sian was brilliantly timed and executed. No word of the rebels' plans reached their enemies until too late. By six o'clock on the morning of December 12 the whole affair was over. Tungpei and Hsipei troops were in control at Sian. The Blueshirts, surprised in their sleep, had been disarmed and arrested; practically the whole General Staff had been surrounded in its quarters at the Sian Guest House, and was imprisoned; Governor Shao Li-tzu and the chief of police were also prisoners; the city police force had surrendered to the mutineers; and fifty Nanking bombers and their pilots had been seized at the airfield.

But the arrest of the Generalissimo was a bloodier affair. Chiang Kai-shek was staying ten miles from the city, at Lintung, a famous hot-springs resort, which had been cleared of all other guests. To Lintung, at midnight, went twenty-six-year-old Captain Sun Ming-chiu, commander of the Young Marshal's bodyguard. Halfway there he picked up two hundred Tungpei troops, and at 3 A. M. drove to the outskirts of Lintung. There they waited till five o'clock, when the first truck, with about fifteen men, roared up to the hotel, was challenged by sentries, and opened fire. Reinforcements soon arrived for the Tungpei vanguard, and Captain Sun led an assault on the Generalissimo's residence. Taken by complete surprise, the bodyguards put up a short fight—long enough, however, to permit the astounded Generalissimo to escape. When Captain Sun reached Chiang's bedroom he had already fled. Sun took a search party up the side of the rocky, snow-covered hill behind the resort. Presently they found the Generalissimo's personal servant, and not long afterwards came upon the man himself. Clad only in a loose robe thrown over his nightshirt, his bare feet and hands cut in his nimble flight up the mountain, shaking in the bitter cold, and minus his false teeth, he was crouching in a cave beside a great rock.

孙铭九向他打了招呼，总司令的第一句话是，"你是同志，就开枪把我打死算了。"孙回答说，"我们不开枪。我们只要求你领导我国抗日。"

蒋介石仍坐在大石上，结结巴巴地说，"把张少帅叫来，我就下山。"

"张少帅不在这里。城里的部队已起义；我们是来保护你的。"

总司令闻此似乎感到放心多了，要派一匹马送他下山。"这里没有马，"孙铭九说，"不过我可以背你下山。"他在蒋介石前面蹲下。蒋介石犹豫了一会就同意了，吃力地趴在这个年轻军官的宽阔背上。他们就这样在军队卫护下下了山，等仆人送来了他的鞋子，然后在山脚下上了汽车开到西安去。

"既往不咎，"孙铭九对他说。"从今开始中国必须采取新政策。你打算怎么办？……中国的唯一紧急任务就是打日本。这是东北人民的特别要求。你为什么不打日本而下令打红军？"

"我是中国人民的领袖，"蒋介石大声说。"我代表国家。我认为我的政策是正确的。"[1]

就这样，总司令虽然流了一点血，却毫不屈服，到了城里，成了杨虎城将军和张学良少帅的阶下囚。

在兵变那天，东北军和西北军的师以上将领联名通电中央政府、各省首脑、全国人民。这封简短的电报说明"为了要促使他觉悟"，已要求总司令"暂留西安府"。同时保证他个人安全。提交给总司令的"救国要求"向全国作了广播，但是到处都遭到国民党的新闻封锁，没有在报上发表。这著名的八点要求是：

（一）改组南京政府，容纳各党派共同负责救国。

（二）立即停止内战，**采取武装抗日政策**。

---

[1] 摘自代我在西安府为伦敦《每日先驱报》采访的詹姆斯·贝特兰访问孙铭九的报道。

Sun Ming-chiu hailed him, and the Generalissimo's first words were, "If you are my comrade, shoot me and finish it all." To which Sun replied, "We will not shoot. We only ask you to lead our country against Japan."

Chiang remained seated on his rock, and said with difficulty, "Call Marshal Chang here, and I will come down."

"Marshal Chang isn't here. The troops are rising in the city; we came to protect you."

At this the Generalissimo seemed much relieved, and called for a horse to take him down the mountain. "There is no horse here," said Sun, "but I will carry you down the mountain on my back." And he knelt at Chiang's feet. After some hesitation, Chiang accepted, and climbed painfully on to the broad back of the young officer. They proceeded solemnly down the slope in this fashion, escorted by troops, until a servant arrived with Chiang's shoes. The little group got into a car at the foot of the hill and set off for Sian.

"The past is the past," Sun said to him. "From now on there must be a new policy for China. What are you going to do? . . . The one urgent task for China is to fight Japan. This is the special demand of the men of the Northeast. Why do you not fight Japan, but instead give the order to fight the Red Army?"

"I am the leader of the Chinese people," Chiang shouted. "I represent the nation. I think my policy is correct."[1]

In this way, a little bloody but unbowed, the Generalissimo arrived in the city, where he became the involuntary guest of General Yang Hu-ch'eng and the Young Marshal.

On the day of the coup all division commanders of the Tungpei and Hsipei armies signed and issued a circular telegram addressed to the Central Government, to various provincial leaders, and to the people at large. The brief missive explained that "in order to stimulate his awakening" the Generalissimo had been "requested to remain for the time being in Sianfu." Meanwhile his personal safety was guaranteed. The demands of "national salvation" submitted to the Generalissimo were broadcast to the nation—but everywhere suppressed in the Kuomintang-censored newspapers. Here are the rebels' eight-points:

1. Reorganize the Nanking Government and admit all parties to share the joint responsibility of national salvation.

2. End all civil war immediately *and adopt the policy of armed resistance against Japan.*

---

1. Part of an interview with Sun Ming-chiu by James Bertram, who was acting for me as correspondent in Sianfu for the *London Daily Herald*.

（三）释放上海爱国（七）领袖。

（四）大赦政治犯。

（五）保证人民集会自由。

（六）保障人民组织爱国团体的权利和政治自由。

（七）实行孙中山遗嘱。

（八）立即召开救国会议。

对这一纲领，中国红军、中华苏维埃政府、中国共产党立即表示拥护。[1] 几天后，张学良派自己的座机去保安，接了3个共产党代表到西安：军事委员会副主席周恩来，东方面军参谋长叶剑英，西北苏维埃政府主席博古。东北军、西北军、红军三方面代表开了联席会议，成了公开的盟友。14日宣布成立抗日联军，有13万东北军、4万西北军和大约9万红军。

张学良当选为联合抗日军事委员会主席，杨虎城为副主席。于学忠将军领导下的东北军12日在甘肃省会兰州，对在那里的中央政府官员和军队也举行了兵变，把那里的南京驻军缴了械。在甘肃的其他地方，红军和东北军共同控制了全部交通要道，包围了该省约5万名南京军队，因此叛军在陕甘两省全境操纵了实际控制权。

事变发生后，东北军和西北军奉新成立的军事委员会的命令立即开到陕晋和陕豫边界。红军也奉委员会之命南进。一周之内，红军就几乎占领了渭河以北的陕西北部全境。红军先遣部队在彭德怀率领下就驻在离西安府只有30英里的三原。另一支红军1万人在徐海东率领下绕过西安府开到陕豫边界。红军、东北军、西北军并肩守在陕西边界上。一方面进行这些防御措施，另一方面三支大军都发表明确的声明，反对发生新内战，重申他们纯政治目标，否认有进攻之意。

---

1. 上述八点要求中有七点是完全符合共产党和苏维埃政府在1936年12月1日发出的通电中所提的"救国"纲领的。因此，张学良和共产党至少早在那个时候已经同意了这个纲领，尽管共产党并没有预料到张学良会采取这样令人吃惊的步骤来使南京对此加以考虑。

3. Release the [seven] leaders of the patriotic movement in Shanghai.

4. Pardon all political prisoners.

5. Guarantee the people liberty of assembly.

6. Safeguard the people's rights of patriotic organization and political liberty.

7. Put into effect the will of Dr. Sun Yat-sen.

8. Immediately convene a National Salvation conference.

To this program the Chinese Red Army, the Chinese Soviet Government and the Communist Party of China immediately offered their support.[1] A few days later Chang Hsueh-liang sent to Pao An his personal plane, which returned to Sian with three Red delegates: Chou En-lai, vice-chairman of the military council; Yeh Chien-ying, chief of staff of the East Front Army; and Po Ku, chairman of the Northwest Branch Soviet Government. A joint meeting was called between the Tungpei, Hsipei, and Red Army delegates, and the three groups became open allies. On the 14th an announcement was issued of the formation of a United Anti-Japanese Army, consisting of about 130,000 Tungpei troops, 40,000 Hsipei troops, and approximately 90,000 troops of the Red Army.

Chang Hsueh-liang was elected chairman of a United Anti-Japanese Military Council, and Yang Hu-ch'eng vice-chairman. Tungpei troops under General Yu Hsueh-chung had on the 12th carried out a coup of their own against the Central Government officials and troops in Lanchow, capital of Kansu province, and had disarmed the Nanking garrison there. In the rest of Kansu the Reds and the Manchurian troops together held control of all main communications, surrounding about 50,000 Nanking troops in that province, so that the rebels had effective power in all Shensi and Kansu.

Immediately after the incident, Tungpei and Hsipei troops moved eastward to the Shensi-Shansi and Shensi-Honan borders, on instructions from the new Council. From the same Council the Red Army took orders to push southward. Within a week the Reds had moved their "capital" to Yenan city and occupied virtually the whole of north Shensi above the Wei River. A Red vanguard under P'eng Teh-huai was located at San Yuan, a city only thirty miles from Sianfu. Another contingent of 10,000 Reds under Hsu Hai-tung was preparing to move over to the Shensi-Honan border. The Red, Northeastern, and Northwestern troops stood shoulder to shoulder along the Shensi border. While these defensive arrangements proceeded, all three armies issued clear-cut statements declaring their opposition to a new internal war.

---

1. Seven of the above eight points corresponded exactly to the program of "national salvation" advocated in a circular telegram issued by the Communist Party and the Soviet Government on December 1, 1936.

为了执行八点要求，立刻采取了种种步骤，对此，红军在其新占地区一丝不苟地加以执行，停止实行土地革命纲领。一切反共的作战命令都予撤销。西安府释放了400多名政治犯，取消了新闻检查，取消了对一切爱国（抗日）团体的取缔。成百上千名的学生可以自由地在人民群众中间进行活动，在各阶层中组织统一战线团体。他们也到农村去，开始在政治上和军事上训练和武装农民。在部队里，政工人员进行了前所未有的抗日宣传。几乎每天都举行群众大会。有一次参加者有10万多人。在所有大会上，口号都是团结抗日、停止内战。——后者对农民有现实的号召力，因为他们的粮食和牛羊已因未来的"剿共"战事而被征用了。

但是这些情况的消息在西北各省以外遭到了扣压。甚至颇受尊重的《大公报》也指出，凡是胆敢刊载西安传出来的消息的编辑无不有立即遭到逮捕的危险。与此同时，南京的宣传机器又抛出了一个烟幕弹，使已经弄得稀里糊涂的公众更是莫名其妙。原来南京政府闻到兵变消息后顿时目瞪口呆，先是召开了国民党（中央执行委员会和中央政治委员会）常委会会议，立即宣布张学良为叛逆者，撤销他一切职务，要求释放总司令，否则将开始讨伐。人们听到这轰动一时的新闻，反应不一，有的因蒋介石被逮高兴万分，有的大惊失色。到处出现了分崩离析的迹象。蒋介石是中国许多敌对势力暂时得到某种程度稳定的中心枢纽。一旦他离开了这个中心地位，这些势力就都失去了向心力，各种意见发生公开冲突，必须寻找新的组合、新的向心力、新的黏合剂。

有3天之久，没有人知道蒋介石的生死下落——除了美联社以外，该社断然宣称，张学良已在电台上报告过他如何把蒋介石杀死，以及杀死他的理由。没有人知道叛军究竟打算干什么，很少人充分了解他们的立场的政治意义；甚至一些同情他们的人也因为错误的报道而谴责他们。南京切断了与西北的一切通讯和交通，西北的报纸和宣言都被检查官烧了。西安整天广播，一再声明不向政府军进攻，解释他们的行动，呼吁各方要有理智和要求和平；但是南京的强有力的广播电台进行震耳的干扰，淹没了他们说的每一句话。在中国，独裁政权对于一切公共言论工具的令人吃惊的威力，从来没有这样有力地表现过。

我本人的许多电讯都遭到大肆删节。我几次尝试要把西北的八点要求发出来，这也许对西方读者澄清这个谜有一点帮助，但是检查官一字也不准发。许多外国记者本人对西北近况一无所知，轻信地把宣传工厂里所制造的一切谎言当作新闻。国民党及其追随者一方面竭力扣压真正的消息和事实，另一方面却向全世界发出一些愚蠢的谎言，使得中国更像是个疯人院一样的地方。竟有这样的消息：叛军把警察局长钉在

Steps were taken at once to carry out the eight points. All orders for war against the Reds were canceled. More than four hundred political prisoners in Sianfu were released. Censorship of the press was removed, and all suppression of patriotic (anti-Japanese) organizations was lifted. Hundreds of students were freed to work among the populace, building united-front organizations in every class. They toured into the villages also, where they began to train and arm the farmers, politically and militarily. In the army the political workers conducted an unprecedented anti-Japanese campaign. Mass meetings were summoned almost daily.

But news of those happenings was suppressed outside the provinces of the Northwest. Editors who dared publish anything emanating from Sian, as even the highly respectable *Ta Kung Pao* pointed out, were threatened with instant arrest. Meanwhile Nanking's propaganda machine threw out a smokescreen that further confused an already befuddled public. Dumfounded by the news, the government at Nanking first called a meeting of the Standing Committee (of the Central Executive Committee and the Central Political Council) of the Kuomintang, which promptly pronounced Chang Hsueh-liang a rebel, dismissed him from his posts, and demanded the release of the Generalissimo, failing which punitive operations would begin.

For three days few people knew whether Chiang Kai-shek was dead or alive—except the Associated Press, which flatly announced that Chang Hsueh-liang had described over the radio how and why he had killed him. Few people knew exactly what the rebels planned to do. Nanking cut all communications with the Northwest, and its papers and manifestoes were burned by the censors.

Hundreds of words were deleted from my own dispatches. I made several attempts to send out the eight demands of the Northwest—which might have helped a little to clarify the enigma for Western readers—but the censors let out not a word. Many of the foreign correspondents were themselves completely ignorant of recent happenings in the Northwest. While real news and facts were rigorously suppressed, the Kuomintang and its adherents released to the world some puerile lies which made China appear much more of a madhouse than it really was: The rebels had nailed the chief of police to the city gates;

城门上；红军占领了西安，洗劫全城，城墙上挂了红旗；张学良遭到自己部下的刺杀。南京几乎每天都说西安发生暴乱。红军诱拐男女少年。妇女被"共妻"。整个东北军和西北军变成了土匪。到处发生抢劫。张学良要求给总司令付赎金8,000万元[1]。日本是张学良的后台。莫斯科是他的后台。他是个赤党。他是个鸦片鬼。他是个"死有余辜的忘恩负义之徒"。他是个土匪。

许多最最荒诞不经的谣言也起源于日本人在中国办的报纸，甚至日本高级官员。关于西安"赤色威胁"的"目击者"的异想天开的报道，日本人特别多产——尽管他们同别人一样同那个城市一无联系。日本人还发现事变后面有苏俄阴谋。但是他们在莫斯科报纸上遇到了他们宣传上的敌手。《消息报》和《真理报》正式否认责任、谴责张学良、赞美蒋介石不算，甚至捏造了一个消息来证明，西安事变是前中国行政院长汪精卫和"日本帝国主义者"共同炮制的，这种谣言同事实如此大相径庭，甚至中国最反动的报纸也不敢想出这一招，因为怕人嘲笑。"撒谎是可以的，先生们，"列宁曾经说过，"但是要有限度！"

谣言攻势连续几天。但是蒋介石被俘一周后，南京光是捏造这一轰动一时的事件的背景新闻已不够了。消息走漏了出来，漏洞越来越大，后来出现了大缺口。秘密报纸普遍刊登了八点纲领，在自由主义和进步人士中间争取到了拥护者，因为这实在是个资产阶级的自由进步纲领。公众开始认识到西北方面并不是要打内战，而是要制止内战。一般的情绪已逐渐开始从为一个军阀的个人安危担心转变为为国家存亡担心，现在打内战不仅不能救蒋介石一命，反而会毁灭中国。

在蒋介石被俘的消息传来后，南京就开始了争夺政权的阴谋活动。野心勃勃的军政部长何应钦与国民党内亲日派政学系有密切关系，当时正掌南京大权，八点纲领主要就是发给他的，但是他竭力主张"讨伐"。在这一点上何应钦得到亲法西斯的黄埔系、蓝衣社、在野的汪精卫系、西山会议派、CC系[2]和南京的德、意顾问的充分支持（"煽动"也许是个更确切的词，因为何应钦将军天生是个易受"煽动"的人）。他们都认为这是夺取全部军权的良机，可以把国民党内的开明派、亲美派、亲英派、亲俄派、统一战线派统统压下去，在政治上降到无足轻重的地位。何应钦将军马上动员

---

1. 蒋介石夫人对这些谣言表示遗憾，她写道，"任何时候都没有提出过钱的问题或加官晋爵的问题。"
2. 两个C是陈立夫和陈果夫，陈氏兄弟控制着国民党的军事装备。

the Reds had occupied Sian, were looting the city and flying Red banners on the walls; Chang Hsueh-liang had been assassinated by his own men. Almost daily it was stated by Nanking that riots were taking place in Sian. The Reds were abducting young boys and girls. Women were being "communized." The entire Tungpei and Hsipei armies had turned bandit. There was looting everywhere. Chang Hsueh-liang was demanding $80,000,000 ransom for the Generalissimo.[1]

Many of the wildest rumors circulated had their origin also with the Japanese press in China, and even with high Japanese officials. The Japanese were especially fertile with imaginary "eyewitness" reports of the "Red menace" in Sian. The Japanese also discovered Soviet Russian intrigue behind the coup. But they met their masters in propaganda in Moscow's press. *Izvestia* and *Pravda* went so far in their official disclaimers of responsibility, denunciations of Chang Hsueh-liang, and hosannas to Chiang Kai-shek that they invented a story showing that the Sian affair was jointly inspired by the former Chinese premier, Wang Ching-wei, and "the Japanese imperialists"—a libel so antipodal to the facts that even the most reactionary press in China had not dared to suggest it, out of fear of ridicule. "Prevarication is permissible, gentlemen," it was Lenin who once exclaimed, "but within limits!"

After the first week of Chiang's captivity Nanking's efforts to cork up the facts proved inadequate. Leaks occurred, and then big gaps. The eight-point program was widely published in the surreptitious press, and the public began to realize that the Northwest did not mean to make civil war, but to stop it. Sentiment slowly began to change from fear for the safety of an individual militarist into fear for the safety of the state. Civil war now could not save Chiang, but it might ruin China.

Intrigue for seizure of power had begun in Nanking with the news of Chiang's capture. Ambitious War Minister Ho Ying-ch'in, closely affiliated with the pro-Japanese "political-science clique" of the Kuomintang, then in high office at Nanking—and against whom the eight-point program was primarily directed—was hot for a "punitive expedition." In this General Ho was fully supported by the pro-Fascist Whampoa clique, the Blueshirts, the Wang Ching-wei (out-of-office) faction, the Western Hills group, the "C. C." faction,[2] and Nanking's German and Italian advisers. Their enemies said that they all saw in the situation an opportunity to seize power, relegating the liberal, pro-American, pro-British, pro-Russian, and united-front groups in the Kuomintang to political nonentity. General

---

1. Mme. Chiang Kai-shek, deploring such rumors, wrote that "no question of money or increased power or position was at any time brought up."
2. The two "C's" were Ch'en Li-fu and Ch'en Kuo-fu, brothers who controlled the Kuomintang Party apparatus.

了南京20师军队，开到豫陕边界。他派了一队队飞机在西安府上空飞翔，派步兵向叛军阵线作试探性佯攻。有些南京飞机（为了抗日送给蒋总司令的"五十寿礼"）在陕西境内的渭南和华县试验性地投了几颗炸弹，据报道炸死了一些工厂工人。蒋介石在日记中写道，他听到轰炸的消息，"很是高兴"。

但是蒋夫人显然并不高兴，她当时对局势比她丈夫要清楚得多。她对这种为"在尸体上开宴会"（南京的人当时认为总司令不可能活着出西安）的准备极感愤怒和震惊，于是去见了何应钦，要他解释。如果他开了战，他还能停下来吗？他能救她丈夫吗？她写道，她丈夫的安全"同国家的继续生存是不可分的"。他要杀死她的丈夫吗？这位将军胆怯心虚了。她坚持要他停止战事，把他的才智用在设法争取蒋先生获释上。她要他活着回来。她的论点占了上风——至少是在蒋介石自己的使者到达南京之前。

同时情况也很显然，如果大规模开战，西北不是没有盟友的！广西、广东、云南、湖南、四川、山东、河北、察哈尔、山西、绥远、宁夏的军政领袖都作壁上观，如果何应钦开战，他们几乎肯定没有一个人会举一个小指头出力协助。他们无论哪一个人，或者甚至他们全体都会靠向叛军一边。在最好的情况下，所有这些省份里的当权政治派系也会要求南京出高价才肯保持中立，他们每个人都想在这场冲突中设法增强自己的势力。这一点到23日就很明显了，当时有势力的宋哲元和韩复榘将军（河北和山东的统治者）发出通电，要求和平解决，明确告诫不要开战，清楚地表明对何应钦将军的计划毫不赞成。

现在问题是：蒋介石在西安身系囹圄，是否还能够在南京纠集到足够的力量防止爆发消耗力量的内战，这场内战很有可能意味着他的政治生命——如果说不是实际生命——的完蛋。在南京和上海，他的妻舅、中央银行董事长宋子文，他的连襟、代理行政院长孔祥熙，蒋介石夫人，把他的亲信召集在一起，竭力设法阻止南京方面更加反动的分子以"反共讨伐"的名义发动进攻。

同时，在西安也发生了迅速的回心转意。总司令在被俘以后不久就开始认识到，他的最大"叛徒"也许不在西安，而是在南京。考虑到这个情况，蒋介石想必作了决定，他不作殉难者，白白让何应钦将军或者任何别人踏着他的尸体爬上独裁者的宝座。

Ho mobilized twenty Nanking divisions and moved them toward the Honan-Shensi border. He sent squadrons of airplanes roaring over Sianfu, and made tentative thrusts at the rebels' lines with his infantry. Some of the Nanking planes (anti-Japanese "fiftieth-birthday gifts" to the Generalissimo) experimentally bombed Weinan and Huahsien, inside the Shensi border, and reportedly killed a number of factory workers.

The big question now became this: whether Chiang Kai-shek could, even from his seat of captivity in Sian, still muster enough support in Nanking to prevent the outbreak of an exhausting war which was likely to mean his own political, if not physical, demise. In Nanking and Shanghai his brothers-in-law—T. V. Soong, chairman of the Central Bank of China, and H. H. Kung, acting premier—and Mme. Chiang rallied Chiang's personal followers and worked frantically to prevent the more reactionary elements in Nanking from initiating an offensive in the name of an "anti-Communist punitive expedition."

Meanwhile, swift changes of heart were taking place in Sian. Soon after his capture the Generalissimo had begun to realize that perhaps his worst "betrayers" were not in Sian but in Nanking. Contemplating this situation, Chiang Kai-shek must have decided that he did not choose to be the martyr over whose dead body General Ho Ying-ch'in or anybody else would climb to dictatorial power.

三、 蒋、张和共产党

中国还不是个民主国家，在政治斗争中常常恢复到纯封建手段。在报纸遭到完全控制，人民被剥夺政治权利的情况下，人人都知道要向南京进言或者改变它的政策，只有一个有效办法，那就是武装示威，即中国人所说的"兵谏"，这是中国政治斗争中公认的一种手段。把感情暂且撇在一边不说，可以认为张学良对独裁政权头子采取直接行动，是选择了最人道的、最直接的办法，来达到自己的目的。所花的生命损失最少，流血最少。不错，这是一种封建的方法，但是张少帅要对付的人物是一个凭直觉就能了解他自己在半封建政治中的枢纽作用的人物。他的行动是根据极端现实主义来考虑的，今天一般人都认为，这一行动的客观历史效果是进步的。

但是蒋介石的生命是不是真的有过严重危险呢？

看来是如此。不过危险不是来自张少帅，也不是来自共产党。有可能来自杨虎城。但是最可肯定的还是来自东北军和西北军的少壮派军官，来自有着不满情绪的桀骜不驯的士兵，来自有组织和武装起来的群众，他们都要求在如何处理总司令的问题上要有发言权。少壮派军官通过决议，要求公审"卖国贼"蒋介石和他的僚属。部队的情绪肯定是赞成把总司令干掉的。奇怪的是，如今却要由共产党人来说服他们饶他一命！

共产党在西安事变中的政策始终没有明确地解释过。许多人认为，共产党为了要报蒋介石对他们进行十年无情战争之仇，现在一定会得意洋洋要求把他处死的。许多人认为，他们会利用这个机会与东北军和西北军勾结，大大地扩大自己的地盘，

3   Chiang, Chang, and the Reds

China was no parliamentary democracy, but was ruled by party or individual dictators. Very often in politics it reverted to feudal practice. With the press completely stifled, and the populace disfranchised, there was but one effective way to censure Nanking, or alter its policies. That was by armed insurrection or armed demonstration, or what the Chinese call *ping chien*—"military persuasion"—a recognized tactic in Chinese political maneuver. Chang Hsueh-liang probably chose the most humane and direct method conceivable by which to achieve his purpose when he used direct action upon the head of the dictatorship. It cost a minimum loss of life, and a minimum of bloodshed. It was a feudal method, but the Marshal was dealing with a personality whose role in semifeudal politics he intuitively understood. Because the objective result of Chang's action was to unite China to confront a national peril, most Chinese I knew came to regard Chang as a patriot.

Was Chiang Kai-shek's life ever really in serious danger?

It appears that it was. Not from the Young Marshal, and not from the Reds. From Yang Hu-ch'eng, possibly. But most certainly from the radical younger officers of the Northeastern and Northwestern armies, from the discontented and mutinous soldiery, and from the organized and arming masses, all of whom demanded a voice in the disposal of the Premier. Resolutions passed by the young officers called for a mass trial of "Traitor" Chiang and all his staff. The mood of the army decidedly favored the Generalissimo's immolation. Curiously enough, it fell to the lot of the Communists to persuade them that his life should be saved.

Communist policy throughout the Sian Incident was never clearly explained. Many people assumed that the Communists, in triumphant revenge for the decade of relentless war which Chiang Kai-shek had waged against them, would now demand his death. Many believed that they would use this opportunity to coalesce with the Tungpei and Hsipei armies, greatly enlarge their base, and challenge Nanking in a great new struggle

与南京进行新的争夺政权的大决斗。实际上他们一点也没有这么做,他们不仅力主和平解决,释放蒋介石,而且还主张由他回到南京去担任领导。甚至蒋介石夫人也写道,"同外界看法恰巧相反,他们(共产党)并不想扣留总司令。"但是为什么不想扣留他呢?

上文经常提到共产党要求停止内战,组成抗日"民族统一战线",在南京建立民主的政体。这些口号是绝对诚实的,原因很简单:这些口号符合一切客观条件迫使共产党采取的战略的内在因素。不论在经济上,政治上,军事上,总之,在一切方面,他们都真正需要和平,真正需要一个代议制的、多方面参加的民主政体,来实现他们当前的目标。他们清楚地看到,这样一种民主政体,是唯一令人满意的结构,可以团结整个民族,对日本进行反帝斗争,谋求独立。而且他们充分相信,必须先有这一斗争,然后才谈得上进一步努力在中国实现社会革命,它们两者是不可分割的,而且前者必须同时带动后者。他们通过切身经验了解到,在势必要灭亡整个民族的外国威胁面前,继续进行革命战争不但会进一步削弱全民族的抗战力量,而且也会随之埋葬革命本身的潜在力量。

毛泽东说,"中国民族解放运动的胜利是国际社会主义胜利的一部分,因为中国打败帝国主义意味着摧毁帝国主义最强大的一个根据地。如果中国赢得了独立,世界革命就会非常迅速地发展。如果我国遭到敌人的征服,我们就丧失一切。**对于一个被剥夺民族自由的人民,革命的任务不是立即实现社会主义,而是争取独立。如果我们被剥夺了一个实践共产主义的国家,共产主义就无从谈起。**"[1]

因此,基本上就是根据这一论述,甚至在蒋介石被俘以前,共产党人就向国民党提出了统一战线的建议。在危机期间,他们始终坚持他们的"路线",这种坚定性令人惊讶,而且他们的冷静客观态度在中国的极度个人化的政治中是罕见的。尽管客观情况显然向他们提供了许多引诱,他们还是表现出党的纪律,凡是公正的观察家,一定会有很深刻的印象。从一开始,他们就看到了,西安事变对他们的中心意义就是有了表示他们提出统一战线纲领具有诚意的机会。他们同逮捕蒋介石没有关系,他们同全国一样感到意外。但是他们对于逮捕的结局却起了不少作用。

苏维埃政府和共产党在听到了事变的消息后,立即召开联席会议,决定支持八点纲领和参加联合抗日军事委员会。不久以后他们就发表通电[2],表示相信"西安领袖

---

1. 在保安接见我时的谈话。着重体是我用的。
2. 《召开和平会议的建议》,1936 年 12 月 19 日保安。

for power. Instead, they not only urged a peaceful settlement, and the release of Chiang Kai-shek, but also his return to leadership in Nanking. Even Mme. Chiang wrote that, "quite contrary to outside beliefs, they [the Reds] were not interested in detaining the Generalissimo." But why not?

Economically, politically, militarily, in every way, they really needed internal peace.

"The victory of the Chinese national liberation movement," said Mao Tse-tung, "will be part of the victory of world socialism, because to defeat imperialism in China means the destruction of one of its most powerful bases. If China wins its independence, the world revolution will progress very rapidly. If our country is subjugated by the enemy, we shall lose everything. *For a people being deprived of its national freedom, the revolutionary task is not immediate socialism, but the struggle for independence. We cannot even discuss communism if we are robbed of a country in which to practice it.*"[1]

Thus it was fundamentally on this thesis that the Communists based their united-front proposals to the Kuomintang, even before the capture of the Generalissimo. In that crisis they recognized an opportunity to demonstrate the sincerity of their offer. If they had nothing to do with the arrest of Chiang Kai-shek, they had much to do with its denouement.

Immediately after hearing of the event, the Soviet Government and the Communist Party called a joint meeting, at which it was decided to support the eight-point program and to participate in the United Anti-Japanese Council. Soon afterwards they issued a circular telegram[2] expressing the belief that "the Sian leaders acted with patriotic sincerity and

---

1. In his interview with me at Pao An. Italics mine.
2. "Proposal for the Convention of a Peace Conference," Pao An, December 19, 1936.

此次行动出诸爱国热诚,希望迅速制定立即抗日的国策。"通电强烈谴责何应钦的讨伐,宣称"如发动内战,全国就会陷入大乱,日本强盗就会利用这个机会侵略我国,亡国奴的命运难逃。"为了要争取和平解决,共产党要求在不打仗的基础上开始谈判和召开各党派和平会议,讨论全国联合抗日的纲领。该电明确表明了张少帅请到西安去的共方代表要遵循的政策——在整个事变期间他在很大程度上依靠他们为他在政治上出主意。

共产党代表团团长周恩来一到以后就去见了蒋介石[1]。不难想象这次会见对总司令产生了什么效果。蒋介石当时身体犹弱,惊魂未定,据说见到周恩来——他原来的政治副手,曾经悬赏 8 万元要他首级——进了房间向他友好地打招呼,吓得脸色发白。他一定以为红军已经进了西安,要把他带去当俘虏了。这样一种恐惧也使蒋介石夫人的标致的脑袋不安过一阵子,因为她说,她"觉得目标(如果蒋介石被带出西安)一定在红军战线后面的某个地方。"

但是周恩来和张少帅两人都马上解除了总司令的疑惧,他们两人都承认他是总司令,坐下来向他解释共产党对民族危机的态度。蒋介石开始时沉默不语,态度僵硬冷淡,后来听着——这是他十年反共战争中的第一次——共产党的观点,态度才慢慢地缓和下来。

宋子文于 20 日飞抵西安。到这时,"原则上"的总协议似乎已经达成。总司令没有提到它,但是张学良少帅在 19 日向外国报界发表了声明,从下述摘要可以看出,至少他是认为解决方案已几乎完全求得了:

> 总司令在此久留不是我们的责任。端纳先生[2]上星期一到达后,总司令的气愤和不愿谈话的心情稍减,他心平气和地讨论了我们面前的问题,至星期二已原则上同意我们所提各点,以便采取明确国策,实行改革,使全国能够在政治上和物质上合理地和自由地发展,符合孙中山博士的遗志。

---

1. 蒋介石自己的记载中没有提到同周恩来的谈话。
2. 澳大利亚人,蒋介石和张学良二人的密友,(在蒋夫人的坚持下)端纳是南京派往西安的第一位代表。

zeal, wishing speedily to formulate a national policy of immediate resistance to Japan." The telegram strongly condemned Ho Ying-ch'in's punitive expedition, declaring that "if civil war is launched, the whole nation will be plunged into complete chaos, the Japanese robbers, taking advantage of this, will invade our nation, and enslavement will be our fate." To secure a peaceful settlement, the Reds urged that negotiations be opened on the basis of no war, and the summoning of a peace conference of all parties, at which would be discussed the program of united national resistance to Japan. This telegram clearly indicated the policy followed out by the Red delegates whom Marshal Chang summoned to Sian.

Shortly after his arrival, the head of the Communist delegation, Chou En-lai, went to see Chiang Kai-shek.[1] One could easily imagine the effect of this meeting on the Generalissimo. Still physically weak and psychologically deeply shaken by his experiences, Chiang was said to have turned pale with apprehension when Chou En-lai—his former political attaché for whose head he had once offered $80,000—entered the room and gave him a friendly greeting. He must have at once concluded that the Red Army had entered Sian, and that he was to be turned over to it as captive. Such a fear also troubled the comely head of Mme. Chiang Kai-shek, who said that she "felt the objective [if Chiang were removed from Sian] would be somewhere behind Red lines."

But the Generalissimo was relieved of this apprehension by Chou and the Marshal, both of whom acknowledged him as commander-in-chief and sat down to explain the attitude of the Communists toward the national crisis. At first frigidly silent, Chiang gradually thawed as he listened, for the first time during his decade of war against the Communists, to their proposals for ending civil war.

By December 20, general agreement "in principle" seemed to have already been reached. The following excerpts from the statement issued to the foreign press by Marshal Chang Hsueh-liang on the 19th indicated that he, at least, regarded the settlement as virtually complete:

> *The Generalissimo's prolonged stay here is not of our doing. As soon as Mr. Donald[2] arrived last Monday, and the Generalissimo had somewhat recovered from his natural indignation, and his reluctance to talk, he calmly enough discussed the problem confronting us all, and by Tuesday had agreed in principle with the points we had in view . . . and in accordance with the will of the late Dr. Sun Yat-sen.*

---

1. In his own account Chiang does not mention having talked to Chou En-lai.
2. An Australian confidant of both Chiang Kai-shek and Chang Hsueh-liang, W. H. Donald was Nanking's first envoy to Sian (sent at Mme. Chiang's insistence).

我因此打电报欢迎南京方面派任何人来听总司令的意见,并与他安排必要措施以防止内战的发展。总司令自然强烈要求释放他回南京,我个人虽然完全相信总司令会履行诺言,但不能贸然让他在回南京后被人劝说继续内战……他同意这一看法,此后他即与我们一样等待南京派有权处理此事(即提供适当保证)的人员前来,以便总司令能回京,但迄今并无结果。

　　情况就是如此。如此贻误,实在令人奇怪。若派员前来,他几天前就早已可以回去……

张学良。[1]

　　但是东北军少壮派军官中间发生了严重问题。他们在张学良的军事委员会中已取得了直接的有力的发言权,他们的意见现在很重要。他们受现在在西北广泛开展的强大群众运动的情绪的影响,起先反对在南京方面开始执行八点纲领以前释放蒋介石。实际上,他们大多数人坚持要召开群众大会,对蒋介石举行"公审",要他的命。

　　这种当众蒙耻的可能性,蒋介石也想到了。没有人比他更了解西北蓬勃发展的这个运动可能干出些什么事来,因为1927年一次类似的起义几乎推翻了他。蒋介石的整个生涯就是同他称为"暴民"的那种骚乱因素进行斗争,不让他们打乱他的如意算盘。"公审"的话甚至挂在他周围岗哨的嘴上。蒋介石写到他听到门外囚卒谈到他的下场的话:"我听到'人民的判决'的话,我就明白,这是他们要用暴民作为借口来杀害我的恶毒阴谋。"

　　但是在这里,共产党代表团起了极大作用。在他们自己与蒋介石会谈后,他们已从他那里得到足够的保证(除了现在看来显然是从客观情况得出的保证以外)可以

---

[1] 这封电报是在12月19日从西安府发给伦敦《泰晤士报》驻上海记者弗雷泽的,要求他散发给其他记者。但南京新闻检查官扣压了这一电报。另有一份抄件交给了端纳先生,本文引用的出于他的来源。

I therefore telegraphed, welcoming anyone to come from Nanking to hear the Generalissimo's views, and arrange with him for the necessary safeguards to prevent the development of civil warfare. The Generalissimo naturally vigorously demanded that he be released to proceed to Nanking, but while I personally had full confidence that the Generalissimo would carry out his promises, it was impossible to risk his being persuaded after his arrival at Nanking to continue with the warfare . . . . He acquiesced in the view, however, and ever since then he has been waiting in vain, as have we, for someone to arrive from Nanking competent to deal with the matter [i. e., to offer adequate guarantees], so that the Generalissimo can return to the capital.

That is all. It is a strange thing that there has been this delay. Had someone come, he could have returned some days ago. . . .

CHANG HSUEH-LIANG.[1]

But serious trouble was developing in the ranks of the radical younger officers of the Tungpei Army. They had acquired strong direct voice in the affairs of Chang's military council, and their views were important. Infected by the temper of the strong mass movement now spreading throughout the Northwest, they were at first fiercely opposed to the release of Chiang Kai-shek before Nanking began to carry out the eight-point program. The majority, in fact, insisted upon giving Chiang a "popular trial" for his life, before an enormous mass meeting which they planned to call.

The possibility of this public humiliation had also occurred to Chiang. No one knew any better than he the potentialities of the movement that had been set afoot in the Northwest, for a similar rising had almost overwhelmed him in 1927. Chiang's whole career had been a struggle against the intervention in his well-ordered chain of events of that disturbing imperative which he called "the mob." Talk of the "popular trial" was even on the lips of the sentries around him; Chiang wrote of listening through the doorway to the conversation of his jailers, in which his fate was discussed: "When I heard [the words] 'the people's verdict,' I realized that it was a malicious plot to kill me by using the mob as their excuse."

Chiang Kai-shek may have been saved from further humiliation only by the Communists' opposition to any such plan. Even before Chou's talk with Chiang, the Communists had begun to state that they had received enough assurances from him (aside from assurances to be inferred from the objective situation) to believe that if released he would be obliged

---

1. This telegram was sent from Sianfu on December 19, addressed to Frazer, London *Times* correspondent in Shanghai with the request that it be given to other correspondents. Nanking censors suppressed it. A copy was also given to Mr. Donald who is the source of this quotation.

相信，他如果获释是会停止内战的，而且总的来说，是会执行全部"统一战线"纲领的。但是要做到这一点，必须保持蒋介石的地位，必须让他在威望无损的情况下回南京去。因此他们清楚地看到，如果他在什么协议上签了字，让人家知道了，或者如果他受到"人民审判"之辱，这些事情会无可挽救地损害他，破坏他的领袖地位。更糟的是，如果他被杀，内战不可避免地会大规模爆发，国共内战的十年僵局就会大大延长，要实现抗日民族阵线的希望就会变得渺茫。这样的前途，对任何一方都没有好处，吃亏的只是中国，得利的只是日本。至少，共产党是这样辩论的。

这样，博古、叶剑英、周恩来和在西安的其他共产党人现在花了好几个小时，常常一谈就是通宵，一再解释他们采取这样的政策的原因。对于东北军的少壮派军官来说，他们的立场是极其费解的，因为这些少壮派原来以为共产党是第一个要蒋介石的命的。他们有的人真的因为这种"叛卖"而气得哭起来——因为他们仰望共产党给他们政治领导，共产党对他们的影响不下于张学良本人。但是，虽然他们多数人——杨虎城与他们一起——仍不相信释放蒋介石是得策的，要他的命的情绪已经稍减。慢慢地，比较讲理的态度抬了头。张学良现在受到要他采取激烈行动的压力减轻以后，在会谈方面就有了较大的进展。

除了宋子文、端纳、南京来的其他两三个人以外，西安现在冠盖云集，其中有陕西、甘肃两省主席、内政部长、军政部次长、军事参议院院长、总司令侍从室主任以及参谋总部的各色成员。他们是同蒋介石一起被扣的。他们大多数参加了同张学良、杨虎城、周恩来及东北军高级将领的谈判。一到正式谈判开始，八项要求中显然没有一项是照原样接受的，因为双方都认识到必须维护政府体制的威信。不过中国人提出要求时总是开价很高，其实并不认为实际上是可以达到的，只是因为开价高了以后，可以从从容容地进行实实在在的讨价还价。西安也不是例外。

拥护八点纲领的人认为八点纲领的实质内容按其重要性次序如下：（一）停止内战、国共合作；（二）执行武装抵抗日本进一步侵略的决策；（三）南京撤换某些"亲日派"官员，采取积极外交，与英、美、苏俄建立更加紧密的关系（如果可能结成联盟）；（四）在与南京军队（在政治上和军事上）同等的基础上改编东北军和西北军；（五）扩大人民政治自由；（六）在南京建立某种形式的民主政体。

蒋介石和张学良离开西安以前所达成的协议主要之点似乎就是这些。蒋介石并亲自保证不再打内战。蒋介石说他没有签任何文件，这说的肯定是实话，因为没有任何证据可以证明他签了什么文件这种说法。但是，虽然南京方面和总司令保全了他们的"面子"，后来的事件却证明，张少帅也没有完全白丢他的面子。

to stop civil war, and in general to carry out the whole "united-front" program. But to do so Chiang's position had to be preserved and he must return to Nanking with his prestige intact. If he were submitted to the indignity of a "people's trial," civil war would inevitably develop, the decade of stalemate in the Red-Kuomintang war would be very much prolonged, and hopes of achieving an anti-Japanese national front would become remote indeed. From such a prospect no party could hope to benefit, only China could suffer, and only Japan gain. So, at least, the Reds explained their policy to me.

By December 22 several envoys and negotiators from the Central Government had arrived in Sian, including T. V. Soong, chairman of the National Economic Council (and Chiang's brother-in-law), the Minister of Interior, the Vice-Minister of War, the president of the Military Advisory Council, the chief aide-de-camp of the Generalissimo—as well as assorted members of the General Staff, who had been "detained" with Chiang Kai-shek. Most of them took some part in the parleys with Chang Hsueh-liang, Yang Hu-ch'eng, Chou En-lai, and high commanders of the Tungpei Army.

The substantial meaning of the eight demands to those who supported them was, in correct order of importance, as follows: (1) cessation of civil war and cooperation between the Kuomintang and the Communists; (2) a definite policy of armed resistance against any further Japanese aggression; (3) dismissal of certain "pro-Japanese" officials in Nanking, and the adoption of an active diplomacy for creating closer relations (alliances, if possible) with Great Britain, America, and Soviet Russia; (4) reorganization of the Tungpei and Hsipei armies on an equal footing (politically and militarily) with Nanking's forces; (5) greater political freedom for the people; and (6) the creation of some sort of democratic political structure at Nanking.

Those seemed to be the main points of agreement between Chiang Kai-shek and Chang Hsueh-liang before they left Sian. Chiang also made a personal guarantee that there would be no more civil war. It is certain that Chiang Kai-shek was quite honest in saying that he signed no document, and there is no evidence to support any claims that he did. But although Nanking and the Generalissimo still had their "face," subsequent events were to show that the Young Marshal had not lost his entirely in vain.

蒋夫人 22 日的抵达，无疑地加速了会谈的结束。而且（像她生动地叙述她在西安三天经过所充分说明的一样），她自己对张学良的规劝和申斥，也加速了蒋介石的获释。她的丈夫自喻为十字架上的耶稣基督，蒋夫人也认为自己在扮演《圣经》中的一个角色，她引述说："耶和华现在要做一件新的事，那就是，他要让一个女人保护一个男人。"25 日那天，蒋夫人还在纳闷"圣诞老人是不是绕过西安而去"，这位尼克老人却以张学良的身份出现，宣布他已说服了他的军官们，当天就派飞机送他们回南京。结果确是如此。

最后，还有最后一幕令人目瞪口呆的保全面子的姿态。张学良少帅坐着自己的座机同总司令一起回首都去自请惩处！

The arrival of Mme. Chiang on the 22nd no doubt hastened the termination of the interviews, and (as in her lively account of her three days in Sian she made abundantly clear) her own importunity and scolding of Chang Hsueh-liang speeded up the Generalissimo's release. Just as her husband compared himself with Jesus Christ on the Cross, so also Mme. Chiang recognized herself in a Biblical role, quoting, "Jehovah will now do a new thing, and that is, he will make a woman protect a man." On the 25th, when Mme. Chiang was wistfully wondering if "Santa Claus would pass by Sian," old St. Nick appeared in the person of Chang Hsueh-liang, who announced that he had won all the arguments with his officers. He would that day fly them back to Nanking. And he did.

Finally, there was that last and flabbergasting gesture of face-saving. Marshal Chang Hsueh-liang, flying in his own plane, went with the Generalissimo to the capital to await punishment!

四、"针锋相对"

现在最后一幕开始演出,对于初次见到东方的装模作样的艺术的人来说,甚至对于有些老资格的观察家来说,这都是最令人惊叹和莫名其妙的一幕。在以后的3个月里,西安事变所引起的政治上错综复杂的关系大部分都一一展现在观众面前,到了最后,局面就完全倒了过来。有人得到了大进展,大胜利,也有人遭到了大挫折,大失败。但是所进行的决斗就像中国旧戏舞台上两个古代武将所进行的决斗一样。他们口中连声呐喊,手中猛舞刀剑,令人心惊胆战,但是实际上却一点也没有碰到对方。最后,战败者颓然倒地,表示阵亡,过了一会儿却又自己爬了起来,大摇大摆地走下舞台,威风凛凛,极其庄严。

这就是在南京打的奇怪的、却完全令人眼花缭乱的太极拳。人人都"得胜"了,只有历史受了骗——给骗掉了一个牺牲品。

"兹汗颜随钧座返京,听候惩处,以昭军纪,"张学良到南京后就对总司令这么说。

蒋介石则慨然答道:"由于本人无德无才,教导部下无方,以致发生此史无前例之事变……汝既有悔过之意,自当转呈中枢,采取适当措施,以挽堕局。"

挽救的措施是什么?留心请看一切严厉措施都何等巧妙地因双方表示谅解而得到宽免,惩罚和赔礼都做得恰到好处。真不愧是妥协折中大师的杰作,完全掌握中国人所说"有实无名"和"有名无实"之间的细微差别。

蒋介石一回到南京,第一个步骤是什么?他发表一篇长篇声明,自认无力防止叛乱,没有尽到行政院长责任。他立即下令把全部政府军撤出陕西——这样就履行

4   "Point Counter Point"

During the next three months most of the political involutions created at Sian were completely unraveled, and in the end the scene was radically altered. Great conquests were made and victories won. Great losses and retreats were recorded too. But the duels fought were like those in a Chinese theater between two warriors of old. They fling out blood-curdling yells, viciously slashing the air but never actually touching each other. In the end, after the loser has acknowledged his demise by languidly draping himself on the floor for a moment, he pulls himself together and stalks from the stage under his own locomotion, a dignified walking corpse.

Such was the fascinating shadowboxing that went on at Nanking. Everybody "won," and only history was cheated—of a victim.

"Blushing with shame, I have followed you to the capital for the appropriate punishment I deserve, so as to vindicate discipline," said Chang Hsueh-liang to the Generalissimo, immediately after reaching Nanking.

"Due to my lack of virtue and defects in my training of subordinates," gallantly responds Chiang, "an unprecedented revolt broke out . . . . Now that you have expressed repentance, I will request the central authorities to adopt suitable measures for rehabilitation of the situation."

And what were the rehabilitation measures? How superbly all acts of severity were commuted by acts of conciliation, how fine the adjustment of punishment and compensation. Here was the work of a master in the strategy of compromise, of perfect knowledge of how to split the difference between what the Chinese call *yu shih wu ming*, the "reality without the name," and *yu ming wu shih*, the "name without the reality."

As Chiang's first move on returning to Nanking he issued a long statement confessing his inability to prevent the revolt, and his failure as Premier. He immediately ordered

了他停止内战的诺言——并提出辞职。他要按照惯例连辞3次。实际上，他和南京方面都并没有把他的辞职真的当一回事，因为在12月29日他就召开了中执会常会紧急会议，"请求"国民党这一最高机构做4件大事：把惩处张学良问题交给军事委员会（他本人是委员长）；把处理西北问题委托给军事委员会；停止对叛军的军事作战行动；撤销（何应钦的）"讨伐"司令部。他的建议得到了采纳。

12月31日，张学良被军事法庭（蒋介石本人没有出席）判处徒刑10年，褫夺公权5年。第二天就获赦免。在这期间他一直是蒋介石的妻舅、最近去西安的使者宋子文的上宾！接着，在1月6日撤销总司令在西安的剿匪总部。两天以后大家就知道了国民党政学系重要领袖、曾在日本留学能说日语的外交部长张群要下台了，他是西北方面攻击南京"亲日派"官员的主要目标。接任的是曾在英国留学的律师王宠惠博士，他是西北军人集团赞成的国民党政客中反日的欧美派的一个领袖。

又是在蒋介石的要求下，国民党中央执行委员会在2月15日举行全会。党的历史上召开这样的会还只是第三次。在过去，它的作用是很容易预测到的，仅仅限于在法律手续上认可统治集团——实际上就是蒋介石独裁政权——事先已决定的党的政策上的重要改变。现在党的政策要作什么重要改变呢？对这个最高机构要提出的决议案成百上千，大多数有关"救国大计"。

在1月间和2月初，蒋介石请了"病假"。他带着张学良隐居到家乡浙江省奉化附近的老家去。他的第一次辞呈遭拒，他又提一次。与此同时，表面上他卸了官职，实际上却完全掌握西北问题的解决大权，完全控制当时与东北军、西北军和红军将领进行的谈判。受到"贬黜"的张学良随侍在侧，实际上是他的阶下囚。在南京，蒋介石的部下忙着搜集情况以供他估计西安事变所造成的拥护他和反对他的力量的新对比，重新估计他的拥护者的实力，把忠于他的人同那些准备在西安炸死他的投机分子区别开来。西安事变真如蒋夫人所说，"因祸得福"。而且不止在一个方面。

the withdrawal of all government troops from Shensi—thus fulfilling his promise to prevent civil war—and offered his resignation (he was to repeat it the traditional three times). In reality he took his resignation no more seriously than did his government, for on December 29 he called an emergency meeting of the standing committee of the Central Executive Committee, and "requested" this highest organ of the Kuomintang to do four important things: to hand over to the Military Affairs Commission (of which he was chairman) the punishment of Chang Hsueh-liang; to delegate to the Military Affairs Commission the settlement of the Northwest problem; to terminate military operations against the rebels; and to abolish "punitive expedition" headquarters which had been set up, during Chiang's absence, to attack Sian. His "recommendations" were "obeyed."

On December 31 Chang Hsueh-liang was sentenced by tribunal (at which Chiang was not present) to ten years' imprisonment and deprivation of civil rights for five years. On the following day he was pardoned. And all the time he was the personal guest of Chiang Kai-shek's brother-in-law and recent envoy to Sian, T. V. Soong. On January 6 the Generalissimo's Sian headquarters for Bandit Suppression (Anti-Communist Campaign) was abolished. Two days later it was already known that the skids were under Japanese-speaking, Japanese-educated Foreign Minister Chang Chun, important leader of the "political-science clique" in the Kuomintang. Chang Chun had been the principal target of the Northwest in its charges of "pro-Japanese" officials at Nanking. He was replaced by Dr. Wang Chung-hui, British-educated barrister, and a leader of the Ou-Mei P'ai, the anti-Japanese "European-American" clique of Kuomintang politicians, whom the Northwest junta regarded with favor.

Again at Chiang's request, a plenary session of the Kuomintang Central Executive Committee was summoned for February 15. In the past its functions had been easily predictable, and confined to legalizing important changes in Party policy decided in advance by the ruling cliques, which in coalition were the Chiang Kai-shek dictatorship. What were the important changes of policy now to be introduced? Hundreds of resolutions were prepared for presentation to that august body. The great majority dealt with "national salvation."

During January and early February, Chiang Kai-shek took "sick leave." He retired, with Chang Hsueh-liang, to rest in the Generalissimo's country home near Fenghua, his native place in Chekiang. His first resignation rejected, Chiang repeated it. Meanwhile, ostensibly freed from official duties, he had complete command of the settlement of the Northwest issue, complete control of the conversations going on with the Tungpei, Hsipei, and Red Army commanders. Chang Hsueh-liang, "in disgrace," was at his side, still a virtual prisoner.

2月10日，共产党中央委员会向南京的国民党政府和国民党中执会三次全会发了一个历史性的电报[1]，向政府祝贺和平解决西安事件和"即将和平统一"全国。它向中执会全会提出在政策方面作4项重大修改：停止内战；保证言论、出版、集会自由和释放政治犯，制订全国抵抗日本侵略计划；恢复实行孙中山遗嘱中的"三大原则"。

如果不论在形式上或实质上，这些建议得到采纳，共产党为了"加速全国统一和抗日"，准备停止一切推翻政府的尝试，采纳下列政策：（一）红军改名为"国民革命军"，隶属军事委员会指挥；（二）苏维埃政府改名为"中华民国边区政府"；（三）在苏区内实行"完全民主的"政体；（四）停止没收土地政策，集中人民力量用在救国——即抗日——的任务上。

但是全会在2月15日召开时没有正式理会这封"匪电"。还有更加重要的事情需要处理。蒋介石在他第一次发言中再一次重述了他在西安被扣的整个过程，（对他来说）感情激动。他有声有色地叙述他拒绝书面保证履行叛军要求。他也谈到叛军怎么转变过来同意他的观点，看到他被抄去的日记中爱国感情的流露而感动得下泪。在说了这一切以后，他最后才十分不经意和轻蔑地把叛军的八点要求向全会提出。全会重申对总司令的完全信任，拒绝了他的第三次辞呈，谴责了张学良，也同样不经意和轻蔑地拒绝了这八点荒唐的要求。

但是且慢，好戏还在后头。与此同时，中央执行委员会却有条不紊地根据自己的安排采取了一些措施。最有意义的也许是在领导集团中地位仅次于蒋介石的汪精卫的开幕词。自从反共战争以来这位汪同志第一次发言中没有说到"安内"（即"剿共"）是全国头等大事，没有重复他的名言"抗战必先统一"。他说，现在全国"首要问

---

1. 见苏维埃刊物《新中国》，1937年3月15日延安。

On February 10 the Central Executive Committee of the Communist Party addressed to the National Government at Nanking, and to the Third Plenary Session, a historic telegram.[1] It congratulated the government on the peaceful settlement of the Sian affair, and on the "impending peaceful unification" of the country. To the Plenary Session it proposed four important changes in policies: to end civil war; to guarantee freedom of speech, press, and assembly, and to release political prisoners; to invoke a national plan of resistance to Japanese aggression; and to return to the "three principles" of Dr. Sun Yat-sen's will.

If these proposals were adopted, in form or in substance, the Communists stated they were prepared, for the purpose of "hastening national unification and resistance to Japan," to suspend all attempts to overthrow the government and to adopt the following policies: (1) change the name of the Red Army to the "National Revolutionary Army," and place it under the command of Chiang Kai-shek's Military Affairs Commission; (2) change the name of the Soviet Government to the "Special Area Government of the Republic of China"; (3) realize a "completely democratic" (representative) form of government within the soviet districts; and (4) suspend the policy of land confiscation and concentrate the efforts of the people on the tasks of national salvation—that is, anti-Nipponism.

But the Plenary Session, when it convened on February 15, took no formal notice of the bandits' telegram. There was much more important business to be accomplished. Chiang Kai-shek in his first speech to the Session once more recounted, in complete and (for him) impassioned utterance, the whole story of his captivity in Sian. Dramatically he described how he refused to sign any pledge to carry out the rebels' demands. He told also how the rebels were converted to his own point of view, and were moved to tears by the revelations of patriotism in his confiscated diary. And not until he had said all this did he at last, in a very offhand and contemptuous manner, submit the rebels' eight demands to the Session. Reiterating its complete confidence in the Generalissimo, the Session rejected his third resignation, condemned Chang Hsueh-liang, and just as casually and contemptuously rejected the impertinent demands.

Meanwhile, however, in its well-trained way, the Central Executive Committee was accomplishing things on its own initiative. Significant above everything else, perhaps, was the opening statement of Wang Ching-wei, second only to Chiang Kai-shek in party leadership. For the first time since the beginning of the anti-Red wars, Comrade Wang made a speech in which he did not say that "internal pacification" (eradication of communism) was the most important problem before the country, in which he did not repeat his famous phrase, "resistance *after* unification." The "foremost question" before

---

1. See *New China*, a Communist publication (Yenan), March 15, 1937.

题"是"收复失土"。此外,全会还真的通过决议要先收复冀东和察北,取消"自治性"的冀察委员会。当然,这并不是说南京要同日本开战。它的意义仅仅是,日本如继续对中国进行军事侵略将会遭到南京方面的武装抵抗。但是这已是向前跃进了一大步。

接着,中执会又在行政院长的建议下,决定在11月12日召开长期拖延未开的"国民大会",在中国实行"民主"。这次是决定要召开了,不再进行拖延。更重要的是,常会受权修改国大组织法,增加"各界"的代表名额。总司令——又是通过汪精卫——宣布全国的第二个大问题是加速实现民主。

最后,在全会的最后一天,蒋介石发了言,保证除了卖国贼以外给大家更大的言论自由,而且他没有提到"文匪"——这还是大家第一次听到总司令要维护新闻自由。他并且答应"释放悔改的政治犯"。另外不声不响地向报界发了一道命令,不再用"赤匪"和"共匪"的字样。少数监狱开始放出一些不太重要的受害者。

然后,好像事后才想到的一样,在这次有历史意义的全会的最后一天,即2月21日,发表了一个长篇宣言,表面上是为了要谴责共产党。宣言概述了十年烧杀破坏的罪行史。这当然是国民党对这十年的观点。宣言问道,这些人曾经是体面的公民,甚至是德行操守无懈可击的国民党的盟友,怎么会堕落至此?要同匪徒、小偷、凶手"和解"是根本谈不上的,这一点岂不明显?但是结果是,这一切空话实际上不过是为宣言末尾提出的和平条件作准备,这使得那些仍旧不惜一切代价反对和平的保守派感到极为反感。

这些建议是什么?全会向共产党提供了一个"改过自新"的机会,不过有四个条件:(一)取消红军,改编为国军;(二)解散"苏维埃共和国";(三)共产党停止与孙中山的三民主义唱反调的宣传;(四)放弃阶级斗争。这样,虽然是用"投降"而不是用"合作"的字眼,国民党接受了共产党提出的"和解"谈判的基础。[1]请注意,这些条件仍把共产党的小小自治国、他们的军队、他们的组织、他们的党、他们的将来"最高纲领"留在共产党的手里。或者说,至少共产党可以这样希望。而实际上他们就是这样希望的。因为在3月15日,共产党、苏维埃政府和红军发表了一个长篇宣言,要求与南京方面重开谈判。

---

1. 这些重要决议的全文见《中国年鉴》(1938年上海)。

the country now, he said, was "recovery of the lost territories." Moreover, the Session actually adopted resolutions to begin by recovering east Hopei and northern Chahar, and abolishing the Japan-made "autonomous" Hopei-Chahar Council. Of course that did not mean that Nanking was to launch a war against Japan. Its significance was simply that further Japanese military aggression in China would meet with armed resistance from Nanking. But that was a real leap forward.

Second, the CEC, again on the Premier's recommendation, decided to convene on November 12 the long-delayed "People's Congress," which was supposed to inaugurate "democracy" in China. More important, the standing committee was authorized to revise the organic laws of the Congress to increase representation of "all groups." The Generalissimo—through Wang Ching-wei again—announced that the second great problem before the nation was the speedy realization of democracy.

Finally, on the last day of the Session, Chiang Kai-shek made a statement in which he promised greater liberty of speech to all but traitors—and he said nothing about the "intellectual bandits." He also promised "release of political prisoners who repent." Very quietly an order went out to the press that no longer were the epithets "Red bandit" and "Communist bandit" to be used. A few prisons began to pour out a trickle of their less important victims.

Then, as if in afterthought, on February 21, last day of the historic Session, a long manifesto was issued, ostensibly to denounce the Communists. The history of ten years of crime and vandalism was recapitulated. Was it not obvious that any talk of "reconciliation" with brigands, thieves, and murderers was out of the question? But all that explosion of wind, it turned out, was actual preparation for the terms of peace which, to the extreme distaste of Tories who still opposed peace at any price, concluded the manifesto.

What were these proposals? The Session offered the Communists a chance "to make a new start in life," on four conditions: (1) abolition of the Red Army and its incorporation into the national army; (2) dissolution of the "Soviet Republic"; (3) cessation of Communist propaganda that was diametrically opposed to Dr. Sun Yat-sen's "three principles"; and (4) abandonment of the class struggle. Thus, though phrased in terms of "surrender" instead of "cooperation," the Kuomintang had accepted the Reds' basis for negotiation of a "reconciliation."[1] Note that those terms still left the Reds in possession of their little autonomous state, their own army, their organizations, their Party, and their "maximum program" for the future. Or so, at least, the Reds could hope. And so, indeed, they did. For on March 15 the Communist Party, the Soviet Government, and the Red Army issued a long manifesto requesting the opening of negotiations with Nanking.

---

1. For full text of these important resolutions see *The China Year Book* (Shanghai, 1938).

蒋介石的这一切复杂的手腕，为了什么目的？显然，这么巧妙地搞这一套手法是为了要既不降低他本人或南京的威望而又能同反对派和解。他的命令和讲话，全会的决议，按其正确的顺序来读一下，就可以看出，他满足了所有各反对派别的政治要求的一部分——刚好使他们不至于团结起来坚决反对他，但又不足在国民党内部引起反叛。内战停止了，很明显，南京终于承担起武装抗日的任务。他答应了扩大政治自由，并为实现"民主"定了一个具体日期。最后，还提出了一个方案，国共可以据此武装休战共处，如果还谈不上"合作"的话。同时，政府在名义上拒绝了叛军的要求和共方的"合作"建议。这都是好得不能再好了。

我们一定会注意到，这些和解措施是蒋介石在南京面临很大敌对意见的情况下强行通过的，而且当时他个人刚刚经历了一场巨变，险遭不测，换了一个不如他有远见的人，很可能怀恨在心，失去理智，轻率采取报复行动——实际上，蒋介石在南京的一些愤愤不平的部下就是这样要求的。但是蒋介石比他们精明。他安然脱险时受到人民极大的欢迎，这不仅是对他个人的拥护，而且也是人民要求和平反对内战，要求团结抗日的有力表示。对此，蒋介石是完全理解的，他也知道他如果对西北方面采取任何惩戒行动都会在一夜之间丧失民心。更重要的是，西安事变暴露了他自己权力结构中的深刻裂痕。他明白这种裂痕很容易扩大为致命的破裂，使整个结构四分五裂。他现在清楚地看到和平对他有极大的好处，可以把这些裂痕一一消除殆尽。他没有收回在西安作出的诺言，他没有对扣留他的人马上进行公开的报复，他软硬兼施，既作了恰如其分的威胁，又作了必要的让步，真不愧是玩弄政治手腕的天才。这样，他终于分裂了西北集团（这是他第一个目标），把东北军安然无事地从陕西调到安徽和河南，把杨虎城将军的西北军整编后划归中央指挥。2月间，南京军队就能够安然无事地未遭任何抵抗占领了西安和西安近郊，到下一月，开始同共产党谈判。

What was the purpose of all these complex maneuvers by Chiang? Obviously they were skillfully interwoven in such a manner as to conciliate the Opposition without weakening the prestige either of himself or of Nanking. Read in their proper sequence, his orders and statements, and the resolutions of the Plenary Session, showed that he *partly* satisfied the political demands of all groups of the Opposition—just enough to shatter their solidarity and resolution in defying him, but not enough to cause a revolt in the Kuomintang. Civil war had been stopped, and it was clear that Nanking had at last shouldered the task of armed resistance to Japan. Promises of greater political freedom had been made, and a definite date had been set for the realization of "democracy." Finally, a formula had been proposed by which the Kuomintang and the Communists might at least live together in armed truce, if not in "cooperation." At the same time the government had nominally rejected the rebels' demands and the Communists' proposals for "cooperation." It was all very wonderful.

One should not fail to note that these conciliatory gestures were forced through by Chiang Kai-shek in the face of considerable antagonism to them in Nanking, and at the conclusion of a terrific personal shock which might have embittered and unbalanced a man less gifted with foresight, and hastened him into precipitate actions of revenge—which, in fact, Chiang's outraged followers in Nanking demanded. But Chiang was shrewder than they. It was real genius of political strategy that he did not ignore the promises made in Sian, that he took no immediate overt revenge against his captors, that he tactfully employed a policy combining just the right weight of threat with the necessary softening of concession. In that way he eventually succeeded in breaking up the Northwest bloc (his first objective), and peacefully transferred the Tungpei Army from Shensi into Anhui and Honan, while the Hsipei Army of General Yang Hu-ch'eng was reorganized under the central command. In February, Nanking troops were able to occupy Sian and its environs without disturbance or opposition, and in the following month—with his guns at their frontiers—Chiang opened negotiations with the Communists.

五、　《友谊地久天长》[1]？

在西安事变期间，红军占领了大批新扩展的地方。在陕西省，它现在占了一半以上的面积，包括渭河以北的几乎所有地方。在他们50来个县份里——面积在6万到7万平方英里之间，大体上等于奥地利面积的两倍——共产党所控制的领域是他们有史以来最大的一块地方。但在经济上这个地方很穷，发展前途极为有限，人口稀少，大约不到200万。

但这个地区战略上极为重要。共产党可以从这里出发封锁中亚的贸易通道，或者打通同新疆或外蒙古的直接联系。假如与日开战，这个边境线的有机价值是很明显的。这是日本无法封锁的仅有的两条中国边境线之一，也是供应来源之一。新疆有一半以上，面积约55万平方英里，已在一个同情中共、半独立于南京、半从属于苏联的半社会主义政体的统治下。在它东北的外蒙古自治共和国，另一个面积达90万平方英里的前中国附属国——中国对它的宗主权至今仍得到名义上的承认，即使俄国也是承认的——现在则肯定是在红旗的统治下，这是1936年与苏联缔结军事同盟（共同防御条约）的结果。

在现在仍可称为"大中华"的这个地方，共产党控制下的这三个地区加起来大约占前中华帝国1/3的面积。把它们三者相互隔开来而没有实际接触的，只是一些政治上态度暧昧的缓冲地区，住的是蒙古人、回民和同南京关系脆弱的边境部落，日本侵略的威胁对他们来说倒是日益现实的。这些地区后来很可能被纳入"抗日统一战线"的圈子，在苏联的影响之下。这样就会形成一个未来的庞大共产党根据地，

---

1. 用名诗人彭斯的诗句谱写的苏格兰著名民歌，又译《美好的昔日》，一般在惜别或旧友重逢时歌唱，此处喻国共重新合作。——译注

5   "Auld Lang Syne"?

During the Sian Incident the Red Army had occupied large new areas. In Shensi it now held the greater part of the province, including nearly everything north of the Wei River. In their some fifty counties—an area between sixty and seventy thousand square miles, or, roughly, twice the size of Austria—the Reds controlled the biggest single realm they had ever ruled. But it was economically poor, very limited in its possibilities of development, and thinly populated, with perhaps less than 2,000,000 inhabitants.

Strategically the area was extremely important. From it the Reds could, if they chose, block the trade ways to Central Asia, or perhaps later themselves make direct connections with Sinkiang or Outer Mongolia. It was one of only two Chinese frontiers, and sources of supply, which Japan could not blockade. More than half of Sinkiang, roughly 550,000 square miles in area, was ruled by a warlord seemingly sympathetic to the Chinese Reds and the U.S.S.R. Northeast of it, Outer Mongolia, another 900,000 square miles of former dependency of China—Chinese suzerainty over which was still nominally recognized, even by Russia—was now definitely under the Red banner, as a result of the military alliance (Mutual Defense Pact) concluded with the U.S.S.R. in 1936.

These three regions of Communist control in what could still be called "Greater China" were altogether about a third the size of the former Chinese Empire. Separating them from physical contact with each other were only politically ambiguous buffer districts inhabited by Mongols, Moslems, and frontiersmen whose ties with Nanking were fragile, and against whom the threat of Japanese conquest was a deepening reality. Those areas might later on be brought into the orbit of the "Anti-Japanese United Front," and under soviet influence. That would close in an immense future Red base extending from Central

从中亚和蒙古延伸到中国的西北腹地。但是这一片地方都很落后，有些部分是贫瘠的草原和沙漠，交通不便，人口稀少。它要在东方政治中起决定性的作用，必须同苏联或华中，或者两者的先进工业军事基地结成紧密的同盟。

中共的当前收获限于这几个方面：停止了内战，南京的对内政策有了一定程度的自由化和容忍，对日态度趋于强硬，苏区不完全地脱离了长期孤立状态。总司令派赴西安的使者张冲将军和共方在西安的代表周恩来谈判的结果，在4、5、6月发生了一些重要的变化。经济封锁取消了。红区和外界建立了贸易关系。更重要的是，双方悄悄地恢复了交通联系。在边界上，红星旗和国民党的青天白日旗象征性地交叉挂在一起。

邮件和电报开放了一部分。共产党在西安买了一批美国卡车，在自己区内的各主要地方之间开办了长途汽车。各种各样必需的技术材料开始运了进来。对共产党来说最珍贵的是书籍。延安新开了一家鲁迅纪念图书馆，全国各地的共产党同志都寄了成吨成吨的新书来。成百上千的中国年轻的共产党人从大城市来到陕北红色新首都延安。到5月间，已有2,000名学员进了红军大学（改名为"抗日大学"），500名进了党校。其中有蒙古人、回民、西藏人、台湾人、苗族、彝族。还有好几十人在一些技术训练班学习。

除了党的久经考验的工作者以外，还有热情的年轻激进分子从全国各地前来，有的长途跋涉，步行而来。到7月间，尽管学习生活很艰苦，伙食是小米白菜，吃不饱肚子是有名的，仍有许多人申请入学，容纳不下。许多人只好请他们回去等下一届，共产党打算再接受5,000名。许多有训练的技术人员也来了，或者当教员，或者从事现已开始的"建设计划"。这，也许是和平所带来的最大的眼前利益：有了一个可以自由地为革命和抗战训练、装备、培养新干部的根据地。

当然，国民党仍继续严密监视共产党同外界的联系。现在对共产党的行动已不是那么有限制了，但是还没有公开承认这个事实。许多非共产党的知识分子团体也到红色中国来考察那里的情况，许多人来了以后就留下工作不走了。6月间，国民党自己也秘密派了一个半官方的代表团，以邵华为首，参观红色首都。他们游历了苏

Asia and Mongolia into the heart of Northwest China. But all that realm was backward, some of it barren steppe and desert, with poor communications, and sparsely populated. It could become a decisive factor in Eastern politics only in close alliance with the advanced industrial and military bases of either the U.S.S.R. or Central China, or both.

Immediate gains of the Chinese Reds were confined to these categories: the cessation of civil war, a certain degree of liberalization and tolerance in Nanking's internal policies, a stiffening toward Japan, and a partial release of the soviet districts from their long isolation. As a result of negotiations conducted between General Chang Chung, the Generalissimo's envoy in Sian, and Chou En-lai, the Reds' delegate there, a number of important changes took place during April, May, and June. The economic blockade was lifted. Trade relations were established between the Red districts and the outside world. More important, communications between the two areas were quietly restored. On the frontiers the Red Star and the Kuomintang White Sun were crossed in symbolic union.

Mail and telegraph services were partly reopened. The Reds purchased a fleet of American trucks in Sian and operated a bus service connecting the principal points in their region. Needed technical materials of all sorts began to pour in. Most precious to the Communists were books. A new Lu Hsun Memorial Library was established in Yenan, and to fill it Communist comrades throughout the country sent in tons of new literature. Hundreds of young Chinese Communists migrated from the great cities to Yenan, the new Red capital in north Shensi. By May over 2,000 students had been accepted for enrollment in the Red University (renamed the "Anti-Japanese University"), and some 500 were in the Communist Party school. Among them were Mongols, Moslems, Tibetans, Taiwanese, and Miao and Lolo tribesmen. Scores were also studying in a number of technical training institutes.

Enthusiastic young radicals as well as veteran Party workers rolled in from all parts of China, some walking over great distances. By July, despite the rigors of student life, there were so many applicants that no more could be accommodated. Scores were turned back to wait for another term, when the Reds prepared to receive 5,000. Many trained technicians also arrived, and were given work as teachers, or in the "construction plan" which was now begun. In this, perhaps, lay the biggest immediate benefit of peace: a base in which freely to train, equip, and discipline new cadres for the ranks of the revolution and the anti-Japanese war.

Of course, the Kuomintang continued strictly to supervise the Reds' connections with the outer world. There was less restriction on the movement of Communists now, but there was as yet no open acknowledgment of the fact. Many parties of non-Communist intellectuals also arrived in Red China to investigate conditions there—and many of them stayed on, to work. In June, the Kuomintang itself secretly sent a semiofficial group of delegates, headed by Hsiao Hua, to visit the Red capital. They toured the soviet districts

区，在盛大的群众大会上发表了相当红色的抗日演说。他们欢迎国共恢复反帝统一战线。不过，国民党报纸是不准刊登这些情况的。

对列宁的拥护者来说，国民党地区的情况也改善了。共产党在名义上仍属非法，但可以扩大影响，扩大组织，因为压迫已有所减弱。监牢里不断放出少量的政治犯。特别宪兵（蓝衣社）仍继续侦查共产党，但是不再绑架和拷打了。还传出消息来说，今后蓝衣社的活动主要集中对付"亲日汉奸"。后者有一些遭到逮捕，有几个领日本津贴的中国特务第一次真的已被处决。

到5月间，作为让步的交换，苏区准备改名为"边区政府"，红军已申请作为国民革命军编入国防部队。党和红军的全国代表大会5月和6月间分别召开了。会上作出了决定，要采取实现同国民党合作的新政策。在这些大会上，列宁、马克思、斯大林、毛泽东、朱德和共产党其他领导人的画像同蒋介石和孙中山的画像挂在一起。

这些现象反映了共产党方面总的来说愿意在形式上和名称上作必要的让步，同时又保留他们在主义上和纲领上的基本内容，和他们的在自治条件下的存在。国民党口头唱得好听的孙中山的三民主义，像在大革命时期一样又受到共产党的尊重。这不是蒋介石的三民主义，因为共产党给了他们自己的马克思主义的解释。很明显，马克思主义，还有社会革命的基本原则，他们是决不会放弃的。他们所采取的每一新步骤、所作的每一变化，都是从马克思主义的角度来进行检查、辩论、决定和结合的，而且也是从无产阶级革命的角度，共产党并没有放弃无产阶级革命，这仍是他们的最终目标。

共产党政策的最重大变化是停止实行没收地主土地，停止反对南京和反对国民党的宣传，答应给一切公民平等权利和选举权，不论他们阶级成分如何。其中最直接影响到红色经济的，自然是停止没收土地。这并不意味着在已重新分配土地的地方把土地还给地主，而是同意在共产党新控制的地区放弃这种做法。[1]

为了补偿由于这种让步而造成经费的短缺，蒋总司令同意——尽管不是正式地——把苏区视作"国防地区"的一部分，并且按这种地位拨给经费。第一笔经费（50万元）是在蒋介石回南京后不久付给共产党的。国民党的货币有一部分用来收回苏区

---

1. 然而，新的地租政策意在惩罚地主，在实践中"民主"政治组织内的这种倾向性对贫农有利。在任何时候，甚至在短暂的两党合作的头几个月里，共产党都没有停止过宣传他们的事业，也没有否定过他们最终的马克思主义道路。

and made appropriate rufescent anti-Japanese speeches before huge mass meetings. They acclaimed the return to the anti-imperialist united front between Communists and the Kuomintang. Nothing of this was allowed to appear in the Kuomintang press, however.

Conditions in the Kuomintang areas also improved for the followers of Lenin. The Communist Party was still nominally illegal, but it became possible to extend its influence and widen its organization, for the oppression somewhat diminished. A small but steady stream of political prisoners was released from the jails. The special gendarmes, the Blueshirts, continued their espionage on Communists, but kidnapings and torture ceased. Word was sent out that Blueshirt activities henceforth should center primarily on "pro-Japanese traitors." A number of the latter were arrested, and several Chinese agents in Japan's pay were reported to have been executed.

By May, in an exchange of concessions, the soviets had prepared to adopt the name Special Area Government, and the Red Army had petitioned to be included in the national defense forces as the National Revolutionary Army. Great "all-China" meetings of Party and Red Army delegates were called in May and June. Decisions were made on measures by which the new policies, calling for cooperation with the Kuomintang, could be realized. At these meetings the portraits of Lenin, Marx, Stalin, Mao Tse-tung, Chu Teh, and other Red leaders appeared beside those of Chiang Kai-shek and Sun Yat-sen.

The most important changes in Red policy were the cessation of the practice of confiscation of the landlords' land, the cessation of anti-Nanking, anti-Kuomintang propaganda, and the promise of equal rights and the voting franchise to all citizens, regardless of their class origin. Cessation of land confiscation did not mean the return of land to the landlords in areas where redistribution had already been realized, but was an agreement to abandon the practice in districts newly brought under Communist control.[1]

On his side, Generalissimo Chiang agreed to consider the soviet districts part of the "national defense area," and pay accordingly. The first payment to the Reds ($500,000) was delivered shortly after Chiang Kai-shek's return to Nanking. Some of the Kuomintang

---

1. New land-rent policies were, however, to penalize the landlords, and in practice the bias in "democratic" political organizations favored the poor peasants. At no time, not even in the early months of the brief lived two-party cooperation, did the Communists cease propagandizing for their cause or repudiate their ultimate Marxist program.

货币，还有一部分购买制成品给合作社（现在存货充沛）和购买必要的装备。这些钱没有一文浪费在薪水上。财政人民委员仍靠5元钱一月生活！南京每月经费的确切数字在本书写作时仍在谈判中——事实上，未来合作的具体工作协议也还在谈判中。

6月间，蒋介石派私人座机到西安接共方首席代表周恩来到中国夏都牯岭。周恩来在那里同蒋介石及其内阁作进一步谈判。讨论的问题有共产党要求参加定于11月召开并通过"民主"宪法的国民大会。据报道，已经达成协议，"边区"可以作为一个地区派9名代表。

但是，极有可能，这些代表不会称为"共产党人"的。南京还没有公开承认这次所谓"复婚"。它宁可把这关系看成是"纳妾"，她行为是否端正还有待证明，而且为了外交的缘故，这种关系在家庭圈子外面还是少谈为妙。但是即使这种偷偷摸摸的"结合"，也是令人震惊地公开反抗日本，这在几个月以前是不可想象的。同时，日本自己的（通过媒人广田）与南京体面地结成"反共"婚姻[1]的要求，终于被拒。这也许是南京外交政策终于有了根本变化的最后的明确迹象。

对于不熟悉中国政治的天真的西方观察家来说，这个结局似乎是完全不可理解的，因此在分析它的意义时可能犯严重的判断错误。当然除了中国以外世上别的地方是不可能发生这种事情的。在经过了十年的最激烈内战以后，红军和白军忽然携手合唱《友谊地久天长》。这是什么意思？是不是红军变白了，白军变红了？谁都没有变。但是总得有人得了利，有人失了利？是的，中国得了利，日本失了利。因为看来似乎是，由于第三方面因素——日本帝国主义——的插手，极其复杂的两方之争，再一次推迟了决战。

因此要大略知道红色的天际上出现的前途，我们必须看一看帝国主义在中国革命中所饰的角色。

---

1. 日本的提议的实质是将中国变为罗马—柏林—东京联盟中的一种卫星伙伴。

money was used to convert soviet currency, to buy manufactures for their cooperatives, and to purchase needed equipment. The exact monthly allowance from Nanking was still under negotiation—as, indeed, was the whole definitive working agreement for future cooperation—while the storm of Japanese invasion was gathering in the North.

In June the Generalissimo sent his private plane to Sian for Chou En-lai, the Reds' chief delegate, who flew to Kuling, China's summer capital. There Chou held further conversations with Chiang Kai-shek and members of the cabinet. Among points discussed was the Communists' demand for representation in the People's Congress—the Congress scheduled to adopt a "democratic" constitution—in November. It was reported that an agreement was reached whereby the "Special Area" would be permitted to elect nine delegates on a regional basis.

However, these delegates in all probability would not be known as "Communists." Nanking had not openly acknowledged the so-called remarriage. It preferred to regard the relationship rather as the annexation of a concubine whose continence had yet to be proved, and one about which, for diplomatic reasons, the less said outside family circles the better. But even this furtive *mésalliance* was an astounding and open defiance of Japan, unthinkable a few months previously. Meanwhile Japan's own offer (through Matchmaker Hirota) of a respectable "anti-Red" marriage[1] with Nanking was finally spurned. In this was perhaps a last and definite indication that Nanking's foreign policy had undergone a fundamental change.

All that seemed an utterly incomprehensible denouement to many an observer, and serious errors were made in its analysis. After a decade of the fiercest kind of civil war, Red and White suddenly burst into "Auld Lang Syne." What was the meaning of it? Had the Reds turned White, and the Whites turned Red? Neither one. But surely someone must have won, and someone lost? Yes, China had won, Japan had lost. For it seemed that a final decision in the profoundly complicated internal struggle had been postponed once more, by the intervention of a third ingredient—Japanese imperialism.

---

1. The essence of Japan's proposals was to make of China a kind of satellite partner in the Rome-Berlin-Tokyo alliance.

六、　　红色的天际

有一个很有造就的社会科学家名叫列宁。他曾写道："一般历史，特别是革命的历史，总是比最优秀的政党、最先进阶级的最觉悟的先锋队所想象的更富有内容，更多种多样，更生动活泼，'更巧妙'。这是不言而喻的，因为最优秀的先锋队也只能表达几万人的意识、意志、热情和想象；而革命却是在人的一切才能特别高度和集中地表现出来的时候，由千百万被最尖锐的阶级斗争所激励的人的意识、意志、热情和想象来实现的。"[1]

中国的历史在哪些方面证明了是比共产党理论家在 10 年左右以前预见到的"更富有内容，更多种多样，更生动活泼，'更巧妙'"呢？具体地来说，为什么红军尽管作了英勇卓绝的斗争，仍没有能够在中国赢得政权？要回答这一问题，我们必须再回顾一下，而且要明确地记住，共产党的中国革命概念及其主要目标。

共产党认为，中国的资本家阶级不是一个真正的资产阶级，而是一个"殖民地资产阶级"。这是一个"买办资产阶级"，是它主要服务对象外国金融和垄断资本的寄生物。它无力领导革命，只有通过完成反帝运动，消灭外国统治，它才能求得本身的自由。只有工人和农民能够领导这样一场革命一直到最后胜利。共产党要做到使工人和农民不会把胜利的果实拱手让给他们通过革命而解放出来的新资本家，像法国、德国、意大利所发生的那样，事实上除了俄国以外，到处都是这样。相反，工人和农民要在一种"新经济政策"时期，一个短短的"有控制的资本主义"历史时期，

---

1. 列宁：《共产主义运动中的"左派"幼稚病》（1934 年伦敦）。

6   RED HORIZONS

There was an accomplished social scientist named Lenin. "History generally," he wrote, "and the history of revolutions in particular, is always richer in content, more varied, more many-sided, more lively and 'subtle,' than the best parties and the most class-conscious vanguards of the most advanced class imagine. This is understandable, because the best vanguards express the class consciousness, the will, the passion, the fantasy of tens of thousands, while the revolution is made, at the moment of its climax and exertion of all human capabilities, by the class consciousness, the will, the passion, and the fantasy of tens of millions who are urged on by the very acutest class struggle."[1]

In what ways had Chinese history proved "richer in content, more varied, more many-sided, more lively and 'subtle,'" than the Communist theoreticians foresaw a decade or so ago? To be specific, why had the Red Army failed to win power in China? In attempting an answer one had to recall again, and keep clearly in mind, the Communist conception of the Chinese revolution, and of its main objectives.

The Communists said that the Chinese capitalist class was not a true bourgeoisie, but a "colonial bourgeoisie." It was a "comprador class," an excrescence of the foreign finance and monopoly capitalism which it primarily served. It was too weak to lead the revolution. It could achieve the conditions of its own freedom only through the fulfillment of the anti-imperialist movement, the elimination of foreign domination. But only the workers and peasants could lead such a revolution to its final victory. And the Communists intended that the workers and peasants should not turn over the fruits of that victory to the neo-capitalists whom they were thus to release, as had happened in France, Germany, Italy—everywhere, in fact, except in Russia. Instead, they should retain power throughout a kind of "NEP" period, a brief epoch of "controlled capitalism," and then a period of

---

1.   V. I. Lenin, *"Left-Wing" Communism: An Infantile Disorder* (London, 1934).

然后在一个国家资本主义时期，保持政权，在这以后才最后迅速过渡到社会主义建设——在苏联的帮助下。所有这一切都很清楚地在《中华苏维埃共和国的基本法律》一书中有所说明[1]。

毛泽东在1934年重复说[2]，"驱逐帝国主义，打垮国民党的目的是要统一中国，实现**资产阶级民主革命**，使得有可能把这一革命转到社会主义革命的更高阶段。这就是苏维埃的任务。"

在中国大革命高潮，在农民群众和无产阶级中间存在着必要的革命情绪。但是同产生俄国革命的情况有许多差异。其中有一种差异十分大。封建主义残余在俄国甚至比中国还要明显，但是中国是一个半殖民地国家，一个"被压迫民族"，而俄国是一个帝国主义国家，是一个"压迫民族"。在俄国革命中，无产阶级只需打败一个阶级，它本国的资产阶级兼帝国主义阶级，而中国革命却要对付一个有双重人格的本国敌人——它本国的新生资产阶级和外国帝国主义的既得利益。理论上来说，在开始的时候，中国共产党人以为他们敌人的这种双重性质会被他们自己的进攻的双重性质所抵消，那就是他们的进攻会得到他们在世界上的"无产阶级盟友"和"苏联劳动者"的援助。

中国产业工人几乎有1/2集中在上海，在六七个世界强国的炮舰瞄准之下。在天津、青岛、上海、汉口、香港、九龙以及帝国主义的其他势力范围中，大概集中了中国产业工人的3/4！上海是个最典型的样本。这里有英国、美国、法国、日本、意大利和**中国的**士兵、水兵、警察，所有国际帝国主义的势力同本地的土匪流氓和买办资产阶级这些中国社会最腐化堕落的成分结合起来，一起"合作"，对赤手空拳的千千万万工人挥舞棍棒。

这些工人被剥夺了言论、集会、组织自由。**只要本国的和外国的警察力量的双重制度存在一天**，要动员中国产业无产阶级采取政治行动，是完全不可想象的。历史上只有一次——在1927年——打破过这种制度，当时在短短的几天里，蒋介石利用工人取得了对北洋军阀的胜利。但是他们马上遭到镇压，这是历史上最使人丧气的一种流血事件，得到了外国列强的认可和外国资本家的财政援助。

---

1. 毛泽东等。
2. 《红色中国：毛泽东主席……》（1934年伦敦）。

state capitalism, followed at last by a speedy transition into Socialist construction, with the help of the U.S.S.R. All that was indicated quite clearly in *Fundamental Laws of the Chinese Soviet Republic*.[1]

"The aim of the driving out of imperialism, and destroying the Kuomintang," repeated Mao Tse-tung in 1934,[2] "is to unify China, to bring the *bourgeois democratic revolution* to fruition, and to make it possible to turn this revolution into a higher stage of Socialist revolution. This is the task of the soviet."

At the apex of the Great Revolution (1924—1927) there was present the necessary revolutionary mood among both the peasant masses and the proletariat. But there were many differences from the situation which had produced the Russian Revolution. One of these was very great. Survivals of feudalism were even more pronounced in Russia than in China, but China was a semicolonial country, an "oppressed nation," while Russia was an imperialist country, an "oppressor nation." In the Russian Revolution the proletariat had to conquer only a single class, its own native bourgeois-imperialist class, while the Chinese revolution had to contend with an indigenous enemy of dual personality—both its own nascent bourgeoisie and the entrenched interests of foreign imperialism. Theoretically, in the beginning, the Chinese Communists expected this dual nature of their enemy to be offset by the dual nature of their own assault, which would be aided by their "proletarian allies" of the world, and the "toilers of the U.S.S.R."

Nearly half of all the industrial workers of China huddled in Shanghai, under the gunboats of the world's great powers. In Tientsin, Tsingtao, Shanghai, Hankow, Hongkong, Kowloon, and other spheres of imperialism were probably three-quarters of all the industrial workers of China. Shanghai provided the classic prototype. Here were British, American, French, Japanese, Italian, *and Chinese* soldiers, sailors, and police, all the forces of world imperialism combined with native gangsterism and the comprador bourgeoisie, the most degenerate elements in Chinese society, "cooperating" in wielding the truncheon over the unarmed workers.

Rights of freedom of speech, assembly, or organization were denied these workers. Mobilization of the industrial proletariat in China for political action was hardly conceivable *as long as the dual system of native and foreign policing power was maintained.* Only once in history had it been broken—in 1927—when for a few days Chiang Kai-shek made use of the workers to secure his victory over the northern warlords. But immediately afterwards they were suppressed in one of the demoralizing bloodbaths of history, with the sanctification of the foreign powers and the financial help of foreign capitalists.

---

1. Mao Tse-tung *et al.*
2. *Red China: President Mao Tse-tung Reports...*

因此，要在城市中举行起义，这种尝试总是注定要失败的。南京政权能够而且事实上也的确依靠外国列强在通商口岸据有的工业基地，依靠他们的军队、大炮、巡洋舰、内陆警察、内河炮艇，依靠他们的财富、报纸、宣传、特务。尽管这些强国直接参与反红军的战争的事例不多，这一点无关紧要。在必要的时候，这种行动确实发生。但是他们的主要贡献是镇压产业工人，为南京提供军火飞机，串通一气，把共产党概称为"土匪"，若无其事地否认内战的存在，使得"不干涉委员会"（像今天在西班牙那样）这个令人为难的问题根本不会出现。

由于工人从一开始就处于这种无力状态，由于在城市中没有能力赢得一个重要的工业基地，无产阶级的先进领导人不得不依靠农村地区，那里的共产主义运动一方面保持着社会主义的目标和思想，在实践中却有了一种土地革命的经济性质。在农村地区，共产党希望最后终于能积聚足够的力量可以先在一些外国势力不那么牢固的城市基地进攻南京政权[1]，然后希望在世界无产阶级的帮助下进攻外国势力在通商口岸的堡垒。

但是帝国主义强国是南京反对共产主义的客观盟友，而共产党希望从世界无产阶级那里得到的援助却没有实现。虽然在《共产国际纲领》[2]中明确地承认，像中国那样的半殖民地国家，无产阶级运动要胜利，"只有从已建立无产阶级专政的国家（即苏联）得到直接援助才有可能"，可是苏联事实上并没有给予中国同志这里所保证的"无产阶级专政的援助和支持"，在程度上与其需要相符。相反，在1927年以前苏联给予蒋介石的相当于干涉程度的庞大援助，却有援助国民党中最反动的分子上台的客观效果。当然，在1927年以后，直接援助中国共产党与苏联所采取的立场是不相容的——这是苏联国家政策的眼前需要同世界革命眼前需要发生矛盾的著名例子，因为这有引起国际战争、危及在一国建设社会主义的整个纲领的危险。尽管如此，必须指出，这个因素影响中国革命至巨。

中国共产党人被剥夺了外国盟友，继续孤军奋战，要争取"资产阶级革命的领导权"，相信国内外政治的深刻变化会带来有利于他们的新力量。他们完全弄错了。结果是引起一场长期的大动乱，为中国人民大众带来了政治分娩的一切痛楚，最后却没有生产子嗣。

---

1. 但是即使在1930年，红军攻占长沙这样一个对外国帝国主义并不十分重要的内陆战争，他们也在英、美、日炮舰的猛烈炮轰下被迫放弃。
2. 1929年伦敦。

The Nanking regime could and did count upon the security of the industrial bases held by the foreign powers in the treaty ports—and on their troops, their guns, their cruisers, and their inland police, the river gunboats—and on their wealth, their press, their propaganda, and their spies. It did not matter that instances of direct participation of these powers in actual warfare against the Red Army were few. They occurred on the occasions when such action was necessary. But their chief services were rendered by policing the industrial workers, by furnishing Nanking with munitions and airplanes, and by entering into a conspiracy which complacently denied the very existence of civil war by the simple device of calling the Communists "bandits," so that the embarrassing question of "nonintervention committees" (as in the case of Spain) was never even allowed to arise.

Communist leaders were obliged to fall back on the rural districts, where the soviet movement, while retaining the aims and ideology of proletarian class consciousness, in practice assumed a peasant-based national social revolution. In the rural areas the Reds hoped eventually to build up sufficient strength to be able to attack urban bases where foreign influence was less firmly established and later—with the help, they hoped, of the world proletariat—to invest the citadels of foreign power in the treaty ports.

But while the imperialist powers were the objective allies of the Chinese bourgeoisie against communism, the assistance that Communists expected from the world proletariat failed to materialize. Although in the *Communist International Programme*[1] it was clearly recognized that successful proletarian movements in semicolonial countries such as China "will be possible only if direct support is obtained from the countries in which the proletarian dictatorship is established" (i.e., in the U.S.S.R.), the Soviet Union in fact did not extend to the Chinese comrades the promised "assistance and support of the proletarian dictatorship" in any degree commensurate with the need. On the contrary, the great help, amounting to intervention, which the Soviet Union gave to Chiang Kai-shek until 1927 had the objective effect of assisting him into power—although, at the same time, it helped create the revolutionary opposition in the Red Army movement that arose later on. Of course, the rendering of direct aid to the Chinese Communists after 1927 became quite incompatible with the position adopted by the U.S.S.R. —for that would have been to jeopardize by the danger of international war the whole program of Socialist construction in one country. Nevertheless, it must be noted that the influence of this factor on the Chinese revolution was very great.

Deprived of material help from an outside ally, the Chinese Communists continued to struggle alone for the "hegemony of the bourgeois revolution," believing that deep changes in internal and international politics would release new forces in their favor. They were quite mistaken.

---

1. London, 1929.

南京的力量在大城市中仍相对牢固，原因已如上述，但在农村中，发展却很慢。矛盾的是——其实也是辩证的——资产阶级的农村贫血症的来源也可以推溯到南京在城市中的力量——即外国帝国主义。因为虽然帝国主义很急于要"进行合作"，防止或镇压城市暴动，或城市暴动的可能性，但同时它却在客观上——主要通过日本，远东这个制度的最大表面张力的焦点——为这种服务勒索高昂的代价，其形式就是并吞新的领土（东北、热河、察哈尔、冀东），胁迫作出新的让步，劫夺属于中国的新的财富。帝国主义侵略的这个最新阶段压在南京政府身上的负担，使国民党不可能在农村地区进行必要的资本主义"改革"——商业信贷、改进交通、集中税收和警察力量等等——其速度可以对付农村不满和农民暴动的扩散。而共产党由于执行土地革命的政策，可以满足很大一部分农民群众的要求，掌握中国一部分农村的领导权，甚至在一种几乎纯农业经济的基础上建立好几个有力的根据地。但是同时，他们在城市中却不得发展，而他们的敌人则继续以城市为根据地。

在这种情况下，共产党认为，国民党进攻苏区妨碍中国人民实现他们要驱逐日本人的"民族解放"的使命，国民党自己不愿保卫祖国证明资产阶级领导的破产。共产党的革命论点由此可见是言之有理的。但国民党老羞成怒，反唇相讥说，共产党企图推翻政府，才使他们不能抗日，而在严重的民族危机的前面继续在内地采取"赤匪"行径，妨碍了国内改革的实现。有趣的是，而且也是辩证的，这两种说法都是对的，也都是错的。中国革命现阶段的这个奇特的僵局，这个根本的软弱性，基本上就在这里。

在过去这十年内，帝国主义压力日益严重，帝国主义为了在城市中保护中国买办阶级利益所索取的代价这么高昂，颇有冲淡资产阶级和地主的政党国民党与工人和农民的政党共产党之间的阶级矛盾之势。正是由于这一原因——也因为本书前章所述及的当前形势——国民党和共产党因此在十年不停内战后，能够重新联合起来，这表现在共同抵抗日本帝国主义这个更高的基础上的必要团结。这种团结由于它的内在矛盾，不是稳定的；不是永久的；只要国内的矛盾超过了目前对外的矛盾，它就可能破裂。但是这种团结的实现，肯定结束了革命战争的时代，而揭开了一个新的时代。

The Kuomintang's power remained relatively secure in the great urban centers, for the reasons mentioned, but in the villages it developed only very slowly. Paradoxically—and dialectically—the rural anemia of the bourgeoisie was traceable to the same source as Nanking's strength in the cities—to foreign imperialism. For while imperialism was eager enough to "cooperate" in preventing or suppressing urban insurrection, or possibilities of it, at the same time it was objectively engaged—chiefly through Japan, the focus of the system's point of greatest stress in the Far East—in collecting heavy fees for this service, in the form of new annexations of territory (Manchuria, Jehol, Chahar, and east Hopei), new concessions, and new wealth belonging to China. The great burdens placed upon the Nanking Government by this newest phase of imperialist aggression made it impossible for the Kuomintang to introduce in the rural areas the necessary capitalist "reforms"—commercial banking, improved communications, centralized taxing and policing power, etc. —fast enough to suppress the spread of rural discontent and peasant rebellion. By carrying out a land revolution the Reds were able to satisfy the demands of a substantial peasant following, take the leadership of part of rural China, and even build several powerful bases on an almost purely agrarian economy. But meanwhile they could grow no stronger in the cities, on which their enemies continued to be based.

In this situation, the Communists argued that the Kuomintang's attacks on the soviets prevented the Chinese people from fulfilling their mission of "national liberation" in driving out the Japanese, and that the Kuomintang's own unwillingness to defend the country proved the bankruptcy of its leadership. But the enraged Nationalists retorted that the Communists' attempts to overthrow the government prevented them from resisting Japan, while the continued practice of "Red banditry" in the interior, despite the grave national crisis, retarded the realization of internal reforms. And here in essence was the peculiar stalemate, the fundamental impotence of this period of the Chinese revolution.

Over this decade the imperialist pressure gradually became so severe, the Japanese price for the protection of the interests of the Chinese compradors in the cities became so excessive, that it tended to neutralize the class antagonisms between the Kuomintang, the party of the bourgeoisie and the landlords, and the Kungch'antang, the party of the workers and peasants. It was precisely because of this—and because of the immediate events described in the foregoing chapters—that the Kuomintang and the Communist Party were thus able, after a decade of ceaseless warfare, to reunite in a synthesis expressed in terms of their essential unity on the higher plane of a common antagonism against Japanese imperialism. This unity was not stable; it was not permanent; it might break up again whenever the internal denials outweighed the external ones. But it began a new era.

这十年政治经验的主要意义是什么？从理论上来说显然是：共产党不得不暂时放弃他们的"只有在无产阶级领导下"资产阶级民主运动才可能发展起来的论点。今天，它承认，**只有**"一个各阶级的联合"才能实现这些目标。其实际意义是，它清楚地承认国民党在民族革命中的**目前**领导——在这里与政权是同义词。对共产党来说，这当然可以认为是从江西时代的"一个大后退"，就像毛泽东坦率地承认的那样，因为在江西时代，他们努力要"巩固工农专政，把它扩大到全国，动员、组织、武装苏维埃和群众打这一场革命战争。"[1] 马上夺取政权的斗争是停止了。今天共产党的口号改为：拥护中央政府，在南京领导下加速和平统一，实现资产阶级民主，组织全国人民抗日。

这种让步所带来的实际好处，前文已有述及。但是要保持这些好处，共产党有什么保证呢？维持国内和平，实现民主诺言，执行抗日政策有什么保证呢？

但是在这种时期里，列宁写道，"有必要把对共产主义思想的严格忠实同作一切必要的妥协、'转变航向'、达成协议、迂回、后退等等的能力结合起来"。因此，虽然在中国共产党人中间发生了这种战略大转变，他们仍相信，现在他们有可能在一种比以前更加有利的气氛中进行竞赛。正如毛泽东所说，双方"互相作了让步"，这种交换是"有具体限度"的。

他继续说："共产党在苏区和红军问题上保持领导权，在同国民党关系中保持独立性和批评自由。在这些问题上是不能作让步的……共产党永不放弃社会主义和共产主义目标，它们将通过资产阶级民主革命阶段达到社会主义和共产主义阶段。共产党保持自己的纲领和自己的政策。[2]"

显然国民党也会充分利用共产党对自己实行新政策的好处。由于南京的权威得到中国唯一能够与之抗衡的政党的承认，蒋介石可以继续在一些军阀势力很强大的

---

1. 《红色中国：毛泽东主席……》第 11 页（1934 年伦敦）。
2. 向共产党作的报告（1937 年 4 月 10 日延安）。

At the end of a decade of class war the Communists had been forced to abandon temporarily their thesis that "only under the hegemony of the proletariat" could the bourgeois democratic movement develop. Instead it was acknowledged that *only* "a union of all classes" could achieve those purposes. Its practical significance was the clear recognition of the *present* leadership—which was here synonymous with power—of the Kuomintang in the national revolution. For the Reds it had certainly to be considered "a great retreat," as Mao Tse-tung had frankly admitted, from the days in Kiangsi, when they fought "to consolidate the workers' and peasants' dictatorship, to extend this dictatorship to the whole country, and to mobilize, organize, and arm the soviets and the masses to fight in this revolutionary war."[1] The armed struggle for immediate power had ceased. Communist slogans became these: to support the Central Government, to hasten peaceful unification under Nanking, to realize bourgeois democracy, and to organize the whole nation to oppose Japan.

Practical gains resulting from these concessions have already been discussed. But what guarantees had the Communists that these gains could be held? What guarantees were there that the internal peace would be maintained, that the promised democracy would be realized, that a policy of resistance to Japan would last?

In such periods "it is necessary," wrote Lenin, "to combine the strictest loyalty to the ideas of communism with the ability to make all necessary compromises, to 'tack,' to make agreements, zigzags, retreats, and so on." And thus, although among the Chinese Communists there was this great shift in strategy, still they believed it was now possible to conduct the contest in a much more favorable atmosphere than in the past. There had been an "exchange of concessions," as Mao Tse-tung said, and an exchange to which "there are definite limits."

He continued: "The Communist Party retains the leadership on problems in the soviet districts and the Red Army, and retains its independence and freedom of criticism in its relations with the Kuomintang. On these points no concessions can be made . . . . The Communist Party will never abandon its aims of socialism and communism, it will still pass through the stage of democratic revolution of the bourgeoisie to attain the stages of socialism and communism. The Communist Party retains its own program and its own policies."

Quite clearly the Kuomintang would utilize to the fullest extent the benefits of the new Communist policy toward itself. With Nanking's authority recognized by the only political party in China capable of challenging it, Chiang Kai-shek would continue to extend his military and economic power in peripheral areas where warlord influence was still strong,

---

1. *Red China: President Mao Tse-tung Reports*..., p. 11.

边缘地区，例如广西、云南、贵州、四川，扩大自己的军事和经济权力。他在共产党周围改善了自己的军事地位以后，就可以同时从共产党那里得到政治上的让步作为他暂时容忍的交换条件。最后，他希望靠巧妙地兼而采取政治和经济策略，在政治上削弱他们，在时机成熟可以最后要求他们完全投降（他无疑仍希望做到这一点）时，他可以把红军孤立起来，利用他们的内部政治分歧来分化他们，把顽固的残部作为纯粹地方军事问题来加以解决。

对此，共产党丝毫不抱幻想。他们同样地也并不以为自己如不积极争取，"民主"的诺言或者反帝运动就会实现。他们决不会放弃实现充分民主和反帝的口号，他们在维护这两个口号时，不惜作出政治上的小让步，因为他们相信，他们的根本政治基础是摧毁不了的。当然，历史上从来没有一个独裁政党出让过一点点政治权力给人民，除非是在极大的压力之下，国民党也不会是例外。如果不是由于这十年来存在着共产党反对派，要实现现在快要在望的那种程度的"民主"也是不可能的。的确，如果没有这种反对派，"民主"就没有必要，现在中国出现的那种程度的中央集权的国家政权也是不可想象的。因为民主政体的发展，就像现代国家本身的成长一样，是一种需要获得权力和体制的表现，以便在这种权力和体制之内调和资本主义社会的基本上不可调和的矛盾——基本阶级对立。这就是资产阶级民主的最简单的说明。

这种矛盾在中国并没有消退，而是在迅速增长，只要这种矛盾保持尖锐化，国家就不能忽视。国内和平的实现本身就必不可免地使得南京方面要更广泛地有各社会阶层的代表，如果这种国内和平要继续保持的话。这并不是说国民党可能真诚地实现资产阶级民主，允许共产党在公开竞选中同自己竞争，这样签发自己的死刑判决书（因为到处都承认，单单农民的选票就可以使共产党获得压倒优势的多数），尽管这是共产党和其他政党的要求，他们并且会继续这么进行宣传鼓动。但是这的确意味着，一小撮垄断国家经济和警察力量的少数人不得不承认大多数人的一些要求。同意苏区代表作为一个地区出席国民大会就是一个迹象。

经济、政治、社会利益的向心发展，所谓"统一"的过程——产生这个制度的一些措施本身——为了本身的存在，同时也要求越来越多的集团把注意力集中于中央，以解决不可解决的难题——阶级利益的日益加深的冲突。南京越是具有代表全国不同的更加广泛的阶级利益的倾向——它越是接近于实现民主——它越是要被迫寻求一种通过恢复国家主权以求自保的办法。

areas such as Kwangsi, Yunnan, Kweichow, and Szechuan. Improving his military position all around the Reds, he would meanwhile extract political concessions from them in return for his temporary toleration. Eventually, by skillful combination of political and economic tactics, he hoped so to weaken them politically that, when the moment was right for the final demand of their complete surrender (which he undoubtedly still aspired to secure), he might isolate the Red Army, fragmentize it on the basis of internal political dissensions, and deal with the recalcitrant remnant as a purely regional military problem.

The Reds were under no delusions about that. Likewise they were under no delusions that the promise of "democracy" could be fulfilled without a continued active opposition of their own. No party of dictatorship in history ever yielded up its power except under the heaviest pressure, and the Kuomintang would prove no exception. The achievement of even the measure of "democracy" now in prospect would have been impossible without the ten-year presence of an armed Opposition. Indeed, without that Opposition no "democracy" would have been necessary, and no state power with the degree of centralization which we now began to witness in China would have been conceivable. For the growth of popular government was, like the maturing of the modern state itself, a manifestation of the need for a power and mechanism in which to attempt to reconcile contradictions inherent in capitalist society—the basic class antagonisms.

These contradictions were not diminishing in China, but rapidly increasing, and, to the extent that they sharpened, the state had to take recognition of them. The achievement of internal peace itself made it inevitable, if that internal peace were to last, that Nanking reflect a wider representation of social stratifications. That did not mean that there was any likelihood of the Kuomintang quietly signing its own death warrant by genuinely realizing bourgeois democracy, and by permitting the Communist Party to compete with it in open election campaigning (for it was quite possible that the vote of the peasantry alone would have given the Communists an overwhelming majority), although that is what the Communists and other parties demanded, and would continue to agitate for. But it did mean that some recognition of peasant demands would have to be made by the tiny minority which monopolized the state economy and policing power. The tentative concession of representation of the soviet areas in the National Congress was an indication of that.

The centripetal spread of economic, political, and social interests, the process of so-called "unification"—the very measures which created the system—at the same time required, for their own preservation, that ever widening groups be focused in the center in an attempt to resolve the insoluble—the deepening conflict of class interests. And the more Nanking tended to represent different and wider class interests throughout the country—the nearer it came to achieving democracy—the more it was forced to seek a solution of self-survival by resistance to the increasingly greedy demands of Japan.

因此，共产党扩大影响、防止将来受到"围剿"的保证，在共产党人看来，是中国的经济、社会、政治有机关系中所固有的——正是这种关系才造成了目前这样的形势。这些保证首先是在武装的和非武装的群众中间普遍地要求继续保持国内和平，改善生活，实现民主，争取民族自由。其次，共产党的"保证"在于它能够对全国争取实现这种要求的运动继续提供领导，在于共产党的实际军事和政治的战斗力量。第三，它依靠中国人民这十年来的政治经验，这经验证明，在资产阶级和无产阶级联合起来的反帝斗争中需要从历史上暂时埋葬阶级分歧。

1937年春，日本对南京压力稍减，侵略内蒙古暂停，英日开始会商"在华合作"，英国政府希望调停中日争执和在远东导致"基本和平"，这使有些人寻思，共产党对政局估计是否错误。把整个战略建筑在中日马上必战中心前提上，是否太冒险了？他们认为，现在中国既有国内和平，共产党既已停止企图推翻国民党，日本也就真的向南京表示和解了。日本帝国主义者已认识到，他们要中国资产阶级走上投降道路操之过急，推之过远了，结果中国的内战已消灭于普遍仇日之中。他们现在已经认识到为了使中国资产阶级可以再次放手去搞国内冲突，对它实行友好新政策是明智得策的。东京和南京这样修好就能消除共产党的政治影响，因为后者是过于依靠抗战了。

但是根据力学原理，历史的洪水必须找到排泄口。它是不能强制倒流到发洪水前的渠道上去的。日本要关上闸门为时已太迟了。共产党人了解即使日本最能干的领导人认识到暂停的必要性，日本也不能在中国转而采取静止政策。共产党的这一预见，在7月8日似乎已得到卢沟桥事变的充分证实。因为在这里，日本改变心意的暂时假面具给戳破了。日本军队在北平以西10英里处的宛平县中国领土上进行"午夜演习"（这是完全非法的），自称受到中国铁路警卫人员的枪击。这一事件给了日本军队借口；它再一次表示了它的真正必要。到7月中，日本已赶调1万名左右的军队到了京津一带，并且提出了新的帝国主义要求，如予同意，等于是接受在华北成立日本的一个保护国。

共产党对这一形势的看法，对这一形势所必然引起的一触即发的事件的看法是，

The guarantees of increased Communist influence, the guarantee against future annihilation campaigns, therefore, were seen by the Communists to be inherent in the organic economic, social, and political relationships of the country—precisely those formations which had resulted in the present situation. These were, first of all, a wide popular demand among both the armed and unarmed masses for continued internal unity, for improved livelihood, for popular government, and for resistance to Japan in a common struggle for national freedom. Second, the Communist Party's "guarantees" lay in the leadership it could continue to give to the movement for those demands throughout the country, and in the actual military and political fighting strength of the Communist Party.

In the spring of 1937 the temporary diminution in Japanese pressure on China, a pause in the invasion of Inner Mongolia, the opening of Anglo-Japanese conversations for "cooperation in China," and the hopes of the British Government to mediate a Sino-Japanese agreement and a "fundamental peace" in the Far East caused some people to wonder whether the Communist estimate of the political scene was not in error. Was it not reckless gambling to pivot a strategy on the central inevitability of an early Sino-Japanese war? Now that internal peace was established in China, now that the Reds had ceased their attempts to overthrow the Kuomintang, Japan was really turning a conciliatory face to Nanking, it was argued. Japan's imperialists realized that they had pushed the Chinese bourgeoisie too far and too fast along the road of surrender, with the result that China's class war was canceled in the universal hatred of Japan. They now saw the wisdom of enforcing a new and friendly policy toward the Chinese bourgeoisie, in order to renew its freedom to engage in internal conflict. And such a Tokyo-Nanking *rapprochement* would destroy the Communists' political influence, which was too heavily based on *k'ang jih*—the "resist Japan" movement.

But history in flood must seek its outlets according to the laws of dynamics. It cannot be forced back into its preflood channels. Japan could not revert to a static policy in China even though Japan's ablest leaders realized the imperative necessity for a halt. And this Red prescience seemed fully vindicated on July 8 by the Liukochiao Incident. Japanese troops, holding "midnight maneuvers" (quite illegally) on Chinese territory at the town of Wanping, about ten miles west of Peking, claimed to have been fired on by Chinese railway guards. The incident gave the Japanese Army the pretext. By the middle of July the Japanese had rushed some 10,000 troops into the Peking-Tientsin area and had made new imperialist demands, capitulation to which would have meant virtually the acceptance of a Japanese protectorate in North China.

The Communists' conception of that situation, and of the kindling events which it must set in motion, was that the growing pressure of the whole nation for resistance, not only

全国日益要求不仅在这里进行抵抗，而且在所有发生新侵略的地方进行抵抗的压力，都会逼使蒋介石政权采取除了战争没有别的出路的立场，如果日本不改变政策、改正过去错误的话。这意味着除了战争没有别的出路。请记住，共产党认为这样一个战争不仅是争取民族独立的斗争，而且是一种革命运动，"因为在中国打败帝国主义意味着摧毁它的一个最强大的根据地"，而且因为中国革命本身的胜利"与中国人民反对日本侵略的胜利是一致的"（毛泽东语）。战争可能明天就开始。也可能一两年内还打不起来。但不会拖得太长了，根据共产党人对日本、中国和全世界政治经济上达到爆发点的紧张形势的分析，他们认为人类命运不可能再长期拖延不解决了。

共产党的预见是，在这场战争中，将有必要武装、装备、训练、动员千百万人民参加一场能够起到一举而割除帝国主义外瘤和阶级压迫内癌这一双重外科手术作用的斗争。照他们的看法，只有最广泛地动员群众，发展一支高度政治化的军队，才能进行这样一场战争。而且这样一场战争只有在最先进的革命领导之下才能**获胜**。它可以由资产阶级来发动。但只有革命的工农才能完成。一旦人民真正大规模武装和组织起来，共产党将尽一切可能来实现对日战争的决定性胜利。只要资产阶级领导抗战，他们就同资产阶级并肩前进。但是只要资产阶级发生动摇，变成"失败主义"，或有愿意屈服于日本的表现——这种倾向他们认为战争一开始遭受重大损失以后一定会马上出现的——他们就准备把领导权接过来。

南京政权当然也充分了解共产党的这些目标，就像中国一切有权有势的人一样，因此他们会寻求一切可能的妥协道路；只要能避免在国内产生后果，他们就会向日本作进一步的让步，至少在暂时是如此，除非条件十分有利，南京政权不仅能有力量开战，而且在战后仍能保持这一力量完整无损，而国内革命仍遭压制。但是共产党充分相信他们自己对于历史发展的分析，认为他们为未来航程所选择的航道是正确的，将来的事件会**迫使**南京为求自己的生存而战。他们预料南京可能继续动摇，日本可能继续多方玩弄各种手段，视当时情况需要，软硬兼施，一直到从外部来说是日本帝国主义的利益与中国的民族利益之间，从内部来说是中国和日本的群众与他们豪绅地主统治者之间的对立达到了极其尖锐的程度，一直到所有实际的克制和压迫都到了绝对不能容忍的地步，历史的障碍终于被冲垮，帝国主义所哺育的巨灾大祸，像科学怪人弗兰肯斯坦[1]一样，终于冲了出来摧毁帝国主义，像洪水般滚滚向前，

---

1. 英诗人雪莱的妻子玛丽·雪莱于1818年所著同名小说中的一个科学家，他制造了一个怪物而毁灭了自己。——译注

here but everywhere that new acts of aggression occurred, would oblige Chiang Kai-shek's regime to take a position in which, if Japan did not reverse her policies and make amends for the past, there was no way out but war. Which meant that there was no way out but war. And the Communists continued to interpret such a war not only as a struggle for national independence, but as a revolutionary movement, "because to defeat imperialism in China means the destruction of one of its most powerful bases" and because *the victory of the Chinese revolution itself* "*will correspond with the victory of the Chinese people against Japanese aggression*" (Mao Tse-tung). According to Mao Tse-tung's analysis of the breaking-point politico-economic tension in Japan, China, and throughout the world, this settlement in human destinies could not be delayed for any important length of time.

The Reds foresaw that in this war it would become necessary to arm, equip, train, and mobilize tens of millions of people in a struggle which could serve the dual surgical function of removing the external tumor of imperialism and the internal cancer of class oppression. Such a war, as they conceived it, could be conducted only by the broadest mobilization of the masses, by the development of a highly politicalized army. And such a war could be *won* only under the most advanced revolutionary leadership. It could be initiated by the bourgeoisie. It would be completed only by the revolutionary workers and peasants. Once the people were really armed and organized on an immense scale, the Communists would do everything possible to establish a decisive victory over Japan. They would march with the Kuomintang as long as it led the resistance. But they would be prepared to take over this leadership whenever the government faltered, turned "defeatist," and exhibited a willingness to submit to Japan—a tendency which they anticipated would appear soon after the first great losses of the war.

Probably the Nanking regime fully understood those objectives of the Communists, and hence they would seek out every possible road of compromise; they would, if they could avoid the internal consequences, make further concessions to Japan, at least until the odds seemed very greatly in favor of the regime's ability not only to enter a war with power, but to emerge from it with that power still intact, and with the internal revolution still in abeyance. But the Communists were sufficiently content with their own analysis of the course of history behind them to be satisfied with the chart of direction which they had chosen for the voyage ahead, through events which would *compel* Nanking to make a stand for its own survival. They foresaw that Nanking might continue to vacillate, that Japan might continue to feint and maneuver in myriad ways, until the utmost agony of antagonism was reached between the interests of Japanese imperialism and the national interests of China externally, and between the Chinese and Japanese masses and their landlord-gentry rulers internally, until the moment when all the physical restraints and oppressions became utterly intolerable, the barriers of history broke down, the mighty catastrophe bred by imperialism was set loose, Frankenstein-like, to destroy imperialism,

一发不可收拾。

因此，只有帝国主义会摧毁帝国主义，因为只有一场帝国主义大战——这场大战几乎肯定具有世界大战的性质——才会把力量解放出来，使得亚洲的各国群众得到他们的武装、训练、政治经验、组织自由、国内警察力量的致命削弱，这都是他们为了要在较近的将来革命成功取得政权所必要的条件。即使到了那个时候，"武装起来的群众"是否会跟随共产党的领导走向最后胜利也取决于许多可变的不可预料的因素——首先是国内的因素，但是也有像美、英、法、德、意等国的东方政策这样的因素。

这，我认为就是共产党对未来局势的看法。人们不一定会全部同意这种看法，但是至少有一点是肯定的，那就是列宁在20多年以前写过的话仍是有效的："不论伟大的中国革命——各种各样的'文明的'鬣狗都在磨牙——的命运如何，世界上没有力量能够在亚洲恢复以前的农奴制度，也不能够在地球的表面上抹去亚洲和半亚洲国家人民群众的英勇的民主政体。"

还有一点看来也是肯定的。中国已有成千上万的青年为了民主社会主义思想捐躯牺牲，这种思想或者这种思想的背后动力，都是不容摧毁的。中国社会革命运动可能遭受挫折，可能暂时退却，可能有一个时候看来好像奄奄一息，可能为了适应当前的需要和目标而在策略上作重大的修改，可能甚至有一个时期隐没无闻，被迫转入地下，但它不仅一定会继续成长，而且在一起一伏之中，最后终于会获得胜利，原因很简单（正如本书所证明的一样，如果说它证明了什么的话），产生中国社会革命运动的基本条件本身包含着这个运动必胜的有力因素。

and *le déluge* swept forward.

Thus "capitalism digs its own grave," thus imperialism would destroy imperialism, in that only a great imperialist war would release the forces that could bring to the Asian masses the arms, the training, the political experience, the freedom of organization, and the mortal weakening of the internal policing power which were the necessary accessories for any conceivably successful revolutionary ascent to power in the relatively near future. Whether or not, even then, the "armed masses" were likely to follow Communist leadership with final success depended upon many variable and unpredictable factors—internal factors first of all, but such factors also as the policies in the East of America, Great Britain, France, Germany, and Italy, and to the very greatest extent the policies of the U.S.S.R.

And that, I believed, was the contour of the Communist picture of the future as China waited for Japan to strike. One might not follow all of it, but this at least seemed certain—that what Lenin had written more than twenty years before was still true: "Whatever may be the fate of the great Chinese revolution, against which various 'civilized' hyenas are now sharpening their teeth, no forces in the world will restore the old serfdom in Asia, nor erase from the face of the earth the heroic democracy of the popular masses in the Asiatic and semi-Asiatic countries."

And another thing seemed equally certain. Neither could the democratic Socialist ideas for which tens of thousands of youths had already died in China, nor the energies behind them, be destroyed. The movement for social revolution in China might suffer defeats, might temporarily retreat, might for a time seem to languish, might make wide changes in tactics to fit immediate necessities and aims, might even for a period be submerged, be forced underground, but it would not only continue to mature; in one mutation or another it would eventually win, simply because (as this book proves, if it proves anything) the basic conditions which had given it birth carried within themselves the dynamic necessity for its triumph.

后记（1944 年）[1]

自从 1937 年 7 月卢沟桥事件爆发、日本开始企图占领中国以来的 7 年间，本书中的中国人的情形如何呢？首先，时间的流逝已经证明了毛泽东和其他共产党领导人的判断，实现全民族的联合抗日比革命运动的其他任何当前目标都重要。

在这一点上，西安事变现在似乎是当代中国历史上一个具有决定性意义的事件。很少有人记得就在西安事变之前，中国曾经距离反共产国际协约有多么近，但现在十分明白的是，东京和南京最后分道扬镳的时刻已经来到。西安确保了中国在即将到来的世界斗争中将站立在反法西斯的一边。

从其他方面来看，时间已证明了本书故事中的革命者所为之战斗和牺牲的思想的正确性。在这场现在行将结束的漫长磨难中，它为幸存者及其大大增加的追随者带来了巨大的声望。一场革命运动要求其领导者必须在知道即将会发生什么方面具有稍稍超过其他人的能力；而在这个方面，毛泽东已经是如此的成功，数以百万计的中国人对他的判断的信任程度丝毫不亚于蒋介石。

无论他们可能会对共产党人怀有什么样的感觉以及他们现在代表着哪一派，大多数中国人都会承认毛泽东准确地分析了有关的国内、国际各方势力，正确地描绘了未来时局的大体走向。内战的确结束了，共产党和红军不仅存活了下来，而且还得到了壮大。毛泽东关于战争发展到一定阶段部分国民党人会背叛中国而成为日本人的傀儡的说法长期以来令人耿耿于怀；但是在地位仅次于蒋总司令的国民党二把手汪精卫叛变之后，谁都不能否认毛泽东对中央政府中的对立成分有着深刻的理解。

---

1. 节选自《西行漫记》（1944 年现代图书馆版）。

Epilogue (1944)[1]

What had happened to the Chinese of this book in seven years since the Liukochiao Incident, when Japan began her attempt to conquer China in July, 1937? For one thing, the passage of time had vindicated the judgment of Mao Tse-tung and other Communist leaders that the achievement of national unity for the struggle against Japan was more important than any other immediate objective of the revolutionary movement.

In this perspective the Sian Incident now loomed as a happening of decisive importance in contemporary Chinese history. Few remembered how close China came to adherence to the Anti-Comintern pact, just before the Sian affair, but it was now quite clear that after it there came the final parting of the ways between Tokyo and Nanking. Sian made certain that China would be on the anti-Fascist side of the coming world struggle.

In other respects time had confirmed the validity of the ideas for which the revolutionaries whose stories were told in these pages had fought and died. It had brought immense prestige to the survivors, and to their greatly increased following, during the long ordeal now drawing to a close. A revolutionary movement demands of its leader the ability to know a little ahead of anyone else what is going to happen; and in this respect Mao Tse-tung had been so successful that millions of Chinese now reposed as much confidence in his judgment as in that of Chiang Kai-shek.

However they might feel about the Communists and what they now represented, most Chinese would admit that Mao Tse-tung accurately analyzed the internal and international forces involved, and correctly depicted the general shape of events to come. Civil war did end and the Communist Party and the Red Army not only survived but were strengthened. Mao's suggestion that at a certain stage in the war part of the Kuomintang would betray China and turn puppet for the Japanese was long resented; but after the defection of Wang Ching-wei, deputy leader of the KMT and second only to the Generalissimo, it could not be denied that Mao had intimately understood the contradictory elements in the Central Government.

---

1. Condensed from *RSOC* (Modern Library edition, 1944).

此外，毛泽东预测说这场战争将会持久而艰难，历史上武装斗争的领导人不向其追随者许诺速胜者凤毛麟角，毛泽东肯定是其中之一。他的坦率事先消除了那种折磨着支离破碎的梦幻的失败主义情绪。另一方面，毛泽东正确地估计了进行革命动员后以中国的人力和物资资源为后盾的强大的持久力，从而帮助增强了人们更为持久的自信。他指明了中国在民族战争融入世界战争之前为了支撑下去而将不得不采取的那种战略和策略，这场世界战争包括日本对英国人、法国人、荷兰人以及美国人的进攻，他警告说世界战争是不可避免的，虽然当时许多欧洲人和美国人并不这么认为。

到 1944 年，中国共产党在华北地区领导的游击组织已成为世界上最大的游击组织。从长江流域到蒙古草原，再到东北地区南部的山山水水，日本封锁线后面的成千上万的村庄构成了这场"人民战争"的格局。它的组织者是主要由第十八集团军——由八路军和新四军合并而成[1]——启发和训练出来的青年。这些部队由朱德、彭德怀以及先前中国红军的其他老战士领导，历经 17 年艰苦卓绝的内战和民族战争，他们创造了令人惊叹的生存与壮大的记录。

1943 年访问过游击区的外国观察家估计，在日本封锁线之后，第十八集团军组织起来进行过粗略训练的民兵人数高达 700 万左右。这些是主力作战部队的预备队。此外，据说还有大约 1,200 万各类抗日团体成员，他们帮助为正规军提供衣服、食物、住所、装备以及交通，是他们的眼睛和耳朵。官方资料显示，游击战渗透进了华北的 455 个县和 52,800 个村庄，涉及人口超过了 6,000 万。有 3/5 到 2/3 的所谓沦陷区在大多数时间都掌握在游击队手中。

将近 7 年的时间，日本人一直在企图消灭这些不知疲倦的军队。1937 年，八路军正规军人数才刚刚 5 万人，仅仅吸引了几个师的日军。但是这支先锋部队向四面八方扩张。1944 年，中国本土（不包括东北）35 万日军中半数以上和约 20 万伪军都在设防地区疲于应付十八集团军，抵挡其讨伐行动。日本军事报告将其兵力定为 50 至 60 万人。

被日军占领的省份的总面积有法国的 3 倍大，游击队在每个省都已经建立起了村级和县级委员会。他们在根据地建立了 4 个"边区"政府，这些根据地除了短暂的失守之外，整个战争期间一直为游击队所控制。每个边区政府都代表着几个相邻省份的解放区。这些敌后政权几乎行使着正规政府的所有职能。它们有自己的邮政系统和无

---

1. 与史实有出入。——编注

Again, Mao predicted that the war would be long and difficult, and this must be one of the few instances in history in which an advocate of armed struggle did not promise his adherents a speedy triumph. His candor disarmed in advance the kind of defeatism that preys upon shattered illusions. On the other hand Mao helped to build up a more durable self-confidence in the nation by correctly estimating the enormous staying power guaranteed by China's own human and material resources, when mobilized in a revolutionary way. And he indicated the kind of strategy and tactics which China would have to adopt to hold on until the national war merged with the world war, including Japanese attacks on the British, the French, the Dutch, and the Americans, which he warned were inevitable in a period when many Europeans and Americans thought otherwise.

By 1944 the Chinese Communists provided the leadership in North China for what was much the largest guerrilla organization in the world. Stretching from the Yangtze Valley to the Mongolian steppe, and to the mountains and rivers of southern Manchuria, thousands of villages behind the Japanese lines made up the pattern of this "people's war." Its organizers were youths chiefly inspired and trained by the Eighteenth Group Army—the combined Eighth Route and New Fourth armies. These forces were led by Chu Teh, P'eng Teh-huai, and other veterans of the former Red Army of China, who now had behind them an amazing record of survival and growth through seventeen years of difficult civil and national war.

Foreign observers who visited the guerrilla districts in 1943 estimated that behind the Japanese lines the Eighteenth Group Army had organized and given crude training to militia numbering about 7,000,000 people. These were the reserves of the main fighting units. In addition, there were said to be some 12,000,000 members of various anti-Japanese associations which helped to clothe, feed, house, equip, and transport the regular troops, and were their eyes and ears. Official data showed partisan penetration in 455 *hsien*, or counties, of North China and in 52,800 villages, with a population of more than 60,000,000. From three-fifths to two-thirds of the so-called conquered territory was in guerrilla hands most of the time.

For nearly seven years the Japanese had been trying to exterminate these tireless enemies. Eighth Route regulars numbered hardly 50,000 men in 1937, and diverted only a few divisions of Japanese troops. But that vanguard multiplied in every direction. In 1944 more than half of Japan's 350,000 troops in China proper (excluding Manchuria) and some 200,000 puppet troops were occupied in defending fortified areas against the Eighteenth Group Army and in fighting punitive actions against it. Japanese military reports put its strength at from 500,000 to 600,000.

In every one of the provinces occupied by the Japanese, which covered an area three times the size of France, partisans had set up village and county councils. They had established four "border" governments in bases held throughout the war, except for brief intervals; and each of these regional governments represented liberated areas of several neighboring provinces. These behind-the-lines regimes performed nearly all the functions of normal administration. They had their own postal

线电通讯。它们发行自己的报纸、杂志和书籍。它们维持着庞大的学校系统，实施了一部经过改良的法律，承认男女平等，给予成年人选举权。它们监管租金，征税，控制贸易，发行货币，开办工业，运营着许多实验农场，发放农业信贷，实行粮食供给制，在少数几个地区还开展了相当大的造林计划。

1944年日军在华所控制的防线在1939年末之前便已经稳定了下来。敌人最初侵入沦陷省份的时候，国民党政府的大多数老官僚和军队都撤到了西部和南方。在他们身后，行政管理机构分崩离析。在城市里，它被日本人及其中国傀儡所取代，但是在敌人驻军缝隙中的偏远城镇和村庄却存在着一种政治真空。先前的中国红军便开进了这片暂时的真空——随之而来的是武器、教师和对人民力量的信任。

这种行动开始时得到了蒋总司令的默许。这之所以可能，首先是因为，正如我们已看到的，少帅张学良稍早一些时候为了劝说总司令停止与红军作战并与其联合抗日，而在西安对他进行的"扣留"。日本侵入华北之后，国共双方达成了一项协议，结束了十年内战。协议规定红军编入国民革命军，取消苏维埃政府，代之以一个代表所有阶层的政府，共产党放弃阶级斗争的口号，停止没收和重新分配土地。北方的红军放弃了红旗和红星，接受了"八路军"的番号。在上海东南方，叶挺和项英两位将军率领的红军余部于1938年被改编为"新四军"。[1]

国共两党这时都宣称自己是中华民国缔造者孙逸仙博士的合法继承人。在革命初期双方都支持过他。然而，即便在1937年以后，双方都没有就实践孙逸仙"民族、民权、民生"的三民主义达成协议。共产党仍然认为孙逸仙是一位社会主义革命者，要求对他的三民主义进行激进的阐释。简而言之，他们想要进行的是"一场彻底的民主革命"，均田地，实现普选权，建立立宪政府，确立人民的权力，即给予共产党权力，最终实现"无产阶级专政"。由于国民党在国内所获得的支持仍然主要来自地主阶级，它自然反对激进的土地革命。大体而言，它想要维持现有的经济和政治关系的完整性，将自己的专政凌驾于中国陈旧的半封建制度之上。如果它承认了其他党派的

---

1. 有关红军改编和1937—1941年期间游击战争的发展的描述，参见埃德加·斯诺所著的《为亚洲而战》（1941年纽约）。

system and radio communications. They published their own newspapers, magazines, and books. They maintained an extensive system of schools and enforced a reformed legal code recognizing sex equality and adult suffrage. They regulated rents, collected taxes, controlled trade and issued currency, operated industries, maintained a number of experimental farms, extended agricultural credit, had a grain-rationing system, and in several places had undertaken fairly large afforestation projects.

The defense perimeter held by Japanese troops in China in 1944 was already stabilized before the end of 1939. When the enemy originally moved into the conquered provinces most of the old officials of the Kuomintang Government, as well as its troops, withdrew to the West and South. Behind them the administrative bureaucracy collapsed. In the cities it was replaced by Japanese and their Chinese puppets, but a kind of political vacuum existed in the hinterland towns and villages, the interstices between enemy garrisons. Into that temporary vacuum moved the former Red Army of China—with arms, with teachers, and with faith in the people's strength.

This movement began with the Generalissimo's acquiescence. It was made possible first of all, as we have seen, by Marshal Chang Hsueh-liang's earlier "detention" of the Generalissimo at Sian, in order to persuade him to stop fighting the Reds and unite with them against Japan. After the Japanese invaded North China, an agreement was reached which ended a decade of civil war. This provided that the Red Army should be incorporated into the national forces, that the soviets should be abolished in favor of a government in which all classes would be represented, and that the Communists would abandon the slogans of class warfare and cease confiscating and redistributing the land. The northern Red forces dropped the Red flag and the Red star and accepted the designation "Eighth Route Army." Southeast of Shanghai other Red remnants under Generals Yeh T'ing and Hsiang Ying were regrouped in 1938 as the "New Fourth Army."[1]

Both the Kuomintang and the Kungch'antang now claimed to be the legitimate heirs of Dr. Sun Yat-sen, founder of the Chinese Republic. Both supported him in the early days of the revolution. Even after 1937, however, there was no agreement over the practical application of Sun Yat-sen's Three Principles of "nationalism, livelihood and democracy." The Communists still regarded Sun as a social revolutionary and demanded a radical interpretation of his principles. Briefly, they wanted a "thoroughgoing democratic revolution," with equalization of land ownership, universal suffrage, and constitutional government establishing the people's power, by which they meant the Communist Party and, ultimately, a "proletarian dictatorship." Since the Kuomintang still drew its chief internal support from the landlord class, it was naturally opposed to radical land reform. In general it wanted to keep economic and political relationships intact and to superimpose its dictatorship on the old Chinese semifeudal structure. If it acknowledged the legality of other parties and their conflicting

---

1. See Edgar Snow, *The Battle for Asia* (New York, 1941), for an account of the reorganization of the Red Army and growth of partisan warfare from 1937 to 1941.

合法性及它们彼此冲突的阐释,尤其是如果它认可了成人选举权,那么几乎可以肯定这个制度将会被推翻。

虽然阶级权力、国家和社会的最终形式等问题出现了短暂的僵持,但是当日本入侵后,共产党和国民党还是至少就"民族主义"达成了共识。红军之后便听从总司令的军令了。1937年,他把他们派往华北前线,许多国民党领导人满以为他们会被日本的进攻所吞噬。然而,红军并没有像北方军阀的军队那样土崩瓦解。他们遭受了攻击,在城市中遭到了挫败,但是他们并没有退却,也没有投降,而是后撤到了村庄和群山之间继续战斗。

北方各省都有经验丰富的游击领导人和政治组织者秘密渗入,逃离城市的难民越来越多,红军很快便从中招募了弥足珍贵的新鲜血液:学生、工人以及各行各业的男男女女,其中包括一些属于非共产党的开明政党的知识分子,他们长期遭受中日当局的双重压迫。被切断了后路的中国战败军队,整师整师地投奔到红军旗下。在华北,国民党正规军被日本逐出之后,民团失去了中央指示和凝聚力。他们的地主豪绅主子要么逃走了,要么留了下来与日本人做交易,民团只好要么成为日本人的伪军,要么逃往蒋统区,要么就加入共产党领导的游击队。**日本人帮了共产党的大忙,他们摧毁或者削弱了维持农村地主豪绅和城市有产者之间的旧有联盟的整个农村警察权力系统。**起初,正是由于这个警察系统的解体,而不是对日作战的胜利,才使得八路军的迅速扩张成为可能。然而,他们的枪支数量稳步增长。到了1939年,他们的要塞已经牢不可破,日军被迫对他们发起一场声势浩大的正式进攻。从此每半年日军便进行一次这样的进攻。

第一个游击政权完全位于沦陷区内部,建立在河东山西东北部的山区,包括的地区向北远至热河(或者内蒙古)。另一个政权的首府位于山西东南部,它指挥着在已被收复的横贯河北南部、山东和向东直至黄海的300英里的土地上的行动。在上海以北的苏北地区还有第三个边区,由新四军的近10万大军控制着。第四个地方政府建立在汉口以上长江以北的多山的乡村,在这里安徽和湖北的边界环绕着河南的最南端。

用于组织人民的政治和军事方法大量地借鉴在陕北老苏区时所形成的模式。1937年,苏维埃政府被取消,"陕甘宁边区政府"取而代之,被誉为"中国游击战之母"的延安城成为其首府。新政府成立后,我于1939年重访延安。这次延安之行成了外国

interpretations, especially if it conceded adult suffrage, that structure would almost certainly be overthrown.

While questions of class power and of the ultimate form of the state and society remained in momentary abeyance, the Communists and Nationalists at least agreed upon the principle of "nationalism" when Japan invaded the country. The Reds then took their military orders from the Generalissimo. In 1937 he sent them into the battle line in North China, where many Kuomintang leaders confidently expected them to be swallowed up in the Japanese drive. They did not disintegrate in that way, however, as some of the northern warlord armies did. They met the attack and were defeated in the cities, but instead of retreating or surrendering they withdrew to the villages and hills and continued fighting.

Infiltrating all the northern provinces with experienced partisan leaders and political organizers, they soon enlisted valuable reinforcements from a thickening stream of refugees fleeing from the cities: students, workers, and various professional men and women, including some intellectuals belonging to the non-Communist liberal political parties, long suppressed by both the Chinese and Japanese regimes. Cut off from the rear, whole divisions of defeated Chinese troops came under Red leadership. In North China the *min-t'uan* lost its central direction and cohesion when Nationalist regulars were driven out by Japan. Their landlord-gentry paymasters fled, or stayed to make deals with the Japanese, and the militia had to become puppet troops for the Japanese, or flee to Chiang Kai-shek's territory, or join the Communist-led partisans. *Japan served the Communists by destroying or demoralizing the whole rural police-power system with which the old rural landlord-gentry alliance with the urban property owners had been maintained.* At the outset it was the disintegration of that police system, rather than victories over the Japanese, that made possible the rapid expansion of the Eighth Route Army. Their rifle power, however, steadily increased. By 1939 their strongholds had become so formidable that the Japanese were compelled to launch a full-dress offensive against them. They went on doing so semiannually from then on.

The first partisan regime entirely inside occupied territory was set up in the mountains of northeastern Shansi, east of the Yellow River, and included areas as far north as Jehol, or Inner Mongolia. Another regime, with its capital in southeast Shansi, directed operations in recovered territory which stretched for over 300 miles across southern Hopei and Shantung eastward to the Yellow Sea. There was a third border region centering in northern Kiangsu, north of Shanghai, which was controlled by the New Fourth Army, with nearly 100,000 troops. A fourth regional government was established in the mountainous country north of the Yangtze River above Hankow, where the borders of Anhui and Hupeh enclose the southern extremity of Honan.

Political and military methods used to organize the people borrowed heavily from the pattern developed in the old soviet districts of north Shensi. After the Soviet Government was abolished in 1937, a "Shensi-Kansu-Ninghsia Border Area Government" took its place and the town of Yenan, the so-called "mother of the Chinese partisans," became its capital. I revisited Yenan in 1939, after

记者造访延安的最后一次，直到1944年才被打破，因为不久之后这个地区便被国民党的军事封锁隔绝了与外界的联系。

在黄河对岸，敌后社会、政治、经济生活的组织自然比延安更为艰难，但是即便没有始终取得同等程度的胜利，不过大体上目标还是相当的。虽然"自由中国"的报纸记者无法调查山西和河北等地区，但是在北平众多外国人逃离了日本人的控制，一路南下穿过了游击区，他们相当详尽地描述了这种成功的体制。在这些观察人士中，有一位便是著名的美国教会学校燕京大学的威廉·班德教授，我在1934至1935年间在燕京大学教课时认识的他。另一位是林迈可，也是燕京大学的教授，他关于游击区情况的报告于1944年发表在《美亚》杂志上。[1] 这是一时间到达外部世界的关于游击区的最为详尽的报告，它被作者的父亲A.D.林赛（牛津大学贝列尔学院院长）公开出版。

据林迈可教授称，游击区政府是从由人民及其组织直接提名的候选人中选举出来的。中国游击队的目标是建立一个包含所有群体的统一战线，因此在任何选举出来的机构中共产党都将自己的人数限制在总数的1/3。这种奇特的政策得到了大力贯彻，据林迈可称。其目的是在政府中给地主（外居地主除外）和商人以代表权，但是最重要的政治领导人的发展要在贫农和工人中进行。按照游击队领导的说法，这叫做"通过实行民主进行民主教育"。

但是，在群众团体中对共产党领导人数并没有限制；这些团体是游击队的中坚生命力的所在。它们包括农民、工人、青年、儿童、妇女等人群的独立协会，各个协会的会员人数都达到了数百万。最重要的是，所有这类组织都是自卫团、民兵和少年先锋队。这些简单的基础军事组织在地方上支持着第十八集团军的主力。

花旗银行北平分行的前任经理G.马特尔·霍尔是最后一个从日本控制区逃出并穿越游击区的美国人。他告诉我他几乎没有其他方式能说明游击队领导人在对待农民方面的成功，"只有通过他们自己的高尚廉洁、他们饱满的爱国热情、他们对实践民主的全心投入、他们对普通人民的信任、他们为激发他们行动起来而作出的不懈努力以及责任感。"

对日本人的共同仇恨为这些狂热者提供了利用人民的爱国热情的氛围，但是伴随

---

1. 1944年3月31日至4月14日纽约。

the new government was established. It remained until 1944 the last trip made there by any foreign newspaper correspondent, for soon afterwards the region was cut off by the Kuomintang's military blockade.

On the other side of the Yellow River, behind Japanese lines, the organization of the social, political, and economic life was naturally more difficult than in Yenan, but in general the goals, if not always the degree of success achieved, were comparable. Although newspaper correspondents in Free China were not able to investigate the Shansi and Hopei areas, the various foreigners who escaped from the Japanese in Peking and made their way southward across the guerrilla territory gave fairly complete pictures of the system which prevailed. Among these observers was Professor William Band, of the famous American missionary institution, Yenching University, whom I knew when I lectured there in 1934—1935. Another was Professor Michael Lindsay, also of Yenching, whose report of conditions there was published in *Amerasia* magazine in 1944.[1] The most comprehensive account of the partisan areas to reach the outside world for some time, it was released for publication by the author's father, A. D. Lindsay, Master of Balliol College, Oxford.

According to Professor Lindsay, the partisan governments were elected from candidates nominated directly by the people and their organizations. The Chinese partisans aimed to establish a united front of all groups and hence the Communist Party limited its own members to one-third of the total of any elected body. This peculiar policy was vigorously enforced, according to Lindsay. The purpose was to give representation in the government to both landowners (except absentee landlords) and merchants, but above all to develop political leaders among the poor peasants and workers. It was "education in democracy by practicing democracy," according to the partisan leaders.

In the mass organizations there were no limitations on Communist leadership, however; and these organizations were the guerrillas' sinew and life. They included separate unions or associations for farmers, workers, youth, children, and women, and membership in each ran into the millions. Most important of all such organizations were the self-defense corps, the militia, and the Young Vanguards. These were crude but basic military organizations which locally supported the Eighteenth Group Army's main forces.

G. Martel Hall, former manager of the National City Bank in Peking, who was the last American to escape from the Japanese across the partisan areas, told me that there was simply no other way he could explain the success of the partisan leaders with the peasants, "except through their own incorruptibility and honesty, their energetic patriotism, their devotion to practical democracy, their faith in the common people, and the continuous effort they made to arouse them to action and responsibility."

Mutual hatred of the Japanese provided the atmosphere in which these zealots exploited the

---

1. New York, March 31 and April 14, 1944.

政治改革推出的是经济和社会变革。在妇女问题上,像一夫一妻制、婚龄男女婚姻自由、免费义务教育以及18岁即拥有选举权这样的法律的实施赢得了惊人的反响。林迈可教授说,游击区的妇女组织的成员在300万以上。许多妇女已被选入村级和镇级委员会,大批年轻姑娘担负着严肃的政治和军事责任。

小学系统在所有的"永久性"游击根据地广泛存在,理论上实行免费义务教育,但是如果由于贫困的话,事实上是鲜有机会实现的。不过在一些地方,高达80%的学龄儿童都识字。基本的改革是迅速削减地租。外居地主的土地为大家共同耕种;目标是耕种所有可以耕种的土地。税收主要以谷物的形式征收,其水平保持在日本人所征收的10%左右。消费者、销售和工业合作社非常普遍。林迈可称山西有4,000多个合作社,而单单在河北中部就有5,000个。

游击组织所走的每一步都伴随着难以想象的艰辛。[1]诚然日本人没能摧毁游击力量,也没能阻止它们的壮大,他们针对游击队进行了差不多数千次大小规模的扫荡。他们到处劫掠,烧毁了成千上万座村庄,奸淫妇女,屠杀了无数平民,在一片恐怖气氛中试图荡清所有抵抗的念头。游击队总是能够想方设法克服这些策略所产生的瓦解士气的后果,但是也并非没有付出像俄国所忍受的那种惨重的牺牲。诚然日本人还无力控制他们在华北铁路和公路沿线驻军范围以外很远地方的任何一座村庄,但是同样不能否认的是他们的据点已经大大增加,现在不付出惨重代价是无法攻克的。

背景就讲这么多。所有这些对美国通过中国击败日本的计划有什么影响呢?

"毕竟,你们拯救了国民党,"我以《星期六晚邮报》的战地记者的身份重返中国(1942—1943)时重庆的一位中国知识分子对我说。"它现在是你们的孩子,你们对它的行动责无旁贷。"

他说的就是美国的金钱、武器和经济援助都给了国民党当局,而不附带任何有关在中国奉行何种政策的条件。美国政府代表多次向重庆表明,我们不赞成在联合抗日的过程中重燃内战战火,但是美国人所做的也仅此而已,并没有寻求解除针对游击区的封锁。

共产党在敌后胜利收复失地令国民党领导人日益恐慌,重庆便布下了针对第十八

---

1. 对战时这些苦难生动而令人心酸的现实主义直击,参见艾格尼丝·史沫特莱的鸿著《中国战歌》。

people's patriotism, but side by side with political reforms went economic and social changes. In the case of women the enforcement of laws like monogamy, freedom of marriage at the age of consent, free education, and suffrage at the age of eighteen won a surprising response. Professor Lindsay said there were over 3,000,000 members of the women's organizations in the partisan areas. Many women had been elected to village and town councils and large numbers of young girls carried serious political and military responsibilities.

The primary school system operated widely in all the "permanent" guerrilla bases and education was free and compulsory in theory if, because of poverty, seldom attainable in fact. Yet in a few places as high as 80 per cent of the younger children of school age were literate. The basic reform was a drastic reduction in land rent. Land of absentee landlords was tilled in common; the aim was to cultivate all cultivable land. Taxes were collected mainly in grain, and were kept at about 10 percent of those demanded by the Japanese. Consumer, marketing and industrial cooperatives were widespread. Lindsay stated that there were over 4,000 cooperatives in Shansi and 5,000 in central Hopei alone.

Unimaginable hardships accompanied partisan organization at every step.[1] While it is true the Japanese failed to destroy the partisan forces, or to stop their increase, they carried out literally thousands of large- and small-scale punitive expeditions against them. They looted and burned thousands of villages, raped the womenfolk and slaughtered countless civilians, in a terror aimed to wipe out all thought of resistance. The guerrillas always found ways to overcome the demoralizing effects of these tactics but not without sacrifices as bitter as any endured in Russia. It was true that the Japanese were still unable to control any village much beyond the range of their garrisons along North China's railways and roads, but it was also true that their fortified points had greatly increased and could now be seized only at a heavy cost.

So much for background. How did all this affect American plans to defeat Japan through China?

"After all, you saved the Kuomintang," a Chinese intellectual in Chungking said to me when I returned to China (1942—1943) as a war correspondent for the *Saturday Evening Post*. "It is your baby now and you cannot avoid responsibility for its actions."

He meant simply that American money, arms, and economic aid were given to the Kuomintang authorities, without any conditions concerning policies pursued inside China. American government representatives had several times made it clear to Chungking that we would disapprove of a renewal of civil strife during the joint war against Japan, but Americans had not gone beyond that nor sought to have the blockade lifted against the partisan areas.

Chungking established its blockade against the Eighteenth Group Army when Kuomintang party leaders became increasingly alarmed by the Communists' success in recovering control of areas

---

1. For a vivid and almost painfully realistic eyewitness account of these sufferings of growth in the midst of war, see Agnes Smedley's powerful book, *Battle Hymn of China*.

集团军的封锁。总司令将他们的活动描述为"非法占领国土"。国民党战区政治和党务委员会所持的态度是所有的游击政权都是"非法的",都应该予以取缔,等待重建国民党的系统。

1940年,总司令命令新四军从其长江以南靠近上海的根据地出发,向完全位于敌后的地区转移,行军途中一些国民党军队与新四军的殿后部队交火。这显然是一场奇袭,据报道游击队只有国民党军队的1/8。4,000人左右的小分遣队不是一个作战单位,很容易遭到包围歼灭。新四军军长叶挺将军(他本人不是共产党员)受伤被俘,战地指挥项英将军与他的许多参谋一同遇害,同时死难的还有医疗队的一些医生和护士、许多正在康复中的伤员、一些军校学员、男女学生以及该军所属的一些工业合作社工人。

这一事变未能肃清新四军,它的主力已经到达了长江北岸,与日军交上了火,但是这实际上标志着国共并肩作战的终结,成为联合抗日过程中公开争夺领导权的开始。总司令作出的裁决是这次事件是由新四军"违抗军令"引起的,因此不仅撤回对新四军的所有援助,而且也撤回了对八路军的所有援助。

在这一悲剧发生前的数月里,第十八集团军所属部队无一拿到军饷。悲剧发生以后,他们不仅拿不到军饷和军火,而且还被一圈强大的政府军切断了从"自由中国"获取补给的路线,他们原本可以从那里的人民手中购买或获赠的。极富讽刺意味的是,执行这项封锁任务的国民党军队的大部分补给居然都来自苏联!有两个集团军(第三十七集团军和第三十八集团军)专门执行这项封锁任务。1942年美国军官建议说在收复缅甸的战役中需要这两个集团军,但是重庆认为它们在西北的"执勤角色"更为重要。

所有这类事实都为在华的美国人所熟知,但是国内很可能没有谁会意识到我们依照《租借法案》提供的援助无一例外都落入了国民党当局的手中。我们在延安没有设立领事馆,也没有军事联络员与游击队联系。[1] 我们提供的所有供给都经过"驼峰航线"空运到了中国——现代轰炸机和战斗机、火炮、运输车辆和弹药,当然支持的只有这一个党。美国产业工会联合会、劳工联合会和铁路工人联合会送往中国的资金援助也都无一例外地进了国民党集团的腰包。

---

1. 直到1944年末,蒋介石才允许一个美国观察团驻进延安,尽管观察团并没有带去任何军事和经济援助,但还是受到了欢迎。

behind the Japanese lines. The Generalissimo described their activity as "illegal occupation of the national territory." The Kuomintang's War Areas Political and Party Affairs Commission took the position that all the guerrilla administrations were "illegal" and should be abolished to await the re-establishment of the Kuomintang system.

In 1940 some Kuomintang troops engaged the rear echelon of the New Fourth Army while it was moving from its base south of the Yangtze River, near Shanghai, to an area entirely behind the Japanese lines to which it was assigned by the Generalissimo. It was apparently a surprise attack and the partisans were reportedly outnumbered eight to one. The little detachment of about 4,000 was not a combat unit and it was easily encircled and destroyed. General Yeh T'ing, the commander of the New Fourth Army (who was himself not a Communist), was wounded and taken prisoner, and General Hsiang Ying, the field commander, was killed together with many of his staff, some doctors and nurses of the medical battalions, a number of convalescent wounded soldiers, some cadets, men and women students, and some industrial cooperative workers attached to the army.

The incident failed to liquidate the New Fourth Army, whose main forces were already north of the Yangtze River, engaging Japanese troops there, but it was the effective end of Nationalist-Communist collaboration in the field and the beginning of an open struggle for leadership in the joint war against Japan. The Generalissimo ruled that the incident was caused by the New Fourth's "insubordination" and thenceforth withdrew all aid not only from that army but also from the Eighth Route.

For some months previous to the tragedy no part of the Eighteenth Group Army had been paid. From this time on they not only received no pay or ammunition but were blockaded by a ring of strong government forces from access to supplies in Free China, which they might have purchased or received as gifts from the people. Ironically enough, the Kuomintang troops enforcing this blockade were largely supplied by Soviet Russia. There were two group armies (the Thirty-seventh and Thirty-eighth) engaged exclusively in the blockading enterprise. American officers in 1942 suggested that they were needed in the campaign to recover Burma, but Chungking considered their "policing role" in the Northwest of greater importance and there they remained.

All such facts were known to Americans in China, but probably few at home realized that our lend-lease aid went exclusively to the Kuomintang authorities. We maintained no consular representation in Yenan and no military liaison with the partisans.[1] All our supplies flown over the Hump into China—modern bombers and fighters, artillery, transport, and ammunition—supported only the one party, of course. Financial aid sent to China by the C.I.O., A.F.L., and Railway Brotherhoods also went exclusively to Kuomintang groups.

---

1. Not until late in 1944 did Chiang Kai-shek grant permission for an American observer team to be stationed in Yenan, where they were welcomed, although they brought no military or economic assistance.

针对中国的这一"内政"我们能做些什么？我们与中国的新条约（1943年）废除了治外法权，将全部主权都交还给了中国政府。我们能告诉现任政府该怎么做而不被打上新帝国主义的烙印吗？但不能避免的是，我们对国民党的经济和军事援助已经使我们陷入其中。我们如果再假装未来给予中国的经济援助不含有任何隐含的重大政治责任，这不是在自欺欺人吗？

一旦日本被打败，蒋介石接着会不会消灭共产党和他们的游击盟友？1937年之前，国民党已经枉费了10年的心机。即便是使用手头的美国轰炸机和战斗机，在与这些身经百战的游击战士作战时，总司令所取得的胜利也不大可能比日本人好到哪里去。除非在盟军的全力支持下进行一场长期而惨烈的战争，重庆政府已经基本不可能摧毁这支反对力量。

到了1944年夏天，局势已经非常明朗了，1928年在偏僻的井冈山上举起红旗的那一小股青年发起的示威行动已经演变为一场讨伐战争，最终上升到了全国性运动的高度，其影响范围之广已令任何一位中国的命运决定者都不能再无视它为广大民众讲话的要求。

What could be done about this "internal affair" of China? Our new treaty with China (1943) renounced extraterritoriality rights and restored full sovereignty to the Chinese Government. Could we now tell the present government how to run its business without being branded neoimperialists? But inevitably the war had already caused us to intervene in support of the Kuomintang, in terms of economic and military aid. Was it not merely playing ostrich to pretend that our future economic help to China did not carry implicit political responsibilities of the gravest kind?

Once Japan was defeated, would Chiang Kai-shek then destroy the Communists and their partisan allies? The Kuomintang spent ten fruitless years in the attempt before 1937. Even with the use of American bombers and fighters on his side, the Generalissimo was not likely to secure greater success than the Japanese had had against these experienced guerrilla warriors. It had become a physical impossibility for the Chungking Government to destroy this opposition in anything short of a long and bloody war, fully backed by Allied troops.

By the summer of 1944 it had thus become manifest that the tiny band of youths who raised the Red flag on the lonely mountain of Chingkangshan far back in 1928 had launched a demonstration which evolved into a crusade which finally rose to the stature of a national movement of such scope that no arbiters of China's destiny could much longer deny its claims to speak for vast multitudes of people.

深访毛泽东

由于篇幅所限，1936年我对毛泽东的访谈笔录并未全部收入初版的《西行漫记》，不过其中大部分都在1937年2月3至5日的《上海晚邮信使》上刊载过。以下节选部分或许会具有一些当代意义。[1]

保安，1936年7月23日

关于共产国际、中国和外蒙古

斯诺：在实践中，如果中国革命取得了胜利，那么苏维埃中国和苏联之间的经济和政治关系会保持在第三国际或者一个类似的组织内呢，还是可能出现某种实际的政府合并呢？中国苏维埃政府在同莫斯科的关系上和现在的外蒙古政府可以相提并论吗？

毛泽东：我认为这是一个纯属假设的问题。我跟你说过，红军现在寻求的不是霸权，而是一个反抗日本帝国主义的统一的中国。

在第三国际这个组织内，世界无产阶级的先锋队将其集体经验汇集起来，使全世界所有的革命人民受益。它既不是一个行政管理机构，在顾问职能以外也没有任何政治权力。从结构上来看，它与第二国际并没有太多差异，不过在实质上差异还是巨大的。但是正如没有谁会说在由社会民主党组成内阁的国家第二国际就是独裁者一样，说在有共产党的国家第三国际就是独裁者也同样是荒谬的。

---

1. 作者在原文中加了斜体，在译文中以黑体代之。——译注

Further Interviews with Mao Tse-tung

Owing to space limitations the text of my interviews with Mao Tse-tung in 1936 was not included in its entirety in the original edition of *Red Star Over China*, although most of it was published in the *Shanghai Evening Post & Mercury*, February 3, 4, 5, 1937. The following extracts may be of contemporary interest. (Italics added.)

Pao An, July 23, 1936

On the Comintern, China, and Outer Mongolia

SNOW: In actual practice, if the Chinese revolution were victorious, would the economic and political relationship between Soviet China and Soviet Russia be maintained within the Third International or a similar organization, or would there probably be some kind of actual merger of governments? Would the Chinese Soviet Government be comparable in its relation to Moscow to the present government of Outer Mongolia?

MAO: I assume this is a purely hypothetical question. As I have told you, the Red Army is not now seeking the hegemony of power, but a united China against Japanese imperialism.

The Third International is an organization in which the vanguard of the world proletariat brings together its collective experience for the benefit of all revolutionary peoples throughout the world. It is not an administrative organization nor has it any political power beyond that of an advisory capacity. Structurally it is not very different from the Second International, though in content it is vastly different. But just as no one would say that in a country where the cabinet is organized by the Social Democrats the Second International is dictator, so it is ridiculous to say that the Third International is dictator in countries where there are Communist parties.

苏联是共产党掌权的国家，不过即便在那里第三国际也没有进行统治，对人民没有任何直接的政治权力。同样地，可以说虽然中国共产党是共产国际的成员，但是这决不意味着苏维埃中国是由莫斯科或者共产国际来统治的。我们为解放全中国而战斗当然不是为了将国家拱手交给莫斯科！

中国共产党在中国只是一个党派，在取得胜利后它必须要替全国人民说话。它不能替苏联人民说话，也不能替第三国际治理这个国家，而是只能服务于中国人民的利益。只有在中国人民的利益和苏联人民的利益重合的时候，才能说"顺了莫斯科的意愿"。不过一旦中国人民掌握了民主权力，并在社会和经济上得到了解放，就像他们的苏联兄弟一样，当然这种共同利益的基础会极大地得到拓宽。

在许多国家都建立了苏维埃政府后，可能会产生国际苏维埃联盟这个问题，到时看如何解决这个问题会非常有趣。但是今天我提供不了解决方案；这是一个尚未出现的问题，不能提前去解决。在今天这个世界上，不同国家和民族之间的经济和文化交流日益紧密，这样一个联盟看起来非常理想，**不过条件是要建立在自愿的基础之上。**

但是，显然最后一点最为重要；这样一个世界联盟要取得成功，就必须让每个国家都有权根据自己人民的意愿加入或者退出联盟，保持各自主权的完整性，当然还有永不"听命"于莫斯科。没有共产党人不是这样想的，"莫斯科主宰世界"这种荒诞的说法只是法西斯和反革命分子编造出来的。

外蒙古和苏联的关系，无论现在还是过去，一直都是建立在完全平等这个原则之上的。在中国的人民革命胜利后，外蒙古共和国将按照其意愿自动成为中华联邦的一部分。同样地，回族和藏族人民也都将在中华联邦之下组建自治的政府。对于少数民族的不公平待遇，正如国民党所实施的，在中国的建国方略中没有位置，它在任何一个民主共和国的建国方略中都不会有位置。

中国的"关键"角色

斯诺：中国共产主义运动取得胜利后，你认为其他亚洲国家或者半殖民地国家，比如朝鲜、印度支那、菲律宾和印度，会迅速爆发革命吗？中国现在是不是世界革命的"关键"所在？

In the U.S.S.R. the Communist Party is in power, yet even there the Third International does not rule nor does it have any direct political power over the people at all. Similarly, it can be said that although the Communist Party of China is a member of the Comintern, still this in no sense means that Soviet China is ruled by Moscow or by the Comintern. We are certainly not fighting for an emancipated China in order to turn the country over to Moscow!

The Chinese Communist Party is only one party in China, and in its victory it will have to speak for the whole nation. It cannot speak for the Russian people or rule for the Third International, but only in the interests of the Chinese masses. Only where the interests of the Chinese masses coincide with the interests of the Russian masses can it be said to be "obeying the will" of Moscow. But of course this basis of common benefit will be tremendously broadened, once the masses of China are in democratic power and socially and economically emancipated, like their brothers in Russia.

When soviet governments have been established in many countries, the problem of an international union of soviets may arise, and it will be interesting to see how it will be solved. But today I cannot suggest the formula; it is a problem which has not been and cannot be solved in advance. In the world today, with increasingly close economic and cultural intimacies between different states and peoples, such a union would seem to be highly desirable, *if achieved on a voluntary basis.*

Clearly, however, the last point is of utmost importance; such a world union could be successful only if every nation had the right to enter or leave the union according to the will of its people, and with its sovereignty intact, and certainly never at the "command" of Moscow. No Communist ever thought otherwise, and the myth of "world domination from Moscow" is an invention of the Fascists and counterrevolutionaries.

The relationship between Outer Mongolia and the Soviet Union, now and in the past, has always been based on the principle of complete equality. When the People's Revolution has been victorious in China, the Outer Mongolian republic will automatically become a part of the Chinese federation, at its own will. The Mohammedan and Tibetan peoples, likewise, will form autonomous republics attached to the China federation. The unequal treatment of national minorities, as practiced by the Kuomintang, can have no part in the Chinese program, nor can it be part of the program of any democratic republic.

On China as the "Key"

SNOW: With the achievement of victory of a Red movement in China, do you think that revolution would occur quickly in other Asiatic or semicolonial countries, such as Korea, Indochina, the Philippines, and India? Is China at present the "key" to world revolution?

毛泽东：中国革命在世界局势中是一个关键因素……中国革命彻底胜利后，许多殖民地国家的人民将会效仿中国，取得他们自己类似的胜利。但是我要再次强调夺取政权不是我们（当前）的目标。我们想要停止内战，同国民党和其他党派一起建立一个人民的民主政府，共同抗日，赢得我们的独立。

保安，1936 年 7 月 19 日

关于土地分配

斯诺：在抗击日本帝国主义的斗争之后，革命最重要的国内任务是什么？

毛泽东：中国革命是资产阶级民主性质的，它的首要任务是重新解决土地问题——实现土地革命。看一下今天中国土地分配的数据，你可能就会对土地革命的紧迫性有所了解。在国民革命时期，我是国民党农民委员会的书记（农民部部长），主管收集 21 个省份的统计数据。

我们的调查显示出的不平等令人震惊。整个农村人口中约 70% 都是贫农、佃农或者半佃农以及农业工人。约 20% 是耕种自己的土地的中农。高利贷者和地主约占农村总人口的 10%。这 10% 之中还包括富农以及军阀、收税官等剥削者。

这 10% 的富农、地主和高利贷者一共控制着约 70% 的耕地。有 12% 到 15% 的土地掌握在中农的手中。剩下 70% 的贫农、佃农和半佃农以及农业工人拥有的土地只占全部耕地的 10% 到 15%……革命主要是由两大压迫引起的——帝国主义者和那 10% 的地主和中国剥削者。所以我们可以说在我们提出民主、土地革命和抗击帝国主义的新要求时，**反对我们的不足农村人口的 10%**。确切地说不是 10%，很可能只有 5% 左右，因为至多也就那么多中国人会当汉奸和日本一起在联合"反共协约"下压迫自己人。

斯诺：苏维埃计划中的其他东西都为了统一战线而延缓了，重新分配土地是不是也能缓一缓呢？

毛泽东：不没收地主的土地，不满足农民的主要民主要求，就不能为成功解放全国的革命斗争奠定广大的群众基础。**为了赢得农民对全国事业的支持，就必须满足他们对土地的要求**……

MAO: The Chinese revolution is a key factor in the world situation. . . . When the Chinese revolution comes into full power the masses of many colonial countries will follow the example of China and win a similar victory of their own. But I emphasize again that the seizure of power is not our (immediate) aim. We want to stop civil war, create a people's democratic government with the Kuomintang and other parties, and fight for our independence against Japan.

Pao An, July 19, 1936

On Land Distribution

SNOW: What is the foremost internal task of the revolution, after the struggle against Japanese imperialism?

MAO: The Chinese revolution, being of bourgeois-democratic character, has as its primary task the readjustment of the land problem—the realization of agrarian reform. Some idea of the urgency of rural reform may be secured by referring to figures on the distribution of land in China today. During the Nationalist Revolution I was secretary of the Peasant Committee [department] of the Kuomintang and had charge of collecting statistics for areas throughout twenty-one provinces.

Our investigation showed astonishing inequalities. About 70 per cent of the whole rural population was made up of poor peasants, tenants or part-tenants, and of agricultural workers. About 20 per cent was made up of middle peasants tilling their own land. Usurers and landlords were about 10 per cent of the population. Included in the 10 per cent also were rich peasants, exploiters like the militarists, tax collectors, and so forth.

The 10 per cent of the rich peasants, landlords, and usurers together owned about 70 per cent of the cultivated land. From 12 to 15 per cent was in the hands of middle peasants. The 70 per cent of the poor peasants, tenants and part-tenants, and agricultural workers, owned only from 10 to 15 per cent of the total cultivated land. . . . The revolution is caused chiefly by two oppressions—the imperialists and that 10 per cent of landlords and Chinese exploiters. So we may say that in our new demands for democracy, land reform, and war against imperialism we *are opposed by less than 10 per cent of the population.* And really not 10 per cent, but probably only about 5 per cent, for not more than that many Chinese will turn traitor to join with Japan in subjugating their own people under the device of the joint "Anti-Red Pact."

SNOW: Other things in the soviet program having been postponed in the interest of the united front, is it not possible to delay land redistribution also?

MAO: Without confiscating the estates of the landlords, without meeting the main democratic demand of the peasantry, it is impossible to lay the broad mass basis for a successful revolutionary struggle for national liberation. *In order to win the support of the peasants for the national cause it is necessary to satisfy their demand for land.* . . .

关于教育和拉丁化汉字

斯诺：你能给我简要介绍一下你们针对……文盲的政策吗？

毛泽东：……至于文盲这个问题，对真心想要提高人民的经济和文化水平的人民政府来说这个任务并不难……

在江西，我们的扫盲协会在教育专员的领导下已经取得了惊人的成就。它在每个村都建立了由青年学生、少共党员和少年先锋队队员领导的团体，教人们读书写字。这些大众教育学校，数百个都是组织起来的农民自己创建的，由热情的红色青年进行授课，他们主动地把自己的时间和精力奉献给这一任务，没有报酬。经过三四年的时间，我们江西苏区的大多数农民都认识几百个汉字，能够阅读简单的文章、讲话稿和我们的报纸及其他出版物。

我们的统计数字在长征途中遗失了，但是我在第二次中华苏维埃全国代表大会[1]上作的报告详尽讲述了教育的进步，这种进步既有人民的大众教育运动的功劳，也有苏区政府开办的正规学校系统的功劳……

在陕西和甘肃也建立了一个扫盲协会。以前这里的文化水平比江西要低得多，今天我们仍然面临着非常艰巨的教育任务……为了加速这里的扫盲进程，我们开始试验新文字——拉丁化的汉字，**现在在我们的党校、红军大学、红军和《红色中华》的一个专栏中使用**。我们相信拉丁化是战胜文盲的一个很好的工具。汉字非常难学，即使最好的基本汉字系统或最优秀的简化教学都无法教会人们真正有效而又丰富的词汇。**我们相信，要创建一种人民充分参与其中的新型社会文化，我们迟早得将汉字统统舍弃**。我们现在广泛使用拉丁化，要是我们在这里能呆上3年的话，文盲问题将会在很大程度上得到解决……

以下节选的是在中国以外从未完整发表过的1939年访谈笔录，这些访谈于1940年1月13日和20日发表在上海的《密勒氏评论报》上。[2]

---

1. 第二次中华苏维埃全国代表大会于1934年1月在江西瑞金举行。参见毛泽东，《红色中国：毛泽东主席……》。
2. 作者在原文中加了斜体，在译文中以黑体代之。——译注

On Education and Latinized Chinese

SNOW: Could you give me a brief statement of policy concerning ... illiteracy?

MAO: .... As for the problem of illiteracy, this is not a difficult task for a people's government which really wants to raise the economic and cultural standard of the masses....

In Kiangsi our Society for the Liquidation of Illiteracy, under the leadership of the Commissioner of Education, has had astonishing successes. It built up in every village groups led by young students, Young Communists and Young Vanguards, to teach people how to read and write. These mass-education schools, hundreds of them, were created by the organized peasantry themselves, and instructed by the enthusiastic Red youths, who freely gave their time and energy to this task, without pay. After three or four years the majority of the peasants in our soviet districts in Kiangsi knew several hundred Chinese characters and could read simple texts, lectures, and our newspapers and other publications.

Our statistics were lost during the Long March, but my report before the Second All-Soviet Congress[1] contained a full account of the progress made in education, both through the people's mass-education movement, and through the regular school system maintained by the soviets....

In Shensi and Kansu there has also been established a Society for the Liquidation of Illiteracy. The cultural level here was formerly much lower than in Kiangsi, and great tasks of education still face us today.... In order to hasten the liquidation of illiteracy here we have begun experimenting with Hsin-Wen-Tzu—Latinized Chinese. *It is now used in our Party school, in the Red Academy, in the Red Army, and in a special section of the* Red China Daily News. We believe Latinization is a good instrument with which to overcome illiteracy. Chinese characters are so difficult to learn that even the best system of rudimentary characters, or simplified teaching, does not equip the people with a really efficient and rich vocabulary. *Sooner or later, we believe, we will have to abandon the Chinese character altogether if we are to create a new social culture in which the masses fully participate.* We are now widely using Latinization, and if we stay here for three years the problem of illiteracy will have been largely overcome....

Following are excerpts from 1939 interviews never fully published outside China, where they appeared in *The China Weekly Review*, Shanghai, January 13 and 20, 1940. (Italics added.)

---

1. The Second All-China Soviet Congress was held in Juichin, Kiangsi, in January, 1934. See Mao Tse-tung, *Red China: President Mao Tse-tung Reports* ....

延安，1939 年 9 月 25 日

"我们从来都不是改良主义者"

斯诺：由于中国共产党已经放弃了强调阶级斗争的宣传，取消了苏维埃政府，接受了国民党和国民党政府的领导，采用了孙逸仙博士的三民主义，不再没收地主和资本家的财产，停止了在国统区（公开）进行组织工作和宣传，许多人现在都断言中国共产党人事实上已经不再是社会主义革命者，只是改良主义者而已——无论在方法上还是目标上都是资产阶级的。你怎么回应这些说法？

毛泽东：**我们一直都是社会主义革命者；我们从来都不是改良主义者**。在中国革命这个问题上，有两大目标。第一大目标是完成民族民主革命的任务。第二大目标是进行社会主义革命。后者必须实现，而且要彻底实现。现在的革命就其目标的性质而言是民族和民主革命，**但是经过一定阶段之后它将转变成社会主义革命**。现在在中国革命这个问题上，社会主义革命者角色的"变化"将会使它成为"现实"——除非我们现阶段的工作不成功，那样的话社会主义革命就不可能早日实现。

进行反攻的准备

斯诺：根据你"持久战"的理论，目前中国的抗战处于什么阶段？已经到了"僵持"阶段吗？

毛泽东：对，战争正处于僵持阶段，但是这有几个特定条件。

在新的国际形势下，在日本处境日益艰难的情况下，而且中国不去寻求妥协，战争就处于僵持阶段……这（对我们来说）就意味着进行反攻的准备。

关于纳粹和苏联签订的《苏德互不侵犯条约》

斯诺：我看了你对苏联和纳粹德国签订的《苏德互不侵犯条约》的评论。你好像认为苏联不太可能被拖入欧洲的战争……你觉得苏联只要不遭受攻击就会保持中立吗，哪怕是纳粹德国眼看就要取得胜利？

Yenan, September 25, 1939

"We Are Never Reformists"

SNOW: Because the Communist Party of China has abandoned propaganda emphasizing class struggle, abolished its soviets, submitted to leadership of the Kuomintang and the Kuomintang Government, adopted the *San Min Chu I* [Dr. Sun Yat-sen's *Three Principles of the People*], ceased confiscating the property of landlords and capitalists, and stopped (overt) organizational work and propaganda in Kuomintang areas, many people now assert that Chinese Communists are in fact no longer social revolutionaries but mere reformists—bourgeois in methods and in aims. How do you answer such claims?

MAO: *We are always social revolutionaries; we are never reformists.* There are two main objectives in the thesis of the Chinese revolution. The first consists of the realization of the tasks of a national democratic revolution. The other is social revolution. The latter must be achieved, and completely achieved. For the present the revolution is national and democratic in the character of its aims, *but after a certain stage it will be transformed into social revolution.* The present "becoming" of the social revolutionary part in the thesis of the Chinese revolution will turn into its "being"—unless our work in the present phase is a failure, in which case there is no early possibility of social revolution.

Preparation for Counterattack

SNOW: In what stage, according to your theory of the "Protracted War," is Chinese resistance at the present time? Has the stage of "stalemate" been reached?

MAO: Yes, the war is in a stage of stalemate, but with certain qualifications.

Under the condition of a new international situation, and under the condition that Japan's position is becoming more difficult, while China will not seek a reconciliation, the war is in a stage of stalemate . . . the meaning of which (for us) is preparation for a counterattack.

On the Nazi-Soviet Pact

SNOW: I read your comment on the signature of the Soviet-German Pact. You seem to think it unlikely that the Soviet Union can be drawn into the European War. . . . Do you think the U.S.S.R. would remain neutral, as long as it is not attacked, even if Nazi Germany appears to be near victory?

毛泽东：苏联不会参加这场战争，因为战争双方都是帝国主义者，这只是一场强盗战争，双方都是非正义的。双方都在争夺力量对比和对世界各族人民的统治权。双方都是错误的，苏联不会卷入这种战争，而会保持中立……至于当前欧洲战争的结果，苏联不会被获胜一方对她的威胁所吓倒，不管获胜的是英国还是德国。一旦苏联遭受攻击，她将获得各国人民的支持，获得殖民地和半殖民地国家少数民族的支持……

关于苏联与希特勒的经济合作

我事先给毛泽东写了一长串问题供他细读。这时我插进了一个不在问题列表中的问题，我问他既然德国是帝国主义，和英、法两国没有什么区别，为什么苏联还要参与德国的帝国主义冒险，将苏联的大量小麦、石油和其他战争物资提供给德国。为什么，顺便说一下，苏联还要继续将库页岛的油田租借给日本，或者给日本以捕鱼权？后者极具价值，使日本可以出口大量的鱼类，借以积累起购买弹药的外汇，然后对"半殖民地的中国"发动一场阻止"民族解放运动"的"强盗帝国主义"战争。

毛泽东回答说，这是一个极为复杂的问题，在没有看到这项政策的结果之前，还无法回答这个问题。他并不清楚苏联向日本出售石油的条件。不管怎样，苏联既没有向德国也没有向日本提供任何战争装备，保持正常的贸易往来并不等于参与战争。

我问在现代战争中向交战一方提供坦克或者飞机用的燃料与提供坦克和飞机本身有什么不同。为什么美国因为卖给日本战争所需的原材料就成为日本帝国主义侵华的参与者，而苏联向德、日两国提供同种物资时却既不是德国帝国主义的欧洲战争的参与者，也不是日本的亚洲战争的参与者？

毛泽东承认战争物资贸易和战争装备贸易之间的差别并不明显。他说，重要的是这个国家是不是在真心地支持革命解放战争。以此进行判断，苏联的立场是无可非议的。她曾经积极地支持过1925至1927年间中国的革命战争，支持过西班牙的革命战争和当前中国的革命战争，**苏联将永远站在正义的革命战争的一边**，而不会支持帝国主义战争，不过她可能会与所有交战方都保持正常的贸易往来。

MAO: The Soviet Union will not participate in this war, because both sides are imperialists, and it is simply robber war with justice on neither side. Both sides are struggling for the balance of power and rule over the peoples of the world. Both are wrong, and the Soviet Union will not become involved in this kind of war, but will remain neutral.... As for the outcome of the present European war, the Soviet Union cannot be frightened by the threat of the victorious power to herself, whether it is England or Germany. Whenever the Soviet Union is attacked it will have the support of the peoples of various countries, and of the national minorities in colonial and semicolonial countries....

On Soviet Economic Cooperation with Hitler

I had submitted a long list of written questions for perusal by Mao in advance. At this point I interpolated a question outside that list, asking why, if Germany was imperialist and no different from Britain and France, the Soviet Union should participate in Germany's imperialist adventure to the extent of making available to Germany Russia's great reserves of wheat, oil, and other war materials. Why, incidentally, did Russia continue to lease oil lands to Japan in Sakhalin, or to give Japan fishing rights? The latter were of great value in enabling Japan to export large quantities of fish, and thus establish foreign credits with which to buy munitions and carry on a "robber imperialist" war against the "national liberation movement" of "semicolonial China."

Mao replied that it was an extremely complicated question, and could not be answered until one saw the end of the policy. The conditions under which the Soviet Union was selling oil to Japan were not clear to him. In any case, the Soviet Union was supplying neither Germany nor Japan with any war instruments, and to maintain ordinary trade did not make her a participant in the war.

I asked whether there was any difference, in modern war, between supplying a belligerent with fuel for tanks or airplanes and supplying the tanks and planes themselves. Why was the United States a participant in Japan's imperialist invasion of China because she sold Japan the raw materials of war, but the Soviet Union not a participant in Germany's imperialist war in Europe, nor Japan's war in Asia, when she supplied the same kind of materials to the two combatants?

Mao conceded that the distinction between trade in war materials and trade in war instruments was not great. What mattered, he said, was whether the country in question was really supporting revolutionary wars of liberation. In that judgment there was no question where the U.S.S.R. stood. She had given positive support to revolutionary wars in China, in 1925—1927, in Spain, and in China at present. *The Soviet Union would always be on the side of just revolutionary wars* but would not take sides in imperialist war, though she might maintain ordinary trade with all belligerents.

关于波兰问题

毛泽东：纳粹入侵波兰将这个问题摆在了苏联面前：要不要听任全部波兰人民都成为纳粹迫害的受害者，或者要不要解放波兰东部的少数民族。苏联选择了第二条行动路线。

波兰东部广阔的国土上定居着 800 万白俄罗斯人和 300 万乌克兰人。这片领土是作为《布列斯特－立陶夫斯克和约》的代价而被强行从年幼的苏维埃社会主义共和国分割出去的，落入了反动的波兰政府的手中。今天的苏联已经不再软弱，不再年幼，收回自己的领土，解放他们……

保安，1936 年 7 月 25 日

毛泽东表扬自己的同伴们

作为讲述完长征时的一种后记，毛泽东将长征的胜利结束归功于党的"正确领导"，接着点出了 18 位同志的姓名。由于这些话看起来多少影响了主要叙述的趣味，当初我并没有采用它们，但是在今天这些话语可能会具有一些历史意义。需要特别注意毛泽东列出这些人时的顺序，特别注意他们中有的毛泽东最近刚刚与其斗争过，以后还会再次斗争，还要特别注意被省略的名字。

毛泽东：（党）不可战胜的另一个原因在于人才——革命干部——卓越的才能、非凡的勇气和绝对的忠诚。朱德、王明、洛甫、周恩来、博古、王稼祥、彭德怀、罗迈、邓发、项英、徐海东、陈云、林彪、张国焘、徐向前、陈昌浩、贺龙、萧克等同志——还有许许多多优秀的同志为革命事业献出了自己的生命——所有这些同志为着共同的目标携手奋斗，缔造了红军和苏维埃运动。这些同志及其他后来者将领导我们走向最终的胜利。

On the Question of Poland

MAO: The Nazi invasion of Poland presented the Soviet Union with this problem: whether to permit the whole Polish population to fall victim to Nazi persecution, or whether to liberate the national minorities of Eastern Poland. The Soviet Union chose to follow the second course of action.

In Eastern Poland there is a vast stretch of territory inhabited by 8,000,000 Byelo-Russians and 3,000,000 Ukrainians. This territory was forcibly seized from the young Soviet Socialist Republics as the price of the *Brest-Litovsk Treaty*, and fell under the domination of the reactionary Polish Government. Today the Soviet Union, no longer weak and young, takes back its own, and liberates them. . . .

Pao An, July 25, 1936

Mao Praises Fellow Leaders

As a kind of postscript to the end of his account of the Long March, Mao attributed its successful conclusion to the "correct leadership" of the Party and then singled out eighteen comrades by name. As the remarks seemed somewhat anticlimactic to the main account I did not use them, but today these sentences may be of some historical interest. Attention need hardly be called to the order in which Mao listed the names, to the fact that they included men with whom Mao had but recently struggled and against whom he would struggle again, and to the names omitted.

MAO: Another reason for its [the Party's] invincibility lies in the extraordinary ability and courage and loyalty of the human material, the revolutionary cadres. Comrades Chu Teh, Wang Ming, Lo Fu, Chou En-lai, Po Ku, Wang Chia-hsiang, P'eng Teh-huai, Lo Man, Teng Fa, Hsiang Ying, Hsu Hai-tung, Ch'en Yun, Lin Piao, Chang Kuo-t'ao, Hsu Hsiang-ch'ien, Ch'en Chang-hao, Ho Lung, Hsiao K'eh—and many, many excellent comrades who gave their lives for the revolution—all these, working together for a single purpose, have made the Red Army and the soviet movement. And these and others yet to come will lead us to ultimate victory.

尾注 关于朱德[1]

不像莎士比亚，孔夫子认为名字具有头等重要性。至少在朱德这个名字上是这样。这个名字叫起来很响亮，英文里应拼作 Ju Deh，因为发音是如此。这个名字很贴切，因为这个名字由于在文字上的奇异巧合，在中文中的两个字正好是"红色的品德"的意思，虽然当他在边远的四川省仪陇县诞生后他的慈亲给他起这个名字时，是无法预见这个名字日后具有的政治意义的。无法预见这样的事，否则他们早就会吓得把他改名了。

在南方的这些年月里，朱德指挥全军，打了几百次小仗，几十次大仗，经历了敌人的5次大围剿，在最后一次中，他面对的敌人，其技术上的进攻力量（包括重炮、飞机和机械化部队）估计超过他自己的部队8倍至9倍，资源超过他许多许多倍。不论如何估计他的胜败，必须承认，就战术的独创性、部队的机动性和作战的多样性而言，他再三证明自己胜过派来打他的任何一个将领，而且无疑建立了中国革命化军队在游击战中的不可轻侮的战斗力。红军在南方所犯的重大错误是战略上的错误，对此，政治领导人必须负主要的责任。但是即使有这种错误也很少疑问，要是红军能够在第五次"围剿"中哪怕以大致相当的条件与敌军对垒，结果就会造成南京的惨败——德国顾问也没有用。

从纯粹军事战略和战术上处理一支大军撤退来说，中国没有见到过任何可以与朱

---

1. 斯诺这次在陕北期间，没有直接见到朱德同志，原写的这一章有一些不确切之处，1938年复社出版中译本时，斯诺根据韦尔斯在1937年去陕北访问朱德同志的记录（这部分以后收在她的《红色中国内幕》，即《续西行漫记》中）重新作了改写。这里用的是他改写过的这一章。——译注

Endnote Concerning Chu Teh[1]

Unlike Shakespeare, Confucius held that names were of first importance. In Chu Teh, at least, there is much. It is a strong sounding name which should really be spelled Ju Deh in English, for so it is pronounced. But it is an appropriate name, because by a strange accident of language these two characters in Chinese mean "Red Virtue," although for the fond parents who yclept him thus when he was born in far-away Yi Lung, Szechuan, it was impossible to foresee the political meaning which that name later on was to acquire. Impossible, or they would surely have changed it in terror.

During these years in the South, Chu Teh led the combined Red armies in hundreds of skirmishes, through scores of major battles, and through the brunt of five great annihilation campaigns, in the last of which he faced an enemy with technical offensive power (including heavy artillery, aviation, and mechanized units) estimated at from eight to nine times greater than his own, and resources many, many times exceeding anything at his disposal. However his degree of success or failure is to be measured, it must be admitted that for tactical ingenuity, spectacular mobility, and richness of versatility in maneuver, he repeatedly proved his superiority to every general sent against him, and established beyond any doubt the formidable fighting power of revolutionized Chinese troops in partisan warfare. The great mistakes of the Red Army in the South were strategic, and for those the political leadership must be held chiefly responsible. Even with such blunders, however, there is little doubt that had the Red Army been able to face their enemy on anything even approximating equal terms in the Fifth Campaign, the result would have been a catastrophic defeat for Nanking—Nazi advisers notwithstanding.

For pure military strategy and tactical handling of a great army in retreat nothing has been seen in China to compare with Chu Teh's splendid generalship of the Long March, already described. And

---

1. This endnote has been inserted at the request of the Party Literature Research Center. It reproduces the text of Chapter 4 of Part Ten of *Red Star Over China*, Edgar Snow, Victor Gollancz Ltd., London, 1937.

德统率长征的杰出领导相比的情况，这在前文已有描述。他部下的军队在西藏的冰天雪地之中，经受了整整一个严冬的围困和艰难，除了牦牛肉以外没有别的吃的，而仍能保持万众一心，这必须归因于纯属领导人物的个人魅力，还有那鼓舞部下具有为一个事业英勇牺牲的忠贞不贰精神的罕见人品。至少我个人是不可能想象蒋介石、白崇禧、宋哲元或者中国任何其他一个国民党将领能够在这样的条件下保全一支军队的，更不用说还能够在这样的考验结束时真的做到卷土重来，发动一场大进攻，在敌军为了防止它突破而从从容容地构筑了好几个月的防线上，打入了一个楔子。我走马西北的时候，朱德在做的正是这样一件事。

难怪中国民间流传他有各种各样神奇的本领：四面八方能够看到百里以外，能够上天飞行，精通道教法术，诸如在敌人面前呼风唤雨。迷信的人相信他刀枪不入，不是无数的枪炮弹药都没有能打死他吗？也有人说他有死而复活的能力，国民党不是一再宣布他已死亡，还详详细细地描述了他死去的情况吗？在中国，许许多多的人都知道朱德的大名，有的把他看成是危险的威胁，有的把他看成是希望的明星，这就看每个人的生活地位了，但是不论对谁来说，这是这十年历史中不可磨灭的名字。

但是大家都告诉我，朱德貌不惊人——一个沉默谦虚、说话轻声、有点饱经沧桑的人，眼睛很大（"眼光非常和蔼"这是大家常用的话），身材不高，但很结实，胳膊和双腿都像铁打的一样。他已年过半百，也许已有五十三四岁，究竟多大，谁也不知道——但是李长林笑着告诉我，就他所记得而言，他每次总说46了。这好像是他爱说的一个小小的笑话。李长林认为，他同现在这位夫人结婚后就不再记年龄了。这位夫人是个骨骼粗壮的农村姑娘，枪法高明，骑术高超，自己领导过一支游击队，把受伤战士背在身上，大手大足像个男人，身体壮实，作战勇敢。

朱德爱护他的部下是天下闻名的。自从担任全军统帅以后，他的生活和穿着都跟普通士兵一样，同甘共苦，早期常常赤脚走路，整整一个冬天以南瓜充饥，另外一个冬天则以牦牛肉当饭，从来不叫苦，很少生病。他们说，他喜欢在营地里转，同弟兄们坐在一起，讲故事，同他们一起打球。他乒乓球打得很好，篮球打个"不厌"。军队里任何一个战士都可以直接向总司令告状——而且也常常这样做。朱德向弟兄们讲话往往脱下他的帽子。在长征途中，他把马让给走累了的同志骑，自己却大部分步行，似乎不知疲倦。

to sheer personal magnetism of leadership, and the rare human quality which inspires in followers that unquestioning faith and devotion that gives men the courage to die in a cause—to this must be attributed the unbroken unity with which the forces under him withstood the terrible winter of siege and hardship, eating nothing but yak meat, on the icy wind-driven plateaus of Tibet. For me at least it is utterly impossible to imagine Chiang Kai-shek, Pai Chung-hsi, Sung Cheh-yuan, or any other Kuomintang general in China surviving with an army under such circumstances, to say nothing of actually staging a comeback at the end of that ordeal, and launching a big attack to drive a wedge right through the defence lines of enemy troops that had been comfortably preparing for months to prevent it, which was what Chu Teh was doing as I rode across the Northwest.

No wonder Chinese legends credit him with all sorts of miraculous powers: the ability to see 100 *li* on all sides, the power to fly, and the mastery of Taoist magic, such as creating dust clouds before an enemy, or stirring a wind against them. Superstitious folk believe he is invulnerable, for have not thousands of bullets and shells failed to destroy him? Others say he has the power of resurrection, for has not the Kuomintang repeatedly declared him dead, often giving minute details of the manner in which he expired? Millions know the name "Red Virtue" in China, and to each it is a menace or a bright star of hope, according to his status in life, but to all it is a name imprinted on the pages of a decade of history.

Yet everybody told me Chu was unimpressive in appearance—a quiet, modest, soft-spoken, old-shoe sort of man, large-eyed ("very kind eyes," was the frequent expression), short, rather stockily built, but with arms and legs of iron. He is now over fifty, perhaps as much as fifty-three or fifty-four, nobody knew exactly—but Li Chiang-lin laughingly told me that he has been saying he is forty-six ever since he could remember. It seemed to be a little jest of his own: and Li thought he had stopped counting his age when he married his present wife—a big-boned peasant girl, who is an excellent shot and an expert rider, an Amazon who has led a partisan brigade of her own, and carried wounded comrades on her shoulder, a woman with big hands and feet like a man, robust, in hearty health, and courageous.

Chu Teh's devotion to his men is proverbial. Since assuming command of the Army he has lived and dressed like the rank and file, has shared all their hardships, often going without shoes in the early days, living one whole winter on squash, another on yak meat, never complaining, rarely sick. He likes to wander through the camp, they say, sitting with the men and telling stories, or playing games with them. He plays a good game of table tennis, and a wistful game of basketball. Any soldier in the Army can bring his complaints directly to the commander-in-chief—and frequently does. Chu Teh takes his hat off when he addresses his men. On the Long March he lent his horse to tired comrades, walking much of the way, seemingly tireless.[1]

---

1. The previous six paragraphs are from *Red Star Over China*, Edgar Snow, Victor Gollancz Ltd., London, 1937.

"我认为他的基本特点就是天性极端温和，"当别人请他的妻子康克清谈一谈她认为她的丈夫有什么与众不同的性格时，她说道，"其次，他对一切大小事情都十分负责。第三，他喜欢跟一般战斗员生活打成一片，经常和他们谈话。

　　"朱德对弟兄们说话非常朴实，他们都能听懂。有时要是他不十分忙，就帮助农民们种庄稼。他常常从山下挑粮食到山上。他非常强健，什么东西都能吃，除了大量辣椒，没有什么特别爱吃的东西，因为他是四川人。他晚上非到十一二点钟不睡，早晨总是五六点钟起床。

　　"他喜欢运动，但是也喜欢读书。他仔细订出读书计划，熟读政治、经济的书籍。他也喜欢跟朋友们谈天，有时也开开玩笑，虽然并不像毛泽东那样幽默。他一般没有脾气，我从没有跟他吵过嘴，但他在战斗中却要发怒。打仗时朱德总是在前线指挥，但没有受过伤。"

　　我没有会见朱德的好运气，因为当他到达陕北的时候，我已经离开了。幸运的是朱德马上就被世界作家所注意，我现在竟有机缘得到一些最近的材料。"西安事变"以后，就有人到苏区去访问，韦尔斯女士是第二个会见中国红军领袖的外国人，康克清上面这番话就是对她说的。下面简述的朱德自传，是朱德亲口对韦尔斯女士说的，这改正了过去许多不确的记载[1]。它里边没有富有戏剧性的叙述，这对于朱德是不公平的。正如韦尔斯女士所说，"朱德决不会写出一部自传，因为他以为自己个人不能离开他的工作而存在。"但作为他的生涯的真实记载，下面的自传仍有无限的价值。朱德这样叙述他一生的经历：

　　"我于1886年生在四川仪陇县一个叫马鞍场的村子里。我家是穷苦的佃农。为着一家20口的生活，我们租了20亩田。我6岁时，进了一个丁姓地主的私塾。他要我

---

1. 本书第一版中关于朱德的一章，虽然根据我在西北时所搜集的材料，而且是朱德的同伴们所供给的，可是其中仍然有许多错误和不确之处。幸蒙韦尔斯女士慨予合作，使我得在中译本里纠正这些错误，不胜欣幸。单从这一个经验，更可证明，写作关于中国革命的复杂情况，除了第一手材料外，都不可靠，这一个规则，始终是对的。

"His primary characteristic, I think, is that he is extremely kind by nature,"[1] said his wife K'ang K'e-ch'ing, when asked what she considered Chu Teh's distinguishing features.[2] "Second, he takes full responsibility for everything, great and small. And, third, he likes to be a part of the life of the common fighters and to spend his time talking with them.[3]

"Chu Teh speaks in a very plain way to the men, and they understand him clearly. Sometimes he helps the farmers to plant their crops when he is not too busy, and he used to carry grain from the valley to the mountain. He is very strong and healthy, eats any kind of food, and doesn't care for any special thing except plenty of pepper, for he is a Szechuan man. He does not go to bed until eleven or twelve at night, but always gets up at five or six.

"He likes athletics, but he is studious, too. He always has a carefully-planned reading schedule of books on politics and economics. He also likes to talk to friends and is not always serious, though he is not humorous like Mao Tse-tung. He has no temper ordinarily, and I have never had a quarrel with him, but he gets angry in battle. In fighting, Chu Teh always takes command at the front, but he has not been wounded."[4]

I was not lucky enough to meet Chu Teh, for I had left north Shensi by the time he arrived there. But he soon attracted the attention of other foreign writers, giving me the opportunity to obtain further material. Visits were made to the Soviet area immediately after the Sian Incident, and Nym Wales was the second foreigner to interview the leaders of the Chinese Red Army. The above words were said to her by K'ang K'e-ch'ing. The short autobiography given below was told to Miss Wales by Chu Teh himself and helped correct many inaccuracies of the past.[5] It is bare of dramatic detail and does not do justice to Chu Teh. But, as Miss Wales put it, "He is one of those persons who could never write an autobiography because for himself his personality does not exist apart from his work." As a true account of his life, the following autobiography was still invaluable. Chu Teh began his life story thus:[6]

"I was born in 1886 in a Szechuan village called Ma-an Ch'ang, which is in Yi Lung *hsien*. My family were poor tenant farmers. For the existence of its twenty members we rented twenty *mou* of land. When I was six years of age I attended the tutorial school of the landlord, named Ting. For this he

---

1. From *Inside Red China*, Helen Foster Snow (Nym Wales), Doubleday, Doran & Company, Inc., New York, 1939.
2. Translated from the Chinese. No record of these words exists in English.
3. From *Inside Red China*, Helen Foster Snow (Nym Wales), Doubleday, Doran & Company, Inc., New York, 1939.
4. The previous two paragraphs are from *Inside Red China*, Helen Foster Snow (Nym Wales), Doubleday, Doran & Company, Inc., New York, 1939.
5. In the first edition of this book, the chapter concerning the life story of Chu Teh was based on information I had collected in the Northwest from his companions. It nevertheless included many mistakes and inaccuracies. Thanks to Miss Wales' generous cooperation, I was able to make a number of corrections in the Chinese edition. This experience shows that only first-hand materials are reliable when reporting on the complex circumstances of the Chinese revolution—a rule that never fails. [Footnote translated from the Chinese. No record of these words exists in English.]
6. Translated from the Chinese. No record of these words exists in English.

缴学费，而且待我很坏，好像这是慈善事业似的。我在家里吃饭睡觉，每天走 3 里路上学。放学后，我干各种活，如挑水、看牛等等。我在这家私塾里读了 3 年书。

"后来在地主的压迫下，我们这个大家庭无法再过下去了，为了经济上的原因分了家。我被过继给一个伯父，到大湾去跟他同住。我自己的父亲待我很坏，但这个伯父却爱我如同亲生儿子一样，送我上学念了六七年古书。全家只有我一个人受教育，因此我一面读书，一面又不得不干各种活。

"我在 1905 年考过科举，在 1906 年到了顺庆县，在一个高等小学里读 6 个月书，又在一个中学里读 6 个月。1907 年，我到成都，在一个体育学校里读 1 年书，后来回到故乡仪陇县，在本县高等小学里教体操。1909 年，我到云南的省会云南府，进了云南讲武堂，直到 1911 年的辛亥革命发生后才离校。我的志愿总是想做个军人，而这个讲武堂恐怕是当时中国最进步，最新式的了。它收学生很严格，我竟被录取，因此感到非常高兴。

"我一向崇拜现代科学，觉得中国需要一个产业革命。我小的时候，太平天国的故事给我很大影响，这是织布匠和别的走村串寨的手艺工人讲给我听的。他们在当时是新闻的传播者。由于有革命的倾向，1909 年我进讲武堂不到几星期，就加入了孙中山的同盟会。

"1911 年，我当时是个连长，我随有名的云南都督蔡锷率领的滇军参加推翻清朝的革命。1911 年的辛亥革命是 10 月 10 日在武昌开始的，20 天后，云南也举行了起义。我在同年被派往四川，与清朝总督赵尔丰作战。我们打败了赵尔丰，次年四五月间回到云南。1912 年下半年，我被任为云南讲武堂学生队长，在校里教授战术学、野战术、射击术和步枪实习。

"1913 年，我被任为蔡锷部下的营长，在法属印度支那边界驻扎了两年。1915 年，我升为团长，被派往四川跟袁世凯的军队作战。打了 6 个月仗，我们获得胜利。我升为旅长，部队驻扎在四川南部长江上的叙府、泸州一带。我的部队是第七师的精锐第十三混成旅（后来改为第七混成旅），当时稍有声誉。不过我们遭受重大的损失，在战争中半旅以上被消灭了。我在这一带地方驻扎了 5 年，不断地跟听命于北京段祺瑞政府的反动军队作战。

demanded a fee and treated me as badly as if it were charity. I ate and slept at home, walking three *li* to the school every day. After school hours I worked at various tasks, such as carrying water and tending cows. I studied in this school for three years.

"Then the large family could no longer survive under the pressure of the landlord, so it was broken up for economic reasons. I was adopted by an uncle and moved to Ta Wan to live with him. Although my own father had been very unkind to me, this uncle loved me as his son and sent me to school to study the Classics for six or seven years. I am the only one in my family who received an education, and in order to achieve this I was obliged to work at various tasks while attending school.

"I took the state examinations in 1905 and in 1906 went to Hsun Ch'ing *hsien*, where I attended a higher primary school for six months and then a middle school for six months. In 1907 I went to an athletic school in Ch'engtu for a year, then returned to my native Yi Lung *hsien* to teach athletics in the higher primary school there. In 1909 I went to Yunnanfu, the capital of Yunnan Province, and entered the Yunnan Military Academy, where I remained until the 1911 Revolution. My ambition was always to be a military man, and this Academy was perhaps the most progressive and modern in China at that time. It had stiff requirements, so I was very happy to be admitted there for study.

"I had always worshiped modern science and felt the need for China to have an industrial revolution. I was also very much influenced as a child by the stories of the T'ai-p'ing Rebellion told by weavers and other itinerant workers, who were news carriers in those days. Having a revolutionary bent, I joined the T'ung Meng Hui, Sun Yat-sen's Revolutionary Party, during my first few weeks at the Academy in 1909.

"In 1911, being then a company commander, I participated in the uprising to overthrow the Manchus as part of the Yunnan troops led by Ts'ai O, the famous Yunnan governor. The 1911 Revolution began on October 10 in Hankow, and twenty days later our Yunnan uprising was held. I was then, in the same year, sent to Szechuan to fight the Manchu governor there, Chao Erh-feng. We defeated Chao and returned to Yunnan the next April or May. In the latter part of 1912 I was ordered to take the post of detachment commander over the students in the Yunnan Military Academy, and there I taught war tactics, field maneuvers, marksmanship and rifle practice.

"In 1913 I was appointed battalion commander in Ts'ai O's troops and stationed on the French Indo-China border for two years. In 1915 I was ordered to Szechuan as regimental commander to fight against Yuan Shih-k'ai's military forces there. After six months of fighting we were victorious. I became a brigade commander, and my troops were stationed at Hsuifu, Luchow, on the Yangtze River in south Szechuan. Mine was the crack 13th Mixed Brigade of the 7th Division (later changed to the 7th Mixed Brigade), which gained some fame at this time. However, we sustained heavy losses, over half the brigade being destroyed in the fighting. I stayed in this region for five years, fighting continually against the old traitor troops under orders of the Peking Government of Tuan Ch'i-jui.

"到1920年底,我回到云南府,打反动的唐继尧,这时蔡锷已经死了。蔡锷是南方最进步的共和派青年领袖之一,他给我很大的影响。1915年袁世凯阴谋称帝,蔡锷首先为保卫民国而独树反帜。

"1921年从9月到10月,我任云南省警察厅长。唐继尧卷土重来,追我追了20天,我终于带一连人逃出来。另外一位同志也带领一连人,跟我一起逃走,但他被唐继尧捉住,拷打致死。我带领一连难兵到了西康,所走的路线正是1935年红军长征的路线。我们渡过金沙江,到打箭炉附近的雅州,在会理州停留一下,然后进了四川。我先到嘉定去,后来又到重庆,受到督军刘湘和重庆警备司令杨森的招待,1922年6月同他们一起看了龙船会。这两个四川军阀,红军后来当然打过他们。但在那时,刘湘并没有悬赏要取我的首级,却急于要给我一个师长的位置,我谢绝了,因为我已决定寻找共产党,为自己寻找新的革命道路。刘湘所以要我为他效劳,是因为我的特殊战术已经出名,使人害怕。我用来对付反动派军队颇具成效的战术,是我驻在印度支那边界时跟蛮子部落和土匪作战的经验得来的机动游击战术。我跟部队的逃兵、流窜的匪帮作战,从这些艰苦经验中学习到的东西特别有价值。当然我把这种游击经验同从书本和学校学到的知识结合起来。

"我的带兵的特殊战术是这样的:我自己体格很强壮,能跟弟兄们共同生活,跟他们密切接触,因而获得他们的信任。每次作战不管大小,我事前总要查勘地形,精密计划一切。我的主要战术一般都很成功,因为我细心处理一切,亲自领导部队。我总是坚持要从一切角度对敌人的阵地有清楚的了解。我跟民众一般也保持很好的关系,这给我不少帮助。蔡锷以其指挥战术著称,他教我许多东西。那时滇军是新式军队,有德国步枪作为武装。我以为对指战员都很重要的另一个因素,是对政治形势的了解。有了这种了解,他们才能有坚决地为主义而战的士气。此外就是经验——你仗打得越多,越能掌握局面。

"我在四川离开刘湘以后,就搭长江轮顺流而下,到上海寻找共产党。这时,中国已回到军阀的封建时期,前途实在黑暗,我很苦闷。我在四川当军官的最后一年,即1920年,我染上了吸鸦片的恶习。但在1920年底回到云南时,在从唐继尧手中逃脱

"At the end of 1920 I returned to Yunnanfu to fight against the reactionary T'ang Chi-yao, as Ts'ai O had died. Ts'ai O, one of the most progressive young republican leaders of the South, had had considerable influence over me. He was first to raise the standard of revolt in defense of the Republic against Yuan Shih-k'ai's plot to become Emperor in 1915.

"From September to October 1921 I was Commissioner of Police of Yunnan Province. Then T'ang Chi-yao staged a successful comeback, and I escaped with only one company of troops, though T'ang pursued me for twenty days. Another comrade who had left with me, taking one company with him also, was caught by T'ang and tortured to death. I led my company of refugees to Sikang [Tibet] along exactly the same route as the Red Army took later in the Long March of 1935. We crossed the River of Golden Sand, went to Yachow, near Tachienlu, stopped at Huilichou and entered Szechuan. I went to Chia Ting and then to Chungking, where I was received by Liu Hsiang, the governor-general, and Yang Sen, Chungking garrison commander, and saw the Dragon Boat Festival with them in June 1922. These two militarists of Szechuan were, of course, later attacked by the Red Army. However, at this time, instead of offering a reward for my head, Liu Hsiang was anxious to give me an appointment as division commander, which I refused because I had already decided to find a new revolutionary way for myself in searching for the Communist Party. Liu Hsiang's interest in procuring my services derived from the fact that my special tactics had already become known and feared. These tactics, which I had used with signal success against the troops of the monarchy, were mobile partisan tactics which I learned mainly from my experience on the Indo-China border and in fighting the Man-tzu tribes and bandits. I learned from a hard school of experience in fighting against mobile groups of bandit deserters from the armies, which was especially valuable. I combined with this guerilla experience, of course, what I had learned from books and in school.

"My own particular tactics in leading an army were these: I was myself physically strong, so I lived with my men and kept the closest contact with them, thus establishing confidence in them. Before any engagement, large or small, I looked over the topographical situation and planned every detail very carefully. My main tactics were usually sound because of careful management and personal leadership of the troops. I always insisted upon getting a clear picture of the enemy position from all angles. I also usually had good relations with the people, which helped me very much. Ts'ai O, who was famous for his commanding tactics, taught me very much. The Yunnan Army then was new and modern and armed with German rifles, of course. I think that the other element important for both commander and men is an understanding of the political situation so they have the morale to fight firmly for a principle. The rest is experience—the more you fight, the better you are able to grasp the situation.

"After leaving Liu Hsiang in Szechuan, I took a boat down the Yangtze River to search for the Communist Party in Shanghai. At this time China had gone back into a period of militarist feudalism, and the outlook was dark indeed, and I was very depressed. During my last year as commander in Szechuan, which was 1920, I had taken up the habit of smoking opium. When I returned to Yunnan, however, at the end of 1920, I bought some medicine to cure myself before making my escape from

出来前，我买了一些戒烟的药品，1921年我向西康作第一次'长征'时，实行戒烟，在到上海的船上，继续戒烟。到上海时，差不多已经戒脱了这个恶习，在上海广慈医院住了一星期，我完全戒绝了烟瘾。

"我在1922年离开四川去寻找中国共产党的时候，一点也不知道怎样同党发生关系，只是决心要同它取得不管是什么的联系。事实上，党刚在几个月前才组织起来，这是我后来知道的。我对于共产主义和布尔什维主义的兴趣，是在我自己阅读有关俄国革命的书籍后引起的。对我的其他影响只有跟法国留学生的几次谈话。我驻在四川的时候，凡是我能够找到的关于世界大战和俄国革命的书籍，我都读了。在这以前，我把全部精力都放在保卫民国和在中国实现孙中山的民主政治的战斗上。但1911年革命的失败和后来全国陷入劳民伤财的军阀混战，使我大失所望。我认识到中国革命必须更进一步，必须像俄国革命一样彻底，俄国革命的不断胜利，给了我以希望。

"我在上海找不到共产党的踪迹，因此我到北京去继续寻找。当时孙中山的机关报《民报》的主笔孙炳文也跟我同去寻找共产党。然而在北京我运气也不好，仍找不到共产党员，我又回到上海。这样，在1922年这一年，我从南方跑到北方，又回到南方，像一匹脱缰的马。北京给我的主要印象是国会的腐败和滑稽可笑。然而在另一方面，我又碰到许多学生，我跟其中有些一同旅行，他们的活动给我很好的印象。

"在回到上海后，我碰到孙中山、汪精卫、胡汉民和其他国民党领袖。孙中山给我的印象是一个非常诚恳、坚毅、聪慧的领袖。他要我去打陈炯明，我没有答应。他又要我到美国去，但我却要到德国去研究军事学，亲眼看看世界大战的结果。我在九月间搭船赴欧，经过新加坡和马赛，到了巴黎，我拍了一张从埃斐尔铁塔俯瞰巴黎全景的照片，感到很得意。

"在柏林，我碰到周恩来[现在是红军军事委员会副主席]和别的同志们。我终于在柏林找到了中国共产党！我在1922年10月间到达柏林，那时年纪36岁左右。我一找到共产党，当场立刻加入，这是1922年10月间的事。

"我在柏林住了1年，学习德文，然后到哥丁根进了一所大学，修了两学期社会科学——一半是掩护我继续呆在德国。我在德国的时期内，经常做党的工作。1924年，我们在柏林组织了一个国民党支部。中国青年党是国家主义的政党，当时学生分裂成

T'ang Chi-yao, and took this cure during my first 'long march' to Sikang in 1921, continuing the treatment on the river trip to Shanghai. I was nearly cured of the habit when I arrived, and after one week of intensive treatment in St Marie's Hospital in Shanghai I was permanently cured.

"When I left Szechuan in 1922 in search of the Chinese Communist Party, I had no idea of how to get into contact with it, but I had determined to make a connection somehow. In fact, the Party had only been organized a few months previously, I learned later. My interest in Communism and Bolshevism developed out of my own reading on the Russian Revolution. My only other influence was a few talks with returned students from France. While I was stationed in Szechuan, I studied everything I could find about the World War and the Russian Revolution. Until this time I had given all my energies to fighting for the Republic and the realization of Sun Yat-sen democracy in China. But the failure of the 1911 Revolution and the reaction into wasteful militarist war into which the country was plunged afterward discouraged me greatly. I realized that the China Revolution must go deeper and be as fundamental as that in Russia, the continuing success of which gave me hope.

"I could not find any trace of the Communist Party in Shanghai, so I went to Peking to continue my search. Sun Ping-wen, the editor of Sun Yat-sen's organ, *The People's Press*, went with me also in search of the Communist Party. In Peking, however, I had no better luck in finding the Communists, so returned to Shanghai. Thus, this year, 1922, I wandered about from south to north and back again like a horse without a bridle. My main impression of Peking was of the corruptness and farcical nature of Parliament. However, on the other hand I met many students, with some of whom I traveled, and their activities made a good impression on me.

"On my return to Shanghai I met Sun Yat-sen, Wang Ching-wei, Hu Han-min and other Kuomintang leaders. Sun impressed me as being a very sincere, determined and intelligent leader. He wanted me to go to Szechuan to fight against Ch'en Chiung-ming, but I refused. Sun then wanted me to go to America, but I was interested in going to Germany to study military science and to see the effects of the great World War for myself. In September I took a boat to Europe, passing through Singapore and Marseilles and then to Paris, where I proudly had my picture taken surveying that city from the Eiffel Tower.

"In Berlin, I met Chou En-lai (now vice-chairman of the Military Council of the Red Army) and other comrades. I had found the Chinese Communist Party at last—in Berlin! I arrived in Berlin in October 1922, being then about thirty-six years of age. I joined the Party as soon as I found it then and there; this was in October 1922.

"I stayed in Berlin one year studying German, then went to Göttingen, where I entered a college and took lectures in social science for two semesters—partly as a protection to permit me to continue my stay in Germany. I carried on Party work steadily while I was in Germany. In Berlin we organized a branch of the Kuomintang in 1924. The Chinese Youth Party was the Nationalist party, and the students were then split into two camps. At the same time I edited a weekly political paper in

两个阵营。我同时主编一个油印的《政治周报》。后来在中国组织第三党的邓演达当时也在那里。我出席世界学生大会，在1925年，因与臧戈夫案件有关，被德国宪警拘捕。臧戈夫是保加利亚的一个反动派，有人在一个大教堂里要炸他，许多人因而被捕，共30名，内有三四个中国人。这是我第一次被人逮捕，不过只有28小时。1925年，我在柏林第二次也是最后一次被捕，那是为了参加共产党为声援五卅运动而召开的大会。这第二次被捕的结果只拘留了30小时。所以我为革命坐牢的记录恐怕并不怎样惊人——一共不过58小时。那时候，我跟许多在德国的印度人一同工作。许多国家的学生出席学生大会，我结识不少朋友。我终于由于这些活动而被逐出德国，我遂环游欧洲，到了苏联，到1926年才回国。

"回国后，我从上海到汉口，再到四川万县。党命令我去领导四川的军事运动，到杨森的军队里做宣传鼓动工作，因为杨森是我的好朋友。这些军队是吴佩孚的旧部，杨森是吴佩孚所任命的，他们反对国民党的北伐。然而我终于把他们改编为国民革命军第二十军。我当二十军政治部主任，兼任国民党党代表，或称政委，但未担任军职。1927年，因杨森态度依旧动摇不定，他的军队表面上改编为国民革命军，实际上依然跟北方的敌人有联络，湖南的唐生智奉令率领国民党军队去打杨森。我在这时离开万县，到了江西。

"1927年1月间，我加入南昌朱培德的军队，被任为南昌军校校长，兼南昌公安局长，这两个职位我一直担任到南昌八一起义。我参加组织这次起义，它是在我这个公安局长保护下策划的。起义后我被举为起事中组成的新九军副军长，该军约有3000人。国民党第十一军、第四军和第二十军也参加了起义。

"当时，我跟周恩来、贺龙、张国焘、刘伯承、林伯渠、林彪、徐特立、叶挺等革命同志们一同工作。毛泽东那时不在南昌，我到后来才见到他。

"我接着率领队伍到了广东海陆丰附近的东江，我是革命军右翼司令。我进攻梅县的三河坝，叶挺、贺龙进攻潮汕和汕头。我们在这些区域同时失败后，我退到福建，然后到江西、湖南。到那时，我第九军大部分弟兄已经牺牲了。我只有1,200个弟兄，其中还有许多从贺龙、叶挺的部队退下来的散兵。

mimeograph. Teng Yen-ta, who later founded the Third Party in China, was also there. I attended the World Student Congress, and in 1925 was arrested by the German police for activities in connection with the Chankoff case. Chankoff was a Bulgarian reactionary whom somebody tried to bomb in a cathedral, causing many arrests to be made. There were thirty arrested, and these included three or four Chinese. This was the first time I was ever arrested, and it was only for twenty-eight hours. My second and last arrest was made in Berlin in 1925 for activities in support of the May Thirtieth Movement during a conference called by the Communist Party. This second arrest resulted in only thirty hours' detention. Therefore, my revolutionary prison record is not very impressive, I fear—only fifty-eight hours in all. At that time I worked with many Indians in Germany. In the Student Congress there were many nationalities among whom I made friends. I was finally driven out of Germany for these activities, so I traveled around Europe and to the U. S. S. R. until my return to China in 1926.

"Home again, I went from Shanghai to Hankow and then to Wan *hsien* in Szechuan. I had been ordered by the Party to conduct a military movement in Szechuan and to do agitation work among Yang Sen's troops, being a good friend of General Yang. These were troops which had been under Wu P'ei-fu, Yang being Wu's appointee, and had opposed the Northern Expedition of the Kuomintang. I succeeded, however, in helping to reorganize them as the 20th Army of the National Revolutionary troops. I was chairman of the Political Department of this 20th Army and was concurrently the Kuomintang Party delegate, or commissar, but held no military position. In 1927, because Yang Sen still wavered in his attitude and his troops, though ostensibly reorganized under the National Revolutionary Army, still kept their connections with the enemy North, T'ang Sheng-chih of Hunan was sent with Kuomintang troops to fight Yang Sen. At this time I left Wan *hsien* and went to Kiangsi.

"In January 1927 I joined Chu P'ei-teh's army in Nanchang and was made principal of the Military Training School in Nanchang as well as Chief of Police of the Nanchang Bureau of Public Safety, which positions I held up to the Nanchang Uprising of August 1. I helped organize this Uprising, which was planned under my protection as Chief of Police! After the Uprising I was made vice-commander of the new Ninth Army, created during the revolt, which consisted of about three thousand men. The 11th, 4th and 20th Kuomintang armies also participated in the Uprising.

"At this time I worked with Chou En-lai, Ho Lung, Chang Kuo-t'ao, Liu Po-ch'eng, Lin Pai-ch'u, Lin Piao, Hsu T'eh-li, Yeh T'ing and other revolutionary comrades. Mao Tse-tung was not in Nanchang, and I did not meet him until later.

"I then led my troops to Tungkiang, the East River district near Hailufeng, Kwangtung, as commander of the right wing of our revolutionary troops. I attacked San-ho-pa in Mei *hsien*, while Yeh T'ing and Ho Lung attacked Ch'aoshan and Swatow. After our mutual failures in these areas, I retreated to Fukien, then to Kiangsi and Hunan. By that time most of my men in the Ninth Army had been sacrificed. I had altogether only twelve hundred troops, which included also many retreaters from Ho Lung's and Yeh T'ing's forces who scattered after their defeat.

"我接着参加组织1928年湘南起义。我们改名为'工农革命军第一师',举起红旗,上有锤子、镰刀与红星。在湘南起义中,我们第一次在我们旗上用了红星。6个月后,1928年5月,我到了江西的井冈山,队伍增到1万人。我们在井冈山下不久就要建立最初根据地,我在这里第一次会见毛泽东。这是一件非常令人兴奋和愉快的事。

"在湘南起义以前,毛泽东的部队在1927年冬季就上了井冈山。当我退出广东东江后,他派他的兄弟毛泽覃来和我取得联络,那是我在1928年前跟毛泽东的仅有一次的联系。1928年在井冈山,毛泽东和我把两部军队合组成新'第四军',所以用这名字,为要保持国民党第四军'铁军'的大名,它在大革命中是我们革命的堡垒。我任第四军军长,毛泽东当政治委员。我们在井冈山上呆了6个月,击退了3次进攻。这时彭德怀在平江起义后,率部到了井冈山。1929年,我们留他守山,毛泽东和我率部到了江西南部、福建、广东、湖南去进行建立苏维埃的长期斗争。从此以后,我的生平不过是红军历史的一部分了。

"关于我个人的私生活问题:我在参加共产党的斗争以前结过两次婚。第一个妻子死了,第二个还活着。第一个妻子生了一个儿子,但我不知道他现在的下落。1935年长征时候,我在报上看到我的儿子,那时18岁,为要保全自己的性命,已逃离他母亲的故乡叙府附近的纳溪[1]。我的第一个妻子是一个师范学校的教员,天足,有赞助革命的进步思想。我们结婚的时候,我25岁,她18岁。我第三个妻子,是1928年湘南起义时期内跟我同居的,名叫吴玉兰[2]。她后来被湖南省主席何键捉住,砍了头。现在的妻子康克清是在1928年同我结婚的。

"关于我有百万家财的传说,并不确实。我在云南有些财产,但并不多,我的妻子也稍稍有一点。但是我1921年被迫逃走时,我的财产全被唐继尧没收了。"

朱德就这样简单地结束了他的自述。但这些朴素的话,是许多年不能想象的最最生动的人生经历的辉煌记录——这是一个大胆无畏和大公无私的故事,一个无比勇敢和智慧的故事,一个难以相信的苦难的故事,一个为着忠于一个为民族的自由解放而斗争的伟大主义而丢弃个人享受、财富和地位的故事。当这一时期的历史完全被写下

---

1. 经查证,"纳溪"疑为"南溪"。——编注
2. 经查证,"吴玉兰"疑为"伍若兰"。——编注

"I then helped organize the South Hunan Revolt in January 1928. We changed our name to the '1st Division of the Peasants' and Workers' Revolutionary Army,' and carried the red banner, the hammer-and-sickle and the red star. We used the red star for the first time on our flag during the South Hunan Revolt. Six months later, in May 1928, I went to Chingkangshan in Kiangsi with troops increased to ten thousand men. Here, at the foot of the mountain, Chingkangshan, where we were to establish our first base, I met Mao Tse-tung for the first time. It was a very exciting and happy occasion.

"Before the South Hunan Revolt Mao Tse-tung's troops had left for Chingkangshan in the winter of 1927. My only connection with him previous to 1928 was when his brother, Mao Tse-t'an, was sent to make connections with me after my retreat from the East River district in Kwangtung. At Chingkangshan in 1928 Mao and I combined our forces into the new 'Fourth Army,' using this name in order to keep the famous name of the Kuomintang Fourth Army, the 'Ironsides,' which had been our revolutionary stronghold during the Great Revolution. I was made commander of the Fourth Army, while Mao was political commissar. We stayed on the mountain Chingkangshan for six months and defeated three campaigns to annihilate us. At this time P'eng Teh-huai, after his uprising in the P'ingkiang region, arrived in Chingkangshan. We left him to garrison Chingkangshan while Mao and I led our forces to South Kiangsi, Fukien, Kwangtung and Hunan, in 1929, to carry on our long struggle for the Soviets. After this my life is merely a part of the Red Army's history.

"To answer questions about my personal life: I was married twice before joining the Communist struggle. My first wife died, but the second is still alive. I had one son by this first wife, but I have no idea where he is now. During the Long March in 1935 I read in the press that my son, then eighteen, had escaped from his mother's native town in Na Ch'i, near Hsuifu, where he was living, in order to save his life. This first wife was a normal-school teacher, with natural feet and progressive ideas in support of the revolution. I married her when I was twenty-five and she eighteen. My third wife, with whom I lived during the South Hunan Revolt in 1928, was named Wu Yu-lan. She was then captured by Ho Chien, governor of Hunan, and beheaded. My present wife is K'ang K'e-ch'ing, whom I married in 1928.

"And no, the legend about my millions of dollars is not true. I had some property in Yunnan but not much, and my wife had a little. However, my property was all confiscated by T'ang Chi-yao when I was forced to run away in 1921."[1]

Chu Teh ended his autobiography with these simple words, concluding a glorious tale spanning many years of extraordinary experiences—a story of boldness and selflessness, unrivalled courage and wisdom, hardships beyond imagination, the renouncing of personal happiness, wealth and position for the sake of a great doctrine devoted to the battle for the freedom and liberation of a nation.

---

1. The previous twenty-three paragraphs are from *Inside Red China*, Helen Foster Snow (Nym Wales), Doubleday, Doran & Company, Inc., New York, 1939.

的时候，上述这个简单的自传将长上血肉，我们就可以看到这部历史的新页上涌现出一个人物——少数真正的时代伟人之一。

朱德的一生经历与中国民众的命运有不可分割的关系，从他的一生中可以看出红军奋斗的原因。请容许我再引用韦尔斯女士的话：

"红军是一支十分年轻的军队，为旧中国前所未有。对这支军队来说，朱德是稳定的象征，是同传统和过去历史间的联系，因为他在内地亲身经历了清朝以来整个革命运动的发展最缓慢和最根本的阶段。他曾经生活在中国内地两个最落后的省份——云南和四川。当沿海一带瞬息万变的变化传到这些一潭死水一样的地方时候，这些变化必须证明是行之有效的才能站得住脚。朱德与中国新军的许多领袖人物不同，他不是日、俄、德等国的'留学生'。他的经历是土生土长，扎根于中国的内地，他所以能获得弟兄们的信任和中国旧式将军的敬重，这未始不是重要的原因。他熟悉内地从北到南的绝大部分地势，熟悉当地的民情风俗。

"朱德是在中国第一批新式军校里受到共和派名将蔡锷的训练的。他接着在法属印度支那边界和四川、云南的山间要塞担任卫戍任务时又学得特殊的游击战术，这后来对红军有很大的贡献。在政治上，他首先在1909年以同盟会会员的身份为民主政治而奋斗，接着加入了国民党，最后完全自发地寻找共产党，在1922成为中国共产党最老的党员之一。从朱德远道跋涉，到上海、北京、柏林找寻共产党这件事，可以看出他日后成为三次革命的领袖所具备的自发精神和坚定目标。

"中国共产主义运动的历史进程，如果没有它的两个孪生天才'朱、毛'，是无法想象的，许多中国人实际上都把他们看作是一个人。毛泽东是这一斗争的冷静的政治头脑，朱德是它的热烈的心，以行动赋予了它的生命。共产党所以能够对红军保持严密的控制，朱德对'文职'领导的忠诚和服从，是原因之一。从朱、毛以下直到各级指挥员和政治委员没有发生军政势力之间的斗争。朱、毛的联合不是互相竞争的，而是相辅相成的。朱德没有任何政治野心，他能接受命令，因此也能发布命令——这是革命军队的领导的一个很有价值的因素。

When the history of this period was written down, the bare autobiography above would be fleshed out and a figure would emerge that came to be seen as one of the few truly great men of the time.

Chu Teh's life was inseparably linked to the destiny of the Chinese people, from which the Red Army's struggle arose. To quote Miss Wales again:[1]

"The Red Army is an army of extreme youth, entirely new to the background of old China. For this army Chu Teh is a symbol of stability and a link with tradition and past history, for he has experienced the whole revolutionary movement since the Manchu Dynasty in its slowest but most fundamental phase, in the interior. He lived in the two most backward provinces, farthest in the interior, Yunnan and Szechuan. By the time the mercurial coastal changes reached these backwaters, they had to be valid and proven. Unlike many dominant figures in modern Chinese armies, Chu Teh is not a 'returned student' from Japan, Russia or Germany. His experience is rooted deep in the bedrock of native interior China, and this is not the least of the reasons why he has the complete confidence of his men, as well as the respect of old-style Chinese generals in China's armies. He knows intimately most of the terrain of this interior from north to south, as well as its people and general conditions.

"Chu Teh was trained under the brilliant Yunnan republican general, Ts'ai O, at one of the first modern military schools in the country. He then learned the special guerilla tactics, which served the Red Army so well later, in his garrison duties on the French Indo-China border and in the mountain fastnesses of Szechuan and Yunnan. Politically, he began fighting for democracy as a member of the T'ung Meng Hui in 1909, later joining the Kuomintang and then, entirely on his own initiative, searching out and becoming one of the earliest members of the Chinese Communist Party in 1922. Chu Teh's expedition in search of the Communist Party in Shanghai, Peking and then Berlin reveals the intellectual initiative and sure determination of purpose that have made him a leader in three revolutions.

"It would be difficult to imagine the course of the history of the Communist movement in China without its twin-genius 'Chu-Mao,' which many Chinese actually think of as one person. Mao Tse-tung has been the cool political brains and Chu Teh the warm heart of the struggle which gave it life-action. One of the reasons for the surprising discipline which the Communist Party maintains over the Red Army is Chu Teh's loyalty and submission to 'civil' control. There is no struggle between the military and political power from Chu and Mao down to the army commanders and their political commissars. The Chu-Mao combination was fortunately not competitive but perfectly complementary. Chu Teh is not politically ambitious in any way; he accepts orders and is therefore able to give them in turn—a factor of no small value in the command of a revolutionary army.

---

1. The previous two paragraphs are translated from the Chinese. No record of these words exists in English.

"朱德的那种难能可贵的个性几乎能立刻博得人人的爱戴。看来产生这种个性的由来是他的谦虚,而这种谦虚也许又是渊源于他个人诚实可靠的品质。"

但是落入红军之手的人无疑把他认为是凶神化身。阶级战争不知慈悲为何物。关于红军暴行的许多传说现在已证明是不确的,但是,如果认为朱德不会由于"革命需要"而下枪决的命令,那就不免过于天真了。要完成他的任务,他必须完全忠于贫苦无依的人,在这个地位上,他不可能比他要授予权力和服从的群众更加慈悲。因此,除非你认为群众也不能杀人,否则,朱德决不是一个手上没有沾血的人,但是,你究竟把这血看作是外科医生的血还是刽子手的血,这就完全要看你本人的世界观、宗教、成见或同情心了。反正朱德不是圣人,但是在他的自己人中间,在穷人——毕竟他们占中国人民的绝大多数——中间,他是个深受爱戴的人,他在一段的时间内,曾经高举解放的火炬,在那些为中国的人权自由而斗争的人中间,他的名字已经永垂不朽。

"Chu Teh has that rare kind of personality which is immediately and universally appealing to nearly everyone. It seems to come from a modesty which perhaps derives from his consciousness of solidity and personal integrity."[1]

Yet people who have fallen victim to the Reds no doubt saw in him a fiend in human form. Class war knows little mercy. Many of the horror stories spread about the Reds have now been discredited, but it would be naive to suppose that Chu Teh has not found it a "revolutionary necessity" to send men to the firing squad. To succeed in his mission he had to transfer his loyalty completely to the disinherited, and in that role he could have been no more merciful than the masses he sought to empower and obey. So unless you believe that the masses cannot also take life, Chu Teh is no man without blood on his hands, but it depends entirely on your own philosophy or religion or prejudice or human sympathy, whether you find it the blood of the surgeon or of the executioner. Chu Teh has been no saint in any case, but still among his own people, among the poor, who are after all the vast majority in China, he has been a deeply loved man who for a while held high a torch of liberation, and his name is already immortalized among those who have fought for human freedom in China.[2]

---

1. The previous four paragraphs are from *Inside Red China*, Helen Foster Snow (Nym Wales), Doubleday, Doran & Company, Inc., New York, 1939.
2. The previous paragraph is from *Red Star Over China*, Edgar Snow, Victor Gollancz Ltd., London, 1937.